Wo Wolman, Benjamin
Handbook of dreams

HANDBOOK OF DREAMS

Research, Theories and Applications

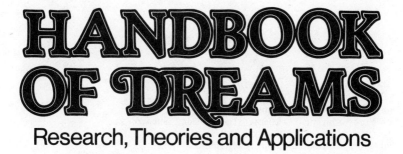

HANDBOOK OF DREAMS

Research, Theories and Applications

Edited by

Benjamin B. Wolman

Consulting Editors

Montague Ullman
Wilse B. Webb

 VAN NOSTRAND REINHOLD COMPANY
NEW YORK   CINCINNATI   ATLANTA   DALLAS   SAN FRANCISCO
LONDON   TORONTO   MELBOURNE

Van Nostrand Reinhold Company Regional Offices:
New York   Cincinnati   Atlanta   Dallas   San Francisco

Van Nostrand Reinhold Company International Offices:
London   Toronto   Melbourne

Library of Congress Catalog Card Number: 79-653
ISBN: 0-442-29592-8

Manufactured in the United States of America

Published by Van Nostrand Reinhold Company
135 West 50th Street, New York, N.Y. 10020

Published simultaneously in Canada by Van Nostrand Reinhold Ltd.

15 14 13 12 11 10 9 8 7 6 5 4 3 2 1

Library of Congress Cataloging in Publication Data

Main entry under title:

Handbook of dreams.

    Includes index.
    1. Dreams—Addresses, essays, lectures.   I. Wolman,
Benjamin B.
BF1078.H28   154.6'34   79-653
ISBN 0-442-29592-8

Contributors

Harry Fiss, Ph.D., Professor of Psychiatry, University of Connecticut School of Medicine, Farmington, Connecticut.

David Foulkes, M.D., Professor of Psychiatry, Emory University.

Leo Gold, Ph.D., Dean, Alfred Adler Institute, New York.

Thayer A. Greene, B.D., S.T.M., Faculty, Jungian Institute, New York.

J. Allan Hobson, M.D., Professor of Psychiatry and Director of Laboratory of Neurophysiology, Harvard Medical School.

Richard M. Jones, Ph.D., Professor of Psychology, The Evergreen State College, Olympia, Washington.

Susan Knapp, Ph.D., Faculty, Post Graduate Center for Mental Health, New York.

Milton Kramer, M.D., Professor of Psychiatry, University of Cincinnati College of Medicine Director, Sleep Disorders Center Cincinnati General Hospital, and Sleep and Dream Laboratory, V.A. Hospital, Cincinnati.

Robert W. McCarley, M.D., Associate Professor of Psychiatry and Co-Director, Laboratory of Neurophysiology, Harvard Medical School.

Thomas Roth, Ph.D., Sleep Disorders and Research Center, Department of Psychiatry, Henry Ford Hospital, Detroit, Michigan.

Patricia J. Salis, M.A., Sleep Disorders and Research Center, Department of Psychiatry, Henry Ford Hospital, Detroit, Michigan.

Charles T. Tart, Ph.D., Professor of Psychology, University of California, Davis.

Jon Tolaas, Lektor in Humanities, Eids Gymnas, Nordfjordeid, Norway.

Montague Ullman, M.D., Faculty, Westchester Center for Psychoanalysis and

Psychotherapy.   Formerly Director, Dream Laboratory, Maimonides Medical Center.

Wilse B. Webb, Ph.D., Graduate Research Professor of Psychology, University of Florida, Gainesville.

Benjamin B. Wolman, Ph.D., Editor-in-Chief, International Encyclopedia of Psychiatry-Psychology, Psychoanalysis, and Neurology.

Preface

Prior to Freud, dreams were either overvalued as augurs of future events or dismissed as meaningless exercises of fantasy. Freud's indefatigable and relentless determinism led to a fruitful and heuristic discovery of the meaning of dreams. There was no room for coincidences in Freud's system of cause and effects, and dreams had to be assigned a proper place in his theory.

Freud ascribed three main features to dreams. The first was the above-mentioned meaningfulness. Although the bricks out of which one's dream is built could be picked from recent experiences of the dreamer, the dream itself carries a message beyond its superficial, manifest façade. The second feature was related to the particular role of a dream as the carrier of hidden, repressed wishes. The third feature was related to the role of dreams as guardians of sleep.

Freud's theory was modified, rewritten, or rejected by psychoanalytic disciples and dissidents. The main revisions were directed to the second feature, namely wish-fulfillment, and instead stressed adaptation and attempts at solving the problems the dreamer was struggling with.

A major breakthrough in dream research was the discovery of Rapid Eye Movement (REM) sleep in 1953. This epoch-making discovery gave rise to innumerable attempts at sleep and dream analysis which went far beyond the data observed by Freud and other analysts. Scores of new theoretical concepts have grown out of the multifaceted experimental studies, and the house that Freud built must undergo serious renovations if it is to survive.

The REM research has proved beyond doubt that sleep is the protector of dreams and not vice versa. While some researchers and theoreticians question other aspects of Freud's theory, it seems that the causal principle has survived all criticism, and the meaningfulness of dreaming is still to stay.

However, what the message of dreams is, and what their organic and psychological corollaries are, are today controversial issues that attract the attention of scores of first-rate research workers and theoreticians.

The purpose of the present volume is to present the wealth of research data, theories, and applications related to dreams and the process of dreaming.

BENJAMIN B. WOLMAN

Contents

HANDBOOK OF DREAMS
Research, Theories and Applications

Part I

HISTORY AND RESEARCH

1

A Historical Perspective
of Dreams

Wilse B. Webb

Because dreams form a natural warp to the woof of our waking thoughts, their curious presence has been a continuous part of mankind's response to itself. The path of these responses, from the earliest writings of the Egyptians to the current experimental probings, has been rich and varied across time and within any given time period. Like man's response to life's mysteries—for example, God, love, death, or fortune—the breadth and imaginative range of responses as these appear in folklore, literature, customs, and finally science, cannot be captured as a whole. Some Procrustean scheme must be used. It is hoped that the broad outlines of the story will remain.

In this background review of dreams, I have chosen to follow the mainstream of Western thought as it has moved from the ancient world to our contemporary scene. I have, consequently, suppressed the Eastern and cross-cultural areas.[1] I have focused on four periods: ancient, pre-Freudian early science, Freudian and post-Freudian concepts, and the new experimental approach to dreaming. While this framework reflects a convenience of resources, it also represents periods of significance in our groping efforts to capture the dream in the net of our waking thoughts.

DREAMS IN ANCIENT TIMES

The most pervasive attitude toward dreams in ancient Greece reflected the fluid relationship between the divine and the secular world. The gods freely interacted in the real world, particularly with heroes. Homer's *Iliad* is replete with the appearance in dreams of gods bearing messages. Nestor visited Agamemnon in a dream and described himself as a "messenger from Zeus." The gods were capricious: in the second book of the *Iliad*, Zeus deliberately deceived Agamemnon with a false dream. Penelope fully recognized this capriciousness. When sent a dream by Minerva about the return of Odysseus, she said, "The truth is we don't know how to deal with dreams; what they tell is uncertain and they do not all come true."

Dreams were divided into two types: those from the Gate of Horn and those from the Gate of Ivory. The former were true and the latter false. In later Grecian times, perhaps because of the difficulties of interpretation and perhaps because of the availability of more reliable auguries, dreams became focused on the cure of illnesses. Throughout Greece, and typically in exotic settings, oracles and shrines evolved where pilgrims with illnesses visited. At their height, there were more than 400 such oracles, dedicated either to gods or heroes. Before each were stelae attesting to earlier cures. The most famous oracles were those of Aesculapius. Pilgrims were cured through the process of incubation (*incubare* = to sleep in the sanctuary). After making offerings and sacrifices and after following prescribed rituals, the petitioner slept in the temple. While sleeping he was visited in a dream by a god or his representative. Through the appropriate dream a cure was effected.

These notions—god visits and incubation—were pandemic in the ancient world. An Egyptian papyrus in the British Museum dated between 2000 and 1790 B.C. recites: "To obtain a vision from (the god) Besa. Make a drawing of Besa on your left hand and enveloping your hand in a strip of black cloth that has been consecrated to Isis (and) lie down to sleep without speaking a word, even in answer to a question. . . . " A number of dream interpretation papyri have been found. In one in the Cairo Museum: "If she gives birth to a cat, she will have many children; if she gives birth to a dog, she will have a boy, etc." In their concern with evil or demonic dreams Mesopotamian and Sumerian records show an interesting variation from Grecian concepts. Demonic dreams were not viewed as predictors of future events. Rather, they indicated a need for exorcistic rituals and magic means.

Throughout the ancient Near East we find in the literary texts the "message" dream. As described by Oppenheim (1966) this type of dream has a characteristic pattern. The dreamer is a man, typically, a king, hero, or priest. In a moment of crisis (of which the dreamer may be unaware), a deity appears and calls the sleeping person. A message is delivered, and the dreamer awakens. The true message dream is delivered "in the clear," i.e., the message is apparent. Jacob returns to his homeland on Yahweh's command, and the Assyrian king Assurbanipal campaigns against the Elamites on the command of Ishtar. A close variant is the "symbolic" dream, such as those experienced by Pharoah and Nebuchadnezzar. These required the interpreter skills of Joseph and Daniel, along with the help of God.

Underlying these views was essentially the Orphic notion that sleep freed the soul from bodily constraints and "noise," thus permitting the perception of higher sources. As noted by Meir (1966), this was a position essentially held by the Pythagoreans, Aeschylus, and Euripides, as well as Pindar and Xenophon, and found in Plato's *Phaedrus*.

Among these concepts are those found in the writings of Aristotle (1933). Aristotle first established in *Parva Naturalia* the fact that we can continue to perceive events after the initial stimulation: "even when (the) external object of perception has departed, the impressions may persist, and are themselves objects of impression." Aristotle viewed these residual sensory impressions as the source of dreams: "whether derived from external objects or from causes within the body," they present themselves during sleep with "even greater impression," since the actions of the intellect and the sense organs do not "extrude them." These sense impressions are "like little eddies which are being formed in rivers . . . often remaining like what they were when they first started, but often, too broken into other forms by collisions." He further notes that if one "violently" disturbs these "residuary movements," they may become distorted and appear confused and weird. This may occur particularly in persons who are "atrabilious, or feverish or intoxicated" (pp. 460–461).

Not surprisingly this essentially naturalistic approach to dreams led Aristotle to scepticism about divination from dreams. "Most (so-called prophetic) dreams are . . . mere coincidences . . . one's mentioning a particular person (in waking) is neither a token nor a cause of this presenting himself, but a mere coincidence. . . . " However, Aristotle noted that dreams can reasonably presage events, " . . . For as when we are engaged in any course of action, or have performed certain actions . . . the dream movement has had a way paved for it and (this in turn) should prove a starting point for action to be performed. . . . " Within sleep, "events" propagated as "movement" in waking may be perceived in the body, since people during sleep are more sensitive to slight sensory movements. However, "such are not sent by gods. If this were the case it would be a gift that would occur in the daytime and to the wise" (pp. 462–463). As for dream interpretation Aristotle wrote a striking passage:

> The most skilful interpreter of dreams is he who has the faculty of observing resemblances. Anyone may interpret dreams which are vivid and plain. But . . . dreams are analogous to forms reflected in water . . . if the motion in the water is great, the reflection has no resemblance to the original. Skilful (is he) who could rapidly discern . . . the scattered and distorted fragments . . . for internal movement effaces the clearness of dreams. (p. 464)

We find Aristotle, writing midst a God-invoking world, yet making constant appeal to observations of nature and attributing events to naturalistic causes. While he is often wrong in detail, the magnificence of the approach remains a marvel of the history of ideas.

One cannot leave the ancient world without a glance at the culminating work of Artemidorus in the second century. This is a remarkable set of five volumes, titled *Oneirocritica* (1603), which collected the entire antique literature of the time and reflected his own experiences with more than 3,000 dreams. Artemidorus was to dreams what Galen was to medicine. Much of these books comprise a direct translation of symbols (a head = father; a foot = slave; the right hand = father, son, friend, brother; the left hand = mother, wife, mistress, daughter) and particular dreams (a dolphin in the water is a good omen; out of the water a bad omen; to have asses' ears is servitude and misery; gold is a good omen except if worn as a necklace, which is a bad omen). It is said that many of the current "dream interpretation" books still carry elements of Artemidorus' work. Artemidorus' writings, however, were far from simplistic. They carry much modern wisdom. He insisted above all that the dream be interpreted in relation to the particular dreamer, whose character and mood must be known. In one instance (cited by Meir [1966]) he gives seven different interpretations of the same dream by seven different pregnant women, all of whom had dreamed of giving birth to a dragon. Each was adapted to the particular circumstances of the dreamer. He noted that the customs of the place and time must be taken into account. Again, as Meir notes, he even adjures the dream analyst to translate the dream pure and simple without trying to impress the dreamer with his scholarliness or intelligence. Freud refers to the *Oneirocritica* as "the most painstaking study of dream interpretation of the Graeco-Roman world." In *The Interpretation of Dreams* (Freud, 1900/1965)[2] he notes that Artemidorus' procedure "takes into account not only the content of the dream but also the character and circumstances of the dreamer . . . " (p. 130). In a footnote to the 1914 edition of *The Interpretation of Dreams*, Freud further writes that Artemidorus used the principle of association in decoding dreams. "(For him) a thing in a dream means what it recalls to mind—to the dream interpreter's mind, it need hardly be said" (p. 138). He adds, however, that he (Freud) had extended this principle to what it means to the dreamer himself.

A scholarly and detailed review of dreams in classical times has been published by Bonuzzi (1975). As the author notes, " . . . practically no classical author, be he a biologist or a man of letters, fails to devote at least a few lines to the problem of dreams. . . . "

PRE-FREUDIAN TIMES

We move forward some 1500 years to the 1800s. There appears to be a general tendency these days to perceive our contemporary interest in dreams as having sprung *de nova* from the head of Freud. A reading of *The Interpretation of Dreams* quickly dispels this notion. The work begins with a chapter on "The Scientific Literature Dealing with the Problem of Dreams." Further this chapter was continuously expanded and updated through successive editions (1909, 1911, 1914, 1919, 1921, 1922) of the book. It is the most comprehensive review I have found and serves as the primary resource for this present work.

Admittedly Freud considered his review to be merely a scholarly exercise: "In the pages that follow I shall bring forward proof that there is a psychological technique which makes it possible to interpret dreams, and that, if that procedure is employed, every dream reveals itself as a psychical structure which has a meaning and which can be inserted at an assignable point in the mental activities of waking life. I shall further endeavour to elucidate the processes to which the strangeness and obscurity of dreams are due and to deduce from those processes the nature of the psychical forces by whose concurrent or mutually opposing action dreams are generated. Having gone thus far, my description will break off, for it will have reached a point at which the problem of dreams merges into more comprehensive problems, the solution of which must be approached upon the basis of material of another kind.

I shall give by way of preface a review of the work done by earlier writers on the subject as well as of the present position of the problems of dreams in the world of science, since in the course of my discussion I shall not often have occasion to revert to those topics. For in spite of many thousands of years of effort, the scientific understanding of dreams has made very little advance—a fact so generally admitted in the literature that it seems unnecessary to quote instances in support of it. In these writings many stimulating observations are to be found and a quantity of interesting material bearing upon our theme, but little or nothing that touches upon the essential nature of dreams or that offers a final solution of any of their enigmas. And still less, of course, has passed into the knowledge of educated laymen. . . ." (pp. 35–36)

Freud in his review cites some 150 earlier sources. His primary citations are drawn from the following books and articles specifically addressing dreams:

Burdach	(1838)—*Die Physiologie als Erfahrungswissenschaft*
Delboeuf	(1885)—*Le sommeil et les rêves*
Fichte	(1864)—Psychologie: Die Lehr vom bewussten Geiste des Menschen
Hilderbrandt	(1875)—*Der Traum und seine Verwertung für's Leben*
Maury	(1853)—Nouvelles observations sur les analogies des phénomènes du rêve et de l'aliéntation mentale
Radestock	(1879)—*Schlaf und Traum*
Spitta	(1882)—*Die Schlaf und Traumzustände der menschlichen Seele*
Strumpell	(1877)—*Die Natur und Entstehung der Traüme*

Volkelt   (1875)–*Die Traum-Phantasie*
Weygandt   (1893)–*Entstehung der Traüme*

These may be best described as essays on dreaming, with arguments supported by example. Only Maury contains "experimental" work, which included his famous use of physical stimuli, e.g., tickling the nose with a feather, to determine the effects on dream context. Supportive or variant statements about a topic are drawn in Freud's review from a wide range of comments in more general books. For example, there are two quotations from Fechner's *Elemente der Psychophysik* (1860), some 10 citations from Wundt's *Grundzüge der physiologischen Psychologie* (1874) and citations of specific articles, such as Calkin's "Statistics of Dreams," in the *American Journal of Psychology* (1893).

Freud organizes his review into topics: Relations of Dreams to Waking Life, Memory in Dreams, Stimuli and Sources of Dreams, Why Dreams are Forgotten, Distinguishing Characteristics of Dreams, The Moral Sense of Dreams, Theories of Dream Functions, Dreams and Mental Diseases. Each section, as Freud states, contains, "many stimulating observations." For example, Strumpell, in analyzing the Forgetting of Dreams, anticipates modern memory theory by saying, "It is in general as difficult to retain what is nonsensical as it is to retain what is confused and disordered" (p. 77). He anticipates the issue of secondary elaboration by noting that, "Thus it may easily happen that waking consciousness unwillingly makes interpolation in the memory of a dream: we persuade ourselves that we have dreamt all kinds of things that were not contained in the actual dreams" (p. 78).

To give a sense of the pre-Freudian period, I will review some of the concepts of two of its major contributors, Maury and Strumpell. Both authors hold to a basically Aristotelian position that dreams are essentially residue of earlier or concurrent sensory impression; both struggle with the apparent problem that much of dream content is not immediately attributable to events in waking memory. Both accept a notion of hypermnesia associated with dreaming. Strumpell states:

> ... we observe how dreams sometimes bring to light, as it were, from beneath the deepest piles of debris under which the earliest experiences of youth are buried in later times, pictures of particular localities, things or people, completely intact and with all their original freshness. ... This is not limited to experiences which created a lively impression when they occurred or enjoy a high degree of psychical importance and return later in a dream as genuine recollections at which waking consciousness will rejoice. On the contrary, the depths of memory in dreams also include pictures of people, things, localities, and events dating from the earliest times, which either never possessed any psychical importance or more than a slight degree of vividness, or which have long since lost what they may have possessed of either, and which

consequently seem completely alien and unknown alike to the dreaming and waking mind till their earlier origin has been discovered. (p. 49)

Maury cites several experiences of his own in which dreams based upon remote sources of childhood events were in fact precise reproductions of them. Even within recent events Strumpell notes that the stimuli of the actual dream may be quite trivial:

> . . . There are cases in which the analysis of a dream shows that some of its components are indeed derived from experiences of the previous day or its predecessor, but experiences so unimportant and trivial from the point of view of waking consciousness that they were forgotten soon after they occurred. Experiences of this kind include, for instance, remarks accidentally overheard, or another person's actions inattentively observed, or passing glimpses of people or things, or odd fragments of what one has read, and so on. (p. 52)

Maury's position on the role of external stimuli on dreams is quite famous in dream theory. Strumpell essentially agrees. But again, both are faced with the wide variety of dreams that emerge from similar events and the elaborate and often remote relation of the dream report to the signal itself. Strumpell invokes the notion that while one is asleep, the sense impressions of the past from without are less clearly perceived and lend themselves to illusory responses. In further efforts to account for the looseness of the apparent relationship to external stimuli, Maury and Strumpell emphasized the role of somatic stimuli: " . . . (In sleep the mind) is obliged to receive and be effected by impressions of stimuli from parts of the body and from changes in the body of which it knows nothing when awake" (p. 66). Thus, for example, dreams of falling may be evoked by the arm falling away from the body or a flexing of the leg.

Strumpell attributed forgetting of dreams to a number of possible causes; e.g., the sensory impression may be too weak, there may be no repetition of the event as it occurs in waking life, the material to be remembered may be disorganized or nonsensical, and, most critically, on awakening the attention may be drawn away from dreams and replaced by the waking world. As Freud practically summarizes Strumpell's thoughts, "dreams give way to the impressions of the new day just as the brilliance of the stars yield to the light of the sun" (p. 78).

Both Maury and Strumpell also attribute the distorted character of dreams to a reduction in higher mental processing. As Maury put it, there is a series of "degradations de la faculte pensante et raisonnante." Strumpell specifically noted the loss of logical relations and connections, and attributed this to the fact that the waking mind uses ideas and thoughts in verbal images, while the dream may resort to only sensory images and "run their course . . . without reflection or common sense or aesthetic taste or moral judgment" (p. 98).

The presence and force of motive systems operating in dreams are noted by Maury: "Thus in dreams a man stands self-revealed in all his native nakedness and poverty. As soon as he suspends the exercise of the will, he becomes the plaything of all the passions against which he is defended while he is awake by his conscience, his sense of honour and his fears" (p. 105).

Freud cites a number of striking quotations related to this theme:

Spitta: "Tell me some of your dreams, and I will tell you about your inner self" (p. 99).

Hilderbrandt: "It is impossible to think of any action in a dream for which the original motive has not in some way or other—whether as a wish, or desire or impulse—passed through the waking mind" (p. 101).

Particularly noteworthy is a statement of Fichte: "The nature of our dreams gives a far more truthful reflection of our whole disposition than we are able to learn from self-observations in waking life" (p. 103).

We can briefly summarize this period of dream history as a time when dreams were viewed as a provocative intellectual puzzle. They represented a state somehow related to our waking life, for which some generally rational and comprehensible explanation could be found if we looked closely enough at the dream itself. The focus was on explanation of the dream, not on understanding of the dream itself. As Freud put it, "As we have seen the scientific theories of dreams leave no room for any problem of interpreting them, since in their view a dream is not a mental act at all, but a somatic process signalizing its occurrence by indication registered in the mental apparatus . . . " (p. 128).

THE FREUDIAN STREAM

This epoch clearly dates from the publication of Freud's *The Interpretation of Dreams.* Published November 7, 1899, it was dated 1900. Freud indicates in his *History of the Psychoanalytic Movement* that his treatise on dreams was written in its essentials as early as 1896, but was not actually written down until 1899. His first published reference to dreams was in a footnote in Breuer and Freud's *Studies of Hysteria* in 1895, and his analysis of his own dream of Irma occurred in 1895. This crucial dream forms the second chapter of *The Interpretation of Dreams.*

The specific concepts underlying Freud's approach to dreams are written about in later chapters of this book. It should be noted, however, that Freud clearly considered that he was making a distinct break from the past.

In his second chapter he states, " . . . My presumption that dreams can be interpreted at once puts me in opposition to the ruling theory of dreams . . . (although) the philosophers and the psychiatrists rule out the problem of dream-interpretation as purely a fanciful task" (pp. 130–132). To the contrary, said

Freud, "I must affirm that dreams really have a meaning and that a scientific procedure for interpreting them is possible" (p. 132).

The initial response to his work was surely disappointing. Only 351 copies of *The Interpretation of Dreams* were sold in the first six years after publication. This is noted in the preface to his second edition, published in 1909:

> If within ten years of the publication of this book (which is very far from being an easy one to read) a second edition is called for, this is not due to the interest taken in it by the professional circles to whom my original preface was addressed. My psychiatric colleagues seem to have taken no trouble to overcome the initial bewilderment created by my new approach to dreams. The professional philosophers have become accustomed to polishing off the problems of dream-life (which they treat as a mere appendix to conscious states) in a few sentences . . . and usually in the same ones; and they have evidently failed to notice that we have something here from which a number of inferences can be drawn that are bound to transform our psychological theories. . . . (p. XXV)

A similar note is struck in his postscript to his initial chapter, which reviews the dream literature:

> The intervening nine years have produced nothing new or valuable either in factual material or in opinions that might throw light on the subject. In the majority of publications that have appeared during the interval my work has remained unmentioned and unconsidered. It has, of course, received least attention from those who are engaged in what is described as "research" into dreams, and who have thus provided a shining example of the repugnance to learning anything new which is characteristic of men of science. In the ironical words of Anatole France, "les savants ne sont pas curieux." If there were such a thing in science as a right to retaliate, I should certainly be justified in my turn in disregarding the literature that has been issued since the publication of this book. The few notices of it that have appeared in scientific periodicals show so much lack of understanding and so much misunderstanding that my only reply to the critics would be to suggest their reading the book again—or perhaps, indeed, merely to suggest their reading it. (p. 125)

However, by the fourth edition (1914), Freud was more optimistic. In referring to the previously noted postscript, he wrote:

> The preceding plea of justification was written in 1909. I am bound to admit that since then the situation has changed; my contribution to the interpretation of dreams is no longer neglected by writers on the subject. The new state of affairs, however, has now made it quite out of the question for me to extend my previous account of the literature. . . . (p. 127)

There are other interesting responses by Freud. In the second paragraph of the postscript to the 1909 edition, Freud wrote: "A large number of dreams have been published and analyzed in accordance with my directions in papers by physicians who have decided to adopt the psychoanalytic therapeutic procedure, as well as by other authors (Jung, Abraham, Riklin, Muthmann and Stekel). But these publications have merely confirmed my views and not added anything to them" (p. 125). This second sentence was modified in the 1911 edition to read: "In so far as these writings have gone beyond a mere confirmation of my views I have included these findings in the course of my exposition" (p. 125).

By the 1914 edition the names had been omitted. However, there are five references to Jung in the 1914 edition. Stekel is also cited seven times. In one citation, referring to Stekel's interpretation of symbols, Freud is impelled to write, "this author's lack of a critical faculty and his tendency to generalization at all costs throw doubts upon his other interpretations or render them unusable; so that it is highly advisable to exercise caution in accepting his conclusions . . ." (p. 393).

To me a most remarkable expression of Freud's thoughts about dreams is found in his *New Introductory Lectures on Psychoanalysis* (1933/1965):

It is therefore of special interest to us, in the particular instance of the theory of dreams . . . to learn what advances it has made in being understood and appreciated by the contemporary world. I may tell you at once that you will be disappointed in both these directions. Let us look through the volumes of the *Internationale Zeitschrift für (arztliche) Psychoanalyse*, in which, since 1913, the authoritative writings in our field of work have been brought together. In the earlier volumes you will find a recurrent sectional heading "On Dream-Interpretation," containing numerous contributions on various points in the theory of dreams. But the further you go the rarer do these contributions become, and finally the sectional heading disappears completely. The analysts behave as though they had no more to say about dreams, as though there was nothing more to be added to the theory of dreams. But if you ask how much of dream interpretation has been accepted by outsiders—by the many psychiatrists and psychotherapists who warm their pot of soup at our fire (incidentally without being very grateful for our hospitality), by what are described as educated people, who are in the habit of assimilating the more striking findings of science, by the literary men and by the public at large— the reply gives little cause for satisfaction. A few formulas have become generally familiar, among them some that we have never put forward—such as the thesis that all dreams are of a sexual nature—but really important things like the fundamental distinction between the manifest content of dreams and the latent dream-thoughts, the realization that the wish-fulfilling function of dreams is not contradicted by anxiety-dreams, the impossibility of interpreting a dream unless one has the dreamer's associations to it at one's disposal, and, above all, the discovery that what is essential in dreams is the process of the dream-work—all this still seems about as foreign to general awareness as it was thirty years ago. (pp. 7–8)

Later, as he concludes his "lecture" he says: "I could have told you all this fifteen years ago, and indeed I believe I did in fact tell it to you then. And now let me bring together such changes and new discoveries as may have been made during the interval. I have said already that I am afraid you will find that it amounts to very little, and you will fail to understand why I obliged you to listen to the same thing twice over" (p. 22).

Years do little to modify the perception of the pure Freudian stream. In the 1951 *Annual Survey of Psychoanalysis*, the editor, J. Frosch, noted that Dream Studies was not a section in the preceding *Annual Review* (which had replaced the *Yearbook of Psychoanalysis*). He states: "It is astonishing . . . to notice the gaps in the recent literature relative to the important contribution to theory and practice of psychoanalysis. The early contributions were devoted to reports of dream phenomena and to confirmation and elaboration of Freud's observations. The elaborations were essentially in clinical observation, not in basic theory."

But these are surface statements and not history. As Hadfield (1954) points out, "It is hardly to be expected that Freud, even with his monumental discoveries regarding dreams, should be able to comprehend the whole truth at once. . . . " He goes on to say, "Freud . . . himself considerably modified his earlier views, but . . . they are largely an adoption of views in the meantime already anticipated by Adler and Jung as against Freud's views . . . one could wish that he had made some acknowledgement of his indebtedness to these authors, for he could not have been unaware of their view . . . " (p. 31).

One may add to Hadfield's listing of Adler and Jung as modifiers of Freud's views, another close and early follower of Freud—Stekel—with a sidelight on Stekel's publication of a position on dreams in 1911 as described in Ernest Jones' *The Life and Works of Sigmund Freud* (1955).

In the spring of 1911 he (Stekel) published a large book on dreams. It contained many good and bright ideas, but also many confused ones. Freud found it "mortifying for us in spite of the new contribution it makes." Ferenczi stigmatized it as "shameful and dishonest." When he proposed that Putnam be asked to review it Freud told him he must do it himself. "We ask so much of Putnam that we cannot possibly expect him to deal with our own dirty linen. . . . " (p. 155)

Later chapters of this book detail the variations that post-Freudian times have brought. A succinct and comparative exposition of the main variation to Freud's interpretive approach is to be found in R. M. Jones' book *The New Psychology of Dreaming* (1970). He reviews the positions of Jung, Adler, Silberer, Lowy, Hall, French, Ullman, Erickson and Boss. Jones points to the writings of Maeder Stekel, Horney, Sullivan, Fromm, Binswanger, and Bonime and commends their work for "many noteworthy and distinctive interpretational nuances." He suggests that, in his opinion, however, no significant or distinctive lead has been lost, since "French has incorporated Maeder; Lowy has included Stekel; Ullman has improved on Horney and Sullivan; Hall has incorporated Fromm; Boss has covered Binswanger; and Bonime has brought to a high clinical polish the roughly presented suppositions of Lowy" (p. 109).

A recent chapter in dream content interpretation has been the publication and wide public acceptance of a book by Ann Faraday, a British psychologist: *Dream Power* (1972). Published in 1972, it had sold over 500,000 copies by 1973. Having done experimental work in the context of the "new biology of dreaming" and having been dissatisfied with the treatment of her own dreams within a Freudian-oriented psychoanalysis, she took the contributions of Jung, Hall, and Frederick Perls and wove them into a self-interpretive procedure.

Finally, note should be taken of the Winget and Kramer review of the tangled but critical efforts of coding—in contrast to decoding—dreams (in press). This is a review of the variety of systems that have been developed to classify or categorize dream content so that they may be compared across groups or conditions. More than 150 dream rating scales developed over a 25-year span are described. For example, dreams have been rated on such dimensions as "distortion," "fantasy," or "imagination; "aggression" or "hostility"; "sexuality" or "gentality"; "activity" or "participation." A widely used system dealing with dream content is a primarily descriptive system developed by Hall and Van de Castle (1966).

THE NEW BIOLOGY OF DREAMING

This period refers to the discovery and exploration of the interrelations between the physiological state of dreaming and the conscious content associated with that state.

The inauguration of this era can be publicly dated from the publication of Aserinsky and Kleitman (1953). The specific interconnection between the states was noted as follows:

> To confirm the conjecture that this particular eye activity was associated with dreaming, 10 sleeping individuals in 14 experiments were awakened and interrogated during the occurrence of this eye motility and also after a period of at least 30 min. to 3 hr. of ocular quiescence. The period of ocular inactivity was selected on the basis of the EEG pattern to represent, as closely as possible, a depth of sleep comparable to that present during ocular motility. Of 27 interrogations during ocular motility, 20 revealed detailed dreams usually involving visual imagery; the replies to the remaining 7 queries included complete failure of recall, or else, "the feeling of having dreamed," but with inability to recollect any detail of the dream. Of 23 interrogations

during ocular inactivity, 19 disclosed complete failure of recall, while the remaining 4 were evenly divided into the other 2 categories.

That these eye movements, EEG pattern, and autonomic nervous system activity are significantly related and do not occur randomly suggests that these physiological phenomena, and probably dreaming, are very likely all manifestations of a particular level of cortical activity which is encountered normally during sleep. An eye movement period first appears about 3 hours after going to sleep, recurs 2 hours later, and then emerges at somewhat close intervals a third or fourth time shortly prior to awakening. This method furnishes the means of determining the incidence and duration of periods of dreaming. (p. 274)

This paper formed the groundwork of the now familiar activated EEG pattern (Stage 1) and rapid eye movements (REM) associated with dreaming. This report had been preceded by associated events which are well reviewed by Snyder (1967). There had been the necessary developments in recordings and analyses of the electroencephalographic characteristics of sleeping subjects (Webb, 1973). A passing observation on the relationship between eye movements and dreams had been noted as early as 1892 (Ladd). In 1935, Max explored the relationship between the muscle action changes in the fingers and forearms of deaf and mutes (Max, 1935). In particular, there had been specific preliminary studies of eye movements in infant sleep by Aserinsky and Kleitman (1955), which were critical predecessors of the discovery of the interrelations between dreams and the physiological state of REM and Stage 1 sleep. Snyder notes that an MA thesis specifically directed toward a study of the EEG and dreaming was written in 1943 (Teplitz, 1943).

The early response also has been reviewed by Snyder (1967). A more extended report of the 1953 paper of Aserinsky and Kleitman appeared in 1955 (Aserinsky and Kleitman). The first "application" of the Stage 1–REM procedure to schizophrenia by Dement (1955) appeared in the same year. In 1957, Dement and Kleitman (1957) essentially formalized the relationship between Stage 1–REM and dreams in their paper, "The Relationship of Eye Movements During Sleep To Dream Activity: An Objective Method For The Study of Dreaming."

The book *Experimental Studies of Dreaming* was published in 1966 (Witkin and Lewis). The yearly number of studies cited in this book from 1957 through 1965 may be seen in Table 1-1.

In perspective, it was this seed of the linkage of the dream to the physiological state of Stage 1–REM that blossomed into the current burgeoning field of sleep research. It fell on rich soil. Kleitman's revision of his *Old Testament of Sleep Research* (1939) was almost complete, and appeared in 1963 (Kleitman). Central nervous system neurophysiology in general was accelerating, and the early

TABLE 1-1.

Year	Number of Publications
1957	5
1958	5
1959	9
1960	15
1961	18
1962	33
1963	43
1964	45
1965	64

work of Ranson, Hess, and Nauta on sleep mechanisms and, in particular, the work of Magoun and Moruzzi which related the reticular activating system to wakefulness in 1949 had prepared the way for the search for central mechanisms. The establishment of the dream analogue of a Stage 1-REM state in the cat by Dement (1958) bound these streams of research. Most critically the seed fell midst ample federal funding of research in the post-Sputnik era.

Again, as seen in Snyder's review (1967), the quest of dreaming in contemporary research was not only an accelerating but a protean process. The sprawling directions can be seen from the subheadings of Snyder's article: Early Confirmations, The Relationship of REM to Dreaming (19 studies involving 2464 REM period awakening), The Nature of Reported REM and NREM Mentation, Facts Affecting Dream Recall and Studies Relating to the Dream Process. This later group of studies are particularly descriptive of the extensions of activity beyond the dream itself: Dreaming as a Psychophysical State, The Effects of "Dream Deprivation," Extending the Physiological Definition, REMs in Other Species, Ontogenic Studies, Factors Affecting REM Occurrences, Neurophysiology of REMs.

It is appropriate to note that in the late 1960s and early 1970s the thrust of research on dreams had reverted, with a slight variation, to Freud's description of the pre-Freudian approach to dreams quoted earlier: " . . . their view of the dream is not a mental act at all, but a somatic process signalizing its occurrence by indications registered in the mental apparatus. . . . " The variation, of course, was that the signal had become Stage 1-REM and the dream an associated verbal report.

The extent to which the focus on REM research had become the dominant theme in sleep research is exemplified by a study of research strategies as revealed in "Sleep" research (Lemaine et al., 1975). Entitled *Strategies et choix dans la recherche: A propos des travaux sur le sommeil*, the study focuses exclusively on the research within and between the REM state and the cognitive associates of that state.

THE DREAM OF TODAY

We in our time and in this book focus on this time. Historical perspectives of recent and continuing times offer the advantages of accessibility, contemporary personages, and one's own experiences. But, accessibility can be overwhelming; persons are highly subjective; elements and experiences bring biases. It is necessary, however, to summarize one's conceptions.

Clearly the joining of the dream as a cognitive state with the physiological state within sleep (1-REM) was a powerful catalyst. The neurophysiological and physiological research focused sharply around the state; the dream report was brought into the laboratory; the function of the dream was pursued by deprivation studies; relations to sleep disorders and other pathological states were explored. REM was indexed across species and age ranges; the effects of drugs and relation to biochemistry and endocrines were probed. For more than a decade the nature and correlates of REM sleep dominated the general area of sleep research. Impressionistically at least, the broad phenomena of sleep and dreams per se were relegated to secondary considerations in the excitement of the new biology of dreams.

This is not to say sleep as so described has not substantially benefited by this era. Sleep had always been, as stated elsewhere (Webb, 1975), " . . . an orphan of uncertain parentage living within a larger family of powerful aunts and uncles who, occasionally, gave sustenance and attention to the waif." Certainly the mere presence of the outpouring of experimental work and the concomitant excitement associated with a sleep state attracted and stimulated workers whose interest were in areas of sleep that extended beyond the REM-based efforts. As we have incorporated and explicated this state within sleep, we have extended our knowledge of sleep. The extent to which this era has enlightened us about dreams, you will examine in this book before you.

FOOTNOTES

[1] The most extensive resource for these areas is *The Dream In Human Societies* (Von Grunebaum and Callois, 1966).

[2] Further references to *The Interpretation of Dreams* and page numbers therein will refer to this reference source.

REFERENCES

Aristotle, *Parva Naturalia* (Ross, W. D., Ed., Beare, J., Trans.). Oxford: Clarendon, 1933.
Artemidori Daldiani. *Oneiocriticia* (Rigaltins, Ed.). 1603 [English trans. (abridged) *The Interpretation of Dreams*. London: R. Wood, 1644].
Aserinsky, E., and Kleitman, N. Regularly occurring periods of eye motility, and concomitant phenomena, during sleep. *Science*, **118**: 273–274, 1953.

Aserinsky, E., and Kleitman, N. A motility cycle in sleeping infants as manifested by ocular and gross bodily activity. *J. Appl. Physiol.*, **8**: 11–18, 1955 (a).

Aserinsky, E., and Kleitman, N. Two types of ocular motility occurring in sleep. *J. App. Physiol.*, **8**: 1–10, 1955 (b).

Bonuzzi, L. About origins of the scientific study of sleep and dreaming. In Lairy, G., and Salzarulo, P. (Eds.), *The Experimental Study of Human Sleep: Methodological Problems.* New York: Elsevier Press, 1975.

Breuer, J., and Freud, S. Studies in hysteria. *Nerv. Ment. Dis. Monog. Ser.*, **61**, 4th ed., 1950, p. 241.

Burdach, K. F. *Die Physiologie als Erfahrungswissenschaft*, Vol. 3 of 2nd ed., 1832–40 (1st ed. 1826–32).

Calkins, M. W. Statistics of dreams. *Amer. J. Psychol.*, **5**: 311, 1893.

Delboeuf, I. *Le sommeil et les rêves*, Paris, 1885.

Dement, W. C. Dream recall and eye movements during sleep in schizophrenics and normals. *J. Nervous and Mental Disorders*, **122**: 263–269.

Dement, W. C. The occurrence of low voltage, fast electroencephalogram patterns during behavioral sleep in the cat. *EEG Clin. Neurophysiol.*, **10**: 291–295, 1958.

Dement, W. C., and Kleitman, N. The relation of eye movements during sleep to dream activity: An objective method for the study of dreaming. *J. Exp. Psychol.*, **53**: 339–346, 1957.

Faraday, A. *Dream Power*. New York: Berkley Medallion Books, 1972.

Fechner, G. T. *Elemente der Psychophysik.* Leipzig, 1860.

Fichte, I. H. *Psychologie: Die Lehre vom bewussten Geiste des Menschen* (2 vols.) Leipzig, 1864.

Freud, S. *The History of the Psychoanalytic Movement* (J. Strachey, Ed. and Trans.). *The Complete Psychological Works of Sigmund Freud.* London: Hogarth Press and The Institute of Psychoanalysis, 1964 (originally published in 1914).

Freud, S. *The Interpretation of Dreams* (J. Strachey, Ed. and Trans.). New York: Avon, 1965 (originally published 1900, 1909, 1911, 1914, 1919, 1921, 1922).

Freud, S. *New Introductory Lectures on Psychoanalysis* (J. Strachey, Ed. and Trans.). New York: Norton, 1965 (originally published 1933).

Frosch, J. *The Annual Survey of Psychoanalysis.* New York: International Press, 1951, p. 231.

Hadfield, J. *Dreams and Nightmares.* Baltimore: Penguin, 1954.

Hall, C., and Van de Castle, R. *The Content Analysis of Dreams.* New York: Appleton-Century-Crofts, 1966.

Hilderbrandt, F. W. *Der Traum und seine Verwertung für's Leben.* Leipzig, 1875.

Jones, E. *The Life and Works of Sigmund Freud* (Vol. 2). New York: Basic Books, 1955.

Jones, R. M. *The New Psychology of Dreaming.* New York: Grune & Stratton, 1970.

Kleitman, N. *Sleep and Wakefulness.* Chicago: University of Chicago Press, 1939, 2nd ed., 1963.

Ladd, G. T. Contribution to the psychology of visual dreams. *Mind*, **1**: 299–304, 1892.

Lemaine, G., Clemencon, M., Gomis, A., Pollin, B., and Salvo, B. *Strategies et choix dans la recherche: A propos des travaux sur le sommeil.* Paris: Groupe d'Etudes et de Recherche sur la Science, 1975.

Maury, L. F. A. Nouvelles observations sur les analogies des phénomènes du rêve et de l'aliénation mentale, Pt. II. *Ann. méd-psychol.*, **5**: 404, 1853.

Max, L. W. An experimental study of the motor theory of consciousness: III. Action-current responses in deaf-mutes during sleep, sensory stimulation and dreams. *J. Comp. Psychol.*, **19**: 469–486, 1935.

Meir, C. A. The dream in ancient Greece and its use in temple cures (Incubation). In Von Grunebaum, G. E., and Callois, R. (Eds.), *The Dreams and Human Societies.* Berkley: University of California Press, 1966.

Oppenheim, A. L. Mantic dreams in the Near East. In Von Grunebaum, G. E., and Callois, R. (Eds.), *The Dreams and Human Societies.* Berkley: University of California Press, 1966.

Radestock, P. *Schlaf und Traum.* Leipzig, 1879.

Snyder, F. In quest of dreaming. In Witkin, H. A., and Lewis, H. B. (Eds.), *Experimental Studies of Dreaming.* New York: Random House, 1967.

Spitta, H. *Die Schlaf und Traumzustände der menschlichen Seele.* Tübingen, 1882 (1st ed. 1878).

Strumpell, L. *Die Natur und Enstehung der Traüme.* Leipzig, 1877.

Teplitz, Z. An electroencephalographic study of dreams and sleep. Unpublished master's thesis, University of Illinois, Chicago, 1943.

Volkelt, J. *Die Traum-Phantasie.* Stuttgart, 1875.

Von Grunebaum, G. E., and Callois, R. *The Dreams and Human Societies.* Berkley: University of California Press, 1966.

Webb, W. B. *Sleep: An Active Process.* Glenn View: Scott Foresman, 1973.

Webb, W. B. *Sleep: The Gentle Tyrant.* Englewood Cliffs: Prentice-Hall, Inc., 1975.

Weygandt, W. *Entstehung der Traüme.* Leipzig, 1893.

Winget, C., and Kramer, M. *Dimensions of Dreams.* Gainesville: University of Florida Press, in press.

Witkin, H. A. and Lewis, H. B. *Experimental Studies of Dreaming.* New York: Random House, 1967.

Wundt, W. *Grundzüge der physiologischen Psychologie.* Leipzig, 1874.

2

Current Dream Research: A Psychobiological Perspective

Harry Fiss

> Sleep is a state in which a great part of every life is passed . . . . Yet of this
> change, so frequent, so great, so general, and so necessary, no searcher has yet
> found either the efficient or final cause; or can tell by what power the mind
> and body are thus chained down in irresistible stupefaction; or what benefits
> the animal receives from this alternate suspension of its active powers . . . .
> And, once in four-and-twenty hours, the gay and the gloomy, the witty and
> the dull, the clamorous and the silent, the busy and the idle, are all over-
> powered by the gentle tyrant, and all lie down in the equality of sleep.

Thus wrote Samuel Johnson more than 200 years ago (Webb, 1975, p. 156). It
would be difficult to find a more eloquent description of the obligatory quality
of sleep. Nor could the ubiquity of sleep have been a secret at that time either:
not only humans require it, but all mammals, birds and reptiles do too. But
these are not the only reasons why one should seek to gain a better understanding of the nature of sleep. As we now know, the brain mechanisms which regulate sleep consist of such a complex network of neuroanatomical structures that
it even boggles the mind of twentieth century man. If this network didn't have
important functions, how could it possibly have survived evolution? The study
of sleep is important also because it provides the neurophysiological and neurochemical background for the experience of dreaming, which, since Freud, has
become the cornerstone of psychoanalysis—the profound influence of which on
contemporary civilization hardly needs to be pointed out. Understanding sleep
and dreaming also has major clinical applications. Just as troubled minds produce troubled sleep, so does troubled sleep produce troubled minds. Knowledge

of sleep and dreaming is thus essential for the effective treatment of sleep disorders and psychopathology. Sleep and dreaming play a critical role in somatic illness too: many medical conditions, such as cardiovascular disease, are known to become exacerbated during sleep, and sleep disturbances, as we all know, frequently accompany pain and other symptoms of physical disorder (Kales and Kales, 1974). It is for these reasons that scientific investigators firmly believe that sleep research is an undertaking without which human functioning—behavior, development, health, and illness—could never be fully understood.

THE "IMPOSSIBLE" DREAM COMES TRUE:
A PRIVATE EXPERIENCE BECOMES A PUBLIC EVENT

Of all the aspects of sleep, dreams have intrigued mankind the most. From earliest times on, probably even before Jacob dreamed of a ladder reaching all the way up to Heaven, dreams have occupied a special, even hallowed place among life's phenomena. All kinds of magic powers have been ascribed to them: that they reveal the will of divine forces; that they foretell the future; that they are therapeutic; that they are a rich source for creative work; and so on. Yet, strangely, it took millennia for this mysterious realm of the human mind to become accessible to scientific investigation. The breakthrough occurred, quite unexpectedly, in the mid-1950s, with the discovery by Aserinsky and Kleitman (1953) and Dement and Kleitman (1957a, b) of regularly occurring rapid conjugate movements of the eyeballs (REMs) during sleep: when the sleeper was awakened during these rapid eye movement periods (REMPs), he would usually report that he had been dreaming. A phenomenon that had lain dormant (if you will pardon the pun) for aeons suddenly became real and measurable. For the first time in history it became possible to determine precisely and objectively when, how long, how frequently, and to a certain extent how and why a person dreams. This discovery ushered in a new era in research and literally opened up a new frontier for scientific exploration. Questions often asked but until then unanswerable suddenly became meaningful. Do dreams have any value, and if so, what is their function? What are they, and what are they like? Do they really occur? These are by no means simple questions. Dreaming, as we know now, is a highly complex biological and psychosocial process. To understand dreaming one must look at it from multiple vantage points, from the firing pattern and chemical composition of single nerve cells all the way to cross-cultural differences. The answers obviously aren't all in yet; but a major incursion into the unknown has undoubtedly been made.

What follows is an attempt to describe, in some detail, the explosive impact the discovery of REMs has had on our knowledge of sleep and particularly dreaming—knowledge that, in little more than two decades, has been advanced

by incalculable years—and to suggest a few directions for adding to this knowledge in the future.

SLEEP: THE OLD AND THE NEW VIEW

One thing the discovery of REMs accomplished was to revolutionize our concept
of the very nature of sleep. Before this momentous event, human existence had
been conceptualized as unidimensional, as a continuum ranging from very deep
sleep on one end to highly alert states, such as mania, on the other. Position on
this continuum was determined by the amount of stimulation the cerebral cortex was receiving from the ascending reticular activating system. In other words,
sleep and waking were believed to be regulated by a single, *unitary* brain mechanism: the reticular formation. When this wakefulness-producing mechanism
was dampened, the person drifted into sleep. Sleep was thus considered to be
an essentially *passive* process, analogous to removing one's foot from the ac-
celerator in order to bring a car to a stop.

   This view has completely gone by the boards and has given way to the principle that sleep, far from being unitary and passive, is *cyclical* and *active*. It is
cyclical because it consists not of one but of two organismic states (REM and
NONREM), which alternate with one another and differ from each other as
much as each differs from wakefulness. This suggests that one should speak of
"sleeps" rather than of sleep; and implies that dreaming, "rather than being an
occasional, unpredictable and ephemeral psychic anomaly . . . devoid of objective correlates . . . is the subjective aspect of an extremely substantial, predictable, universal, and basic biological function" (Snyder, 1966). Snyder
found the physiological characteristics of this phenomenon so distinctive that
he called it "a third state of existence."[1]   The full implications of this statement will soon become clearer. Regarding the active-passive dimension of
sleep, recent neuroanatomical, neurophysiological, and biochemical work (also
described below) has clearly shown that sleep is induced by a mechanism which
actively suppresses the state of wakefulness, very much in the manner of a person applying the brakes in order to stop a car. We don't drift asleep—we *fall*
asleep.

POLYSOMNOGRAPHY: A NEW TECHNOLOGY

The Sleep Laboratory

A dream may be a complex affair, but a sleep laboratory, paradoxically, really
is not. Basically all it requires is a sleeper, a bed to sleep on, a polygraph for
electrically recording sleep, a technician, and a miscellaneous assortment of
supplies and hardware. To prepare a subject for sleep-recording, electrodes are

attached to the subject's face and scalp, and wires leading from each electrode are plugged into a terminal box at the head of the bed, slightly above and behind the subject. From this box a cable runs to an adjacent room where a polygraph produces a write-out of the subject's brain waves, (electroencephalogram or EEG), eye movements (electro-oculogram or EOG), and muscle activity (electromyogram or EMG). Other parameters, such as respiration, blood pressure, pulse rate, and so on, are also frequently recorded; but the EEG, EOG, and EMG (the last usually recorded from the chin) are essential for accurate sleep stage measurement. To "capture" a dream, the subject is typically awakened during an REM period and instructed to report his dream into a microphone, which is connected to a tape recorder. The technique not only makes it possible to correlate electrophysiological activity directly with mental activity; it also vastly increases dream retrieval: subjects recall on the average three or four times as many dreams in the laboratory as they normally do, and their dreams are usually far more complete and detailed. Laboratory dreams are also more likely than home dreams to correspond to the actual dream experience itself, since the awakening takes place in close temporal proximity, allowing far fewer distortions and substantially less forgetting to occur. (On the other hand, there is also a common phenomenon called the "first night" effect, which makes dreams an artifact of the laboratory. Most sleep studies have to take this effect into account.)

The Five Sleep Stages

The EEG is so ideally suited for recording and measuring sleep that it has virtually become synonymous with sleep and sleep stage: it is continuous, unobtrusive, sensitive, stable, economical, and easy to use. The principal distinguishing EEG, EOG, and EMG characteristics of each sleep stage and the state of wakefulness are summarized below. Stages 1, 2, 3, and 4 are all NONREM. Stages 3 and 4 are also called slow wave sleep (SWS).

Stage W: Refers to drowsy waking state, just prior to sleep onset. EEG is characterized by "alpha" waves, which are regular in form, have a frequency of *8-12 cycles per second* (c.p.s.), and a fairly *low amplitude* or voltage (about 50 μv). EMG and REMs are both present.

Stage 1: Also called sleep onset stage. EEG is more irregular, has a somewhat lower frequency *(4-8 c.p.s.)*, but *amplitude* remains *low*, at 50 μv. EMG is present and so are eye movements, but these are slow (SEMs) and rolling.

Stage 2: Most characteristic of this stage are the "spindles"—brief bursts of fast (12-14 c.p.s.), low voltage waves, and "K-complexes," which are sharply rising and falling high amplitude waves. The spindles and K's are interspersed amidst an irregular, low frequency (3-4 c.p.s.), low amplitude pattern. EMG is present, but eye movements are absent.

Stage 3: Contains a moderate amount (20-50%) of very low frequency (*1-2 c.p.s.*), *high voltage* (75 μv) waves called "delta." Spindles and K-complexes continue to appear occasionally. EMG is present, but there are no eye movements.

Stage 4: Record is dominated by (contains more than 50%) *slow, high amplitude* delta waves. EMG is present, but eye movements are not.

Stage REM: Characterized by Stage 1 EEG, bursts of rapid conjugate eye movements (REMs), and EMG suppression.

A look at these sleep stages reveals that progression from Stage W to Stage 4 is characterized by a general *slowing of the frequency spectrum* and an overall *increase in wave amplitude.* This has often been taken to mean that a person progresses from "light" to "deep" sleep. Depth of sleep, however, depends entirely on the particular criterion used to define it. Thus, REM sleep can be called "light" in terms of EEG activation, but "deep" if the EMG is used as criterion. In fact, REM sleep is also called "paradoxical sleep" for this very reason. To avoid this kind of confusion, therefore, it is probably best to abandon the concept of sleep "depth" altogether, and instead to consider each sleep stage a unique configuration of physiological activity, probably serving different organismic functions.

The Sleep Cycle

As Figure 2-1 illustrates, the five sleep stages reviewed above are organized into cycles, i.e., they alternate with each other in rhythmic fashion. Thus in a typical night's sleep, a young adult would "descend" from NONREM Stage 1 to NONREM Stages 2, 3, and 4 and then "ascend" back up until "emerging" into REM. A complete cycle lasts on the average 90 minutes. This means that the first REMP of the night can be expected to occur roughly an hour and a half following sleep onset. Once completed, the cycle repeats itself approximately five times per night, with NONREM sleep, which takes up about 75% of the night, always *preceding* REM sleep,[2] which takes up about 25%. The cycles are not completely symmetrical, of course. Very often a stage may be skipped, or a

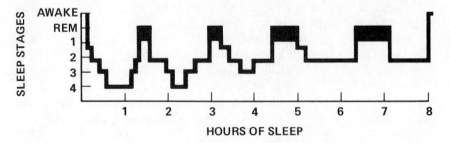

Figure 2-1. A typical night of sleep in a young adult.

person may wake up. Of special importance is the fact that delta or slow wave sleep tends to occur early in the night and gradually drops out, so that later at night the shifts occur mainly between REM and Stage 2. REM sleep, on the other hand, predominates during the later part of the night, the early REMPs generally being much shorter than the later ones. This is why it is usually the dreams from the later REMPs (particularly the last one) that we remember upon rising in the morning. The average length of an REMP is about 20 minutes.

The sleep cycle is not only a human phenomenon: it characterizes pretty much the entire mammalian species, including the opossum, which is so primitive it has been called a "living fossil" (Snyder, 1966).[3] Having survived millions of years of evolution, the sleep cycle is thus fairly stable. On the other hand, it is also sensitive to change. A mother who wakes up when her baby whimpers will sleep soundly through a roaring thunderstorm. Jet lag and shift work will alter the cycle radically; but if a new work schedule is maintained for a while, the cycle resumes its original shape. Only when stress is extreme or chronic, as in certain psychiatric or medical conditions, will changes in the sleep pattern persist. We then speak of insomnia. All conditions or situations that keep us awake a long time will affect our sleep: in general, the longer we are kept awake, the stronger our tendency to go to sleep and the longer our tendency to stay asleep. Individual differences also determine variations in sleep pattern. Some people called "short" sleepers simply seem to require less sleep than "long" sleepers; however, these differences do not seem to arise from personality traits (Webb, 1975, p. 68). Personality as a variable, however, does discriminate between "good" and "poor sleepers," the latter showing significantly higher pathology on the MMPI (Monroe, 1967).

A study by Fiss and Ellman (1973) clearly demonstrates that psychological factors can influence sleep patterns. For two consecutive nights, Ellman and I interrupted every REMP with an unpleasant task about 10 minutes after the onset of REM. The subjects however, were not REM-deprived, and no dream reports were elicited. The interruption nights were preceded by four to five baseline nights and followed by two recovery nights. During these nights subjects were not awakened. The results showed that all subjects continued to have significantly shorter than normal (approximately 10 minute) REMPs during their first recovery night. These shortened REMPs even occurred at a time of night when REMPs normally become much longer. However, by the second recovery night, the interruption effect had worn off and subjects again had a normal sleep cycle. The finding suggests that subjects can be *conditioned* to have significantly shorter than normal REMPs, and that therefore people can *learn* to modify their sleep cycle.

In summary, prolongation of wakefulness, changes in work routine and life style, stress, changes in the immediate sleep environment, and individual differences can all result in modifications of the sleep cycle. It is equally clear, however, that these modifications occur only under special or extreme conditions. We are therefore forced to conclude that Samuel Johnson, quoted above, was quite insightful when he dubbed sleep a "gentle tyrant." As Webb (1975, pp. 164-165) puts it, "being gentle, he permits us certain freedoms; being a tyrant, he will not permit us to live in total freedom . . . . Sleep . . . is remarkably *adaptive*, within limits . . . . When permitted and not pushed, it unfolds and proceeds to perform effectively . . . . When pushed by our real or presumed needs, it yields and bends, but remembers and reminds us of its nature."

There is one sleep determinant, however, to which sleep, no matter how gentle a tyrant, never yields, and that is aging. And although there is very little we can do about it, it does behoove us to know a little bit about what has been called the "ontogenesis" of sleep.

It probably does not come as a great surprise that the requirement for sleep diminishes throughout life. Children simply require more sleep than old folk, whose sleep pattern often resembles that of insomniacs. One may say that the intensity of the sleep process is greatest early in life and minimal in old age. What is more interesting, however, is that REM and NONREM sleep show distinctly different patterns of change with age. The newborn spends at least twice as much of his total sleep time (50%) in REM as the average adult. This high proportion of REM time decreases rapidly during the first year of life, stabilizing at approximately adult levels (20-25%) by age five. Then it more or less remains at a plateau level until old age, when it declines slightly (to 18% or less). In contrast to the steep decline of REM sleep during the early years of development, the quantity of NONREM sleep remains relatively constant throughout life until it too declines in old age. This pattern also holds up for most mammals: most young mammals, for instance, sleep more than the adult and have an especially high REM%. This and other considerations led Roffwarg et al. (1966) to theorize that REM sleep is an endogenous source of stimulation by providing large quantities of excitation to higher brain centers. Such stimulation is especially necessary in utero (when REM% has been found to be even higher than 50%) and during the early postnatal period, before sufficient exogenous stimulation becomes available to the central nervous system. Thus, according to Roffwarg et al., REM sleep facilitates the structural differentiation and maturation of the central nervous system, preparing the young organism to handle the enormous quantities of stimulation to which it is exposed during the early stages of its growth.

THE NEUROPHYSIOLOGY OF SLEEP AND DREAMING

REM vs NONREM Sleep

It can be said that the degree of physiological activation during REM sleep, no matter what the particular parameter may be, is substantially greater and resembles the waking state considerably more than the amount of physiological arousal associated with NONREM sleep. The most important differences are listed below. Note again how strikingly the absence of muscle tonus (EMG) during REM sleep contrasts with the enormous amount of central nervous system activation that is simultaneously present during this so aptly called "paradoxical" sleep state.

Respiration, heart rate or pulse, blood pressure: more elevated and irregular (varied) in REM than in NONREM.

Oxygen consumption, brain temperature, cortical blood flow: increased in REM, decreased in NONREM.

Penile erections, middle ear muscular activity, twitches of small muscles of face and limbs: all very much in evidence during REM, absent or rare during NONREM.

Tonic vs. Phasic Sleep Characteristics

Up to now we have emphasized differences between REM and NONREM sleep characteristics. We now come to a different class of neurophysiological events, one that cuts across the traditional classification of sleep into stages. I am referring to the "tonic" and "phasic" sleep events.

Tonic events are those electro- and neurophysiological components of sleep that are *continuously* maintained. They are the *long-lasting* characteristics of sleep. Examples of tonic activity are most of the EEG patterns defining the various sleep stages, EMG activation and suppression, and brain temperature changes. Phasic events, on the other hand, are *discontinuous, episodic flurries* of activity, such as the REMs themselves, small muscle twitches, cardiovascular and respiratory irregularities, and middle ear muscular activity. In short, tonic events are stable background characteristics upon which momentary bursts of physiological activity—phasic events—are intermittently superimposed.[4]

A phasic characteristic of sleep that has attracted particular attention in recent times is the PGO (pontine-geniculo-occipital) spike observed in the cat. PGO spikes are prominent bursts of sharp, monophasic, high amplitude waves recorded directly from the pons, the geniculate nuclei, and the occipital cortex. They have been found to be temporally related to nearly all phasic activity, precede all REMPs by about 10–30 seconds, and have their highest discharge rate during REM sleep, even though a scattering of PGOs (roughly 15%) also occurs during NONREM sleep.

Why all the fuss about PGOs? For one thing, there are some indications that they may reflect the activity of a more central regulatory mechanism than the one presumably producing tonic events. This is suggested by the finding that depriving cats of PGOs leads to substantially larger REM "rebounds" (compensatory increases in REM time) than does depriving cats of REM sleep alone

(Ferguson et al., 1968). Since a "rebound" effect expresses a biological need for whatever it is that has been eliminated, it is possible to conclude from this finding that phasic activity is biologically more vital than the REM sleep stage. A second reason why sleep researchers have been getting excited about PGOs is that they have produced evidence suggesting that phasic events may be more specifically related to the experience of dreaming than the REMPs themselves. This inference is based on experiments by Rechtschaffen et al. (1972) and Watson (1972) which show that PIPs (periorbital phasic integrated potentials) in human subjects tend to be associated with dreamlike mentation regardless of whether they are accompanied by REMs or not. While the validity of the claim that PIPs (which are derived from muscle activity of the human eye) are human PGO-equivalents has by no means been established, the finding seems consistent with the fact that some dreaming does occur in NONREM sleep.

A third reason for the recent interest in pontine spiking activity is that this activity has rekindled our hope of coming a step closer to solving the riddle of mental illness, in particular schizophrenia. Thus, we may at last have arrived at the interface between two major disciplines: schizophrenia research and sleep research. Two studies lend credence to this optimistic feeling. One of these, by Watson et al. (1976) shows a close positive relationship between severity of schizophrenic symptomatology and frequency of *NONREM*-PIPs. In the other study, reported by Dement (1969, p. 256), the occurrence of PGO spikes in the *waking* cat was found to be accompanied by behavior strikingly reminiscent of human psychotic behavior: the animals seemed to be continuously preoccupied with internal stimulation and acted as if responding to hallucinations. How have the advocates of the PGO spike pieced this jigsaw puzzle together? In the "normal" person, they contend, phasic discharges are pretty well confined to REM sleep. The psychological correlate of these discharges is the experience of dreaming. In psychosis, owing to some defective "safety-valve" mechanism, these discharges "spill over" into other sleep stages and also into the waking state, where presumably they give rise to hallucinations, delusions, and other psychotic manifestations. Since, moreover, the phasic activity has "leaked out" of the REM state and with it its accumulated discharge potential, there is no further need for REM, and REM deprivation is ineffective—no rebound occurs. The obvious implications of all this for some kind of reciprocal relationship between dreaming and mental illness are hard to ignore. We shall come back to this point later.

A further implication of the above considerations is that they point to a biochemical basis of schizophrenia. The defective "safety-valve" which may be responsible for the "leakage" of phasic discharges into wakefulness may be serotonergic, especially since serotonin is known to regulate phasic events.

These of course are but fascinating speculations. However, the work on phasic activity that I have briefly described represents one of the furthest outposts in sleep and dream exploration, as well as a major new refinement in our current conception of sleep and dream physiology. No presentation should be considered complete without containing at least some reference to it.

THE BIOCHEMISTRY OF SLEEP AND DREAMING

Just as our notion that sleep is merely the absence of wakefulness has yielded to the concept that sleep is a biological activity in its own right, so has the idea that the brain is an electric switchboard given way to the recognition that the brain is a chemical plant. Few would question today that the primary sleep-regulating brain mechanisms are biochemical in nature, and that they involve the biogenic amines, in particular *serotonin* (5-hydroxytryptamine or 5-HT) and the catecholamine *noradrenaline* (also known as norepinephrine). Both are hypnogenic neurotransmitter substances which are found in heavy concentrations in various parts of the brain stem. It is widely believed today that these two chemical substances play an essential—though by no means exclusive—role in the regulation of sleep. Their action, however, is highly complex and as yet not fully understood. Nevertheless, because of new advanced techniques, such as histofluorescent microscopy and tracer labeling, we know a great deal more about them today than we did a decade ago, and will undoubtedly continue to make inroads into this area at an ever accelerating pace.

A number of different viewpoints are held today, many of them conflicting, concerning the manner in which the bioamines control sleep and interact with each other and other biochemical systems. One of them is the *monoamine theory of sleep-waking behavior*. It is largely the product of Jouvet and his colleagues at Lyon, and it is with their experimental work that we will primarily concern ourselves here (Jouvet, 1969, 1972, 1973, 1974). This is not to say that their work should be accepted as gospel truth. No theory should, and this one undoubtedly too will still have to undergo many revisions.[5]

The theory states quite simply that serotonin-containing nuclei and pathways play a dominant role in regulating NONREM sleep, while noradrenergic systems are principally involved in the control of REM sleep.

Serotonin and NONREM Sleep

The brain center that controls NONREM sleep is said to be a collection of nerve cells in the brain stem known as the *raphé* nuclei. These cells contain heavy concentrations of serotonin, which acts as a brake on the reticular activating system. Neurophysiologically speaking, this means that in inducing sleep, serotonin blocks eye movements and fast cortical activity (EEG) but does *not* block muscle tonus. This concept is based on evidence that includes the following results, all based on animal work, of course: (1) Surgical lesion (i.e., destruction) of the raphé nuclei induces total insomnia. (2) Complete insomnia is also brought about by intravenously injecting the animal with a chemical substance that inhibits serotonin synthesis (PCPA or parachlorophenylalanine). (3) This PCPA-induced effect is reversed, i.e., sleep is induced, when the animal is injected with a serotonin precursor: 5-HTP (hydroxytryptophan).

Noradrenalin and REM Sleep[6]

The part of the brain that presumably regulates REM sleep is also located in the brain stem but consists of a set of nerve cells known as the nuclei of the *locus coeruleus.* These cells contain noradrenalin, which, when released, supplants the action of the serotonergic mechanism and reestablishes effects that resemble normal wakefulness: it unblocks, i.e., restores, eye movements and fast cortical activity; at the same time, however, it also acts as an inhibitory mechanism on the body's motor system—it *blocks* muscle tonus. Evidence in support of this conception consists of the following: (1) Lesions of the neurons in the locus coeruleus abolish REM sleep and lead to hyperactive behavior which very much looks as if the animal were acting out a dream or responding to hallucinations. For example, the animal will suddenly and without apparent reason attack some imagined enemy. (2) REM suppression is also brought about by injecting the animal with AMPT (alpha-methylparatyrosine), a substance that inhibits noradrenalin synthesis. (3) This AMPT-induced effect is reversed, i.e., REM sleep is reestablished, when the animal is injected with dopa, a noradrenalin precursor.

Interrelationships between Serotonergic and Noradrenergic Systems

The dualistic character of the monoamine theory makes it look deceptively simple. Actually, the theory is extremely complicated and requires an extensive background in neuropharmacology and neurochemistry to be fully appreciated. Therefore, to give a complete account of it would be far beyond my ability and the scope of this chapter. However, I will touch upon some of the major interrelationships that are believed to exist between the two biochemical systems, and also venture a foray or two into yet other systems (cholinergic, for example) which have been found to play an important role in sleep regulation. For a more detailed account of this complex issue, the reader is advised to turn to Morgane and Stern (1974, 1975), and Hobson et al. (1975).

The interrelationships between serotonin and adrenalin are believed to be both facilitative and inhibitory:

Facilitative Interrelationships.   Serotonin has not only an "executive" function, i.e., it does not only "trigger" NONREM sleep; it also has a "priming" function, i.e., it has a "priming" effect on *REM* sleep. This is suggested, for example, by the fact that a certain critical minimum amount of slow wave sleep (16%) seems to be necessary before REMs can appear. Morgane and Stern (1975) speculate that the priming mechanism is a growth hormone which is only released during SWS.

Inhibitory Interrelationships. The two systems—serotonin and noradrenalin—also act antagonistically in relation to each other. Since noradrenalin has an arousing effect, it is necessary for serotonergic neurons, in order to induce sleep, to exert an inhibitory action on noradrenergic neurons. This is probably why destruction of the raphé nuclei leads to insomnia. Conversely, noradrenalin, in order to trigger REM sleep, must inhibit the sleep-inducing action of serotonin. That is probably why any chemical that deactivates noradrenalin, such as AMPT, will induce hypersomnia.

The Role of Cholinergic Mechanisms in Regulating Sleep

One of the shortcomings for which the monoamine theory has been criticized is that it is simplistic, that it is naive to implicate only two biochemical systems in a process as complex as sleep. This seems to contradict my earlier statement that the theory is highly complex. Actually, there is no contradiction: the theory *is* complex, but it probably is not complex enough. To illustrate this point: cholinergic substances have also been located in the brain stem and found to interact with the monoamines in ways that are still largely unknown (Hobson et al., 1975). We know, for example, that acetylcholine injected into the brain stem will trigger both NONREM and REM sleep, whereas atropine, which is anticholinergic, suppresses sleep and leaves the animal behaviorally awake. Atropine also abolishes PGOs, while eserine, a cholinergic agent, reverses this effect and induces PGOs. Thus cholinergic mechanisms also play a key role in the phasic regulation of sleep.

Protein Synthesis and Sleep

To add further to the confusion, evidence is now beginning to accumulate which implicates neuroproteins in the regulation of sleep. Much of it comes from Russia. It has been reported there, for instance, that even brief REM deprivation markedly decreases protein levels in cerebral neurons (Demin and Rubinskaya, 1974) and that protein synthesis in the brain drops during SWS and rises during REM sleep (Kogan et al., 1975). More recently, Adam and Oswald (1977), both from Edinburgh University, have published evidence that protein synthesis is maximal during REM sleep, suggesting that REM sleep is closely linked to general body metabolism.

THE FUNCTIONS OF SLEEP:
BIOLOGICAL THEORIES OF WHY WE SLEEP AND DREAM

Sleep and dreaming—although by no means identical, as I shall take great pains to emphasize later—are nonetheless extremely closely interwoven, and much of what holds true for sleep holds true for dreaming. Furthermore, we know a great deal more about the biology than we do about the psychology of sleep and dreaming, a state of affairs which once prompted a well known sleep researcher to quip that we seem to have learned a great deal about the biology of dreaming without really knowing what dreaming is the biology of (Rechtschaffen, 1964). The point is well taken. But it does not mean that we should ignore the biology of sleep and dreaming. A good deal of it is necessary background information, especially for some of the material that will be presented later.

There are two ways of looking at causation. We can seek an explanation in terms of *how* a thing works, or we can try to find out *why* something happens. We can look at a process mechanistically, or we can approach it teleologically, i.e., by asking what function or purpose it serves. Whether we choose one or the other is purely volitional. Freud could not do without either; so he felt compelled to construct a meta-psychological superstructure on top of his clinical theory. Whether he needed to do this or not has been debated in psychoanalytic circles for years. The truth, as it so often does, probably lies somewhere in the middle; sometimes we need one type of explanation, at other times the other, and sometimes both. I suspect we need both for the subject under discussion here. I think we need to know both how we dream and why we dream. This is a question that has always guided my own research efforts. Let us first, however, address ourselves to the issue of why we sleep.

A few explanatory attempts of varying generality have already been mentioned (Roffwarg et al., 1966; Snyder, 1966; Ephron and Carrington, 1966). To this group one might also add Berger's (1969) rather circular formulation that REM sleep serves to innervate the oculomotor system, which is a little bit like saying we move our eyes in order to move our eyes. As our data base has steadily expanded, however, our theoretical formulations about sleep have likewise become increasingly comprehensive.

Sleep and dreams affect us all; they are deeply personal; and we all seem to require them. All of us have suffered at some point in our lives because of lack of sleep. Sleeplessness is one of the most prevalent physical complaints. Some 30 million Americans are afflicted with it to some degree. There is a certain face validity, therefore, to the widely held belief that sleep is something we cannot do without.

But what exactly does sleep do for us? Is it some form of restitution or restoration to make up for something "used up" during the day? Or is it a form of adaptation necessary for survival? Is it both? One way we can try to find out is by removing it and seeing what happens—hence, the popularity of sleep deprivation studies.

Effects of Total Sleep Deprivation: Experimental Insomnia

Although studies too numerous to mention have been performed on the effects of total sleep (TS) deprivation, the outcome has been disappointingly inconclusive. Webb, who has done an extensive review of the literature on TS deprivation (1971; 1975, pp. 119-127), has concluded quite seriously that "the effect of sleep deprivation is to make the subject fall asleep." To be sure, there are effects; but they are hardly breathtaking. In a study of his own, in which subjects were kept awake continuously for over 50 hours, the most frequent behavioral changes he reports were "transient inattentions, confusions, or misperceptions." No really "strange" or "crazy" behavior occurred. Hartmann (1973, p. 46), in a parallel review of the problem, comes to essentially the same conclusion. Even studies exceeding 100 hours of TS deprivation show an extremely low incidence of severely disturbed behavior. In a single reported case (Gulevich et al., 1966), even 264 hours of sleep deprivation failed to produce any unusually deviant response! This does not mean that aberrant behavior of psychotic proportions never occurs; but it does so extremely rarely. By and large, the subjects continue to function. They are simply "flattened" or "dulled" by the experimental procedure. Animal studies have on the whole confirmed this impression.

Effects of REM Deprivation

It is of course possible that the inconsequential results of TS deprivation are due to the fact that the TS deprivation procedure deprives subjects of two totally different states of sleep, and that the effects of one type of deprivation cancel out the effects of the other. The next logical step therefore is to look at the effects of *selective* sleep deprivation, i.e., of eliminating particular sleep stages. Let us first consider the effects of REM deprivation.

The classical REM deprivation experiment was performed by Dement (1960) and resulted in the "rebound" effect mentioned before: after about five consecutive nights of being awakened at the onset of every REMP, Dement's subjects showed a marked increase in REM time (as compared to their normal baseline durations) during a subsequent uninterrupted recovery night. A control group which was awakened an equivalent number of times during NONREM sleep gave no evidence of any compensatory increase in REM time. Dement also observed that his REM-deprived subjects attempted to engage in REM sleep a greater number of times as REM deprivation increased. These findings, which have since been replicated innumerable times, give clear evidence that there is a biological need for Stage 1 REM sleep. They also led Dement to the theory that REM sleep serves the function of clearing the central nervous system of toxic metabolic substances that accumulate during wakefulness. One can agree or disagree with this theory, but the "rebound" effect is a firmly established sleep phenomenon.

Not so dramatic were the psychological effects on waking behavior that Dement noted: anxiety, irritability, increased appetite, and difficulty in concentrating. True, these changes were merely anecdotally recorded; no psychometric tests were used. Subsequent studies, however, *did* employ precise measurements of REM deprivation effects on behavior (Sampson, 1966; Clemes and Dement, 1967; Agnew et al., 1967; Kales et al., 1964). Yet, *not a single one of them* came up with any striking results. Again there were indications of heightened drive and some cognitive impairment, but no gross personality disorganization resulted from the procedure.

Suppose one REM-deprived subjects for much longer periods of time: would the results differ? Fisher (1974) accomplished nearly total REM deprivation in three subjects for a total of six months (!) by administering Nardil. The result? Essentially negative: none of the subjects evidenced any marked impairment of ego-functioning. Vogel (1975) reports REM-depriving a depressed patient for 25 consecutive nights: she actually improved! This and other findings on depressives are consistent with an earlier report by Vogel et al. (1968) that REM deprivation, rather than being harmful, actually brings about marked clinical improvement in endogenously depressed patients. The same year, Vogel and Traub (1968) REM-deprived chronic schizophrenics and found no significant symptom aggravation. Small wonder then that Vogel concludes that "REM sleep deprivation does not produce psychological harm."

Is there *anything* that REM deprivation can teach us about the function of REM sleep? The answer is probably no as long as we keep looking for extreme and gross disturbances in personality functioning as the outcome. If, on the other hand, our studies are designed in ways meant to answer specific questions relating to specific functions, such as information processing, or mastery of stress, then our efforts are much more likely to be rewarded. A case in point is a study by Greenberg et al. (1972) in which subjects were shown the same stressful movie in the evening and again in the morning. Some of the subjects were REM-deprived, some were awakened an equal number of times during NONREM sleep, and some were permitted to sleep through the night between the viewings. The REM-deprived subjects responded with significantly more anxiety to the second viewing of the film than all the other subjects. The authors concluded from this that REM sleep aids adaptation to anxiety-provoking stimulation. In a related study (Grieser et al., 1972), subjects who were not REM-deprived had better waking recall of threatening verbal material than REM-deprived subjects. A similar result is reported by Cartwright et al. (1975a): again memory loss was significantly more pronounced after REM deprivation than after control awakenings, but only when the recall material was personally relevant. When the material to be recalled is neutral, i.e., not affectively charged, REM deprivation has generally not been found to interfere with retention (Feldman and Dement, 1968; Muzio et al., 1971; Ekstrand et al., 1971; Chernik, 1972; Allen, 1974). Thus there has been some though by no means consistent confirmation of the notion that REM sleep has adaptive value, specifically with respect to adaptation to stress and the consolidation of memory in humans.

Animal work along these lines, though plentiful, is more difficult to evaluate. In a review of REM sleep deprivation studies, Albert (1975) lists more than a dozen recent animal studies on the effects of REM deprivation on memory and learning. Of these, eight resulted in positive findings. However, even they seem to contain so many methodological flaws that one probably has to agree with the author that "it has not been clearly demonstrated that learning and memory in animals are reliably influenced by REM deprivation." It is very difficult therefore, at the present time, to draw any firm conclusions regarding the function of REM sleep on the basis of REM deprivation studies. The technique has yielded a great deal of suggestive but relatively unpersuasive information on this subject. All we can say with certainty at this point is that REM sleep must serve some vital function, since there is an obvious need for it. Other experimental approaches to this problem are clearly called for.

Studies of REM Sleep Function Not Involving Sleep Loss

By and large, studies using less invasive procedures than REM deprivation seem to have lent more convincing support to the adaptational hypothesis of REM sleep. With respect to the presumed information storage and information processing function of REM sleep, for instance, a number of investigators appear to have succeeded in demonstrating a remarkably consistent relationship across a wide range of conditions and subjects (human as well as animal) between REM amounts and the retention and learning of new or difficult tasks. Thus it has been shown that aphasic patients who are relearning their speech have higher proportions of REM sleep than patients who are not recovering their speech function (Greenberg and Dewan, 1969). A somewhat similar relationship between REM sleep and cognitive activity is suggested by the observation that severely retarded adults and children have lower-than-normal REM sleep proportions, delayed REM sleep onset, and fewer-than-normal eye movements, with those scoring lowest on IQ tests showing the least amount of REM activity (Feinberg, 1968; Feinberg et al., 1969; Castaldo, 1969). A study by Barker (1972) with normal subjects is a further case in point. Barker's subjects were college students who were given a visual memory test immediately before and after a brief sleep period. Those who had spent the time interval in REM did far better on the retest than those who had been in NONREM during the intervening sleep period. It has also been reported (Zimmerman et al., 1970) that complex, novel, or stressful input, requiring substantial organismic readjustment, increases the proportion of time spent in REM sleep. The adaptive task in this particular study consisted of wearing prismatic glasses that reversed the visual field.[7] During the initial period of adjustment, which is the most difficult, REM was noted to increase. Once the subjects got used to the glasses, and the surroundings started to look normal again, REM time dropped back to normal. Unfortunately, a subsequent attempt to replicate this study failed (Allen et al., 1972). However, a different stressful situation, in which subjects were given difficult and frustrating tasks to perform (Lewin and Gombosh, 1972), did significantly elevate REM time; and Greenberg et al. (1972) report a significant relationship between traumatic experiences and increased proportions of REM sleep.

These findings suggest that REM sleep does have a role to play in the consolidation of such ego functions as learning, coping, memory, and problem solving. But, as Cartwright (1974b) points out, this role is probably more significant when the material that has to be remembered or learned is emotionally or personally meaningful. To prove her point, she gave a group of students three types of problems, ranging from neutral to emotional (crossword puzzles, word-associations, and story-completions), under two experimental conditions: one condition had a waking interval, the other a REM sleep interval between the time the subjects began working on a problem and the time they finished it. The results confirmed two of Cartwright's hypotheses: (1) the more emotional the material, the more REM sleep influenced the subjects' performance on it; and (2) only REM sleep altered the way subjects viewed the emotional problem. The way in which the subjects changed their perception of the problem, however, came as a surprise: themes of failure followed the REM interval, while themes of successful resolution followed the waking interval. This could mean, the author speculated, that REM sleep helped subjects face up to reality, which during the waking state they tried to avoid.

Finally, it should be noted that a whole series of studies with animals show very clearly that REM time becomes significantly elevated as a function of new learning. This relationship holds up for a wide variety of species ranging from rats, mice, and cats to newly hatched chicks, and for virtually any kind of appropriate task, be it the learning of a conditioned avoidance response, a maze, a discriminatory response, or whatever (Greenberg et al., 1969; Fishbein et al., 1974; McGinty, 1969; Smith et al., 1974; Lucero, 1970; Leconte et al., 1973, 1974). Studies using implanted animals, which implicate the locus coeruleus, have likewise furthered our understanding of the role of REM sleep in adapta-

tion. We already know that the locus coeruleus is a key brain region for initiating and maintaining the REM state. Since REM sleep appears to play a critical
role in memory consolidation, the locus coeruleus should too. That is precisely
what has recently been reported: lesions of the locus coeruleus have been shown
to impair memory and response acquisition (Zornetzer and Gold, 1976; Crow
and Wendlandt, 1976). The reader will recall that the locus coeruleus contains
concentrations of noradrenergic cells. This whole complex interplay between
biochemical neurotransmitter substances, neuroanatomical brain structures,
sleep, and adaptive behavior all comes together in a bold attempt at synthesis,
which we will be shortly discussing (see Hartmann, 1973, below).

In conclusion, it appears that experimental studies, have on the whole, been
somewhat more successful in demonstrating the adaptive role of REM sleep
when they have *not* employed the methodologically troublesome technique
of REM deprivation. It must be kept in mind, however, that the results obtained by investigators using relatively noninvasive techniques are also by and
large correlational in nature, and a correlation, as we all know, does not necessarily signify a cause-and-effect relationship. We are still very much on the
edges of a frontier here. But, as the reader can see, we are moving forward.

Studies of NONREM Sleep Function

Among sleep researchers a certain schism seems to have evolved between the
advocates of REM sleep and those espousing the virtues of NONREM sleep. At
times this division reaches somewhat polemic proportions, as in the case of an
article by Horne (1976) entitled "Hail Slow Wave Sleep, Goodbye REM." The
title may sound like wishful thinking, but it also contains a grain of truth: interest has in fact tended to focus mainly on REM, with NONREM sleep strictly
taking second place. Whether this has occurred because REM is the more glam-
orous of the two or because REM is, in fact, more worthy of scientific investigation is for the future to decide. As things stand now, we know far less about
NONREM sleep than about its more favored rival.

One thing we can be certain of, however: just as there is a biological requirement for REM sleep, so there exists a biological need for NONREM sleep. This
information we owe largely to the work of Agnew, Webb, and Williams (1964,
1967), who were able to demonstrate a Stage 4 "rebound effect." In a design
similar to Dement's (1960) REM rebound paradigm, the subjects in this study
had several baseline nights followed by two nights of Stage 4 deprivation[8] and
two recovery nights. All subjects showed a highly signficant increase in Stage 4
sleep on the recovery nights when compared with their baseline nights. Again,
however, the procedure failed to produce any clear-cut behavioral results, even
after seven days of total Stage 4 deprivation. The authors, however, did note

that Stage 4-deprived subjects tended to be physically lethargic and depressed, in contrast to REM-deprived subjects, who appeared to be irritable and emotionally labile. This suggests that sleep may have important mood-regulating functions, a point recently underscored by Kramer et al. (1976). The point is well taken, since mood, drive, and energy are all part and parcel of the adaptive process.

What do studies not involving sleep loss tell us about the function of NONREM sleep? Here the evidence is somewhat more informative, though still meager by comparison. The strongest single finding so far has been that physical exercise, probably by inducing fatigue, elevates SWS time in both humans and animals (Baekeland and Lasky, 1966; Hobson, 1968; Matsumoto et al., 1968; Zloty et al., 1973), though even here there are contradictory reports (Hauri, 1968; Horne and Porter, 1975; Webb, 1975, p. 53). In the male rat, sexual activity has been found to increase SWS (Boland and Dewsbury, 1971). And Oswald (1972) and MacFayden et al. (1973) report that starvation has an elevating effect on SWS. These effects suggest a pattern different from that involving REM sleep. To help us understand what this difference tells us about the question we posed at the beginning of this section about the functions of sleep, we had better turn to Hartmann (1973), who has formulated a tentative answer.

Theoretical Formulations

Hartmann's Theory.   Hartmann's (1973) theory probably is the most ambitious attempt made to date to integrate the enormous data base that has accumulated in sleep research since its inception. It takes into account not only the kinds of experimental data which I have presented above, but also many variations in nature, for example the observation that "long" sleepers, who are "worriers," require more REM sleep than "short" sleepers, who are more self-confident. Aside from being comprehensive, the theory also has the advantage of being specific; in fact, it is two theories: one about the function of REM sleep, and one about the function of NONREM sleep.

Concerning REM sleep, the theory states (1) that *REM sleep restores our mental functioning* after the trials and tribulations of our waking hours. By helping us consolidate our memory and other cognitive abilities, and by elevating our mood, REM sleep enables us to adapt both intellectually and emotionally to the world around us. (2) It accomplishes this function by *providing recuperation of the catecholamine-dependent neuronal systems in the brain* which have become depleted in the course of our activities during wakefulness. Here Hartmann draws heavily on two well-documented sets of observations: (a) that the catecholamines (norepinephrine and dopamine) play a critical role in adaptive functioning: in psychomotor coordination, learning, memory, vigilance, attention, and so on; and (b) that brain catecholamine levels vary inversely with "REM pressure";[9] drugs that raise CA levels lower REM pressure, and drugs that lower CA levels increase REM pressure.

While according to Hartmann REM sleep is psychologically restorative, *NON-REM sleep is physically restorative* and involves not the synthesis of monoamines but of *proteins*. These are subsequently utilized by REM sleep in fulfilling *its* function. In other words, NONREM sleep restores the physical effects of waking and prepares for the action of REM sleep. Its function is essentially biological, related to "growth or regeneration of body tissues."

Webb's Theory.   Webb takes an entirely different approach to the question of why we sleep. Webb does not concern himself with the separate functions of REM and NONREM sleep. His model is applicable to sleep in general. Furthermore, he does not conceptualize sleep as restorative, as a response to some loss or deprivation that needs to be made up. Instead Webb views sleep as an *instinctive response to environmental change* or rather a "non-response," which protects us from harm. "We do not sleep because we are exhausted but rather to avoid exhaustion" (1975, p. 162). According to Webb, sleep is part of our innate biological heritage, an automatic built-in unlearned pattern of behavior which ensures that we sleep and wake in ways appropriate to our environment. It is *reflexive rather than purposive.*

This *ecological* view, I think, fits very nicely the fact that the primary effect of sleep deprivation (total and selective) appears to be on sleep itself (as shown by the universality of the rebound phenomenon) rather than on our waking behavior. Like a "gentle tyrant," sleep can be pushed just so far; when push comes to shove, it will make its authority known and will ultimately prevail.

Webb's theory owes its uniqueness also to its *evolutionary* outlook. If sleep has evolved as an adaptive form of non-response to the environment, it must have done so by increasing the organism's survival chances; and, to survive, an organism must be able to obtain food as well as avoid being food (for predators). Webb succeeds in demonstrating this vividly by ample illustrations from the animal kingdom. For instance, grazing animals and elephants both sleep very little (about 2 in 24 hours), but for entirely different reasons: the former do so because they are low in the predator hierarchy, and have no safe place to sleep, while the latter have to stay active to avoid starving. This adaptational difference also explains why grazing animals sleep in brief bursts and elephants sleep for more sustained periods. The evolutionary point of view is consistent with recent experimental findings, for it suggests that even though sleep may not be vital in the artificial setting of the laboratory, it might be vital from an evolutionary perspective.

Comparison of the Two Theories.   Webb calls his theory "adaptive" in contrast to so-called restorative theories of Dement or Hartmann. I do not believe this distinction is helpful. Both purposive and instinctive behavior can be adaptive or nonadaptive, as the case may be. I am therefore inclined to consider both theories adaptive, each covering and emphasizing different classes of phenomena. In other words, I see them as *complementary, rather than conflicting*. And, just like Jouvet's theory, or any existing theory of sleep and dreaming, neither Webb's nor Hartmann's should be regarded as the last word on sleep. Data contradicting one or the other, or not explained by either, have been and will continue to be found. Yet, even with these limitations, the two models will in all probability exert a profound influence on sleep and dream research in the years to come.

THE PLACE OF DREAM PSYCHOLOGY IN CONTEMPORARY SLEEP RESEARCH: A CRITICAL APPRAISAL

Near the end of his book *The Functions of Sleep*, Hartmann has this to say about the dream: "The experienced dream . . . is of interest to us here as a concomitant . . . of important events taking place in the brain . . . a sort of window into these processes . . . . I believe that *the psychological experience of dreaming, like any psychic experience, cannot be studied scientifically in its own right*, but rather as an indicator of what may be going on" (1973, p. 132). Since what is "going on" during REM sleep, according to Hartmann, is "a process of repair and restoration of certain catecholamine-dependent brain systems that are necessary during waking" (p. 136), we are left with the inevitable conclusion (p. 138) that *dreams "show us the functioning of the brain when the catecholamine influence is removed."* Hartmann does not explicitly say so, but it certainly is difficult to escape the implication that dreaming is something like the subjective equivalent of a poorly functioning cortex—in other words, a form of low-grade thinking.

It is possible that the dream has no function at all; that it is a mere "epiphenomenon," a "psychic appendix," the result of a "fortuitous choice of subject matter to account for the direction, size, and velocity of eye movements" (Dement, 1964)—a series of meaningless random images produced by an activated brain (Hobson and McCarley, 1977). Evans and Newman (1964) have likened dreams to the residue of a memory filter: disposable bits of irrelevant information.

However, it seems more plausible that dreams serve not only a function, but a very important and useful one. Given the universality of dreaming, the insistence with which it occurs, and the obvious interrelatedness and thematic coherence of any group of dreams collected from any one person in the course of a night (Kramer et al., 1964), it appears to be extremely difficult to avoid the conclusion that dreams *qua* dreams play a vital role in human functioning and that they help us live more fully integrated lives.

At the crux of the matter, it seems, is the issue whether or not dreaming is a process that exists independently of its neurophysiological correlates. I would like to submit that it does: that *dreaming not only exists as a separate process,* but that *it also has functions of its own, quite apart from REM sleep*; that *there exists a psychological need for certain sleep experiences, just as there exists a biological need for certain sleep stages; and that the content and quality of dreaming—how we dream, what we dream about—are as vital for adaptation as the amout of REM we get.*

As long as we operationally defined dreaming as REM sleep and left it at that, then obviously there would be no point in studying dreaming as a separate process; we could simply stop right at that point, having said all there was to be said. One could argue, however, that doing so would be tantamount to committing *a common epistemological error: the error of confusing simultaneity with isomorphism.* In other words, just because two processes—REM sleep and dreaming—are co-terminously active does not necessarily indicate that they are identical in nature (Globus and Gardner, 1968; Stoyva and Kamiya, 1968).

Is it because of this confusion, perhaps, that we have been steadily "physiologizing the dream out of existence?"—as Hall (1966) puts it. Or is it because of some unwritten credo that only biological research is respectable and can satisfy the canon of scientific rigor and precision?

This, of course, is a question for historians and philosophers to answer. But the enormous prevalence of reductionism in the field of sleep research should be quite apparent to readers by now and would become even more evident were they to start perusing the literature. They would discover, for instance, that REM-deprivation is frequently called *dream*-deprivation (Dement, 1960), and that REM sleep has been christened the *D*-state (Hartmann, 1973)—to give only two out of many examples. The literature abounds with such isomorphisms. Yet, such isomorphisms are by no means foregone conclusions. "Although it is true to say that we dream when we REM, that does not mean the same as we REM when we dream" (Cartwright, 1977, p. 51).

The fact that sleep researchers have thus emphasized the biological substratum of dreaming and by and large neglected the psychological experience of dreaming has given rise to a curious paradox: despite the monumental achievements in sleep research in recent years, our prevalent notions of dreaming continue to be derived principally from clinical practice and psychoanalysis—as if REMs had never been discovered. In brief, *the technological breakthrough of the fifties and sixties has had relatively little impact on our understanding of dreaming.* Much of the testimony to the dream's psychological importance comes from sources other than the sleep lab and continues to be based on clinical, anecdotal, and even anthropological data.[10] How reassuring, therefore, that in a recent overview of sleep research, Dement and Mitler (1975) state that "much future work is needed to establish and clarify the role of the psychological side of dreams . . . . *The dream must regain its status as a psychological event*, while at the same time retaining its position as a neurophysiological process." Considering that the average person regularly has about five REM dreams per night alone, spends about four years of his life in REM sleep, and experiences about 150,000 dreams during his or her lifetime, this statement seems highly appropriate.

We shall shortly return to this important issue. But first, let us briefly review a few fundamental facts that we *have* learned about dream psychology in the laboratory.

DREAMS: FACTS AND FICTION

What Is a Dream? Psychological Characteristics of Sleep Mentation

With the incidence of dream reports elicited from REMPs shortly after the discovery of REMs ranging as high as 88% of awakenings, it is not surprising that dreaming during REM sleep was at first considered to be the only existing kind of nocturnal mental activity. However, as usually happens after a new phenomenon is discovered, simplistic conceptions about it are quickly forced to give way to more sophisticated ones. Thus, other investigators soon reported an incidence ranging up to 74% of dreamlike reports from NONREM sleep awakenings (Foulkes, 1962; Rechtschaffen et al., 1963). However, there are distinct qualitative differences between REM and NONREM dream reports. Although REM-like dreams can occur in NONREM sleep and NONREM-type dreams in REM sleep, in general it can be said that the content of REM-related dreams, in contrast to NONREM-related dreams, tends to be: more perceptual–hallucinatory, vivid, bizarre, irrational, emotional, complex, elaborate, and symbolic. NONREM-related dreams, on the other hand, are more likely to be thought like, rational, conceptual, and realistic. Following a model outlined by Jones (1970, p. 37), one could liken the quality of REM mentation to primary process thinking and the quality characteristic of NONREM mentation to secondary process thinking. Rechtschaffen (1978) describes REM dreams as "singleminded." By that he is referring to the peculiar state of the ego during REM sleep, a state perhaps akin to what Rapaport describes as "ego passivity" (Rapaport, 1967). The ego's uncritical acceptance of extremely bizarre and unusual events, which is so typical in REM dreams, would be an extreme example of such ego-passivity. I vividly recall one such dream of my own, in which I was bitten by a dead dog. The fact that dead dogs can't bite never entered my mind while I was having this dream. I accepted the occurrence with a matter-of-factness that could only have been described as psychotic had I been awake. Another aspect of "single-mindedness" is the lack of control over attention, which is another form of ego-passivity, and perhaps may be likened to Piaget's concept of egocentrism. During wakefulness, it is quite normal to have two or more thoughts simultaneously present in one's mind; during dreaming, this hardly ever occurs. Whatever the train of thought may be, it seems to preempt all others.

While these characteristics by no means exhaust all the formal differences which have been found to exist between REM and NONREM sleep mentation, they do represent the principal ones, and clearly indicate that what distinguishes REM from NONREM sleep is not so much the presence or absence of mental activity, but the uniqueness of the formal thought properties associated with each sleep state. The validity of this statement is based on the fact that REM and NONREM reports are indeed discriminable by blind judges who have no knowledge of the conditions under which reports are obtained (Monroe et al., 1965). The judges in the Monroe et al. study were able to do so with better than 90% accuracy. One may safely conclude, therefore, that there is a continuum of sleep mentation ranging from more or less realistic, conceptual ideation to the bizarre and hallucinatory content which we generally attribute to dreams. In short: *although dreaming is a special kind of sleep mentation that typically occurs during REM sleep, some form of mental activity seems to be present during NONREM sleep stages as well.* Thus, the mind is never at rest.

With these observations in mind, it is now possible for the first time to give a definition of dreaming that fits the facts: *a dream is a form of thought, usually occurring during sleep, having specifiable properties. The quality of these properties depends on the sleep state during which this thought process occurs.*

Do Dreams Really Exist?

None of the above comments, however, tells us whether or not dreams actually occur. Although dreaming is widely reported, the certainty of its occurrence and the identity assumed to exist between the dream experience and its subsequent report still needs to be established. Perhaps, as Snyder (1969) once remarked, there is no psychic life at all during sleep: perhaps the effects of the REM state carry over into the waking state, as a study by Fiss et al. (1966) suggests, and simply enhance the capacity for confabulation after waking up. Or perhaps "upon awakening, the subject constructs a report of a dream experience which he falsely attributes to the preceding REM period" (Rechtschaffen, 1967). These and sundry alternatives must be ruled out before we can be sure of the reality of the dream.

To establish this reality, to confirm the validity of the dream report, so to say, it is necessary to carry out experiments that will demonstrate certain consistent and specific relationships between REM sleep variables and dream variables. Thus, it has been shown that dreams and REMPs are approximately equal in duration—in other words, that REM time equals dream time. For example, Dement and Wolpert (1958), by introducing external stimuli into ongoing dreams, were able to demonstrate that the portion of the dream between the transformed appearance of the stimulus and the awakening was approximately equal in length to the corresponding electrophysiological epoch. This experiment and others like it thus permanently put to rest the ancient and popular myth that dreams are instantaneous. These same authors were also able to show that active REMPs, i.e., REMPs containing many eye movements, tended to be associated with active dreams, while relatively quiescent REMPs, containing very few eye movements, tended to be associated with inactive dreams.

A particularly detailed and controlled analysis of the relationship between REMs and specific dream content has been reported by Roffwarg et al. (1962). In this study, one experimenter awakened the subject immediately following the appearance of a distinct eye movement pattern. A second experimenter independently obtained a detailed dream report from the same subject and then postdicted from the dream report how the subject must have moved his eyes while having his dream. For example, a subject reported dreaming that she walked up a flight of five or six steps, looking up at every step. The experimenter correctly postdicted that the subject's EOG would show a series of five vertical upward eye movements. For 80% of the instances when the dreamer rated his dream recall as "good," there was a high degree of correspondence between postdicted and actual eye movements. This relationship between dream content and directionality of eye movements has led to the speculation that the REMs show the dreamer "scanning" the events of his dream. Unfortunately, the methodological problems inherent in this kind of experiment leave it open to much criticism and make replication difficult. Thus, the "scanning hypothesis" still needs to be confirmed. Nevertheless, the study of Roffwarg et al. (1962) represents one of the milestones in the history of dream research.

Another study, this one by Arkin et al. (1966), approaches the problem of the reality of the dream from yet a different angle. Arkin et al. gave one of their subjects, prior to sleep, the post hypnotic suggestion that he talk in his sleep, without awakening, whenever he was having a dream, and that he describe his dream while it was going on. In 87% of awakenings after such REMP sleep speeches, an extremely close correspondence was observed between dream content and sleep speech content! This study obviously also needs to be replicated. It is certainly the closest anyone has ever come to *observing a dream as it occurs.*

Obviously, we still do not know *for certain* whether or not dreams occur. But the bulk of the evidence we have reviewed clearly indicates that they do. In the final analysis, the dream experience, if nothing else, will probably always remain the most parsimonious and plausible explanation of that elusive phenomenon the dream report.

Factors Influencing Dream Recall

The fact that in all likelihood we are going to be stuck with the dream report as our sole "window" into the dream dictates that we had better learn all we can about the myriad factors which can influence dream recall. I doubt whether anyone would seriously recommend that we wait for someone to invent a technique for directly observing dream *content*, though, of course, anything is possible.

We routinely forget the bulk (about 90%) of our nightly dream experiences. Even in the sleep laboratory, which is the most effective device for "trapping" dreams known today, 10 to 20% of REM awakenings will fail to yield a dream report. How can we account for this enormous attrition? And if dreaming, as some would say, is such a rich source of potentially valuable material, what, if anything, can we do to improve this unfortunate poverty of recall?

Unfortunately, necessity forces us to be brief and selective in our discussion; for a more thorough coverage of this far-reaching subject, the reader will have to look elsewhere, particularly at the work of Goodenough and his co-workers, who have concentrated a great deal of their research efforts on this issue (Goodenough et al., 1959; Shapiro et al., 1963; Shapiro et al., 1965; Goodenough et al., 1965a,b; Lewis et al., 1966; Goodenough, 1969; Goodenough et al., 1974). Here we can only summarize some of the main conclusions that can be drawn from this large body of work.

Aside from the more obvious fact that *sleep state* is a major determinant of dream recall, one of the first factors which come to mind is *motivation:* when we want to, we remember more dreams. I think most of us are aware of this. Even people who claim they never or very rarely dream can be stimulated, at least temporarily, to pay more attention to their dream life and thereby remember more dreams. Since we now know that everyone has several dreams per night, this should not come as a surprise. Even before this knowledge became common, psychotherapists always understood that patients would bring more dreams into their sessions if they had formed a therapeutic alliance with their therapist. People can also be trained to increase their recall of dreams in experimental situtations (Cartwright, 1977, p. 40). Since learning generally requires a desire to learn, such laboratory training effects lend additional support to the notion that motivation is one of the variables we must pay attention to in considering the various determinants of dream recall.

If the forgetting of dreams is such a normal occurrence, then *repression* can hardly be considered to be as general an explanation as Freud made it out to be (Freud, 1900). While repression undoubtedly can affect dream recall—few would deny that—sleep research has indicated that the primary factors responsible for the recall and forgetting of dreams are the same as or similar to those which operate in memory consolidation in ordinary waking life: *serial position effects*, such as primacy and recency, and especially *salience* and *interference*, as recently suggested by Cohen (1974).

Concerning salience, Cohen (1974) writes that dreams are more likely to be recalled if they are accompanied by high autonomic arousal, for instance irregular breathing, REM "density," penile erections, and other phasic events, and if the dreams themselves are more imaginative, vivid, interesting, self-involving, and so on. Fiss et al. (1974) likewise found that active dreams are more salient: when REMPs were experimentally shortened, the associated dream reports became not only more "dream-like" but also longer. Support for the interference hypothesis comes from the well-documented observation that abrupt awakenings from REMPs tend to yield more dream reports than gradual awakenings. This indicates that *method of awakening* is a major dream recall parameter.

How much and how well we recall our dreams also depends on *how much sense dreams make to us*. Since most dreams are forgotten in the normal course of events, it may be that most dreams are cast in a "language" which makes it difficult to "translate" them into the more conventional terminology of our waking lives. This argument does not necessarily support the Freudian view that dreams are meant to conceal. Rather, it seems far more consistent with the Piagetian view of things (Jones, 1970, pp. 134–166). Jones proposes that the frequently incomprehensible character of dreams results from the activation of more primitive, i.e., "preoperational schemas," in which "assimilation" takes precedence over "accomodation." This occurs not because going to sleep promotes regression in the Freudian sense, but because it induces a shift to a form of thought organization characteristic of an earlier stage of cognitive development. In short, dreams are so often obscure to adults because they are forms of thinking that are not readily "assimilable" by waking consciousness, and not because of some presumed "censor" transforming repressed infantile drives seeking "discharge." Again, we are led to a structural, ego-psychological formulation, rather than one couched in energy terms. Of course, this is not the only explanation that can be offered for the difficulty we all have in understanding "the forgotten language" of the dream. Cartwright (1977, p. 64) offers an alternative explanation: "Part of the problem of getting good dream reports is that whereas dreams are largely products of right-brain activity experienced in nonverbal, imagistic language, we inquire about them in verbal terms, which requires the dreamer to translate his experience into left-brain (verbal) terms." Other equally intriguing explanations can probably be found. One thing most contemporary dream researchers would probably agree on however is this: dreams are hard to understand because they are *different*, *not* because they are *distorted*.

Personality and individual differences have also been found to be significantly related to dream recall. Good recallers, as compared to poor recallers, have been reported to be more anxious (Tart, 1962); field-independent (Schonbar, 1965); inner-directed and self-aware (Lewis et al., 1966; Cohen, 1974); light sleepers (Zimmerman, 1970); and so forth.

The *social* climate in which we live—the importance of dreams in our *culture*—must likewise be considered. The Senoi, who greatly prize their dreams, are infinitely better dream recallers than we in America, where dreams are generally not considered to be of much consequence. The list of factors influencing dream recall could easily be extended. This is obviously an area in which there is still a great deal of room for further research.

Factors Influencing Dream Content

Having considered *when* and *whether* we dream and *how much* dreaming we recall, we are now ready to focus on *what* we dream about: why it is we dream the dreams we dream. This last question is usually answered by studying or "tracing" the effects of presleep stimulation on dream content. (The question of *why* we dream will be taken up last.)

The variety of different presleep stimuli to which experimental subjects have been exposed is bewildering. They include, to name only a few: real-life stress situations (Breger et al., 1971); all sorts of emotionally arousing films (Witkin and Lewis, 1967; Foulkes and Rechtschaffen, 1964; Cartwright et al., 1969); a conscious drive—thirst (Bokert, 1968); a conscious wish—to be different (Cartwright, 1974a); and a host of suggestions—hypnotic and otherwise—to dream about specific topics, to have short and long dreams, pleasant and unpleasant ones, and so on (Fisher, 1953; Barber and Calverley, 1962; Barber et al., 1973; Albert and Boone, 1975; Tart, 1964; Brunette and DeKoninck, 1977).

In the opinion of this writer, the overall result of this massive effort has been disappointing. To be sure, we have learned that it is relatively easy to influence dream content and to influence it in a predictable fashion. Thus, when Barber et al. (1973) suggested to their subjects that they dream about the death of President Kennedy, those subjects who received the suggestion dreamed about the topic significantly more often than those who did not receive it. The manner in which the suggestion was given also proved to be an important variable, and interacted with hypnotic induction; specifically, the presleep suggestion had the greatest effect when given authoritatively to hypnotic subjects and when given permissively to nonhypnotic subjects. Their work on the effect of stress on dreams led Breger et al. (1971) to conclude, among other things, that "it is affect-related or emotionally arousing information of personal relevance that one dreams about" (p. 186), and to speculate, on the basis of this finding, that dreams serve the purpose of assimilating affectively aroused information into solutions embodied in existing memory systems (p. 22). Cartwright, in generalizing from the results of some of her work, proposes that dreams fulfill an identity-preserving function, in line with ideas put forth earlier by Erikson (1954) and Jones (1962): her subjects' dreams, especially the ones that followed an erotic film (Cartwright et al., 1969) and the wish to be different (Cartwright, 1974a), "provided emotional support for the dreamer's self-identity . . . and reaffirmation of the salient features of the self" (Cartwright, 1977, p. 88). Dreams, she concludes, appear to fulfill the function of "restating *who we are*."

It is always tempting to speculate on the function of dreaming. It is also understandable why we would be thus tempted: when we ask *why* subject S_1 has dream D_1 and subject S_2 has dream D_2, we are, in fact, asking whether D_1 and D_2 are doing S_1 and S_2, respectively, any good. In other words, we want to know what D_1 and D_2 accomplish, what *functions*, if any, they serve. The problem with the strategy of studying the influence of presleep stimuli, however, is that using the dream as a dependent variable can get us only so far and no further. This is so because, in order to test the hypothesis that dreams have a function—any kind of function—we have to assume that *dreaming not only reflects what is going on in us* but that *it actively influences our waking behavior*. Such a test requires a different experimental strategy: one in which the dream is not the dependent but the *independent* variable. Such work has, in fact, already been undertaken, and will be described in a later section of this chapter, on the effects of dreaming on wakefulness.

Nightmares and Night Terrors: Two Birds of Different Feathers

Although it is not the purpose of this chapter to deal with sleep pathology, one more useful lesson which the sleep laboratory has taught us and which has helped us distinguish fact from fiction should be mentioned. I am referring to the relatively recent discovery that there are not one but two entirely different forms of "mental disturbance" during sleep: the anxiety dream and the night terror or *pavor nocturnus*. Until fairly recently, the distinction between these two sleep phenomena was blurred. But now, thanks to the work of Fisher et al. (1968, 1970, 1973, 1974), Gastaut and Broughton (1963), Broughton (1968, 1970), and others, we know in great detail what the principal distinguishing features of these two kinds of sleep pathology are. A brief review of these characteristics follows.

1. *Night terrors occur predominantly out of stage 4 SWS.* They are not dreams at all. *Nightmares, on the other hand, occur during normal REM sleep* and are the usual garden variety of anxiety dreams.

2. A person always awakes from a night terror, less frequently from a nightmare, and when awakened by a nightmare, goes back to sleep more readily than when awakened from a night terror attack. This is why *night terrors are considered disorders of arousal rather than disorders of sleep.*

3. *Night terrors are generally of shorter duration* (1 or 2 minutes only) than nightmares, *and occur earlier in the night* (15 to 30 minutes after sleep onset).

4. *Night terrors occur most commonly in early childhood*; in fact, 2 to 5% of all children suffer from attacks of pavor nocturnus at one time or another. *Nightmares occur in all ages.*

5. In comparison with nightmares, night terrors are far more disruptive: *night terrors are characterized by much more intense anxiety and greater panic, more extreme levels of autonomic discharge* (with heart rates of 200 beats per minute not uncommon), *and greater amounts of motility and vocalization.* Hearing the blood-curdling screams of a person who has just awakened from a night terror is an experience one does not easily forget. Sitting and standing up and even walking around are likewise not uncommon concomitants of night terror awakenings.

6. *Very little content is generally recalled from night terror episodes;* the most recall one usually gets is a single fleeting, frightening image or thought. *In contrast, the content recalled from nightmares tends to be much richer, more elaborated and sequential.*

7. *Following a night terror, a person is much more confused* than he is after awakening from a nightmare *and less responsive* to external stimulation.

Further details on these and other common disorders of sleep can be found in review articles by Kales and Kales (1974), Williams et al. (1974), Dement and Guilleminault (1973), and Dement and Mitler (1975).

REM AND DREAMING: TWO SEPARATE PROCESSES

We are now ready to consider the experimental evidence which supports the proposition, advanced before, that dreams are not simply reducible to the basic biological processes which have been described earlier; that, in fact, dreams have an existence of their own.

That this is a fundamental point of view shared by some and not by others goes without saying. In essence, it is a matter of philosophical conviction, of dualism vs. monism. It is the everlasting mind-body problem surfacing once again, keeping us on our toes and stimulating debate such as one that took place at a recent symposium of the Association for the Psychophysiological Study of Sleep. The symposium was appropriately called "Mind-Body Isomorphism and Dream Theory." Robert McCarley, who spoke on behalf of isomorphism, proposed that we reduce dreaming to the spontaneous activity of a pontine (not even a cortical!) generator and dispense with clinical conceptions altogether. In brief, he proposed a new language, one completely devoid of any mentalistic concepts. In this new language, symbols would be translated as "synchronous" neuronal activity, images as "intensity" of neuronal activity, and so forth. Milton Kramer was the spokesman for the dualistic position: biology can't explain everything, even in 1976, and isomorphism is premature (what are the neurophysiological correlates of empathy? of attitude?) ... psychological phenomena still require psychological explanations, explanations in terms of meaning ... elaboration of mental content must involve the cortex (the pons may generate REMs but how could it generate dreams?) ... and so on.

To this observer, the discussion was an event of historical significance. Only a poet could have expressed more eloquently the present status—or rather dilemma—of dream research:

> One mystery alone remains
> Of my beloved's sleep:
> We've solved the movement of her eyes
> And why they do repeat,
> We know what brings her breath in sighs,
> We've tracked her EEG.
> The haunting doubt that still remains
> Is does she dream of me?[11]*

But let us try to be haunted no longer and start looking at the experimental evidence in support of the argument that dreams do have an independent existence.

Occurrence of Dreamlike Mentation Outside of REM

A good place to begin is with evidence that REM-like mental activity during sleep can occur in the absence of REM sleep. Reference has already been made to the observation by Foulkes (1962) and others that a good deal of mental activity occurs during NONREM sleep; but the quality of NONREM mentation has generally been found to be so different from REM sleep mentation that not only are judges able to discriminate one from the other but subjects are too (Antrobus and Fisher, 1965; Antrobus, 1967). Not so with respect to NONREM Stage 1 (sleep onset). The type of mental activity found associated with this particular NONREM sleep stage, called *hypnagogic*, though supposedly less continuous, elaborate, and affect-charged, does share many of the features commonly ascribed to REM dreams: bizarreness, sexual and aggressive content, hedonic tone, and so forth (Foulkes and Vogel, 1965)—so many, in fact, that trained judges given the task of discriminating sleep onset and REM reports had difficulty doing so: they called 50% of REM reports "sleep onset" reports and 25% of sleep onset reports "REM" reports (Foulkes and Vogel, 1974). Dreamlike episodes have also been reported from naps (Slap, 1977).

*Reproduced with permission of Dr. Milton Miller and Charles C Thomas, Publisher, Springfield, Illinois.

Evidence that dreamlike mental activity occurs outside of sleep altogether has also been found. In a study of drug-induced hallucinations, Cartwright (1966) reports striking and consistent similarities between subjects' REM dreams and waking hallucinations: both were highly visual, obviously related to subjects' current concerns, and rapidly forgotten; and in both, reality testing was impaired, thinking symbolic and loose, and attentional control lacking. Blind judges' matchings of subjects' dream and drug experiences likewise attested to their similarity. Even the subjects' brain state was similar in the two conditions: it was highly aroused in both.

Dreamlike thinking in the waking state has also been observed by Fiss et al. (1966). This study employed a method of retrieving sleep mentation that circumvented the necessity of relying on recall: instead of asking our subjects to report dreams in the traditional way, we showed them a TAT card immediately following each awakening and instructed them to make up a story about it. The awakenings occurred from both REM and NONREM sleep. The results showed that stories produced after interrupted REMPs were significantly longer, more complex, elaborate, visual, vivid, emotional, and bizarre than stories obtained after interrupted NONREMPs. The latter, in contrast, were remarkably impoverished, unimaginative, and much more thoughtlike. In short, the narratives following REMP awakenings tended to be dreamlike, while those following NONREM awakenings resembled NONREM mentation. We also obtained dream reports from these subjects: they were strikingly similar in thematic content to their corresponding waking fantasies. These findings led us to postulate that the distinguishing properties of REM sleep mentation, rather than being automatically "switched off" upon awakening, will persist into the waking state. This "carry over effect," as we have called it, clearly refutes the REM definition of dreaming.[12]

Substitution Phenomena

Another phenomenon that does so is the "substitution" phenomenon, which represents mainly the work of Cartwright and her associates (Cartwright et al, 1967; Cartwright and Monroe, 1968; Cartwright and Ratzel, 1972; Cartwright, 1972). The take-off point for this series of investigations is the above-mentioned drug study (Cartwright, 1966), which found not only that drug-induced hallucinations resemble dreams, but also that the drug experience may actually have served as a *substitute* for dreaming: The night following the drug experience, there was a sizeable reduction in the proportion of time these subjects spent in REM. To carry this line of investigation a step further, Cartwright et al. began to concentrate on individual differences in response to REM deprivation and discovered two types of responders: "rebounders" and "substituters." Psychological testing of these two groups revealed that those who show the rebound effect are less differentiated (more field-dependent) than those who do not. The latter, the substituters, apparently have easier access to dreamlike material outside of REM and therefore less need to make up for lost REM time. A direct test of this hypothesis was then performed on a group of REM-deprived subjects: some of them were given a neutral task, others a fantasy task during their deprivation period. As predicted, the neutral task group made up for more REM time than the fantasy group. These results clearly show that REM deprivation does not necessarily prevent dreaming, nor is it always an accurate measure of dream deprivation.

Results of studies with schizophrenic patients, especially patients in the acute phase of their illness, lend additional support to the substitution hypothesis, and are remarkably consistent with the findings of Cartwright's drug study. Thus, acute schizophrenic symptomatology has been found to be associated with decreased REM time (Kupfer et al., 1970; Feinberg et al., 1964), while remission of symptoms has been related to increased REM time (Gulevitch et al., 1967). Also consistent with the substitution hypothesis is the observation that the content of schizophrenics' dreams tends to be duller, blander, simpler, more static, and less bizarre than normal subjects' dreams (Dement, 1955; Cartwright, 1972; Okuma et al, 1970; Kramer et al., 1970). Actively symptomatic schizophrenics have also failed to show REM rebounds (Zarcone et al., 1968). Perhaps there is some truth after all to the ancient belief that madness is dreaming during the day and that dreaming at night preserves our sanity during the day. The reader will recall that this question came up earlier in the context of our discussion of the displacement of phasic activity into states of consciousness other than REM sleep (Ferguson et al., 1968; Watson et al., 1976). The notion that dreaming and psychosis are closely related has been popular for a long time and has been expressed at various times by Hughlings Jackson, Freud, Jung, Bleuler, Frieda Fromm-Reichmann, and others. In their review article, Dement and Mitler (1975) caution us against taking such aphorisms too seriously. I am very much in agreement with them on this in general. One should definitely not throw caution to the winds. On the other hand, one can also be too cautious and adopt too atheoretical a stance. These are not only aphorisms we are dealing with; they are also sound empirical findings. And while I appreciate, along with Dement and Mitler, that "the overall results in animals and man indicate that REM sleep deprivation per se is not harmful," I also find it difficult to ignore those studies (some from their own lab) which suggest a relationship between REM rebounds, phasic displacement, and psychopathology. All I am really saying is that we should not abandon this ancient "aphorism" prematurely. There may be a kernel of truth in it after all. But let us once more get back to dreaming as a normal, everyday type of process.

STUDIES OF THE ADAPTIVE FUNCTION OF DREAMING

In the preceding pages, an attempt has been made to establish the credibility and utility of two ideas, among others: (1) that REM sleep and dreaming are two generally concurrent but nonetheless essentially separate organismic events; and (2) that REM sleep serves an adaptive function. This still does not tell us, however, that dreaming *per se* serves an adaptive function. Dreaming and REM may indeed exist independently of each other, and REM may indeed be vital for adaptation—yet, as several writers whose work has been discussed have seriously suggested, the possibility still exists that dreams are essentially non-functional: incidental, discardable by-products or concomitants of sleep. It still needs to be demonstrated, therefore, that dreams in and of themselves serve adaptive needs.

But how can this be accomplished? Again, the REM deprivation paradigm comes to mind: if we could remove dreaming, then we could perhaps find out *why* we dream.

Unfortunately, this cannot be done: there is simply no way in which we can remove dreaming without at the same time removing REM sleep. Regardless of whether we use awakenings or some other method (for example REM-suppressing drugs) of REM deprivation, the psychological process of dreaming will remain hopelessly confounded with the neurophysiological event of REM sleep. Some other way must be found.

A Study of Recurrent Dreams

Some time ago, my colleague and friend the late George Klein, I and other collaborators had the idea that the study of recurrent dreams might provide us with an answer (Klein et al., 1971). Our reasoning simply was that recurrent dreams must be particularly important dreams, judging by the urgency with which they seem to seek expression. Hence, if we studied important dreams, we might find out why dreams are important. Unfortunately, although all our subjects, who had been carefully screened, had reported extremely high rates of recurrence, we were able to "capture" only a single repetitive dream in its entirety. (Fisher, personal communication, experienced similar difficulties recruiting subjects with nightmares: for reasons about which we can only speculate, a very high proportion of his volunteers simply failed to report any nightmares once they settled down in the sleep laboratory.) We obtained only *fragments* of recurrent dreams and some unanticipated data suggesting that the recurrent dream—perhaps like the equally unpleasant nightmare—seems to have very little adaptive value, that in fact it may result from a *failure of adaptation*. Perhaps we should have persevered longer. But the question of *importance* never ceased to preoccupy us.

The Need to Complete One's Dreams

If dreams are important, i.e., have a function, isn't it reasonable, we once thought, that people would want to *complete* their dreams?

As it turned out, this question led to more promising results, and probably not coincidentally so, for it arose out of a rather well-established theoretical context: once again that of ego-psychology. As we soon discovered, the notion of some sort of completion gradient has been around for some time; in fact, it dates as far back as the end of the nineteenth century, when a German psychologist, Robert (1886), declared that "the instigators of dreams are things which are in our minds in an uncompleted shape." While this translation leaves a lot to be desired, its message is unmistakable and must have been clear to Freud too, for it was the same unfinished business, the same unresolved problems of the preceding day, that he had in mind when he proposed his concept of the "day residue." What is of even greater interest to us, however, is that he frequently used the term "unerledigt" (meaning incomplete) rather than "unbefriedigt" (meaning unfulfilled) in describing this residue—the very term Zeigarnik used some 30 years later (Zeigarnik, 1927).[13] The connection is not fortuitous, since Freud, who coined the term "ego," could hardly have been completely oblivious of the ego-psychological implications of his theories. Furthermore, it is the Zeigarnik phenomenon—the recall of uncompleted tasks—that Hartmann, Kris, and Loewenstein, who are as ego-psychological as can be, cite in drawing attention to the psychic disequilibrium resulting from prevention of what they call "completion of the act" (Hartmann et al., 1964). Spitz, another major contributor to ego-psychology, likewise believes that "a damaging influence is exerted through the repeated interruption of action cycles prior to their consummation" (Spitz, 1964). According to Spitz, dreaming occurs to protect the mental apparatus from such impairment. Klein has similarly proposed that dreams and thoughts be conceptualized as "self-closing cycle-completing series of ideomotor events" (Klein, 1970).

In brief, we felt we had ample reasons to consider the need to dream as a need to complete an important adaptive task, and to expect that this uncompleted task would constitute a problem which would continue toward completion throughout the night. But how could we demonstrate the existence of a need to complete one's dreams? Except for a single pilot study by Rechtschaffen (1964), who reported that REMP interruptions resulted in a degree of thematic continuity rarely observed in the dreams of a single night, there was little to be found in the literature that suggested a direct method for demonstrating this need experimentally. It occurred to us then to use the same story-telling technique with which we had earlier demonstrated the "carry-over" of REM sleep mentation into wakefulness (Fiss et al., 1966); only instead of obtaining our narratives post-REM and post-NONREM, as we had done earlier, we redesigned our experiment in such a way that stories were elicited during REM sleep only, but in three different conditions: one night at the very beginning (REM prevention condition), one night in the middle (REM interruption condition), and one night at the end of a REMP (REM completion condition). In brief, our purpose was to compare the "carry-over effects," not of REM interruption and NONREM interruption, as we had done in the previous study, but of REM interruption, REM completion, and REM prevention. (We chose the term "prevention" because our procedure was not intended to deprive subjects of any appreciable amount of REM sleep. Actually, subjects were awakened only twice during each experimental laboratory night).

The results of this investigation (Fiss, 1969; Fiss et al., 1969) clearly confirmed our hypothesis that the carry-over effect would be strongest in the REMP-interruption and not in the REMP-prevention or REMP-completion condition. They show unequivocally that the tendency to continue dreamlike mentation into the waking state is strongest when we have been awakened in the middle of an *already ongoing* dream experience. Our results showed more than that, however: they showed—and this came as surprise to us—that the stories obtained after interrupted REMPs contained the greatest amount of projected feelings of frustration, annoyance, irritability, anger, and hostility. Apparently, our subjects felt much more psychologically disturbed when awakened in the middle of a REMP than they did when awakened either at the beginning or the end of a REMP. This serendipitous finding suggests even more strongly that awakenings from ongoing dreams have a far greater psychological impact than awakenings from beginning or concluding dreams. We also obtained an unexpected Zeigarnik effect: interrupted dreams were significantly better recalled than completed dreams! In summary, the study left little doubt in our minds that being prevented from completing a dream is far more disruptive than not being allowed to dream at all, and that therefore *the need to complete a dream must be psychologically more important than sheer amount of dreaming.* It clearly supports a conception of dreaming in structural rather than in instinctual or energy terms, and again suggests that dreams be regarded not as psychic representations of forces (physiological or otherwise) pressing for discharge, or processes that tune up the brain or remove toxic substances in the nervous system, but as organized, meaningful, integrating, and synthesizing experiences.

"Dream Intensification" Effects: A Compensation Phenomenon

Another approach that we found fruitful in testing the adaptational hypothesis of dreaming derived from the Fiss-Ellman (1973) study, described earlier in this chapter, which demonstrated the modifiability of the sleep cycle by means of a REMP interruption procedure that succeeded in "conditioning" REMP durations. We were able to accomplish this because our subjects apparently "learned" that they could avoid an unpleasant awakening by slipping into NONREM sleep at just about the time the experimenter was to have awakened them. It intrigued us to know what motivated these subjects to learn this response. Was it that they wanted to avoid being prevented from completing their dreams? There was no way to answer this question on the basis of the 1973 study, since that study had not been designed with this purpose in mind. But it did sustain our curiosity about the effects of prolonged REMP interruptions. If, by means of repeated REMP interruptions, subjects can "learn" to shorten their REMPS, would they also "learn" to speed up or intensify their dream experience to compensate for this attenuation? If they could, then dreaming certainly must be of importance to them. In order to find this out, we needed to know what the effects of massive REMP interruptions carried out over several nights would be on dream *content*. If dreams are important, vital, or useful, such intensification effects should occur, and subjects could be expected to make up for their dream losses by compressing a more elaborate dream experience into their shortened REMPs. A further motive for our undertaking this difficult study was the hope that the dream intensification, should it occur, might serve to "highlight" some of the dream's *specific* functions. It is not enough to know that dreams are important. We also need to know *why* dreams are important.

The method we (Fiss et al., 1974) employed this time included clinical as well as experimental procedures, with the clinical ones (open-ended interviews, projective tests) intended to provide us with a detailed life-history and an in-depth understanding of each subject's personality and basic conflicts. This combined procedure represented a departure from the more traditional method of studying dreams: instead of studying the dreamer via his dreams, we intended to study the dream process via the dreamer. Each subject spent 15 consecutive nights in the lab: six baseline nights of uninterrupted sleep, four REM-completion nights, four REM-interruption nights, and one uninterrupted recovery night. As in the Fiss-Ellman (1973) study, we controlled for REM deprivation during the interruption nights by requiring each subject to remain in the laboratory until he had accumulated REM sleep amounts approximately equal to his normal REM requirement, as determined by his baseline total. Each dream report was blindly scored for length, for dreamlike properties (affect intensity, vividness of imagery, bizarreness, and so on), and for conflictful content.

A summary of our results is as follows: (1) Dream reports following inter-rupted REMPs were on the average *equal in length* to dream reports following completed REMPs. Thus, our prediction that REM interruption would bring about a compensatory increase in the length of dream reports was confirmed: the subjects must have "compensated" for the repeated interruptions by "cram-ming" more and more dream activity into the experimentally shortened REMPs. And since the subjects were not REM-deprived, they must have made up for lost dreaming and not for lost REM time. (2) REM-interruption reports were more "dreamlike," i.e., more vivid and emotional, than REM-completion reports. This finding confirmed our initial hypothesis that sustained REMP interruptions would bring about a compensatory intensification of the dream process.[14] On the other hand, our hypothesis that interrupted dreams would be more bizarre than completed dreams was not confirmed; in fact, the exact opposite turned out to be true: interrupted dreams were significantly *less* bizarre than completed dreams. Not only that, but interrupted dreams were also narrated with significantly greater coherence and clarity of expression. It was as if the interruption procedure had helped bring the subjects' major preoccupations into ever sharper focus, revealing more and more of their focal conflicts. Thus, one of our subjects, a young male who had many conflicts over homosexuality and sexual impotence, initally reported such dream symbols as a bottle top breaking off, or the seat of a motor cycle inflating. However, his later interruption night dreams were much more transparent and self-revealing. "It ended up in bed with somebody (a man) . . . I was carrying on with somebody."[15] (3) We also found that interrupted REMPs contained significantly more eye movement activity (greater REM "density") than completed REMPs. Yet, despite this indication of heightened dream activity, the interrupted REMPs contained *fewer* signs of associated sleep disturbance, such as body movements, alpha, or NONREM intrusions (spindles, K-complexes, and so forth). This phenomenon, which had also been observed by Fiss and Ellman (1973), suggests that REMPs tend to become "purer," more typically REM–like, as a function of repeated interruptions, and not, as one would expect if interruption had an arousing or disruptive effect, more disorganized and irregular. What all this seems to add up to is that experiencing vivid, emotional, and conflictful dreams does not necessarily disturb sleep, and that such material need *not* be extensively transformed and distorted by primary process mechanisms in order to "guard" sleep, as Freud always insisted. On the contrary: *perhaps we dream in order to concentrate periodically on what troubles and ails us, and to work out some kind of solution.* As Greenson (1970) puts it, *"maybe sleep is necessary in order to safeguard our need to dream."*

It is difficult on the basis of these observations to avoid the temptation to speculate that dreaming is not only generally important—for maintaining our psychic balance, as Jung (1933), for example, might have put it—but also, as I have pointed out, that dreaming serves *specific* ego functions. For example, the results of the study just described could be interpreted as demonstrating a *problem or conflict solving* function, or possibly a *defensive* function. We could also interpret our data as suggesting a *communicative* function (Bergmann, 1966). Practically all our results could be interpreted as indicating a need to communicate a dream, not just a need to have a dream. The disproportionately lengthy dreams reported in the interruption condition (which allowed subjects less than half as much REM time as the completion condition!) could be attributed to increased pressure to *report* dreams rather than to an acceleration of the dream process alone. The greater transparency of the dreams reported during the interruption nights could easily suggest that dreams are messages enabling a person to "give away" his problems behind the safe and protective cloak of seemingly innocent story-telling. The absence of the conditioning effect (short REMPs all night long) previously observed by Fiss and Ellman (1973) also points to a communicative function, especially since the same subjects participated in both studies. Both studies employed essentially identical procedures, with one exception: in the Fiss-Ellman (1973) study, subjects were not permitted to report their dreams, while in the Fiss et al. (1974) study, subjects were required to report their dreams. The mere fact of reporting could therefore have made the difference—an assumption given additional support by the fact that in the earlier study, in which dream reporting was not a task requirement, subjects learned to avoid being awakened by entering another sleep state, whereas in the present study, in which dream reporting was required, subjects learned to *awaken spontaneously* just as the experimenter was about to awaken them. Had they learned this time to awaken themselves in order to tell their dreams?

The data at hand, intriguing though they are, do not permit us to answer these questions definitively. The inference that they offer evidence of functional specificity is unwarranted because it is one which can only be made *a posteriori*. Consequently, they do not constitute *prima facie* evidence of the adaptive hypothesis of dreaming. As I emphasized before, such a critical test is possible only if we link dream content to *postsleep* behavior. In the section that follows, we will consider a few representative studies which do fulfill this requirement.

Effects of Dreaming on Waking Behavior

Dreaming and the Process of Ego-Integration. In a general way, what we have been asking all along is whether dreams, if not necessarily springboards to feats of artistic and scientific creation, can at least help us live better-integrated lives. Since psychotherapy has essentially the same objective—that of augmenting the individual's capacity for adaptation and personal growth—it should not come as a surprise that "effective dreaming may be likened to effective psychotherapy" (Jones, 1970, p. 133). It is hardly necessary for me to point out, I'm sure, that dreams have for this very reason always played a key role in the psychological treatment of mental and emotional disturbances. Bearing this in mind, a number of sleep researchers, including this author, have recently become interested in providing empirical validation for this so widely held but poorly substantiated belief. Two of these investigators are Greenberg and Pearlman

(1975a,b), who have attempted to relate dream content to the content of psychoanalytic sessions held immediately prior to and following laboratory dreaming. Their preliminary findings with this clinical-experimental model, though highly tentative, suggest that *dreaming about a problem raised during presleep analytic hours will positively influence the way in which patients deal with the problem during their subsequent morning sessions.*

A series of investigations still in progress by Cartwright et al. (1975b, 1977) take a somewhat different approach to this problem. Cartwright's subjects are patients who have been referred to a university counseling service and have been designated poor risks. Before starting therapy, those who have volunteered for the study are randomly assigned to one of three preparatory laboratory training programs in dream recall: a program consisting of REM awakenings and dream reports, a program consisting of comparable NONREM awakenings and dream reports, and a daytime dream workshop. A fourth group of patients who receive no preparatory training in dream recall serve as a control group. Aside from dream retrieval, the training consists also of morning sessions with an experimenter in which the content of the dreams is discussed. It is thus primarily a technique for bringing a larger than normal amount of dream content into awareness. Results so far have consistently favored the REM training condition: *patients who have been trained in attending to their REM dreams stay longer in treatment* (have a lower drop-out rate), *make better progress* (as rated by patients, therapists, and objective judges), *and show greater depth of self-exploration and access to feelings* (again as determined by ratings) *than patients in any of the other training groups.* This outcome is not dependent on the extra attention given to the patients in the training groups, nor is it due to the therapists' empathic responses to them; it appears to be strictly due to REM preparation. This suggests that REM dreams contribute more to ego-consolidation than other forms of mental activity.

A related pilot study by Fiss and Litchman (1976) comes to essentially the same conclusion: that dream-awareness is therapeutically beneficial. These authors have developed a technique which they have called "dream enhancement," a method of focusing as much waking attention on one's dream life as possible, consisting of the following steps: (1) inducing a positive dream set; (2) suggesting that subjects try to dream about what troubles them most and also about possible solutions to their problem; (3) laboratory dream recording to maximize dream recall; (4) playing the recorded laboratory dreams back to the subjects the next day to reduce dream forgetting; and (5) encouraging subjects to reflect as much as possible on the meaning of their dreams and their possible usefulness for solving their problem, without, however, offering them any interpretations. The entire procedure is intended to be a sort of "crash" or "total immersion" program designed to give the dream every conceivable opportunity to show what it can accomplish. To measure the effect of this procedure, we have used several commonly employed clinical instruments for evaluating psychopathology (symptom distress, anxiety, and depression), as well as the degree of insightfulness expressed during psychotherapy sessions and clinical interviews. To control for the attention lavished on the subjects and other possibly confounding factors such as subjects' positive expectation that this procedure will help them, the enhancement procedure is carried out with both REM and NONREM dream reports, each subject serving as his own control. Our results so far, although based on a very limited sample, are extremely encouraging: *REM dream enhancement, in contrast with NONREM dream enhancement, has been found to be significantly associated with increased self-awareness and decreased psychopathology.* Our subjects have also found REM dream enhancement to be more enlightening, stimulating, and helpful than NONREM dream enhancement. In summary, we now have at least preliminary evidence from three separate lines of investigation showing that directing one's waking attention to REM-related mental activity is of some value in maintaining and even improving one's state of mental health.

Dreaming and the Consolidation of Memory. In order to determine whether dreaming has a memory-consolidating function independently of REM sleep, a study was done by Fiss et al. (1977), which demonstrated that *incorporating a presleep stimulus into dream content facilitated the subsequent recall of the stimulus in the waking state.* The subjects, who had been preselected for good dream recall, spent two consecutive nights each in the sleep laboratory, during which they were awakened from every REMP exceeding ten minutes in duration, and reported their dreams. The procedure for the two nights was identical, except that on the second (the stimulus) night, before going to bed, the subjects read a brief but vivid story about a sea monster attacking a sinking ship. The subjects were instructed to visualize the scene while falling asleep and to try to dream about it. The next morning, after their final dream report, the subjects were asked, much to their surprise, to recall the story. A checklist was used to measure incorporation of story elements in subjects' dreams. Self-ratings and sleep onset latency were used to measure the extent to which the subjects thought about or rehearsed the story while awake. The data analysis revealed that stimulus-night dreams received significantly higher checklist incorporation scores than control-night dreams. This provided evidence that the story influenced the subjects' dreams. A large and significant correlation between dream incorporation and story recall provided evidence that *dreaming about the presleep stimulus facilitated its recall.* Thus, our principal hypothesis was confirmed. An interesting but unexpected finding was a significant correlation between overall dream productivity and story recall. Apparently, having richer, more varied dreams and dreaming about a specific subject matter can both facilitate recall. No relationship was found between story recall and either eye movement density or story rehearsal. Thus, dream content and dream productivity predicted story recall, while story rehearsal and REM physiology did not. It is clear from these findings that dreaming has a mnemonic function which is *analogous to but not identical with* the mnemonic function of REM sleep.

Dreaming, Mood Regulation, and Environmental Mastery. Two major experimental investigations have dealt with the relationship between dream content and adaptation to stress, one by Cohen and Cox (1975), and one by DeKoninck and Koulack (1975). In the Cohen and Cox study, subjects were assigned to either a positive or a negative (stressful) presleep condition and then slept for one laboratory night of both REM and NONREM awakenings and dream reports. Before and after sleep, subjects rated themselves on a variety of mood scales. In the positive presleep condition, subjects were treated in a friendly and personal manner, given lots of information, and made to feel competent. In the stressful presleep situation, they were treated impersonally and perfunctorily, given no explanations, and made to feel inadequate. The authors predicted that the negative condition would be associated with a higher percentage of dream recall, and that subjects who dreamed about the negative presleep laboratory situation (the "incorporators") would show a greater improvement in mood from presleep to postsleep than nonincorporators. Both hypotheses were confirmed, indicating that amount of dreaming as well as specific dream content are related to affect change. Dream preoccupation with the negative presleep experience also affected the subjects' attitude toward it: *not only were those who dreamed about the unpleasant experience in a better frame of mind the next morning, they were also more predisposed to tackle it again*; after having been debriefed, only the incorporators expressed willingness to participate in future studies!

In the study by DeKoninck and Koulack (1975), the stressful experience was a gory film about workshop accidents. It was shown to the subjects before they went to sleep and again in the morning. A mood adjective checklist was administered to the subjects before and after each showing of the film. Contrary to expectation, film incorporation *interfered* with adaptation to stress in this experiment: those who incorporated film elements in their dreams tended to be more anxious at the second presentation of the film than the nonincorporators. This finding, of course, contradicts the outcome of the study by Cohen and Cox (1975). It is also at variance with the findings reported by Greenberg et al. (1972).

To account for these discrepancies would be beyond anybody's capacity at this point. The studies simply differ on too many levels. Some focus on REM sleep, others on dream content; some use one kind of stressor, others use a different kind. Perhaps it is more adaptive in some situations to dream about a particular stress experience, while in other instances it may be more adaptive to dream about something pleasant. There is a difference between a film depicting an ugly incident in which we are not directly involved and a failure experience that affects us on a deeply personal level. It would be easier, therefore, to deny the former than the latter. If not dreaming about something is indicative of denial, as not thinking about something is, then perhaps some of the differences make sense. We obviously have a long way to go yet before we understand the relationship—if there is any—between dreaming and coping behavior.

CONCLUDING REMARKS

Our odyssey is now complete. It has taken us over lands whose existence was not even suspected barely 25 years ago. Ours was a Cook's tour, of course, and the voyagers are cordially invited to return for more extended visits to places of their own choosing. But we did at least get a glimpse or two of most of the major landmarks of this vast and varied territory. We have been introduced to the modern technology of studying sleep and dreaming: the sleep lab. We have become acquainted with the formal properties of sleep, the background of dreaming: its two principal states, its five stages, and the manner in which it is organized into cycles. We have become a little bit familiar with the physiology and biochemistry of sleep and dreaming and the principal brain structures underlying both. We have speculated about the functions of sleep and dreaming, both in psychological and in biological terms; i.e., in terms of meaning and purpose and in terms of mechanism and process. We have assessed the overall status of the dream in the sleep literature and come away with the impression that the recent explosion of knowledge to which we have just been exposed has had far more of an impact on the biology than on the psychology of sleep and dreaming. Yet, despite this onesidedness, we *have* learned a great deal about dream psychology that we did *not* know before. We have learned to make certain distinctions, for example, that we probably would not have been able to make: between REM sleep and NONREM sleep; between REM sleep and REM dreams; between REM dreams and NONREM dreams; between nightmares and night terrors; between dreaming as a reflection and dreaming as a determinant of what goes on in our waking lives; and between the dream as a perceptual experience, as a memory, and as a communicated report. During all this, I hope that I as your guide have led, not *misled* you, and succeeded in keeping my opinions separate from the facts, which I have tried to present in as comprehensive and up-to-date a manner as possible.

A final comment or two about the functions of sleep and dreaming. Although I am firmly convinced that both serve adaptive functions, I do not wish to imply, of course, that sleep and dreaming are necessary *and* sufficient conditions for adaptation. All I am saying is that both significantly *contribute* to the adaptive process. Whether their functions are analogous, different, or overlap is still an open question. My hunch is that the functions of sleep and dreaming overlap. For instance, I find it difficult to believe that sleep can help a person gain better self-understanding. It is far more likely that dreams can help accomplish this. But does this mean that dreams, to be adaptively useful, must be reported, or can they fulfill their function as private, unreported experiences? And if they have to be communicated, is it sufficient simply to report dreams, or do they have to be laboriously worked over before they do us any good? We are now in the process of investigating whether the "dream-enhancement" effect described above can occur merely by having subjects listen to the playback of their recorded dreams *without* reflecting on their meaning. Perhaps dreams need merely to be brought into awareness, without having to be actively integrated into waking thought.

The practical applications of these considerations to the process of psychotherapy are not inconsequential. For one thing, they have a lot to do with the key issue of interpretation. If dreams merely need to be dreamed or recalled, without additional input or effort on our part, then interpretation may not be as necessary as it has been deemed to be in the past. Second, if REM dreams are adaptively more useful than NONREM dreams, as Cartwright et al. (1975b, 1977) and Fiss and Litchman (1976) have indicated, then therapists and patients perhaps should concentrate on REM dreams only—something that should not be much of a problem, since it has been shown that REM dreams can readily be discriminated from NONREM dreams (Monroe et al., 1965; Antrobus, 1967). Third, the therapeutic manipulation of dreams becomes a possibility—i.e., making dreams work better for us, as Garfield (1974) has suggested. The presleep suggestion to dream about a specific problem, which has been used by the author and many other investigators, appears to be a step in that direction. The sleep lab began as a place for conducting basic research on the nature of sleep and dreaming. Today, it has become a major center for diagnosing sleep disorders. In the future, it may serve therapeutic purposes as well. Finally, the sleep lab can also teach us a great deal about the process of psychotherapy itself. If dreaming is conducive to increased self-awareness, as Fiss and Litchman (1976) and Cartwright et al. (1977) have demonstrated, then isn't the sleep lab also teaching us something about the process of insight—the very core of therapeutic personality change?

One thing we can be pretty certain of: dreams probably have not *a* function but multiple functions. Just as breathing provides oxygen for the body, is necessary for speaking and singing, and also serves to express feelings, so dreaming may be "of as many different sorts as the process of waking thought; in one case it would be a fulfilled wish, in another a realized fear, or again a reflection persisting on into sleep, an intention, or a piece of creative thought . . . ." And this by none other than Freud (1905, p. 68) himself! Freud never seriously entertained this notion and continued to favor his wish-fulfillment concept, but had he been aware of what research has brought to light in the past two and a half decades, he might well have agreed that the entire spectrum of ego-functions (self-awareness, self-esteem, memory, learning, mood, mastery, and so on), in short, how we think, feel, and act, even creativity, can all be strongly influenced by what we dream about. This is not say that *all* dreams have to have a function. There is good reason to assume that some dreams, like some waking thoughts, are trivial; that they can fail to accomplish their work, as in the case of the nightmare, or the recurrent dream perhaps (Klein et al., 1971); that under certain circumstances, they can even be noxious. Just as not all sleep is physiologically restorative, so not all dreams are necessarily psychologically restorative. I think we should and will know someday why some dreams "work" and others do not. We will know the answer to this and many other questions, not by studying the biology of dreaming, but by means of a rigorous experimental psychology of dreaming. For that, we are only at the threshold of a new era.

FOOTNOTES

[1]This statement should not be taken too literally. While it is entirely correct to say that REM and NONREM sleep are qualitatively distinct organismic states, the reader should not be misled into assuming that what is necessarily true for one state cannot possibly be true for the other, for example: if mental activity is associated with REM sleep, then it cannot be associated with NONREM sleep. As the discussion below on mental activity during sleep will show, such a statement would be entirely false. After all, both REM and NONREM sleep represent the same brain doing two different things. The brain simply is not all that compartmentalized: a lot goes on in the brain that is common to both sleep states. Equal precaution is advised concerning recent speculations linking the right hemisphere to REM sleep mentation and the left hemisphere to NONREM and waking mentation (Cartwright, 1977, pp. 6 and 124). Intriguing though this possibility is, the data are not yet in to confirm it.

[2]This observation has given rise to the speculation (Ephron and Carrington, 1966) that REM and NONREM sleep are homeostatic mechanisms which regulate "cortical tonus." During NONREM sleep, a state of "deafferentation" occurs in response to stimulus overload during wakefulness. This state, however, leads to loss of "cortical tonus." To make up for this loss, the REM state acts to restore "cortical tonus" by periodic "afferentation", i.e., by internally generating sensory input.

[3]The fact that the REM state is clearly a mammalian phenomenon has suggested to Snyder (1966) that it is an important survival mechanism, serving a vital "vigilance" function by

providing the sleeping animal a period of preparatory activation for fight or flight. Some support for this theory comes from a study by Fiss et al. (1966), who found significantly longer reaction times and greater paucity of ideation following awakenings from NONREM sleep than after REM sleep awakenings.

[4] The critical distinction to keep in mind is quantitative rather than qualitative: it has to do primarily with continuity-discontinuity. Thus, for example, even though EMG changes tend to be long-lasting, brief instances of EMG suppression do occur and would be called phasic. Certain EEG characteristics, such as the K-complex, would also be considered phasic.

[5] In fact, the theory has already come under attack from several quarters. While undoubtedly there is a great deal of evidence supporting it, many findings contradict it. Hobson (1969), one of the severest critics of the theory, reports that electrical stimulation of the raphé nuclei does not enhance NONREM sleep, and that stimulation of the nucleus locus coeruleus does not increase REM sleep. He also questions the validity of the lesion effects reported by Jouvet on the ground that they are too nonspecific. It seems to me, however, that electrical brain stimulation suffers from the same defect. Other findings seem more damaging to the monoamine theory: for example, nearly normal amounts of slow wave sleep have been observed in serotonin-depleted animals (Ferguson et al., 1970). More recently, Hobson et al. (1975) have proposed an entirely new model, a "reciprocal interaction" model, according to which the basic regulatory mechanisms of sleep cycle oscillation are not aminergic but *cholinergic* and located in single neurons in the pontine gigantocellular tegmental field (FTG). Much attention has been focused since this chapter was written on the activity of these important "giant" cells. A comprehensive account of this activity and its implications for dream theory is given in Hobson and McCarley (1977).

[6] The reader may have noticed that the catecholamine dopamine has not been included in this presentation. The reason for this omission is that very little literature exists yet on the role of dopamine in the regulation of the sleep wakefulness cycle.

[7] For a detailed description of this technique and how it was originally developed, see H. Fiss (Transl.), "Formation and Transformation of the Perceptual World" by I. Kohler, *Psychological Issues*, Mon. No. 12, New York: International Universities Press, 1964.

[8] Stage 4 deprivation was accomplished not by awakening the subject but by sounding a buzzer whenever the EEG indicated the onset of a Stage 4 sleep period. The buzzer was loud enough to alter the subject's sleep stage, but not loud enough to awaken him. Without this ingenious method, the procedure would not have been possible, as the use of awakenings would have produced only total sleep deprivation. Obviously, REM deprivation is technically easier to achieve.

[9] "REM pressure" or the need for REM is variously defined as REM latency (the time elapsed between sleep onset and onset of the first REMP), REMP frequency, duration of first REMP, eye movement "density," and the size of the REM rebound itself. Thus, REM pressure is high when REM latency is short, when the first REMP is long, when REMP frequency and REM density are high, or when the REM rebound is large, and vice versa.

[10] This statement should not be misconstrued as meaning that contemporary psychologists have not attempted to generate theories compatible with those arising from the sleep laboratory. Quite the contrary. It only says that relatively few sleep laboratories have been devoted to experimental studies of dream function. In fact, a good many psychological theories of dream function have recently been advanced, theories that for the most part have tended to move away from Freudian to *ego-psychological* concepts of dream function.

Thus they are all pretty much in agreement that meaning is *revealed* rather than concealed by dreams and that dreams occur not so much to protect sleep, fulfill wishes, and discharge libido, but to promote specific *adaptive* functions, including, among others: environmental mastery, conflict and problem solving, information storage and processing, mood regulation, self-awareness, self-esteem, and ego-integration or consolidation. Some contemporary theorists have also approached the contribution of dreams to creativity. It would be far beyond the scope of this paper to present these views in any detail. An excellent review of contemporary dream theory is presented by Dallett (1973), but for an understanding in greater depth, readers should familiarize themselves especially with the following: Ullman (1959, 1960, 1961, 1962), Breger (1967), French and Fromm (1964), Fisher (1965), Cartwright (1977), Hawkins (1966), Jones (1962, 1970), Lerner (1967), Greenberg (1970), Pearlman (1970), and Krippner and Hughes (1970). For a fascinating anthropological documentation of the adaptive value of dreaming, the work of Stewart (1972) on the dream practices of the Senoi is particularly recommendable.

[11]Written by Dr. Milton Miller in the preface to *Dream Psychology and the New Biology of Dreaming* (M. Kramer, Ed.), Charles C Thomas, Publisher, Springfield, Illinois 1969.

[12]A subsequent related study (Starker, 1970) has demonstrated a similar effect.

[13]This choice of words by Freud became apparent to me while reading a recent German edition of his *Interpretation of Dreams* (Freud, 1961).

[14]An *acoustic* analysis of the dream reports of one of the subjects also revealed that *nonverbal* measures, such as voice amplitude, are more sensitive indicators of the emotional quality of dream reports than verbal measures. For example, we found that voice amplitude correlated more highly with both eye movement activity and conflictful content than any of the content ratings (Fiss et al., 1969). Future investigators might well bear this in mind.

[15]A study by Greenberg et al. (1970) on the psychological effects of REM deprivation (erroneously, in my opinion, called "dream deprivation" by the authors) led to remarkably similar results. They report that "material which had been well defended against in baseline tests appeared, after dream deprivation, in a much more open fashion," adding that ". . . the dream may serve the purpose of bringing new perceptions or new experiences into contact with old memories or patterns of behavior." This addendum of course is quite consistent with other recent formulation about dream function (see footnote 10).

REFERENCES

Adam, K., and Oswald, I. Sleep is for tissue restoration. *Journal of the Royal College of Physicians*, 11: 376–388, 1977.

Agnew, H. W., Webb, W. B., and Williams, R. L. The effects of stage four sleep deprivation. *Electroencephalography and Clinical Neurophysiology*, 17: 68–70, 1964.

Agnew, H., Webb, W., and Williams, R. Comparison of stage 4 and 1-REM stage deprivation. *Perceptual Motor Skills*, 24: 851, 1967.

Albert, I. B. REM sleep deprivation. *Biological Psychiatry*, 10: 341–351, 1975.

Albert, I. B., and Boone, D. Dream deprivation and facilitation with hypnosis. *Journal of Abnormal Psychology*, 84: 267–271, 1975.

Allen, S. REM sleep and memory. *Proceedings of the Second European Congress of Sleep Research*, Rome, Italy, 1974.

Allen, S., Oswald, I., Lewis, S., and Tagney, J. The effects of distorted visual input on sleep. *Psychophysiology*, 9: 498–504, 1972.

Antrobus, J. S. Discrimination of two sleep stages by human subjects. *Psychophysiology*, 4: 48–55, 1967.

Antrobus, J. S., and Fisher, C. Discrimination of dreaming and nondreaming sleep. *Archives of General Psychiatry*, 12: 395–401, 1965.

Arkin, A., Hastey, J. M., and Reiser, M. F. Post-hypnotically stimulated sleep-talking. *Journal of Nervous and Mental Disease*, 142: 293–309, 1966.

Aserinsky, E., and Kleitman, N. Regularly occurring periods of eye motility and concomitant phenomena during sleep. *Science*, 118: 273, 1953.

Baekeland, F., and Lasky, R. Exercise and sleep patterns in college athletes. *Perceptual Motor Skills*, 23: 1203–1207, 1966.

Barber, T. X., and Calverley, D. S. Hypnotic behavior as a function of task motivation. *Journal of Psychology*, 54: 363–389, 1962.

Barber, T. X., Walker, P. C., and Hahn, K. W. Effects of hypnotic induction and suggestions on nocturnal dreaming and thinking. *Journal of Abnormal Psychology*, 82: 414–427, 1973.

Barker, R. The effects of REM sleep on the retention of a visual task. *Psychophysiology*, 9: 107, 1972.

Berger, R. J. Oculomotor control: A possible function of REM sleep. *Psychological Review*, 76: 144–164, 1969.

Bergmann, M. S. The intrapsychic and communicative aspects of the dream. *International Journal of Psychoanalysis*, 47: 356–363, 1966.

Bokert, E. The effects of thirst and a related verbal stimulus on dream reports. *Dissertation Abstracts*, 28: 122–131, 1968.

Boland, B. D., and Dewsbury, D. A. Characteristics of sleep following sexual activity in male rats. *Physiological Behavior*, 6: 145–149, 1971.

Breger, L. Function of dreams. *Journal of Abnormal Psychology Monograph*, 72 (No. 5, Part 2, Whole No. 641): 1–28, 1967.

Breger, L., Hunter, I., and Lane, R. W. *The Effect of Stress on Dreams*. New York: International Universities Press, 1971.

Broughton, R. Sleep disorders: Disorders of arousal? *Science*, 159: 1070–1078, 1968.

Broughton, R. The incubus attack. In Hartmann, E. (Ed.), *Sleep and Dreaming*. Boston: Little Brown, 1970, pp. 188–192.

Brunette, R., and DeKoninck, J. The effect of pre-sleep suggestions related to a phobic object on dream affect. Paper presented at meeting of the Association for the Psychophysiological Study of Sleep, Houston, Texas, 1977.

Cartwright, R. Dreams and drug-induced fantasy behavior. *Archives of General Psychiatry*, 15: 7–15, 1966.

Cartwright, R. Sleep fantasy in normal and schizophrenic persons. *Journal of Abnormal Psychology*, 80: 275–279, 1972.

Cartwright, R. The influence of a conscious wish on dreams. *Journal of Abnormal Psychology*, 83: 387–393, 1974 (a).

Cartwright, R. Problem solving: Waking and dreaming. *Journal of Abnormal Psychology*, 83: 451–455, 1974 (b).

Cartwright, R. *Night Life*. Englewood Cliffs, New Jersey: Prentice-Hall, 1977.

Cartwright, R., Bernick, N. Borowitz, G., and Kling, A. The effect of an erotic movie on the sleep and dreams of young men. *Archives of General Psychiatry*, 20: 262–271, 1969.

Cartwright, R., Lloyd, S., Butters, L., Weiner, L., McCarthy, L., and Hancock, J. The effects of REM time on what is recalled. *Psychophysiology*, **12**: 149–159, 1975 (a).

Cartwright, R., Lloyd, S., Tipton, L., Wicklund, J., and Brown, J. Effects of lab training in dream recall on psychotherapy behavior, Part II. Presented at meeting of Association for the Psychophysiological Study of Sleep, Houston, Texas, 1977.

Cartwright, R., and Monroe, L. The relation of dreaming and REM sleep: The effects of REM deprivation under two conditions. *Journal of Personality and Social Psychology*, **10**: 69–74, 1968.

Cartwright, R., Monroe, L., and Palmer, C. Individual differences in response to REM deprivation. *Archives of General Psychiatry*, **16**: 297–303, 1967.

Cartwright, R., and Ratzel, R. Effects of dream loss on waking behavior. *Archives of General Psychiatry*, **27**: 277–280, 1972.

Cartwright, R., Weiner, L., and Wicklund, J. Effects of lab training in dream recall on psychotherapy behavior, Part I. Presented at meeting of Second International Sleep Research Congress, Edinburgh, 1975 (b).

Castaldo, V. Down's syndrome: A study of sleep patterns related to level of mental retardation. *American Journal of Mental Deficiency*, **74**: 187, 1969.

Chernik, D. Effect of REM sleep deprivation on learning and recall by humans. *Perceptual Motor Skills*, **34**: 283, 1972.

Clemes, S., and Dement, W. Effect of REM sleep deprivation on psychological functioning. *Journal of Nervous and Mental Disease*, **144**: 485, 1967.

Cohen, D. Toward a theory of dream recall. *Psychological Bulletin*, **81**: 138–154, 1974.

Cohen, D., and Cox, C. Neuroticism in the sleep laboratory: Implications for representational and adaptive properties of dreaming. *Journal of Abnormal Psychology*, **84**: 91–108, 1975.

Crow, T., and Wendlandt, S. Impaired acquisition of a passive avoidance response after lesions induced in the locus coeruleus. *Nature*, **259**: 42–44, 1976.

Dallett, J. Theories of dream function. *Psychological Bulletin*, **80**: 408–416, 1973.

DeKoninck, J., and Koulack, D. Dream content and adaptation to a stressful situation. *Journal of Abnormal Psychology*, **84**: 250–260, 1975.

Dement, W. Dream recall and eye movements during sleep in schizophrenics and normals. *Journal of Nervous and Mental Disease*, **122**: 263–269, 1955.

Dement, W. The effect of dream deprivation. *Science*, **131**: 1705–1707, 1960.

Dement, W. Experimental dream studies. In Masserman, J. H. (Ed.), *Science and Psychoanalysis*. New York: Grune & Stratton, 1964, pp. 129–162.

Dement, W. The biological role of REM sleep. In Kales, A. (Ed.), *Sleep Physiology and Pathology*. Philadelphia: Lippincott Co., 1969.

Dement, W., and Guilleminault, C. Sleep disorders: The state of the art. *Hospital Practice*, 57–71, 1973.

Dement, W., and Kleitman, N. Relation of eye movements during sleep to dream activity: Objective method for study of dreaming. *Journal of Experimental Psychology*, **53**: 339–346, 1957 (a).

Dement, W., and Kleitman, N. Cyclic variations in EEG during sleep and their relation to eye movements, body motility, and dreaming. *Electroencephalography and Clinical Neurophysiology*, **9**: 673–690, 1957 (b).

Dement, W., and Mitler, M. An overview of sleep research: Past, present, and future. In *American Handbook of Psychiatry* (Revised Edition, Vol. VI), New York: Basic Books, 1975, pp. 130–191.

Dement, W., and Wolpert, E. The relation of eye movements, body motility, and external stimuli to dream content. *Journal of Experimental Psychology*, **55**: 543, 1958.

Demin, N. N., and Rubinskaya, N. L. *Doklady Akademii Nauk*, 214: 940, 1974.

Ekstrand, B., Sullivan, M., Parker, D., and West, J. Spontaneous recovery and sleep. *Journal of Experimental Psychology*, 88: 142, 1971.

Ephron, H. S., and Carrington, P. Rapid eye movement sleep and cortical homeostasis. *Psychological Review*, 73: 500-526, 1966.

Erikson, E. The dream specimen of psychoanalysis. *Journal of the American Psychoanalytic Association*, 2: 5-55, 1954.

Evans, C. R., and Newman, E. A. Dreaming: An analogy from computers. *New Scientist*, 419: 577-579, 1964.

Feinberg, I. Eye movement activity during sleep and intellectual function in mental retardation. *Science*, 159: 1256, 1968.

Feinberg, I., Braun, M., and Schulman, E. EEG sleep patterns in mental retardation. *Electroencephalography and Clinical Neurophysiology*, 27: 128, 1969.

Feinberg, I., Koresko, R., Gottlieb, F., and Wender, P. Sleep encephalographic and eye movement patterns in schizophrenic patients. *Comprehensive Psychiatry*, 5: 44-53, 1964.

Feldman, R., and Dement, W. Possible relationships between REM sleep and memory consolidation. *Psychophysiology*, 5: 243, 1968.

Ferguson, J., Cohen, H., and Barchas, N. Sleep and wakefulness: A closer look. *Proceedings of the Federation of the American Society of Experimental Biology*. New York: Academic Press, 1970.

Ferguson, J., Henriksen, S., McGarr, K., Belenky, G., Mitchell, G., Gonda, W., Cohen, H., and Dement, W. Phasic event deprivation in the cat. *Psychophysiology*, 5: 238-239, 1968.

Fishbein, W., Kastaniotis, C., and Chattman, D. Paradoxical sleep: Prolonged augmentation following learning. *Brain Research*, 79: 61-75, 1974.

Fisher, C. Experimental induction of dreams by direct suggestion. *Journal of the American Psychoanalytic Association*, 1: 222-255, 1953.

Fisher, C. Psychoanalytic implications of recent research on sleep and dreaming. *Journal of the American Psychoanalytic Association*, 13: 197-303, 1965.

Fisher, C. Experimental and clinical approaches to the mind body problem through recent research in sleep and dreaming. Paper presented at meeting of the Michigan Psychiatric Society, Aruba, 1974.

Fisher, C., Byrne, J., and Edwards, A. NREM and REM nightmares. *Psychophysiology*, 5: 221, 1968.

Fisher, C., Byrne, J., Edwards, A., and Kahn, E. A psychophysiological study of nightmares. *Journal of the American Psychoanalytic Association*, 18: 747-782, 1970.

Fisher, C., Kahn, E., Edwards, A., and Davis, D. A psychophysiological study of nightmares and night terrors. *Archives of General Psychiatry*, 28: 252-259, 1973. Also in *Psychoanalysis and Contemporary Science*, New York: International Universities Press, 1974, pp. 317-398.

Fiss, H. The need to complete one's dreams. In Fisher, J., and Breger, L. (Eds), *The Meaning of Dreams: Some Insights from the Laboratory*. California Mental Health Research Symposium Mon. No. 3, 1969, pp. 38-63.

Fiss, H., Alpert, M., Klein, G. S., Shollar, E., and Gwozdz, F. Acoustic analysis of the voice during dream reporting. *Psychophysiology*, 6: 252, 1969.

Fiss, H., and Ellman, S. J., REM sleep interruption: Experimental shortening of REM period duration. *Psychophysiology*, 10: 510-516, 1973.

Fiss, H., Ellman, S. J., and Klein, G. S. Waking fantasies following interrupted and completed REM periods. *Archives of General Psychiatry*, 21: 230-239, 1969.

Fiss, H., Klein, G. S., and Bokert, E. Waking fantasies following interruption of two types of sleep. *Archives of General Psychiatry*, 14: 543–551, 1966.

Fiss, H., Klein, G. S., and Shollar, E. "Dream intensification" as a function of prolonged REM period interruption. In *Psychoanalysis and Contemporary Science*, New York: International Universities Press, 1974, pp. 399–424.

Fiss, H., Kremer, E., and Litchman, J. The mnemonic function of dreaming. Presented to the Association for the Psychophysiological Study of Sleep, Houston, Texas, 1977.

Fiss, H., and Litchman, J. Dream enhancement: An experimental approach to the adaptive function of dreams. Presented to the Association for the Psychophysiological Study of Sleep, Cincinnati, Ohio, 1976.

Foulkes, D. Dream reports from different stages of sleep. *Journal of Abnormal and Social Psychology*, 65: 14–25, 1962.

Foulkes, D., and Rechtschaffen, A. Presleep determinants of dream content: Effects of two films. *Perceptual Motor Skills*, 19: 983–1005, 1964.

Foulkes, D., and Vogel, G. Mental activity of sleep onset. *Journal of Abnormal Psychology*, 70: 231–243, 1965.

Foulkes, D., and Vogel, G. The current status of laboratory dream research. *Psychiatry Annals*, 4: 7–27, 1974.

French, T., and Fromm, E. *Dream Interpretation*. New York: Basic Books, 1964.

Freud, S. *The Interpretation of Dreams* (1900). In Strachey, J. (Ed.), *Standard Edition of the Complete Psychological Works of Sigmund Freud*. London: Hogarth Press, 1953.

Freud, S. *Die Traumdeutung* (1900), Vol. 2/3. *Gesammelte Werke*. Frankfurt a/M: S. Fischer Verlag, 1961.

Freud, S. (1905). *Fragment of an Analysis of a Case of Hysteria. Standard Edition*. London: Hogarth Press, 1953.

Garfield, P. *Creative Dreaming*. New York: Simon & Schuster, 1974.

Gastaut, H., and Broughton, R. Paroxysmal psychological events and certain phases of sleep. *Perceptual Motor Skills*, 17: 362, 1963.

Globus, G., and Gardner, R. CNS function underlying states of waking, sleeping, and REM sleep: A trireme model. Presented at meeting of Association for the Psychophysiological Study of Sleep, Denver, Colorado, 1968.

Goodenough, D. R. The phenomena of dream recall. In *Progress in Clinical Psychology*. New York: Grune & Stratton, 1969, pp. 136–153.

Goodenough, D. R., Lewis, H. B., Shapiro, A., and Sleser, I. Some correlates of dream reporting following laboratory awakenings. *Journal of Nervous and Mental Disease*, 140: 365–373, 1965(a).

Goodenough, D. R., Lewis, H. B., Shapiro, A., Jaret, L., and Sleser, I. Dream reporting following abrupt and gradual awakenings from different types of sleep. *Journal of Personality and Social Psychology*, 2: 170–179, 1965(b).

Goodenough, D. R., Shapiro, A., Holden, M., and Steinschriber, L. A. A comparison of dreamers and nondreamers: Eye movements, electroencephalograms, and the recall of dreams. *Journal of Abnormal Psychology*, 59: 295–302, 1959.

Goodenough, D. R., Witkin, H. A., Lewis, H. B., Koulack, D., and Cohen, H. Repression, interference, and field dependence as factors in dream forgetting. *Journal of Abnormal Psychology*, 83: 32–44, 1974.

Greenberg, R. Dreaming and memory. In Hartmann, E. (Ed.), *Sleep and Dreaming*. Boston: Little Brown, 1970, pp. 238–267.

Greenberg, R., and Dewan, E. Aphasia and rapid eye movement sleep. *Nature*, 223: 183, 1969.

Greenberg, R., Kelty, M., and Dewan, E. Sleep patterns in the newly hatched chick. Paper presented to the Association for the Psychophysiological Study of Sleep, Boston, 1969.

Greenberg, R., and Pearlman, C. A psychoanalytic dream continuum: The source and functions of dreams. *International Review of Psychoanalysis*, 2: 441–448, 1975(a).

Greenberg, R., and Pearlman, C. REM sleep and the analytic process: A psychophysiologic bridge. *The Psychoanalytic Quarterly*, 44: 392–403, 1975(b).

Greenberg, R., Pearlman, C., Fingar, R., Kantrowitz, J., and Kawliche, S. The effects of dream deprivation: Implications for a theory of the psychological function of dreaming. *British Journal of Medical Psychology*, 43: 1–11, 1970.

Greenberg, R., Pearlman, C., and Gampel, D. War neuroses and the adaptive function of REM sleep. *British Journal of Medical Psychology*, 45: 27–33, 1972.

Greenberg, R., Pillard, R., and Pearlman, C. The effect of REM deprivation on adaptation to stress. *Psychosomatic Medicine*, 34: 257–262, 1972.

Greenson, R. The exceptional position of the dream in psychoanalytic practice. *Psychoanalytic Quaterly*, 39: 519–549, 1970.

Griesser, E., Greenberg, R., and Harrison, R. The adaptive function of sleep: the differential effects of sleep and dreaming on recall. *Journal of Abnormal Psychology*, 80: 280–286, 1972.

Gulevitch, G., Dement, W., and Johnson, L. Psychiatric and EEG observations on a case of prolonged wakefulness. *Archives of General Psychiatry*, 15: 29–35, 1966.

Gulevitch, G., Dement, W., and Zarcone, V. All night sleep recordings of chronic schizophrenics in remission. *Comprehensive Psychiatry*, 8: 141–149, 1967.

Hall, C. S. Processes of fantasy. *Science*, 153: 626–627, 1966.

Hartmann, E. *The Functions of Sleep*. New Haven: Yale University Press, 1973.

Hartmann, H., Kris, E., and Loewenstein, R. M. Papers on psychoanalytic psychology. *Psychological Issues*, Mon. No. 14. New York: International Universities Press, 1964, pp. 42–43.

Hauri, P. Effects of evening activity on early night sleep. *Psychophysiology*, 4: 267–277, 1968.

Hawkins, D. R. A review of psychoanalytic dream theory in the light of recent psychophysiological studies of sleep and dreaming. *British Journal of Medical Psychology*, 39: 85–104, 1966.

Hobson, J. A. Sleep after exercise. *Science*, 162: 1503–1505, 1968.

Hobson, J. A. Sleep: Biochemical aspects. *New England Journal of Medicine*, 281: 1468–1470, 1969.

Hobson, J. A., and McCarley, R. W. The brain as a dream state generator: An activation-synthesis hypothesis of the dream process. *The American Journal of Psychiatry*, 134: 1335–1348, 1977.

Hobson, J. A., McCarley, R. W., and Wyzinski, P. W. Sleep cycle oscillation: Reciprocal discharge by two brainstem neuronal groups. *Science*, 189: 55–58, 1975.

Horne, J. A. Hail slow wave sleep: Goodbye REM. *Bulletin of the British Psychological Society*, 29: 74–79, 1976.

Horne, J. A., and Porter, J. M. Exercise and human sleep. *Nature*, 256: 573–575, 1975.

Jones, R. M. *Ego Synthesis in Dreams*. Cambridge, Massachusetts: Schenkman, 1962.

Jones, R. M. *The New Psychology of Dreaming*. New York: Grune & Stratton, 1970.

Jouvet, M. Biogenic amines and the states of sleep. *Science*, 163: 32–41, 1969.

Jouvet, M. Some monoaminergic mechanisms controlling sleep and waking. In Karczmar, A. G., and Eccles, J. C. (Eds.), *Brain and Human Behavior*. New York: Springer Verlag, 1972, pp. 131–161.

Jouvet, M. Monoaminergic regulation of the sleep-waking cycle. In *Pharmacology and the Future of Man.* Basel, Switzerland: Karger, 1973, pp. 103–107.

Jouvet, M. The role of monoaminergic neurons in the regulation and function of sleep. In Petre-Quadens, O., and Schlag, D. J. (Eds.), *Basic Sleep Mechanisms.* New York: Academic Press, 1974, pp. 207–236.

Jung, C. G. *Modern Man in Search of a Soul.* New York: Harcourt, Brace, & World, 1933.

Kales, A. Holdemaker, F., Jacobson, A., and Lichtenstein, E. Dream deprivation: An experimental appraisal. *Nature*, 204: 1337, 1964.

Kales, A., and Kales, J. D. Sleep disorders: Recent findings in the diagnosis and treatment of disturbed sleep. *New England Journal of Medicine*, 290: 487–499, 1974.

Klein, G. S. Peremptory ideation: Structure and force in motivated ideas. In Klein, G. S., *Perception, Motives, and Personality.* New York: Knopf, 1970, pp. 357–412.

Klein, G. S., Fiss, H., Shollar, E., Dalbeck, R., Warga, C., and Gwozdz, F. Recurrent dream fragments and fantasies elicited in interrupted and completed REM periods. *Psychophysiology*, 7: 331–332, 1971.

Kogan, A. B., Brodsky, V. Y., Feldman, G. L., and Gusatinsky, V. N. Comparison of electrical and metabolic indices of sleep processes. In Moiseeva, N. I. (Ed.), *Proceedings of Symposium "Self-Regulation of the Sleep Process."* Leningrad: Academy of Sciences of the USSR, 1975.

Kramer, M., Roehrs, T., and Roth, T. Mood change and the physiology of sleep. *Comprehensive Psychiatry,* 17: 161–165, 1976.

Kramer, M., Whitman, R., Baldridge, B. J., and Lansky, L. M. Patterns of dreaming: The inter-relationship of the dreams of a night. *Journal of Nervous and Mental Disease*, 139: 426–439, 1964.

Kramer, M., Whitman, R., Baldridge, B., and Ornstein, P. Dream content in male schizophrenic patients. *Diseases of the Nervous System*, 31: 51–58, 1970.

Krippner, S., and Hughes, W. Dreams and human potential. *Journal of Humanistic Psychology*, 10: 1–20, 1970.

Kupfer, D., Wyatt, R., Scott, J., and Snyder, F. Sleep disturbance in acute schizophrenic patients. *American Journal of Psychiatry*, 126: 1213–1223, 1970.

Leconte, P., Hennevin, E., and Bloch, V. Analyse des effets d'un apprentissage et de son niveau d'acquisition sur le sommeil paradoxcal. *Brain Research*, 49: 367–379, 1973.

Leconte, P., Hennevin, E., and Bloch, V. Duration of paradoxical sleep necessary for the acquisition of conditioned avoidance in the rat. *Physiology and Behavior*, 13: 675–681, 1974.

Lerner, B. Dream function reconsidered. *Journal of Abnormal Psychology.* 72: 85–100, 1967.

Lewin, I., and Gombosh, D. Increase in REM time as a function of the need for divergent thinking. Report to the First European Congress of Sleep Research, Basel, Switzerland, 1972.

Lewis, H. B., Goodenough, D. R., Shapiro, A., and Sleser, I. Individual differences in dream recall. *Journal of Abnormal Psychology*, 71: 52–59, 1966.

Lucero, M. A. Lengthening of REM sleep duration consecutive to learning in the rat. *Brain Research*, 20: 319–322, 1970.

MacFayden, V. M., Oswald, I., and Lewis, S. A. Starvation and human slow wave sleep. *Journal of Applied Physiology*, 35: 391–394, 1973.

Matsumoto, M., Nishisho, T., Sudo, T., Sadahiro, T., and Miyoshi, M. Influence of fatigue on sleep. *Nature*, 218: 177–178, 1968.

McGinty, D. J. Effects of prolonged isolation and subsequent enrichment on sleep patterns in kittens. *Electroencephalography and Clinical Neurophysiology*, 26: 332–337, 1969.

Monroe, L.   Psychological and physiological differences between good and poor sleepers. *Journal of Abnormal Psychology*, **72**: 255, 1967.

Monroe, L., Rechtschaffen, A., Foulkes, D., and Jensen, J.   Discriminability of REM and NREM reports. *Journal of Personality and Social Psychology*, **2**: 456–460, 1965.

Morgane, P., and Stern, W.   Chemical anatomy of brain circuits in relation to sleep and wakefulness. In Weitzman, E. (Ed.), *Advances in Sleep Research*, Vol. 1. New York: Spectrum Publications, 1974, pp. 1–131.

Morgane, P., and Stern, W.   The role of serotonin and norepinephrine in sleep–waking activity. In Barnard, B. K. (Ed.), *Aminergic Hypotheses of Behavior: Reality or Cliché?* N.I.D.A. Research Mon. No. 3, Rockville, Md., 1975, pp. 37–60.

Muzio, J., Roffwarg, H. Anders, C., and Muzio, L.   Retention of rote-learned verbal material and alterations in the normal sleep EEG. Paper presented to Association for the Psychophysiological Study of Sleep, Bruges, Belgium, 1971.

Okuma, T., Sunami, Y., Fukuma, E., Takeo, S., and Motoike, M.   Dream content study in chronic schizophrenics and normals by REMP-awakening technique. *Folia Psychiatrica et Neurologica Japanica*, **3**: 151–162, 1970.

Oswald, I.   Report to the First European Congress of Sleep Research, Basel, Switzerland, 1972.

Pearlman, C.   The adaptive function of dreaming. In Hartmann, E. (Ed.), *Sleep and Dreaming*. Boston: Little Brown, 1970, pp. 329–334.

Rapaport, D.   Some metapsychological considerations concerning activity and passivity. In Gill, M. (Ed.), *Collected Papers of David Rapaport*. New York: Basic Books, 1967.

Rechtschaffen, A.   Discussion of W. Dement's "Experimental dream studies." In Masserman, J. H. (Ed.), *Science and Psychoanalysis*. New York: Grune & Stratton, 1964, pp. 162–171.

Rechtschaffen, A.   Dream reports and dream experiences. *Experimental Neurology*, Suppl. 4: 4–15. 1967.

Rechtschaffen, A., The singlemindedness and isolation of dreams. *Sleep*, **1**: 97–109, 1978.

Rechtschaffen, A., Verdone, P., and Wheaton, G.   Reports of mental activity during sleep. *Journal of the Canadian Psychiatric Association*, **8**: 409–414, 1963.

Rechtschaffen, A., Watson, R., Wincor, M., Molinari, S., and Barta, S.   The relationship of phasic and tonic periorbital EMG activity to NONREM mentation. Paper given at meeting of the Association for the Psychophysiological Study of Sleep, Lake Minnewaska, New York, 1972.

Robert, W. *Der Traum als Naturnotwendigkeit erklaert*. Hamburg, Germany, 1886.

Roffwarg, H., Dement, W., Muzio, J. N., and Fisher, C.   Dream imagery: Relationship to rapid eye movements of sleep. *Archives of General Psychiatry*, **7**: 235, 1962.

Roffwarg, H., Muzio, J. N., and Dement, W.   Ontogenetic development of the human sleep-dream cycle. *Science*, **152**: 604–619, 1966.

Sampson, H.   Psychological effects of deprivation of dreaming sleep. *Journal of Nervous and Mental Disease*, **143**: 305, 1966.

Schonbar, R.   Differential dream recall frequency as a component of life style. *Journal of Consulting Psychology*, **29**: 468–474, 1965.

Shapiro, A. Goodenough, D. R., and Gryler, R. B.   Dream recall as a function of method of awakening. *Psychosomatic Medicine*, **25**: 174–180, 1963.

Shapiro, A., Goodenough, D. R., Lewis, H. B., and Sleser, I.   Gradual arousal from sleep: A determinant of thinking reports. *Psychosomatic Medicine*, **27**: 342–349, 1965.

Slap, J. W.   On dreaming at sleep onset. *The Psychoanalytic Quarterly*, **46**: 71–81, 1977.

Smith, C., Kitahama, K., Valatx, J., and Jouvet, M.   Increased paradoxical sleep in mice during acquisition of a shock avoidance task. *Brain Research*, **77**: 221–230, 1974.

Snyder, F. Toward an evolutionary theory of dreaming. *American Journal of Psychiatry*, 123: 121–136, 1966.

Snyder, F. The physiology of dreaming. In Kramer, M. (Ed.), *Dream Psychology and the New Biology of Dreaming*. Springfield, Illinois: Charles C. Thomas, 1969.

Spitz, R. A. The derailment of dialogue: Stimulus overload, action cycles, and the completion gradient. *Journal of the American Psychoanalytic Association*, 12: 752–775, 1964.

Starker, S. Effects of sleep state and method of awakening upon TAT productions at arousal. *Journal of Nervous and Mental Disease*, 150: 188–194, 1970.

Stewart, K. Dream theory in Malaya. In Tart, C. (Ed.), *Altered States of Consciousness*. New York: Doubleday, 1972.

Stoyva, J., and Kamiya, J. Electrophysiological studies of dreaming as the prototype of a new strategy in the study of consciousness. *Psychological Review*, 75: 192–205, 1968.

Tart, C. Frequency of dream recall and some personality measures. *Journal of Consulting Psychology*, 26: 467–470, 1962.

Tart, C. A comparison of suggested dreams occurring in hypnosis and sleep. *International Journal of Clinical and Experimental Hypnosis*, 12: 263–289, 1964.

Ullman, M. The adaptive significance of the dream. *Journal of Nervous and Mental Disease*, 129: 144–149, 1959.

Ullman, M. The social roots of the dream. *American Journal of Psychoanalysis*, 20: 180–196, 1960.

Ullman, M. Dreaming, altered stages of consciousness, and the problem of vigilance. *Journal of Nervous and Mental Disease*. 133: 529–535, 1961.

Ullman, M. Dreaming, life style and physiology: A comment on Adler's view of the dream. *Journal of Individual Psychology*, 18: 18–25, 1962.

Vogel, G. W. A review of REM sleep deprivation. *Archives of General Psychiatry*, 32: 749–761, 1975.

Vogel, G. W., and Traub, A. REM deprivation: Effect on schizophrenic patients. *Archives of General Psychiatry*, 18: 287–300, 1968.

Vogel, G. W., Traub, A., Ben-Horin, P., and Meyers, G. REM deprivation: The effect on depressed patients. *Archives of General Psychiatry*, 18: 301–311, 1968.

Watson, R. Mental correlates of periorbital potentials during REM sleep. Unpublished doctoral dissertation, University of Chicago, 1972.

Watson, R., Liebmann, K., and Watson, S. Comparison of NONREM PIP frequency in schizophrenic and nonschizophrenic patients. Paper presented to the Association for the Psychophysiological Study of Sleep, Cincinnati, Ohio, 1976.

Webb, W. B. Paper presented at a symposium of the First International Congress of the Association for the Psychophysiological Study of Sleep, Bruges, Belgium, 1971.

Webb, W. B. *Sleep: The Gentle Tyrant*. Englewood Cliffs, New Jersey, 1975.

Williams, R., Karacan, I., and Hursch, C. Clinical sleep disorders—Dyssomnias. In *Electroencephalography of Human Sleep: Clinical Applications*. New York: Wiley, 1974, pp. 119–160.

Witkin, H., and Lewis, H. Presleep experiences and dreams. In Witkin, H. and Lewis, H. (Eds.), *Experimental Studies of Dreaming*. New York: Random House, 1967.

Zarcone, V., Gulevich, G., Pivik, T., and Dement, W. Partial REM phase deprivation and schizophrenia. *Archives of General Psychiatry*, 18: 194–202, 1968.

Zeigarnik, B. Das Behalten erledigter und unerledigter Handlungen. *Psychologische Forschungen*, 9: 1–85, 1927.

Zimmerman, J., Stoyva, J., and Metcalf, D. Distorted visual feedback and augmented REM sleep. *Psychophysiology*, 7: 298, 1970.

Zimmerman, W.   Sleep mentation and auditory awakening thresholds.   *Psychophysiology*, 6: 540, 1970.

Zloty, R. B., Burdick, J. A., and Adamson, J. D.   Sleep of distance runners.   *Activ. Nerv. Sup.*, 15: 217–221, 1973.

Zornetzer, S., and Gold, M.   The locus coeruleus: Its possible role in memory consolidation.   *Physiology and Behavior*, 16: 331–336, 1976.

3

The Form of Dreams and the Biology of Sleep

Robert W. McCarley and J. Allan Hobson

I. INTRODUCTION AND STATEMENT OF THE ACTIVATION-SYNTHESIS HYPOTHESIS FOR DREAM FORMATION

This chapter has two purposes: the first is the traditional task of surveying its assigned field of purview, "organic" or brain-oriented models of dream generation; this we do briefly. The second task is to go beyond survey and to sketch a unified theory of mind and brain activity in sleep, the *activation-synthesis hypothesis of dream generation*. This latter attempt has been prompted by the explosion of knowledge in both general neurobiology and the specific neurobiology of the brain stem and of the sleep cycle.

Our theory does not attempt to suggest the mechanisms for all aspects of dream construction; we restrict ourselves to those aspects for which there are plausible matches with the physiology of the desynchronized sleep state (D sleep). These concern more the formal, universal aspects of the dream experience and less the content particular to one individual. But in the creation of dreams as in the creation of other human works, the distinction between form and content is a very blurred one, and many aspects of content may follow from the form.

The activation-synthesis model of dream formation is a straightforward notion that can be put simply: during the desynchronized sleep state (D sleep), sensory input from the external world is constricted, but the brain is activated internally by motivationally neutral activity arising from the pontine reticular formation. Brain areas activated include both sensory and motor systems. The sensations and the feedback from neuronal command signals for muscular activity so engendered play preeminant roles in the construction of the dream experience. The generation of successive dream plots is temporally isomorphic with the successive sequences of activity of pontine reticular neurons and the consequent activation of different motor pattern generators and sensory systems. The synthetic aspects of dream formation are the knitting together of these often disparate elements, and the resulting combinations of incongruous elements causes some of the bizarreness of the dream experience. Throughout this chapter the strategy followed is to look for possible matches between D state physiology and dreaming, to seek isomorphisms or instances of similar form between the mental and the physiological domains during dreaming sleep. We do *not* assert the primacy of either, nor do we assert that events in one domain cause events in the other. They represent different conceptualizations.

Such a program of looking at both mind and body requires the reader, as well as the authors, to examine modern neurophysiology as well as dream content. For the reader accustomed to staying firmly planted on one side or the other of the hyphen in psycho-physiology, this may prove demanding or even discouraging. To facilitate traversing the conceptual tightrope symbolized by the hyphen, we summarize the more technical details of the physiological story at the beginning of the appropriate sections. The reader may wish to use the following list of section topics to chart his course of initial reading and to facilitate later use of the chapter as a reference.

- *The Mind-Brain Problem* (II) is a brief statement of the philosophical issues involved in the consideration of both mind and body.
- *The Neurobiologically Based Dream Theory of Sigmund Freud* (III) shows that Freud's neural model of dreams in the *Project* and the psychological model of The *Interpretation of Dreams* are based in the neurobiology of the 1890's.
- *The Physiology of Desynchronized Sleep State Generation* (IV) surveys the physiology of the D state and modern knowledge about its generation.
- *Visual and Motor System Physiological Processes during D Sleep of Special Relevance to Dream Theory* (V) is a fairly detailed physiological survey of: the varieties of information coding in the visual and oculomotor systems and their implications for information transfer in the dream state; the concept of the motor pattern generator and how activation of motor pattern generators is an important substrate for dream construction.
- *Contemporary Theories of Mind-Body Relationships during Dreams* (VI) surveys recent history, theories, and data on the relationship between mind and brain activity during sleep.
- *Dream Form and Dream Content: The Activation-Synthesis Hypothesis Applied to Dream Reports* (VII) examines the congruence of this hypothesis with actual dream reports.

- The *Summary* gives an overview of the essential physiological processes of the D state and the correspondences with the psychological events of dreams.

The reader unfamiliar with the activation-synthesis hypothesis may wish to scan first the summary and then turn to the section on dream form and dream content to find the specific ways in which this new hypothesis can be applied to dream interpretation.   Most of the sections can be read independently of each other.

II. THE MIND-BRAIN PROBLEM

Whether of a philosophical inclination or not, the researcher combining work with the mind (dreams) and with the body and brain (the desynchronized sleep state) cannot avoid traversing the thicket of philosophical issues surrounding the relationship of mind and body, or to phrase it more properly in view of today's knowledge, the relationship of mind and brain.   Thus the researcher would do well to be aware of the various philosophical viewpoints on the mind-brain problem so as to know the difficulties, strengths, and some of the implications of each.   Otherwise the researcher may awaken and be shocked to find that he or she, in a situation epistemologically analogous to that of the bourgeois gentilhomme, has been speaking central state materialism all his or her scientific life.   Our outline is brief and general and intended as a series of signposts rather than a definitive lexicon.   Further reading can be found in our sources for this section (Smart, 1963; Feigl, 1967; White, 1967; Shaffer, 1968; Presley, 1971; Globus et al., 1976).

The idea of a distinction between mind and body may have had its origins in the observation that mind or mental operations were quite different from material objects which occupied space, and were substantive.   Most of the modern differences in thinking on the mind-body problem were evident even in Greek culture.   Democritus, the prototypical materialist, postulated that there existed nothing but atoms (matter) in space, and that mind was reducible to particular combinations of matter.   Plato's insistence on the immateriality of the psyche is equally well known.   The fundamental positions that one can take about the mind-brain problem, as we shall term it, are quite simple variants of these two positions.   (1) The *immaterialist* believes that there is nothing but mind; (2) the *materialist* holds that there is nothing but matter; (3) the *dualistic* position asserts that there are both mind and matter; (4) *neutral monism* holds that there is some neutral other substance of which mind and matter are manifestations; (5) finally, the *philosophical linguistic* position is that the difficulties which arise in the consideration of the mind-brain problem are really problems arising from different kinds of linguistic categories, from use of different conceptual models.   This is the viewpoint that we shall adopt in our exposition of scientific questions and investigations relevant to sleep research. We now turn to a sketch of the various schools.

Immaterialism.   This is the theory most vigorously championed by and associated with Bishop Berkeley, who held that there is no matter, only minds. Material objects in this viewpoint are the creation either of a single mind (absolute idealism) or a multiplicity of minds whose concepts are unified by the fact that God created minds in the same way, and thus produced a uniformity of perceptions and viewpoints (subjective idealism, Berkeley's viewpoint). It is perhaps not necessary to state that this viewpoint has not found favor with scientists. Because of this and other inherent problems, we shall not consider it further.

Dualism.   This is the viewpoint of Descartes, which postulates that both mind and body exist and neither is preemminent. The chief difficulty in this philosophical stance is specifying how mind and body interact, if they do. Descartes belived in *interactionism*, the notion that mind and body do causally affect each other. In order to make this doctrine plausible, Descartes felt that he must specify a place in the brain where this occurred; he chose the pineal. Of course, modern neurophysiology and anatomy have found no evidence for the pineal being in any way specialized for this function, and this belief in interactionism is not popular today.

Psychophysical parallelism is a doctrine that the mind and body exist independently but operate concomitantly, like two perfect clocks ticking simultaneously, although neither causally affects the other. Most scientists, operating on a conscious or unconscious approval of the principle of Ockham's razor that one should not multiply entities needlessly, have not seriously considered psychophysical parallelism. The great English physiologist Sherrington was a distinguished exception: "It is not inherently more implausible, I suppose, that there should be two kinds of fundamental reality, mind and matter, than one" (see Granit, 1967). Finally, there is a variant of dualism called *epiphenomenalism*, which asserts that while the body can causally affect the mind, mental events cannot effect brain events. It asserts that mental events are really shadows, by-products or "epiphenomena" of the determining physical events. This viewpoint is closely related to the next, eliminative materialism.

Materialism.   *Eliminative materialism* is a position that no such things as sensations, images, perceptions, or emotions really exist. They either are described as useless or meaningless noise from the workings of the causal material processes, or are outmoded prescientific notions or descriptions with no truth value. Apart from the difficulty in consistently maintaining such a theory on an existential and experiential basis, it appears unlikely that any students of dreaming will believe that the subject of their interest lies beyond scientific description, although some may believe that dreams are indeed "noise" and without meaning. *Reductive materialism* asserts that mental phenomena exist but are now or will be in the future reducible to material events, to particular combinations of matter. A currently very strong trend in materialism theory is labeled *central state materialism*. This theory is also sometimes called the *identity thesis*, and simply asserts that mental events, states, and processes are all really reducible to brain states, processes, and events. Much of Herbert Feigl's writing has espoused a variant of this kind of position. We suspect that most contemporary reductionists fall into this category, and a recent discussion of consciousness includes arguments for and against this position (Globus et al., 1976).

One of the reasons for the strong interest in the philosophy of mind in modern philosophical thought was an extremely provocative and influential book by Gilbert Ryle (1949) called *The Concept of Mind*. In it, Ryle takes what might be termed an *analytical behaviorist position*. This states that in talking about the mind one is not really talking about an actual entity or "a ghost in the machine" but a notion of how people are disposed to behave, i.e., talking about the probability of various kinds of behavior. The analytical behaviorist suggests that when one says "I have a pain," what one is really doing is giving a verbal surrogate for a wince; and, similarly, to feel angry is to have a disposition to exhibit angry behavior. Analytical behaviorism is a logical position and as such, is not connected at all with the psychological theory of behaviorism.

Neutral Monism.   This theory asserts that neither mental nor physical events are fundamental, but both are aspects of some other more fundamental substance. Closely linked to this viewpoint is the theory of some *linguistic philosophers* that the real differences between mind and body lie in the use of two different kinds of language to describe them, two different kinds of conceptual systems. One is a physical science language with a conceptual analytic model, and the other is the world of "person talk," in which moral responsibilities and ethical values enter in. Our emphasis on mind–body conceptual systems is closely related to the philosophical linguistic viewpoint.

Mind–Body Isomorphism.   We suggest that the most useful strategy in the scientific study of mind–brain relations is to regard mind and brain concepts as coming from different linguistic and conceptual systems. In accord with the phenomenologists, we see the common origin of all percepts, whether of objects or of motions, in raw experiential consciousness, and suggest this initial event furnishes the foundation for elaboration of both mind and body or brain concepts. The domain of physiological theory and data is one example of a particular logical and conceptual system, while the domain of the study of mental events or psychology is another. We do not seek to reduce physiological to psychological events or psychological to physical events. Nor do we view psychological events as causing physiological events or vice versa. Instead we view the proper strategy in mind-brain study as seeking areas of contact between the conceptualizations of physiological and psychological theory. Mind-body isomorphism is our name for this strategy; it implies a conviction that such matching or mapping between operations and objects in the two conceptual systems of mind and brain can be found.

Isomorphism literally means "of the same form" and has been used in mathematics to indicate correspondences between different algebraic systems, composed of objects and operations on these objects. We believe that the search for mind-brain isomorphisms will be particularly fruitful in the effort to link dream theory and D state physiology. We further suggest that most dream theories, historical or current, can be analyzed in terms of the kind of isomorphisms their proponents believe exist between mind and brain theory. The next section will discuss Freud, who believed in the virtual identity of mind and brain concepts and often used the same kind of conceptual language to discuss events in both domains. In this context it is interesting also that a contemporary theorist, E. Hartmann, believes in a simple isomorphism between the effects of a neurochemical transmitter (dopamine) and the psychoanalytic mental concept of "psychic energy."

III. THE NEUROBIOLOGICALLY BASED DREAM THEORY OF SIGMUND FREUD

While the prevailing view for many years was that Freud's *The Interpretation of Dreams* (Freud, 1900) was a purely psychological theory, the discovery and publication of Freud's manuscript of a *Project for a Scientific Psychology* (Freud, 1895) has revolutionized our understanding of the roots of Freud's psychoanalytic model of the mind. The *Project* shows that Freud's dream theory was derived from a model of the brain that in turn was shaped by the neurobiological theories current in 1895, when the *Project* was written (McCarley and Hobson, 1977, and McCarley, 1979a, discuss this topic in more detail).

It should be appreciated that Freud spent most of his early career working in neurobiology as a medical student, as a resident in neurology, and as a researcher at the Physiological Institute of the University of Vienna. Even after leaving academic medicine for a private practice, Freud maintained an active interest in neurobiology, as evinced by his being asked to write an article on the brain in a medical encyclopedia (Freud, 1888) and by his 1891 volume on aphasia (Freud, 1891).

It may be that Freud's efforts at mind-body integration were spurred by a

book published in 1894 by Sigmund Exner, the head of the University Physiological Institute and Freud's one-time co-worker (Exner, 1894). Exner's book,
A Physiological Explanation of Psychic Events, was intended to show that "life
processes can be explained on the basis of chemical and physical processes,"
and that no vitalistic doctrines were necessary. Freud espoused a similar faith
in scientific method and began his *Project* with an explicitly materialist position,
quoting Lucretius to the effect that nothing exists except atoms in motion and
space. Freud commented on his view of the problems of validation of psychological theories by noting he was writing the *Project* using physiological language
as much as possible in order to make his brain and mind model "perspicacious
and free from contradiction." Although Freud began the *Project* with a philosophical stance akin to reductive materialism, he later adopted a variant of mind-
body isomorphism: a belief in simple isomorphisms between physical and mental
processes that came close to asserting their identity. Freud therefore often did
not find it necessary to tell the reader when he was describing a mental event
and when a physical event. It is an interesting confirmation of our viewpoint
of the influence of neurology on Freud's mind theory that a recent computer
modeling of Freud's mental schema found that the model would not work, was
incomplete, unless brain concepts were also included (Wegman).

We begin our brief survey of Freud's *Project* by noting that Freud had problems in correctly conceptualizing fundamental aspects of neuronal function.
This is, of course, quite understandable, since the neuron doctrine was less than
five years old when he was working, and most of these properties were not
discovered until much later. Freud had to base his notions on the limited knowledge of 1895. In so doing, Freud mistakenly thought of neurons as passive
receptacles of electrical energy. Freud, again erroneously, believed that this
energy was always derived from extraneuronal sources and that neurons stored
this energy in a fashion analogous to capacitors in electric circuits. Furthermore, Freud did not conceive of neurons as signal elements as we would today,
but rather as nervous system elements adapted for passing on their entire supply
of energy, and being capable of being charged or occupied with nervous energy
("cathected" is the translation of Freud's term *Besetzung*) from the external
world and from somatic, extracerebral sources. Finally, Freud included no
inhibitory neurons in his model; there were only excitatory elements, and he
thus had difficulty in modeling diversion of neural activity (Figure 3-1). Even
at the cellular level Freud's model of the brain and mind was such that one
might easily suppose that the organism constructed from these elements would
run into difficulty with an energy overload. Energy was immutable; it could
be transferred from one element to another, but could never be canceled, inhibited, or quenched.

In fashioning the neurons into a complete nervous system, Freud also followed

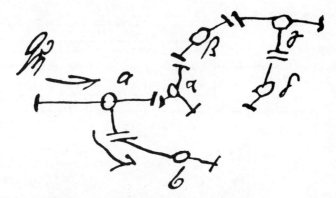

Figure 3-1. Freud's sketch illustrates his concept of diversion of neural energy through a "side cathexis." The normal flow of energy (labeled *Qn* in Freud's script) is to neuron *b*: Freud postulated that a side cathexis of neuron alpha would attract *Qn* and divert the flow from neuron *b*. Freud believed this postsynaptic attraction of energy or side cathexis (for which there is no experimental support) to be the neuronal mechanism underlying repression. If Freud were doing the *Project* today, repression could not be realistically modeled by a "side-cathexis" of immutable neural energy. Substitution of modern physiological concepts would have profound consequences for the isomorphic psychological models of psychoanalytic theory (McCarley and Hobson, 1977).

the theories current in the biology of his day. His fundamental guideline was an organism operating according to the principle of reflex action (see Figure 3-2). Energy entered the nervous system from outside the brain and was passed along through the various internal systems to be discharged in motoric activity. Like individual neurons, neuronal systems had no independent energy, for all of nervous energy was ultimately derived from outside the brain. This concept seems surprising today in view of our awareness of the brain's capacity to provide its own energy sources for signaling and its capacity to modulate and regulate itself. Freud believed that the nervous system on both the cellular and systems level operated on the basis of the "nirvana" principle, a principle of tension reduction. Again we emphasize that motoric activity was the only path of discharge of the immutable nervous or psychic energy (Freud used these terms interchangeably, believing in an equivalence isomorphism in this instance between mind and body.)

The essence of Freud's dream theory was created during 1895, when he was also writing the *Project* (Freud, 1887-1902; Freud, 1900; Jones, 1959). His idea of the dream theory became complete, he tells us, when he had analyzed only one dream, his own Irma dream. That the brain and mind theory of the *Project* is virtually identical with what is labeled as a model of the mind in *The Interpretation of Dreams* is not surprising in view of this close temporal link,

FREUD'S NEURAL MODEL

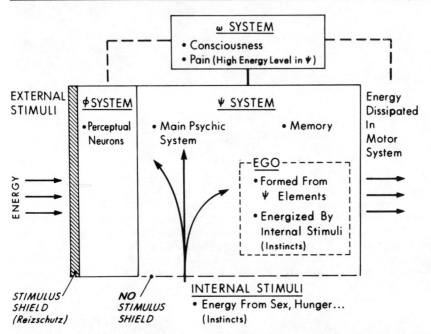

Figure 3-2. Freud's model of the nervous system as outlined in the *Project*. The driving energy is from sources outside the brain, principally the instincts (McCarley and Hobson, 1977).

and because the *Project* is a distillation of Freud's entire theoretical thought of this period. As a matter of fact, although Freud labels the model in *The Interpretation of Dreams* as a psychological model, he gives ample hints as to its origins in the *Project* in the theoretical seventh chapter of *The Interpretation of Dreams*.

Freud's theory of dreaming was quite straightforward. The ego wishes to sleep (the causal basis for this wish was not clear); it withdraws its cathexes from the motor system, resulting in sleep paralysis; the dream process begins when something in the day's experience stirs up a repressed wish in the unconscious. Wish and residue pair forces and seek to move in the usual direction of the flow in Freud's model (see arrow in Figure 3-3) toward the preconscious system. Entry of the undisguised wish is blocked by the censor, and there is a regressive movement of the "currents of excitation" toward the mnemic elements of the psyche, which, as in the model of the *Project*, are close to the perceptual side of the apparatus. There the "dream's work" of condensation, displacement, and symbol formation takes place with a disguise of the wish by the imagery of those

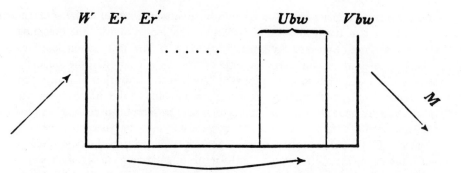

Figure 3-3. Freud's model for the psyche in the seventh chapter of *The Interpretation of Dreams* (1900). *W* is the German abbreviation for the perceptual system. The constituent elements of the main or psychic system (not labeled as such in the original figure) are as follows: *Er*, memory; *Ubw*, unconscious; and *Vbw*, preconscious. *M* indicates the motoric system. Note the isomorphism with the *Project* model as outlined in Figure 3-2: the energy source is from outside the brain, there is a perceptual to motor (left to right) reflex model of normal energy flow, and discharge of energy is through motoric activity. Both models provided for "regressive" energy flow (right to left) when discharge was impeded by psychic censorship. Both model dream imagery as resulting from such a regressive flow of wish-derived neural energy processing to the memory elements, where the dream disguise is formed by associative links.

mnemic elements with the strongest associative links to the wish. The disguised wish thus becomes acceptable to the censor and is passed into consciousness. Freud believed that the dream functioned as a guardian of sleep by preventing the intrusion of undisguised and unacceptable wishes into this conscious system, with subsequent arousal.

The essential features of Freud's dream theory were isomorphic to his brain model: dreaming was not an affair of the brain, but it was rather always triggered by energy from drives external to the brain. Freud believed that the brain and mind struggled even in sleep with dealing with the problem of the press of energy toward motoric discharge.

Freud has the same psychic and neural agencies in his *Project* model and in his *The Interpretation of Dreams* model; their organizational sequence and function are the same, direction of flow of energy is the same, and the reflex model is retained. The psychic elements of *The Interpretation of Dreams* share the property of the *Project's* neurons in that *excitation* is *transmitted* according to *conductive resistance* of various pathways. Associative links result from *facilitation* of pathways between simultaneously excited elements, and Freud even talked about *currents of excitation* in *The Interpretation of Dreams*.

Even before going into the modern cellular physiology of desynchronized sleep state generation, one can see that the modern discoveries of the sleep-dream cycle have made Freud's wish fulfillment–disguise model of dreaming incomplete in that it provides no explanation whatsoever of why the dreaming state and dreams occur on a rhythmic, periodic basis. The next section describes cellular studies which show that the impetus for the generation of the dreaming state is not a wish, but rather a motivationally neutral activation of neurons in the pontine reticular formation. If the neural impetus to the dreaming state is motivationally neutral, then the corresponding or isomorphic psychological process creating the dream imagery cannot be described as being based on a need for disguise. Freud believed that every properly interpreted dream would reveal a wish; the dream *manifest content* was the result of an attempt to disguise a single wish, and the process of dream interpretation involved extracting the *latent content* (the wish) from the manifest content. It should be emphasized at this point that while there is absolutely no evidence that the basic impetus to dream generation is wishes, this does not at all mean that dreams are not connected with the characteristic feelings, thought, and personality style of the dreamer; dreams have meaning in the sense that they can be placed in the context of an individual's history and personality. It must also be emphasized that modern psychophysiological investigations of dreams are very much in the tradition pioneered by Freud in his *Project* and of Freud's hopes in seeking to unite mind and body theory.

IV. THE PHYSIOLOGY OF DESYNCHRONIZED SLEEP STATE GENERATION

This section reviews modern physiological studies on the pontine brain stem mechanisms of generation of desynchronized sleep (D sleep). We also present a model for the events underlying the periodic generation of the D sleep phase: this model incorporates data and specific predictions about the anatomy, physiology, pharmacology, and time of events during the sleep cycle and, as such, is a source of predictions and suggestions about very specific linkages between brain events and mind events during the sleep cycle.

Summary. Readers unfamiliar with physiology may wish to orient themselves with the following summary of the *reciprocal interaction model of sleep cycle control:* the critical event for the generation of many of the events of D sleep is the activation of pontine reticular neurons, especially those in the gigantocellular pontine reticular field (FTG). These cells are cholinergic and cholinoceptive. Their activity may underlie the D sleep phasic events of rapid eye movements, ponto-geniculo-occipital (PGO) electroencephalographic waves, and muscle twitches. They may indirectly influence tonic events such as the paralysis of muscle tone via connections with the bulbar reticular formation and the cortical electroencephalographic (EEG) desynchronization through their actions on mesencephalic reticular cells. FTG cell activation before and during D sleep is caused by a decrease in inhibition stemming from a reduced discharge rate of cells in the locus coeruleus (LC) that are noradrenergic and dorsal raphé nucleus (DRN) cells that are serotonergic. Excitability of the aminergic cells is maximal in waking, while that of the pontine giant cells is maximal in D sleep. The alternate waxing and waning of activity in each population results from their direct interaction and the feedback of each population upon itself. It is this reciprocal interaction that determines the rhythmic occurrence of the desynchronized sleep phase.

What Brain Region Controls the Periodic D Sleep Episodes Associated with Dreaming?

Early lesion and stimulation experiments pointed to the pontine brain stem as the site of the rhythmic generation of desynchronized sleep. One of the most remarkable lesion preparations demonstrating the sufficiency of the pontine brain stem in generating periodic phenomena of REM sleep is Jouvet's pontine cat preparation (see Moruzzi, 1972, for a review). This preparation has all brain rostral to the pons removed, save for a hypothalamic island to preserve endocrine function. This preparation shows rhythmic episodes of: (1) muscle atonia, (2) rapid eye movement (the abducens nucleus is intact), and (3) PGO waves recordable in the pons. This evidence is important because it implicated pontine brain stem structures as sufficient for most of the defining phenomena of REM sleep. Forebrain structures, although they may modulate the brain stem activity, are not themselves sufficient for D sleep (McGinty, 1971).

How Is The Pontine Brain Stem Organized So As to Generate Sleep?

With these data as a guide, it was natural to begin cellular investigation of the mechanisms of D sleep generation by recordings in the pons. In a series of experiments utilizing extracellular recordings of the discharges of pontine brain stem cells, the authors of this chapter and their collaborators (McCarley and Hobson, 1971; Hobson et al., 1974a) have demonstrated the regular modulation of activity of these cells over the sleep cycle (see Figure 3-4 for anatomical schema). As seen in Figure 3-5 this modulation is most dramatic in the gigantocellular tegmental field (FTG) of the pontine reticular formation where increases of activity are phase-linked to the occurrence of the desynchronized phase of sleep: units in the pontine reticular formation begin to increase their discharge several minutes before the onset of D sleep as defined electrographically (Hobson et al., 1974b). There is a further explosive increase of activity with D onset, a high level of activity throughout D, and a precipitous decline of activity with the

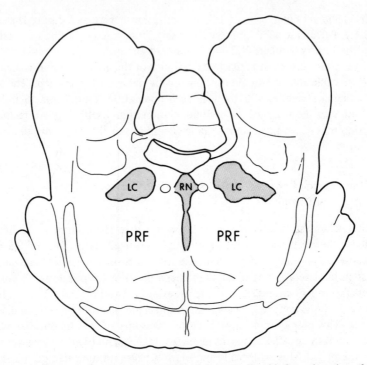

Figure 3-4. Schematic anatomy of the pontine brain stem. On this frontal section of the cat brain stem the cells that are activated in D sleep are in the pontine reticular formation (PRF) or gigantocellular tegmental field. Shaded areas indicate the cell populations that are inactivated in D sleep and may be inhibitory to the PRF cells. The inhibitory cells lie dorsally in the region of the locus coeruleus (LC) and medially in the region of the raphé nuclei (RN). The same cell groups are sketched in a sagittal section in Figure 3-11 (Hobson and McCarley, 1977(b)).

termination of D sleep. During the course of D sleep, cells in the gigantocellular reticular formation show discharges that are phase-leading and have the longest phase lead for the rapid eye movements (Pivik et al., 1977) and the PGO waves of this state (McCarley and Hobson, 1976). Units with projections to the spinal cord (demonstrated by the method of antidromic activation) have discharges that are phase-leading and correlated with the phasic muscle twitches of D sleep; thus there is evidence that these cells may generate the phasic muscle twitches (Wyzinski et al., 1978).

FTG cells thus satisfy the necessary *temporal latency* criteria for generator cells showing earliest lead time over putative controlled events, including both tonic events (D onset) and phasic events within D. It is apparent that neurons whose discharge causes events must have discharge changes preceding the events they generate, and the cells that are the initiators of events should have the long-

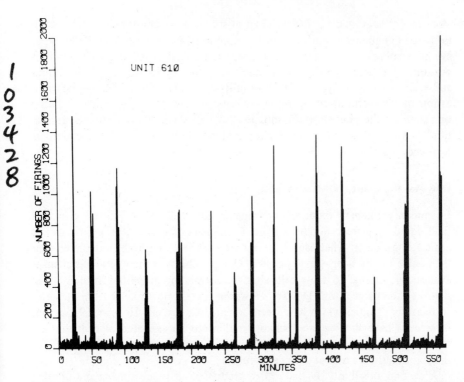

Figure 3-5. Discharge activity of a pontine reticular giant cell neuron recorded over multiple sleep–waking cycles. Each peak corresponds to a desynchronized sleep episode, and a regular trend of discharge activity over a cycle is observable: a peak in desynchronized sleep; a rapid decline at the end of the desynchronized sleep episode; a trough, often associated with waking; a slow rise (in synchronized sleep and preceding all electrographic signs of desynchronized sleep); and an explosive acceleration at the onset of desynchronized sleep. Note also the extreme modulation of activity and the periodicity (McCarley and Hobson, 1975b).

est latency. These reticular cells further show *selective modulation* of activity in relation to the controlled events.

How Might Activation of the Giant Cells Determine Sleep Events?

There is further strong evidence indicating that pontine giant cells satisfy the *connectivity criterion* for the causation of events. Early Golgi and Gudden technique studies suggested that the giant cells had very wide-ranging projections, extending both rostrally and caudally, and Golgi studies further indicated extensive intra–brain stem connections, with many cells having extensive branching.

More recent anatomical and physiological studies have confirmed direct projections to: (1) abducens nuclei, with the functional possibility of initiating rapid eye movements of desynchronized sleep; (2) spinal cord, with the resultant possibility of mediating the phasic muscle twitches of REM sleep; (3) midbrain and even more rostrally, with the possibility of mediating the EEG desynchronization of desynchronized sleep; and (4) medulla, with the possibility of initiating some of the phenomena of muscle atonia via the inhibitory reticular formation. (Anatomical and physiological evidence detailing these connections is reviewed in McCarley, 1978).

How Are the Giant Cells Activated?

In summary, there is quite strong evidence that cells in the pontine giant cell field could mediate a number of the phenomena of D sleep. The obvious but critical question is: what causes the activity of these cells to be modulated over the course of the sleep–waking cycle? One possibility is that metabolic changes exclusively internal to these cells alter the membrane properties in such a way that they discharge during D sleep. However, there is no evidence from the auto-correlational studies which have been done (McCarley and Hobson, 1975a) that these cells have the regular discharge pattern to be expected of cells that are spontaneously depolarizing. Since there is no positive evidence whatsoever for this hypothesis, we do not consider it further.

A second possibility is that other groups of cells are driving the pontine reticular cells. However, with respect to the time of onset of deep sleep itself, non-reticular cells do not show such long lead times, and with respect to the phasic phenomena outlined above, cells in the reticular formation of the pons have the longest lead times for the rapid eye movements and PGO waves of D sleep. It should further be remembered that the FTG cells begin to increase their discharge rate at a time before D sleep onset when there is no muscle inhibition and where there are no movements, either rapid eye movements or somatic body movements. Thus this increase in these cells' discharge cannot simply be attributed to their being driven in the course of commands for movement.

How Is Giant Cell Activity Turned On?

The third class of model, the reciprocal interaction model, proposes that the increased excitability of FTG cells just before and during the occurrence of desynchronized sleep is a result of progressive tonic disinhibition by inhibitory cells which decrease discharge rate with the approach of desynchronized sleep (McCarley and Hobson, 1975b). This model proposes that it is the release from inhibition during desynchronized sleep which causes the marked increase of FTG

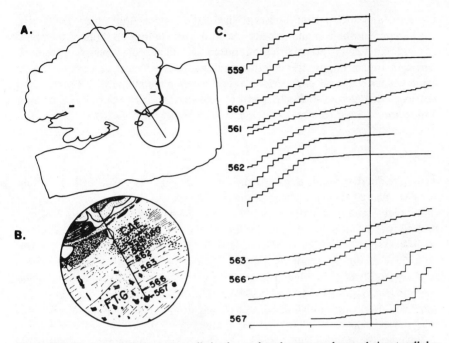

Figure 3-6. Reciprocal discharge by cells in the nucleus locus coeruleus and gigantocellular fields of the anterior pontine brain stem. (A) Outline tracing of a sagittal section of the cat pontine brain at 2.5 mm lateral to the midline, showing the path of an exploring microelectrode which passed through the anterior lobe of the cerebellum into the dorsal brain stem. (B) Detailed drawing of the histology in the zone circled in (A), showing the location of the seven successive recording sites in the penetration. The diameter of the circle is 5 mm. The cell fields of interest are LC, nucleus locus coeruleus, and FTG, the gigantocellular tegmental field. (C) Cumulative rate histograms of the cells recorded at the seven sites shown in (B), during the transition period beginning 2 minutes before desynchronized sleep onset (vertical line) and ending 1 minute thereafter. Each activity curve shows the cumulative percentage of discharge for as much of the epoch as was free of arousal (Hobson et al., 1975).

population discharge activity during D sleep. (As discussed later, the model does not specify that FTG cells are totally inactivated during waking. In this state, although less excitable than during D sleep, they can be driven by inputs and thus discharge in relationship to various kinds of specific activation.) The finding that cells in the locus coeruleus and subcoeruleus (LC) have a reciprocal time course of activity to that of FTG cells over the sleep cycle provides strong evidence supporting the reciprocal interaction model (Hobson et al., 1975). LC cells radically decrease rate with the approach of D sleep episodes (D-off cells, see Figure 3-6); as this LC neuronal activity decrease occurs, FTG activity increases. Chu and Bloom (1974a, b) have confirmed the finding of D-off

LC cells, and their histofluorescent histology suggests that these D-off cells are norepinephrine-containing cells. Such norepinephrine-containing cells have been shown to have long-lasting inhibitory effects at their synapses in cerebellum and hippocampus. Furthermore, there is anatomical and physiological evidence of reciprocal connections between the populations of FTG cells and the locus coeruleus D-off cells and of recurrent feedback connections of each population on itself (McCarley, 1978).

What Is the Chemistry of Dreaming Sleep Generation?

There is a body of consistent evidence indicating that the giant cells are likely to be cholinergic (i.e., use acetycholine as a neurotransmitter) and cholinoceptive (have acetylcholine synapses), and that they have generally excitatory effects (see Figure 3-7). In this regard one of the most convincing demonstrations of the cholinoceptive nature of the giant cells and their ability to either mediate directly or recruit other populations in the generation of REM sleep phenomena, is the possibility of eliciting D sleep-like episodes with carbachol, a cholinergic agent (see Amatruda et al., 1975; Vivaldi et al., 1978). In recent experiments in this laboratory, hour-long episodes of muscle atonia, rapid eye movement, cortical desynchronization, hippocampal theta, and PGO waves have been elicited from injection of a few micrograms of carbachol into the pontine reticular formation. Figure 3-7 illustrates our structural model of the interaction between this FTG population and the population of inhibitory cells. Although we use the LC population as an example of an inhibitory population, it is to be emphasized that serotonergic dorsal raphé neurons also decrease discharge rate with D sleep onset (McGinty et al., 1973), and thus could have similar inhibitory roles with respect to FTG cells.

Prey-Predator Interaction: Parallels with Brain Stem Neuronal Interaction in Dreaming Sleep Generation

The interaction of the FTG (excitatory) and locus coeruleus (inhibitory) populations can be mathematically modeled by equations of the Lotka-Volterra type, originally used to describe the interaction of prey (analogous to FTG) and predator (analogous to LC) populations. The time course of activity predicted by the model is in good agreement with actual physiological recordings. According to this model the events of the sleep cycle can be qualitatively described as follows: During waking, giant cell activity is low because of tonic inhibition from the LC population of cells. This inhibitory influence gradually decreases because of inhibitory feedback of the LC population on itself. With this disinhibition, giant cell activity increases, at first gradually, then rapidly and exponentially as

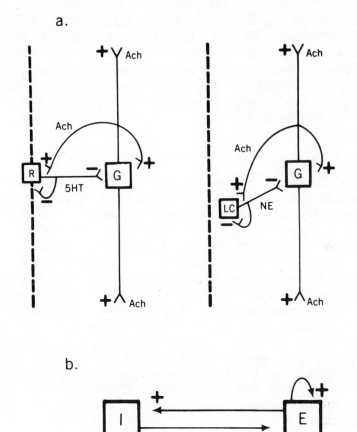

Figure 3-7. Reciprocal interaction model of generator process. The G cells (pontine reticular giant cells) are seen as executive elements; they excite with and are excited by acetylcholine (Ach). They interact reciprocally with two aminergic cell groups, the LC and raphé (R), which utilize norepinephrine (NE) and serotonin (5HT) respectively. Both amines are hypothesized to be inhibitory to the G cells. D sleep will therefore be enhanced by increasing giant cell excitability, and this can occur by either adding cholinergic drive or subtracting aminergic inhibition. Conversely, D sleep will be suppressed by subtracting cholinergic drive or by adding aminergic inhibition. Formal reduction of the elements in the top portion of the figure yields the general model of reciprocal interaction, of inhibitory (I, –) and excitatory (E, +) populations, each of which contains a self-loop as well as a projection to the other set. The resulting oscillation of activity in the two sets can be mathematically described by the Lotka-Volterra equations (Hobson and McCarley, 1977b).

self-excitation becomes prominent in the giant cell population. This rapid increase of activity marks the onset of a D sleep episode. With the attainment of a high level of giant cell activity, more activity is induced in the LC population. The inhibitory influence of the LC population ends the high level of giant cell activity and the D phase of sleep, and the cycle starts anew. The specific details of the mathematical model have been described elsewhere (McCarley and Hobson, 1975b; McCarley, 1978).

Why Do We Dream Every 90–100 Minutes?

Figure 3-8 summarizes the reciprocal interaction model and describes the fit between a theoretical curve derived from the model and actual FTG data. The goodness of fit is apparent from the figure. With respect to possible differences of influence between LC-norepinephrine-containing cells and the raphé-serotonin-containing cells, it should be noted that there is evidence that LC effects have a longer time duration. LC effects may be mediated by cyclic AMP, which acts as a "second messenger" and has effects on the cellular metabolism and/or membrane properties that account for the long duration of LC effects and the long duration of the D sleep cycle. In contrast, it now appears that serotonin acts as a more conventional, short-duration transmitter. Thus LC inhibition may be especially involved in long-term events of the D sleep cycle, while the serotonin-containing raphé cells may be especially involved with shorter-term periodicities, such as those involved in PGO wave generation (see McCarley, 1978, for a summary of evidence supporting this formulation). This statement of the reciprocal interaction model provides a description of the anatomical structure, pharmacology, and the time course of activity relevant to generation of the "free-running" sleep cycle. This basic version of the model does not attempt to include the mechanisms by which disturbances in the free-running sleep cycle oscillation could operate. In fact, it is important to note that the data were derived from an animal preparation that, because of head restraint, was able to do very little else except go through its sleep–waking cycle.

Why Don't We Dream During Waking?

We emphasize that the basic version of the reciprocal interaction model provides an explanation for the *modulation* of excitability in the FTG and LC-raphé *populations*. It is the time course of population excitability changes over the sleep–waking cycle that this model is concerned with. By excitability we mean the propensity of a neuron to discharge; an increase in excitability means an alteration of membrane properties of a cell in such a way as to increase the probability of discharge. Note that the model predicts that when a sufficiently high

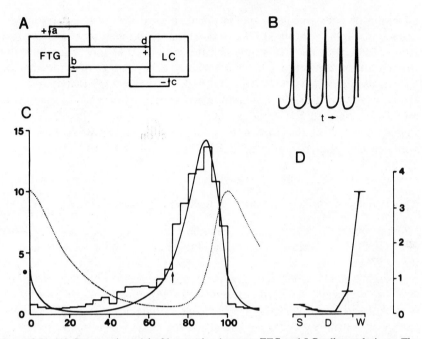

Figure 3-8. (A) Structural model of interaction between FTG and LC cell populations. The plus sign implies excitatory and the minus sign inhibitory influences. (B) Theoretical curve derived from the model that best fits the FTG unit in Figure 3-5. (C) The solid line histogram is the average discharge level of FTG unit 568 over 12 sleep–waking cycles, each normalized to constant duration. The cycle begins with the end of desynchronized sleep, and the arrow indicates the bin with the most probable time of desynchronized sleep onset. The solid curve describes the FTG fit, and the dotted line the LC fit derived from the model. The dot in the ordinate scale indicates the equilibrium values for the two populations. (D) Geometric mean values of the discharge activity of ten LC cells before (synchronized sleep, S), during (desynchronized sleep, D), and after (waking, W) a desynchronized sleep episode. Each time epoch is equal to one-quarter of a desynchronized sleep period. Note that, as predicted by the model, the discharge rate increase begins in the last quarter of D (McCarley and Hobson, 1975b).

level of excitability is reached in the total pontine reticular giant cell population, then D sleep will ensue, and will persist as long as this level of excitability is maintained.

This concept of population modulation is basic to an understanding of why D sleep does not ensue in waking when, for example, one can record activity from individual FTG cells during eye movement or somatic muscle activity (Henn and Cohen, 1976; Siegel et al., 1977). During the instances of waking activation only a small subset of the FTG population is being activated at any one time by a specific motor command. In waking there remains a suppressive background of inhibition on other members of the population. It is both an interesting fact and supportive of the reciprocal interaction model that repetitive electrical stimulation of inputs to the FTG can hasten the onset of REM, most likely by acting to increase the level of excitability in the FTG population (see, for example, Frederickson and Hobson, 1970). The model further predicts that activation of the population of FTG cells by local injection of an agonist of the neurotransmitter excitatory to FTG cells should produce a state resembling D sleep, and the confirmation of the prediction is now clear in the results of experiments with injection of carbachol into the FTG (Amatruda et al., 1975; Vivaldi et al., 1978).

What Happens If We Turn Off the "Off Switch" for Dreaming Sleep?

Another approach to experimental modification of the population excitability of FTG cells is to decrease the activity of the inhibitory population, to turn off the "off" cells. The prediction of the reciprocal interaction model is that this also should result in REM sleep. This prediction has been dramatically confirmed recently by Cespuglio and associates in the Lyon group (1976, 1978), who observed the rapid onset of REM sleep following "switching off" either the raphé or locus coeruleus by cooling. Vivaldi and the authors of this chapter (1978) have observed in pilot experiments that the beta-adrenergic blocking agent, propranalol, injected into the FTG, will also cause the onset of REM sleep, presumably by blocking the inhibitory norepinephrine synapses on FTG cells.

What Happens If We Turn On the "Off Switch" for Dreaming Sleep?

The detailed and specific nature of the reciprocal interaction model can lead to generation of testable hypotheses about other important aspects of phenomena of the sleep cycle that may be related to dreams. A specific example is the effects and mechanisms of D sleep deprivation, and possibly that of sleep onset itself. Based on the reciprocal interaction model, we suggest the following course of events during D sleep deprivation. Extended periods of waking and thus of D sleep deprivation can result (1) from natural, external input to the organism; (2) from internal stimuli such as hunger or thirst leading to self-generated, goal-directed activity; or (3) from experimental manipulation. We propose that the population of LC cells is "clamped" at high levels of activity by input attendant upon these various conditions. It should be noted that one source of excitatory input to the LC population during waking may be the FTG population. As any of these conditions persist, the negative feedback of LC cells upon themselves will gradually lower the membrane potential in the LC population and thus make these cells more and more difficult to keep activated. Thus, stronger and stronger stimuli would be required to keep the cells at a high level of activity and to prevent the onset of sleep. With the cessation of strong input to LC cells, this population will shut off quite abruptly because of the already present inhibition in the population. This shutting off will, in turn, disinhibit the FTG population with a time course that is much more rapid than normal. The result is a shortened D sleep latency and increased D sleep intensity, the well-known experimental findings in D sleep deprivation. The well-known persistence of deprivation effects over numerous sleep cycles, the apparent "memory" of deprivation, could be accomodated in the model as a result of cyclic AMP–induced changes in cellular metabolism, perhaps even in the rate of neurotransmitter synthesis. The predictions about deprivation effects should, of course, be regarded as ideas needing to be checked against actual experimental data and with quantitative modeling of the time course of the LC and FTG populations.

V. VISUAL AND MOTOR SYSTEM PHYSIOLOGICAL PROCESSES DURING D SLEEP OF SPECIAL RELEVANCE TO DREAM THEORY

How Do We See and Move in Dreams?

Introduction and Summary. The main argument of the activation-synthesis model of dream generation is that the brain is first internally activated and then synthesizes this information to form the physiological concomitants of the dream experience. Since one of the defining and primary characteristics of dreams is the visual experience, knowing the kinds and transmission pathways of visual information is especially important. The physiological data to be presented will illustrate the detail and extent of visual information coding and transfer in the nervous system and the consequences of activation of this system during D sleep. In some instances we will draw on psychophysical data to make clear the possible conscious concomitants of such activation.

Although much remains to be learned about the details of physiological processes during both D sleep and waking, there is quite powerful evidence that the visual system is both intensively and extensively activated during desynchronized sleep and that these physiological phenomena may be isomorphic with the visual phenomena in dreams. Part B will discuss the relationship between neuronal motor pattern generators and body movements in dreams. Figures 3-11 and 3-12 (below) provide an anatomical and physiological overview of the activation-synthesis model and should be consulted while reading this section.

A. VISUAL PHENOMENA IN DREAMS

How Do Visual Centers Keep Track of Eye Movement?

Lesion and stimulation studies indicate that a region of the pontine reticular formation ventral and just rostral to the abducens nuclei is critical for horizontal

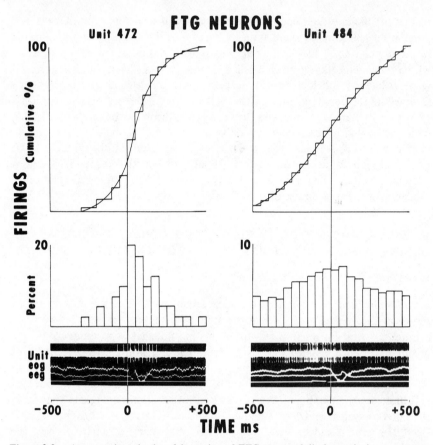

Figure 3-9a. Average phase lead and intensity of FTG neuronal discharge during eye movement in desynchronized sleep. Cumulative (upper graph) and sequential interval (lower graph) histograms of average discharge in relation to ten isolated eye movements for each of two units. For each eye movement, time 0 (t_0) was established as the point of eye movement onset in the filmed records; the number of discharges was registered in 50-msec bins preceding and following t_0. The percent of the total number of discharges is shown for each bin and cumulated in the graphs. Note the phase leads of 300 msec and peaks coincident with eye movement for both units. Owing to the virtual absence of the background discharge, the graphs of unit 472 are more sharply inflected than those of unit 484 (Pivik et al., 1977).

conjugate gaze movements. There is anatomical evidence for direct projections from this region to the abducens nucleus and some evidence for direct projections to the oculomotor nucleus. Extracellular recordings of neurons in this area in alert animals by a number of investigators (Cohen and Henn, 1972; Luschei and Fuchs, 1972; Keller, 1974; Henn and Cohen, 1976) have demonstrated the pre-

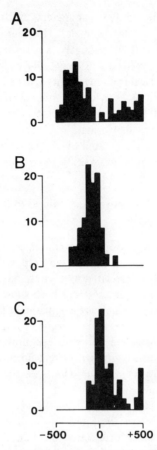

Figure 3-9b. Temporal sequence of discharge minima (*A*), inflection points (*B*), and maxima (*C*) in a population of 49 eye movement positive pontine giant cell field (FTG) neurons relative to the onset of an isolated eye movement in desynchronized sleep. Ordinate is percent of the population. Note the extent of population synchrony: discharge in the FTG cell population is suppressed 300–350 msec before eye movement onset, accelerates rapidly 250 msec before eye movement onset, and peaks at the onset of the eye movement. The levels of synchrony are highly statistically significant (Pivik et al., 1977).

sence of units that encode and direct changes in eye position, magnitude of position change, and the direction of eye movement. Some neurons in this area discharge long before (in the 100 msec range) the start of eye movement. Recordings of neurons in this area during desynchronized sleep (Pivik et al., 1977) have demonstrated similar long leads between unit discharge and eye movements recorded during D sleep (Figure 3-9). A recent study of Büttner et al. (1977)

has found neurons coding similar parameters in the rostral mesencephalic reticular formation (MRF) in alert animals. The neurons in this area that code position changes or movement direction have a preferred direction of movement that is always close to the vertical axis, suggesting that MRF neurons code the critical information for vertical eye movements. No neurons in the mesencephalic reticular formation had lead times as long as those in the pontine reticular formation, implying that initiation of eye movement in this class of premotor cells may begin in the pontine reticular formation. There is thus quite strong evidence that eye movements may be generated by the activity of neurons in the brain stem reticular formation both during waking and during desynchronized sleep.

How Is Information About Eye Movement Utilized to Construct the Visual World?

The next question is how the information contained in the discharges of these neurons is relayed to other areas of the brain, especially those forebrain areas whose activity is presumably correlated with conscious experience. In response to this kind of question much interest has been shown in the ponto-geniculo-occipital waves (PGO waves), which are stigmatic EEG waves that appear just before and during D sleep episodes and are named for the sites at which they are recorded. D sleep PGO waves and the rapid eye movements of D sleep usually appear together but, although highly correlated, do not have a one-to-one relationship (Hobson and McCarley, 1971). The D sleep PGO waves (PGO_D) occur before the onset of the rapid eye movements, generally showing a phase lead of the order of 15–20 ms (Sakai and Cespuglio, 1976). PGO_D appear first in the pons and from there travel to the lateral geniculate nucleus (LGN) and, by separate pathways, to the visual cortex (Hobson et al., 1969).

During waking, similar, but smaller, EEG waves occurring after eye movements (PGO_W) can be recorded from the same areas as the PGO_D (Brooks, 1968). The anatomical sites where PGO waves are recorded suggest that information contained in the events underlying PGO waves might play a role in adjusting the sensory visual system to the consequences of eye movement. Thus there was great interest upon the discovery of the PGO_W as to whether these potentials could be recorded in the dark—if they could not, then the implication was that the PGO_W might be generated as a result of retinal discharge attendent on the rapid motion of images on the retina during an eye movement. Recent work has provided substantial evidence that the PGO_W are not entirely dependent on retinal discharge and thus may be signs of a central process transmitting information about eye movements (Bartlett et al., 1976).

There are two general kinds of hypotheses about information transmission during PGO_W: saccadic blanking and visual constancy. Psychophysical experiments have convincingly demonstrated that perception is markedly diminished during saccades (very rapid eye movements): could the PGO_W be a sign of the neural process underlying such a blanking? The best modern evidence indicates that most of the blanking during saccades is a consequence of processes exclusively in the retina, and thus that the PGO waves must be concerned with other phenomena (see review in Bartlett et al., 1976).

What Does the Pons Tell the Forebrain Visual System?

Extracellular neuronal recordings during desynchronized sleep have shown that the PGO_D are associated with generalized cellular activation, and a recent study by Kasamatsu (1976) has shown that the PGO waves are rather specifically excitatory for complex cells in the visual cortex. Recordings in the LGN indicate a generally excitatory effect associated with PGO waves and with the analogous waves evoked by mesencephalic reticular formation (MRF) stimulation. MRF stimulation producing such waves appears to act by disinhibition (suppression of inhibition) in LGN relay cells (Singer, 1977). Earlier observations (Bizzi, 1966) that interpreted the optic tract depolarization associated with PGO_D waves as evidence for presynaptic inhibition have been thrown into doubt. Recent studies show no anatomical evidence for this kind of interaction, and there is further clear physiological evidence that transmission through the LGN, rather than being inhibited, is actually enhanced during the PGO_D of desynchronized sleep (see Singer, 1977).

The brain stem neurons that likely form the set of "output neurons" for the PGO wave generation system show consistent, stereotyped bursts of discharges before PGO waves recorded in the LGN (McCarley et al., 1978). These PGO burst neurons (located in the midbrain in close approximation to the brachium conjunctivum) show markedly increased excitability in D sleep, and thus directly indicate the greater openness of the brain stem to forebrain pathway for visual system information transmission during D sleep.

Eye Movement: The Mind's Eye View

There is an important body of psychophysical evidence relating to the effects and nature of feedback from eye movements. Some late nineteenth century physiologists (Wundt, Helmholtz, and Mach) believed in a direct consciousness of muscle nerve activation, or as they phrased it, "feelings of innervation" (see Festinger et al., 1967). Both Sherrington in England and William James in America successfully opposed this view, the latter arguing that " . . . *all our ideas of movement*, including those of the effort which it requires as well as those of its direction, its extent, its strength, and its velocity are images of peripheral sensation . . . " (James, 1890, emphasis his). For all the immediate success of this argument it now appears that James and Sherrington were mistaken. The source of confusion in this debate is instructive: conflict arose because they chose the narrowly defined issue of whether feedback from eye movements was conscious, rather than focusing on the more appropriate and more general issue of whether the brain had any kind of information available to it about eye movement, conscious or not. Today we know of abundant evidence that there are "central programs" for directing behavior or movement that operate largely independently of sensory feedback, with sensory feedback being used only in the case of unexpected inability to complete a planned and preprogrammed movement. These central programs or dispositions to respond can sometimes influence conscious perception, although consciousness is not invariably present. James' argument that "feelings of innervation" cannot exist because they are not conscious thus appears to miss the point. Evidence regarding the situations in which consciousness is influenced has been discussed by Festinger et al. (1967) for the visual system. For example, the wearing of curved lenses leads to a reprogramming of perceptual tracking strategies and to an altered conscious perception of the curvature or linearity of objects.

The World Moves With the Eyes

A more direct and immediately convincing example of the effect of eye movement on perception and the presence of feedback about eye movement comes from stimulation experiments done on the human visual cortex for the development of a visual prosthesis (Brindley, 1973). An electrical point stimulation produces a glowing spot, a phosphene. The stimulation site in this case is obviously anatomically fixed and continues to excite the same neuronal elements. If feedback from eye movements did not alter the relative perceptual position of objects during eye movement, then exciting the same fixed sets of neurons during eye movement should produce no subjective sense of movement of the phosphene. The demonstration that such a phosphene does move with eye movement, although the stimulation site remains fixed in the visual system, indicates conclusively that the perception of the visual world is fundamentally dependent upon information derived from eye movements. Since such apparent movement takes place in eye movements done with the eyes closed or open, it is apparent that *central* processes must be responsible for the active alteration of the visual world. For the physiologist interested in dream construction, the important message is that eye movement, or rather information about commands for eye movement, may be as powerful in generating parts of the dream story as it is in shaping perception.

B. ACTIVATION OF MOTOR PATTERN GENERATORS AND DREAM CONSTRUCTION

How the Movement Machinery Works in D Sleep

The thesis developed here is simple: during D sleep, pattern generators for various kinds of stereotyped behavior are activated, and information about the motor commands of these generators is used in dream construction. As with the discussion about information from eye movement commands, a critical concept is that the source of information for dream construction is a "corollary discharge" of motor pattern generator neurons; that the actual execution of muscle movement is blocked in sleep does not alter this critical source of information.

How the Movement Machine is Turned On and Regulated

Grillner (1975) and Shik and Orlovsky (1976) have recently surveyed the large body of evidence supporting the concept of central neuronal pattern generators for movement. An important portion of the argument for our purposes is that *unspecific* activating input can set a pattern generator into motion and produce a quite *specific* sequence of motor behavior for the stimulus duration. For example, in cats with brain stems transected at midbrain level, electrical stimulation applied immediately ventral to the inferior colliculus in the lateral pontine tegmentum produces walking movements in the animal.

The precise parameters of the step cycle in walking are comparable to those seen in walking in intact cats, and increasing the strength of the stimulation leads smoothly to increased walking speed and then to a gallop, always with the same excellent coordination and sequencing of muscle activity found in the intact animal. Again, the critical feature for the argument that motor pattern generators play a critical role in dream construction is that the brain interprets activation of the step generator (i.e., for walking) as indicating walking is taking place, even if the limbs are paralyzed as they are during D sleep. Although it is not necessary for control, absence of the usual sensory consequences of movement in D sleep may contribute in part to the bizarreness of dreams.

There are many other examples of generators for stereotyped movements at both the brain stem and spinal cord level. Henry Head, at a 1923 symposium, gave a beautiful description of the variety of "adaptive" behavior that can be observed in the decerebrate preparation:

> If the brain is removed just in front of the anterior colliculi the cat is capable of a large number of discriminative reflexes. Water placed in the pharynx is swallowed in a normal manner, and when a small quantity of alcohol is added the tongue makes a wide sweeping movement, curling at the tip as if to lick

the lips. Several different reflexes can be evoked from the pinna, each of which is adapted to the nature of the stimulus: if it is pricked it falls down; touching the hairs within the ear causes a movement that would be effective in dislodging a flea. A drop of water placed in the pinna is followed by a rotation of the head which brings a stimulated ear downwards followed by a rapid shake admirably adapted to displace fluid.

Turning On More Complex Behavior

At higher levels there are also important hierarchically ordered and stereotyped behavioral patterns that can be elicited from subcortical sites, such as sham rage at the hypothalamic level. After removal of all cerebral cortex, cats still retain large portions of their behavioral repertoire, including feeding, sexual behavior, rage, defensive behavior, and so forth (Grillner, 1975; Brady, 1960). A distinction should be drawn between motor pattern generators and other higher-level behavioral pattern generators, although for convenience, we will often refer to both as "behavioral sequence generators." We believe that activation of both is important for dream construction.

Releasing the Movement Normally Blocked in Dreaming Sleep

There is now fairly strong evidence for activation of behavioral sequence generators in D sleep (Sastre and Jouvet, 1977; Hendricks et al., 1977). Placing lesions in the pontine tegmentum between the locus coeruleus and gigantocellular tegmental field (FTG) leads to a syndrome in which there is no muscle atonia, but the other phenomena defining D sleep are present. During the episodes in which the cats show behavioral sequences, they have the following phenomena also present in normal REM sleep: unresponsiveness to visual stimuli, myotic pupils, relaxed nictating membranes, PGOs, rapid eye movements, facial and somatic muscular twitches, hippocampal theta in the EEG, and, finally, the absence of thermoregulation. Behaviors in this preparation include immobility and stalking movements and cage "exploration," albeit without visual guidance. These cats vividly demonstrate their unresponsiveness to visual stimuli by bumping into the walls, a behavior of vanishingly low probability in the waking cat. There are also "pseudo-emotional" behavioral sequences, such as an attack posture with the ears folded back and paws reaching out, sometimes combined with a pounce like that used to capture a mouse. One also sees posturing with the ears back, mouth open, and hair standing erect on an arched back that closely mimics defensive behavior in the waking cat. Sometimes one sees cats reaching out a paw to toy with an (imaginary) object, much as waking cats do with a captured mouse or a ball of yarn. Sometimes there is grooming, just as in waking. It is reasonable to imagine that D sleep in the human is accompanied by activation of similar sequences of behavior, but they simply are not observed because of the muscle inhibition that normally accompanies D sleep. Figure 3-10 shows the temporal sequences of pontine reticular activity that we postulate to be isomorphic with dream sequences.

Do Dreams Reveal the Activation of Central Movement Pattern Generators?

If the activation-synthesis model of dream generation is correct, one might suspect that even with powerful muscle inhibition there might be some association between observed movements during D sleep and dream content. Gardner and Grossman (1975) and Gardner et al. (1975) have found evidence that there is a positive association between movement in the upper and lower extremity muscles and movements as a whole in the dream sequence. There are also specific associations between upper and lower extremity movement and dream content. The percentage of variance explained in these studies is a relatively low 25%; this may be a result of the fact that what one is able to observe breaking through the D sleep muscle paralysis is a poor reflection of the actual events programmed in central pattern generators. We emphasize again that the brain does not need execution of the movement to be fed information about the activity of neurons generating the movement. In fact, all of the current evidence is that movement sequences are usually predominantly centrally programmed and depend very little on feedback from specific sensory consequences of the movement: the crucial event for the brain is not execution of the movement but activation of the neurons which direct the movement.

   If the activation-synthesis model of dream construction is correct, and dreams are partially generated from a substrate of information about pattern generators for movement and behavior sequences, then one would expect dreams to be full of activity. This is a testable hypothesis and one whose verification in dream content will be discussed later in this chapter.

VI. CONTEMPORARY THEORIES OF MIND-BODY RELATIONSHIPS DURING DREAMS

The association of the state of desynchronized sleep with the mental activity of dreaming must be regarded as the most fundamental advance in this field (Aserinsky and Kleitman, 1953). Following this discovery there was a period wherein researchers hoped to find simple, direct links between physiology and psychology, only to find the relationships were not so simple. Our treatment of these and later studies is not intended to be comprehensive, but is meant to outline for the reader the considerable work that has taken place in the field and to focus upon some persistent difficulties and ambiguities in the relationships between physiology and psychology.

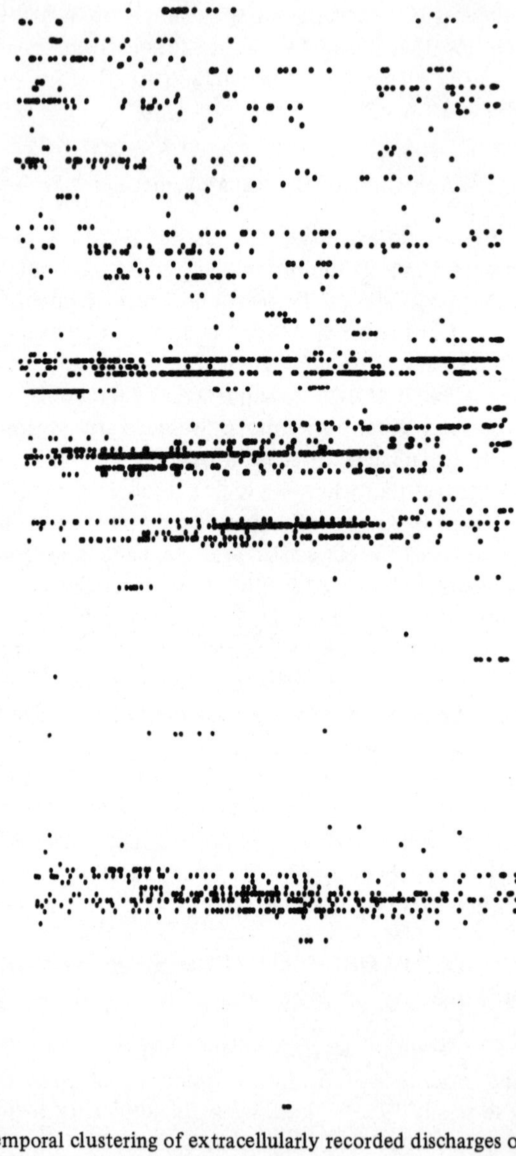

Figure 3-10. Temporal clustering of extracellularly recorded discharges of cat giant cell field neurons during D sleep. Each discharge is represented by a dot; the time sequence runs left to right and top to bottom, with each line 1 second in duration. The figure encompasses about 200 seconds of D sleep activity. Clustering is visible as closely spaced dots and, over longer durations, as "bands" of activity, some of which appear to occur rhythmically. Note the various durations of clusters and the presence of shorter-duration clusters of activity within longer-duration clusters. Clusters are delimited by periods of relative inactivity.

Rapid Eye Movements and Dream Content. The "scanning" hypothesis of Roffwarg and associates (1962) argued that the rapid eye movements (REMs) are a result of the dreamer's scanning the visual image of the dream. Two facts indicate that dream visual images cannot be the cause of eye movements. First of all, the acceleration in neuronal discharge in visual cortex follow the REMs, rather than REM's following the visual cortex excitation (Hobson and McCarley, 1971). Even humans without visual cortex have REMs (as do pontine cats), indicating that the chain of activation runs from brainstem to visual cortex, rather than in the reverse direction. Moscowitz and Berger (1969) have cast doubt on whether there is even a simple, direct link between REM sequences and subjective dream gaze sequences. In a study similar to that of Roffwarg et al., except that blind scoring of results was employed, Moscowitz and Berger could find no association between runs of eye movements in a particular orientation (i.e., horizontal or vertical) and dream gaze sequences. Jacobs et al. (1972) were also unable to replicate the findings of Roffwarg et al.

There is, however, farily consistent evidences that REM *intensity* and visual *intensity* are correlated: that is, even if individual eye movements do not correspond with the dreamer's shifts of gaze, there is still a significant association between the amount of REM activity and the amount of the dreamer's visual activity (Dement and Wolpert, 1958; Berger and Oswald, 1962; Molinari and Foulkes, 1969). A recent study by Firth and Oswald (1975) has suggested that such an intensity relationship, while existing, is quite weak, perhaps accounting for less than 5% of the variance. As noted in the previous section, it is our contention that further progress in their field will come through increased sophistication and precision of data analysis and reduction procedures. For example, Firth and Oswald could have observed only a weak intensity association simply because their scoring was not precise enough: they did not count REMs, but depended on the global score of presence or absence in 2-sec epochs during 5 minutes prior to awakening. Their psychological variable was also global: whether dreams were visually active or passive. We believe that investigations using computer-generated "scan fields" indicating the sequence, pattern, and velocity of gaze changes may prove to be helpful in further studies of REMs and dream content.

PIPs, MEMA, and Dream Content. Two sets of investigators have sought to improve psychophysiological correlations by focusing on developing measures

---

Such sequences of giant cell neuronal activity are temporally associated with runs of eye movements and ponto-geniculo-occipital waves, and similar sequences of executive neuron discharges may represent the neuronal substrate of dream sequences in man (Hobson and McCarley, 1977b).

for detection of phasic events in humans that might be analogous to the easily defined and quantified PGO waves in animals. The Chicago group has examined phasic integrated muscle potentials (PIPs) in extraocular (E-PIPs), facial, and lip sites. An important recent finding is that E-PIPs and PGO waves in cats are highly correlated (81% congruence) (Rechtschaffen, 1978). A preliminary study of the relationship between dream content and human E-PIPs shows that dream bizarreness, i.e., distortion and discontinuity, is the mental event associated with intense phasic activity (Watson et al., 1978); unfortunately this relationship does not appear to hold in all subjects.

Roffwarg and associates have documented the presence of another D sleep phasic event in man, middle ear muscle activity (MEMA) (Pessah and Roffwarg, 1962; Roffwarg et al., 1975). On the basis of whether dream content contained loud noises (or similar stimuli that evoked MEMA in waking), raters were able to predict the presence or absence of MEMA in the 12 seconds prior to awakening with 68% success (52% was chance level); in instances where dream content was rated most clearly of the type associated with waking MEMA, the predictive ability rose to 82%. Details of the MEMA pattern (burst or repetitive) could not be predicted on the basis of content. This report is, of course, in accord with the notion of an intensity isomorphism for subjective auditory sensation and auditory system activation, and with the activation-synthesis hypothesis in general.

Dream and Physiological Intensity Correlations with Autonomic Variables.   Hobson et al. (1965) found that dream intensity—as measured by vividness, emotionality, and physical activity—was associated with episodically high and variable respiratory rates. The phasic variable of respiratory rate was highly correlated with REM rates. Only a single finding suggested a specific association between respiratory activity and specific dream content: respiratory apnea and similar subjective dream events. Hauri and Van de Castle (1973) confirmed these results and noted similar associations between dream emotionality and heart rate variability and skin potential fluctuations. There are, however, some conflicting reports (Aserinsky, 1967; Baust and Engel, 1970) on the relationship between autonomic physiological variables and dream intensity. These differences may be related to subject variability as to preferred mode of autonomic response; this variability of response has been documented in alert subjects, and some subjects were found to respond to emotions with heart rate changes, some with skin potential alterations, and some with other patterns (Lacey, 1950). Studies utilizing autonomic variables might thus find it useful to measure the subjects' waking autonomic response signature before proceeding to psychophysical dream correlations.

Phasic Events and Dream Content. On balance, there does appear to be a correlation between intensity of phasic events and intensity of mentation variables within REM, but the specificity of these correlations has proved extremely difficult to establish.

Incorporation of External Stimuli in the Dream. One methodological problem facing the dream psychophysiologist is knowing at what time prior to awakening he should begin his cross-correlation. It was early thought that one might be able also to insert a time marker in the dream by delivering a calibrated stimulus during dreaming sleep and then observing at what point and how the stimulus appeared in the dream. One also might learn about the symbolic transformations in dreams. Unfortunately for this simple and logically flawless idea, the phenomenon of dream incorporation itself has proved to be highly capricious (Dement and Wolpert, 1958; Koulack, 1969; Foulkes and Shepherd, 1973; see Arkin and Antrobus, 1978, for a detailed review). In general the rate of "dream incorporation" is about a rather low 25%, making it difficult to get enough data for comprehensive study. Higher and lower figures have been obtained; they are directly related to how specific or general one is in the definition of what constitutes incorporation. The trade-off is clear: high specificity means low yield; low specificity means high uncertainty about whether one is dealing with an incorporation or not. The unfortunately low incorporation rate is probably related to the physiological inhibition of external sensory input in D sleep.

It is important, from the standpoint of dream grammar and symbolic transformation, that all investigators are agreed there is usually a "seamless" incorporation of the stimulus into the ongoing dream; incorporation procedes in a way that is usually indistinguishable from the way other elements in the dream are introduced. It is often highly symbolic and metaphorical (see Berger, 1963; Cartwright, 1977), as with other dream elements. We suggest that the seamless "incorporation" of external stimuli into the dream implies that the inhibition-free "internal" activation of sensory systems may form an important foundation for dream construction. A dream with external stimulus incorporation is presented in Section VII.

Hemispheric Specialization and Dreams. Several writers have proposed (D. Cohen, 1975; Broughton, 1975; Antrobus and Erlichman, 1978) that the dream phenomena of predominance of imagery, "primary process thinking," and primitive nature of the processes are a result of the physiological preeminance of activity from the minor (nondominant) hemisphere during D sleep. Nondreaming sleep reflects the activity of the dominant hemisphere (verbal, intellectual kinds of activity). This hypothesis is primarily founded on the similarity of psychological processes during dreaming and those thought to be associated with nondominant hemisphere activity; physiological support in terms of evidence for a shift of hemisphere activity in the course of sleep and waking is so tenuous and indirect as to be almost nonexistent.

Berlucchi's study is sometimes quoted as supporting the possibility of unrestrained dominance of one hemisphere over the other during D sleep because of the abolition of callosal activity (and thus interhemispheric transfer) during this state (Berlucchi, 1965). We believe Berlucchi's data do not support this contention, and, because of the recent interest in this kind of theory, we think it worthwhile to specify in detail what Berlucchi did and did not show. Berlucchi measured tonic levels of callosal activity in cats by the method of integration of filtered multiunit activity from semi-microelectrodes; he did not use more precise techniques of recording individual fibers that would have allowed quantification. He reported that tonic integrated activity was maximal in waking, diminished during desynchronized sleep, and minimal during D sleep. However, as Berlucchi himself is careful to state, the significance of his results must be considered somewhat questionable in view of the fact that the method cannot give a true quantitative sampling of callosal activity and because he did not measure at all the peaks of very prominent phasic activity that occurred during D sleep and that are clearly visible in the figures in his paper.

It should also be emphasized that the numerous studies using recordings of individual cortical units, while not specifically testing differences in left–right hemisphere activity during D sleep in cats and monkeys, have never reported any left–right differences in neuronal activity level or patterns in D sleep (see Hobson and McCarley, 1977a). Further arguing against this notion of the origin of dreamlike activity in hemispheric differences is recent evidence from a study of dream reports in patients who have undergone commissurotomy of both the corpus callosum and anterior commissure (Greenwood et al., 1977). This study found no evidence whatsover for selective visual dream mediation by the dominant hemisphere. In conclusion, although hemispheric differences as a source of dream phenomena remains a testable hypothesis, it is quite clear that there is at present no solid physiological support.

A Neurochemical Approach.   Ernest Hartmann has studied the relationship between mind and brain functioning during dreaming from the standpoint of possible links between neurochemical transmitters and mind events. Hartmann believes that the concepts of psychoanalytic psychology will ultimately prove to be shorthand descriptions of physiological events, and in this respect his faith in a simple isomorphism between psychoanalytic and physiological concepts is a direct translation of Freud's.

Hartmann's pharmacological theory and that of the reciprocal interaction model of sleep cycle control outlined in this chapter are very closely related in that Hartmann uses pharmacological evidence to indicate that increased D sleep time is associated with conditions of decreased effective brain norepinephrine (Hartmann and Schildkraut, 1973). (It will be remembered that norepinephrine is one of the suggested inhibitory neurotransmitters in the reciprocal interaction model.) Hartmann goes on to suggest that one of the functions of sleep may be to restore the efficacy of norepinephrine systems depleted during waking.

Hartmann (1973) suggests that it is possible to associate certain mental states with states of increased or decreased brain norepinephrine, and that the diminished level of norepinephrine in D sleep offers a window on the brain and mind during conditions of low levels of this transmitter. States with high levels of norepinephrine are associated with the mental states of focused attention, good reality sense, "feedback modulated self-guidance," and a continuing sense of the self. In contrast, dreaming and states of low norepinephrine are associated with opposite conditions. Hartmann, consistent with his position that psychoanalytic concepts will prove shorthand for physiological processes, believes that the psychoanalytic concept of *ego strength* may be directly related to norepinephrine activity.

For another neurotransmitter, dopamine, Hartmann suggests that dopamine may be related to "un-neutralized psychic energy," and this biogenic amine may be increased in D sleep and thus account for some of the vividness of dreams. He goes on to suggest that the pattern of increased dopamine release and decreased norepinephrine release that he believes occurs during dreaming may also be present in schizophrenics and account for some of the fundamental similarities of the two mental states (Hartmann, 1976). From a physiological viewpoint the theses of Hartmann about norepinephrine and dopamine levels during D sleep are testable through examination of whether cells containing these neurotransmitters show increased or decreased discharge activity during D sleep. It is more difficult to develop an animal model for the complex psychic states that Hartmann sees as isomorphic with or reducible to the physiological transmitter states. In view of the multiplicity of brain systems, we ourselves feel that it is most unlikely that any single neurotransmitter will be found to subserve or be isomorphic with any single complex psychic function, such as "ego strength" or "psychic energy." From a physiological point of view it is unlikely, for example, that dopamine systems in the retina have the same relationship to psychological functioning that dopamine systems in the caudate nucleus have. It thus seems imperative to specify in which neuronal system transmitter level alteration affects psychic functioning. Furthermore, as our discussion of the concept of psychic energy in Freud's theory makes clear, the notion of psychic energy itself is one that appears to be a relic of antique neurophysiology rather than a precisely defined and operational psychological concept.

A Genetic and Developmental Hypothesis about the Function of D Sleep.   Jouvet (1973, 1975) has suggested that the function of D sleep in the developing animal is to organize and/or to program instinctive behavior. Jouvet bases his argument on the activation of various innate behaviors in the course of D sleep, a position that is akin to our emphasis on the activation of various motor pattern generators and of other hierarchically organized behavioral sequences as the substrate for dream construction. Jouvet points out that the activation of these systems during embryonic life may constitute an important factor in their ultimate development, and that D sleep may serve thus to program or organize the integration of all the complicated sequences of motor behavior that are necessary for the genetically constituted behaviors. In the adult Jouvet believes that dreaming may serve the function of "reprogramming" some innate behavior.

VII. DREAM FORM AND DREAM CONTENT: THE ACTIVATION-SYNTHESIS HYPOTHESIS AS APPLIED TO DREAM REPORTS

The activation-synthesis hypothesis postulates that principal elements of dreams derive from a synthesis of information generated by activation of motor pattern generators and of sensory systems. The general strategy of seeking mind-brain isomorphisms suggests that we should examine dreams for specific matches between the physiology of the dream state and the content and form of dreams as revealed in dream reports. We will use two time-honored forms of dream evaluation. First will be the clinical approach, featuring narrative samples of dreams, followed by a comment on their "interpretation." (By interpretation is meant presentation of a theory about the generation of the dream.) The second part of this section will deal with dream reports in a statistical, quantitative manner. Figure 3-11 and 3-12 provide an overview of the anatomy and physiology of the activation-synthesis hypothesis and should be examined while reading this section.

   The following examples and preliminary data from dream reports are derived from a pilot study currently in progress (McCarley, 1979b). The data base is dream reports derived from 12 male college students aged 20–24 who were awakened at the end of the first four REM periods of each of 20 consecutive nights spent in the sleep laboratory in conjunction with another study conducted at the Cincinnati sleep and dream laboratory (Kramer et al., 1976). The subsample of this dream report set used for the pilot study was derived from consecutive nights of all subjects during the middle portion of this study. In accordance with the literature, reports of mental activity on awaking were scored as dreams if they exceeded 50 words in length (Hall and Van de Castle, 1966). We found shorter reports either were not dreamlike or were not sufficiently detailed to be useful in the analysis. No maximum length was placed on dream reports.

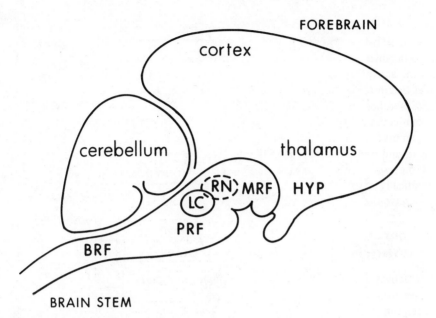

Figure 3-11. Schematic sagittal section of brain showing location of structures involved in dream state generation.   Legends: bulbar reticular formation (BRF), pontine reticular formation (PRF), midbrain reticular formation (MRF), hypothalamus (HYP), locus coeruleus (LC), and dorsal raphé nucleus (RN).

Some comment is required as to why we will use the narrative form of dream reports. While this presentation is by definition nonsystematic, we believe it to be informative and necessary in counteracting many prejudices about what dreams are and are not. Many of these notions are derived from a palimpsest marked with residues of dream reports selected to illustrate various theories of dream content interpretation. The selection bias of the dream theories in these reports is often further compounded by the use of reports not derived from D sleep awakenings; there is thus added both the selection bias of the dreamer and the alteration of dreams attendant upon the quirks of memory and the social setting in which the dreams are reported.

Presentation of the dreams in narrative also allows us to give examples relating to the issue of how a dream is made. The activation-synthesis theory suggests that the primary events are sensory and motor system behavioral sequence activation and then a knitting together in a way that includes the dreamer's experience. In this view the manifest content transparently shows the impetus to the dream, in contrast to the wish fulfillment–disguise model of psychoanalytic theory, according to which dream elements are merely part of the disguise of the unacceptable wish.

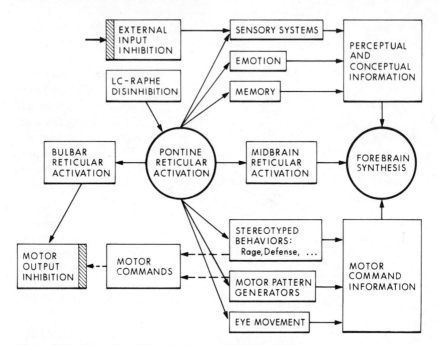

Figure 3-12. Schematic of the activation-synthesis hypothesis of dream state generation.

We again caution the reader that our approach to dream analysis focuses on the primary impetus to dream formation and the formal, universal aspects of the dream, although we believe our approach is compatible with the use of dreams to learn about the personality and concerns of the dreamer. In fact, we believe the relative absence of disguise of motivational themes, as will be seen in some of the dream samples, is an asset in this examination.

It is, however, our view that what is particularly dreamlike is the form of the dream, and the form, as with other human creations and syntheses, often dominates the content. Robbe-Grillet offers a similar view in his comments on the translation of his novel *Last Year at Marienbad* (1962) to the screen:

This is precisely what makes the cinema an art; it creates a reality with forms. It is in its form that we must look for its true content. The same is true of any work of art, of any novel, for instance: the choice of a narrative style, of a grammatical tense, of a rhythm of phrasing, of vocabulary carries more weight than the actual story . . . . The initial idea for a novel involves both the story and its style; often the latter actually comes first in the author's mind, as a painter may conceive of a canvas entirely in terms of vertical lines before deciding to depict a skyscraper group.

1. Dreams with a Dominant Sensory Stamp. Since the activation-synthesis model suggests that part of the stuff of dreams is internally generated sensory activation, production of a pure or nearly pure sensory-dominant dream would both be in accord with such a theory and further show the kind of dream transformation such sensory activations might undergo. By choosing a sensory mode with an extreme of sensation rarely experienced during the day (vestibular activation), we will be able to argue that the origin of this representation in the dream is unlikely to lie in a memory or in a day's residue. A plausible assumption is then that the source is the activation of the sensory system during D sleep, and a later statistical study will also be of benefit to us in this argument. The following dream, given in its entirety, appears unlikely to reflect a memory of the day's events:

> I was spinning, my body was spinning around. The circus performers put the bit in their horses and they spin around. The trapeze was spinning like that. Hands at my sides and yet there was nothing touching me. I was as nature made me and I was revolving at 45 rpm record (speed). Had a big hole in the center of my head. Spinning, spinning, and spinning. And at the same time, orbiting. Orbiting what, I don't know. I'd stop for a second, stop this orbit and spinning. (Dream 1651)

Both dream form and dream content in this instance are dominated by a sensory experience, the sensation of whirling in space. As such, this dream illustrates what is likely a relatively pure form of inclusion of an internally generated vestibular sensory experience into the dream. We note there is ample physiological evidence of activation of the vestibular system during D sleep, since microelectrode recordings (Bizzi et al., 1964) indicate that individual cells are intensely activated, and there is further evidence that the vestibular nuclei may play an important role in generating PGO waves (Morrison and Pompeiano, 1966). In terms of our hypothesis about generation of many of the active phenomena of D sleep by the pontine reticular formation, there also is anatomical and physiological evidence for direct excitatory input to the vestibular nuclei from the pontine reticular formation.

Some critical theoretical issues of dream interpretation can be taken up with this dream. The interpretation we have given is that the dream is built on a dominant sensory experience, and an unusual one at that, one that is unlikely to be in the day's residue or even in memory. It should be clear that, whatever other interpretations one wishes to make, one must come up with an explanation as to *why and how this particular form of sensory representation was chosen*—the activation-synthesis model of dream content provides the most parsimonious hypothesis and thus satisfies the principle of Ockham's razor. The following dream report (presented in its entirety) also suggests vestibular system activation as a primary event:

I was on the floor in some kind of house . . . an apartment or someplace and, ah . . . I sort of ah . . . like floating along and came to a stairway . . . about four or five flights of stairs I could see and just sort of floating down. You know, still like lying floating down, right above the stairs and ah . . . and that's all I remember is going down the stairs. You know, I don't know where I went or anything after that. (Dream 8582)

Note that it may be possible to make other "interpretations" of these dreams. On a superficial level, the hole in the center of the head in the first dream is obviously appropriate for a record and may represent a dreamer's association that is appropriate to the vestibular sensory input. Still other interpretations are possible, including one directly in the Jungian/Freudian tradition: the erect revolving person with the hole in the center of his head could suggest a representation of a phallus, and as such, is reminiscent of Jung's childhood dream [as reported in his autobiography, *Memories, Dreams, Reflections* (Jung, 1963)] and may also be linked to the dreamer's sexual concerns. Note that these further interpretations are not contradictory to the activation-synthesis hypothesis. This hypothesis suggests only that the usual first temporal event in dream formation is activation of sensory/motor systems, and that idiosyncratic and personal elements in the dream are the ones later retrieved from the dreamer's memory because they most closely match the input from a motor sequence or sensory activation. (Figure 3-12 illustrates the possibility that, in some instances, memory systems may be directly activated. Absence of a detailed physiology of memory makes this hypothesis difficult to test.)

We now turn to a relatively pure report possibly derived from *auditory stimulation:*

I heard music in my head and it was thunderous music of the cosmos . . . Guitars are screaming. Drums are pounding. I heard a voice over it. A very mild mannered Indian voice. Said something to the effect "We will maintain the highest degree of virtue at all costs." It sounded like his speech was this music . . . it was really recorded. It had been programmed in his words he had taken off paper. I don't know who he was, but I think I made a face to go with him. Something that was across my path once or twice. Of no importance. (Dream 0627)

Possible *somesthetic system* activation is illustrated in the next dream portion:

There were just thousands of tennis balls all over where the grass had been. You know they had been there all the time, but the grass was too high so I couldn't see them. So I started to pick the tennis balls up, and all of a sudden I also notice there were just hundreds of thousands of frogs all over. All over the grass. When I'd stoop over to pick up a tennis ball, they'd get all over my hands and everything. And they were crawling all over me and everything. (Dream 1727)

Elements of visual form abound in dreams, but the purity and intensity of the visual in the following report suggest a primary activation. The motoric activity will also serve as an introduction to the next topic.

> Walking along, I came upon a rainbow. I don't remember if I was alone or not. But the rainbow was three dimensional and it touched earth. The rainbow was three dimensional so I took off on the rainbow just like I would a beanstalk. I continued along the steps which I can describe to be like layer cake of different colors in shape of steps. Little action except there were two couplets spoken. The one spoken by myself, "What am I doing down here?" And the reply, "come back tomorrow." It's a very existential dream. (Dream 7619)

2. Evidence of Motor Pattern Generator Activity in Dreams. Repetitive motor activity, while occurring frequently in dreams, rarely occurs alone, as a solo theme. Instead, like Baroque figured bass, it often runs throughout the dream as a continuing theme, combined, sometimes rather bizarrely, with other elements. It is clearly apparent when pointed out, and we italicize for emphasis in the following examples.

> I was *riding* around on a bicycle in a field. Just like on a truck, like where they cleared away to build a road. I was *going* a little fast, like this was a motorcycle. And . . . *riding* past people. A lot of people were walking on it. And it was just mud . . . curved around mostly, you know, in this same area. I don't remember going anywhere on it. Just *riding* it around more or less. (Dream 9556)

The next dream illustrates both the continuing of a repetitive motor movement and the phenomenon of change of dream plot (emphasis ours).

> I was sitting in front of a piano . . . I remember I wasn't playing the piano, I was just sort of *putting my fingers on the keys and moving them around* . . . I was at an amusement park. I got in line, they were having pizzas . . . the line big and long . . . and I wasn't in too good of shape so I got out of the line . . . *we were just walking around* . . . there was another scene. There was a band . . . (a drum major tossed a baton as high as he could) . . . it landed on top of some chair and it started bouncing toward me. I grabbed it and threw it back at him. . . . then I *walked* over to someone that I knew . . . then I left the band. I *walked* up, it sort of changed real quick; I was *walking* up these steps . . . there was going to be a robbery . . . I was just *walking* through, the map showed me how I was supposed to walk and I could see this happen. Then there were all these rocks in the water, big, there was a big slab of marble. . . . I don't know how a 20 pound rock floats but some of them were. We were just filling this hole up with marble slabs. (Dream 4099)

3. External Stimulus "Incorporation."   We think this phenomenon is important because the fate of external stimuli in dream construction (in terms of the dream transformation) may be analogous to the fate of internally generated sensory stimuli. Such stimuli are frequently said to be "incorporated" into the dream; but we believe a more accurate statement is that the dream is built on these elements, and that they may be regarded as foundations of the dream.

The following dream, edited because of its length, offers an interesting example of how much of a dream appears to be constructed on the basis of an external stimulus, in this case mucous in the throat. Note that as in the first vestibular dream, this element of mucous in the throat is not only represented in the dreamer as actor in the dream, but also is represented in the other characters, suggesting that a rule for sensory transformation is that representation may include other characters as well as the self. (Material in parentheses is our summary of these events.)

> (The dreamer argues with two janitors) . . . Finally it came to—they started spitting on the floor, the two of them, like to demonstrate what they could get away with, just what I dare not do, you know? It was also like they were spitting on the floor in front of me like daring me to come closer, you know? Or warning me to keep my distance. All the time I should mention in this spitting business, my throat was full of mucous, and I couldn't cough it up. I wanted to spit. I was trying to, or at least was trying to cough this stuff up. It was uncomfortable. *It still is now that I'm telling you the dream too.* [emphasis ours] (The dreamer is confronted by his supervisor who) . . . accused me of spitting on the floor, got upset that I spit on the floor, that I even would consider spitting on the floor. I immediately jumped on him and said, "You son-of-a-bitch . . . that's unfair. . . . " . . . all this was while we were going up on the elevator. Essentially that was the end of the episode except that I was still trying to swallow the stuff in my throat or cough it up somehow . . . it was bothering me. (Dream 0019)

Clearly evident in this dream is the joining of the stimulus (mucous) with idiosyncratic and personality characteristics of the dreamer.

4. Examples of Abrupt Scene Shifts.   This dream phenomenon may be isomorphic with a run of pontine reticular cell activity, then a period of quiescence, then another outburst of activity (Figure 3-10). Different dream sequences may be constructed with the activation of another motor pattern generator or sensory system. The next dream illustrates a rapid scene shift to a segment that appears to be related to vestibular sensation.

> I was out in this big house or something, kind of like out in the country. A real big yard. I didn't know much about the people there. And something, you know, like started happening for the people. I don't know what it was. But it made them really strange. It was like, it affected their minds. They

were, you know, able to think thoughts between them, instead of talking and things like that. It was like a science fiction movie and, I don't know how they did it, you know, they could make somebody else be like that or—it was contagious or something. I kept on and you know, the people that weren't like that, sort of freaking out, and the people that were, you know, trying to get everybody else like that and that went on for a while [*dream sequence change*]. And the dream changed into a thing where I was on this stage, you know, holding the guide rope for someone who was flying around on wires, you know, hanging from the ceiling. That went on until I got real dizzy from turning around all the time. So I stumbled off and set down at a table right cff the stage. (Dream 2229)

5. Bizarreness. Part of the bizarreness and strangeness of dreams may result from the simultaneous combination of internally generated sensory activation and behavioral sequence activation which is rarely encountered in waking. The different nature of internally generated stimuli (as compared with the usual external ones) may also contribute to the bizarreness, which the dreamer labels as such only in retrospect.

Note in the following dream that the motoric (pattern generator) activity of walking continues throughout the dream; this banal activity is combined with the extraordinary and exotic in the first segment, then goes to the everyday in two further plot shifts. (We italicize for emphasis.)

The first part of the dream, I was an investigator policeman and we were looking for vampires . . . so the very first place I *walk* into was a john, must have been some public building. *I walk* in and there is a man on the wall with a stick going up through his chin. I turned around and walked out the door and *turned around* and said to whoever I was with, "Who's been in here?" So I *walked* back in again and he was definitely dead. Then I heard something in one of the stalls, the toilet stalls. So I *walk around*, but just as I was getting ready to look down through the top of it, this lady bites this man in the neck. They both drop dead right there. Blood flowing freely. . . . *Then the dream changed sort of. I was walking* along some street. . . . There were four little people yelling out, each one of them, "Help me! My mommy's doing something!" They were all screaming and I was trying to decide which one sounded the most serious. Which to help first. Then the one up in the fourth room started climbing out the window. Then the dream changed. I was a door-to-door salesman of some books or something. . . . this car pulls up and started following me along the street and I thought to myself, "They're trying to sell books too." I'm doing all the work peddling doors while they just drive along and make a sale. (Dream 1064)

In the next dream there is again a repeated motor activity (driving); a bizarre effect is achieved by the use of a familiar character in an unfamiliar setting.

That I was sitting on and *driving* at times, a fork-lift truck like we have at the warehouse. Again, this dream involved this woman who was to be my wife, my fiance. Sometimes I was *driving* this truck around and sometimes I was lifting things onto it, like wooden skids. And she was, sometimes I was *driving around* her, or passed her or something. And setting some things down on a point. (Dream 4773)

As this theory of dream interpretation is elaborated, and it is now only at the beginning of its development, we hope to discover the general rules relating sensory and motor system activation to the subjective dream experience, to discover the dream syntax and grammar. Undoubtedly, there will also be better methods developed for ascertaining what kind of physiological activation is taking place and associating it with dream content. For example, with DC recordings of eye movement and a projection of the scan sequence mapped out over a portion of the dream, one might then be able to examine very carefully dream content, and see how, if indeed at all, information about eye movements was fed into the construction of the dream. Improved methods for detection of other D sleep phasic physiological events in humans are also critical, and we again stress the significance of the efforts of Rechtschaffen (PIPs), and Roffwarg (MEMA) and their coworkers and the previously cited studies of somatic movements in D sleep. The next section deals quantitatively with the preservation of rank order of sensory experience in the physiological domain and the intensity of activation of various sensory and motor systems.

Quantitative Analysis of Dream Phenomena and the Activation-Synthesis Hypothesis. The activation-synthesis hypothesis predicts a correspondence between the frequency and intensity of subjective sensations in dreams and the extent and intensity of physiological activation of brain nuclei related to these sensations. We have proposed a specific isomorphism (McCarley, 1979a): rank order of intensity is preserved in mappings between the physiological and psychological domain. As will be seen, much more data must be collected on both the physiological and psychological side to test this isomorphism fully; but it provides a simple, testable, and rather comprehensive hypothesis about the ordering of dream and physiological data. In this section we continue our report of a pilot study and describe new information relating to this particular isomorphism; and, in later portions of this section, we turn to other aspects of the activation-synthesis hypothesis.

McCarley (1978b) scored 80 dreams in the Cincinnati collection for the presence of a word indicating a particular sensory phenomenon. This word could be spoken by or applied to any dream character. As an example of the scoring process, we note that a dream was scored as having an auditory sensation present if there were present in the dream words such as "heard," "talk," "noise," "sound," or any explicit descriptions of the characteristics of a sound. The dif-

TABLE 3-1. FREQUENCY OF EXPLICIT REPORTS OF DIFFERENT SENSORY MODES
AND EMOTION IN 80 DREAMS. ALL DREAMS HAD VISUAL IMAGERY.
THE MOST FREQUENT EMOTION WAS ANXIETY.

System	Visual	Auditory	Vestibular	Gustatory	Somesthetic	Pain	All Emotions	(Anxiety)
N Reports	80	44	6	5	2	0	10	5
%	100	55	7.5	6.25	2.5	0	12.5	6.25

ference between this scoring and that of the Hall–Van de Castle scale should be noted; in the latter, vocalizations are scored separately from auditory sensations. In this category and others we were conservative in inclusion, and *specific references* to a sensation had to be present. We also note that in this particular study the dreamers were not questioned about sensation; so it is possible that there is under-reporting. All dream reports had, in their description of the dream activity, evidence for visual elements in the dream. Vestibular sensations were scored when, as in our dream examples, there was evidence of spinning, floating, or repetitive changes in position in space, such as ascending or descending.

The results of this tabulation are presented in Table 3-1. Note that the rank order or predominance was: visual > auditory > vestibular > taste > touch > temperature (cold). There are already physiological data on two comparisons, and the visual > vestibular subjective sensation corresponds to the intensity of physiological activation of these systems. No pain sensation was present in this dream set, and the preliminary analysis of one hundred additional dreams shows no pain reports there either. Unfortunately for the sake of testing our isomorphism hypothesis, the central pathways for pain are presently unclear and thus have not been recorded during sleep; we unequivocally predict that they will not be activated during D sleep. In this dream subsample no sexual feelings were reported, although they were included in other dreams in this collection.

Emotion.   While the central physiology of emotional behavior remains unknown, it is useful to have baselines for comparison when knowledge of the physiology is developed, and a test of the isomorphism theory can be accomplished. Emotions were scored as present when the dreamer or any character described the presence of pleasure, sorrow, anger, or anxiety (which included reports of fear, terror, and fright). Presenting statistical studies of the presence of emotion is also important because the majority of the dreams reported anecdotally for an interpretation of dream content include strong emotions. Table 3-1 also gives the prevalence of reports of emotions in dreams; the percentage is relatively low ($12\frac{1}{2}\%$) and suggests that the predominance of dreams involving emotions in anecdotal reports may reflect a selection bias. It can be seen that emotions related to anxiety are most prominent in these dreams.

Dream Activity and the Motor Pattern Generator Activation Hypothesis.   If the activation-synthesis hypothesis is correct, then one must find evidence of motor activity in dreams that corresponds to the activation of motor centers discovered physiologically. Note that this is a necessary but not sufficient condition for the activation-synthesis hypothesis to be true. If we do not find strong evidence of motor activity in dreams, it means that the activation-synthesis is probably false; but if we do, there may be other explanations. The examination, however, is a necessary preliminary step to any serious consideration of the activation-synthesis hypothesis.

McCarley (1979b) scored motor activity in dreams by looking at lower extremity activity as reported in a second set of 50 dreams from the Cincinnati collection. Lower extremity activity was indicated exclusively through the use of verbs. Verbs included were: walking, running, stepping, climbing, driving (i.e., driving a bike and driving all motor vehicles, for lower extremity action is necessarily involved), dancing, skipping, and so on. We also scored lower extremity activity as present when there was in the dream the use of a verb, such as "go," that describes the changing of location of a dreamer from one clearly defined and specified spot to another in which no other form of muscular activity other than lower extremity movement could accomplish the location change, i.e., "go up the stairs," "go down the road." It should be noted that our method of scoring has important differences from the Hall–Van de Castle scale; these authors score an activity only once even though there are repeated verbs describing the same activity; only if there is a different intervening activity does the same activity get scored again. In our opinion, intensity of movement is best scored using the entire dream information available, and the dreamer's report of repeated muscle activity is important because it signifies that this activity is recurring throughout a large portion of the dream.

In this analysis we wished not only to indicate the presence or absence of lower extremity activity, but also to obtain a measure of the frequency of this occurrence within the dream. To compute this measure we used the number of verbs indicating lower extremity movement in comparison with the total number of verbs of all kinds in the dream (after eliminating the purely descriptive verbs "to be" and "have").

The results are quite strongly in support of the activation-synthesis hypothesis, since a high proportion, 80%, of the dreams contained reports of lower extremity activity. Furthermore, if one looks at the frequency of verbs indicating lower extremity activity as compared with all verbs, one finds it to be rather surprisingly high, at 33% (this was with the probabilities conditioned on each dream). In Figure 3-13 we have tabulated the frequency of occurrence of lower extremity movement as a proportion of all verbs in each of 50 dreams. Note that the histogram is bi-modal, reflecting the ten dreams with no report of

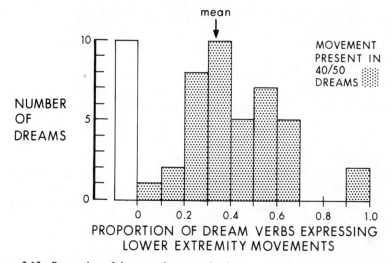

Figure 3-13. Proportion of dream verbs expressing lower extremity movements. See text for further description.

locomotor activity combined with the smooth-appearing, almost gaussian, distribution of the probability of lower extremity movement verbs in the other part of the distribution. This suggests that two processes may be at work, one determining whether or not lower extremity movement is reported at all and the second determining the frequency of reports. When lower extremity movement is reported, the mean probability that any verb in the dream report will refer to this movement climbs to a rather high figure of about .41. The data are consistent with the notion that motor pattern generator activity may underlie the construction of dreams.

Clearly, many more variables relevant to our hypothesis remain to be studied. We will, for example, determine if the frequency of lower extremity movement reports remains constant from subject to subject over nights, suggesting either a constant physiological or psychological variable, or whether it varies widely, suggesting the presence of important day-to-day factors. We also will enlarge the sample and include a scoring reliability measure. Finally, we should note that since the dreams used in this report were not done using questions about the specific variables that we are interested in, some under-reporting probably exists in all our categories. The great counterbalancing positive aspect of using a set of dreams collected for another purpose is that there was absolutely no question of interviewer bias toward a confirmation of the hypothesis discussed here. We thus believe our conclusions are quite supportive of the activation-synthesis hypothesis, that they are conservative, and that further work may well indicate even stronger support.

VIII. SUMMARY

We are at the point of making significant links between dreams and the physiological events of sleep. This chapter has outlined the evidence for the following unifying hypotheses about dreams and the desynchronized sleep state.

There is a good working model of the clock that times and controls the periodic occurrence of the brain state of desynchronized sleep and its isomorphic mind state of dreaming sleep: the basis of this clock lies in the reciprocal interactions of two neuronal populations, excitatory pontine reticular cells and inhibitory biogenic amine-containing cells in the locus coeruleus and raphé. Activity in these two populations alternately waxes and wanes during the sleep cycle, and they interact with each other to produce this modulation. Desynchronized sleep occurs when the population levels of pontine reticular formation neuronal activity rise sufficiently high, as a result of disinhibition by biogenic amine-containing cells. Many of the physiological events of desynchronized sleep result from the activation, direct or indirect, of other groups of cells by this pontine reticular formation activity.

The activation-synthesis hypothesis of dream generation proposes the following links or isomorphisms between the physiological activation of desynchronized sleep and the psychological events of dreams:

- The high intensity of dream experiences is isomorphic with the intense neuronal activation of D sleep. In particular, the predominance of visual imagery in the dream is linked to the most intense activation of the visual and oculomotor systems.
- Specific kinds of information about the commands for the eyes to move may play an important role in dream construction also; shifts in the dream visual world may reflect a synthesis of information about eye movements.
- Specific information about commands for somatic movement may also play an important role in dream construction. Although output of commands for somatic motor movement is normally blocked by an output motor neuron inhibition in D sleep, there is evidence that during desynchronized sleep the command centers for motor pattern generators are activated. Thus the dream event of stepping or walking may be linked to activation of the brain stem pattern generator for locomotor movement.
- Activation of higher brain regions concerned with controlling stereotyped instinctive behaviors, including those connected with emotions such as anger and defensive behavior, also furnishes important plot and content substrates for dream construction.
- Brain systems concerned with memory may be activated independently or may function in a pattern analogous to their usual mode in waking; they

may retrieve memories that most closely match the pattern of activation in motor systems and sensory systems. Much of the idiosyncratic and specific personality-linked aspects of the dream could enter in this fashion.

- The frequent bizarreness of dream content may reflect the knitting together of contradictory elements that occur in dreams because of the different mode of activation in dreams as compared with waking—i.e., internal instead of external activation—and also may reflect the fact that during dreams, and unlike waking, there is simultaneous activation of many different systems.

- The frequent scene shifts and plot changes in dreams, typically occurring abruptly and without transitional bridges, may reflect the temporal course of activation of the pontine reticular cells. This consists of long runs of activity during which one set of sensory and motor elements could be activated, followed by another run of activity during which different sets of sensory or motor systems might be activated.

- As for the final step in our process, that of synthesis, we suggest that it occurs in much the same fashion as it does during waking. Information from sensory systems, motor systems, information about the affective states of the organism are all linked together and compared with information about the organism's experiences in the past, its memories. Dreams are not a result of an attempt to disguise but are a direct expression of this synthetic effort.

ACKNOWLEDGMENTS

We thank Dr. John P. Nelson for his comments on an earlier version of the manuscript and Ms. Sharon Haugen and Eve Melnechuk for their secretarial and bibliographic assistance. Portions of this chapter have appeared in the *American Journal of Psychiatry*, Vol. 134: 1211-1221, 1977 and Vol. 134: 1335-1348, 1977. Copyright 1977, the American Psychiatric Association. Reprinted by permission.

REFERENCES

Amatruda, T. T., Black, D. A., McKenna, T. M., McCarley, R. W., and Hobson, J. A. Sleep cycle control and cholinergic mechanisms: Differential effects of carbachol at pontine brain stem sites. *Brain Res.* 98: 501-515, 1975.

Antrobus, J. S., and Erlichman, H. The dream report: Attention, memory, functional hemispheric asymmetry and memory organization. In: Fishbein, W. (Ed.), *Sleep, Dreams, and Memory*. New York: Spectrum, in press.

Arkin, A. M., and Antrobus, J. S. The effects of external stimuli applied prior to and during sleep on sleep experience. In: Arkin, A. M., Antrobus, J. S., and Ellman, S. M. (Eds.), *The Mind in Sleep*. Hillsdale, New York: Lawrence Erlbaum Assoc., 1978.

Aserinsky, E. Physiological activity associated with segments of the rapid eye movement period. *Res. Publ. Assoc. Res. Nerv. Mental. Dis.* 45: 338-350, 1967.

Aserinsky, E., and Kleitman, N. Regularly occurring periods of eye motility, and concurrent phenomena during sleep. *Science*, 118: 273–274, 1953.

Bartlett, J. R., Doty, R. W., Sr., Lee, B. B., and Sakakura, H. Influence of saccadic eye movements on geniculostriate excitability in normal monkeys. *Exp. Brain Res.* 25: 487–509, 1976.

Baust, W., and Engel, R. Korrelation von Herzfrequenz, Atmung and Trauminhalt. *Pflügers Arch.* 319: 139, 1970.

Berger, R. Experimental modification of dream content by meaningful stimuli. *Brit. J. Psychiat.* 109: 722–740, 1963.

Berger, R. J., and Oswald, I. Eye movements during active and passive dreams. *Science*, 137: 601, 1962.

Berlucchi, G. Callosal activity in unrestrained, unanesthetized cats. *Arch. ital. Biol.* 103: 623–634, 1965.

Bizzi, E. Changes in the orthodromic and antidromic response of optic tract during the eye movements of sleep. *J. Neurophysiol.* 29: 861–870. 1966.

Bizzi, E., Pompeiano, O. and Somogti, I. Spontaneous activity of single vestibular neurons of unrestrained cats during sleep and wakefulness. *Arch. ital. Biol.* 102: 308–330, 1964.

Brady, J. V. Emotional Behavior. In Field, J., and Magoun, H. W. (Eds.), *Handbook of Physiology*, Section 1. Washington, D.C.: Amer. Physiol. Soc., 1960, pp. 1529–1552.

Brindley, G. S. Sensory effects of electrical stimulation of the visual and paravisual cortex in man. In Jung, R. (Ed.), *Handbook of Sensory Physiology*, Vol. VII/3, Central Processing of Visual Information, Part B. New York: Springer-Verlag, 1973, pp. 583–594.

Brooks, D. C. Waves associated with eye movement in the awake and sleeping cat. *Electroenceph. Clin. Neurophysiol.* 24: 532–541, 1968.

Broughton, R. Biorhythmic variations in consciousness and psychological functions. *Canadian Psychological Rev.* 16: 217–239, 1975.

Büttner, U., Büttner-Ennever, J. A., and Henn, V. Vertical eye movement related unit activity in the rostral mesencephalic reticular formation of the alert monkey. *Brain Res.* 130: 239–252, 1977.

Cartwright, R. D. *Night Life*. Englewood Cliffs, New Jersey: Prentice-Hall, 1977.

Cespuglio, R., Walker, E., Gomez, M. E., and Musolino, R. Cooling of the nucleus raphe dorsalis induces sleep in the cat. *Neurosci. Letters*, 3: 221–227, 1976.

Cespuglio, R., Gomez, M. E., Walker, E., and Jouvet, M. Effect of localized cooling of the locus coeruleus upon the sleep cycle of the cat. Presentation at the Association for the Psychophysiological Study of Sleep, 18th Annual Meeting, Stanford, California, 1978.

Chu, N.-S. and Bloom, F. E. Activity patterns of catecholamine-containing pontine neurons in the dorsolateral tegmentum of unrestrained cats. *J. Neurobiol.* 5: 527–544, 1974(a).

Chu, N.-S. and Bloom, F. E. The catecholamine-containing neurons in the cat dorsolateral pontine tegmentum: Distribution of the cell bodies and some axonal projections. *Brain Res.* 66: 1–21, 1974(b).

Cohen, D. B. Dream content, eye movement, and EEG changes during the night: Implications for extending cortical specialization theory to sleep. *Sleep Res.* 4: 182, 1975.

Cohen, B., and Henn, V. Unit activity in the pontine reticular formation associated with eye movements. *Brain Res.* 46: 403–410, 1972.

Dement, W. C. and Wolpert, E. A. The relation of eye movements, body motility, and external stimuli to dream content. *J. Exp. Psychol.* 55: 543–553, 1958.

Exner, S. *Entwurf zu einer Physiologischen Erklärung der Psychischen Erscheinungen*. Vienna: Deuticke, 1894.

Feigl, H. *The "Mental" and the "Physical": The Essay and a Postscript.* Minneapolis: University of Minnesota Press, 1967.

Festinger, L., Ono, H., Burnham, C. A., and Bamber, D. Efference and the conscious experience of perception. *J. of Exp. Psychology Monograph.* **74**, no. 4: 1-36, 1967.

Firth, H., and Oswald, I. Eye movements and visually active dreams. *Psychophysiology* **12**: 602-606, 1975.

Foulkes, D., and Shepherd, J. Children's dream recall: contribution of sleep, adaptation, demographic, and ability variables. *Sleep Res.* **2**: 112, 1973.

Frederickson, C. J. and Hobson, J. A. Electrical stimulation of the brain stem and subsequent sleep. *Arch. ital. Biol.* **108**: 564-576, 1970.

Freud, S. Gehirn. In *Handwörterbuch der gesamten Medizin*, Stuttgart: F. Enke, 1888.

Freud, S. *The Interpretation of Dreams. Complete Psychological Works*, standard ed., Vols. 4 and 5 (J. Strachey, Trans.). London: Hogarth Press, 1966.

Freud, S. *Die Traumdeutung* (1900). In *Gesammelte Schriften*, Vol. II. Vienna: Internationaler Psychoanalytischer Verlag, 1925.

Freud, S. *Project for a Scientific Psychology* (1895). *Complete Psychological Works*, standard ed., Vol. 1 (J. Strachey, Trans.). London: Hogarth Press, 1966, pp. 294-397.

Freud, S. *Zur Auffasung der Aphasien.* Vienna: Deuticke, 1891.

Freud, S. *The Origins of Psychoanalysis: Letters to Wilhelm Fliess, Drafts and Notes: 1887-1902.* New York: Basic Books, 1954.

Gardner, R., Jr., Grossman, W. I., Roffwarg, H. P., and Weiner, H. The relationship of small limb movements during REM sleep to dreamed limb action. *Psychosomat. Med.*, **37**: 147-159, 1975.

Gardner, R., Jr., and Grossman, W. I. Normal motor patterns in sleep in man. In Weitzman, E. (Ed.), *Advances in Sleep Research*, Chapter 3, Vol. 2. New York: Spectrum Publications, Inc., 1975.

Globus, G., Maxell, G., and Savodnik, J. (Eds.) *Consciousness and the Brain.* New York: Plenum Press, 1976.

Granit, R. *Charles Scott Sherrington.* Garden City, New York: Doubleday & Co., 1967.

Greenwood, P., Wilson, D. H. and Gazzaniga, M. S. Dream reports following commissurotomy. *Cortex*, **13**: 311-316, 1977.

Grillner, S. Locomotion in vertebrates: Central mechanisms and reflex interaction. *Physiological Rev.* **55**: 247-304, 1975.

Hall, C. S. and Van de Castle, R. *The Content Analysis of Dreams.* New York: Appleton-Century-Crofts, 1966.

Hartmann, E. *The Functions of Sleep.* New Haven: Yale University Press, 1973.

Hartmann, E. Schizophrenia. A theory. *Psychopharmacology*, **49**: 1-15, 1976.

Hartmann, E., and Schildkraut, J. J. Desynchronized sleep and MHPG excretion: An inverse correlation. *Brain Res.* **61**: 412-416, 1973.

Hauri, P. and Van de Castle, R. L. Psychophysiological parallels in dreams. In Jovanovic, U. J. (Ed.), *The Nature of Sleep.* Gustave Fischer Verlag, 1973, pp. 140-143.

Head, H. The conception of nervous and mental energy (II). *Brit. J. Psychology*, **24**: 126-147, 1923.

Hendricks, J. C., Bowker, R. M., and Morrison, A. R. Functional characteristics of cats with pontine lesions during sleep and wakefulness and their usefulness for sleep research. In: Koella, W. P., and Levin, P. (Eds.), *Sleep 1976.* Basel: Karger pp. 207-210, 1977.

Henn, V., and Cohen, B. Coding of information about rapid eye movements in the pontine reticular formation of alert monkeys. *Brain Res.* **108**: 307-325, 1976.

Hobson, J. A., Alexander, J., and Frederickson, C. J. The effect of lateral geniculate lesions on phasic electrical activity of the cortex during desynchronized sleep in the cat. *Brain Res.* 14: 607–621, 1969.

Hobson, J. A., Goldfrank, F., and Snyder, F. Respiration and mental activity in sleep. *J. Psychiat. Res.* 3: 79–90, 1965.

Hobson, J. A. and McCarley, R. W. Cortical unit activity in sleep and waking. *Electroenceph. Clin. Neurophysiol.* 30: 97–112, 1971.

Hobson, J. A., and McCarley, R. W. *Neuronal Activity in Sleep. An Annotated Bibliography.* UCLA Brain Information Service, 1977(a).

Hobson, J. A. and McCarley, R. W. The brain as a dream state generator: An activation-synthesis hypothesis of the dream process. *Am. J. Psychiat.*, 134: 1335–1348, 1977(b).

Hobson, J. A., McCarley, R. W., Freedman, R., and Pivik, R. T. Time course of discharge rate changes by cat pontine brain stem neurons during sleep cycle. *J. Neurophysiol.* 37: 1297–1309, 1974(b).

Hobson, J. A., McCarley, R. W., Pivik, R. T., and Freedman, R. Selective firing by cat pontine brain stem neurons in desynchronized sleep. *J. Neurophysiol.* 37: 497–511, 1974(a).

Hobson, J. A., McCarley, R. W., and Wyzinski, P. W. Sleep cycle oscillation: Reciprocal discharge by two brain stem neuronal groups. *Science*, 189: 55–58, 1975.

Jacobs, L., Feldman, M., and Bender, M. B. Are the eye movements of dreaming sleep related to the visual images of the dreams? *Psychophysiology*, 9: 393–401, 1972.

James, W. *The Principles of Psychology*, Vol. II. New York: MacMillan, 1890, pp. 493–494.

Jones, E. *The Life and Work of Sigmund Freud*, Vols. 1–3. New York: Basic Books, 1959.

Jouvet, M. Essai sur le rêve. *Arch. ital. Biol.* 111: 564–576, 1973.

Jouvet, M. The function of dreaming: A neurophysiologist's point of view. In *Handbook of Psychobiology*, New York: Academic Press, 1975.

Jung, C. G. *Memories, Dreams, Reflections.* (Recorded and edited by Aniéla Jaffe. Trans. by Richard and Clara Winston.) New York: Vintage Books, 1963.

Kasamatsu, T. Visual cortical neurons influenced by the oculomotor input: Characterization of their receptive field properties. *Brain Res.* 113: 271–292, 1976.

Keller, L. Participation of medial pontine reticular formation in eye movement generation in the monkey. *J. Neurophysiol.* 37: 316–332, 1974.

Koulack, D. Effects of somatosensory stimulation on dream content. *Arch. Gen. Psychiat.* 20: 718–725, 1969.

Kramer, M., Hlasny, R., Jacobs, G., and Roth, T. Do dreams have meaning? An empirical inquiry. *Am. J. Psychiatry*, 133: 778–781, 1976.

Lacey, J. L. Individual differences in somatic response patterns. *J. Comp. Physiol. Psychol.* 43: 338–350, 1950.

Luschel, E. S. and Fuchs, A. F. Activity of brain-stem neurons during eye movements of alert monkeys. *J. Neurophysiol.* 35: 445–461, 1972.

McCarley, R. W. Control of sleep–waking state alteration in *Felix domesticus. Neurosci. Symposia*, Vol. 3, 1978.

McCarley, R. W. Mind–body isomorphism and the study of dreams. In: Fishbein, W. (Ed.), *Advances in Sleep Research*, 1979a, in press.

McCarley, R. W. Manuscript in preparation, 1979b.

McCarley, R. W., and Hobson, J. A. Single neuron activity in cat gigantocellular tegmental field: Selectivity of discharge in desynchronized sleep. *Science*, 174: 1250–1252, 1971.

McCarley, R. W., and Hobson, J. A. Discharge patterns of cat pontine brain-stem neurons during desynchronized sleep. *J. Neurophysiol.*, 38: 751–766, 1975(a).

McCarley, R. W., and Hobson, J. A. Neuronal excitability modulation over the sleep cycle; a structural and mathematical model. *Science*, **189**: 58-60, 1975(b).

McCarley, R. W., and Hobson, J. A. PGO waves: Phase locked firing by pontine reticular neurons. *Neurosci. Abstracts*, **2**: 894, 1976.

McCarley, R. W., and Hobson, J. A. The neurobiological origins of psychoanalytic dream theory. *Am. J. Psychiatry*, **134**: 1211-1221, 1977.

McCarley, R. W., Nelson, J. P., and Hobson, J. A. PGO burst neurons: Correlative evidence for neuronal generators of PGO waves. *Science*, **209**: 269-272, 1978.

McGinty, D. J. Encephalization and the neural control of sleep. In Sterman, M. B., McGinty, D. J., and Adinolfi, A. M. (Eds.), *Brain Development and Behavior*. New York: Academic Press, 1971.

McGinty, D. J., Harper, R. M., and Fairbanks, M. K. 5-HT-containing neurons: Unit activity in behaving cats. In Barchas, J., and Usdin, E. (Eds.), *Serotonin and Behavior*. New York: Academic Press, 1973, pp. 267-279.

Molinari, S., and Foulkes, D. Tonic and phasic events during sleep: Psychological correlates and implications. *Percept. Mot. Skills*, **29**: 343-368, 1969.

Morrison, A. R., and Pompeiano, O. Vestibular influences during sleep. IV. Functional relations between vestibular nuclei and lateral geniculate nucleus during desynchronized sleep. *Arch. ital. Biol.* **104**: 425-456, 1966.

Moruzzi, G. The sleep-waking cycle. *Ergebn. Physiol.* **64**: 1-65, 1972.

Moskowitz, E., and Berger, R. J. Rapid eye movement and dream imagery: Are they related? *Nature*, **24**: 613-614, 1969.

Pessah, M. A., and Roffwarg, H. P. R. Spontaneous middle ear muscle activity in man: A rapid eye movement sleep phenomenon. *Science*, **178**: 773-776, 1972.

Pivik, R. T., McCarley, R. W., and Hobson, J. A. Eye movement-associated discharge in brain stem neurons during desynchronized sleep. *Brain Res.* **121**: 59-76, 1977.

Presley, C. F. (Ed.) *The Identity Theory of Mind*. 2nd Ed. St. Lucia: University of Queensland Press, 1971.

Rechtschaffen, A. Phasic EMG in human sleep: I. Relation of EMG to brain-stem events. Presentation at 18th Annual Association for the Psychophysiological Study of Sleep Meeting, Palo Alto, California, 1978.

Robbe-Grillet, A. *Last Yeat at Marienbad*. (Trans. by Richard Howard.) New York: Grove Press, Inc., 1962, pp. 7-8.

Roffwarg, H. P., Dement, W. C., Muzio, J. N., and Fisher, C. Dream imagery: Relationship to rapid eye movements of sleep. *Arch. Gen. Psychiatry,* **7**: 235-258, 1962.

Roffwarg, H., Herman, J., and Lamstein, S. The middle ear muscles: Predictability of their phasic activity in REM sleep from dream recall. *Sleep Res.* **4**: 165, 1975.

Ryle, G. *The Concept of Mind*. New York: Barnes & Noble, 1949.

Sakai, K., and Cespuglio, R. Evidence for the presence of eye movement potentials during paradoxical sleep in cats. *Electroenceph. Clin. Neurophysiol.*, **41**: 37-48, 1976.

Sastre, J. P. and Jouvet, M. Les schemes moteurs du sommeil paradoxal. In Koella, W. P., and Levin, P. (Eds.), *Sleep 1976*. Basel: Karger, 1977, pp. 18-23.

Shaffer, J. A. *Philosophy of Mind*, Englewood Cliffs, New Jersey: Prentice Hall, 1968.

Shik, M. L., and Orlovsky, G. N. Neurophysiology of locomotor automatisms. *Physiological Rev.* **56**: 465-501, 1976.

Siegel, J. M., McGinty, D. J. and Breedlove, S. M. Sleep and waking activity of pontine gigantocellular field neurons. *Exp. Neurol.* **56**: 553-573, 1977.

Singer, W. Control of thalamic transmission by corticofugal and ascending reticular pathways in the visual system. *Physiological Rev.*, **57**: 386-420, 1977.

Smart, J.-C. *Philosophy and Scientific Realism*. New York: Humanities Press, 1963.

Vivaldi, E., McCarley, R. W., and Hobson, J. A. The D sleep state and the D-carb state: A quantitative comparison. *Sleep Res.*, 7: 118, 1978.

White, A. R. *The Philosophy of Mind*. New York: Random House, 1967.

Watson, R., Bliqise, D., Friedman, L., Wax, D., and Rechtaschaffen, A. Phasic EMG in human sleep: II. Periorbital potentials and REM mentation. Presentation at the 18th Annual Assoc. for the Psychophysiological Study of Sleep meeting, Palo Alto, California, 1978.

Wegman, C. A computer simulation of Freud's "counterwill" theory. Report 76 SO 01, Dept. of Psychology, Nijmegen Univ., The Netherlands, no date.

Wyzinski, P. W., McCarley, R. W., and Hobson, J. A. Discharge properties of pontine reticulospinal neurons during the sleep–waking cycle. *J. Neurophysiol.* **41**: 821–834, 1978.

4

Children's Dreams

David Foulkes

I will be pursuing here a particular approach to the organization of fact and theory regarding the dreams of children. My main assumption is that the only reliable and representative evidence we now have (or are likely to develop in the future) about children's dreams has come (or will come) from laboratory investigations of physiologically monitored dream periods (including both rapid eye movement [REM] sleep and non-REM sleep). It is appropriate that I begin this review by justifying my assumption, on both conceptual and empirical grounds.

RESEARCH STRATEGIES IN THE STUDY OF CHILDREN'S DREAMS

With the discovery by Aserinsky and Kleitman (1953) of REM sleep and of its correlation with particularly vivid and organized dream narratives, students of dreaming for the first time had solid evidence to indicate that a substantial portion of human sleep is accompanied by full-blown dream experience. REM periods were observed to occur regularly at the termination of 90-minute EEG cycles within sleep, and to range in duration from 5-10 minutes (early in the night) to 30-60 minutes (late in the night). Altogether, roughly a fourth of a young-adult human's standard sleep period is regularly spent in REM sleep.

Normative studies (e.g., Roffwarg et al., 1964) have indicated neonatal REM-sleep percentages considerably in excess (e.g., 55-80%) of the 20-30% range observed in young adults, with a decrease to approximately 30% by the end of the first year of postnatal development. It is unlikely that REM sleep could, in this period of life, be accompanied by any mental experiences approximating dreams as we know them. Children at ages (e.g., 2–3) at which the presence of mental imagery can be demonstrated in waking life (Flavell, 1963; Piaget and Inhelder, 1966), however, also have a REM-sleep incidence on the order of 30% of total sleep time (Williams et al., 1974), a figure which declines only slightly from early childhood to late adolescence (ibid.). Thus children who *are* potential dreamers do not seem to be exceptions to the general rule that REM sleep comprises a significant portion of the total human sleep period.

Moreover, as we shall see below, even young children report dreams, as do adults, significantly more often from REM than from non-REM sleep. Their ability to recollect dreams on experimental arousals from REM sleep is, however, impaired, relative to that of adults, in both sleep periods. There are many reasons, relating to both slowly developing cognitive/memorial skills and task-motivational deficits, why this finding seems unsurprising. It seems most reasonable to assume that the true *incidence* of dream imagery is no different in children with some capacity for internal representations from what it is for adults (although the *form* of that imagery might be expected to covary with waking refinement of skills of mental representation and manipulation). Thus we probably will not be seriously misled to assume that children also are not exceptions to the general rule that REM sleep is accompanied by mental experiences which we could characterize as "dreamlike."

Thus, for both adult and child, there is much more dream activity going on every night than we might have suspected from other methods of dream study (e.g., dream episodes reported in therapeutic interviews or in everyday conversation, dream reports collected in response to daytime administrations of questionnaires). In fact, as I have thus far presented it, this discrepancy has been stated most conservatively, for it now is know (Foulkes, 1966; Rechtschaffen, 1973) that dreamlike imagery of a generally less narrative form often is reported from non-REM sleep, in fact, may be pervasive throughout sleep. And yet, in the absence of deliberate arousals during sleep, we only infrequently are aware of the dreams, REM or non-REM, that we experience. One of the earliest findings of systematic research on REM dreams was the demonstration that, if awakenings are not made during, or within a few minutes following, REM periods, the content of REM dreams is forgotten (Wolpert and Trosman, 1958).

Taken together, the above findings pose, I think, a fatal objection to any method of dream study other than the representative sampling of dreams across different time periods of the night and across the different psychophysiological components of the 90-minute sleep cycle. The objection surely is fatal if we are interested in children's spontaneously-*occurring* mental activity during sleep, rather than merely in spontaneously-*remembered* dreams. The latter topic is, of course, of some interest in its own right, but it deals more with a series of selective mechanisms through which our access to dreaming is drastically and systematically reduced, and by which dream experiences themselves probably are quite systematically altered, than it does with dreaming itself as a mental process. At any rate, the perspective that will guide the remainder of this chapter is not a concern with which dreams children, for a variety of reasons and through a series of selective mechanisms, spontaneously manage to recall, but an interest in the autonomous processes of children's sleeping thoughts themselves, whether or not the products of those processes would have captured the attention of waking thought in the absence of appropriate experimental interventions.

The alternative is to base our understanding of the workings of the child's sleeping mind on a sample of dreams which is only a small portion of all the dreaming that children experience, and, more importantly, to have a dream sample which is doubly biased: (1) the selectivity of memorial processes (e.g., Bartlett, 1932) has had ample time to work its full effects upon the dream experiences actually "recalled"; and (2) those dream experiences so recalled probably constitute a quite *unrepresentative* sample of all those dreams the child actually experienced.

With regard to the latter point, there is some evidence that REM dreams (and perhaps non-REM dreams) systematically vary in quality across the night (Foulkes, 1966; Rechtschaffen, 1973). If we restrict ourselves to REM (or other) dreams "spontaneously" recalled, we run the risk of sampling only those dreams that occur about the time of the spontaneous termination of sleep in the morning. Or, if the "spontaneously recalled" dreams actually did occur earlier in the night, there is a high probability that the child "woke up with them" because they were unrepresentative, e.g., because they, unlike most mid-night dreams, generated anxiety sufficient to be associated with a spontaneous termination of sleep.

With respect to the former point, it seems quite likely that people remember their dreams long enough to be able to recount them later to therapists or interviewers only to the extent that they rehearse their content while awake. Many dreams are likely to impress us—both adult and child—as scarcely deserving such effort. A few dreams, systematically different from the data pool from which they were selected, merit (or force) such attention: dreams with intense affective components, for example, or dreams with particularly vivid or bizarre or personally meaningful imagery.

There is still a further bias in relying upon *clinical* dream samples. It has been demonstrated that, within "normal" subject populations, adults with personality-test indices suggestive of borderline psychopathology (e.g., high MMPI profiles, high MMPI schizophrenia scale scores) have laboratory-monitored dreams of relatively greater intensity, unpleasantness, and so on, than do subjects with more normative personality test scores (e.g., Foulkes and Rechtschaffen, 1964; Pivik and Foulkes, 1966, 1968; Cartwright and Ratzel, 1972). That this finding generalizes to children as well is suggested by two studies: Foulkes (1967) found, in a case-study design, that the laboratory-monitored dreams of a boy with poor waking "ego-control" mechanisms were especially bizarre in comparison to those of other boys in the same study; more systematically, it also has been found (Foulkes et al., 1969) that adolescent boys institutionalized for emotional disturbance had laboratory-monitored dreams which were more bizarre and unpleasant than those of a control group of working-class boys living at their own homes. It thus seems highly likely that clinical dream samples will, even as compared with the biases inherent in questionnaire studies using normal children, systematically overstate the unpleasant and bizarre features of typical childhood ideation during sleep.

It may be objected that there is a "catch" in the evidence thus far adduced in support of a laboratory strategy for studying children's dreams. Won't the dreams children report in a laboratory setting be systematically different from those which they report in their more usual sleep environments? Won't the peculiar features of the laboratory setting (e.g., the experimenter as a novel and "untested" adult; the necessity that electrodes be attached, and worn throughout the night, so that EEG sleep stages can be monitored; fears and fantasies about "electrocution" engendered by these techniques; and so forth) so alter the form and content of what is dreamed that laboratory-sampled dream mentation will, in fact, be unrepresentative of home-experienced dream mentation?

These questions need, I think, to be answered in the order given. *First*, of course, we have every reason to expect that laboratory-monitored children's dreams will differ systematically from those spontaneously reported at home. That is why we are in the laboratory. There we can sample dreams according to a more representative sampling scheme than we generally could hope to achieve anywhere else. (There is, of course, the possibility, now feasible, of electrophysiological monitoring at one's own home [Breger, 1969].) We expect differences. They should not, as such, either surprise or concern us. As to the *second* question: if, however, there were evidence that, with similar dream-sampling plans both at home and in the laboratory, dreams still differed systematically according to their locus of collection, then we would have reason to doubt the representativeness of our laboratory-collected dreams. We are in the laboratory to implement a new, and better, sampling plan, not to "influence" dreams by means of the laboratory environment.

There are two ways in which this second objection may be countered: (1) dream theory (Freud, 1900) suggests that the basic concerns of dreams, and the basic mechanisms of their construction, will not vary because of nontraumatic fluctuations in the quality of dream-day activity. Manifestly, children adapt readily to sleeping in a laboratory setting. Manifestly, few of their dreams make much reference to that setting, or to the persons or objects encountered there.

Presumptively, then, this objection does not carry much force. (2) Fortunately, however, we are not limited to such theoretical arguments, whose persuasiveness will vary with our degree of commitment to the underlying theory. There are empirical data on precisely the question at hand, and they strongly suggest that, at least in the sort of laboratory investigations whose results will be presented below, experimenter-effects, laboratory-environmental-effects, and physiological-recording-effects do *not* hopelessly contaminate, in fact, are *not* a systematic influence upon, children's laboratory-monitored dreams.

Specifically, Foulkes and Shepherd (1972b) found that, when dream-sampling procedures were constant across home–laboratory setting dimensions which differed otherwise in all of their characteristic ways (e.g., laboratory subjects had their sleep physiologically monitored), home- and laboratory-sampled dreams did *not* differ systematically from one another. Groups of 4- and 5-year olds ($n = 14$) and 10- and 11-year olds ($n = 14$) slept for several nights in both settings until a standard arousal time. The younger subjects then were questioned about their dreams (in the laboratory, by the experimenter; at home, by a parent), while the older subjects spontaneously wrote out their dreams (in both settings). Dream effects were assessed with a reliable, comprehensive scoring system specifically developed for children's dreams (Foulkes and Shepherd, 1971). The findings of this investigation thus indicate that the sampling-schedule advantages of laboratory dream studies need not be purchased at the cost of any untoward effects upon dream content of the setting in which that sampling schedule most often must be implemented.

This same study indicated, in precise quantitative terms, the magnitude of typical biases of studies of spontaneous dream recall in childhood. On 42 subject-nights these younger subjects spent at home, only 12 dreams were reported. While recall on REM awakening nights in the laboratory also was relatively poor for these subjects, with three REM awakenings per night, these same subjects recalled dreams at a rate approximating one dream a night. For the older subjects, dreams were reported spontaneously at home, on the average, every other night. On REM awakening nights in the laboratory, with three awakenings per night, these same subjects recalled dreams at a rate approximating two dreams per night. Thus, one's access to children's sleep mentation is amplified three- or fourfold by employing even a relatively low-key schedule of laboratory dream sampling.

In the Foulkes and Shepherd (1972b) study, subjects *knew*, in both settings, that they would be asked about their dreams. It may be objected that, in truly spontaneous home recall, there would be much less chance for reactive effects to occur than in *either* condition of their study. However, it is difficult to see how dreams ever can be studied systematically in the absence of foreknowledge and deliberate sampling. Otherwise, the sampling bias becomes horrendous. For example, in a later study employing Foulkes and Shepherd's group of younger subjects (the children were ages 6-7), children's parents were asked to note down the first two dreams their child spontaneously reported at home. After 91 days, only 11 dreams had been collected for the entire group of 14 children. By conservative estimate, the children experienced 5096 separate dreams (i.e., REM periods) on those nights. What conclusions about the workings of the child's mind in sleep, or about individual differences in these workings, could possibly be based on nonrandom, incomplete sampling of this kind? The dream student's choice cannot be dreams which are reported "truly spontaneously"; the only reasonable question facing such a student is where and how to study dreams deliberately and systematically. The Foulkes and Shepherd results suggest that, since the undoubted gains in representative sampling in the laboratory are in no significant way jeopardized by losses in the representativeness of the dreams being sampled, the most reasonable answer to this question is: "in the laboratory."

METHODOLOGICAL PROBLEMS IN THE STUDY OF CHILDREN'S DREAMS

Regardless of the research strategy employed to collect children's dreams, there are any number of special problems in interpreting the dream data which one collects—"special," in that they either are unique for the child case, or are much exaggerated there as compared to the adult case.

One such problem is that of the validity of the child's report. By what right does one treat the child's report as if it had a correspondence with an experience that actually occurred during sleep? This is, of course, in one form or another, a chronic problem of *all* dream psychology, where we must, perforce, use verbal reports to study private experiences (Rechtschaffen, 1967). But in the child case, there are special complications. Can we be sure, for instance, that the child understands what a dream is? That the child understands what it is to "report" a dream to another person? That the child has language adequate to communicate a dream to us? That even if able to do so, the child will be motivated to report a dream to us? That the child has a sufficient discrimination of fantasy and reality to know or care what is dream and what is not, in the accounts we receive? And, in the laboratory, how do we bestir the child from her or his profound sleep and obtain the attention and acquiescence requisite to our request that a delicate task of introspection be performed in a conscientious manner?

It is well to recognize that these are problems not capable of definitive resolution. Even more than at the adult level, any extrapolation from our analysis of particular dream reports of particular children must be tentative, whether those extrapolations are to the presumed underlying dream experiences of the same children or to other children's dreams.

A dash of common sense is our first remedy for the kinds of problems mentioned above. We should not assume, in questionnaire studies, for instance, that all children are sufficiently attuned to their own dreams to be able to report even a single dream to us, on demand. "Tell me the last two dreams you remember having had" is an instruction obviously containing a biased demand-characteristic (Orne, 1962). In sleep-laboratory studies, our knowledge that the child has been awakened from REM sleep should not force us into the stance that: "I know you had a dream, damn it, and I won't let you go back to sleep until you tell it to me." In this context, it is reassuring that REM dream-recall figures reported below from studies of preschool and early school-age children are as low as they are.

Common sense also dictates that reliable reporting can not be so readily assumed for children as for young adults who have been socialized to middle-class values. In sleep laboratory studies in which large numbers of young-adult college students are studied for a brief span of nights, one never gets to know particular subjects very well. Their reports generally are believed because these people are the sort of people in whom one routinely tends to believe. It probably is wise not to tender the same credibility routinely to children, especially to children who have not yet passed through the objectivity-oriented system of extrafamilial education prevalent in Western societies. It is important to *know* children in more than a passing way in order to know what to make of what they say. Parents probably are less gullible listeners of children's speech than are adult strangers. By studying children intensively and extensively, as in longitudinal study designs (Foulkes, 1971), one perhaps gains the same sort of advantage by coming to serve *in loco parentis.*

But we have recourse to more than common sense in determining the appropriate manner in which we should interpret a report of a purported dream experience by a child. We can collect data relevant to the interpretive problem. With respect to the question of the child's understanding of dreams, Piaget (1926) indicates that the child's accession to a mature understanding of the concept "dream" follows a definite pattern of qualitative development. Laurendeau and Pinard (1962) have developed and standardized a reliable test for determining a child's precise "level" of understanding of "dream." The levels they have identified are:

Stage 0: The child does not comprehend what a dream is, or refuses to discuss what a dream is.

Stage 1: The child believes that dreams are as real as waking life experience, and expects, for example, that a visitor in her or his bedroom also will be able to witness the dream.

Stage 2: The child is in transition from an externalized conception of the dream as a worldly fact to an internalized conception of the dream as an imagining.

Stage 3: The child recognizes the dream as a mental experience, rather than as an external, material fact.

On the basis of a child's performance on this test, one should be able (a) to better shape interrogation strategies so as not to approach the child with inappropriate questions and (b) to better assess potential error in assuming that a child's dream report means, in regard to associated private experience, what an adult's dream report does. In the longitudinal study of children's dreams to be described below (Foulkes et al., 1974), it was not until ages 5 and 6 that all children reached at least Laurendeau and Pinard's level 2, that is, that they recognized dreams as being at least partly internal in origin and nature. Because earlier (ages 3–4) understandings of dream were relatively primitive, lesser weight was attached to findings at those ages. However, having several times administered the Laurendeau and Pinard test, the authors could demonstrate that the bulk of their dream data at *both* age levels came from subjects with, in comparison to peers, *relatively* more mature dream concepts. This finding indicates some potential value for the dream observations made even at ages 3 and 4.

Also relevant to the interpretation of children's dream reports in a laboratory setting is whether these reports discriminate pre-arousal physiological state as do adult reports. In the longitudinal study described below, for instance, at all ages at which children were studied, they reported significantly more dreams on REM- than on non-REM-sleep arousals. That is a finding also made with adults (Foulkes, 1966; Rechtschaffen, 1973), a consideration which increases the belief we likely will accord the bulk of the dream reports in the particular study in question. In addition, at ages 10 and 11, children in this study reported, to a "blind" interviewer and as assessed by "blind" judges, significantly more visual activity ascribed to the dreamer character on awakenings made during REM bursts than on awakenings made during REM-quiescent epochs of REM periods. This finding both makes conceptual sense and accords with similar findings for adults (Berger and Oswald, 1962; Roffwarg et al., 1962). In unwittingly having performed this discrimination, the children in question have, therefore, enhanced the credibility we likely will accord their dream reports.

To address the question as to whether children are able adequately to translate the pictorial imagery of dreams into words, it is possible to perform control tests in wakefulness, in which children at various ages are asked to describe *known* pictorial stimuli (e.g., projective test cards, moving-picture episodes). A pattern of stimulus-report correspondence can be determined independently of the dream context. At an individual level, such tests can be used to determine whether the most detailed dream reports come from those subjects most adept at waking description (this was, in fact, the case for subjects in the longitudinal study described below). More generally, the data generated by such tests are relevant to the hypothesis that waking increases in descriptive skill accompany increases in complexity of dream reports (this also was observed in the same study). This last finding could be used to argue that apparent age differences in dream phenomena in childhood may, in fact, reflect no age difference in dream phenomena as such, but, rather, only a difference in dream-reporting skills. On this hypothesis, one may imagine the mind of the very young child brimful of elaborate dream scenarios, but believe that the child possesses such a limited vocabulary for describing these scenarios that we are led to conclude erroneously that her or his dream experiences are quite primitive in quality. This hypothesis cannot be disproved. If it is correct, it points to an inherent limitation in research on children's dreams, a limitation one cannot circumvent by any refinement of research technique presently imaginable.

However, I want to argue that this hypothesis is, on the face of it, highly implausible. It scarcely seems possible that children of different ages dream similar dreams but only report them differently. It surely would be a remarkable exception to our general knowledge of the human mind were the tightly structured dramatic unity of adult dreams to have no developmental history, to spring full-blown at the time we dream our first dream. Dreaming is a cognitive process; its manifestations at the adult level are considerable developmental achievements. The process of developing dream "competence" must, in fact, be much like that of developing linguistic competence (Chomsky, 1957, 1965, 1972, 1975). In both cases, there is a problem of accounting for the mature capacity to generate an infinite number of novel representations from a finite base of past learning experiences. Dreaming is, like language, a prime instance of the creativity of the human mind. We do not, as very young children, while awake, speak or think as adults do; there is no good reason for believing that, asleep, we should be able to think-in-images as adults do. Elsewhere (Foulkes, 1978), I have argued that the development of the skills of producing and manipulating iconic representations in sleep proceeds in parallel with the development of the skills of producing and manipulating linguistic symbols in wakefulness. If this argument is correct, then it is not an unfortunate artifact, but a reflection of the nature of dream phenomena themselves, that the growth of dream-report competence parallels that of waking verbal competence more generally.

Another set of methodological issues in the study of children's dreams relates to how we should *analyze* the dream data we collect. This is, of course, also a major issue more generally in dream psychology. Available alternatives range from impressionistic qualitative analysis (e.g., as applied in child dream research: Foulkes, 1967; Breger, 1969) to ordinal dream rating scales (e.g., as applied in child dream research: Foulkes et al., 1967; Foulkes et al., 1969) and objective content-analysis systems (e.g., as applied in child dream research: Foulkes, 1971; Hall and Nordby, 1972). Each alternative has characteristic advantages and disadvantages: qualitative analysis is maximally sensitive to "deep" dream meanings, but maximally unreliable; rating scales are reliable, and sensitive to the overall trends in a given dream, but somewhat superficial; content analyses are reliable, and detailed in their scope of application (Hall and Van de Castle, 1966; Foulkes and Shepherd, 1971), but tend hopelessly to fragment individual dreams so that their larger pattern is obscured. While each alternative will, sensibly, I believe, continue to be used, and will, productively, I hope, be subject to further refinement, there is reason to believe that qualitatively different approaches ultimately will be required.

What is needed, particularly, is some technique that can combine the sensitivity to private meanings and deep semantic structure which presently is said to characterize the better of the qualitative techniques with the reliability and generality of today's objective dream-analysis systems. Elsewhere (Foulkes, 1978), I have tried to develop such a technique, a system which can coordinate the reliable scoring of dreamer associations with that of the dream itself so as to capture the private, connotative meaning of dream symbols and so as to permit the reliable modeling of "dream-work" processes (Freud, 1900). Unfortunately for its relevance to children's dreams, however, application of this system depends on concurrent scoring of dreams *and free-associations to those dreams.* As is well known, it is difficult to induce children, especially young children, to associate in any thorough or meaningful way to their dreams (e.g., Foulkes, 1967). Perhaps the nearest approximation we can achieve to the kind of data free association yields for adult dreamers is to work toward objectifying our collection and organization of collateral life-history data for children. This strategy would argue, once again, for studying either children whom one initially knows well (e.g., Breger, 1969) or children whom one arranges, in an extended case-study design, to get to know well (e.g., Foulkes, 1971). But its implementation will, no doubt, be exceedingly difficult, and will require a kind of patience heretofore conspicuously absent in contemporary dream study.

Thus the current situation is that we have no truly reliable, appropriate way of analyzing children's dreams the way we know that they should be analyzed. We have reliable methods that are not fully appropriate to our model of dreams as surface-level representations of deeper semantic structures as transformed by dream-work mechanisms, secondary revision, and so on, and we have methods that claim to be appropriate to that model of dreams but which are, as yet, generally unreliable. Because dream psychologists are under constant pressure, both internally and externally generated, to discover underlying truths about their subject matter, it is wise to remind ourselves that, at present, we are rather poorly equipped, methodologically, to achieve such a goal. Our current techniques are not, by any means, altogether worthless. With them we can begin, and have begun, to make some sense of our subject matter. We know more now than we ever have before about children's dreams, but what we know is not nearly enough, and not nearly so much as we sometimes might wish to affect. Thus, in reading the "results" section of this chapter, the reader will be advised to consider what is said as being only tentative, and to ponder the larger scope of those things that, at present, must remain unsaid.

Person-sampling, as well as dream-sampling within persons, is another persistent problem in dream psychology. We have seen that there is evidence to indicate that disturbed adults or children, the sources for "clinical" dream material, are likely to report dreams which are less realistic and more unpleasant than the dreams of "normal" volunteers. But it also is appropriate to remember that not every adult or child is equally likely to want to participate in laboratory studies of physiological dream-monitoring (nor, for young children, are all parents equally likely to want to commit their children to such study). At present, we simply have no way of knowing how children who volunteer (or who are volunteered) for sleep-laboratory dream study differ from those who do (or are) not. But, because there may be a systematic difference, we must be aware of the limits which that difference may impose on generalization from laboratory-collected data on children's dreams.

There is, however, some reason to believe that volunteer/nonvolunteer differences may be *less* pervasive for children than for adults. In my experience, children are less self-conscious about the content of their dreams than are adults. They are seldom sufficiently sophisticated to realize the kinds of meanings psychologists impute to dream imagery. They seem not to appreciate in any continuing way that they are responsible for the form and content of their dreams. Even where, on test measures, they indicate that dreams are the imaginings of their own mind, they do not bring this abstract knowledge to bear on their response to particular dream images. Rather, they are more likely to be under the sway of the ego-alien phenomenological quality of dream experience: dreams happen to one, rather than being things one does with her or his own mind. In this sense, it is my suspicion that fewer children than college students shy away from dream studies because of the embarrassing things dreams might be imagined to reveal about one's personality, mind, and so on. It also is my suspicion that fewer dream reports are "sanitized" for presentation to the interviewer than is true at the college-student level. Fortunately, children have not read enough adult dream theory to be as wary as adults sometimes seem to be about the "hidden personal meanings" of their dreams.

As will be seen below, a further possible limitation of extant data on laboratory-collected children's dreams is that with two exceptions (Kales et al., 1968; Breger, 1969), they have been generated by children sampled from a single community. Because that community (Laramie, Wyoming) lies in what might be considered a cultural backwash of American society, it is possible that results obtained there may not generalize well to more "urban" or "sophisticated" environments (Breger, 1969). I personally do not feel that this is, in fact, a significant limit on the generality of currently available data. There probably are remarkably few areas of America left that still have the insulated, small-town quality that one pictures on the basis of novelistic and sociological exposés of the 1920s and 1930s. For better or worse, American children now generally are subjected to the same cultural innovations according to pretty much the same timetable. Nevertheless, the nature of the community upon which we now depend for most of our knowledge of children's dreams should be borne in mind when considering the data presented below.

THE STUDIES

Table 4-1 indicates the sources that will be relied upon in subsequent characterizations of children's dreams. For each separate study, the following information is given: number, age, and sex of subjects studied; number of nights for which the children were studied; awakening plan implemented (number of awakenings per night; stages of sleep from which awakened); recall frequency (number of awakenings on which dreams were recalled divided by number of awakenings made); methods of dream analysis; any "special" features of experimental design; and references from which more detailed information may be obtained. Early studies presenting purely impressionistic conclusions (e.g., Roffwarg et al., 1964) have not been included in the table. Also omitted is one study (of 2-year-olds) which did not characterize the few (16) dream reports collected therein (Kohler et al., 1968).

The data of Table 4-1 reveal that over 150 different children aged 3–15 have had their dreams collected in electrophysiological sleep-monitoring studies. These subjects have been studied for over 1500 separate nights, and have been awakened to report dreams on well over 4000 separate occasions. This clearly is not an insubstantial base upon which to draw some tentative conclusions about children's dreams. Although the bulk of the awakening-night data comes from the Laramie longitudinal study, data analysis for which has not yet been completed or comprehensively documented in published monograph form, these data are relied upon extensively in the account below.

RESULTS

General Impressions

The first questions to come to the reader's mind are unlikely to be highly specific ones. Rather, he or she will want to know what, in general, children's dreams are like. What are their typical contents, themes, or, insofar as can be gleaned,

TABLE 4-1. ELECTROPHYSIOLOGICALLY MONITORED STUDIES OF CHILDREN'S DREAMS.

Subjects	Nights Studied	Awakening Plan	Recall Frequency	Methods of Dream Analysis	Special Features	References
32 boys (16 ages 6–9, 16 ages 10–12); middle class; paid volunteers	2 per subject, (non-consecutive)	4 REM awakenings per night	72% REM recall	Rating scales; ad hoc content analysis	Presleep film manipulation (violent vs. non-violent film); group mental test and projective test administered to each subject	Foulkes, et al. (1967)
4 boys selected for high (2 sibs) vs. low (2 sibs) dream bizarreness from among subjects in the previous study; ages 8–12; paid volunteers	6 per subject, (non-consecutive)	4 REM awakenings per night	85% REM recall	Qualitative serial analysis	Associations collected from boys and from their mothers; WISC administered to each subject	Foulkes (1967)
5 boys and 5 girls, ages 5–12, only 9 of whom were studied for dream recall	Not stated	Not stated	61% REM recall, 10% Non-REM recall	Not stated		Kales et al. (1968) [abstract]
5 boys and 3 girls, ages 6–10; 2 subjects were the investigator's own children and the others came from two families well-known to him; unpaid volunteers, above average IQ and social class	One adaptation night, followed by 4 dream-collection nights per subject, "carried out within periods ranging from two weeks to two months"	Interruption of all REM periods after the first	87% REM recall	Qualitative case study of one boy, whose dreams are reproduced approximately verbatim, and are discussed in detail	Children studied in their own homes or while "sleeping over" at a friend's house	Breger (1969)

TABLE 4-1. (Continued)

Subjects	Nights Studied	Awakening Plan	Recall Frequency	Methods of Dream Analysis	Special Features	References
6 boys and 6 girls, ages 3–5, paid volunteers; middle class	2 per subject (nonconsecutive); additional night for attempted influence of REM content via tactile stimuli for 4 of the subjects, with 2 further Non-REM awakening nights for one subject	7 REM awakenings over the 2 nights; generally 3 the first night, 4 the second	44% REM recall	Qualitative analysis (dream reports were sufficiently brief to permit an inclusive enumeration of their contents)	Parents remained with child until sleep onset, sometimes staying for the entire night and conducting dream interviews; Laurendeau-Pinard test, Blacky test collected from children; Traditional Family Ideology Scale responses collected from parents	Foulkes et al. (1969)
7 boys ages 13–15 from an institution for emotionally disturbed adolescents; 7 working class control boys ages 13–15; paid volunteers	2 per subject (nonconsecutive)	4 REM awakenings per night	73% REM recall	Rating scales; content analysis as per Foulkes et al. (1967)	WISC and objective personality test (CPI) administered to all subjects	Foulkes et al. (1969)
40 10–12-year-old boys, selected from 105 volunteers on the basis of high (n = 20) vs. low (n = 20) prior exposure to televised violence; paid volunteers	One adaptation night, plus two experimental nights per subject (nonconsecutive)	3 REM awakenings on adaptation night; 4 REM awakenings per experimental night	73% REM recall	Rating scales, word counts, content analysis; primary focus on the variables of: general dream intensity; hedonic quality; aggression and hostility; and defensiveness and guilt	Questionnaire assessment regarding leisure-time activities, sleep disturbances, school performance, peer-group integration etc.; film manipulation (violent vs. nonviolent) on experimental nights, films viewed in experimentally manipulated focal vs. incidental involvement conditions	Foulkes et al. (1971)

Subjects	Procedure		Results	Method	Comments	References
Initially, 7 boys and 7 girls, ages 3–4, and 8 boys and 8 girls, ages 9–10 (two subjects in latter group dropped out at conclusion of first year of study, and two at conclusion of third year of study); samples augmented at starts of years 3 (6 11–12-year-old boys) and 5 (7 7–8-year-old girls), all these subjects continuing to termination of year 5; paid volunteers; a majority of the children were middle class with a substantial working-class minority	9 nonconsecutive nights per normative year (years 1, 3, and 5) of longitudinal study; variable but comparable investigation during years 2 and 4, which were devoted to a series of special studies of psychophysiological, situational, and other determinants and correlates of dream content	In normative years, 3 per night; over each such year, 15 REM awakenings, 9 Non-REM and 3 Sleep-Onset awakenings were scheduled; 2711 awakenings were actually made during these years, and 1151 dreams collected	*Ages 3/4:* 27% REM 6% Non-REM 18% Sleep-Onset *Ages 5/6:* 31% REM 8% Non-REM 31% Sleep-Onset *Ages 7/8:* 48% REM 21% Non-REM 31% Sleep-Onset *Ages 9/10:* 66% REM 32% Non-REM 61% Sleep-Onset *Ages 11/12:* 66% REM 31% Non-REM 67% Sleep-Onset *Ages 13/14:* 67% REM 40% Non-REM 67% Sleep-Onset	Primarily: Scoring System for Children's Dreams (Foulkes and Shepherd, 1971), an objective method yielding reliable word counts, ratings, and content analysis	Numerous supporting sleep/dream studies in years 2 and 4; extensive program for collecting collateral waking-test and observational data, including interrogation of parents and teachers; during normative years, two nights devoted to stimulus-incorporation trials	Foulkes (1971); Foulkes and Shepherd (1972a, b); Foulkes et al. (1974); Trupin (1976); Foulkes, (1977a, b)

meanings? In what ways do they accord with, and in what ways do they differ from, our prior expectations? With which general theories of dreaming or development are they most (or least) consistent?

The sources of our prior expectations regarding children's dreams are likely to be our recollections of our own dreams from childhood and/or the dreams our own children have reported to us. America's preeminent student of dreams, Calvin Hall (1966), whose own research largely has been built around the technique of collecting spontaneously recalled dreams, undoubtedly has reflected the personal and parental experience of many in his proposition that

> Systematic studies of children's dreams should reveal startling information about the inner life of the child. What little knowledge we have of children's dreams suggests that their dreams are much more complex and much more dreadful than has previously been thought. (p. xx)

As we have seen, however, the sampling biases attaching to the spontaneous-recollection procedure are enormous. And the expectations generated by that procedure are far from uniform. In *The Idiot*, for example, Dostoyevsky (1869) speaks thusly of the dreams of Alexandra Ivanovna Yepanchin:

> . . . her dreams were always remarkable for their extraordinarily vacuous and innocent character, like the dreams of a seven-year-old child. (p. 350)

Are children's dreams dreadful, or innocent?

It is not clear that general psychological theory provides more valid or more consistent bases for generating realistic expectations about the nature of children's dream-life. Freud's (1900) anecdotal observations initially led him to propose that

> The dreams of young children are frequently pure wish-fulfilments and are in that case quite uninteresting compared with the dreams of adults. They raise no problems for solution, but on the other hand they are of inestimable importance in proving that, in their essential nature, dreams represent fulfilments of wishes. (p. 127)

We are informed, in the Strachey variorum text, however, that the qualifier "frequently" was added to Freud's text in 1911, and explained by Freud in 1925 in the following way:

> Experience has shown that distorted dreams, which stand in need of interpretation, are already found in children of four or five; and this is in full agreement with our theoretical views on the determining conditions of distortion in dreams. (1900, p. 127, n. 1)

Evidently, continuing experience with children's dreams led Freud to discount any simplistic interpretation of them as "purely" wish-fulfilling. Their wish-fulfilling character was more often "latent" than "manifest," i.e., more a matter of analytic interpretation than experiential fact.

Jungian psychology generates reasonably strong expectations about the nature of children's dreams. Kirsch (1968) predicted, from the perspective of analytical psychology, that

> The dreams of young children, aged four to seven, would have a mythological character to a significantly greater extent than in adults. Also, one would expect to see mandala symbolism in their dreams. . . . one would predict that there would be a difference [between children's and adults' dreams] because of the child's greater immersion in the world of primitive motifs, magical relatedness, and animistic thoughts. (p. 1462)

Fordham (1969) is more cautious about the role of the collective unconscious in children's dream-formation, but he too divines archetypal imagery in children's dreams.

Stated quite simply, the best *evidence* now available on typical dream imagery in children refutes the hypotheses: (1) that children's dreams are especially "dreadful"; (2) that children's dreams are more manifestly wish-fulfilling than those of adults; and (3) that children's dreams employ archetypal or other exotic forms of symbolism beyond the reach of the child's direct experience with her or his own personal world.

Children's dreams generally are not particularly frightening or unpleasant. The child who falls asleep is not thereby cast into a sea of poorly socialized impulses or terrifying fantasies beyond her or his feeble control. With the admitted qualification that we cannot possibly know all of the child's suppressed daytime (or repressed life-history) wishes, it does not appear that her or his dreams openly (or disguisedly) gratify such wishes any more often than is true for young adults. At *both* age levels, in fact, our independent access to festering wishes is limited, and at both age levels, we have little direct justification in manifest dream imagery for the hypothesis that unfulfilled wishes are peremptory organizers of sleeping thought. Finally, the symbolism of children's dreams draws fairly directly from the child's waking life experience. Fantastic characters or settings and bizarre action sequences are observed very rarely, and to the extent that "mythological" themes are observed, it generally is not difficult to trace them back to the child's direct exposure to the prefabrications of the adult world's mass media.

Thus the typical child dream is much like the typical REM dream of the young adult, as it has been described by Snyder (1970):

> a clear, coherent, and detailed account of a realistic situation involving the dreamer and other people caught up in very ordinary activities and preoccupations. (p. 148)

The most commonly occurring characters in the child's dream are nuclear family members, known persons—often peers, and strangers who function much as do persons known to the dreamer. Where animals appear in the child's dream, they are likely to be from species directly known to her or him. The most commonly observed settings in the child's dream are home and various outdoor/ recreational areas. The most common plot sequences in the child's dream involve everyday forms of social interaction, with a particularly strong emphasis on play activity. Plot resolutions in dreams tend to be realistic and appropriate, rather than grandiosely self-serving.

Origins of Dreaming

Several of the subjects in the Laramie longitudinal study actually commenced service before age 3. In addition, I studied my elder son for a series of six nights beginning before his third birthday. It is, of course, especially difficult to know what degree of credibility one should accord reports from such young children. One bright young two-year-old girl, for instance, who was under considerable maternal pressure to perform "well" in the laboratory, immediately began producing a sterotyped series of domestic-animal scenarios that could reasonably be interpreted only as waking confabulations, as she herself sometimes admitted. The only dream collected from this period to which I attach much belief is that of a young boy who dreamed that he saw himself playing with blocks. He spontaneously remembered that account a month and a half later, and seemed somewhat surprised at it (he thought, evidently, that he would dream of his mother or his pet).

Much interest attaches, of course, to the question of when, and how, dreaming begins as any kind of organized psychological process. It is difficult to imagine dreaming occurring before the age at which mental representations can be reliably demonstrated in wakefulness, but it is not clear that current formulations about the precise age at which that is possible (approximately the second birthday, according to Piaget and Inhelder [1966]) are yet ready to be etched in stone. Still, it is necessary, I think, in addressing questions about the origins of dreaming, to approach them as Piaget has—namely, to see dreams as reflections of a mental process that can only develop concomitantly with other (waking) mental processes. And, because waking representations are much more easily studied than those in sleep, our best answers to questions about the ontogenesis of dreaming ultimately may have to rest on inferences from waking observations.

It is reasonably clear, moreover, that two kinds of evidence traditionally used to push the origins of the dreaming process back toward early infancy are suspect. *Sleep-talking* (e.g., the famous "Anna Fweud, stwawbewwies" episode [Freud, 1900, p. 130]) does not, at the adult level, reliably occur in REM sleep or reliably index representational processes (Rechtschaffen et al., 1962). Speech occurring during, or arising following partial arousals from, sleep might reflect a disinhibition of centers responsible for speech inhibition, rather than any cognitively mediated dreamlike construction. *Night-terrors*, in which children "awaken" in a delirium accompanied by considerable anxiety, do not reliably occur from REM sleep, and any accompanying mental content (which is rare, and sparse, when present) most likely must be assigned to the state of delirium, rather than to the preceding sleep period (i.e., the night-terror is a "disorder of arousal" [Broughton, 1968]).

From experience with very young children, moreover, it is evident that sleep-laboratory studies are unlikely to be highly productive in determining when dreamlike imagery commences or what its early nature might be. However varied and subtle the interrogation procedure, the two-year-old is likely only to be annoyed or amused at it. "Recall" of any kind is likely to be extremely rare. Thus, at very early ages, the electrophysiological dream-monitoring procedure loses the very advantage it has elsewhere in the human life span: it no longer gives the investigator any assurance that he or she is sampling dreams representatively. Added to this, of course, are the inherent limitations imposed by any use of a direct-interrogation strategy with very young children. Piaget's relative success in probing the mental life of the "sensorimotor" and "early preoperational" child has come precisely from his abandonment of that strategy. As much as we would like to know how and when dreaming begins, this is a question whose answer eludes research techniques currently at our disposal.

Piaget (1945), who has as much experience in such matters as anyone, remarks that

> We know, from experience gained from the clinical method of free conversation, that it is almost impossible to question children of three, because of their lack of coherence of thought in following a conversation. After the age of four, on the other hand, it is possible to pursue an enquiry (this does not of course mean that it can be as fruitful as after the age of seven or eight). (p. 136)

Bearing in mind Piaget's qualifier ("almost"), I would agree that it is only in the later preschool years (ages 3-4) that one can begin to learn much about children's dream content by way of direct interrogation, which is, of course, the only way we now have of knowing about anyone's dream content. Even at these ages, moreover, one must bear in mind that report–experience correspondences are, at best, likely to be only approximate.

Developmental Patterns in Dream Experience

At *ages 3 and 4*, children give REM dream "reports" which are quite brief (a sentence or two), and which are relatively lacking in dynamic, thematic quality.

The experiences they purport to describe are not, apparently, likely to be accompanied by much affect. Dream characterization is minimal, and what activities are carried out are likely to be executed by characters other than the dreamer her- or himself. Play activity is relatively frequently dreamed of. Settings tend to be familiar home or outdoor settings, or to be described vaguely. The most distinctive feature of REM-sleep dreams of this age is the relative predominance of animal, rather than of family, characters.

One might, of course, explain the incidence of animal characters in children's dreams in terms of the fantasy materials to which young children especially are exposed in wakefulness (cartoons, comics, fairy tales). Students of the mass media (e.g., Wolf and Fiske, 1949; Riley and Riley, 1954) have hypothesized that animal characters are appealing to children because they allow the child to escape from a world in which impulse control by others is a dominant feature to a world in which impulses and conflicts are more freely expressible in quasi-familial settings. Clinical data, for example on children's phobias, are consistent with this hypothesis (e.g., Freud, 1909; Jones, 1931). Support for an anthropomorphic interpretation of animal figures in children's fantasies also comes from results of a survey of British children who watched zoo programs on television (Morris, 1967). It was found that the popularity of an animal was directly related to the degree to which it possessed humanoid features, and it was suggested that, for younger children, animals often function as parent surrogates. Likewise, as Bellak and Adelman (1960) observe, "The primitivity of animal drives also increases their symbolic proximity for children" (p. 60).

Contextual evidence does support the idea that children's dream animals either are family figures or the child's own "animal" drives. The overwhelming majority of these animals come from domesticated or familiar species, and they often appear in homelike contexts, suggesting that human familial themes simply have been transposed to the animal world. In other cases, it clearly is plausible to read dream animals as animal impulses. For example, the child in the Laramie longitudinal study who had the largest number of animal dreams as a three-year-old had, so far as could be told, no deeper waking interest in animals, and no more waking exposure to animal stories, than any other child in his group. What did distinguish his waking experience, as it was observed in the laboratory and in a nursery-school setting specifically designed to assess waking play patterns of the study's preschoolers, was assertive behavior, hyperactivity, a low threshold for frustration, and a reputation for quarrelsomeness. His animal dreams shifted between themes of containment (a fish moving around in a bowl on the side of a river; a dog in his doghouse, barking) and those of relatively more unrestrained aggression or exhibitionism (kittens eating up a mouse with a pink nose; watching, with his father, a big elephant in a parade). In one dream, he fused the impulsivity and control themes: he was in his "office," doing "cat-work"; meanwhile, a cat hopped around in a cage. The subject's father was a professional, whose office the boy occasionally visited to play "work." In the dream, he cages the animal (but does not abolish its active nature) and identifies with the controlling father (but in a particular work context in which impulsivity still figures).

While it sometimes is plausible to interpret young children's animal-impulse dreams in terms of a "genital" form of sexuality, that plausibility seldom extends to hypotheses couched in terms of "pregenital" stages of psychosexual maturation. The world of dreams, even for preschoolers, generally is more of an interpersonal (or interspecific) one, rather than one of body parts. While organic drives (hunger, thirst, and, interestingly, sleep) are more frequently portrayed in young children's dreams than in those of older children, this portrayal is more in the terms of conventional psychological theory than the theory of psychosexual development (Freud, 1905). While more preemptive, a child's hunger in dreams is not unlike an adult's in its conceptualization. And, "animal impulsivity" is expressed in contexts that suggest an interpersonal, rather than a body-centered, frame of reference. (Waking evidence also suggests precocious genital sexuality in children rather more strongly than it does specifically oral and anal preoccupations [Kohlberg, 1966; Chodoff, 1966; Salzman, 1967; Mussen et al., 1969]). In preschoolers' REM dreams, no significant sex differences have been observed, possibly owing to a common developmental task faced by both sexes: bringing one's own egoistic impulses under social- (and self-) control (but at least equally possibly owing to other reasons, such as the paucity of dream data available for such comparison).

Children's REM dream recall in the preschool years is partially predictable from the child's level of understanding of the concept "dream" (Laurendeau and Pinard, 1962) and from her or his waking descriptive abilities. Within the particular ranges of dream recall and IQ variability investigated, it is not predictable from IQ as such. Factors of motivation and cognitive "style" evidently overshadow psychometric intelligence in determining the young child's laboratory access to her or his own dreams.

Stimulus-incorporation trials have revealed that preschoolers' REM dreams are not influenced more frequently by tactile stimuli applied during sleep than are those of adults (e.g., Dement and Wolpert, 1958). Furthermore, when incorporated, such stimuli are subjected to symbolic transformations much like those observed with adults. In particular, passive → active and self → other transformations are typical. Thus a young girl whose hair was *being sprayed* with water reported a dream of *spraying* a fire; when *her* face was stroked with a soft cotton puff, she reported a dream that *her sister* was playing with a cuddly stuffed animal. Freud (1917) noted that a child's dream does not "reproduce" a disturbing stimulus, but "deals with it" in terms of hallucinatory transformations.

He used such cases to argue the role played by wishes in dream formation. They might, however, equally appropriately, be used to argue for an impressive degree of ego-competency in coping with sleep disturbers. In this context, the stimulus-incorporation data redirect our attention to the primary finding of the study of preschoolers' REM dreams occuring in the *absence* of disturbing stimuli. At the youngest age at which we possess any reliable data, children's dreams are competently controlled fantasy excursions. Neither in terms of manifest dream imagery nor in terms of a more interpretive analysis of themes that might plausibly be imagined to be symbolized by this imagery, does the child lose sight of the nature of her or his true situation in the waking world. There is no descent, at REM-sleep onset, into a state in which impulse obliterates ego. There is no developmental primacy in sleep for unrealistic, wish-dominated, "primary-process" thinking (Freud, 1900), any more than there is in wakefulness. By having attended for too long to those conspicuous, but infrequent, dreams in which the child's adaptive mastery of her or his own thoughts, feelings, and motives fails, we have vastly underestimated the extent to which the mind of the sleeping child is competent at realistically managing its own affairs.

At *ages 5 and 6*, theoretical expectations are generated about possibly significant shifts in the nature of dream experience. Cognitive (i.e., Piagetian) developmental theory suggests that, as children begin to approach the possibility of (concrete) operational thinking, the organization and integration of dream imagery should become qualitatively better (more "adultlike"). Freudian theory suggests that, at least for boys, a developmental crisis is occurring, in which Oedipal strivings for the opposite-sex parent ultimately must be renounced as a function of intolerable anxiety over bodily integrity. As we shall see, expectations generated by each of these different observational perspectives are at least partially confirmed in the dreams of kindergarteners and first-graders.

Compared to ages 3-4, dream reports at ages 5-6 have more than doubled in average length and are markedly more dynamic in quality: increases are noted in both "physical" and "interpersonal" activities within the dream report. No longer do reported dreams have a static, constricted quality; rather, they now begin to approximate in form to adult dreams. The increasing elaboration and organization of dream content evidences a qualitative shift in the competency with which dreams (dream reports?) are constructed.

In terms of specific content, typical dream characters are nuclear family members, known persons, persons unknown who act in the familiar ways of known persons, and animals from species directly known to the dreamer. The most frequently observed settings are recreational or home ones. As is true more generally throughout childhood, the strictly tutorial, as opposed to peer-related or recreational, side of the educational experience finds scant representation in the dreams of early school-aged children. Perhaps the most striking *general* feature of children's dreams at ages 5 and 6 is the relatively passive role ascribed the self-character. The significant increases in activities and interactions as compared to ages 3-4 are largely limited to those ascribed to other dream characters. The newly dynamicized dream world at ages 5-6 is one in which events happen about the child, but in which he or she is not directly involved. It seldom is the case, in particular, that the child is either the initiator or recipient of unfriendly acts.

Despite the increasing cognitive competency reflected in the early school-aged child's dreams, cognition itself (e.g., wondering, reflecting) seldom is present in dream content. Socially directed actions now clearly overshadow object-directed actions in the service of bodily needs such as hunger, thirst, and sleep. Affect is relatively infrequent, particularly negative affect.

An interesting pattern of *sex differences* emerges in dream content at ages 5-6. As compared to ages 3-4, *girls'* dream reports are more pleasant, the girls have assumed more active roles in their own dreams, their dreams show reduced character distortion as animal figures are replaced by familial ones, they dream more often of home settings, and their dreams show marked increases in friendly interaction, positive feelings, and happy outcomes. In these respects, their dream content has become very much like that of older girls. On the other hand, as compared to ages 3-4, *boys'* dream reports are more unpleasant, the boys have assumed markedly more passive roles in their own dreams, their dreams show increased character distortion as animal characters increase in frequency while familial figures (and home settings) continue to be infrequently portrayed, and their dreams show only small increases in friendly interaction, positive feelings, and happy outcomes. In these respects, their dream content remains quite different from that of older boys.

Direct comparisons at ages 5-6 indicate that male strangers and indigenous (untamed) animals appear more often in boys' dreams, while friendly interaction and happy outcomes appear more often in girls' dreams. The girls' dreams are "nice" ones, while those of the boys seem more preoccupied with conflict. Both the nature and timing of the observed boy-girl differences in dream content are consistent with the hypothesis of Oedipal crisis for the boys. Hall (1963), for instance, identifies male strangers in dreams as symbols of the Oedipal father. His reasoning is that the father is a resented and feared stranger in infancy and that, for boys, this early role is strengthened during the Oedipal period (while for girls it is muted by later, more positive feelings to him). Since strangers represent feared properties in one's environment, he reasons that the strangers of the adult male's dreams should be mostly male (while, for adult females, they could be of either sex). He reports empirical confirmation of this prediction. In the present context, it is interesting to observe that, uniquely in the span of childhood years, it is ages 5-6 that sex differences appear in the *overall quality* of dream content, and that the incidence of male strangers is one marker variable for these differences.

It is important, however, to put these differences in context. Even "Oedipal-aged" boys retain significant competence in managing their dream constructions. Their dreams are not "flooded" with unsocialized impulses or unpleasant affect. In fact, they evidence very little self-initiated or self-received hostility. It is only in quite *relative* terms (relative to girls of the same age and/or to boys of other ages) that male dreams at age 5–6 are at all unique. The general impression, even here, is of dreams that are reasonably well-controlled fantasies. Thus, even where dream content is manifestly unrealistic, the boy arranges it so that personal involvement is minimal and that symbolic-level plot resolutions are appropriate, rather than magically wish-fulfilling. For instance, the boy some of whose animal dreams at age 3 were cited above, at age 5 had dreams in which what might be interpreted as castration imagery was displaced, without affect, to animals (somebody cut a caterpillar in half); in which paternal control of animal impulsivity was portrayed, without affect, in a relatively familiar, socialized way (his father caught a jumping frog and put him in the family's gerbil cage); in which open aggression was displaced, without negative affect, to stereotyped fantasy molds (cat-and-mouse episodes, pirates fighting one another); and in which his acceptance of the classical Oedipal resolution might be imagined to have been reflected in animal imagery (a caged turtle goes into its shell, at the grocery store [the "Safe-way"]).

It is revealing, I think, that another, more mundane perspective was not terribly predictive of children's dream imagery at ages 5 and 6. Rather than following psychological theory, one might simply note that children of this age have taken a significant step toward leaving their family of orientation: large portions of their time now are spent with female teachers and peers in a school setting. And yet there is little direct reflection in children's dreams of this momentous (and occasionally traumatic) change. The waking world reflected in children's dreams is not always that which is evident to the untutored naked eye of "common sense." Waking–sleeping continuities are plausible only when we look through the corrective lenses of a developmental theory which goes beyond common sense in its organization of the behavioral phenomena of childhood. If the data of children's dreams strongly suggest that we must view dreaming as a not inconsiderable cognitive competency, they also indicate that dreaming is a form of cognition we cannot fully understand without reference to motivational dynamics, and, particularly, without reference to a theory of unconscious drives and conflicts which, heretofore, cognitive psychologists have rejected as anathema.

At *ages 7 and 8*, the two distinctive features of dream reports at ages 5–6 are reversed: dreamers now are active participants in their own dreams, and boys' dreams now are much like those of girls and of boys at older ages. Specifically, there are significant increases in activities, interactions, and outcomes accruing to dreamers themselves. This is particularly true for boys. The sex differences which remain are not in the general quality of dreaming, but in specific contents dictated by different lines of sex-role development. Female peers, for instance, appear more often in girls' than in boys' dreams.

Boys now dream of family members and known male peers more often than they do of animal figures. There is no longer a specific preoccupation with male strangers. Both boys and girls show a marked increase in the incidence of male strangers. This can be viewed, I think, as indicating the major underlying theme of children's dreams throughout preadolescence—and beyond—namely, the striving for an appropriate sexual identity (Breger, 1969). Males figure prominently in this process for both sexes because boys strengthen their sex-role identification by acting like males and girls strengthen their sex-role identification by learning to act toward males. Or, as Kohlberg (1966) states it:

> ... girls have the option of playing a feminine role in a man's world, whereas boys do not have the option of playing a masculine role in the woman's world. In other words the girl can have "opposite sex" interests, and yet maintain her same-sex values more readily than the boy. (p. 121)

The increased assumption by preadolescents of active roles in their own dream scenarios clearly is consistent with the idea that they are actively modeling adult roles. In fact, an alternate way of indicating the major theme of preadolescent dreaming stresses the primacy of concerns for world-mastery, with differentially prescribed pathways, according to sex, for achieving that mastery as a subsidiary theme. What Freud states for play often may be equally true of dreaming: it is determined by the child's "single wish—one that helps in his upbringing—the wish to be big and grown up" (1908, p. 146). Or, as he later (1931) observed in another context:

> It can easily be observed that in every field of mental experience, not merely that of sexuality, when a child receives a passive impression it has a tendency to produce an active reaction. It tries to do itself what has just been done to it. This is part of the work imposed on it of mastering the external world and can even lead to its endeavouring to repeat an impression which it would have reason to avoid on account of its distressing content. Children's play, too, is made to serve this purpose of supplementing a passive experience with an active piece of behaviour and of thus, as it were, annulling it. (p. 236)

In dreams, this assumption of an active posture is a developmental achievement, one that follows the "Oedipal period" for boys while progressing with more continuity since early childhood for girls.

Earlier passivity in dream representations can be viewed both as a direct reflection of the child's real situation and as a cognitive skill. The young child lives in a world whose features are far from being under her or his control. And yet preschoolers are not without coping mechanisms for dealing with that world (e.g., Murphy, 1962). From an unsystematic examination of preschoolers' play fantasies, Gould (1972) suggests that one of these strategies is a distancing mechanism, whereby "I'm angry" is represented as "There's a monster; it's angry." Realistic coping cannot, of course, end at this point. If early childhood is a period in which the separation of feeling or impulse from ego permits rapid ego development, later childhood is a period in which the ego must begin to attempt to master, rather than displace or deny. Sex-role differentiation interposes here because the learning of sex roles "serves to define for boys and girls the kinds of competence that are most appropriate for them" (White, 1963, p. 120).

In formal terms, the dream reports of 7–8 year olds have fairly well approached the level attained by older children and young adults. They no longer differ significantly in length or elaboration from those of older children, and they come close to having the thematic properties of the dreams of older children.

It is in the heart of preadolescence, i.e., *ages 9 to 12*, that children's dreams have been studied most exhaustively, and it is this period upon which most of the literature's broad characterizations of childhood dreaming have rested. At these ages, children's dreams are formally competent dramatic episodes including a relatively wide range of motoric, cognitive, and interpersonal activities. Their "ego-level" is well predicted by, and, in fact, is at the same level as, concurrent assessments of waking ego functioning (Trupin, 1976). The child's dreams are "peopled" by real people, rather than by animals, with particularly frequent representations of family members, peers, and, especially for male dreamers, male strangers. Home and recreational/outdoor settings are common, with a relative increase, compared to earlier ages, in school settings. Friendly interactions are scored relatively more often than unfriendly ones, with aggressive interactions mostly being both initiated by and directed at characters other than the dreamer her- or himself. Self-ascribed happiness is significantly greater than at earlier ages. The dreamer is increasingly actively involved in her or his own dream scenarios. While the children's dreams are not simply direct reflections of their own waking activity and thought, they do contain relatively realistic portrayals of events and contingencies found in external reality. They are not especially frightening or exciting. In one study (Foulkes et al., 1967), preadolescent subjects characterized as "good" four times as many of their dreams as those they called "bad."

During these years, peer characterization increases as familial characterization declines. This is especially true of female characters and for female dreamers; that is, it is female family members who tend to drop out of the older children's dreams (mothers, female sibs), and it is girl dreamers who tend to dream increasingly often of female peers. During these same years, there is an increasing bias in character selection toward including known peers and persons from one's own sex. Feelings, particularly sad feelings, decrease in dreams collected over this period of childhood, as do unhappy outcomes. Friendly social activity, happy outcomes, and dream pleasantness, on the other hand, increase. As children move toward the end of preadolescence, then, their dreams might well be described as increasingly well-managed, pleasant fantasy excursions.

Sex differences within this period are in line with the children's waking sex-role development. There is, as already noted, an increasing tendency for children to include own-sex friends and persons in their dream scenarios. That is, sex-role concerns are increasingly mapped into peer-world realizations. Early on, male and female dreamers also differ significantly in the amount of gross loco-motor activity present in their dream reports, but girls then "catch up," toward late preadolescence, with a "growth spurt" in self-ascribed motor activity. The literature on waking child development, interestingly enough, also suggests a growth-spurt of physical activity and assertive behavior for girls in late pre-adolescence (Blos, 1962; Kohen-Raz, 1971). As sex differentiation decreases along dimensions of sheer amount of physical activity, however, a new dimension of difference emerges. Manifestly aggressive behavior in dreams decreases for girls, while it increases for boys, so that late preadolescent boys have roughly twice as many dreams containing some aggressive act as do their female counterparts. (But, absolutely, well under half of even their dreams contain such an act, and such acts continue to be mostly other- rather than self-initiated.) The suggestion is, then, that sex-role conceptualizations in dreams in early pre-adolescence are built around the sheer quantity of activity, while later they largely concern the socialized vs. unsocialized quality of activities, rather than activity level per se. In terms of the "ethos" underlying sex-role differentiation in late preadolescence, Trupin (1976) was able to show that boys' REM dreams were more "agentic," and girls' more "communal" (Bakan, 1966).

Much support can be found within particular narrative sequences of children's dreams for the hypothesis that sex-role identity is a major concern of the mind of the sleeping preadolescent. A good portion of the recreational content of boys' dreams, for instance, involves activities (such as hunting, fishing, or other adult sports) which help to define for preadolescents what it means to be a "man." A 10-year-old boy, for instance, watches a male adult stranger bowl a perfect game, buys the man a soft drink, and gets his autograph. Or recreational activities become the focus of frankly pedagogical exercises in the art of growing up: the same boy dreamed that his Little League baseball team lost a game to a group of older players; when he and his teammates were "poor sports" about the loss, the other team offered to "give" them a victory if they wanted one so badly; their own coach, however, returned the victory to its rightful possessors, since his own players had acted so immaturely.

As already suggested, girls' vicarious role playing transpires in a world peopled by both adult males and adult females. Thus a 10-year-old girl dreams of accompanying her father on a trip; she peels potatoes and helps the wife of her father's friend to prepare dinner. Or, more rebelliously, she joins a violent demonstration at a supermarket, where her mother is protesting to the male manager over the high cost of food. Occasionally, sexual development seems to be symbolically represented in more starkly anatomical terms; the same girl, for instance, dreams that it is her birthday (which it isn't); she opens a jewel box to discover some really pretty jewelry. Or, anatomical and social growth seemingly can be jointly portrayed in the same symbolism. A 10-year-old boy whose father is a skilled artisan to whom tools are useful, for example, dreams of having a bag attached to his belt; he fiddles around with it, trying to determine what it contains; it breaks open, and wrenches and a pocket knife fall out. A rather mechanistic portrayal of adult competence is, incidentally, quite common in boys' dreams. Further accounts of preadolescent dream imagery as reflecting concerns with sex-role identification can be found in Foulkes (1967) and Breger (1969).

At *ages 13-15*, theoretical expectations arise once again about significant shifts in the form and substance of dream content. At least some of the children sampled at these ages should be passing from concrete-operational to formal-operational thinking, and many of them will have entered both physiologically and socially defined adolescence. And, once again, expectations generated by these theoretical perspectives seem at least partially confirmed. Formally, for example, REM dreams begin to have a less concrete character; settings become more vague, and overt representations of motoric activity and of organic needs decrease. And, from a content perspective, REM dreams appear to be somewhat less competently controlled, more "disturbed." For instance, there is, in comparison to late preadolescence, a significant increase in anger ascribed to characters other than the dreamer and a significant decrease in the general incidence of prosocial behavior and of happy interpersonal outcomes. Character distortion increases significantly.

Family members figure less often in early adolescent dreams than in late preadolescent ones, and it now is male family members whose salience declines, particularly for male dreamers. Like-sex biases persist in the selection of known peers for dream representation, but they no longer are statistically significant. Home remains an important setting for girls, but not for boys. Girls' dreams now are significantly more pleasant than those of boys. Thus the negative impact of adolescence on dream content seems greater for boys than for girls.

Recent empirical research suggests that early adolescence is, in general, a more placid period for girls than for boys (Kohen-Raz, 1971; Bardwick, 1971). Such research also contests the characterization of adolescence as involving massive psychological upheavals for children of either sex (Douvan and Adelson,

1966; Offer, 1969).   And, the limited nature of the "disturbance" of early adolescent dreaming is consistent with this revisionary characterization of adolescence.   For example, the modal boys' dream is not unpleasant; it merely is less pleasant than the modal girls' dream.   Angry emotions remain relatively infrequent, characterizing less than one of ten adolescent dreams.   Prosocial interaction still occurs more often than aggressive interaction, and happy outcomes mediated by others occur to the self almost twice as often as do unhappy outcomes mediated by others.

Thus neither the "crisis" period at ages 5-6 for boys nor the "crisis" period for both sexes (but more for boys than for girls) at ages 13-14 significantly disrupts the general competency that children more generally display in the organization and control of their nocturnal fantasies.   The relative shifts in dream content observed at these two points in development are theoretically interesting and of some practical value in understanding both waking and dream development.   They should not, however, be misread as indicating fundamental disruptions of otherwise orderly developmental sequences.   In fact, for girls, the dream data suggest very little disruption anywhere along the line.   A large-scale survey of the waking experiences of adolescent boys and girls reported that

> . . . our findings point to the conclusion that the [sex] drive is so successfully excluded from consciousness by the large majority of girls that they do not in any relevant psychological sense confront an impulse problem comparable to boys' during the adolescent years. (Douvan and Adelson, 1966, p. 347)

This generalization probably applies with almost equal force to the mental activity of sleep as to waking experience.

Boys' development, both waking and sleeping, on the other hand, seems somewhat less continuous.   From the point of view of sex-role identity, the boys' task is the harder one.   The basic fact of early childhood is a primary identification with the mother (Stoller, 1973), a feminization of both boys and girls (Mitchell, 1974).   Boys must renounce that tie in a way that never is imposed on girls.   They must model on more distant father figures and must renounce tenderness and other species of "childish" ("feminine") behavior sooner and more definitely than girls have to.   Furthermore, whether one is considering either hostility or sexuality, it seems quite likely that the impulses one must learn to manage while growing up are stronger in male children than in female children (Maccoby and Jacklin, 1974; Bardwick, 1971; Sherman, 1971).

It is in adolescence that we have our first evidence of social-class differences in dream content.   Hostile interactions are more frequent than friendly ones in the dreams of working-class adolescent boys; this does not seem to be true for middle class adolescents (Foulkes et al., 1969; Foulkes, 1977b).   This seems to be especially true, on the other hand, for disturbed working-class adolescent boys (Foulkes et al., 1969). The pattern is not, of course, unexpected, in terms of the different values social classes attach to the "acting out" of aggressive feelings.

Sources and Meanings

Specification of why children dream the things they do and of the underlying semantic structure of their dreams is an inherently risky business. This has not prevented me from hazarding a few speculations above, which I feel to be strongly suggested by the data at hand. But it should be admitted that these are speculations, rather than conclusions. Knowledge of the ultimate sources and meanings of children's dreams can only come from studies in which we have more comprehensive knowledge than we generally do of children's waking activities and fantasies and when we have relatively inclusive samples of their dreams. Case-study (Breger, 1969) and longitudinal (Foulkes, 1971) designs seem especially promising in this regard.

There are advantages for dream psychology, I think, in approaching general questions about dream meanings and functions with observations made in childhood. We have as yet no generally useful theories about adult development. There are fewer plausible theories to which we may refer in trying to fill in missing details of adult dreamers' case-history formulations than we have at our disposal when we need to synthesize children's waking situations. In child psychology we have some reasonable grasp on what the major developmental issues are, on when they are likely to be salient, and on how their salience is likely to vary as a function of variables such as sex and social class. Thus, even granted that children are likely to be less able to tell us directly the information we need to interpret their dreams, it seems that both empirical research and theory built upon such research are more suitable at the child than at the adult level to permit us plausibly to fill in these informational gaps. And, it also seems likely that, as Freud (1900) suspected, children's dreams are enough simpler (less varied in their range of contents, less complexly determined) than adult dreams to permit us to begin addressing meaning and function questions in a more substantial way at the child level. The bridge to adult complexity must, of course, someday be built, but it is more reasonable to start on the side closer to ground level.

In this respect, as relatively "simple" as they are, as relatively realistic as their portrayals often seem to be, and as relatively easily as we can demonstrate correlations of their content with waking events, even children's dreams serve to remind us of why dreaming has been a favored topic more for psychodynamic psychologies than for psychologies devoted to examining only the surface structure of behavior or experience. Without some conceptualization of motives of which individuals are only sporadically or imperfectly aware, but which are required to explain the disorganizations and peculiar organizations of human experience, it is difficult to see how one could begin to explain dreaming as a mental process. From this perspective, the advantage of studying children's dreams is that, despite the child's general failure to recognize some of the programs directing her or his experience, the programs themselves are not so inaccessible as they often seem to be in later life. Our inferences as to their nature are likely to be more direct, and therefore, more reliable. While one might take exception to particular details of Breger's (1969) formulation of the meaning of the dreams of his child-subject "Jake," for instance, the overall synthesis is relatively satisfying. It has the formal properties of a "good" explanation, and sets a standard against which alternative explanations might be evaluated in terms of their consistency, accuracy, subsumptive power, generality, and so on (Sherwood, 1969). It is my belief that, at present, such "good" explanations are more likely to emerge for children's dream series than for those of adults. Both dream *and* waking-history data are more manageable for children than for adults.

Empirical research on the sources of children's dream imagery makes relatively clear the fact that such imagery is no more likely to be explained extrinsically or superficially than is adult dream imagery. External stimuli applied during sleep, as already noted, are neither reliable nor potent determinants of children's dream content. Presleep stimulus manipulations (e.g., the film studies of Foulkes et al., 1967, 1971) do not suggest either powerful or direct determination of children's dream content by mass-media stimuli. While it is clear that children who are relatively addicted to unrealistic fantasy in the media rely upon these sources in constructing their dreams (Foulkes, 1967; Breger, 1969), it is the child's mind which shapes the medium's fantasy, rather than vice versa (Foulkes et al., 1971).

Similarly, relatively superficial catalogs of features of the child's real-world situation and relatively superficial assessments of her or his own traits have only limited predictive value for understanding dream imagery. We know, for example, that early adolescents living away from home (in institutions; Foulkes et al., 1969) dream very seldom of nuclear family members. In this respect, their dreams are like those of college students similarly removed from their families. But this cannot mean, in either case, that family relationships no longer play any active role in children's minds, either awake or asleep. Rather, I think, we must imagine that these concerns merely are expressed in terms of a more readily accessible iconic vocabulary.

Similarly, while overall styles of waking deportment are reliably reflected in children's dreams (e.g., Foulkes, 1967; Breger, 1969), this carryover does not tell us much more than that similar adaptive or defensive strategies tend to be applied, other things being equal, in waking behavior and in sleeping fantasy.

Other things often are not equal, however, and one gets little sense from such general correspondences of the particular contexts in which these strategies are being employed. To know, for instance, that disturbed children have more bizarre dreams than nondisturbed children, or that socially active children play more dominant roles in their own dream scenarios than do socially passive ones (Foulkes et al., 1969), is to know something of importance about children's dreams, but it is far from knowing either the sources or the meanings of particular dreams in which these features appear.

More satisfying answers to questions as to the sources and meanings of children's dreams, then, can only come from comprehensive studies of children's dream series made in conjunction with relatively inclusive analyses of their waking situations. These studies necessarily must be conducted at an individual level, and with due regard for the fact that dream meanings are likely to be private or connotative rather than public or denotative (Foulkes and Vogel, 1974). That is, the surface-level features of dream experience can only be understood in terms of another level of meaning which is not superficial and cannot be accessed solely by inspection of manifest dream content (Freud, 1900). The characterization of this other level need not be hopelessly unreliable (Foulkes, 1978), but it will involve sensitivity to underlying trends of emotional/motivational development in addition to more mundane accounts of current dreamer functioning.

CONCLUSION

A popular stereotype of children's dreams holds that deteriorated ego functioning in sleep often thrusts the child into nightmarish situations well beyond her or his control. Thus children's dreams are frequently unpleasant, and they derive from unresolved instinctual conflicts which outstrip the child's relatively meager resources for coping. There can be no doubt but that this is true of many dreams of some children, and of some dreams of many children (Foulkes, 1967). Few among us, child or adult, have competently mastered the lessons of past experience to such a degree that our sleeping minds are totally free of the influence of childish fears and impulses. Occasionally, for both adult and child, these factors can overwhelm our sleeping minds, with those uncomfortable results with which we are all too familiar.

But as a *general* characterization of dreams, either for adults or for children, this stereotype is seriously misleading. In childhood, dreams generally are competently executed thought sequences betraying considerable cognitive skill. They bear testimony to the power and resilience of the developing human mind. When appropriately sampled, children's dreams are not particularly disturbing or frightening. Even when children, rather than their dreams, are representatively sampled, this is so. Roberts and Baird (1971), for instance, used data from the

National Health Survey, with a probability sample of children aged 6-11 not living in institutions. Over 7000 children were examined. More than half "never" were reported to have had unpleasant dreams; only 1.8% "frequently" had such dreams. From this perspective, then, dreams have as much to tell us about the development of ego-competency or of cognitive skills as they do about the developmental fate of childish fears and unsocialized impulses.

On the other hand, we also must avoid a complementary stereotype in our evolving understanding of children's dreams. They are not simply "ego-processes"; they are not simply realistic reflections of current conscious concerns; they are not simple extensions of developing cognitive competencies to another psychophysiological state. Dreams are cognitive processes, but they are not cognitive processes by any means entirely comprehensible from frameworks which have evolved in conventional scientific studies of waking cognition. Students of waking development tend to study thought and language growth in relatively sterile contexts in which "machinery" growth as such overshadows the deeper motivational/emotional settings in which the child often must use such machinery. The student of dreaming cannot so deftly separate conation from cognition. The explanation of children's dreams, and of children's developmental accession to adult-level dream competency, cannot be achieved without according considerable attention to the underlying motivational tasks of childhood. For example, one needs, I think, in understanding the dreams of early childhood, to comprehend the problems of infantile impulse management, and, in understanding the dreams of preadolescence and of early adolescence, to understand the vital significance to the child of forming a gender-appropriate adult identity. Perhaps the particular value of dreams to our overall understanding of human development is that here is a phenomenon so clearly and so simultaneously both cognitive and motivational that it affords us the opportunity to synthesize the best of developmental approaches otherwise so divergent as psychoanalysis and academic developmental psychology in a truly integrative way.

REFERENCES

Aserinsky, E., and Kleitman, N. Regularly occurring periods of eye motility, and concomitant phenomena, during sleep. *Science*, **118**: 273-274, 1953.

Bakan, D. *The Duality of Human Existence.* Chicago: Rand McNally, 1966.

Bardwick, J. M. *Psychology of Women: A Study of Bio-cultural Conflicts.* New York: Harper & Row, 1971.

Bartlett, F. C. *Remembering.* Cambridge: Cambridge University Press, 1932.

Bellak, L., and Adelman, C. The Children's Apperception Test (CAT). In Rabin, A. I., and Haworth, M. R. (Eds.), *Projective Techniques with Children.* New York: Grune & Stratton, 1960, pp. 62-94.

Berger, R. J., and Oswald, I. Eye movements during active and passive dreams. *Science*, **137**: 601, 1962.

Blos, P. *On Adolescence: A Psychoanalytic Interpretation.* New York: Free Press, 1962.

Breger, L. Children's dreams and personality development. In Fisher, J., and Breger, L. (Eds.), *The Meaning of Dreams: Recent Insights from the Laboratory.* Sacramento: Dept. of Mental Hygiene, State of California, 1969, pp. 64–100.

Broughton, R. J. Sleep disorders: Disorders of arousal? *Science,* 159: 1070–1078, 1968.

Cartwright, R., and Ratzel, R. Effect of dream loss on waking behaviors. *Archives of General Psychiatry,* 27: 277–280, 1972.

Chodoff, P. Feminine psychology and infantile sexuality. In Miller, J. B. (Ed.), *Psychoanalysis and Women: Contributions to New Theory and Therapy.* New York: Brunner/Mazel, 1973 (orig. 1966), pp. 157–172.

Chomsky, N. *Syntactic Structures.* The Hague: Mouton, 1957.

Chomsky, N. *Aspects of the Theory of Syntax.* Cambridge, Massachusetts: M.I.T. Press, 1965.

Chomsky, N. *Language and Mind* (enlarged ed.). New York: Harcourt Brace Jovanovich, 1972.

Chomsky, N. *Reflections on Language.* New York: Pantheon, 1975.

Dement, W., and Wolpert, E. A. The relation of eye movements, body motility, and external stimuli to dream content. *Journal of Experimental Psychology,* 44: 543–555, 1958.

Dostoyevsky, F. *The Idiot.* New York: New American Library, 1969 (orig. 1869).

Douvan, E., and Adelson, J. *The Adolescent Experience.* New York: John Wiley & Sons, 1966.

Flavell, J. H. *The Developmental Psychology of Jean Piaget.* Princeton, New Jersey: D. Van Nostrand, 1963.

Fordham, M. *Children as Individuals.* London: Hodder & Stoughton, 1969.

Foulkes, D. *The Psychology of Sleep.* New York: Charles Scribner's Sons, 1966.

Foulkes, D. Dreams of the male child: Four case studies. *Journal of Child Psychology and Psychiatry,* 8: 81–98, 1967.

Foulkes, D. Longitudinal studies of dreams in children. *Science and Psychoanalysis,* 19: 48–71, 1971.

Foulkes, D. Children's dreams: Age changes and sex differences. *Waking and Sleeping,* 1: 171–174, 1977(a).

Foulkes, D. *Children's Dreams: Year 5 of a Longitudinal Sleep-Laboratory Study.* Atlanta: author (mimeo) 1977(b).

Foulkes, D. *A Grammar of Dreams.* New York: Basic Books, 1978.

Foulkes, D., Belvedere, E., and Brubaker, T. Televised violence and dream content. In Comstock, G. A., Rubinstein, E. A., Murray, J. P. (Eds.), *Television and Social Behavior. Vol. 5. Television's Effects: Further Explorations.* Washington, D.C.: Government Printing Office, 1971, pp. 59–119.

Foulkes, D., Larson, J. D., Swanson, E. M., and Rardin, M. W. Two studies of childhood dreaming. *American Journal of Orthopsychiatry,* 39: 627–643, 1969.

Foulkes, D., Pivik, T., Steadman, H. E., Spear, P. S., and Symonds, J. D. Dreams of the male child: An EEG study. *Journal of Abnormal Psychology,* 72: 457–467, 1967.

Foulkes, D., and Rechtschaffen, A. Presleep determinants of dream content: Effects of two films. *Perceptual and Motor Skills,* 19: 983–1005, 1964.

Foulkes, D., and Shepherd, J. *Manual for a Scoring System for Children's Dreams.* Laramie: author, 1971.

Foulkes, D., and Shepherd, J. *Children's Dreams at Ages 3-4 and 9-10: A Sleep-Laboratory Study.* Laramie: author, 1972(a).

Foulkes, D., and Shepherd, J. *Children's Laboratory Dreams: Four Methodological Studies.* Laramie: author, 1972(b).

Foulkes, D., Shepherd, J., and Scott, E. A. *Children's Dreams: Year 3 of a Longitudinal Sleep-Laboratory Study*. Laramie: author, 1974.

Foulkes, D., and Vogel, G. The current status of laboratory dream research. *Psychiatric Annals*, **4**, (7): 7–27, 1974.

Freud, S. *The Interpretation of Dreams*. New York: Basic Books, 1955 (orig. 1900).

Freud, S. Three essays on the theory of sexuality. *The Standard Edition of the Complete Psychological Works of Sigmund Freud* (*S.E.*), Vol. VII. London: Hogarth Press, 1953 (orig. 1905), pp. 123–245.

Freud, S. Creative writers and day-dreaming. *S.E.*, Vol. IX. London: Hogarth Press, 1959 (orig. 1908), pp. 141–153.

Freud, S. Analysis of a phobia in a five-year-old boy. *S.E.*, Vol. X. London: Hogarth Press, 1955 (orig. 1909), pp. 1–149.

Freud, S. Introductory lectures on psycho-analysis. *S.E.*, Vol. XV–XVI. London: Hogarth Press, 1961–63 (orig. 1917).

Freud, S. Female sexuality. *S.E.*, Vol. XXI. London: Hogarth Press, 1961 (orig. 1931), pp. 221–243.

Gould, R. *Child Studies Through Fantasy*. New York: Quadrangle, 1972.

Hall, C. S. Strangers in dreams: An empirical confirmation of the Oedipus complex. *Journal of Personality*, **31**: 336–345, 1963.

Hall, C. S. *The Meaning of Dreams*. New York: McGraw-Hill, 1966.

Hall, C. S., and Nordby, V. J. *The Individual and his Dreams*. New York: New American Library, 1972.

Hall, C. S., and Van de Castle, R. L. *The Content Analysis of Dreams*. New York: Appleton-Century-Crofts, 1966.

Jones, E. *On the Nightmare*. New York: Liveright, 1971 (orig. 1931).

Kales, J. D., Kales, A., Jacobson, A., Po, J., and Green, J. Baseline sleep and recall studies in children. *Psychophysiology*, **4**: 391, 1968 (abstract).

Kirsch, T. B. The relationship of the REM state to analytical psychology. *American Journal of Psychiatry*, **124**: 1459–1463, 1968.

Kohen-Raz, R. *The Child from 9 to 13: Psychology and Psychopathology*. Chicago: Aldine-Atherton, 1971.

Kohlberg, L. A cognitive-developmental analysis of children's sex-role concepts and attitudes. In Maccoby, E. (Ed.), *The Development of Sex Differences*. Stanford: Stanford University Press, 1966, pp. 82–173.

Kohler, W. C., Coddington, R. D., and Agnew, H. W. Sleep patterns in 2-year-old children. *Journal of Pediatrics*, **72**, 228–233, 1968.

Laurendeau, M., and Pinard, A. *Causal Thinking in the Child*. New York: International Universities Press, 1962.

Maccoby, E. E., and Jacklin, C. N. *The Psychology of Sex Differences*. Stanford: Stanford University Press, 1974.

Mitchell, J. On Freud and the distinction between the sexes. In Strouse, J. (Ed.), *Women and Analysis: Dialogues on Psychoanalytic Views of Femininity*. New York: Grossman, 1974, pp. 27–36.

Morris, D. *The Naked Ape*. New York: Dell, 1969 (orig. 1967).

Murphy, L. B. (and collaborators). *The Widening World of Childhood: Paths toward Mastery*. New York: Basic Books, 1962.

Mussen, P. H., Conger, J. J., and Kagan, J. *Child Development and Personality* (3rd ed.). New York: Harper & Row, 1969.

Offer, D. *The Psychological World of the Teen-ager: A Study of Normal Adolescent Boys*. New York: Basic Books, 1969.

Orne, M. T. On the social psychology of the psychological experiment: With particular reference to demand characteristics and their implications. *American Psychologist*, 17: 776-783, 1962.

Piaget, J. *The Child's Conception of the World*. New York: Harcourt, Brace, 1929 (orig. 1926).

Piaget, J. *Play, Dreams, and Imitation in Childhood*. New York: W. W. Norton, 1962 (orig. 1945).

Piaget, J., and Inhelder, B. *Mental Imagery in the Child*. New York: Basic Books, 1971 (orig. 1966).

Pivik, T., and Foulkes, D. "Dream deprivation": Effects on dream content. *Science*, 153: 1282-1284, 1966.

Pivik, T., and Foulkes, D. NREM mentation: Relation to personality, orientation time, and time of night. *Journal of Consulting and Clinical Psychology*, 32: 144-151, 1968.

Rechtschaffen, A. Dream reports and dream experiences. *Experimental Neurology*, Suppl. 4: 4-15, 1967.

Rechtschaffen, A. The psychophysiology of mental activity during sleep. In McGuigan, F. J., and Schoonover, R. A. (Eds.), *The Psychophysiology of Thinking*. New York: Academic Press, 1973, pp. 153-205.

Rechtschaffen, A., Goodenough, D. R., and Shapiro, A. Patterns of sleep talking. *Archives of General Psychiatry*, 7: 418-426, 1962.

Riley, M. W., and Riley, J. W. A sociological approach to communications research. In Schramm, W. (Ed.), *The Process and Effects of Mass Communication*. Urbana: University of Illinois Press, 1954, pp. 389-401.

Roberts, J., and Baird, J. T. *Parent Ratings of Behavioral Patterns of Children: United States*. Washington, D.C.: Public Health Service, 1971.

Roffwarg, H. P., Dement, W., and Fisher, C. Preliminary observations of the sleep-dream pattern in neonates, infants, children and adults. In Harms, E. (Ed.), *Problems of Sleep and Dream in Children*. New York: Pergamon, 1964, pp. 60-72.

Roffwarg, H. P., Dement, W. C., Muzio, J. N., and Fisher, C. Dream imagery: Relationship to rapid eye movements of sleep. *Archives of General Psychiatry*, 7: 235-258, 1962.

Salzman, L. Psychology of the female: A new look. In Miller, J. B. (Ed.), *Psychoanalysis and Women: Contributions to New Theory and Therapy*. New York: Brunner/Mazel, 1973 (orig. 1967), pp. 173-189.

Sherman, J. A. *On the Psychology of Women: A Survey of Empirical Studies*. Springfield, Illinois: Charles C Thomas, 1971.

Sherwood, M. *The Logic of Explanation in Psychoanalysis*. New York: Academic Press, 1969.

Snyder, F. The phenomenology of dreaming. In Madow, L., and Snow, L. H. (Eds.), *The Psychodynamic Implications of the Physiological Studies on Dreams*. Springfield, Illinois: Charles C Thomas, 1970, pp. 124-151.

Stoller, R. J. Facts and fancies: An examination of Freud's concept of bisexuality. In Strouse, J. (Ed.), *Women and Analysis: Dialogues on Psychoanalytic Views of Femininity*. New York: Grossman, 1974 (orig. 1973), pp. 343-364.

Trupin, E. W. Correlates of ego-level and agency-communion in stage REM dreams of 11-13 year old children. *Journal of Child Psychology and Psychiatry*, 17: 169-180, 1976.

White, R. W. Ego and reality in psychoanalytic theory. *Psychological Issues*, 3, #3, 1963.

Williams, R. L., Karacan, I., and Hursch, C. J. *Electroencephalography (EEG) of Human Sleep: Clinical Applications*. New York: John Wiley, 1974.

Wolf, K. M., and Fiske, M. The children talk about comics. In Lazarsfeld, P. F., and Stanton, F. N. (Eds.), *Communications Research 1948-1949*. New York: Harper & Brothers, 1949, pp. 3-50.

Wolpert, E. A., and Trosman, H. Studies in psychophysiology of dreams. I. Experimental evocation of sequential dream episodes. *Archives of Neurology and Psychiatry*, 79: 603-606, 1958.

5

Extrasensory Communication and Dreams

Jon Tolaas and Montague Ullman

HISTORICAL BACKGROUND

As far back as we have written records, there have been accounts of the unusual phenomena occurring in connection with dreams. The ancients typically believed that dreams were divinely inspired experiences providing counsel and instruction for their waking lives. In the oldest dream book extant, the Egyptian papyrus of Deral-Madineh dating back to 2000 B.C., there are examples of divine revelation. The Egyptians practiced dream incubation, i.e., sleeping in temples in a deliberate effort to induce divinely inspired dreams which would supply answers concerning the state of health and the future of the dreamer. Oracular dreams even affected affairs of state (Woods, 1947). So-called paranormal phenomena often seemed to have an affinity for dreams. Woods (1947) notes that the Egyptians tried to communicate with others through their dreams, believing that homeless spirits carried the message. This suggests that there was some familiarity with the idea of telepathic communication.

In Judeo-Christian and Islamic scriptures the divinely inspired dream is a well-known theme. Van de Castle (1971) notes that there are about 70 references to dreams and visions in the Bible. One well-known dream, possibly suggestive of telepathic influence, is the dream of Nebuchadnezzar (Daniel 2:1-35). The king awoke one morning and was unable to remember a dream he felt was oracular in nature. His dream interpreters were frustrated. When Daniel was consulted, he turned to God in prayer, and Nebuchadnezzar's dream was revealed to him in a night vision. He then related the dream to Nebuchadnezzar, who recognized it as his own.

In contrast to the Egyptians and the Jews, Orientals did not attribute dreams to the interference of gods, but to the dreamer's own soul. In ancient Vedic literature (1500–1000 B.C.) dreaming is seen as an intermediate state of the soul between this world and the other. In the sleeping state the soul leaves the body in "breath's protection" and roams in space, where it sees both this world and the other.

This belief, which seemingly gives credence to telepathy, was introduced in Greece as early as 500 B.C. (Van de Castle, 1971) and is well-known in European folklore (Tylor, 1871). The Greeks, however, were more inclined to the tradition of the divine message dream, a tradition favored by their Eastern neighbors (Dodds, 1957). They distinguished between oracular dreams without symbolism and symbolic ones whose divine message had to be unraveled by professional interpreters.

Most of the dreams that have come down to us from antiquity are prophetic or precognitive, only a few of these available dreams lending themselves to a telepathic explanation. The word telepathy (from the Greek roots *tele*, or distant, and *pathe*, or feeling) was coined in the nineteenth century by F. W. H. Myers (1903).

With Democritus and Aristotle there began what may be called the naturalization of the supernatural dream. Democritus (460–370 B.C.) is credited with the first physical theory of dream telepathy (Dodds, 1971). His view of telepathy is derived from the thesis that everything, including the soul, is made up of innumerable, indivisible, minute particles called atoms. These atoms constantly emit images of themselves, which in turn are composed of still other atoms. He postulated that the images projected by living beings, when emotionally charged, could be transmitted to a dreamer (percipient). When the images reached their destination, they were believed to enter the body through the pores. Images emitted by people in an excited state were especially vivid and likely to reach the dreamer in an intact and undistorted form because of the frequency of emission and the speed of transmission. The importance he assigned to the emotional state of the agent or sender is certainly in keeping with both present-day anecdotal and experimental findings.

Aristotle (384–322 B.C.) rejected the notion of a divine origin of dreams. In his essay "On Divination In Sleep" (Woods, 1947) he discussed veridical dreams and took issue with Democritus' atomist thesis. The topic of his essay is precognitive dreams, but his theory appears to be primarily applicable to instances of telepathy. He compared what happens in telepathic transmission with the ripple effect created by a stone thrown into water. Waves are propagated through the air of the night and "nothing hinders but a certain motion and sense may arrive to souls that dream . . . ." There are motions during the daytime as well, but the night is more tranquil so that the motions are not so easily dissolved.   Besides, "those that are asleep have a greater perception of small inward motions than those that are awake."   Aristotle and Democritus thus made the paranormal dream an object of scientific inquiry and postulated a physical carrier for the information.

For the most part their ideas were neither accepted nor further developed by later thinkers.   Stoics like Poseidonius (135-50 B.C.) again relegated oracular dreams to the divine sphere (Dodds, 1971).   Still later the Roman orator Cicero (104-43 B.C.) tried to demolish both the arguments of the Stoics and Democritus.   In a caustic comment on Democritus, he writes, "I never knew anyone who talked nonsense with greater authority . . ." (On "Divination," quoted from Woods, 1947).   In Artemidorus' *Oneirocritica* (about 200 A.D.), the main source of dream philosophy in antiquity, there is no more Democritian "nonsense."

In the Middle Ages the Icelandic sagas were a rich source of prophetic dreams (Turville-Petre, 1958; Glendinning, 1974).   The old Norsemen seem to have had a pragmatic attitude to such dreams, acknowledging them as an integral and useful part of reality, but they offered little in the way of explanation or theory. Thinkers like Thomas Aquinas, Descartes, and Pascal, among others, addressed the subject of dreams, but made no significant contribution to our understanding of those dreams that challenge our concepts of time and space.

In 1819, Weserman published what is probably the first report of experimentally induced dream telepathy (reviewed later).   His ideas did not arouse sufficient interest to spur further efforts by contemporary investigators.   There are scattered references to paranormal dreams in many later sources, notably in the writings of the German physician C. G. Carus (Meier, 1972).   Not until the foundation of the Society for Psychical Research in 1882 in England, did dream telepathy become an object of genuine scientific inquiry.

Comment

The evidential value of historical material of this kind cannot be assessed.   Such reports, however, do convey the thread of persistent belief in the link between dreaming and the paranormal.   Throughout the ages and in a wide variety of cultural settings, man has been fascinated by dreams that seem to convey telepathic or precognitive content.

PRELITERATE SOCIETIES

In preliterate societies, we find either the belief that the dreamer's soul can quit the body and go for a nocturnal excursion, or that human souls from without can visit the sleeper and appear to him in his dream.   The Maoris thought that the dreamer's soul could travel to the abode of the dead and talk with its friends there (Tylor, 1871).   The Ibans of Borneo conversed with their special protectors, the spirits of the deceased, who came to visit them in their sleep (MacDougall and Hose, 1912). These two beliefs are not incompatible and can exist side by side, as was the case with some North American Indians (Devereux, 1957; Tylor, 1871, Wallace, 1958). These beliefs suggest that dream telepathy was considered something natural and useful. The Melanesians on the Trobriand Islands also believed in induced telepathic dreams. A suitor could cast a spell over his beloved and induce her to dream a dream that would make her "desire the exchange" (Malinowski, 1927).

Comment

Many of the anecdotes on record are insufficiently corroborated, and many of the ideas and beliefs are often quite esoteric. Nevertheless, there is sufficient evidence to suggest some factual distillate. Freud (1933) suggested that telepathy might be a kind of prototypic language, a language before language. So-called primitive peoples may have preserved some of this archaic means of communication. To our knowledge no experimental work has been done on dream telepathy with non-Western subjects. Three researchers, Foster (1943), Rose (1956), and Van de Castle (1970, 1975) have tested such populations using ESP cards. Foster obtained significant results (in one of two conditions) in tests administered to Plains Indian children, as did Rose in tests given to aboriginal subjects in Australia and New Zealand. Van de Castle obtained results at chance level testing Cuna Indians. However, the results were significant when the subjects were differentiated by sex and dream content scores.

ANECDOTAL MATERIAL

The founders of the Society for Psychical Research faced the formidable task of defining and classifying a wide range of unexplainable phenomena and setting standards for observation and reporting. In 1886, three of the founders, E. Gurney, F. W. H. Myers, and F. Podmore, published their historic work, *Phantasms of the Living*. Among the 1300 pages of case histories, the book contains 149 cases of dream telepathy. Myers defined the term telepathy as "the extrasensory communication of impressions of any kind from one mind to another." These men were astute investigators and were very exacting in their search for evidentiality. In the 1880s, however, less was known about the vicissitudes of memory and dream processes than today, so that not all the material they collected would meet modern evidential standards.

Nevertheless, *Phantasms of the Living* is still an invaluable source book. A typical example in this collection (Gurney et al., 1886) follows:

> My brother and father were on a journey .... I dreamt ... I saw father driving in a sledge, followed in another by my brother. They had to pass a

cross-road on which another traveller was driving very fast, also in a sledge with one horse.   Father seemed to drive on without observing the other fellow, who would . . . have driven over father if he had not made his horse rear, so that I saw my father drive under the hoofs of the horse.   Every moment I expected the horse to fall down and crush him.   I called out: "Father! Father!" and awoke in great fright. (vol. 1, p. 202).

It was later discovered that the dream corresponded in great detail with the actual event.

Characteristically, the theme of this dream is one of imminent danger to someone close to the percipient. The common pattern that emerged from a review of the 149 cases of dream telepathy indicated that:

1. Over half of the dreams concerned the theme of death.
2. Another large group was concerned with the occurrence of an emergency.
3. A smaller group focused on trivial matters.
4. In the majority of cases, the agent-percipient pairs were either related or friends.
5. The percipients generally had no special psychic experiences or abilities before the dream in question, so that these dreams were rare and puzzling experiences.

We find the same common features in the major modern surveys of uncorroborated spontaneous cases by Rhine (1962), Sannwald (1959a, b), Prasad and Stevenson (1968), and Hanefeld (1968), and in a survey of 300 cases by Green (1960).   Surveys of the frequency and modalities of psychic experiences by Brockhaus (1968) and Palmer and Dennis (1975) and analysis of corrobated cases by Dale (1951) and Dale et al. (1962) produced results in keeping with the pattern described above.   Others who have published related material are Flammarion (1900), Prince (1931), Stevens (1949), and Priestley (1964).

There are, of course, obvious reasons why dreams of death and serious accidents might occur more frequently.   Dreams with high anxiety content or any very disturbing feeling tone would tend to be more readily recalled, recorded, and possibly reported to others.   It might also be that dreams of death are so common that chance coincidence alone would explain the high incidence of apparently veridical dreams dwelling on this theme. The authors of *Phantasms of the Living* considered this objection and distributed a questionnaire to 5360 persons asking if they had had a vivid dream of the death of someone known to them in the past 12 years.   Only one of every 26 persons queried had had such a dream, a fact that spoke against the chance hypothesis. (For discussion, see Ullman et al., 1973, p. 12.)

The frequency analysis of manifest dream content (Hall and Van de Castle, 1966) also indicates that the subject of death does not occur frequently in dreams.   If chance or coincidence can be discounted, then dreams involving danger to or the death of someone known to the dreamer may reflect the basic nature and function of telepathy as an emergency communicative mechanism somehow linked to the dreaming state. This notion is discussed in a later section.

Referring to the high proportion of reported paranormal experiences occurring between friends and relatives, Honorton (1975) notes that this would be expected because of the greater probability of confirmation than if the occurrence involved remote acquaintances.   Furthermore, unless the relationship permitted "some degree of intimacy, it would be unlikely that either would be sufficiently uninhibited to share unusual personal experiences."   These considerations aside, there may be more basic issues involved having to do with the biological significance of closeness and intimacy. The prototype of closeness is, of course, the early mother–child relationship.   In the postnatal period closeness ensures protection and a chance of survival for a number of species, man included.   It is also the basis of growth and personal development. If psi* abilities manifest themselves early in life, and there is reason to believe that they do (Schwarz, 1971), they would exert their effect within a matrix of closeness and intimacy, a fact which may be related to the incidence of paranormal phenomena occurring between parents and children as well as friends and relatives in later life.

It is difficult to assess the true incidence of telepathic dreaming because of the variability of factors involved in their being reported. Cultural factors such as the low priority given to dreams and general skepticism concerning what might appear to be the occult, would also tend to lower the incidence of such reports.

Another factor at work may be the failure to recognize the telepathic component in a dream.   Rhine (1967) distinguishes between realistic and unrealistic telepathic dreams, the difference being that in the latter the message is carried by the meaning of the fantasy, not by the exactness of the imagery. Where this is the case, many such dreams would probably go unnoticed.

Analyses of anecdotal material strongly suggest that the dreaming state is particularly favorable for the occurrence of paranormal phenomena.   In the cross-cultural surveys quoted, dreams (precognitive or telepathic) account for 64.6% of the 7119 cases reported by Rhine (1962), 63% of the 1000 cases reported by Sannwald (1959a, b), 37% of the 300 cases analyzed by Green (1960), 52.4% of the 900 experiences of Indian school children reported by Prasad and Stevenson (1968), and 38% of several hundred cases collected by Hanefeld (1968) and considered to be paranormal.

Most of the paranormal dreams on record are precognitive (Van de Castle,

*Psi is a generic term to designate parapsychological phenomena.

1977). In addition to the sources already quoted (Green, 1960), Saltmarsh (1934) reported 281 cases of precognition, of which 116 occurred in dreams. Based on intensive studies of his own dreams, Dunne (1927) became convinced that precognition occurred in dreams, and went on to develop a multidimensional theory of time to account for the phenomenon. Two experimental attempts at testing the theory by Besterman (1933) produced inconclusive results. In a third series, Dunne himself served as subject. Of the 17 dreams he forwarded to Besterman in the course of four months, four were suggestive of precognition (Besterman, 1933). Stevenson (1960, 1965) and Barker (1967) published reports describing the precognition of two disasters. Stevenson reported ten cases of precognition related to the sinking of the *Titanic*, eight of which involved dreams. Barker collected 35 cases of precognition of the Aberfan coal slide in 1965, 25 of which occurred in dreams. From a collection of 1300 dreams from one person, collected over a period of many years, Bender (1966) reported a 10% incidence of precognitive elements. Tenhaeff (1968) reported on precognitive elements in another collection of dreams from a single individual. Priestley (1964) provides a number of interesting anecdotal accounts of precognitive dreams called to his attention following a television broadcast.

SHARED DREAMS

Shared dreams form an interesting subcategory. They are defined by Hart (1965) as "those in which two or more dreamers dream of each other in a common space-time situation, and independently remember more or less of their surroundings, their conversation, and their interactions within the dream" (p. 17). Numerous examples have been reported by Hart (Hart and Hart, 1933; Hart, 1959), in which he and his wife seemed to experience such shared dreams. More recent examples are given in accounts by Faraday (1975) and Donahoe (1974). Dream telepathy in a group setting was observed by Randall (1977). He worked in a group setting where there was an unusual degree of rapport and where telepathic correspondences seemed to occur among the group members.

Comment

Interesting though the spontaneous case reports may be, they do not provide hard evidence for the reality of extrasensory effects in dreaming. Despite great care taken to verify them, loopholes can generally be found that raise questions concerning any paranormal explanation. The interest and value of the anecdotal reports lie in the meaningful patterns that may appear from their analyses. The real-life context, especially as noted in cross-cultural surveys, serves as a source of ideas for experimental research and broadens the theoretical framework within which such research is conducted. These accounts strongly suggest that the dreaming state is the psi-conducive state. Psi correspondences in dreams were found to be more complete and less fragmentary than in reports of waking psi experiences (Honorton and Krippner, 1969).

EXPERIMENTAL STUDIES: HISTORICAL PRELUDE

Weserman (1819) is credited with the first published report on experiments with telepathically induced dreams. Serving as agent himself, he attempted to project his "animal magnetism" into the dreams of friends who later reported their dreams to him. Weserman claimed to have been successful on five occasions.

G. B. Ermacora (1895), an Italian psychiatrist, attempted to induce telepathic dreams in a rather strange experimental arrangement. His star subject was a medium in Padua, Signorina Maria Manzini, who had a trance control called Elvira. When Signorina Manzini went into a trance, Dr. Ermacora would suggest to Elvira the specific topic of a dream she was to induce telepathically in Angelina, Maria's four-year-old cousin. The latter would then relate her dream in the morning to the medium, who, in turn, informed Dr. Ermacora. There were, indeed, striking correspondences, but judged by modern standards, the experiments were seriously lacking in precautions against sensory leakage. They remain only of historical interest.

EXPLORATORY STUDIES

In the early 1950s, Wilfred Daim (1953), an Austrian psychotherapist, attempted to transmit a target to a sleeping percipient. The target material consisted of a geometrical symbol and a color in random combination. Target–dream correspondences were reported in 75% of 30 trials. At about the same time, exploratory dream telepathy studies were being initiated by Ullman and Dale (Ullman and Krippner, 1970). These studies were designed to explore possible paranormal correspondences between recorded dreams and events in each of their lives. The results were encouraging and led to a series of exploratory studies using the all-night REM monitoring technique to determine the onset and termination of recurring dream sequences (Aserinsky and Kleitman, 1953). This technique freed the investigator from relying on the uncertainty of spontaneous dream recall in a dream telepathy experiment.

Pilot studies along these lines were initiated in 1960. Two rooms were used. The subject or percipient went to sleep in one, and an agent or sender and EEG technician remained in a second room. A variety of target materials was used including free-hand drawings, pictures taken from magazines, movie clips, and three-dimensional objects. The subject was awakened after several minutes of REM sleep and reported his dream over an intercom to the experimental team.

The working hypothesis was that the agent's preoccupation with the target material during the night might bring about the inclusion of such material or aspects of it in the manifest content of the subject's dreams. The following is an example of the kind of correspondences that occurred:

A dentist was serving as subject and Ullman as agent. The target material during the first part of the night was a toy model of a yellow Citroen car, and during the latter part of the night a picture showing an Oriental garden bordered with diamond-shaped stones and monk who was meditating at one corner. In the second dream of the night, the subject mentioned a road that was yellow in color and referred to a tractor-like vehicle. There were references to diamond shapes in four of the subsequent dreams.

Subjects differed widely in their sensitivity and ability to incorporate telepathic stimuli. Of particular interest was the fact that three disbelievers in ESP, so-called goats (Schmeidler, 1945), did not succeed in incorporating target material. When the correspondences did occur, they came about in a number of different ways, varying from direct incorporation to the selective incorporation of certain elements of form or color as well as correspondences based on symbolic relationships.

Comment

These studies pointed to the usefulness of the REM monitoring technique as a way of experimentally approaching the subject of dream telepathy. The results supported the working hypothesis that psi effects could be incorporated into both manifest and symbolic dream content. Further refinement of the design was indicated:

1. To eliminate all possibilities of sensory cues relating to the target reaching the subject.
2. To arrange for the independent blind outside judging of possible correspondences between target and dream.
3. To work out appropriate statistical techniques to evaluate any matching process.

In 1962, with the establishment of a Dream Laboratory at Maimonides Medical Center in Brooklyn, it became possible to pursue the work along these lines.

FORMAL EXPERIMENTAL STUDIES

Formal experimental studies involving standardized EEG-EMG-EOG monitoring began at Maimonides in June, 1964. Two formats were used; each will be illustrated in detail. The first one involved a screening study of 12 subjects (Ullman et al., 1966) and two agents, one male and one female.

Correspondences between target material and dream reports were evaluated by each of the 12 subjects and three outside judges who independently ranked the pool of 12 targets for correspondences to each dream protocol. A dream protocol consisted of all the dreams of a single night. Confidence ratings were also obtained. The dream material was matched alone and in combination with the subject's postsleep associational material. There were seven males and five females in the study. They had no history of ESP, but expressed a positive attitude to the possibility of its existence. Each subject slept in the laboratory for one night. The targets were postcard-size reproductions of well-known paintings. They were selected on the basis of emotional content, vivid colors, simplicity, and distinctness of detail.

The subject met with the agent prior to the application of the electrodes. Once the subject was in the sleep room, they had no further contact. The agent remained in a room 40 feet away from the subject's room. He had with him one of 12 randomly selected art prints from the 12 prepared for the experiment. He familiarized himself with the picture and wrote his associations down. He would continue to concentrate on the picture whenever the experimenter signaled to him that the subject was going into a REM phase. The same target was used throughout the night.

The subject was awakened toward the estimated end of each REM period and asked to relate his dreams, which were taken down on tape and later transcribed. The agent would listen to the subject reporting his dream, but could not communicate with either the experimenter or the subject.

The transcripts of the dreams as well as the subject's associative data were sent to three outside judges along with copies of the 12 art prints used in the experiment. The judges, working blindly, compared all 12 targets to each dream transcript. A fourth judge compared all 12 dream protocols to each target picture. The mean of the three judges' ranks and ratings were analyzed by two-way analysis of variance (for targets and nights) according to the Scheffé (1959) method. Similarly, the rankings made by the 12 subjects were subjected to two-way analysis of variance. These rankings were further evaluated by the application of the binomial expansion theorem. Ranks from one through six were referred to as "hits" and the rankings from seven to twelve as "misses."

Evaluation of the mean scores for rankings and ratings did not attain statistical significance, but the results were in the predicted direction. Analysis of the ratings of the fourth judge were significant at the .01 level. The rankings did not attain significance. Analysis of the subjects' rankings produced ten "hits" and two "misses," significant at the .05 level (two-tailed test). The ratings were higher for the subjects working with the male agent.

Example

A young female teacher served as subject. The randomly selected target picture was Tamayo's *Animals*. This picture depicts two dogs howling and flashing their teeth. Bones picked clean lie about in the foreground. A huge black rock can be seen in the background. The points of correspondence are noted in the following excerpts:

Second Dream Report: "The name of the dream was *Black Wood*, Vermont or something like that . . . . Well, there's this group of people . . . and they have an idea that they're picked out for something special . . . and that these other people were threatening enemies . . . ."

Third Dream Report: "I was at *this banquet* . . . and I *was eating something like rib steak*. And this friend of mine was there . . . and people were talking about how she wasn't very good to invite for dinner because *she was very conscious of other people getting more to eat than she got—like, especially meat*—because in Israel *they don't have so much meat* . . . . That was the most important part of the dream, that dinner . . . . It was probably Freudian like all my other dreams—you known, eating, and all that stuff, and a banquet. . . . Well, there was another friend of mine also in this dream. Somebody that I teach with, and she was *eyeing everybody to make sure that everybody wasn't getting more than she was too. And I was chewing a piece of rib steak*. And I was sitting at the table and other people were talking about this girl from Israel, and they were saying that she's not very nice to invite to eat because *she's greedy*, or something like that.

From the Subject's Associations: "It was about *a banquet* and *we were eating meat*, and people were telling me that *this Israeli friend of mine was not nice to invite to a banquet because she was always afaid she wasn't getting enough* . . . . I was invited because I'm polite and not demanding, but I just tried to keep my mouth shut in the dream. I tried not to say anything about her, even though in a way I was glad that she was finally being found out . . . . And the second one . . . was about Vermont, *Black Rock*, Vermont . . . . Yesterday, I was at the beach and I was sitting on one of the rocks . . . and I felt like that mermaid from *Black Rock* . . . ."

The references to *Black Wood* in the second dream and *Black Rock* in the associations are suggestive of information conveyed concerning the sensory qualities of the picture. The voraciousness of the dogs comes through in the sequence describing the avariciousness of the friend at dinner. Elsewhere, Ullman (1975b) comments:

Presumably both the sensory image and the emotional message have a significance for the dreamer which could be tapped if the dreams were dealt with analytically. The level, nature, and degree of correspondence are probably determined by other still unknown factors, in addition to the way in which they lend themselves to the expression of the idiosyncratic needs of the dreamer. This factor of idiosyncratic choice of precisely what is extracted from the target picture and incorporated into the dream is quite puzzling. (p. 164)

The First Erwin Study

In the second format, the same subject was used on repeated nights. The highest scoring subject in the preceding screening study, Dr. William Erwin, was paired with the male agent from that study in a seven-night series, using the same basic experimental design and evaluation procedure (Ullman et al., 1966).

The rankings of the judges of the dreams alone and in combination with the associative material were significant ($F = 8.30, p < 0.01; F = 18.14, p < 0.001$, respectively; 1 and 35 degrees of freedom). Significant results were also obtained from the judges' ratings as well as from the subject's rankings and confidence ratings.

Example

The target picture was Chagall's "Paris From a Window," a colorful painting depicting a man observing the Paris skyline from a window. Certain unusual elements stand out very clearly: a cat with a human face, several small figures of men flying in the air, and flowers sprouting from a chair.

Second Dream Period: "Well, I was dreaming of bees. I guess it was bees. Sort of bees *flying around flowers.*"

Third Dream Period: "I was walking. For some reason, I say *French Quarter* .... And I was walking through different departments in a department store ... talking with a group of Shriners that were having a convention. *They had on a hat that looked more like a French policeman's hat, you know the French* .... *I said French Quarter earlier, but I was using that to get a feel... of an early village of some sort* .... *It would be some sort of this romantic type of architecture—buildings, village, quaint.*"

Fifth Dream Period: "... The memory I remember is a man, once again walking through one of *these villages, these towns.* It would definitely be in the nineteenth century. *Attire. French attire.* And he would be walking through one of these towns as though he were walking up the side of a hill above other layers of the town.

Excerpts From the Associative Material: "*The thing that stands out is the dream where I described the village* .... *It's a festive thing* ... *the Mardi Gras-ish type* .... Well, the area must be—I mean, just basing it on the costumes and

all–the nineteenth century. Early nineteenth century . . . either the Italian or
French or Spanish area . . . . *A town of this area* . . . . *It would be of the . . .
of this village type* . . . . *Houses very close covering the hills.*"

A number of minor modifications in procedure were introduced in the experiments that followed in order to encourage the agent to be more involved with
the theme of the target picture; a series of objects relating to the mood of the
target picture were prepared and coded in connection with the target. Such
props afforded the agent the opportunity to get involved with the target picture
in a multisensory fashion. The subsequent studies are briefly summarized.

The Second Erwin Study

As in the case of the first Erwin study, the results confirm the telepathy hypothesis (Ullman and Krippner, 1969). Analysis of the three judges' means for the
correspondences between the targets and the entire protocol produced significant
results ($F = 6.43$; $p < 0.001$ with 7 and 21 degrees of freedom). Judgings on
the basis of the dreams alone were also significant.

To counter the allegation that dreams are so vague that any dream can correspond with any picture, a further analysis was made by a fourth judge. He
compared the seven targets used for the first study and one target used for a
pilot session with the eight transcripts of the second study. The target ratings
were analyzed using the Scheffé (1959) technique. This analysis produced
statistically significant data for the correct target–dream combinations, whereas
the "control" combinations produced chance results.

The Hypnosis Study

Sixteen subjects were divided into two groups of eight subjects each, a hypnosis
group and a nonhypnosis "relaxed" group. Each subject was assigned one of
four agents and was asked (a) to generate waking imagery in the laboratory,
(b) during or immediately after a rest period in the laboratory, and (c) to keep a
dream diary at home. The judges' evaluations produced significant results with
the hypnosis group in condition (b) and for the nonhypnosis group in condition
(c). The subjects' evaluations were significant for the nonhypnosis group in
condition (a) (Krippner, 1968).

The Second Screening Study

This was a 12-night screening study utilizing 12 different subjects and two
agents. The results did not attain statistical significance, but were in the predicted
direction. In contrast to the first screening study, no agent differences emerged
(Ullman, 1969b).

The Posin Study

R. Posin, a female psychologist, had done well in the second screening study and was singled out for an eight-night series. Both the judges' and the subject's results were at chance level although there were interesting correspondences (Ullman and Krippner, 1970).

The Grayeb Study

Miss Grayeb, a young secretary, was selected for a 16-night study on the basis of her results in the second screening study. For eight of the nights the agent concentrated on a target; for the remaining nights there was neither agent nor target. The condition was determined on a random basis. Results for both conditions were at chance level (Krippner, 1969).

The Van de Castle Study

Robert Van de Castle, a dream researcher as well as a parapsychologist, served as the subject for an eight-night series. Earlier he had produced highly significant results in a similar experiment at another laboratory (Hall, 1967). In this study more emphasis was placed on motivational and psychodynamic factors than in the earlier work. The subject was allowed to choose his own agent from among the laboratory staff. He worked with a total of three agents. A female psychologist served as agent for the first two nights. Ullman was the agent for the second session, and a female social worker for the remaining five nights. The fact that both women were young and attractive made for easier rapport.

After each experimental session the motivational and psychodynamic aspects of the dreams of the night before were explored with the subject.

The results were evaluated by the subject and one judge. The subject's rankings produced eight "hits" and no "misses." This distribution is significant at the 0.004 level (binomial method). The ratings were significant at the 0.003 level (Mann-Whitney U Test). The judge's results were also significant. The analytically oriented interview revealed that the telepathic effect was strongest in dreams with aggressive and sexual content (Ullman and Krippner, 1970).

The Vaughan Study

Four subjects were used in this study, each spending eight nights in the laboratory. For four nights the agent concentrated on the same target [target condition (a)]; for the remaining four nights a different randomly selected target was used each time the subject experienced a REM state [target condition (b)]. Three of the subjects evaluated their own results, which were significant for target condition (b). Evaluation by an outside judge was significant for one subject in target condition (b).

This study was designed to investigate the hypothesis that the telepathic stimulus may "build up" over the course of a night and come through more in one of the late REM periods or at the end of the series. However, none of the results in connection with target condition (a) attained significance, indicating that there was no "build up" effect. The agents reported being bored by trying to get involved with the same target for the four nights. The results seem to favor the "mutual-resonance" hypothesis, which postulates that a spontaneous resonance effect occurs in the brains of agent and subject in response to a novel stimulus (Honorton et al., 1971).

The Hypnotic Clairvoyant Dream Study

Sixty subjects were divided equally into high- and low-suggestible hypnosis groups. This was a clairvoyant study, and no agent was used. All the subjects attempted to incorporate the target material (art prints) clairvoyantly, either in a hypnotically induced dream or in the course of an imaginative daydream. The subjects evaluated their own material. Results were significant for the high-suggestible hypnosis group (Honorton, 1972).

The First Bessent Study

In an eight-night precognitive study the British sensitive Malcolm Bessent attempted to dream about an experience that was to be structured for him the following morning, and only after all of his dreams had been collected. A dream theme would be randomly selected on the following morning from among the themes described in *The Content Analysis of Dreams* (Hall and Van de Castle, 1966), and a visual and auditory display relating to this theme would then be shown to the subject upon his awakening.

To determine whether the subject had precognitive dreams about his morning's experience, three outside judges rated correspondences between each dream protocol and the written description of the waking experience. The mean of the judges' ratings were subjected to binomial testing. There were five direct "hits" out of the eight nights ($CR = 3.74, p = .00018$) (Krippner et al., 1971).

The Second Bessent Study

A target pool of ten slide-and-sound sequences was created for this study. On odd-numbered nights the subject was instructed to dream about the target, which would be randomly selected the following evening. On even-numbered nights one of the ten sequences was randomly selected, and the subject was exposed to the slides and the taped sound accompaniment. He was then told to dream about this target material.

Three outside judges working blindly and independently were exposed to the eight slide-and-sound sequences that had been selected for use. In addition, they read all 16 dream protocols and then rated all the protocols against all eight targets. When the eight odd-numbered or precognitive nights were inspected, it was found that the target for those nights received higher ratings than any of the other pairings for that target in five out of eight instances ($p = .0012$, one-tailed). When the eight even-numbered nights were inspected, it was found that the targets for these nights had not received higher ratings than any of the other pairings for that target (Krippner et al., 1972a).

Extrasensory and Presleep Incorporation of Target Material

In this study, Honorton et al. (1975) attempted to compare extrasensory and presleep incorporation of target material in dreams. Forty agent–subject pairs were involved. The targets were two emotionally arousing and two emotionally neutral films. One emotional and one neutral film served as targets for each condition (ESP and presleep). There were two nights in each condition, beginning with two ESP nights to avoid stimulus residues from earlier sessions. On each of the two ESP nights the agent was shown a different film which the percipient attempted to dream about. On the two presleep nights, there was no agent. The subject was shown one of the two remaining target films each night before falling asleep, and was then awakened at the end of each REM period for a dream report.

For the presleep conditions there was significant incorporation of both the emotionally arousing and emotionally neutral films, but the difference between the two target types was not significant. For the ESP condition, none of the stimuli was incorporated to a significant degree. Mean incorporation scores of field independent subjects, as measured by Witkin's Rod-and-Frame Test and Embedded Figures Test, were significant in the ESP condition for the emotionally arousing films ($p = .008$).

Of the thirteen formal experimental studies described above, nine yielded statistically significant results.

Replication Studies

Thus far, six replication studies have been reported. Two produced significant results (Hall, 1967; Ross, 1972), three produced nonsignificant results (Belvedere and Foulkes, 1971; Foulkes et al., 1972; and Strauch, 1970), and one produced equivocal results (Globus et al., 1968). Commenting on five of these studies, Krippner (1975, p. 177) notes: "All five studies represented the investigators' initial attempts to study this phenomenon, and it is difficult to predict what the results would have been had long-range studies been planned."

Keeling (1971) reported a study involving hypnotic dreaming and telepathy. He trained three highly susceptible hypnotic subjects to dream hypnotically and then had each subject serve in turn as agent while the other two served as percipients. The agent was given a one- or two-sentence description as the hypnotic dream stimulus, which the percipients were to incorporate in their hypnotically induced dreams. The overall results were reported as significant.

Rechtschaffen (1970) worked with two subjects under hypnosis, one serving as agent, and one as percipient in an exploratory telepathy experiment. The agent was given a suggestion to dream about the subject's dream. The experiment involved six pairs of subjects and a total of 47 pairs of dreams. Dream-dream matchings produced significant overall results.

Interesting results of informal studies have been reported by Van de Castle (1971, 1977).

Comment

The experimental studies buttress the evidence from other sources for the occurrence of extrasensory effects in dreams. Additional findings that have emerged from the experimental work thus far are as follows:

1. Orientation and expectancy on the part of the subject appear to be necessary for the incorporation of telepathic effects into dreams. When subjects were not informed that an agent was trying to influence their dreams telepathically, the results were at a chance level (Krippner, 1975). In another study a subject was asked to clairvoyantly dream about a randomly selected art print concealed in a box. Without his knowledge, an agent was at the same time concentrating on another target picture. The judges detected clear-cut target–dream correspondences for each of the clairvoyant targets, but not for the telepathy targets (Krippner and Zirinsky, 1971). A long-distance study gave similar results. This involved using as agents 2000 members of the audience attending six concerts of a rock-and-roll group. On all six nights the audience was shown a six-slide sequence on the screen and were told to attempt to transmit the picture to Malcolm Bessent, who was asleep at the Maimonides Dream Laboratory 45 miles away. Without their knowledge, the dreams of a second subject were recorded at the same time. The judges' evaluations produced significant results for Malcolm Bessent and chance results for the other subject (Krippner et al., 1973).

2. An analysis of all available first night sessions between 1964 and 1969

showed that males did better than females as subjects. They also did better when paired with a male agent compared with a female agent (Krippner, 1970). This is at odds with the various surveys of spontaneous cases (Green, 1960; Rhine, 1962; Sannwald, 1959a,b), which show that women far outnumber men in reporting ESP experiences. There is some evidence to suggest that the laboratory setting is more anxiety-provoking to women (Lawrence and Shirley, 1970), which may account for their poor showing in the laboratory situation. These authors have also noted women to be more reluctant to report their dreams as fully as men do.

3. Distance did not seem to affect the ability of subjects to incorporate target material telepathically. Significant results have been obtained in studies involving distances of 98 feet, 19 miles (Krippner, Honorton, Ullman, Masters, and Houston, 1971), and 45 miles (Krippner et al., 1973).

4. Telepathic incorporation is more apt to occur with target material that is emotional in nature (Krippner and Davidson, 1970). When multisensory objects were introduced to enhance the emotional impact of the target, uniformly positive results were obtained (Ullman and Krippner, 1969; Krippner, Ullman, and Honorton, 1971; Krippner et al., 1972b; Krippner and Goldsmith, 1971; Krippner, 1971; Krippner, Honorton, Ullman, Masters, and Houston, 1971).

5. The two Bessent studies based on proposals by Dunne (1927) and Jackson (1967) have provided suggestive evidence that precognitive dreaming can be demonstrated in an experimental setting.

DREAM TELEPATHY IN THE CLINICAL CONTEXT

Clinical interest in dream telepathy began with the advent of psychoanalysis. The initial impetus of Freud's writings on this subject (Freud, 1922, 1925, 1934, 1941) and a volume by Stekel (1920) was followed by confirmatory reports (Hollós, 1933; Deutsch, 1926; Roheim, 1932; Burlingham, 1935; Servadio, 1935), as well as skeptical and critical ones (Zulliger, 1934; Hann-Kende, 1953; Hitschmann, 1924; Schilder, 1934, Saul, 1938). Contemporary interest in the subject was stimulated by the writings of Ehrenwald (1948, 1954), Eisenbud (1946, 1947, 1970), Servadio (1935, 1956), Meerloo (1949, 1968), and Ullman (1959, 1966, 1973). Devereux (1953) proveded an anthology of the earlier psychoanalytic contributions and the controversies that ensued. Three review articles have appeared summarizing the psychiatric and psychoanalytic contributions to our knowledge of dream telepathy (Ullman, 1974, 1975a, 1977).

Despite a lingering skepticism, Freud interested himself in the "occult," particularly from the point of view of the understanding that psychoanalysis could shed on these phenomena. His exploration of reports of paranormal dreams led to a number of speculative hypotheses concerning their dynamics.

He felt that such exchanges occurring at an unconscious level were subject to the same laws of transformation as other unconscious content before making their way into the dream.

The early writers alluded to stressed the libidinal and affective aspects of the telepathic contact (Stekel, 1920), the connection of the message with a repressed wish (Hollós, 1933), the facilitating influence of positive transference (Hann-Kende, 1953; Servadio, 1935), and the role of counter-transferential factors in triggering a telepathic dream (Eisenbud, 1970). Burlingham (1935), Meerloo (1968), and Ehrenwald (1971a) speculated on the role telepathy may play in the early mother-child relationship.

Eisenbud (1970), made explicit use of the telepathy hypothesis in his interpretive exchanges with patients. He (Eisenbud, 1947) and others (Fodor, 1947; Coleman (1958) also noted that in the working through of the dynamics of these events, more than one patient at a time might be involved in a telepathic exchange.

When a dream having reference to the therapist is encountered in the clinical context, it must meet a number of criteria before it can be considered as presumptively telepathic. Although no criterion is sufficient by itself, when taken together the criteria can lead to the strong, subjective sense that something other than chance or coincidence was at work. These criteria are:

1. The items of correspondence in question must be unusual; i.e., must be represented by elements that do not ordinarily appear in dreams.

2. The events in the life of the therapist that these elements have reference to could not have been known to the patient by any ordinary means. They could not have been learned through inadvertent behavioral or subvocal cues, and could not have been inferred based on the knowledge the patient could have had of the personal life of the therapist.

3. A close temporal relationship should exist between the relevant events in the life of the therapist and the patient's dream that depicts these events.

4. Judgments concerning correspondences must include, but not necessarily be limited to, correspondences apparent at the level of the manifest content.

5. The final criterion is that of psychological meaning. The intersecting points of correspondence, when subjected to analysis, must emerge as dynamically meaningful to both patient and therapist.

Clinical Example

An example of presumptively telepathic dream occurring in the clinical context is as follows:

The patient is a 40-year-old woman who had been under analysis for 15 months at the time of the occurrence of the dream. She had been divorced three years earlier, at which time she had also terminated a one-year analysis with another therapist. She felt that she had received some help, but that her basic problems concerning men were unchanged. She had a tendency to slip into relationships with married men, and then to feel guilty and helpless in the situation and unable to extricate herself.

Her husband, whom she did not hold in high regard, had been a physician. This, plus her disillusionment around her previous analysis, made for a considerable amount of caution and withdrawal in her relationship to the therapist (one of the present authors). Her strategy in the main was to attempt to convince the therapist that this was the way she was and that nothing could be done about it. In many devious ways she was out to prove that the therapist was well intentioned but inept, or not really interested in her.

The patient presented the following dream on awakening on a Saturday morning:

> I was at home with John. There was a bottle on the table that contained part alcohol and part cream. It was sort of a white foamy stuff. John wanted to drink it. I said, "No, drink it later." I looked at the label. It read: "Appealing Nausea." I meant to drink it when we went to bed, although we seemed to be in bed at the time.

The patient presented another fragment occurring the same night:

> I had a small leopard. It was very dangerous. I wrapped him up and put him in a large bowl. Mother told me to take him out or he would die.

The patient was seen on a subsequent Tuesday and began the hour by remarking spontaneously that perhaps there was something to extrasensory perception. This was the first time that the term had come up in the analytic situation. She stated that on the previous Friday she had received a phone call from a physician whom she had known several years before, but with whom she had had no contact during the past two years. She had been thinking about him just before he phoned, and she could not recall the last time he had entered her consciousness. She did not attribute any real significance to this and made the remark in jest.

In connection with the dream, the only thing she could think of was that the alcohol-cream mixture reminded her of crème de menthe, a drink that makes her slightly sick. The label "Appealing Nausea" reminded her of her own revulsion in connection with sexual activity. "When I get very excited, I get sick."

On the evening of the preceding Friday, the night the patient had the dream, my wife and I (the therapist) attended a meeting at the New York Academy of Medicine to hear a paper presented on animal neurosis. Part of the film showed the technique of creating a state of alcohol addiction in cats. One scene showed two cats being offered a choice between a glass containing milk and another containing milk and half alcohol. The alcoholic cat, in contrast to the normal cat, went straight for the alcohol–milk mixture, and completely ignored the glass containing the milk alone.

The most striking feature of the dream was the temporal coincidence between the unusual symbolism of a bottle containing part alcohol and part cream with the scene in the film showing a glass containing half milk and half alcohol. The second fragment seemed to supplement the first by introducing a member of the feline family, a leopard. Also suggestive were her introductory remarks indicating her preoccupation with the possibility of extrasensory perception in connection with someone she hadn't seen for a number of years. Assuming the validity of the telepathic factors and integrating them into the analysis of the dream, the interpretation may be outlined as follows:

Her identification is with the leopard—the animal whose spots cannot be changed. She has not resolved the question of trust and hope in therapy. In the dream a physician is trying to get her to drink the mixture just as in the film the experimenter is responsible for the cat seeking out the mixture rather than the whole milk and just as, in reality, she looks with suspicion on the therapist's efforts to force her out of her withdrawal. The release and spontaneity associated with the alcohol are experienced in a conflicting way as attractive and repulsive at the same time. The milk, which is normally sought after by a cat, is symbolic of her blandness and her dependency. In the second dream, the patient, faced with the dilemma of protecting the leopard, attempts to do so by isolating techniques, but is warned by a parental figure of the dire consequences unless some of the control is removed. The patient is in conflict because the whole weight of her past experience has been to equate release and freedom with disaster and control and isolation with safety. The scene in the film provides an appropriate concept in the form of visual imagery expressing the idea that the therapist is as omnipotent in relation to her as the experimenter was to the cats, and that seeking sensual gratification under these circumstances would make her vulnerable to further hurt and exploitation. She is also making a statement about the detachment and omnipotence of the therapist as she experiences him.

The clinical setting, as well as the anecdotal reports, implicates the dream as the state most frequently associated with a telepathic event. There are aspects of dreams and dreaming that suggest possible reasons for this connection. Motivational systems closer to the core of the individual come into operation in the dream, compared to waking hours. The spontaneous occurrence of telepathy in crisis situations suggests that, in some way, the mobilization of vital needs is implicated. Dreaming as a state of heightened activation suggests that a vigilance function is operative and oriented (in the human, at any rate) more to the detection of threats to the symbolic system, linking the individual to his social milieu, than to threats involving his state of bodily intactness. We have, in the dreaming state, the possible advantage of an altered state of consciousness combined with a state of high arousal and one in which basic motivational systems are activated.

Comment

The psychodynamic context in which telepathic events are apt to arise may thus be related to both patient and therapist. Attention has been called to the facilitating influence of the strong emotional bond generated in psychoanalytic therapy. From the patient's point of view, what might be called the telepathic maneuver seems to be a ploy called into operation (1) as a means of deflecting attention from himself when, in the context of a positive transference, conflictual material directed at the therapist begins to surface; and (2) as a reaction to what the patient senses as a withdrawal of interest on the part of the therapist, under which circumstances it then becomes a strategy for dramatically refocusing that interest back to the patient.

From the therapist's standpoint, a somewhat different constellation of predisposing factors appears to be operating. Interest in and belief in the reality of telepathic events seems to favor their occurrence. Several writers (Pederson-Krag, 1947; Ullman, 1959) on the subject have noted the appearance of telepathic dreams in their patients when they themselves, pursuing their own interest, had further need for such material. There is also general agreement that temporary distractions and preoccupations, deflecting the therapist's attention from the patient, often becomes the focal point of a telepathic experience for the patient. Counter-transferential tensions are particularly apt to be unmasked by a telepathic maneuver on the part of the patient. Servadio (1958) notes this in connection with the thoughts the analyst may have that are prejudicial or inimical to the patient.

The conditions outlined as favoring the occurrence of telepathic dreaming may, in each instance, be experienced as prejudicial by the patient. In one way or another the patient may sense the interest, need, and tension of the analyst as adversely influencing the relationship or as interfering with the maintenance of the analyst's clear focus on the therapeutic situation. The occurrence of a telepathic dream under these circumstances constitutes a safe way of "needling" the therapist insofar as it both exposes the patient's awareness of the therapist's dereliction and at the same time does so in a way that leaves the therapist impotent to do anything about it unless he owns up to the manner in which his own preoccupations and concerns may at the moment obstruct the progress of the analysis.

Various generalizations have been proposed to account for the appearance of telepathy in the analytic context. Freud (1933), Meerloo (1949), and Ehrenwald (1971b) regarded telepathy as an archaic communication system available for use when other forms of communication were blocked.

Ehrenwald (1971a) implicated the early mother–child symbiosis as the nexus out of which telepathic exchanges evolved. He also suggested (1971b) that psi events tend to occur on occasions when, for external or internal reasons, we experience a shift away from a time- and space-oriented existence (a Newtonian frame of reference suitable for our everyday waking lives) toward a nonlinear form of consciousness, as in the occurrence of sleep and dreams. He likened this to a relativistic mode and referred to the change in level of adaptation as an existential shift. This can be transitory, incidental, and subtle in the course of our waking lives or occur in the form of sharp qualitative shifts, as in the case of dreaming or drug-induced alterations in consciousness. In either instance, the shift seems to favor the recrudescence of paranormal powers originating in an earlier relational context.

Ullman (1949, 1952) noted that patients who function on schizoid or obsessional levels manifest psi ability in the therapeutic context more frequently and more consistently than do other patients. It is as if having used language so long in the service of maintaining distance from others, they reach a point of no return in their efforts to maintain meaningful communicative bonds with others, including the therapist. This appears to be the circumstance under which telepathic faculties are mobilized.

In his biographical reminiscences Jung (1963) revealed a life-long interest in the paranormal and recounted many incidents occurring throughout his life of both ESP and psychokinesis. In his effort to provide some kind of fit for these experiences, he boldly postulated the existence in nature of a second principle equal in importance to the principle of causality. He referred to this as the principle of synchronicity and defined it to mean that in addition to the existence of a causal order which links external events to subjective impressions, there can exist another order effecting such linkages on the basis of meaning alone. Paranormal events were thus defined as acausal, meaningful coincidences. This principle became operative when, in a given context, there occurred a dovetailing of external events with the realization of "constellation" of an upsurging archetypal impression. Jung thus sought to establish a dynamic link between a paranormal event and the emergence of a specific archetype at a given moment.

The role psi effects play in dream formation, the emergence of psi factors in the context of transference and counter-transference, the interpretive use of the telepathy hypothesis, the characterologic significance of psi abilities, and the possible role that psi plays in the evolution and manifestation of psychopathology are some of the areas where beginning explorations have taken place and where much more clinical and investigative work will have to be done before a full account can be given of the relevance of psi factors to psychiatry.

THEORETICAL CONSIDERATIONS

Quite apart from the question of the validity of parapsychological data in relation to dreaming, there is a need for a holistic approach to the data we now have on the psychology and physiology of dreaming. In the absence of any unifying concept, the newer findings are apt to remain atomistic and perhaps more puzzling than they need be. This particularly applies to any artificial separation of human and animal data. The mounting evidence supporting the reality of extrasensory communication in dreaming makes it all the more incumbent to seek out a unified way of viewing the various manifestations of the dreaming phase of the sleep cycle.

A holistic view emphasizes the fact that parts relate to the whole on the basis of a system principle governing the whole (Angyal, 1941). Part functions and part structures are organized according to and are subordinate to the main system principle. In the case of dreaming, for example, our task would be to identify the main system principle and then explore the way in which the findings of the various experimental studies contribute toward actualizing this principle. In what follows the concept of vigilance is explored as the organizing or leading system principle in relation to which the phenomenology of the REM state and dreaming can be ordered. The question being addressed is: What are the vigilance needs of the sleeping organism? This approach was first developed by Ullman (1956) on clinical grounds and later considered in relation to the recent experimental work on sleep (Ullman, 1958, 1969a, 1973), and the investigative work on dream telepathy (Ullman, 1969b, 1972). A similar approach was taken by Snyder (1963, 1966) in his interpretation of the phylogenetic and evolutionary meaning of REM sleep. Tolaas (1976, 1978) reviewed these formulations and presented an expanded view of vigilance theory to accommodate the human and animal data as well as the pertinent data concerning extrasensory communication and dreaming.

Dreaming and Social Vigilance

Ullman (1973) conceived of dreaming sleep as repetitive cycles of heightened vigilance manifested along both physiological and psychological dimensions. He suggested that, while dreaming, the organism is involved in the process of assessing the impact of recent intrusive novel events in terms of the linkage of these events to past experience and their implication for the immediate future. Although clinically derived, this view seemed in keeping with later work interpreting the REM state as a state of readiness for the urgencies of waking life (Hernandez-Péon, 1966; Ruffwarg et al., 1966).

The vigilance process unfolds in two phases, an exploratory one to assess the implications of the issues being raised, and a reconstituted one where through internal rearrangements personality resources are mobilized to cope with the unsettling event. The dreamer may have the resources necessary to arrive at a creative resolution, or he may have to resort to habitual defensive responses. There are two possible outcomes to these operations. Depending on the degree of tension generated in the dream, either the dreaming cycle continues without interruption or awakening occurs.

For the human organism, the nature of the threat has shifted from a concern with physical danger to a concern with the safeguarding of his status as a social being. Man, as a species, has accumulated enough cultural artifacts to offer protection against most physical threats to his existence. His nighttime concerns have come to focus on his continuing sense of intactness as a social organism. Vigilance operations, accordingly, become more subtle, sophisticated, and social in nature. The content of the dream is defined by this fact. The intrusive events giving rise to the dream range from the trivial to the critical, but they all involve unexpectedness, unpreparedness, and a change in the status quo.

The initiating focus in a dream evolves from a recent event in our lives, having the qualities of being both intrusive and novel. The novelty either may be defined in terms of the qualities intrinsic to the external circumstance (as in the case of exposure to a totally unfamiliar life situation), or it may be defined by the existence of internal strategies of self-deception that limit our ability to cope with a situation that should ordinarily offer no difficulty. Since there tend to be many gaps and lacunae in our emotional development, the latter is the more frequent source of dream content. Our dreams then confront us with some of the unintended consequences of our defensive operations. Therein lie their therapeutic value.

One of the characteristics of dreaming is a backward scanning into remote memory stores in an effort to link the impact of a present situation to past experience. The result of this information search is organized along lines of emotional contiguity rather than in temporal and spatial categories. The data pertaining to dream telepathy and precognitive dreaming suggest that this scanning process can, on occasion, bridge temporal and spatial gaps to provide information independently of any known communication channel (Ullman, 1972).

Dreaming and Survival Needs

REM sleep is regarded as the phylogenetically older phase of sleep (Snyder, 1966) and is found throughout the mammalian species. In the pre-REM era, Rivers (1923) suggested that the dream state in animals served to awaken the animal in the presence of danger, thus anticipating Snyder's sentinel thesis (1965, 1966).

The latter holds that repetitive bouts of physiological arousal provide the necessary critical reactivity enabling the organism to cope with threats on awakening. There can be little doubt that a sleep stage which enabled the animal to adapt to external danger while still asleep, would have great survival value.

Tolaas (1976, 1978) raised a number of objections to Snyder's thesis. It does not account for the high proportion of REM sleep in the neonatal mammalian organism. It does not account for the loss of muscle tonus characteristic of the REM state, a finding which seems to be incompatible with preparation for fight or flight. Finally, the presence of a warning system interspersed in sleep presupposes some kind of synchrony between external dangers and the REM periods, but says nothing about the response to dangers appearing between REM periods. Emphasizing the need of the organism to heed potentially threatening environmental stimuli, the sentinel thesis does not address itself to why there is such a need during the REM periods; nor does it account for the paradoxical loss of tone in the anti-gravity muscles combined with high cortical arousal.

Addressing these questions, Tolaas (1978) has suggested that while dreaming, the organism remains selectively aware of meaningful or threatening environmental stimuli while at the same time fulfilling another aspect of vigilance by attending to the dream imagery that is being produced. The pattern is one of interaction between two orientations—toward environmental stimuli and toward the dream imagery. Motor activity is inhibited in connection with this inward orientation. Tolaas suggests that when dreaming occurs, it must be attended to, a fact which then exposes the dreaming organism to possible physical danger and involves a need for an alerting mechanism.

It is implicit in this view that REM sleep is associated with imagery in infrahuman organisms as well as in man. Writing about dream imagery in very young children, Doob (1972) suggests that dream imagery may occur even before the dreams can be reported verbally and hence "images may be as primordial as any nonphysiological function that can be postulated" (p. 313). This thesis can be extended to include animals as well as humans. Doob's point is that images are ubiquitous and reflect a human ability that has survived from an earlier evolutionary stage. Is this image-forming an exclusively human phenomenon? Through imagery the organism can confront the environment on a symbolic level and be in contact with its own past.

Beritashvili (1969) concludes from animal studies that when higher vertebrates first perceive food in a given place, they form an image or concrete representation of the food and its environmental location. This image, which is improved with every new perception of the object, is not obliterated but is preserved and is reproducible whenever a given environment or some component of it is perceived. It has been pointed out that Beritashvili's concept of image behavior is highly reminiscent of Tolman's concept of cognitive maps (Cole and Maltzman, 1969).

Further studies are beginning to shed light on the representational processes of animals (Mason, 1976). In anthropoids the evidence of image behavior in Beritashvili's sense is very strong. These animals have good memories and do seem to remember selectively. Evidence suggestive of visual imagery in other species may be subsumed in four categories:

1. There is suggestive anecdotal evidence. Anyone who has observed a pet during REM sleep will have noticed movements and twitches of the limbs, tail, ears, and facial muscles. The animal seems to be acting out an inner experience very suggestive of dreaming. Such observations are in keeping with a reasonable interpretation of the REM phase in cats reported by Jouvet (1961).

2. Studies by Evarts (1962), involving implanted microelectrodes in the visual pathways and the visual cortex in the unrestrained cat, have shown unusually high rates of unit discharge during REM sleep similar to those in the active waking state. Similar findings have been reported by Huttenlocher (1961) and by Arduini et al. (1963) in the pyramidal tract.

3. As in humans (Kety, 1965), REM sleep in animals is associated with a marked increase in cortical blood flow comparable to the level of the active waking state (Kanzow et al., 1962).

4. A finding by Vaughan (1966) is also suggestive of visual imagery in monkeys. He trained rhesus monkeys to press a bar whenever images were flashed on a screen, to avoid shock. During REM periods, but not during non-REM periods, these monkeys were observed to press the bar as if they were watching internal imagery.

Snyder (1966) suggests that animals dream about their instinctual repertoire. If this is so, it is hard to see what functional role it serves. If animals do have imagery during REM sleep, that imagery might serve a bidirectional, orienting purpose, as alluded to earlier. It might reflect significant stimuli reaching the organism through sensory or extrasensory means. The imagery would have to be on target and intense enough to arouse the organism to take action. This would represent the environmental direction of the dreaming process.

The other direction of the process is concerned with the intrinsic role of spontaneously generated imagery. More and more dreaming appears to be linked with learning. The all-inclusiveness of this term tends to complicate any discussion of the relevant data. However, some workers (Greenberg and Pearlman, 1974; Pearlman and Becker, 1974) have adopted the distinction between prepared learning, or species-specific learning that occurs quickly and involves little adaptive change, and unprepared learning, or species-specific learning taking longer and involving extensive adaptive change. If this distinction is applied to the mass of apparently conflicting data on REM sleep and learning in humans and animals, a meaningful pattern appears. Learning of novel, unmastered tasks (i.e., unpre-

pared learning) turns out to require posttrial REM sleep in animals and is frequently followed by an increase in REM sleep in humans (Tolaas, 1978). Learning of habitual reactions (i.e., prepared learning), on the contrary, appears to be
REM-independent. Thus REM sleep or dreaming sleep is associated with species-
specific events/tasks involving surprise and unpreparedness. In the dreaming state
the main concern of the organism is exploration of problems and hitches bearing
on its relatedness with its environment, and not on manipulation of the environment through motor activity as in the waking state. This explains the lack of
tonus associated with REM sleep. However, the adaptive function of the dreaming process needs protection through enhanced sensitivity to threats (predators,
fires, floods, and so on) and an increase in critical reactivity. Therefore, vigilance operations point in two directions, toward the dream drama (internal
direction) and the outside world (external direction) in a pattern serving emotional adaptation.

At hardly any other time in life is emotional adaptation and unprepared learning as important as in the early postnatal period, when most of the time is spent
in sleep and a significant proportion of the total sleep time in REM sleep, both in
humans and animals. The young, who must pay attention to the dream imagery,
do indeed need an alerting mechanism (enhanced sensitivity to threats). However, this mechanism would be of no use if it did not help them reach the significant adult. This would certainly be true of the "great dreamers," i.e., those
species who spend more time in REM sleep than others. Interestingly, these are
the species whose central nervous systems are immature at birth, e.g., rats, cats,
rabbits, and humans, and who are consequently helpless (Jouvet, 1969). The
"great dreamers," when young, are unable to cope with physical threats by themselves. In the absence of protective adults, an approaching predator may mean
death, particularly if the young are asleep and dreaming, as they often are. Tolaas
(1978) suggests that circumstances such as these may be the source and origin of
the telepathic bonding between mother and infant. Once the dreaming young
locates the threat, incorporates it into dream imagery, and interprets it as threatening, it may wake up and call the significant adult. But when the mother/parents
are away gathering food and out of hearing range, as they often must be, the
young organism asleep and dreaming would be the easy prey of an approaching
predator. Dream telepathy may serve the important function of bridging the gap
between a vulnerable dreaming organism exposed to threats and a protective
adult, in most cases the mother, as fathers tend to leave the mothers long before
the birth.

Extrasensory communication is not limited to the REM periods, nor is it likely
that it is involved only in major crises; but as REM sleep is phylogenetically and
ontogenetically more primitive than slow-wave sleep (Jouvet, 1969), dream

telepathy may be conceived of as the original means of maintaining communicative ties in the early symbiotic period in all mammalian species when "ordinary" sensory channels are unable to bridge the spatial and temporal gap to the mother/parents.

REFERENCES

Angyal, A. *Foundations for a Science of Personality*. New York: The Commonwealth Fund, 1941.

Arduini, A., Berlucchi, G., and Strata, P. Pyramidal activity during sleep and wakefulness. *Archives Italiennes de Biologie*, **101**: 530–544, 1963.

Aserinsky, E., and Kleitman, N. Regularly occurring periods of eye motility and concomitant phenomena during sleep. *Science*, **118**: 273–274, 1953.

Barker, J. C. Premonitions of the Aberfan disaster. *Journal of the Society for Psychical Research*, **44**: 169–181, 1967.

Belvedere, E., and Foulkes, D. Telepathy and dreams: A failure to replicate. *Perceptual and Motor Skills*, **33**: 783–789, 1971.

Bender, H. The Gotenhafen Case of correspondence between dreams and future events: A study of motivation. *International Journal of Neuropsychiatry*, **2**: 398–407, 1966.

Beritashvili, I. S. Concerning psychoneural activity of animals. In Cole, M., and Maltzman, I. (Eds.), *Contemporary Soviet Psychology*. New York: Basic Books, 1969, pp. 627–670.

Besterman, T. Report of an inquiry into precognitive dreams. *Proceedings of the Society for Psychical Research*, **41**: 186–204, 1933.

Brockhaus, E. Possibilities and limits for research in paranormal phenomena in West Africa. *Papers presented for the Eleventh Annual Convention of the Parapsychological Association*. Freiburg, Germany: Institut fur Grenzgebiete der Psychologie und Psychohygiene, 1968.

Burlingham, D. T. Child analysis and the mother. *The Psychoanalytic Quarterly*, **5**: 69–92, 1935.

Campbell, J. *Myths, Dreams and Religion*. New York: Dutton, 1970.

Cole, M., and Maltzman, I. (Eds.) *Contemporary Soviet Psychology*. New York: Basic Books, 1969.

Coleman, M. L. The paranormal triangle in analytical supervision. *Psychoanalysis and the Psychoanalytic Review*, **45**: 73–84, 1958.

Daim, W. Studies in dream-telepathy. *Tomorrow*, **2**: 35–48, 1953.

Dale, L. A. A series of spontaneous cases in the tradition of *Phantasms of the Living*. *Journal of the American Society for Psychical Research*, **45**: 85–101, 1951.

Dale, L. A., White, R., and Murphy, G. A selection of cases from a recent survey of spontaneous ESP phenomena. *Journal of the American Society for Psychical Research*, **56**: 3–47, 1962.

Deutsch, H. Occult processes occurring during psychoanalysis. *Imago*, **12**: 418–433, 1926.

Devereux, G. (Ed.) *Psychoanalysis and the Occult*. New York: International Universities Press, 1953.

Devereux, G. Dream learning and individual ritual in Mohave shamanism. *American Anthropology*, **60**: 234–248, 1957.

Dodds, E. R. *The Greeks and the Irrational*. London: Beacon Press, 1957.

Dodds, E. R. Supernormal phenomena in classical antiquity. *Proceedings of the Society for Psychical Research*, **55**: 189–237, 1971.

Donahoe, J. *Dream Reality.* Oakland: Bench Press, 1974.

Doob, L. W. The ubiquitous appearance of images. In Sheehan, P. W. (Ed.), *The Nature and Function of Imagery.* New York: Academic Press, 1972, pp. 311-332.

Dunne, J. W. *An Experiment with Time.* New York: Macmillan, 1927.

Ehrenwald, J. *Telepathy and Medical Psychology.* New York: W. W. Norton, 1948.

Ehrenwald, J. *New Dimensions of Deep Analysis.* London: George Allen and Unwin, 1954.

Ehrenwald, J. Mother-child symbiosis: Cradle of ESP. *Psychoanalytic Review,* 58: 455-466, 1971 (a).

Ehrenwald, J. Psi phenomena and the existential shift. *Journal of the American Society for Psychical Research,* 65: 162-173, 1971 (b).

Eisenbud, J. Telepathy and the problems of psychoanalysis. *The Psychoanalytic Quarterly,* 15: 32-87, 1946.

Eisenbud, J. The dreams of two patients in analysis interpreted as a telepathic rêve à deux. *The Psychoanalytic Quarterly,* 16: 39-60, 1947.

Eisenbud, J. *Psi and Psychoanalysis.* New York: Grune & Stratton, 1970.

Ermacora, G. B. Telepathic dreams experimentally induced. *Proceedings of the Society for Psychical Research,* 2: 235-308, 1895.

Evarts, E. Activity of neurons in visual cortex of cat during sleep with low voltage fast EEG activity. *Journal of Neurophysiology,* 25: 812-816, 1962.

Faraday, A. *The Dream Game.* London: Temple Smith, 1975.

Flammarion, C. *The Unknown.* New York: Harper, 1900.

Fodor, N. Telepathy in analysis. *The Psychiatric Quarterly,* 21: 171-189, 1947.

Foster, A. A. ESP tests with American Indian children. *Journal of Parapsychology,* 7: 94-103, 1943.

Foulkes, D., Belvedere, E., Masters, R. E. C., Houston, J., Krippner, S., Honorton, C., and Ullman, M. Long-distance "sensory bombardment" ESP in dreams: A failure to replicate. *Perceptual and Motor Skills,* 35: 731-734, 1972.

Freud, S. Dreams and telepathy. *Imago,* 8: 1-22, 1922.

Freud, S. The occult significance of dreams. *Imago,* 9: 234-238, 1925.

Freud, S. *New Introductory Lectures on Psychoanalysis.* New York: W. W. Norton, 1933.

Freud, S. Dreams and the occult. In *New Introductory Lectures on Psychoanalysis.* London: Hogarth Press, 1934.

Freud, S. Psychoanalysis and telepathy. Schriften Aus dem Nachlass, *Gesammelte Werke,* Vol. 17. London: Imago Publishing Co., 1941, pp. 25-40.

Glendinning, R. J. *Traüme und Vorbeudeutung in der Islendinga Saga Sturla Thordarsons.* Bern: Herbert Lang & Co. AG, 1974.

Globus, G. S., Knapp, P. H., Skinner, J. C., and Healy, G. An appraisal of telepathic communication in dreams. *Psychophysiology,* 4: 365, 1968.

Green, C. E. Report on enquiry into spontaneous cases. *Proceedings of the Society for Psychical Research,* 53: 97-161, 1960.

Greenberg, R., and Pearlman, C. Cutting the REM nerve: An approach to the adaptive role of REM sleep. *Perspectives in Biology and Medicine,* 17: 513-521, 1974.

Gurney, E., Myers, F., and Podmore, F. *Phantasms of the Living* (2 vols.). London: Trübner Co., 1886.

Hall, C. Experimente zur telepathischen Beeinflussung von Traümen. *Zeitschrift für Parapsychologie und Grenzgebiete der Psychologie,* 10: 18-47, 1967.

Hall, C., and Van de Castle, R. L. *The Content Analysis of Dreams.* New York: Appleton-Century-Crofts, 1966.

Hanefeld, E. Content analysis of spontaneous cases. *Proceedings of the Parapsychological Association*, 5: 7–8, 1968.

Hann-Kende, F. On the role of transference and counter-transference in psychoanalysis. English translation in Devereux, G. (ed.), *Psychoanalysis and the Occult*. New York: International Universities Press, 1953, pp. 158–167.

Hart, H. *The Enigma of Survival: The Case For and Against an After Life*. London: Rider & Co., 1959.

Hart, H. *Towards a New Philosophical Basis for Parapsychological Phenomena*. New York: Parapsychology Foundation, Inc., 1965.

Hart, H., and Hart, E. B. Visions and apparitions collectively and reciprocally perceived. *Proceedings of the Society for Psychical Research*, 40: 205–249, 1933.

Hernandez-Péon, R. The nature of sleep and dreams. In *Health*. New York: Lippincott, 1966.

Hitschmann, E. Telepathy and psychoanalysis. *International Journal of Psychoanalysis*, 5: 423–438, 1924.

Hollós, I. Psychopathologie Alltaglicher Telepathischer Erscheinungen. *Imago*, 19: 529–546, 1933.

Honorton, C. Significant factors in hypnotically-induced clairvoyant dreams. *Journal of the American Society for Psychical Research*, 66: 86–102, 1972.

Honorton, C. Has science developed the competence to confront claims of the paranormal? Presidential Address delivered at the Eighteenth Annual Convention of the Parapsychological Association, University of California, Santa Barbara, August 21, 1975.

Honorton, C., and Krippner, S. Hypnosis and ESP performance: A review of the experimental literature. *Journal of the American Society for Psychical Research*, 63: 214–252, 1969.

Honorton, C., Krippner, S., and Ullman, M. Telepathic transmission of art prints under two conditions. *Proceedings of the 80th Annual Convention of the American Psychological Association*, 1971, pp. 319–320.

Honorton, C., Ullman, M., and Krippner, S. Comparison of extrasensory and presleep influences on dreams: A preliminary report. In Morris, J. D., Roll, W. G., and Morris, R. L. (Eds.), *Research in Parapsychology 1974*. Metuchen, New Jersey: Scarecrow Press, 1975, pp. 82–84.

Huttenlocher, P. R. Evoked and spontaneous activity in single units of medial brain stem during natural sleep and waking. *Journal of Neurophysiology*, 24: 451–468, 1961.

Jackson, MacD. P. Suggestions for a controlled experiment to test precognition in dreams. *Journal of the American Society for Psychical Research*, 61: 346–353, 1967.

Jouvet, M. Telencephalic and rhombencephalic sleep in cat. In Wolstenholme, G., and O'Connor, M. (Eds.), *Ciba Foundation Symposium on Nature of Sleep*, London: Churchill, 1961, pp. 188–208.

Jouvet, M. Biogenic amines and the states of sleep. *Science*, 163: 33–41, 1969.

Jung, C. *Memories, Dreams, Reflections*. New York: Pantheon, 1963.

Kanzow, E., Krause, D., and Kühnel, H. Die Vasomotorik der Hirnrinde in den Phasen desychronisierter EEG-Activitat in naturlichen Schlaf der Katze, *Pflugers Archiv fur die gesamte Physiologie des Menshen und der Tiere*, 274: 593–607, 1962.

Keeling, K. Telepathic transmission in hypnotic dreams: An exploratory study. *Journal of Parapsychology*, 35: 330–331, 1971 (abstract).

Kety, S. Relationship between energy metabolism of the brain and functional activity. Paper presented at the 45th Annual Meeting of the Association for Research in Nervous and Mental Disease, New York, 1965.

Krippner, S. An experimental study in hypnosis and telepathy. *American Journal of Clinical Hypnosis*, 11: 45–54, 1968.

Krippner, S. Investigations of extrasensory phenomena, in dreams and other altered states of consciousness. *Journal of the American Society of Psychosomatic Dentistry and Medicine*, 16: 7–14, 1969.

Krippner, S. Electrophysiological studies in dreams: Sex differences in seventy-four telepathy sessions. *Journal of the American Society for Psychical Research*, 64: 277–285, 1970.

Krippner, S. "Clairvoyant" perception of art prints in altered conscious states. *Proceedings, 79th Convention, American Psychological Association*, 1971, pp. 423–424.

Krippner, S. Dreams and other altered conscious states. *Journal of Communication*, 25: 173–182, 1975.

Krippner, S. (Ed.) *Advances in Parapsychological Research. 2. Extrasensory Perception*. New York: Plenum Press, 1978.

Krippner, S., and Davidson, R. Religious implications of paranormal events occuring during chemically-induced "psychedelic" experience. *Pastoral Psychology*, 21: 27–34, 1970.

Krippner, S., and Goldsmith, M. A multisensory approach to telepathic communication in dreams. *A.R.E. Journal*, 6: 183–186, 1971.

Krippner, S., and Ullman, M. Telepathy and dreams: Controlled experiment with electro-encephalogram-electro-oculogram monitoring. *Journal of Nervous and Mental Disease*, 151: 394–403, 1970.

Krippner, S., Honorton, C., Ullman, M., Masters, R., and Houston, J. A long-distance "sensory bombardment" study of ESP in dreams. *Journal of the American Society for Psychical Research*, 65: 468–475, 1971.

Krippner, S., Honorton, C., and Ullman, M. A second precognitive dream study with Malcolm Bessent. *Journal of the American Society for Psychical Research*, 66: 269–279, 1972 (a).

Krippner, S., Honorton, C., and Ullman, M. A sixteen-night study of pre-experience and post-experience dreams. *Psychophysiology*, 9: 114, 1972 (b) (abstract).

Krippner, S., Honorton, C., and Ullman, M. A long-distance ESP dream study with the "Grateful Dead." *Journal of the American Society of Psychosomatic Dentistry and Medicine*, 20: 9–17, 1973.

Krippner, S., Ullman, M., and Honorton, C. A precognitive dream study with a single subject. *Journal of the American Society for Psychical Research*, 65: 192–203, 1971.

Krippner, S., and Zirinsky, K. An experiment in dreams, clairvoyance, and telepathy. *A.R.E. Journal*, 6: 12–16, 1971.

Lawrence, B. E., and Shirley, J. T. Napping habits of a college student population. *Psychophysiology*, 1: 294–295, 1970 (abstract).

MacDougall, W., and Hose, C. *The Pagan Tribes of Borneo*. New York: Macmillan, 1912.

Malinowski, B. *Sex and Repression in Savage Society*. New York: Harcourt, Brace & World, 1927.

Mason, W. A. Environmental models and mental modes. Representational processes in the great apes and man. *American Psychologist*, 31: 284–293, 1976.

Meerloo, J. A. M. Telepathy as a form of archaic communication. *Psychiatric Quarterly*, 23: 691–704, 1949.

Meerloo, J. A. M. Sympathy and telepathy: A model for psychodynamic research in parapsychology. *International Journal of Parapsychology*, 10: 57–83, 1968.

Meier, C. A. *Die Bedeutung des Traumes*. Freiburg: Walter-Verlag Olten, 1972.

Myers, F. W. H. *Human Personality and Its Survival of Bodily Death* (2 vols.). London: Longmans, Green & Co., 1903.

Palmer, J., and Dennis, M. A community mail survey of psychic experiences. In Morris, J. D., Roll, W. G., and Morris, R. L. (Eds.), *Research in Parapsychology 1974*. Metuchen, New Jersey: Scarecrow Press, 1975, pp. 130-133.

Pearlman, C. A., and Becker, M. REM sleep deprivation impairs serial reversal and probability maximizing in rats. *Physiological Psychology*, 2: 509-512, 1974.

Pedersen-Krag, G. Telepathy and repression. *The Psychoanalytic Quarterly*, 16: 61-82, 1947.

Prasad, J., and Stevenson, I. A survey of spontaneous psychical experiences in school children of Uttar Pradesh, India. *International Journal of Parapsychology*, 10: 241-261, 1968.

Priestley, J. B. *Man and Time*. Garden City, New York: Doubleday, 1964.

Prince, W. F. Human experiences. *Bulletin of the Boston Society for Psychic Research*, 14: 5-328, 1931.

Randall, A. Dreaming, sharing, and telepathy in a short term community. Unpublished doctoral dissertation. New York: Teachers College, Columbia University, 1977.

Rechtschaffen, A. Sleep and dream states: An experimental design. In Cavanna, R. (Ed.), *Psi Favorable States of Consciousness*. New York: Parapsychology Foundation, 1970, pp. 87-120.

Rhine, L. E. Psychological processes in ESP experiences. Part II. Dreams. *Journal of Parapsychology*, 26: 172-199, 1962.

Rhine, L. E. *ESP in Life and Lab*. New York: Macmillan, 1967.

Rivers, W. H. R. *Conflict and Dream*. London: Harcourt, 1923.

Roheim, G. Telepathy in a dream. *Psychoanalytic Quarterly*, 1: 227-291, 1932.

Rose, R. *Living Magic: The Realities Underlying the Psychical Practices and Beliefs of Australian Aborigines*. Chicago: Rand McNally, 1956.

Ross, C. *Telepathy and Dreams: An Attempt at Replication*. Princeton, New Jersey: Princeton University, 1972 (mimeo).

Ruffwarg, H., Muzio, J., and Dement, W. C. Ontogenetic development of the human sleep-dream cycle. *Science*, 152: 604-619, 1966.

Saltmarsh, H. F. Report on cases of apparent precognition. *Proceedings of the Society for Psychical Research*, 42: 49-103, 1934.

Sannwald, G. Statistische Untersuchungen an Spontanphänomenen. *Zeitschrift für Parapsychologie und Grenzgebiete der Psychologie*, 3: 59-71, 1959 (a).

Sannwald, G. Zur Psychologie Paranormaler Spontanphänomene: Motivation, Thematik und Bezugspersonen "okkulter" Erlebnisse. *Zeitschrift für Parapsychologie und Grenzgebiete der Psychologie*, 3: 149-183, 1959 (b).

Saul, L. Telepathic sensitiveness as a neurotic sympton. *The Psychoanalytic Quarterly*, 7: 329-335, 1938.

Scheffé, H. *The Analysis of Variance*. New York: John Wiley, 1959.

Schilder, P. Psychopathology of everyday telepathic phenomena. *Imago*, 20: 219-224, 1934.

Schmeidler, G. Separating the sheep from the goats. *Journal of the American Society for Psychical Research*, 39: 47-49, 1945.

Schwarz, B. E. *Parent-Child Telepathy*. New York: Garrett/Helix, 1971.

Servadio, E. Psychoanalysis and telepathy. *Imago*, 21: 489-497, 1935.

Servadio, E. A presumptively telepathic-precognitive dream during analysis. *International Journal of Psycho-Analysis*, 37: 1-4, 1956.

Servadio, E. Telepathy and psychoanalysis. *Journal of the American Society for Psychical Research*, **52**: 125–133, 1958.

Snyder, F. The new biology of dreaming. *Archives of General Psychiatry*, **8**: 382–392, 1963.

Snyder, F. Speculations about the contribution of the rapid eye movement state to mammalian survival. Paper presented at symposium on "Activité onirique et conscience," Lyon, 1965.

Snyder, F. Toward an evolutionary theory of dreaming. *American Journal of Psychiatry*, **123**: 121–142, 1966.

Stekel, W. *Der telepathische Traum.* Berlin: Johannes Baum, 1920.

Stevens, W. O. *The Mystery of Dreams.* New York: Dodd, Mead, 1949.

Stevenson, I. A review and analysis of paranormal experiences connected with the sinking of the *Titanic. Journal of the American Society for Psychical Research*, **54**: 153–171, 1960.

Stevenson, I. Seven more paranormal experiences associated with the sinking of the *Titanic. Journal of the American Society for Psychical Research*, **59**: 211–225, 1965.

Strauch, I. Dreams and psi in the laboratory. In Cavanna, R. (Ed.), *Psi Favorable States of Consciousness.* New York: Parapsychology Foundation, 1970, pp. 46–54.

Tenhaeff, W. H. C. Personality structure and psi research. *Papers presented for the Eleventh Convention of the Parapsychological Association.* Freiburg, Germany: Institut fur Grenzgebiete der Psychologie und Psychohygiene, 1968.

Tolaas, J. Dreaming—A psi modality? *Psychoenergetic Systems*, **1**: 185–195, 1976.

Tolaas, J. REM sleep and the concept of vigilance. *Biological Psychiatry*, **13**: 135–148, 1978.

Turville-Petre, G. Dreams in Icelandic tradition. *Folklore*, **69**: 93–111, 1958.

Tylor, E. B. *Primitive Culture.* London: John Murray, 1871.

Ullman, M. On the nature of psi processes. *Journal of Parapsychology*, **13**: 59–62, 1949.

Ullman, M. On the nature of resistance to psi phenomena. *Journal of the American Society for Psychical Research*, **46**: 11–13, 1952.

Ullman, M. Physiological determinants of the dream. *Journal of Nervous and Mental Disease*, **124**: 45–48, 1956.

Ullman, M. Dreams and arousal. *American Journal of Psychotherapy*, **12**: 671–690, 1958.

Ullman, M. On the occurrence of telepathic dreams. *Journal of the American Society for Psychical Research*, **53**: 50–61, 1959.

Ullman, M. A nocturnal approach to psi. *Proceedings of the Parapsychological Association*, **3**: 35–62, 1966.

Ullman, M. Dreaming as metaphor in motion. *Archives of General Psychiatry*, **21**: 696–703, 1969 (a).

Ullman, M. Telepathy and dreams. *Experimental Medicine and Surgery*, **27**: 19–38, 1969 (b).

Ullman, M. Vigilance, dreaming and the paranormal. In Muses, C., and Young, A. (Eds.), *Consciousness and Reality.* New York: Outerbridge and Lazard, 1972, pp. 35–56.

Ullman, M. A theory of vigilance and dreaming. In Zykmund, V. (Ed.), *The Oculomotor System and Brain Function.* London: Butterworth, 1973, pp. 453–466.

Ullman, M. Psi and psychiatry. In Mitchell, E. D., and White, J. (Eds.), *Psychic Exploration.* New York: Putnam's, pp. 247–267, 1974.

Ullman, M. Parapsychology and psychiatry. In Freedman, A., Kaplan, H., and Saddock, B. (Eds.), *Comprehensive Textbook of Psychiatry*, vol. 2, 2nd ed. Baltimore: Williams and Wilkins, 1975 (a), pp. 2552–2561.

Ullman, M. The role of imagery. *Journal of Communication*, 25: 162–172, 1975 (b).

Ullman, M. Psychopathology and psi phenomena. In Wolman, B. B. (Ed.), *Handbook of Parapsychology*. New York: Van Nostrand Reinhold, 1977, pp. 557–574.

Ullman, M., and Krippner, S. A laboratory approach to the nocturnal dimension of paranormal experience: Report of a confirmatory study using the REM monitoring technique. *Biological Psychiatry*, 1: 259–270, 1969.

Ullman, M., and Krippner, S. Dream studies and telepathy. *Parapsychological Monographs No. 12.* New York: Parapsychological Foundation, 1970.

Ullman, M., Krippner, S., and Feldstein, S. Experimentally-induced telepathic dreams: Two studies using EEG-REM monitoring technique. *International Journal of Neuropsychiatry*, 2: 420–437, 1966.

Ullman, M., Krippner, S., and Honorton, C. A review of the Maimonides dream-ESP experiments, 1964–1969. *Psychophysiology*, 7: 354–355, 1970 (a) (abstract).

Ullman, M., Krippner, S., and Honorton, C. A review of the Maimonides dream-ESP experiments 1964–1969. *Mysterious Worlds* (Tel Aviv), 16: 36–37, 1970 (b).

Ullman, M., and Krippner, S., with Vaughan, A. *Dream Telepathy*. New York: Macmillan, 1973.

Van de Castle, R. Psi abilities in primitive groups. *Proceedings of the Parapsychological Association*, 7: 97–122, 1970.

Van de Castle, R. *The Psychology of Dreaming*. Morristown, New Jersey: General Learning Press, 1971.

Van de Castle, R. The Cuna Indians of Panama. *Journal of Communication*, 25: 183–190, 1975.

Van de Castle, R. Sleep and dreams. In Wolman, B. B. (Ed.), *Handbook of Parapsychology*. New York: Van Nostrand Reinhold, 1977, pp. 667–686.

Vaughan, C. J. The development and use of an operant technique to provide evidence for visual imagery in rhesus monkeys under "sensory deprivation." *Dissertation Abstracts*, 26: 6191, 1966.

Wallace, A. F. Dreams and wishes of the soul . . . among the 17th century Iroquois. *American Anthropology*, 60: 234–248, 1958.

Weserman, H. M. Versuche willkürlicher Traumbildung. *Archives f. d. Tierischen Magnetismus*, 6: 135–142, 1819.

Woods, R. K. (Ed.) *The World of Dreams*. New York: Random House, 1947.

Zulliger, H. Prophetic dreams. *International Journal of Psycho-Analysis*, 15: 191–208, 1934.

6

Drugs, REM Sleep, and Dreams

Thomas Roth, Milton Kramer,
and Patricia J. Salis

Historically, man's interest in sleep has to a great extent been determined by his interest in dreams. This tradition was followed when the modern era of sleep research began in 1953 with the discovery by Aserinsky and Kleitman of rapid-eye-movement (REM) sleep. It was the new knowledge that REM sleep represents the stage during which most true dreaming occurs that excited researchers and stimulated them to launch the research endeavor that continues actively today. (Aserinsky, 1967, reported that there was more than a 900% increase in publications on dreaming in the ten years after 1953.) The initial excitement was related to the fact that with polygraphic monitoring of electroencephalographic (EEG) and electro-oculographic (EOG) activity it was possible to detect REM sleep and therefore maximize the chances of obtaining immediate reports of dream content from an awakened sleeper. It was also related to the fact that periods of REM sleep occur regularly every 90–120 minutes throughout a normal night of sleep. The frequency and pervasiveness of the dreaming process assured that sufficient material was available for the systematic, scientific study of dreams. Clearly, given the importance assigned since Freud's time to dreams in the mental life of both healthy and disturbed persons, the ability to study dreams in a rigorous manner might have important implications for understanding the dynamics of both normal and abnormal psychological states.

Along with the discovery of REM sleep and its association with dreaming, it was also learned that the rapid eye movements signal a distinct physiological state which differs dramatically from non-REM (NREM) sleep and, in fact, resembles wakefulness: the REM state is characterized primarily by desynchronized cortical activity and autonomic nervous system activation in the form of increased levels and variability of heart rate, respiration rate, blood pressure, and numerous other measures, whereas NREM sleep, which is subdivided into four distinct sleep stages, is characterized by increasing levels of cortical synchronization and relative physiological quiescence (Snyder and Scott, 1972). This discovery had consequences equally as important as the discovery of the REM-dreaming association, for it initiated an interest in the physiology of sleep itself and of its two constituents, active REM sleep and quiet NREM sleep. (Again, Aserinsky, 1967, found an increase of over 600% in publications on sleep in the ten years after 1953.) Thus, the discovery of REM sleep served as a window that provided a view of the vast psychological and physiological terrain which remained to be explored and that, with the aid of the polygraph, was now able to be explored. Among many other things, dream researchers were provided an opportunity to investigate the relationship between the psychological events of the dream and the distinct physiological events of the REM state.

Interest in the effects of drugs on dreams derives primarily from the importance that has been attached by psychologists and psychiatrists to the dreams of the mentally ill. With the widespread use of psychotropic drugs to treat mental illness, there has developed a need to explore how the drugs either influence or work through the patient's dreams. The technology of the sleep and dream laboratory permits systematic pursuit of this line of research. Perhaps the most important opportunity is that of testing the hypothesis that changes in dreams aid or at least accompany changes in clinical state. On the other hand, there is, as will be seen, no question that most psychotropic drugs affect the physiological concomitants of dreams—REM sleep and even the rapid eye movements themselves. If it were demonstrated that these changes are accompanied by predictable changes in dream content, there would be strong evidence of a parallelism between the psychological and the physiological events of the dreaming process.

In this chapter, we assess the progress made to date in the study of the effects of drugs on dreams. We first review existing work on the effects of selected drugs on EEG-EOG sleep patterns, and especially on REM sleep. We then consider the effects of drugs on dreams. The quantity of information on sleep-pattern effects has permitted selection of what are considered to be definitive studies. By contrast, the paucity of information on dream effects has mandated a rather exhaustive, all-inclusive review. In our conclusions, we present recommendations for future research that may aid fulfillment of the original promise presented by the discovery of REM sleep.

PROCEDURES AND TERMINOLOGY

The procedures we used in selecting studies for review require some explanation. The effects of drugs on sleep patterns have been comprehensively reviewed recently by Kay et al. (1976). For the present review, only fully reported studies that met minimal design requirements have been included (our criteria for these definitive studies conform to those of Kay et al.). Specifically, subjects were homogeneous in type, numbered at least five, and were taking no drugs except that under study. When more than one drug dosage or type was administered in a study, there was at least a three-day washout period between discrete drug periods. Conditions included a placebo control condition, a predetermined drug and dosage administration schedule, a constant study environment, and an adequate statistical analysis and report of probability levels. Once the definitive studies had been determined, we selected for review the drugs for which there were at least two definitive studies and which were representative of the major classes of psychotropic medications. Application of these criteria resulted in the inclusion of approximately 25% of the available studies. The effects of drugs on dreams have been examined in nine studies, and all these studies are reviewed here. When we report a result for any study, it can be assumed that the result was statistically significant, unless we label it as nonsignificant or only a tendency ($p < .10$).

Some explanation of our terminology is also required. Each study may be categorized as one of three types, depending on the length of the drug administration period. In a *dose-effect study* the period is a single day or night, in a *short-term study* it is 1–14 days, and in a *long-term study* it is 15 days or more (this terminology is also consistent with that of Kay et al.). Many studies included examination of a placebo period following discontinuation of drug

TABLE 6-1. EEG-EOG SLEEP-PATTERN MEASURES.

Category	Measure	Definition[a]
Efficacy	Sleep latency	Time from recording onset to sleep onset
	Total sleep time	Time in REM and NREM sleep
	Number of awakenings	Number of waking periods after sleep onset
	Amount of wakefulness	Minutes or percent of time awake (either total or after sleep onset)
NREM	Amount of Stage 1	Minutes or percent of time in Stage 1 sleep
	Amount of Stage 2	Minutes or percent of time in Stage 2 sleep
	Amount of Stage 3	Minutes or percent of time in Stage 3 sleep[b]
	Amount of Stage 4	Minutes or percent of time in Stage 4 sleep[b]
REM	Amount of Stage REM	Minutes or percent of time in Stage REM sleep
	Latency of Stage REM	Time from sleep onset to first REM period
	Number of REM periods	Nuber of sustained periods of REM sleep
	REM density	Incidence of eye movements per unit time of REM sleep

[a]Representative; precise definitions vary among studies.
[b]Often combined as amount of slow-wave sleep.

administration; in these studies *drug period* refers to the period of administration of active drug, and *recovery period* refers to the postdrug period. The term *initial effect* refers to an effect that lasts at most one week during a drug or recovery period; the term *persistent effect* refers to an effect that lasts throughout the period. In the studies of dreams, the content was examined either by awakening subjects from REM sleep or by having the subjects recall their dreams when they awoke in the morning. The former, almost by definition performed in the laboratory, are called *REM-recall studies*, and the latter, typically performed at home, are called *morning-recall studies*. The measures examined for the studies of sleep patterns are listed and defined in Table 6-1. *Efficacy measures* are those related to amounts of wakefulness and total sleep, *NREM measures* are the amounts of the four NREM stages of sleep, and *REM measures* include several different descriptors of the REM state. For the studies of dreams, two general measures have been employed and are described: the frequency of dreams recalled per night, and the quality of the dream content in terms of scores on scales of manifest or latent content.

EEG-EOG SLEEP PATTERNS

Sedative-Hypnotic Agents

Pentobarbital. The characteristics of the three definitive sleep studies of pentobarbital (Baekeland, 1967; Hartmann, 1968; Kay et al., 1972) are summarized in Table 6-2. Studies of this drug have been dose-effect studies of normal subjects or ex–opiate addicts; doses have ranged from 75 to 300 mg/70 kg body weight. There has been no definitive study of recovery from pentobarbital. In the normal subjects, changes in various efficacy measures indicated a hypnotic effect for the drug (i.e., reduced sleep latency, increased total sleep time, reduced number of awakenings, and/or reduced amount of wakefulness); these changes were not apparent in the ex-addicts. Total NREM sleep was elevated by pentobarbital in the one study of normal subjects in which it was examined, but amount of Stage 2 and amount of Stage 3 + Stage 4 were not affected. By contrast, in the ex-addicts amount of Stage 2 increased, amount of Stage 3 tended to decrease, and amount of Stage 4 was unchanged. In all studies amount of REM sleep was reduced by the drug; in two (including that of ex-addicts) of the three studies, there were also an increase in REM latency, a decrease in number of REM periods, and a decrease in REM density. These changes are characteristic of full-blown REM suppression. Studies of experimental REM suppression (Dement, 1960) and of REM suppression by other drugs (see below) suggest that it is typically followed on recovery nights by REM rebound, or levels of REM sleep that exceed baseline levels. Nondefinitive studies of pentobarbital (reviewed in Kay et al., 1976) leave unclear whether REM rebound characterizes recovery from pentobarbital administration.

TABLE 6-2. CHARACTERISTICS OF EEG-EOG STUDIES OF BARBITURATE SEDATIVE-HYPNOTIC AGENTS.

Authors and Year	No. and Type of Subjects	Dose (mg)	Intake Time[a]	Drug Period Length[b]	Recovery Period Length[b]	Comments
Pentobarbital						
Hartmann, 1968	7 normal	100	30' *a hs*	1 day	0	
Baekeland, 1967	15 normal	100	*hs*	2 NC days	0	
Kay, Jasinski, Eisenstein, and Kelly, 1972	8 ex-opiate addicts	75, 150, and 300 mg/ 70 kg body weight	?	1 day/dose	0	
Secobarbital						
Lehmann and Ban, 1968	10 normal	100	*hs*	1 day	0	
Allnutt and O'Connor, 1971	8 normal	100	60' *a hs*	2 NC days	0	Bedtime 8 P.M.; arising 3 A.M.
Kales, Hauri, Bixler, and Silberfarb, 1976	8 insomniac	100	??	14 C days	4 C days	Drug period recordings: nights 1-3 and 12-14
Lester, Coulter, Cowden, and Williams 1968	14 normal	200	30' *a hs*	1 day	1 day	

[a] *a hs*—before bedtime; *hs*—bedtime.
[b] NC—nonconsecutive; C—consecutive.

Secobarbital.   The four definitive studies of secobarbital (Allnutt and O'Connor, 1971; Kales, Hauri, Bixler, and Silberfarb, 1976; Lehmann and Ban, 1968; Lester et al., 1968) are also summarized in Table 6-2. There have been three dose-effect studies of normal subjects and one short-term study of insomniacs. Doses have been 100 and 200 mg. Recovery following drug administration was examined for one and four days, the latter following a 14-day drug period. Two of the four studies revealed improvements in efficacy measures. In the study of insomniacs, the drug initially reduced amount of wakefulness, especially after sleep onset; this effect had become nonsignificant at the end of two weeks. An increase in amount of Stage 2 was the only striking change in NREM measures: it was observed initially, but not after two weeks, in the insomniacs, and on the single night when 200 mg was administered to normal subjects. The 200-mg dose also tended to reduce amounts of Stages 3 and 4. Amount of REM was reduced in one dose-effect study of 100 mg and in the study of 200 mg; in the latter study, REM density was also reduced. There were no recovery effects on the night following the 200-mg dose. In the insomniacs, amount of wakefulness returned to baseline levels, amount of Stage 2 dropped below baseline levels, and amount of Stage 3 exceeded baseline levels. In neither of the studies of the recovery period was amount of REM signficantly different from baseline levels.

Flurazepam.   Five reports have described definitive studies of flurazepam (Hartmann, 1968; Itil et al., 1974; Johns and Masterton, 1974; Kales, Bixler, Scharf, and Kales, 1976; Vogel et al., 1976); they are summarized in Table 6-3. Only dose-effect studies of 15 and 30 mg were performed with normal or non-insomniac subjects; short-term and long-term studies of 30 mg included insomniac patients and examined recovery periods.   With initial administration, flurazepam increased total sleep time and usually reduced number of awakenings and amount of wakefulness. By the second or third day in insomniacs it also reduced sleep latency. With longer administration to insomniacs, the effects on number of awakenings and amount of wakefulness gradually disappeared, but the reduction in sleep latency persisted. There were few first-night effects of the drug on NREM measures. By the second or third night, insomniacs exhibited reduced amounts of Stage 1 and of Stage 3 and/or 4, and increased amount of Stage 2. These changes persisted with long-term administration to insomniacs. A single administration also produced no significant changes in REM sleep, but with continued administration to insomniacs amount of REM decreased and REM latency increased (number of REM periods and REM density were not described). Study of recovery periods suggested carry-over effects on the first one or two nights. Efficacy measures remained improved relative to baseline, but significantly so only in isolated cases. Initial recovery was characterized primarily by the continued reduction in amount of Stages 3 and 4 sleep; by the second week of recovery from long-term drug administration this effect had disappeared. There was no evidence of significant REM rebound during initial or extended recovery from flurazepam.

Nitrazepam.   Nitrazepam has been examined in six definitive studies (Adam et al., 1976; Allnutt and O'Connor, 1971; Haider and Oswald, 1971; Lehmann and Ban, 1968; Nakazawa, Kotorii, Ohshima, Horikawa, and Tachibana, 1975; Risberg et al., 1977); their characteristics are listed in Table 6-3. Normal subjects were evaluated in all studies. Doses were 5 mg (one dose-effect and one long-term study) and 10 mg (three dose-effect and one short-term study). Recovery periods were examined in the short- and long-term studies. Efficacy measures were not always reported; the available data do not provide a clear picture of the drug's effects. In two dose-effect studies (one at each of the doses), sleep latency was reduced. In the long-term study of 5 mg in middle-aged subjects, the drug persistently increased total sleep time and reduced amount of wakefulness. Similar effects were not significant in the short-term study of 10 mg in younger subjects. There were no apparent effects of either dose on amount of Stage 1. Amount of Stage 2 was generally increased by 10 mg, and this effect persisted for 10 days of drug administration. Long-term administration of 5 mg produced a reduction in amount of Stage 3 and Stage 4. Two of the four studies of 10 mg confirmed this effect; in the short-term study it was most evident at the end of the 10-day drug period. Virtually all studies revealed a decrease in amount of REM sleep and an increase in REM latency. When it was examined, the number of REM periods was unchanged from baseline levels. There was a persistent decrease in REM density in the 10-day study of 10 mg. During recovery from long-term administration of 5 mg, there was a reduction in total sleep time and an increase in amount of wakefulness relative to baseline. The short-term study of 10 mg revealed nonsignificant trends for this disruptive effect of discontinuation of nitrazepam. In both studies, amounts of Stages 2, 3, and 4 gradually returned toward baseline levels. REM sleep descriptors that had been changed by the drug also returned to baseline levels. There was no evidence of recovery REM rebound.

Glutethimide.   Table 6-4 tabulates the major characteristics of the two definitive studies of glutethimide; the results of these studies have been presented in four reports (Allen et al., 1968; Goldstein et al., 1970; Goldstein et al., 1971; Kales, Preston, Tan, and Allen, 1970). Both studies were short-term studies in which glutethimide, 500 mg, was administered for three consecutive nights, and there was a recovery period of two to four nights. Normal subjects were examined in one study, and chronic insomniacs were evaluated in the other. Total

TABLE 6-3. CHARACTERISTICS OF EEG-EOG STUDIES OF BENZODIAZEPINE SEDATIVE-HYPNOTIC AGENTS.

Authors and Year	No. and Type of Subjects	Dose (mg)	Intake Time[a]	Drug Period Length[b]	Recovery Period Length[b]	Comments
Flurazepam						
Johns and Masterton, 1974	6 normal	15	15' *a hs*	1 day	0	1 recovery night available for $N = 4$
Hartmann, 1968	10 normal	30	30' *a hs*	2 NC days	0	
Itil, Saletu, and Marasa, 1974	12 slight to moderate anxiety	30	*hs*	1 day	0	
Vogel, Barker, Gibbons, and Thurmond, 1976	12 insomniac	30	30' *a hs*	4 C days	2 C days	
Kales, Bixler, Scharf, and Kales, 1976	23 insomniac	30	?	3 C days	–	Separate analysis of various conditions of a study series; subjects listed below are subsets
	11 insomniac	30	?	14 C days	–	Drug nights 13 and 14 reported
	5 insomniac	30	?	28 C days	–	Drug nights 27 and 28 reported
	16 insomniac	30	?	3–28 C days	3 C days	Recovery nights after varying drug period lengths reported
	5 insomniac	30	?	28 C days	15 C days	Recovery nights 13–15 reported

Nitrazepam

Allnutt and O'Connor, 1971	8 normal	5	60' *a hs*	2 NC days	0	Bedtime 8 P.M.; arising 3 A.M.
Adam, Adamson, Březinová, Hunter, and Oswald, 1976	10 normal	5	30' *a hs*	9 C weeks	2 C weeks	Recordings: drug weeks 5, 6, 11, 12; recovery weeks 1, 2
Lehmann and Ban, 1968	10 normal	10	*hs*	1 day	0	
Haider and Oswald, 1971	6 normal	10	*hs*	2 NC days	0	
Nakazawa, Kotorii, Ohshima, Horikawa, and Tachibana, 1975	5 normal	10	30' *a hs*	1 day	2 C days	Recovery results not reported
Risberg, Henricsson, and Ingvar, 1977	8 normal	10	30' *a hs*	10 C days	4 C days	Drug period recordings: nights 1, 2, 9, 10

[a] *a hs*—before bedtime; *hs*—bedtime.
[b] NC—nonconsecutive; C—consecutive.

TABLE 6-4. CHARACTERISTICS OF EEG-EOG STUDIES OF OTHER SEDATIVE-HYPNOTIC AGENTS.

Authors and Year	No. and Type of Subjects	Dose (mg)	Intake Time[a]	Drug Period Length[b]	Recovery Period Length[b]	Comments
Glutethimide						
Allen, Kales, and Berger, 1968; Kales, Preston, Tan, and Allen, 1970	5 normal	500	*hs*	3 C days	2 C days	
Goldstein, Graedon, Willard, Goldstein, and Smith, 1970; Goldstein, Stoltzfus, and Smith, 1971	10 insomniac	500	*hs*	3 C days	4 C days	
Methaqualone						
Kales, Kales, Scharf, and Tan, 1970	5 normal	150	*hs*	3 C days	2 C days	
Risberg, Risberg, Elmqvist, and Ingvar, 1975	6 normal	250	*hs*	2 NC days	0	
Itil, Saletu, and Marasa, 1974	12 slight to moderate anxiety	300	*hs*	1 day	0	
Kales, Kales, Scharf, and Tan, 1970	5 normal	300	*hs*	3 C days	2 C days	
Goldstein, Graedon, Willard, Goldstein, and Smith, 1970; Goldstein, Stoltzfus, and Smith, 1971	10 insomniac	300	*hs*	3 C days	4 C days	

[a] *hs*—before bedtime; *hs*—bedtime.
[b] NC—nonconsecutive; C—consecutive.

sleep time was not reported for either study, but other efficacy measures were described for the insomniacs: the drug failed to significantly reduce sleep latency, number of awakenings, or amount of nocturnal wakefulness. In both studies, it increased amount of Stage 2 and had no significant effects on amounts of other NREM stages. It reduced amount of REM sleep in the normal subjects and tended to do so in the insomniacs. It elevated REM latency in both studies, but had no significant effect on number of REM periods. In the insomniacs it reduced REM density. The recovery period suggested subtle effects on efficacy measures in insomniacs, for in comparison to the drug period it was characterized by an increased number of awakenings and total amount of wakefulness; values for these measures equaled or exceeded those for the baseline period. Recovery for insomniacs was also characterized by a reduction to baseline levels of Stage 2; a similar trend was apparent for the normal subjects. A cumulative effect of the drug of Stage 4 sleep was suggested by a significant reduction of amount of this stage on the first recovery night for the normal subjects. In both studies there was evidence of recovery REM rebound: amount of REM was elevated above baseline levels, and, for the normal subjects, REM density was greater than at baseline. REM latency returned to baseline levels or below, while number of REM periods remained unchanged.

Methaqualone. Table 6-4 shows the characteristics of the five definitive studies of methaqualone (Goldstein et al., 1970, 1971; Itil et al., 1974, Kales, Kales, Scharf, and Tan, 1970; Risberg et al., 1975). Doses between 150 and 300 mg have been evaluated on single nights and on three consecutive nights; two to four consecutive recovery nights have been examined. Non-insomniacs were evaluated in four studies, and insomniacs were studied in the fifth. Efficacy measures were examined in only three studies and were changed during drug administration only with insomniacs: sleep latency decreased, but number of awakenings and amount of nocturnal wakefulness did not change significantly. Results for amounts of NREM stages are not all consistent, but if the drug affects these stages, it is likely to be in the direction of increasing amount of Stage 2 and reducing amount of Stage 4, especially with higher doses. Little or no effect should occur with Stage 1 or Stage 3. Two of the five studies (normal subjects, 250 and 300 mg) revealed a significant reduction by methaqualone of REM amount, while the remaining studies found no change. REM latency and number of REM periods have never changed significantly. In the two single-night studies, the drug reduced REM density. The study of insomniacs demonstrated the greatest number of recovery effects: amount of Stage 2 returned to baseline levels; amount of Stage 4, which in this study was reduced by the drug, remained significantly reduced; and amount of REM which had not changed with drug administration, nevertheless increased during the recovery period. A similar recovery elevation of REM amount occurred in the multiple-night study of 300 mg in normal subjects.

Antidepressant Agents

Amitriptyline. Table 6-5 summarizes the major characteristics of the five definitive studies of amitriptyline (Hartmann, 1968; Hartmann and Cravens, 1973b; Nakazawa, Kotorii, Kotorii, Horikawa, and Ohshima, 1975; Nakazawa et al., 1977; Saletu et al., 1974). All studies involved healthy subjects, not depressed patients. All but one study were dose-effect studies. Recovery periods of 1-2 or 32 nights were evaluated. Doses ranged from 25 to 75 mg; the single long-term study examined 50 mg. There is some evidence that the drug initially increased total sleep time in normal subjects. Whether this effect resulted from reduced sleep latency and/or from reduced amount of nocturnal wakefulness was not clearly established. The most consistent initial effect on NREM stages was increase in amount of Stage 3. There was also some evidence that the drug initially reduced amount of Stage 1 and increased amount of Stage 2; amount of Stage 4 has never been shown to change significantly with administration of amitriptyline. In the single long-term study, elevations in amounts of Stages 2 and 3 sleep persisted throughout the 28-day drug period. It has universally been found that amitriptyline reduces amount of REM sleep. In the long-term study, this REM suppression was greatest during the first week of drug administration, but persisted uniformly at a somewhat higher level for at least three weeks; REM latency was also persistently elevated, and the number of REM periods was persistently reduced. Recovery effects were comprehensively examined in one dose-effect study of 25 mg and in the long-term study of 50 mg. The dose-effect study revealed an increase, relative to baseline, in total sleep time on the first of two recovery nights, a decrease in amount of Stage 2 on the second night, an increase in amount of Stage 3 on the first night, and an increase in REM density on both nights. In the long-term study, the initial week of recovery was characterized by increased sleep latency, amounts of wakefulness, Stage 1, and Stage REM, and number of REM periods; and by reduced amount of Stage 2 and latency to Stage REM. Amounts of Stage 4 and of Stage 3 + Stage 4 were reduced throughout the recovery period, and especially during the first week.

Antipsychotic Agents

Chlorpromazine.   The characteristics of the five definitive studies of chlorpromazine (Hartmann and Cravens, 1973c; Kaplan et al., 1974; Lester et al., 1971; Lester and Guerrero-Figueroa, 1966, Saletu et al., 1974) are shown in Table 6-6. Doses between 50 and 400 mg have been examined in dose-effect and long-term studies. Four studies involved normal subjects. The fifth study involved chronic schizophrenic inpatients; in contrast to the other studies, where a baseline condition was included, drug effects in the patients were compared to those

TABLE 6-5. CHARACTERISTICS OF EEG-EOG STUDIES OF ANTIDEPRESSANT AGENTS.

Authors and Year	No. and Type of Subjects	Dose (mg)	Intake Time[a]	Drug Period Length[b]	Recovery Period Length[b]	Comments
Amitriptyline						
Nakazawa, Kotorii, Kotorii, Horikawa, and Ohshima, 1975	5 normal	25	30' *a hs*	1 day	2 C days	
Nakazawa, Kotorii, Kotorii, Ohshima, and Hasuzawa, 1977	15 normal	25	30' *a hs*	1 day	1 day	Only REM % reported
Saletu, Allen, and and Itil, 1974	10 normal	35	*hs*	1 day	0	
Hartmann and Cravens, 1973b	10 normal	50	20' *a hs*	28 C days	32 C days	Recordings: drug nights 1–5, 12, 18, 25; recovery nights 1–6, 14, 21, 27
Hartmann, 1968	8 normal	75	30' *a hs*	2 NC days	0	

[a] *a hs*—before bedtime; *hs*—bedtime.
[b] NC—nonconsecutive; C—consecutive.

at the end of a four-week postdrug placebo period. Recovery periods of 1 and 32 days were examined for chlorpromazine in normal subjects. The single-night studies failed to reveal changes in any efficacy measure in normal subjects, but the long-term study indicated an initial increase in total sleep time. In the schizophrenic patients, total sleep time was also increased, and sleep latency and number of awakenings were reduced. Amounts of Stages 1 and 2 were unchanged in two of the three studies of normal subjects in which these measures were examined; in the long-term study of normal subjects, amount of Stage 1 was reduced in the second half of the drug period, and amount of Stage 2 was increased on the first night. Minutes, but not percent, of Stage 2 were also elevated in the schizophrenic patients. All studies suggested some effect of chlorpromazine on Stage 3 and/or Stage 4 sleep: amounts of one or both stages were elevated. In the long-term study of normal subjects, amount of Stage 3 was persistently elevated during the drug period, but amount of Stage 4 was essentially at baseline levels. The definitive studies have not revealed any strikingly consistent effects of chlorpromazine on REM sleep. Amount of REM sleep was changed (elevated) in only one dose-effect study of normal subjects (50 mg); it was unaffected by the drug in both long-term studies. REM latency was reduced in two of the dose-effect studies of normal subjects (100 and 150 mg) and elevated in the schizophrenic patients. Number of REM periods was rather persistently reduced in the long-term study of normal subjects, but was unchanged in other studies. Only in the schizophrenic patients did REM density change: it was increased in comparison to the postdrug period. The recovery period has so far been found to be characterized by relatively few changes. In the long-term study of normal subjects there was an increase in amounts of Stage 1 and Stage 3 on the first recovery night and a decrease in amount of Stage 4 on the fourth through sixth nights; number of REM periods was reduced, especially during the last half of the four-week period. With the highest dosage used in normal subjects (150 mg), the reduction in REM latency that had been seen in the drug period continued on the following recovery night.

Reserpine. There have been five definitive studies of reserpine (Coulter et al., 1971; Hartmann and Cravens, 1973a; Hoffman and Domino, 1969; Murri and Cerone, 1972); their characteristics are listed in Table 6-6. Four studies examined normal subjects; two were dose-effect, one was short-term, and one was long-term. The fifth was a long-term study of chronic schizophrenic patients. Doses have ranged from 0.5 to about 10 mg. Recovery periods were examined in all studies except that of the schizophrenic patients. Efficacy measures were only rarely considered in these studies. The 0.5-mg dose initially reduced sleep latency in the long-term study of normal subjects, but the 0.04- and 0.14-mg/kg doses reduced total sleep time in the dose-effect study. Amount of Stage 1 was

TABLE 6-6. CHARACTERISTICS OF EEG-EOG STUDIES OF ANTIPSYCHOTIC AGENTS.

Authors and Year	No. and Type of Subjects	Dose (mg)	Intake Time[a]	Drug Period Length[b]	Recovery Period Length[b]	Comments
Chlorpromazine						
Saletu, Allen, and Itil, 1974	10 normal	50	hs	1 day	0	
Hartmann and Cravens, 1973c	9 normal	50	20' *a hs*	28 C days	32 C days	Recordings: drug nights 1-5, 12, 18, 25; recovery nights 1-6, 14, 21, 27
Lester and Guerrero Figueroa, 1966	6 normal	100	?	1 day	0	
Lester, Coulter, Cowden and Williams, 1971	12 normal	150	30' *a hs*	1 day	1 day	
Kaplan, Dawson, Vaughan, Green, and Wyatt, 1974	13 chronic schizophrenic	400	4 divided doses	28 C days	28 C days	Recordings: at ends of drug and recovery periods
Reserpine						
Hartmann and Cravens, 1973a	11 normal	0.5	20' *a hs*	28 C days	32 C days	Recordings: drug nights 1-5, 12, 18, 25; recovery nights 1-6, 14, 21, 27
Coulter, Lester, and Williams, 1971	10 normal	1.0	30' *a hs*	1 day	1 day	
Hoffman and Domino, 1969	10 normal 15 normal (5/dose)	1.0 0.01, 0.04, and 0.14 mg/kg body weight	30' *a hs* hs	3 C days 1 day	1 day 3 C days	
Murri and Cerone, 1972	7 chronic schizophrenic	1.0, 3.0, and 5.0 mg	3 divided doses	20+ C days	0	Recordings: nights 2 (1 mg), 20 (5 mg)

[a] *hs*—before bedtime; *hs*—bedtime.
[b] NC—nonconsecutive; C—consecutive.

slightly increased late in the long-term administration of 0.5 mg, it was increased in the dose-effect study of 0.04 and 0.14 mg/kg, but it was unchanged in other studies. Amount of Stage 2 was reduced by doses of 0.04 and 0.14 mg/kg, but increased by the initial 1-mg dose in the schizophrenic patients. Most studies failed to reveal an effect of the drug on Stages 3 and 4, but amounts of these stages combined were reduced with three-day administration of 1 mg, and amount of Stage 4 was reduced by the 0.14-mg/kg dose on one day. Amount of REM sleep was elevated after the first day or two by doses of 0.5 and 1 mg. In the long-term study of 0.5 mg, this increase persisted. In both studies it was accompanied by an increase in the number of REM periods and a nonsignificant decrease in REM latency, and in the three-day study of 1 mg by a reduction in REM density. The single dose of 0.14 mg/kg, by contrast, reduced amount of REM. In the schizophrenic patients, the 1- and 3-mg doses significantly increased the number of REM periods but had no other significant effects on REM measures. Recovery from long-term administration of 0.5 mg was accompanied by a delayed reduction in sleep latency and an initial reduction in amount of Stage 2. In both studies of the 1-mg dose, there was a decrease in amount of Stages 3 and 4 on the recovery night. A reduction in amount of Stage 2 was also observed on recovery from the 0.04- and 0.14-mg/kg doses, and a reduction in amount of Stage 4 was observed with the latter dose. In virtually all studies there was an initial recovery increase in amount of REM and a decrease in REM latency. In the two studies of 1 mg, there was also an increase in the number of REM periods and a decrease in REM density.

DREAMS

Sedative-Hypnotic Agents

Seven of the nine available studies of drugs and dreams deal at least in part with sedative-hypnotic agents. This research emphasis stems from the fact that the primary clinical activity of this class of drugs is on sleep. The accumulated data on the effects of sedative-hypnotic agents on REM sleep led researchers to question whether a reduction in frequency of dreams recalled paralleled the suppression of REM sleep.

Non-laboratory morning-recall studies of drugs such as amobarbital (Morgan et al., 1970), glutethimide (Kales et al., 1969), and methyprylon (Kales et al., 1969; Shaskan et al., 1970) seemed to confirm the prediction that frequency of dream recall would be reduced by sedative-hypnotic agents. In addition, for glutethimide and methyprylon it was found that the number of details in recalled dreams was reduced (Kales et al., 1969). Results in these non-laboratory studies were generally not analyzed statistically, so their conclusions are necessarily only tentative.

A laboratory REM-recall study of meprobamate (in a single subject) also suggested that the frequency of recall was reduced (Whitman, 1963). However, more extensive REM-recall studies of drugs such as phenobarbital (Whitman, 1963), amobarbital (Firth, 1974), an unspecified barbiturate (Carroll et al., 1969), and nitrazepam (Firth, 1974) failed to reveal any significant reduction in the number of dreams recalled.

Examination of the quality of dream content with sedative-hypnotic agents has also produced diverse results. One major contributor to the diversity has been the use of different scales to assess quality of content. For example, non-laboratory morning-recall studies (most without statistical analysis) suggested that amobarbital and nitrazepam reduced hostility but not anxiety (Morgan et al., 1970), that glutethimide reduced unpleasantness and that its cessation increased unpleasantness (Kales et al., 1969), and that methyprylon reduced unpleasantness (Kales et al., 1969) or, by contrast, reduced the number of pleasant dreams and, on withdrawal, reduced the number of unpleasant dreams (Shaskan et al., 1970).

REM-recall studies revealed that phenobarbital increased dependency and homosexuality and reduced intimacy (Whitman, 1963), that an unspecified barbiturate made dreams significantly more conceptual and less perceptual (Carroll et al., 1969), and that meprobamate, given to one subject, increased motility and dependency (Whitman, 1963). Firth (1974) failed to confirm most of the previous results in his study of amobarbital and nitrazepam, but found that amobarbital significantly reduced the number of characters in dreams, and nitrazepam made dreams significantly less bizarre.

Antidepressant Agents

The effect of an antidepressant drug on dreams has been examined in only two studies; the drug was imipramine in both cases. When imipramine, 25 mg, was administered to 10 normal subjects on one night (Whitman, 1963), there were a significant reduction in the frequency of REM-recall dreams and a significant increase in amount of hostility in the dreams. There were also increases in content scores for anxiety and dependency and a decrease in the score for intimacy. Kramer et al. (1968) evaluated the short-term (one week) and long-term (three weeks) effects of imipramine on the REM-recall dreams of seven depressed patients. There was no change from pretreatment placebo levels of recall frequency at either drug evaluation period. The content of dreams after one week of imipramine was characterized by significantly greater hostility and anxiety. These results paralleled those from the study of normal subjects (Whitman, 1963). On the other hand, after three weeks of imipramine the dreams of the depressed patients were characterized by more hostility and anxiety than on placebo nights. There is no immediate explanation for the reversal of the drug effect with long-term administration. Further, it is difficult to separate the drug effect from effects that might be related to the patients' clinical improvement.

Antipsychotic Agents

Only one study of antipsychotic agents was located. Ornstein et al. (1969) in a pilot study evaluated the effects of antipsychotic drugs (type unspecified) on the dreams of schizophrenic patients. They were unable to detect any differences between dreams at the "height of illness" and those at the first evidence of clinical improvement.

SUMMARY AND CONCLUSIONS

Our intention in reviewing the literature on the effects of drugs on sleep patterns was, through presentation of the data on representative drugs, to give the flavor of what is now known about drugs and their effects on the electrophysiological component of dreams, REM sleep. At the same time we attempted to place the findings on REM sleep in their proper context by describing concomitant effects on wakefulness and total sleep and on NREM sleep. With the caveat that allowances must be made for differences in degree of effect among various drugs, among various doses of the same drug, and among various types of subjects, we can summarize data from EEG-EOG studies of sleep patterns by stating that a majority of drugs have at least an initial effect on some measure of total wakefulness and sleep, increase amount of Stage 2 sleep, reduce amounts of Stages 3 and/or 4 sleep, and suppress REM sleep (e.g., decrease amount, increase latency). With discontinuation of the drugs, there may be at least initial continuation of the drug effects (e.g., flurazepam), disruption of sleep patterns (e.g., nitrazepam, glutethimide), or REM rebound (e.g., glutethimide, amitriptyline, reserpine, possibly methaqualone).

Out intention in reviewing the literature on the effects of drugs on dreams was to examine all that is presently known about drugs and their effects on the frequency of dream recall and the quality of dreams. With the caveat that the data are insufficient to provide any firm conclusions, we can infer that the frequency of dreams recalled in the morning is reduced by various drugs, but the frequency of dreams recalled from REM awakenings is not. Further, it appears that some sedative-hypnotic and antidepressant agents may affect the quality of dreams, but the precise nature of the effect is yet to be determined.

The first impression on reviewing the literature on drugs, REM sleep, and dreams is the disparity between the quantity of work performed on the electrophysiology of REM sleep and that on dreams. Even when criteria for adequate methodology were applied in selecting the studies of REM, there were over four times as many studies available for REM as for dreams. The reason for the lack of systematic work on the effects of drugs on dreams is not clear, but perhaps it is related to the relative difficulty of obtaining, scoring, and interpreting valid dream material. In any event, what is clear is that the excitement originally stimulated in 1953 in the systematic study of dreams has not been manifested in adequate work in this promising area.

In spite of the apparent solidity of the research on drugs and REM sleep, a number of criticisms can still be made of this body of work. First and foremost is the frequent failure to employ even minimally adequate research methodology: recall the fact that we deemed only about 25% of available studies worthy of review. Perhaps the greatest shortcoming in this respect has been the use of insufficient numbers of subjects. Another defect has been the failure in many cases to perform sound studies with the drug's target populations in addition to studies of normal subjects. Still another has been the failure to perform dose-response studies. Such studies provide information on specific drug effects, and they are especially needed in this area because of the commonality of the electrophysiological effects observed across various types of drugs. Similarly, there is a need for more studies of the recovery period following discontinuation of drug administration. There are generally more diverse patterns of electrophysiological effects during recovery periods than during drug periods, and greater study of these differences might also contribute to the isolation of drug-specific effects. Finally, only rarely are data from different studies entirely consistent for a particular drug; so for all drugs there is a need to resolve the discrepancies in the existing literature. It is to be hoped that correction of the defects we and others (e.g., Kay et al., 1976) have noted may aid attainment of this goal.

The primary shortcoming of the research on drugs and dreams is, of course, simply the lack of sufficient data. Few if any of the existing studies were more than pilot studies. There has been a failure to examine even one drug in depth, or to follow up on the only seemingly reliable finding, the difference in frequency of dream recall between morning and REM awakenings. Finally, the lack of standardization of methods of assessing quality of dream content has resulted in isolated bits of information that do not yet form a coherent picture.

A number of research questions can and should be explored if we are to understand the effects of drugs on dreams. First are questions of a methodological nature. Perhaps most pressing is the need to examine the relationship between morning and REM recall, both in normal situations and when subjects are taking a drug. Is frequency of recall in the morning some predictable function of frequency of REM recall, or not? Do drugs alter the relationship between the two types of recall? If so, what is the nature of the alteration, does it vary according to class of drug, and what is the mechanism of this effect?

Two major questions with respect to the quality of dream content require attention. First is how best to assess content, especially in drug studies. A number of methods of scoring content exist, but we need to know whether some are more sensitive to drug effects than others. An answer to this question might lead to more standardization in the scoring of content and enhance the likelihood of producing consistent results among studies. Second is the nature of the relationship between scored quality of content and frequency of recall. Obviously, if frequency of recall is reduced, frequency of individual content items may also be reduced. Is the effect of reduced recall frequency nonspecific, or does it selectively affect certain types of content? If this question were answered, it might then be possible to develop a set of correction factors that could be applied when recall frequency is reduced.

The last methodological question concerns the relationship between drug effects and clinical improvement. When patients are administered a drug of therapeutic value, one must automatically wonder whether any changes, in this case in the frequency and nature of dreams, are due to the drug or to changes in the patients' clinical status. Examination of two types of control groups should help resolve this question—normal subjects and the patients during a period of remission or clinical improvement. Use of the patients as their own controls would be especially indicated when the disorder has a suspected biochemical basis.

Another set of questions has to do with more systematic use of existing and forthcoming information on the effects of drugs on REM sleep. This information can be used to generate numerous testable hypotheses. At the most basic level, drugs that are known to suppress REM sleep significantly should be studied for their effects on dreams. In addition, detailed changes in REM density should be examined in relation to changes in frequency of recall and quality of content. Further, for some drugs (e.g., amitriptyline) and amount of REM suppression changes with long-term administration, and it would be of interest to determine whether or not effects on dreams change in an analogous manner. Recovery from drugs that are characterized by recovery REM rebound should receive particular attention, both because it provides an additional opportunity to investigate the parallelism between electrophysiological and psychological events and because of clinical speculation about a relationship between postdrug REM rebound and nightmares (Kales et al., 1969). Finally, as with electrophysiological studies of drug effects, there should be a determination of the specific and nonspecific effects of the various classes (e.g., sedative-hypnotic vs. antidepressant agents) and subclasses (e.g., barbiturates vs. benzodiazepines) of drugs. The dose-response study is one method of approaching this problem.

Our conclusion must be that much work remains to be done in the area of the effects of drugs on dreams. The work will be difficult, but not impossible. It should be facilitated by the existence of reasonably good information on one part of the problem, REM sleep. What researchers must do is seize the opportunities this information affords, and get on with it!

REFERENCES

Adam, K., Adamson, L., Březinová, V., Hunter, W. M., and Oswald, I. Nitrzaepam: Lastingly effective but trouble on withdrawal. *British Medical Journal*, 1: 1558-1560, 1976.

Allen, C., Kales, A., and Berger, R. J. An analysis of the effect of glutethimide on REM density. *Psychonomic Science*, 12: 329-330, 1968.

Allnutt, M. F., and O'Connor, P. J. Comparison of the encephalographic, behavioral and subjective correlates of natural and drug-induced sleep at atypical hours. *Aerospace Medicine*, 42: 1006-1010, 1971.

Aserinsky, E. Drugs and dreams, a synthesis. *Experimental Medicine and Surgery*, 25: 131-138, 1967.

Aserinsky, E., and Kleitman, N. Regularly occurring periods of eye motility, and concomitant phenomena, during sleep. *Science*, 118: 273-274, 1953.

Baekeland, F. Pentobarbital and dextroamphetamine sulfate: Effects on the sleep cycle in man. *Psychopharmacologia*, 11: 388-396, 1967.

Carroll, D., Lewis, S. A., and Oswald, I. Effect of barbiturates on dream content. *Nature*, 223: 865-866, 1969.

Coulter, J. D., Lester, B. K., and Williams, H. L. Reserpine and sleep. *Psychopharmacologia*, 19: 134-147, 1971.

Dement, W. The effect of dream deprivation. *Science*, 131: 1705-1707, 1960.

Firth, H. Sleeping pills and dream content. *British Journal of Psychiatry*, 124: 547-553, 1974.

Goldstein, L., Graedon, J., Willard, D., Goldstein, F., and Smith, R. R. A comparative study of the effects of methaqualone and glutethimide on sleep in male chronic insomniacs. *Journal of Clinical Pharmacology*, 10: 258-268, 1970.

Goldstein, L., Stoltzfus, N. W., and Smith, R. R. An analysis of the effects of methaqualone and glutethimide on sleep in insomniac subjects. *Research Communications in Chemical Pathology and Pharmacology*, 2: 927-933, 1971.

Haider, I., and Oswald, I. Effects of amylobarbitone and nitrazepam on the electrodermogram and other features of sleep. *British Journal of Psychiatry*, 118: 519-522, 1971.

Hartmann, E. The effect of four drugs on sleep patterns in man. *Psychopharmacologia*, 12: 346-353, 1968.

Hartmann, E., and Cravens, J. The effects of long term administration of psychotropic drugs on human sleep: II. The effects of reserpine. *Psychopharmacologia*, 33: 169-184, 1973 (a).

Hartmann, E., and Cravens, J. The effects of long term administration of psychotropic drugs on human sleep: III. The effects of amitriptyline. *Psychopharmacologia*, 33: 185-202, 1973 (b).

Hartmann, E., and Cravens, J. The effects of long term administration of psychotropic drugs on human sleep: IV. The effects of chlorpromazine. *Psychopharmacologia*, 33: 203-218, 1973 (c).

Hoffman, J. S., and Domino, E. F. Comparative effects of reserpine on the sleep cycle of man and cat. *Journal of Pharmacology and Experimental Therapeutics*, 170: 190-198, 1969.

Itil, T. M., Saletu, B., and Marasa, J. Determination of drug-induced changes in sleep quality based on digital computer "sleep prints." *Pharmakopsychiatrie, Neuro-Psychopharmakologie*, 7: 265-280, 1974.

Johns, M. W., and Masterton, J. P. Effect of flurazepam on sleep in the laboratory. *Pharmacology*, 11: 358-364, 1974.

Kales, A., Bixler, E. O., Scharf, M., and Kales, J. D. Sleep laboratory studies of flurazepam: A model for evaluating hypnotic drugs. *Clinical Pharmacology and Therapeutics*, 19: 576-583, 1976.

Kales, A., Hauri, P., Bixler, E. O., and Silberfarb, P. Effectiveness of intermediate-term use of secobarbital. *Clinical Pharmacology and Therapeutics*, 20: 541-545, 1976.

Kales, A., Kales, J. D., Scharf, M. B., and Tan, T.-L. Hypnotics and altered sleep-dream patterns. II. All-night EEG studies of chloral hydrate, flurazepam, and methaqualone. *Archives of General Psychiatry*, 23: 219-225, 1970.

Kales, A., Malmstrom, E. J., Kee, H. K., Kales, J. D., and Tan, T.-L. Effects of hypnotics on sleep patterns, dreaming, and mood stage: Laboratory and home studies. *Biological Psychiatry*, 1: 235-241, 1969.

Kales, A., Preston, T. A., Tan, T.-L., and Allen, C. Hypnotics and altered sleep-dream patterns. I. All-night EEG studies of glutethimide, methyprylon, and pentobarbital. *Archives of General Psychiatry*, 23: 211-218, 1970.

Kaplan, J., Dawson, S., Vaughan, T., Green, R., and Wyatt, R. J. Effect of prolonged chlorpromazine administration on the sleep of chronic schizophrenics. *Archives of General Psychiatry*, 31: 62-66, 1974.

Kay, D. C., Blackburn, A. B., Buckingham, J. A., and Karacan, I. Human pharmacology of sleep. In Williams, R. L., and Karacan, I. (Eds.), *Pharmacology of Sleep*. New York: Wiley, 1976.

Kay, D. C., Jasinski, D. R., Eisenstein, R. B., and Kelly, O. A. Quantified human sleep after pentobarbital. *Clinical Pharmacology and Therapeutics*, 13: 221-231, 1972.

Kramer, M., Whitman, R. M., Baldridge, B., and Ornstein, P. H. Drugs and dreams III: The effects of imipramine on the dreams of depressed patients. *American Journal of Psychiatry*, 124: 1385-1392, 1968.

Lehmann, H. E., and Ban, T. A. The effect of hypnotics on rapid eye movement (REM). *International Journal of Clinical Pharmacology, Therapy, and Toxicology*, 1: 424-427, 1968.

Lester, B. K., Coulter, J. D., Cowden, L. C., and Williams, H. L. Secobarbital and nocturnal physiological patterns. *Psychopharmacologia*, 13: 275-286, 1968.

Lester, B. K., Coulter, J. D., Cowden, L. C., and Williams, H. L. Chlorpromazine and human sleep. *Psychopharmacologia*, 20: 280-287, 1971.

Lester, B. K., and Guerrero-Figueroa, R. Effects of some drugs on electroencephalographic fast activity and dream time. *Psychophysiology*, 2: 224-236, 1966.

Morgan, H., Scott, D. F., and Joyce, C. R. B. The effects of four hypnotic drugs and placebo on normal subjects' sleeping and dreaming at home. *British Journal of Psychiatry*, 117: 649-652, 1970.

Murri, L., and Cerone, G. Effet de réserpine et de L-tryptophane sur le sommeil des malades schizophrénes chroniques. In Jovanović, U. J. (Ed.), *The Nature of Sleep*. International Symposium, Würzburg, September, 1971. Stuttgart: Gustav Fischer Verlag, 1972.

Nakazawa, Y., Kotorii, T., Kotorii, M., Horikawa, S., and Ohshima, M. Effects of amitriptyline on human REM sleep as evaluated by using partial differential REM sleep deprivation (PDRD). *Electroencephalography and Clinical Neurophysiology*, 38: 513-520, 1975.

Nakazawa, Y., Kotorii, M., Kotorii, T., Ohshima, M., and Hasuzawa, H. Individual variations in response of human REM sleep to amitriptyline and haloperidol. *Electroencephalography and Clinical Neurophysiology*, 42: 769-775, 1977.

Nakazawa, Y., Kotorii, M., Ohshima, M., Horikawa, S., and Tachibana, H. Effects of thienodiazepine derivatives on human sleep as compared to those of benzodiazepine derivatives. *Psychopharmacologia*, 44: 165–171, 1975.

Ornstein, P. H., Whitman, R. M., Kramer, M., and Baldridge, B. J. Drugs and dreams IV: Tranquilizers and their effects upon dreams and dreaming in schizophrenic patients. *Experimental Medicine and Surgery*, 27: 145–156, 1969.

Risberg, A.-M., Henricsson, S., and Ingvar, D. H. Evaluation of the effect of fosazepam (a new benzodiazepine), nitrazepam and placebo on sleep patterns in normal subjects. *European Journal of Clinical Pharmacology*, 12: 105–109, 1977.

Risberg, A.-M., Risberg, J., Elmqvist, D., and Ingvar, D. H. Effects of dixyrazine and methaqualone on the sleep pattern in normal man. *European Journal of Clinical Pharmacology*, 8: 227–231, 1975.

Saletu, B., Allen, M., and Itil, T. M. The effect of Coca-Cola, caffeine, antidepressants, and C chlorpromazine on objective and subjective sleep parameters. *Pharmakopsychiatrie, Neuro-Psychopharmakologie*, 7: 307–321, 1974.

Shaskan, D. A., Miller, E. R., and Sears, D. R. Does Noludar (methyprylon) change dreams? *Behavioral Neuropsychiatry*, 1: 22–24, 1970.

Snyder, F., and Scott, J. The psychophysiology of sleep. In Greenfield, N. S., and Sternbach, R. A. (Eds.), *Handbook of Psychophysiology*. New York: Holt, Rinehart, and Winston, 1972.

Vogel, G. W., Barker, K., Gibbons, P., and Thurmond, A. A comparison of the effects of flurazepam 30 mg and triazolam 0.5 mg on the sleep of insomniacs. *Psychopharmacology*, 47: 81–86, 1976.

Whitman, R. M. II. Drugs, dreams and the experimental subject. *Canadian Psychiatric Association Journal*, 8: 395–399, 1963.

7

From Spontaneous Event to Lucidity: A Review of Attempts to Consciously Control Nocturnal Dreaming

Charles T. Tart

Within Western culture, dreams have been and are still generally regarded as events that just happen to people, bizarre nocturnal events that seldom bear any discernible relation to the waking life of the dreamer. If dreams are given any positive value, they are seen as unsolicited gifts. When not particularly valued, the more usual situation in our culture, they are seen as mostly meaningless, chance events. The occasional relationships between life events and dreams tend to be fitted into what Hadfield (1954) charmingly called the "pickled walnut theories" of dreaming: if you ate something that disagreed with you, it might result in the bizarre mental activity of dreaming.

A major shift in the attitude in our culture resulted from Freud's claim, in 1900, that dreams are valuable clues to our unconscious mental life (Freud, 1954). He argued that rather than being spontaneous happenings, dreams are reliably and lawfully related to recent events (day residue), as modified by our fundamental drives and personal developmental history. Life events influence dreams in a transformed, rather than a direct way. He argued that the technique of free association could be used to trace the subtle connections between daily life and dream experience, showing that life experience, interacting with unconscious dynamics, makes the dream a lawfully determined, rather than a spontaneous event. Although most of the evidence supporting Freud's claim is a *post*dictive fitting of life events and dream content together from association in analytic sessions, and so open to alternative explanations, some studies have claimed *pre*dictive validation of this theory.

With the birth of the modern era of sleep research, starting in 1953 with the publication of Eugene Aserinsky and Nathaniel Kleitman's "Regularly occurring periods of eye motility and concommitant phenomena during sleep," more direct tests of whether the content of nocturnal dreams could be directly influenced by presleep operations, such as specific suggestions as to what to dream about, began to be carried out. These studies showed that some direct, untransformed *presleep control of dream content* was possible. Further, publication of Kilton Stewart's paper, "Dream Theory in Malaya," and Frederick van Eeden's "A Study of Dreams" in my widely read *Altered States of Consciousness* (Tart, 1969a) dovetailed with extensive professional and public interest in altered states of consciousness and suggested to many individuals that they could learn to achieve an altered state of consciousness termed "lucid dreaming," a state in which they could exercise conscious control over the events of their dreams *while they were dreaming*, what I shall term *concurrent control of dream content*.

Rather than viewing dream content as either a spontaneous activity or one postdictable (but seldom predictable) only through complex and subtle Freudian dynamics, evidence now demands that we view it as an activity which can be clearly influenced to at least some extent by an individual's presleep desires. Indeed, the psychological quality of dreaming can sometimes be transformed into a discrete state of consciousness (d-SoC)* in which direct, volitional control of content is possible.

I shall review the literature on the control of the content of nocturnal dreaming and on lucid dreams, with special emphasis on methodological considerations relevant to creating a sound scientific knowledge of this area. This review will not deal with ways of affecting the more general process of dreaming, such as shifts in the timing of Stage 1–REM periods, but will focus on content changes. Some of this material has been reviewed from other perspectives also in the last 14 years, and the interested reader should see review papers by Arkin (1966), Evans (1972), Garfield (1974b), Moss (1967), Tart (1965a, b; 1967; 1969b), and Walker and Johnson (1974).

Almost all of the laboratory studies reviewed in this paper have accepted the widely held theory that the d-SoC we call dreaming (a *psychological* construct) is uniquely associated with stage 1–REM periods, or at least that "dreamlike" reports of mental activity are far more frequently associated with awakenings from Stage 1–REM periods than with awakenings from NREM stages of sleep.

---

*The term discrete state of consciousness (d-SoC) will be used throughout this chapter as a scientific term to cover the stabilized patterns of interacting psychological factors called by such common names as "waking state," "hypnosis," "dreaming" "hypnagogic state," and so on, in accordance with its definition and usage in my systems approach to consciousness (see primarily Tart, 1975). The more common term, "state of consciousness," has been used in too general a manner to be scientifically useful.

The latter kinds of awakenings often yield either no recall or reports of more "thoughtlike" activity.

While this assumption will not be explicitly questioned in this review, we should be aware that there are data contradicting this dichotomy (see, Rechtschaffen, 1973, for a review). Some subjects report quite dreamlike activity from NREM awakenings. As an especially striking example, Brown and Cartwright (1978) instructed subjects to press a microswitch taped to one hand whenever they were aware, during sleep, of experiencing visual images. The experimenter then awakened the subject for a report. Eight subjects' reports were scored for their dreamlike quality on a reliable (judges correlated .90) five-point scale. There were as many switch presses by the subjects in NREM sleep as in Stage 1–REM sleep, and the ratings of the reports on dreamlike quality showed that the subjects' own judgments as to when they were experiencing visual imagery in sleep were almost twice as dreamlike as control awakenings initiated on other nights by the experimenter, for both Stage 1–REM and NREM awakenings. A further case study of one high-responding NREM signaler again obtained very dreamlike reports from his NREM awakenings. I believe the next decade of research will have to focus much more closely on the question of just what are the physiological correlates of the psychological d-SoC of dreaming, as our current conceptions are probably too simplistic; but in this review I shall generally use the assumption that the psychological d-SoC we label dreaming is rather uniquely associated with the discrete physiological state we label Stage 1–REM periods.

METHODOLOGICAL CONSIDERATIONS

As we shall see in some detail below, there are a very large number of variables that can potentially affect how attempts to influence nocturnal dream content eventually succeed. The vast majority of these variables have only been studied infrequently and unsystematically. Affecting dream content is a complex, multi-step process, but most of the steps are very poorly specified and understood.

Partially, this is due to the nature of laboratory sleep research: it is an expensive undertaking, and not many variables can be manipulated at one time. Owing to the ambiguous specifications of most of these many variables, I can do little more in the present review than indicate what sorts of things are important to look out for, rather than reach any kind of firm conclusions about the effects of various variables on affecting dream content. Thus, the empirical studies later reviewed can, at this date, do little more than roughly outline *possibilities* about dream content control.

To begin our discussion of the many variables affecting the way attempts to influence dream content exert their effect, consider Figure 7-1. This diagram is deliberately complex in order to illustrate the many variables involved only at the start of the process we consider, namely the giving of some kind of specific presleep suggestions as to what a subject should dream about, either in the context of the sleep laboratory or at home. We shall consider other variables that occur if an altered d-SoC such as hypnosis is added to the process, and the physiological/psychological state transitions inherent in the process of sleeping later.

Figure 7-1 has two major sections. The lower-right-hand series of labeled psychological process blocks and interconnecting arrows represents a systems approach to understanding the major functioning of ordinary, waking consciousness, as described elsewhere (Lee et al., 1975; Tart, 1974a, 1975, 1976, in press). The variables at the upper left, shown as impinging on the subject through his exteroceptors (eyes, ears, and, to some extent, touch, in the laboratory situation), represent the external experimental variables.

To begin with, any experiment is never carried out in isolation, but within a cultural context. Both the experimenters and the subjects have been enculturated within a specific culture to share a relatively common set of views, including attitudes about the importance of dreams, their nature, and the degree to which they can be deliberately manipulated. While we have some historical and anthropological data on different cultural attitudes toward dreams and volitional control of them, I know of no direct experimental data on possible differences; so the most we can do with those cultural variables at the present time is be sensitive to the fact that in many important ways any results we have may be culture-bound. This is a particularly hard point to keep in mind: we tend to think we are investigating basic biological culture-free aspects of man because we are taking physiological measures.

Within the overall cultural context of the experiment, we have a quite complex specific situation which we have long been fooling ourselves into believing is quite simple. We have liked to believe that: (a) the laboratory is a rather neutral setting; (b) a clearly defined experimental manipulation, the independent variable, is applied to a subject; and (c) the behaviors observed, the dependent variables, are either exclusively functions of the independent variable or of the independent variable and random variation. In the latter case, we believe that by running a number of subjects this random variation cancels out, so that we can ascertain the true relationship between the independent and dependent variables. This oversimplified view has now been amply demonstrated to be incorrect for most experimental studies; I recommend Silverman's recent review book (1977) for an excellent overview of the complexities inherent in running a subject in a psychological or physiological) laboratory. A more realistic view is to assume that any subject is an active problem solver, forming his own conclusions about what is expected of him in an experiment. Thus many unknown, covert, or even incidental variables can be potentially more important than formal independent variables.

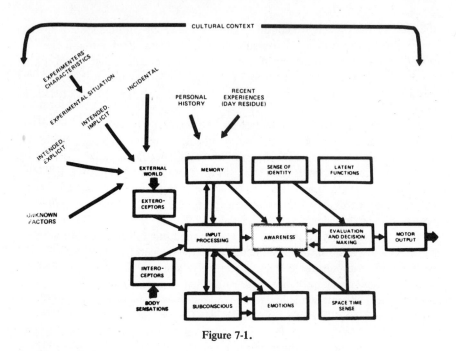

Figure 7-1.

Demand Characteristics

Among the main variables influencing the subject, we must consider the experimenter (or experimenters) and the experimental situation they create. The experimenter's personal characteristics and manner can generally affect the way he treats subjects and probably thus affect their dreams. Experimenter characteristics are almost never described in the reports. What is likely to be described in an experimental report is the formal experimental variable, labeled the "intended, explicit" stimulation that the subject receives in Figure 7-1. Perhaps even more important, experimenters usually have an intellectual and often an emotional investment in verifying a particular hypothesis, and so implicitly and covertly *deliberately* (rather than randomly) affect subjects in ways likely to make this hypothesis come true. This influence is what Orne (1962) has called so nicely the "demand characteristics" of the experimental situation, a covert demand on the subject to please the experimenter by verifying the experimenter's hypothesis. Let us consider a specific example.

Stern and Saayman (in press) carried out a sophisticated study of the effects of implicit demand characteristics of the type likely to be commonplace in sleep research. Both laboratory (two nights) and home dream reports (12 nights) were collected from 12 subjects. All subjects filled out a form asking specific questions about the *settings* of their dreams in addition to asking for a general account of the dream. Half the subjects had forms asking about outdoor/nature settings, half about urban settings: this was the only experimental treatment. The experimenter who interacted with the subjects in the laboratory was blind as to which report-form treatment group the subjects were in. Postexperimental inquiry revealed that none of the subjects consciously guessed that the report form was designed to affect the content of their dreams. A statistically significant effect was found, however, equally spread over the home and laboratory dreams.

The effects of the report forms were assessed both in a global rating of outdoor/nature vs. urban environment, on which two independent judges correlated .80, and with two setting-relevant word-count indices, on which the independent judges correlated .91 and .70. Both types of measure showed a significant increase in suggested settings in the groups receiving each of the two reporting forms, compared to their own baseline dreams. The absolute sizes of the changes were small by the overall rating, about a one-point change on a seven-point scale. The word index measure change was stronger, indicating a three- to fourfold increase in appropriate setting-relevant words.

Although the absolute magnitude of the significant changes in the Stern and Saayman study does not seem large, the potential importance of demand characteristics in affecting other studies about the effects of various presleep suggestions on dream content may become clearer when we realize that the magnitudes of Stern and Saayman's changes were larger than what is reported in many of these other studies.

General Situational Effects

There are many incidental aspects of the experimental situation not directly related to the formal independent variable or the experimenters' covert demands, which have been labeled "incidental" in Figure 7-1. As some examples, the so-called first night effect was recognized early in the era of modern sleep research (Agnew et al., 1966; Domhof and Kamiya, 1964; Kales et al., 1967; Mendels and Hawkins, 1967; Rechtschaffen and Verdone, 1964), and sleep researchers have routinely treated the first laboratory night as an adaptation one without analyzing its data as a consequence. The particulars of a laboratory situation may affect dream content for more than a single night, however (see, e.g., Dement et al., 1965; Hall, 1967; Whitman et al., 1962). The general characteristics of the experimenter who works with a subject may directly or indirectly affect dream content (Fox et al., 1968; Keith, 1962; Tart, 1964a; Whitman et al., 1963). Further, it is not clear how much the content of dreams reported in the laboratory is representative of home dream content, and there have been some demonstrations that content characteristics of laboratory and home dreams differ (see, e.g., Domhof and Kamiya, 1964; Hall and Van de Castle, 1966).

Day Residue

Subjects do not enter the sleep laboratory from a vacuum: they have had a whole developmental history of their own which is likely to influence the kind of dreams they have, and, even more specifically, they have had a variety of experiences over the past few days which may influence their dreams. We may lump these influences together as "day residue," understanding that it is not necessarily limited to only the previous 24 hours. There is typically no specification or attempts to even assess what kinds of day residues subjects may bring to the laboratory with them; so this is a very uncontrolled variable. As with the other variables discussed, it is a poor (albeit common) assumption to believe that the particulars of subjects' day residues cancel out in a random fashion, given the small number of subjects in most dream studies.

The Subject's Internal Processes

Considering now the subject himself, the lower-right-hand portion of Figure 7-1 is a diagram of my systems approach to understanding ordinary consciousness. No attempt will be made to explain it in full here, but it will simply be used to illustrate several important points. First, consciousness is not simply "there"; it is an active, ongoing, constructive process. Second, while we can identify components of it for convenience of analysis (for instance the various labeled processes in Figure 7-1), we must also recognize that, as in any system, consciousness as a whole has emergent system properties that are not straightforward predictions from a knowledge of component psychological processes. Thus the subject is in the laboratory situation, and a variety of stimuli are impinging on his exteroceptors, but this in no way results in a "simple perception" of what we naively assume is there. Our sensory input goes through complex, nonconscious, automated construction processes, processes resulting from our personal socialization. The complex constructions we naively take as simple perceptions thus reflect our personal history, and are influenced by the total system properties, including our needs, at the moment. Thus Figure 7-1 shows all stimuli passing through the Input Processing subsystem before they result in any kind of awareness. Input Processing itself is influenced by our permanent characteristics as embodied in memory, by various kinds of processes we call subconscious or unconscious, by our emotions, by our sense of identity, and so forth. This highly processed construction of what is going on may sometimes bear little resemblance to what an outside observer or the experimenter would say is going on in the laboratory.

In terms of experimental design, what we as experimenters think is the essential nature of the stimuli applied to the subject may not be the way the subject perceives these things at all; so our interpretation of results may be very misleading. Further, it must be emphasized how *active* this process is: while much of the construction/perception of the experimental situation and experimental demands is automated, the subject also actively attempts to understand it, evaluates the situation, and makes some decisions about how he should behave. Usually there is no motor output, as the subject does not actively behave at the time he is getting sleep suggestions, but only later in reporting dream content.

By and large most experiments have been done with an implicit assumption that the "ordinary consciousness" of each subject, the results of this complex systems interaction, is pretty much the same and/or is lawfully related to a few, specifiable personality variables. Considering the number of emergent system properties that can occur, given just what we know currently about psychology, this is a grossly oversimplified assumption.

At the start of the process of attempting to influence nocturnal dreaming then, what we have, as sketched in Figure 7-1, is a quite complex situation, full of implicit demands and many important unknowns as well as an overtly described experimental procedure, to which quite unique individual subjects actively react in ways for which there are usually not even attempts at assessment, much less assessment in any adequate detail. The simple question, "What did you believe we really expected from the laboratory procedure?", for example, is distinguished in sleep research by its rarity. Familiarity with the research on experimenter bias and demand characteristics, excellently reviewed in Silverman's (1977) book, will reveal that this kind of question is a necessary even if a minimal start; and we must move toward sophisticated postexperimental inquiry in this area, toward specifying what the laboratory situation is and what the subjects have made of it.

The Addition of an Altered State Procedure

We shall now consider the additional complexities introduced into affecting dream content when an altered state of consciousness, such as hypnosis, is used to influence the subject. We shall simplify the systems diagram of consciousness used in Figure 7-1 into four more global processes, as sketched in Figure 7-2, namely, Input Processing, Cognitive Processes, Memory Processes (the effects of the various experimental variables and particularly the presleep suggestions must be carried in memory for some time before they become effective), and Motor Output to represent some sort of final behavior, typically the reporting of mental activity during sleep. Figure 7-3 is a simplified diagram of what happens between the time the presleep suggestion about dream content is given and the time when a subject is told to go to sleep. In the simplest situation, illustrated in the top third of the figure, the conscious, overt presleep suggestion/stimulation is given; the subject is, in his own constructed way, aware of what it is that is expected of

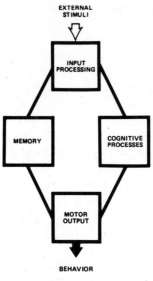

EXTERNAL
STIMULI

INPUT
PROCESSING

MEMORY

COGNITIVE
PROCESSES

MOTOR
OUTPUT

BEHAVIOR

Figure 7-2.

him, such as "Dream about X tonight in all your dreams"; and he stores this suggestion/expectation in memory. I have represented this storage by the black dot in the left-hand box, which represents memory in the simplified systems sketch. A varying period of time then passes in which no other major events (as far as the *experimenter* is concerned) happen, and the subject is told to go to sleep. Subjects, however, are probably trying various types and intensities of procedures to influence their later dreams. Typically there is no experimental assessment at all of what subjects do during this time!

A large class of experiments, which will be discussed briefly later, is what we might call nonconscious or implicit presleep suggestion/stimulation, in that a subject is not overtly told that he is expected to dream about certain kinds of stimuli which have been presented to him before he goes to sleep. Here the stored content is represented in the bottom third of Figure 7-3 as dissociated from what a subject *presumably* could consciously verbalize about the purpose of the experiment: dissociation is represented as a partial wall in the memory subsystem in the figure. Note that I emphasize the "presumably" here: given what we have looked at about demand characteristics and the active, problem-solving approach of many subjects, subjects might quite often be able consciously to verbalize what the experiment was about if they thought it was all right to do so; but here we consider the special case where a subject is not consciously aware of the presleep stimulation pattern that is intended to affect him, but neverthe-less it has some kind of effect. I shall give a few examples later on. As with overt

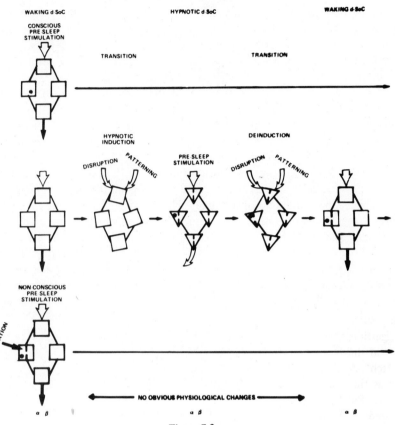

Figure 7-3.

presleep suggestion, there are no other experimental manipulations carried out before the subject is told to go to sleep.

Now let us consider the case where hypnotic suggestion is used to give a suggestion about dream content that is intended to be acted upon posthypnotically during sleep. The subject starts the experiment in his ordinary state of consciousness, represented by the simplified systems diagram at the left of the middle third of Figure 7-3. A hypnotic induction procedure is carried out. In terms of my systems approach, this consists of applying various psychological stimuli, which disrupt the stability of the subject's ordinary d-SoC. Patterning stimuli are also applied, which, following successful disruption of the ordinary d-SoC, restructure the subject's conscious functioning into the d-SoC we call hypnosis. There is a brief transitional period between this disruption and the formation of the hypnotic d-SoC, whose nature is largely unknown. I have indicated it in Figure 7-3 by tilting the boxes representing the various subsystems to show a temporary change in the relationships or systems properties of consciousness. If the hypnotic induction is successful, the altered d-SoC of hypnosis results, with its stabilized but altered psychological functioning represented by the triangular boxes for the simplified systems diagram of consciousness.

Presleep suggestions as to what to dream about are then given to the subject in the hypnotic d-SoC. If, as is often the case, amnesia for these presleep suggestions is also suggested, the presleep content suggestion is stored in memory in a dissociated fashion. This is represented by the partial wall on the memory subsystem, and, just to remind ourselves of the many dissociative phenomena characteristics of hypnosis, the partial wall representing dissociation has been shown in other subsystems. A procedure is then gone through to dehypnotize the subject, the deinduction procedure. This is similar to the induction procedure in that disrupting stimuli to destabilize the hypnotic state are given, and patterning stimuli to reinduce the ordinary state of consciousness are applied. A poorly understand transitional period results, represented by tilting the boxes representing the various hypnotic d-SoC subsystems here, and the subject's ordinary state of consciousness is reinduced. If amnesia has been suggested, the presleep suggestions exist in memory, but in a dissociated form. The nature of the process of inducing any altered state of consciousness, especially hypnosis, is discussed at greater length elsewhere (Lee et al., 1975; Tart, 1974a, 1975, 1976, in press). The subject is now ready to go to sleep.

State Changes Resulting from Sleep

Figure 7-4 represents the various states and transitions to consider in sleep that may affect the action of the presleep content suggestion. Once a subject is told to go to sleep, after a varying period of time he will enter a hypnagogic period, which, in the systems approach, is usually viewed as a transition into sleep rather than as a stabilized d-SoC itself. This transition is represented at the left of Figure 7-4. The quality we call "sleepiness" as well as other factors such as lying down in a quiet place and deciding to go to sleep, constitute disrupting and patterning forces which destabilize the waking state and produce the hypnagogic state. Motor output is shown as blocked, as a subject lies still in order to go to sleep. The EEG shows a pattern of mixed alpha and theta, and eventually a clear stage 1 pattern.

A "successful induction," successfully going to sleep, leads to the d-SoC of "dreamless" sleep, usually associated with Stages 2, 3, and 4 of the EEG with no rapid eye movements (NREM). The EEG is characterized by theta, spindles, and delta, depending on the stage. This different physiological state and correspondingly different d-SoC are represented in Figure 7-4 by a change in the

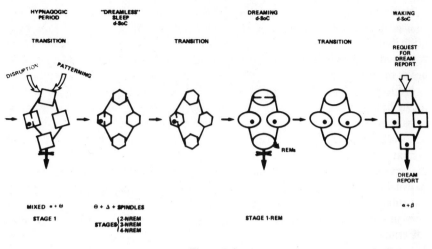

Figure 7-4.

shape of the systems diagram again. Note that in both the hypnagogic transition into sleep and the NREM sleep which results, the presleep content suggestion is still being carried along in memory, in a dissociated form if amnesia has been suggested.

Although possible physiological correlates of this have not been established yet, the systems approach predicts a brief transition period in going from NREM sleep into Stage 1–REM sleep where the psychological activity of dreaming usually occurs. This transition period is again represented in the figure by tilting the subsystem boxes. Then a physiological and psychological state change occurs and the Stage 1–REM state associated with nocturnal dreaming occurs (is induced), stabilizes, and persists for some period of time. Rapid eye movements, usually correlated with dream imagery, characterize this state, although other motor output is actively inhibited by a paralysis of neuromuscular junctions. Sensory input is rather strongly blocked from the d-SoC of dreaming, and this condition is represented by a partial wall across the Input Processing subsystem. If it is effective, the presleep content suggestion is now not only active in the memory subsystem but active in various cognitive and emotional subsystems where the experienced dream content is created and reacted to. A dot representing this has been put in these other subsystems.

In order to find out to what extent the presleep suggestion has been effective, we usually deliberately awaken the subject or allow the subject to awaken himself. Figure 7-4 illustrates an awakening from Stage 1–REM dreaming, but is also applicable to awakenings from NREM sleep. We apply some stimulus to awaken a subject, or it happens naturally; there is again some kind of brief transitional period where the system properties of the dreaming d-SoC become unstable and break down; and the system goes through a reorganization to produce the waking d-SoC where we request a dream report. The presleep suggestion and/or its effects are now active in memory and cognitive processing, and being expressed via the Motor Output subsystem to produce the dream report which we observe.

A large number of changes have taken place prior to our getting our *first* dream report. Memory, which we tend implicitly to assume holds the presleep suggestion rather steadily, has had to carry the presleep suggestion through a variety of transitions, a variety of physiological state and psychological d-SoC changes, any one of which might presumably have some effects on it. Each of the various state changes may also have effects on how the experimental task is perceived, the subject's desires as to how to react to it, how to understand it, and so on. We do not have sufficient knowledge even to begin to speculate on the various effects of this wide variety and number of state changes, but clearly we shall have to be sensitive to them in future experimental research. Later awakenings involve even more of these changes. The major point here is that it is relatively easy at the current state of our knowledge to conceptualize a very large number of variables which may affect our results, and we cannot even begin to specify or speculate on the effects of many of them at this stage of our knowledge.

Inquiry Variables

The action of asking the subject for a report of mental activity preceding an awakening is not the simple one it seems to be. Early in the era of modern sleep research, for example, it was discovered that "simply" asking "Were you dreaming?" was a complex question, involving *simultaneously* asking (1) whether any mental activity could be remembered, and (2) whether the subject would then classify that mental activity as "dreaming," according to his own, idiosyncratic norms. Asking the more neutral question "Was anything going through your mind just before I awakened you?" produced different sorts of answers, such as a much higher percentage of recall from NREM awakenings. Similarly, the questioning process designed to elicit whether there was compliance with the presleep content suggestion can introduce many variables. Practically all experiments now start with a relatively neutral question on the order of "What was going through your mind just before I awakened you?", as it would be obviously biased to ask "Were you dreaming about X?" Almost all of the experiments, however, ask for "clarification" and "further details" on dream reports, and there is considerable possibility of subtly and implicitly exerting psychological pressure on subjects to distort their report to comply here. This was an obvious problem with the early psychoanalytically oriented studies in this area (Fisher, 1953, 1954, 1960;

Malamud and Linder, 1931; Nachmansohn, 1925; Poetzl, cited by Ramsey, 1953; Schrötter, 1912). Full reporting of experimental inquiry procedure here is a must, and further specification of possible implicit demands in this procedure is in order. Outside observers' evaluation of demands would be a methodological advance. By and large there is no standardization of the way requests for greater detail and clarification are carried out from experiment to experiment.

Analysis Variables

Experiments never stop with reports of mental activity, the raw data. They are *analyzed* as to what they "mean," especially in terms of the presleep content suggestions. Except for all-too-occasional repetitions of an experiment in the same laboratory (see, e.g., Tart, 1964b, 1966; Tart and Dick, 1970), there are no standardized analysis procedures for judging how well the subject has complied with the presleep content suggestions. Two general types of analysis procedures have been used, one a general measure of overall thematic compliance, the other an attempt to count the number of times specific elements of the suggestion appear in the reports. Sometimes the degree of reliability of the analysis/judging procedures is not specified. Questions of the validity of the analysis procedures, reliable or not, have seldom even been raised. In reviewing specific studies later, I shall try to make some comparisons of the strength of the content suggestion effect, but these must be very rough because of this lack of standardization or comparability of analysis procedures.

To reiterate the main point of this section on methodological considerations, the number of actual studies of control of the content of dreams is far too small to assess adequately the effects of even a small number of the many variables which are probably important in affecting the content control process. The empirical studies which we now turn our attention to, then, must be seen as illustrating possibilities rather than drawing conclusions.

CONTROLLING DREAM CONTENT BY IMPLICIT SUGGESTION

Many studies have been carried out in which the experimental treatment consisted of exposing subjects to some stimulus condition before they went to sleep, with later awakenings for reports, in order to see if the stimulus condition affected their reported dream content. Subjects were not overtly instructed to have dreams about the experimental treatment, nor were they overtly told that the purpose of the experiment was to see if the experimental treatment would affect their dreams; so the investigators have usually conceptualized these studies as being about relatively direct and nonconscious effects on dreams content. Many of them seem to be based on implicit stimulus-response or physiological models, where a treatment, like giving a drug, is conceptualized as having a direct effect on the biological organism, which is then reflected in dream content reports or physiological variables. From our modern understanding of the active, problem-solving orientation of many experimental subjects, however, it is clear that it may be more profitable to view these kinds of studies as ones involving *implicit presleep suggestion* to dream about a particular topic, the experimental treatment. The effects of such implicit suggestion, mixed with varying (and almost always unassessed) degrees of conscious understanding of and reaction to the suggestion by the subjects, are thus confounded with any more direct effects the experimental treatments may have had. In terms of the methodological points sketched in Figure 7-3, we have unknown degrees of reactive responses to the treatment: how much, e.g., might a subject have self-instructed himself to dream about the specified topic while falling asleep?

I shall make no attempt to review this quite large literature here, but merely give two examples to illustrate the procedures.

In a study by De Koninck and Koulack (1975), 16 subjects slept three non-consecutive nights in the laboratory. They viewed a stressful film of industrial accidents before sleep. The film showed two workers losing fingers in machine accidents and another killed by a flying board shot from a circular saw because of another worker's carelessness. Half the subjects saw only the film before sleep, the other half had the sound track from the film played softly to them during Stage 1–REM periods, as well as a presleep viewing of the film. Mood assessment showed the film was an effective stressor. No overt suggestions to dream about the film were made.

Only subjects in the film-plus-sound group showed statistically significant incorporation of the film in their reported dreams (baseline mean of .27 identifiable film elements vs. a mean of .89 elements on the experimental night). The magnitude of the effect is quite small, even if statistically significant. This very small magnitude of effect is typical of the implicit suggestion studies.

Although most of the implicit suggestion studies seem blithefully unaware of experimenter effects, a series of studies by Roffwarg and his colleagues (Roffwarg et al., in press) shows a fine sensitivity to the implicit demands of the laboratory situation. Subjects wore red goggles for prolonged periods before sleep in order to test the hypothesis that this prolonged change in the quality of visual input would affect the visual qualities of reported State 1–REMP dreams. The goggle effects were quite strong, producing many visual dream worlds that were tinted the way the ordinary world was experienced while wearing the goggles. Roffwarg and his colleagues realized that the subjects would undoubtedly make some kind of connection between wearing the goggles and being asked about color in their dreams, and so the subjects were asked to keep track of their expectations about the experiment as it progressed. The goggle effect was shown as strongly by subjects who formed incorrect hypotheses as to what the purpose of the studies really was as by those who correctly stated its purpose. As a further control, one or more subjects (the rough version of the chapter available to me at this time is ambiguous as to how many subjects were actually used) were deliberately biased to expect the greenish *after-image* experienced after removing the goggles while awake to dominate the colors of their dreams, but the usual, reddish goggle effect was seen in the dream reports. This study is reassuring in showing that effects on dream content do not necessarily have to be mediated through suggestion!

OVERT PRESLEEP SUGGESTION STUDIES

We shall now review a number of studies in which subjects were overtly told to try to dream about a specific, suggested topic just before they went to sleep.

Cartwright (1974) had 17 college student subjects rate various self vs. ideal self characteristic traits with a Q sort. A discrepant trait was individually selected for each subject, and, after being wired for physiological recordings, the subject was instructed to try to dream about having a valued (or in other conditions *not* having a *non*valued) trait by repeating over and over to himself as he fell asleep a suggestion to that effect. After each Stage 1-REM period awakening for dream recall, the subjects were reminded to repeat the suggestion again as they went back to sleep.

Judges averaged 87% agreement on rating the presence or absence of the experimental traits in the dream reports. Two control traits were also scored for, one of about equal discrepancy between self and ideal self, the other of zero discrepancy: neither had any suggestions given to dream about it.

Fifteen of the 17 subjects showed at least one instance of the appearance of the experimental trait in their four Stage 1-REM period dream recalls. Control traits also appeared rather frequently, however, and Cartwright comments that the incorporations of the suggested traits were typically weak and indirect.

In the same year Garfield (1974a) reported a case study of self-conditioning of home recalled dream content in a practiced dream recaller who could regularly awaken several times per night and recall dreams. The subject tried to increase the frequency of images of his hands appearing in dreams (I presume this was inspired by the technique for *dreaming* described by Castaneda, 1971, 1973, 1974, 1977) for five months, and the frequency of flying dreams for twelve months. Compared to a baseline month, the frequency of hand images stayed about the same (14%), but a subset of them took on a quality of extraordinary vividness. The frequency of flying dreams went from 2% in a one-month baseline period to 4% in the experimental period, again with a marked qualitative change involving intense kinesthetic sensations as part of the dreams of flying.

In a brief clinical note, Garfield (1975a) reports teaching students in "creative dreaming" (Garfield, 1974b) classes to "confront or conquer danger in your dreams." If threatened or attacked by a dream character, students were to move toward it and/or counterattack. The presleep suggestion is here a general admonition, carried out by the subjects at home over many nights. Although no quantitative data are presented, Garfield reports that a large majority of her students found themselves occasionally able to recall these instructions while dreaming and were thus able to confront and master fearful dream images. She recommends this as a tool for assertion training, as there was some carryover of a more positive attitude into threatening waking life situations. Other clinicians (Greenleaf, 1973; Latner and Sabini, 1972) have reported similar observations from this kind of active, group dream discussion work.

Foulkes and Griffin (1976), stimulated by Garfield's (1974a,b) work, attempted to see how much subjects could deliberately influence their dream content working under their usual sleep-at-home conditions. Twenty-three college students who professed an interest in dream control along the lines outlined in Garfield's (1974b) popular book each submitted a list of six dream topic suggestions of a simple subject-verb-object type. The experimenters randomly selected one of the six as a constant dream goal for a given subject for all his or her 10 consecutive nights of attempting to influence dreams. For a subgroup of 10, the randomly selected suggestion came from the submitted list of a like-sexed peer. These measures controlled for dreaming about a selected topic resulting primarily from personal preoccupations.

Each subject's collection of home dream reports, ranging from one to ten dreams each, was carefully edited for contaminating information (such as reference to the presleep topic suggestion) and given, along with the list of six possible suggestions, to each of two psychologist judges with long experience in dream research. The judges' task was to identify which suggestion was intended to influence a particular subject's dream reports.

For 23 subjects and a sixfold matching task like this, we would expect about four correct matches by chance alone. One judge got six correct, and the other got three, with only one common correct match between them; so there was no evidence for deliberate control of reported dream content among this group of subjects.

Griffin and Foulkes (1977) repeated the Foulkes and Griffin (1976) study with several improvements which they believed would make successful dream control more likely. With 29 new subjects and four judges, we would expect about 7.25 correct matches per judge by chance alone. The four judges got nine, six, five, and five correct matches, with only two joint hits among the four judges; so the replication again gave no evidence for conscious dream control.

These two studies, questioning the reality of deliberate presleep control, bear an interesting parallel to two studies by Foulkes and his colleagues (Belvedere and Foulkes, 1971; Foulkes et al., 1972) in which they failed to replicate the rather successful ostensibly telepathic content control effects reported from the Maimonides Medical Center laboratory and elsewhere (see Van de Castle, 1977, for a recent review of that literature). Foulkes (as reported in Van de Castle, 1977, p. 491) reports that he and his staff had an air of aggressive skepticism that might have inhibited possible telepathic effects in those studies: could a similar bias have existed in the studies of deliberate presleep content control? Although space considerations preclude further consideration of ostensible telepathic effects on dreams here, it should be noted that the magnitude of that effect often seems to exceed the magnitude of the effects of presleep suggestion through ordinary sensory channels; so it deserves a careful examination.

A number of other studies have given postive evidence for deliberate presleep content control. Hiew (1976a) had 16 college student subjects try to influence the content of their dreams at home. Student experimenters who were acquaintances of the subjects gave one of four possible topic suggestions (riding a bicycle; going on a fishing trip; involvement in a car accident; hearing about a world war breaking out) on three consecutive nights, following an adaptation night. The subjects recorded their own dreams in the morning. Control subjects recorded their dreams, but received no suggestion of a topic. Four judges worked independently to score the presence or absence of each suggested topic in the dream reports. They collaborated on final scoring, but no data are presented on their initial degree of agreement.

Ten of the 19 dreams reported by the experimental subjects contained the suggested topics, while only one of the 15 dreams reported by the control group did. Seven of the compliant experimental dreams were about the pleasant suggested topics, and only three about the unpleasant ones. Subjects who reported themselves as likely to linger in bed after awakening in the morning, to waken by themselves, and to be introspective tended to show more compliance with the experimental suggestions. No data are given that would allow the magnitude of the experimental effect to be assessed.

In another study, Hiew (1976b) requested 70 subjects to suggest to themselves as they fell asleep at home that they would dream about eating a pleasant meal. Each subject recorded his own dreams on alarm-clock-initiated arousal in the morning. Hiew presents no data on the degree of content control *per se*, but rather on the relation of degree of control to other variables, studied through correlational and factor analytic techniques. Since significant relationships are reported, there must have been some content control. He found that those better at dream control generally recalled dreams more frequently and with higher vividness, and considered dreaming to be a meaningful activity. They tended to introspect about their own life and to daydream more frequently.

Immediate presleep factors like mood or degree of activation were not related to success in dream control.

Hiew's study is important in highlighting the importance of subjects' attitudes toward the task of controlling dreaming: we probably should not expect very good results from subjects who do not consider the task very important. Hiew's finding here may be stronger than was empirically found, as the correlations obtained would probably underestimate the true population correlations, owing to a fair number of dreams about such a common topic as eating a pleasant meal probably occurring by chance.

Hiew and Short (1977) investigated the effects of suggested dream topics on dreams reported from laboratory awakenings. Although they woke subjects from NREM as well as Stage 1–REM periods, for a total of four awakenings per subject, their initial analyses do not segregate reports from these different kinds of awakenings; so we will simply call them sleep awakenings here. Twenty-four subjects were used with four subjects each in a 3 X 2 factorial design. The three main conditions were a positive affective tone to the suggested topic (dream about eating a pleasant meal) vs. an unpleasantly toned suggestion (eating an unpleasant meal and getting sick from it) vs. no specific topic suggestion. All of the subjects heard a repeated tone every 30 seconds as they were falling asleep: half of them were instructed that it was a reminder for them to think about the suggested topic; the other half were told it was merely a timing signal they could ignore.

Although details on the scoring of content compliance are sparse, each dream could apparently receive zero to four points, depending on the number of elements of the suggested topic incorporated. No data on judging reliability are presented. The suggestion of eating was apparently something likely to be dreamed about anyway, and so a poor choice as a stimulus, as half of the subjects who had no topic suggested to them dreamed about it at least once, as I suggested earlier. The count of the number of suggested elements in the sleep awakening reports clearly discriminated the positive affect suggestion group from both the negative affect and no suggestion groups (total elements of 30, 7, and 9, respectively, over all subjects). The highest number of elements scored for a single subject was seven: over a total of four awakenings, this is not quite two elements of the suggested topic per report. The tone cue did not seem to have any clear effect on compliance with the suggested topic, but the affective dimension did, with positive affect eliciting much more compliance. Since Hiew and Short report that all the suggestions were given in a permissive, nonauthoritarian manner, the subjects might have not tried very hard to dream about the unpleasant topic.

Brunette and De Koninck (1977) had 24 female subjects who strongly disliked snakes sleep for four nonconsecutive nights in the laboratory. After an adaptation and baseline night, presleep content suggestions were administered on the last two nights, and dream reports were obtained from Stage 1–REM awakenings. Six subjects received suggestions to have pleasant dreams involving a snake, six to have pleasant dreams involving a neutral object, six to have unpleasant dreams involving a snake, and six to have unpleasant dreams involving a neutral object. Dream reports were analyzed with the Hall and Van de Castle (1966) scales. The two pleasant dream suggestion groups reported dreams that had significantly higher levels of tranquility, happiness, friendliness, surgency, and social affection, and significantly lower levels of anxiety, sadness, and aggression. While the authors report statistically significant ($P < .05$) incorporation of the elements of the suggestion, no quantitative data on its magnitude are given, but we can guess that it was probably small and in line with other studies averaging one element or less per dream. No data are reported on differences between the neutral and snake condition.

Reed (1976) reports what is probably the most active attempt to influence dream content, a modern form of ancient *dream incubation* rituals. Many ancient and traditional cultures had special ceremonies, usually in conjunction with healing needs, where, after ritual preparation, a person (the incubant) would have a specially meaningful dream that would give indications for working through his physical or psychological health problems. Reed carefully selected potential incubants, largely on the basis of their current recalled dreams suggesting they could profit from this kind of treatment. After several days of preparation, involving growth- and therapeutic-oriented discussions of current problems, as well as symbolic preparations reinforcing the expectation that the incubant would receive dream help from his own inner resources, the incubant spent the night alone in a special setting, a tent set aside for these incubation procedures. Reed's report of results is preliminary, but he reports important growth benefits obtained by almost all incubants, especially as the dreams recalled on the special night were worked through and integrated into daily living.

Many incubants also reported what seemed like altered d-SoC experiences which they labeled "visions," rather than dreams. One of these was so profound that Reed temporarily discontinued using the dream incubation technique until better understanding of the basic processes was available. It is instructive to quote Reed's description of this "vision," which occurred in addition to a number of meaningful dreams:

> She awoke, startled to find that a strong wind was blowing, and that the tent had blown away. A small, old woman appeared, calling out the incubant's name, and commanded her to awaken and pay attention to what was about to happen. The woman said that she was preparing the incubant's body for death, and that the winds were spirits which would pass through her body to check the seven glands. The incubant was at first afraid, then took comfort

in the old woman's aura of confidence and authority, and finally yielded her body to the experience, almost pleased with the prospect of death. During this time the incubant saw before her a large luminous tablet, containing many columns of fine print, detailing her experiences in her past and future lives. The vision ended abruptly, and the incubant found herself lying within the tent as if she had awakened from a dream. She reported that this experience was qualitatively different, however, from any of her other dreams or psychedelic experiences. (Reed, 1976, pp. 22–23)

I am impressed with the remarkable similarity of this experience to anthropological accounts of the initiatory and training visions of shamans in traditional cultures (see, e.g., Eliade, 1964). There may have been idiosyncratic factors in this particular case, but Reed's general experiences suggest that quite powerful and personally meaningful control can be exercised over dreams.

One additional study of overt presleep content suggestion, a group in the Barber et al. (1973) study, will be discussed in the next section.

POSTHYPNOTIC CONTROL OF DREAM CONTENT

A number of older studies carried out within a psychoanalytic framework (Fisher, 1953, 1954, 1960; Malamud and Linder, 1931; Nachmansohn, 1925; Poetzl, cited by Ramsey, 1953; Schrötter, 1912) took it for granted that hypnotic suggestion was a highly effective method for implanting a posthypnotic dream suggestion in the unconscious, and thus used hypnosis primarily as a tool for studying the specifics of dream formation along psychoanalytically predicted lines. A modern example of this approach is that of Whitman et al. (1964). Their procedure used trained hypnotic subjects, capable of posthypnotic amnesia. On an experimental day, a subject was hypnotized in the morning, and one of 25 structural conflicts was randomly selected from a prepared list and suggested as a dream stimulus. A hypnotic dream was sometimes immediately elicited, but it was expected that the suggested structural conflict would influence later sleep dreams. Amnesia was suggested, and tested for effectiveness. Following an immediate psychiatric interview, the subject went about his daily routine until reporting to the sleep laboratory that evening. Stage 1-REM dream reports and associations to them were collected during the night. The dream reports and associations were later examined blind by the research team to see if the focal conflict suggestion could be identified and the mechanisms of dream formation discovered. The technique is in principle quite interesting, but only an initial case report has been published. Other results obtained with it were complex and contradictory, although clinically useful; so the study was discontinued (Whitman, personal communication, 1978).

As I suggested in my earlier review of attempts deliberately to control dream content (Tart, 1965a), the appearance of classic psychoanalytic transformations in the posthypnotically suggested dreams of the older studies could very likely have been due to the implicit demand characteristics of the experiments. The older studies thus present evidence that presleep content suggestions *can* be transformed along classic psychoanalytic dream work lines, affecting the latent rather than the manifest content, but they do not prove that this is a "normal" mechanism. In the more modern studies to be reviewed below, experimenters who were not analysts seem to have expected to affect dream content *directly* with posthypnotic suggestions, and they got direct effects.

Stoyva (1965), in a 1961 dissertation, was the first to investigate the effects of posthypnotic suggestion of content on dreaming with modern sleep laboratory procedures. Using 16 college student subjects who showed at least a moderate degree of hypnotic responsiveness, Stoyva would hypnotically suggest that they would posthypnotically dream about some simple topic, such as climbing a tree, or beating a drum, on a specified laboratory night. The subjects were generally awakened for dream reports near the estimated end of early Stage 1-REM periods. Seven of his 16 subjects reported dreams that were clearly influenced by the posthypnotic suggestions between 71 and 100% of the time, with some subjects dreaming about the suggested topic in every one of their Stage 1-REM periods. All but two of the 16 subjects had at least an occasional dream about the suggested topics. Stoyva also found some influence of the suggested topics on the "thinking" reports obtained from NREM periods. Since Stoyva usually used single-element suggestions, we may estimate a peak effect of about one element per dream.

Tart (1946b) trained 10 selected college student subjects to reach a deep hypnotic state, defined by successful posthypnotic amnesia and high reports on a self-report scale of hypnotic depth (see Tart, 1970, 1972a, for a review of such scales). Each subject's response to hypnotic suggestions to dream in the hypnotic state, as well as posthypnotic suggestions to dream during sleep for a single night, was studied. We shall focus on the responses from Stage 1-REM awakenings here, as the study conclusively showed that dreams in the hypnotic state were not the same physiologically as Stage 1-REM nocturnal dreams (see Tart, 1965b, for a review of the literature on hypnotic dreams).

Subjects received either of two complex dream narratives as a posthypnotic suggestion. Each narrative was exciting, had a fearful affective tone, and contained 23 scorable elements. Two blind judges correlated .99 on element scoring. Five of the 10 subjects showed at least one Stage 1-REM dream report with at least one suggested element appearing in it, with one individual having all five of his Stage 1-REM reports contain at least seven suggested elements in each. The highest number of suggested elements in a single dream report was 13.

This study was also concerned with whether Freudian-type transformations of the suggested content occurred, as had been reported in the older studies: this was the reason for the strong, negative affective tone of the suggestions. No indication of any such transformations occurred in the obvious ways it had been reported in the older studies. Stoyva (1965) made the same observation.

Data on content effects in an additional, selected subject are presented by Tart as part of a study primarily designed to study the effects of posthypnotic suggestion on the process, rather than the content, of Stage 1–REM dreaming (Tart, 1966). On three laboratory nights this subject averaged 45% of the suggested elements from the complex (23-element) dream suggestions in his reported dreams. He tended to dream quite literally along the lines of the suggestions. The affective tone of the suggestions (strong negative affect as in the earlier study vs. two neutral topics added for this study) had no obvious effect.

The most extensive exploration of the posthypnotic content effect and its relation to hypnotizability was carried out by Tart and Dick (1970). Thirteen highly hypnotizable subjects, initially selected to be in the upper 16% of the population by the norms for Form C of the Stanford Hypnotic Susceptibility Scale (Weitzenhoffer and Hilgard, 1962), received several hypnotic training and assessment sessions prior to spending two nights each (after an adaptation night) in the sleep laboratory. A different stimulus narrative was used each night. Both were very positive in tone, and contained 40 and 43 scorable elements, respectively. Judges counted the number of these elements in dreams reported from Stage 1–REM awakenings: they correlated .98 with each other.

To illustrate more concretely the way posthypnotic suggestion can influence dream content, what follows is the text of one of the stimulus narratives, and two dreams in response to it:

> It had been raining continuously for a week: the earth is soggy, and there are large puddles all along the path you are walking along. The water level has risen in the wells, and the frogs had been having a splendid time, croaking tirelessly all night long. Now, however, it is slowly clearing up. There are patches of blue sky just overhead, and the morning sun is scattering the clouds. It will be months before the leaves of the newly washed trees will again be covered with fine, red dust. The blue of the sky is so intense that it makes you stop and wonder. The air has been purified, and in one short week the earth has suddenly become green. In this morning light, peace lies upon the land, as you walk along the forest path.
>
> A single parrot is perched on a dead branch of a nearby tree and you stop to look at it. It isn't preening itself, and it sits very still, although its eyes are moving and alert. Its color is a delicate green with a brilliant red beak and a long tail of paler green. You want to touch it, to *feel* the color of it, but if you move it will fly away, so you, too, stand perfectly still, eyes fixed upon the parrot. Though it is completely still, a frozen green light, you can feel that it is *intensely* alive, and it seems to give life to the dead branch on which it sits. It is so astonishingly beautiful that it takes your breath away, and you

dare not take your eyes off it, lest in a flash it be gone. You have seen parrots before, but this single bird seems to be the focus of all life, of all beauty, of all perfection. There is nothing but this vivid spot of green on a dark branch against the blue sky. There are no words, no thoughts in your mind; you aren't even conscious that you aren't thinking. You hardly even blink, although the intensity of it almost brings tears to your eyes. Even blinking might frighten the bird away!

But it remains there, unmoving, so sleek, so slender, with every feather in its place.

Five minutes pass as you stand completely still yourself, never taking your eyes from this still vision, but these minutes cover the day, the year, all time: in these few minutes all life is, was, will be, without an end, without a beginning. It is not an experience to be stored up in memory, a dead thing to be kept alive by thought, which is also dying: it is totally alive, and so cannot be found among the dead.

And after this five minutes of eternity someone calls from a house near the path and the dead branch is suddenly bare.

Then you awaken . . . .

The following dream report was rated as containing 3.25 elements in the averaged rating of the two judges:

Technician: Martha, can you recall any dreams?

S: Yes. We went to—my great grandfather and I went to a field— to pick up wood to bring for the fire and as we were going away we got chased by some cattle that lived on the farm and it was kind of fun because they were just calves and they were fooling around with us but they were sort of frisky and everything. And as we were carrying the firewood away, there was a bird in the trees. A green bird—I didn't look at it—but it just kept saying, "Oh, you're taking it away," and it just kept announcing the fact that we were taking the firewood and we wanted it to be quiet because we weren't really sure it was all right for us to be taking this firewood off this land, but this bird just kept saying, "Oh, they're taking it away," and my grandfather was unconcerned, but it bothered me in a way because I was afraid of being caught by a farmer or something like that. There was—the fields were in this—the land was relatively barren. It was kind of dry and the trees had no foliage on them and the fields were dry and there was a lot of dead wood about and everything was rather still—there was no life really around except there was this cattle—there were two calves who were kind of fooling around and running about, but they were kind of far away and we left them. As we were walking away from them to take the firewood to the truck we encountered the bird as we were almost to the truck. And the farmhouse was nearby—that's why I was worried about being caught. But it wasn't really an unpleasant feeling—it was just sort of let's hurry because here's the bird announcing that we were taking firewood. I think that's about it.

Technician: Okay, fine. Did you have any feelings or anything like that? You mentioned the fright—anything else about the day or anything?

S: Oh, I really felt free. It was such a nice feeling because it was such a nice day, even though there was no foliage in the trees and it was kind of a barren atmosphere. It was just so pleasant. I don't know how to explain it. Everything was so clear and really crisp—not crisp, like crisp and cold, but like sharp outlines and everything like that. It was really beautiful to be there. That's why it was so pleasant, I think. I just had this feeling of real happiness there. I think that's all.

This report also illustrates a shortcoming of the element-counting type of measure of compliance, for thematically this report is clearly centered around the posthypnotic suggestion.

The second example illustrates just how detailed and pervasive an effect the posthypnotic suggestion can have: the averaged rating of the judges was 14 elements.

Technician: Peggy, can you remember any dream?

S: It's really broken. There I was talking to my roommate and then I was looking at bugs, and then there were things about legs and sticks, then I was walking along the path and there were puddles on each side—it had been raining for a long time, and the frogs were croaking, and it was getting sunny and the sky was all blue and I walked along and there was a parrot, and I just watched the parrot and he was so green, I just got lost, and I started thinking—oh, then I thought of something else and I never went back to the parrot. I wasn't finished dreaming when you called me, was I?

Technician: I think so, Peggy. Maybe not, but I think so. Can you think of anything else?

S: Because I can't remember if there was anything maybe it just stopped. Oh, I guess it was just green. I was watching the parrot and it was just the greenness and either I went on from there or I just stopped there at green. That's about the last thing I can remember.

Technician: Okay, and how did you feel?

S: Really disoriented. I felt—it was really kind of strange—skipping around from talking to my roommate in one scene and then seeing bugs and legs and sticks—I don't even know how I got on the path and it was (long pause).

Technician: Are there any other details you want to mention before you go back to sleep?

S: No.

Overall for the 13 subjects, there was a range of zero to 25 of the suggested stimulus elements appearing in reported individual Stage 1-REM dream reports.

There was considerable variation across subjects, with the mean effect per subject running between $2\frac{1}{2}$ and $4\frac{1}{2}$ elements, depending on the narrative. The effects were quite comparable to the earlier Tart (1964b) study, in spite of some differences in experimental procedure. The peak effect of 25 elements in a single dream suggests great potential for posthypnotic content control. Tart and Dick also note that after other laboratory work on the effects of posthypnotic suggestion on dream process, some of the subjects reported that they had learned to control the content of their home dreams on their own.

Because quite extensive measures of hypnotic susceptibility had been given to all the subjects, useful correlations with the extent of content effect in the reported dreams could be carried out. They suggested that the more deeply hypnotizable the subject in general (hypnotic *susceptibility*) and/or the more deeply hypnotized a subject felt at about the time the posthypnotic suggestions were given (hypnotic *depth*, a momentary state measure), the greater the degree of content control seen. The "ability" aspects of hypnotizability seemed more related to the content effect than the "compulsion" qualities of hypnosis.

One of the most extensive studies of the effects of posthypnotic suggestion on dream content was by Barber et al. (1973), using 77 student nurse subjects who slept two nights each in the laboratory. For each subject there were a sleep onset awakening, two Stage 1-REM awakenings, and two NREM awakenings. After each report the subject herself classified it as a "thought" or a "dream." We shall deal only with the reports classified as "dreams" here. In a 2 × 3 factorial design, the effects of (1) administering vs. not administering a standardized hypnotic induction *procedure* and (2) permissive topic suggestions vs. authoritarian topic suggestions vs. no specific topic suggestions, were studied on the second night. The suggested topic was dreaming about the death of President Kennedy.

Neither of the no-suggestion topic groups dreamed about this topic. One quarter of the subjects in the other four groups had at least one report they called a dream from their several Stage 1-REM and NREM awakenings that was reliably (99% agreement between two judges) judged as about Kennedy's death. For three of the four treatment groups, this broke down to two or three of the 13 subjects in each group giving at least one (but not more than two) report about this; so the suggestions were effective for about a quarter of the subjects. The suggested topic affected six of the 13 subjects in the permissive suggestion-no hypnotic induction procedure group.

The magnitude of the effect was assessed by counting the number of elements in the dream reports clearly related to Kennedy's death. In the groups administered the hypnotic induction procedure, authoritative suggestions seemed more effective (a total of 16 elements over three subjects) than permissive suggestions (three elements over two subjects), while in the groups not administered the hypnotic induction procedure, the permissive suggestion procedure seemed superior (a total of 21 suggested elements over six subjects) to the authoritarian suggestions (three elements over two subjects). This gives a maximum average effect (in the hypnotic induction group) of about five elements per subject from five awakenings, about one element per report on the average. Since no subject gave more than two dream reports containing suggested elements, the magnitude may have averaged more like two or three elements in a particular dream: these are my rough estimates.

Barber et al.'s data analysis does not discriminate Stage 1-REM awakenings from NREM awakenings, although it does discriminate between reports labeled as "thoughts" or "dreams" by the subjects themselves.

It should be noted that this study's procedure was quite different from most other studies of the effects of posthypnotic suggestions on dreaming in several major ways. First, the "hypnosis" variable is the experimenter's administration of a standardized induction *procedure*, rather than the presence or absence of a diagnosed hypnotic *state* resulting from that procedure. Barber has frequently argued that there is no hypnotic d-SoC, but other hypnosis researchers note that carrying out an induction procedure does not necessarily do anything to a subject; so some of Barber et al.'s subjects in the hypnotic induction procedure group *might* have been hypnotized, while some might not (see, e.g., Tart, 1977). Second, subjects in the hypnotic induction procedure group apparently did not know they were going to be hypnotized until after they were in the sleep laboratory, and this might have been an upsetting procedure to subjects who did not know they were volunteering for more than sleep research. Third, while the experimenters administered five suggestibility test items following the hypnotic induction procedure, and reported that this measure did not correlate with sleep performance, this is a rather small number of items to measure hypnotizability with, and so may be unreliable. Fourth, any comparison of the effectiveness of presleep dream content suggestion in subjects' waking d-SoC vs. the administration of a hypnotic induction procedure might be biased to an unknown degree by Barber's well-known conviction that "hypnosis" does not increase suggestibility. Thus it is difficult to compare the Barber et al. findings with other studies of the effects of posthypnotic suggestion on dreaming.

Some researchers (Barber, 1962; Moss, 1967) have expressed doubt as to whether Stage 1-REM dreams apparently affected by posthypnotic suggestion are what they seem to be: perhaps the subjects (with or without momentarily entering a hypnotic state) fabricate the dreams they report just after they are awakened from a Stage 1-REM period and before reporting. Stoyva and Budzynski (1968) tried to investigate this by correlating the length of the Stage 1-REM period before awakening and the length of the reported dream: a high correlation would argue for the genuineness of the report. They worked with eight subjects who were preselected to report dreams in compliance with simple posthypnotic content suggestions in at least 50% of their Stage 1-REM awakening reports. They found no correlation between Stage 1-REM time and the length of the reported dreams. However, they did note that short reporting latencies yielded long dream narratives, exactly the opposite of what would be expected if the subjects needed time to confabulate or hypnotically dream the suggested narrative. This finding was completely consistent across all eight subjects, and supports the hypothesis that posthypnotic content suggestions affect Stage 1-REM mental activity.

In two yet unpublished studies, I investigated concurrent content alteration of Stage 1-REM dream content by giving tape-recorded suggestions as to what to dream about while the subjects were in Stage 1-REM sleep, after posthypnotic priming. The subjects were preselected for high responsiveness to posthypnotic dream content control, being the more successful ones from the Tart and Dick (1970) study reviewed above. The content suggestions in each study consisted of three element suggestions (such as "Being with a famous person as you smell perfume in an arena," or "Being with some aunts who are carrying beams around on an airfield," or "Being with a group of men who are digging up mounds in a railroad yard") with each element having been picked from the Hall and Van de Castle (1966) norms on home dreaming to have a frequency of occurrence in ordinary dreaming of less than 1%. Thus the priori probability of dreaming about all three elements of the suggestion by chance alone was about one in a million.

In the first study, the subjects were given posthypnotic suggestions just before going to sleep that they would hear the content suggestion which would be played to them during their dreams that night without waking up, and would dream about the suggested topics. While some clear compliance with the suggestions resulted, there were frequent awakenings when the suggestions were presented, thus invalidating some of the trials. In the second study, basically the same procedure was used except that the tape-recorded suggestions were introduced at an almost inaudible volume and then slowly raised to a soft, but clearly audible level. The awakening problem disappeared, and a very high level of compliance appeared. The dream reports obtained from awakenings a few minutes after the suggestions indicated that spontaneous (unrelated to the experiment) dreaming would be going on and then the dream action would rather suddenly change to be about the suggested topic. The following dream report, in response to the suggestion to dream about "Being with a group of lady welders who are applying ointment to the hull of a submarine," is illustrative of typical responses:

> . . . had to do with Dolores, who is my friend from home, I think. She and I
> were planning to go to some little dinky town to see her grandmother (she

really doesn't have a grandmother in a dinky town). Anyway, like it was some place that was real far away. We decided that we were going to do it, but we didn't have a chance to tell her. So we decided to call, and for some reason we called the operator and decided just to talk to her. Because we thought her grandmother wouldn't be there or something. We called the operator and we talked to her for a while. But the funny thing is we talked to her about submarines, not about Dolores' grandmother. I don't know why, but we just did. It cost $5.40. Then we figured out that her grandmother still wouldn't know we were coming. We were going on Mother's Day, so we decided that she wouldn't be doing anything anyway. That is all I can remember about the second part, and I still can't remember the first part.

(Q: What about submarines? What did you say about them?)

Something about how if they were welded properly they were safe, but otherwise they just fell apart like the *Thresher* and the other one that was lost.

(Q: Was this a long conversation?)

No. It was just very short and really out of context with the rest of the dream.

Classic psychoanalytic theory predicts that the more threatening a suggested presleep dream topic is, the more need for dream work to make the manifest dream content innocuous and so preserve sleep, even though the latent dream content must deal with the threatening material. As discussed in a previous section, the early studies purporting to demonstrate this experimentally seemed to have strong implicit demand characteristics forcing this sort of result. In recent years Witkin and his colleagues (Witkin, 1969; Witkin and Lewis, 1965, 1967) have carried out a number of experiments in which subjects are shown one of several highly threatening films before sleep in what I have earlier described as an implicit presleep suggestion procedure: there are no formal instructions to dream about the films, but it must be obvious to the subjects that this is expected. A stimulus film of particular interest is an anthropological documentary film showing subincision rites of Australian aborigines, with closeups of quite bloody operations performed with sharp stones on the penises of adolescent boys being initiated into manhood. Witkin and his colleagues have reported many transformed elements of the film appearing in dream reports but, as expected from psychoanalytic theory, no direct incorporations of the film.

In a still unpublished study, designed to test the potential power of posthypnotic suggestion to control dream content, I asked my selected hypnotic subjects described above if they would volunteer for an unpleasant, but scientifically meaningful, experiment in dreaming about unpleasant material. Several volunteered, received a posthypnotic suggestion to dream explicitly about the film they were to see, and were then shown the subincision film. Most of the subjects dreamed directly about the film, despite its threatening nature.

LUCID DREAMING

Lucid dreaming is an altered d-SoC characterized by the lucid dreamer experiencing himself as located in a world or environment that he intellectually knows is "unreal" (or certainly not ordinary physical reality) while *simultaneously* experiencing the overall quality of his consciousness as having the clarity, the lucidity of his ordinary waking d-SoC. As discussed at length in my systems approach to understanding altered states of consciousness (Lee et al., 1975; Tart, 1974a, 1975, 1976, in press), this characterization of the overall configuration of his consciousness as practically identical to his waking state by the lucid dreamer is the crucial defining element of lucid dreaming.

If you were to answer seriously the question, "Are you dreaming right now?" (to which I assume most, of not all readers' answers would be no), and examine the process(es) by which you arrive at your answer, two basic types of experiential examination processes can be discerned. You might look at some particular quality of consciousness/experience, such as continuity of memory, e.g., and say that since you can continuously remember all of your day up to the present moment, but one of your criteria of dreaming is a lack of such continuity, then you must be awake. Or you might simply scan the gestalt, holistic, pattern qualities of your ongoing experience and well nigh instantly classify that pattern as characteristic of your waking state. Either or both of these basic experiential examination operations can occur when a dreamer questions whether he is dreaming.

A dreamer decides he is experiencing a lucid dream by the results of either or both of these two basic classifications operations: the overall, gestalt quality of his conscious functioning is that of ordinary waking, even though he is located in a dream world, and/or he notices specific aspects of his mental functioning that are characteristic of his waking state and not of his dream state. It is important to note in the latter case that while a particular aspect of mental functioning may trigger the *recognition* that he is having a lucid dream, the lucid dreamer then usually goes on to notice that the overall pattern of his mental functioning, many aspects of it, are more like waking. The appearance of an isolated characteristic of waking thought is *not* the criterion of lucid dreaming, even though it may serve as a convenient indication of the presence of the lucid dream d-SoC to the dreamer. Lucid dreaming is a d-SoC involving a complex pattern change where many of the components of mental functioning we feel characterize waking consciousness come into play together. These methodological aspects of defining a d-SoC are discussed further in Tart (1975).

The feeling of a lucid dream, judging from my own few experiences of them as well as the descriptions of others, is that it feels just like your mental functioning feels right now, except that you know the world you perceive around you is some sort of clever imitation, no matter how real it seems, because you know you are asleep and dreaming.

Lucid dreaming often (but not always) starts from an ordinary dream when the dreamer (in ordinary dream consciousness) notices that some dream event does not "make sense" by ordinary consciousness standards, leading to the realization that he is dreaming. Following this realization, a major change in his pattern of mental functioning, usually quite rapid, is felt, and the dreamer "wakes up" in terms of his general pattern of consciousness; but he still experiences himself as located in the dream world.

I find that a frequent confusion about the concept of lucid dreaming centers around the realization that the dreamer has that he is dreaming. Simply experiencing the dream thought, "This is a dream," or some variant of it, is a necessary but not a sufficient condition for a lucid dream to occur. This thought can be a part of the ordinary dreaming d-SoC. A reorganization of the state of consciousness into a d-SoC pattern that feels like/is experienced as "waking" consciousness is the crucial defining pattern of a lucid dream.

In terms of the systems approach to altered states, a lucid dream is of special theoretical interest. The "higher" mental processes that we think of as characterizing waking consciousness, such as memorial continuity, reasoning ability, volitional control of cognitive processes, and volitional control of body actions (at least for the dream body), all seem to be functioning at a lucid, waking level. Yet the physiological/psychological mechanisms that serve to construct the ordinary dream world are also still functioning; so the lucid dreamer experiences himself in an "external world," one that usually is as vidid and real-seeming as the world of ordinary consciousness, in spite of his intellectual knowledge that it is unreal. Lucid dreamers often make minute examinations of the texture of the dream world to see how closely it resembles (their apparently clear memory of) the ordinary physical world. We should be able to discover specific physiological correlates of lucid dreaming that would arise from the apparent waking level activation of some brain processes combined with the dream level activation of others. In what they characterize as very preliminary exploratory work, Ogilvie et al. (1978), working with two lucid dreamers in the laboratory, suggest that lucid dreams may begin in Stage 1–REM periods but show a shift toward an increase in alpha dominance of the EEG and fewer REMs.

The following description of one of his lucid dreams by the Dutch physician, Frederick van Eeden, gives the flavor of a typical lucid dream:

> On Sept. 9, 1904 I dreamt that I stood at a table before a window. On the table were different objects. I was perfectly well aware that I was dreaming and I considered what sorts of experiments I could make. I began by trying to break glass, by beating it with a stone. I put a small tablet of glass on two stones and struck it with another stone. Yet it would not break. Then I took a fine claret-glass from the table and struck it with my fist, with all my might, at the same time reflecting how dangerous it would be to do this in

waking life; yet the glass remained whole. But lo! when I looked at it again after some time, it was broken.

It broke all right, but a little too late, like an actor who misses his cue. This gave me a very curious impression of being in a *fake-world*, cleverly imitated, but with small failures. I took the broken glass and threw it out of the window, in order to observe whether I could hear the *tinkling*. I heard the noise all right and I even saw two dogs run away from it quite naturally. I thought what a good imitation this comedy-world was. Then I saw a decanter with claret and tasted it, and noted with perfect clearness of mind: "Well, we can also have voluntary impressions of taste in this dream-world; this has quite the taste of wine."

Lucid dreams are generally considered pleasant and important by those who have them, although they are sometimes initiated as a response to unpleasant or threatening situations in ordinary dreaming. The lucid dreamer frequently has volitional control over this lucid dream world to some extent, frequently performing actions which are "magical" by waking life standards, such as willing changes in the "physical" qualities of the dream world, a kind of "experiential psychokinesis." Unpleasant dream situations, e.g., can be conquered or turned into friendly ones along the lines of Senoi dream work discussed later (Stewart, 1953-54, 1954, 1962, 1969). Note that while control over dream situations and characteristics is a frequent aspect of lucid dreaming, control of a dream situation is not *per se* a sufficient indicator of lucidity. Dreamers can sometimes learn partially volitional control in dreams without experiencing the overall shift in state of consciousness that constitutes the d-SoC of lucid dreaming. The high degree of apparent volitional control of content often manifested in lucid dreaming suggests it is the ultimate form of concurrent content control.

Experience in lucid dreams can seem as real or even more vivid and real than ordinary experience. Unlike ordinary dream experience, which may seem real at the time but is rapidly discounted on waking, lucid dream experience usually retains its feeling of reality. This can lead lucid dreamers to entertain serious philosophical questions about the nature of reality. One of the best illustrations of this was the lucid dreams of Ram Narayana, a British-educated editor of Indian medical periodicals. In numerous lucid dreams, e.g., he engaged other dream characters in debates about the nature of reality, even though he knew at the time that they were only dream characters! An interesting and amusing example is the following:

One night when he (Narayana) went to sleep, the dreamer found that during the dream he was walking in a street which appeared quite new to him, and while enjoying this beautiful scene and knowing full well that it was his dream experience he thought of finding out the name of the place he was walking in. He stopped a passerby and enquired of him the name of the street. The man simply laughed and went away, saying that he was in a hurry to go to his office and had no time to waste in idle gossiping. The dreamer then stopped another person and put the same question. This man replied by addressing the dreamer by name: "Don't you recognise this street, it is the same in which you have your own house? Are you mad, what is the matter with you?" Thus speaking, he laughed and went away. The dreamer on hearing the name of the street at once recognised it, but he could not trace his own house. He then approached another person who appeared to be a well-known friend and thus addressed him: "Friend, I feel giddy at this time, would you oblige by taking me to my house?" The man took the dreamer by the arm, left him outside his house and went away. On entering the house, the dreamer did not recognise it as his own and began to talk aloud: "What a fine building I am looking at in my own dream." He then saw the inmates of the house in a group, weeping with downcast faces. The dreamer wondered why were they all weeping and when he enquired the cause of it none of them spoke. He then forcibly raised up the face of one of them, when to his great surprise, he recognised in him the face of his own son, and being very angry the dreamer said, "Why are you so silent my son, and why do you not tell me the cause of all this weeping?" The boy said, "We are weeping, father because you have become mad, and not only do you not recognise us—your own family members—but say that it is a dream." The dreamer then understood why they were weeping and thought it foolish of him to talk of its being a dream scene in their presence. He pacified them by telling that he was all right and that it was his mistake to call it a dream. However, he felt grieved over his people's condition and tried to put an end to that unpleasant dream, but could not succeed in wakening himself. He now fully recognised his home and went to his own room, where he found all the articles exactly in the same condition in which they were in his waking state. He touched and held them up in his hand to see if they were real and found nothing unusual in them. (Narayana, 1922b, pp. 10–11)

An important comment about lucid dreams, which this example illustrates, is in order. Note that the dreamer did not recognise some familiar aspects of the dream, such as the street his own house was on at first, a fact that seems to contradict the notion of (complete) lucidity. For clarity of presentation, I have oversimplified the concept of the d-SoC of lucid dreaming so far, as if were a quite stable, all-or-none phenomenon. It is not. There are variations in the degree of lucidity and the components of lucidity from time to time within a lucid dream, often but not always recognized by the lucid dreamer. Reports are typical, e.g., in which a dreamer reports a minute or so of lucid dreaming and then reports he slipped back into ordinary dreaming, without recognizing this while it happened, but recognizing it a minute later when lucid dreaming resumed. Thus while we can postulate a "pure case" of lucid dreaming at an extreme, one in which *all* cognitive functions work at waking levels while the dream world still seems real in spite of the dreamer's intellectual knowledge that it is not real, future research will have to deal with some variation within this category and the fact of rapid transitions between ordinary dreaming and lucid dreaming. I have dealt elsewhere with the methodological problems of researching the "depth" or "intensity" dimension of a d-SoC (Tart, 1972a, 1975).

There is very little literature on lucid dreaming of any kind, scientific or literary, in Western culture. I suspect the reason is the cultural rejection of dreams in general as well as the specific rejection of the possibility of this kind of dreaming, resulting in a reluctance to report on it. I have talked to numerous people who have reported experiencing at least one lucid dream in their life once I have made them feel confortable about reporting unusual experiences, and I would make a rough guess that at least 10% of the population has experienced lucid dreaming.*

Most of the sparse literature on lucid dreaming consists of self-reports by lucid dreamers, sometimes embedded in a literary matrix. Space limitations preclude any detailed review of the bulk of it here; so I shall simply note the main sources that the interested reader can turn to. Mrs. H. Arnold-Forster (1921) was an English writer who described her lucid dreaming in a small book. Carlos Castaneda describes lucid dreaming as a technique taught him under the name of *dreaming* by his mentor, the Yaqui shaman don Juan (Castaneda, 1971, 1973, 1974, 1977). The Frenchman DeLage (1919) describes his lucid dreams in a book devoted to sleep and dreams. Faraday (1973) describes a few lucid dreams of her own and some of those of her patients in a popular book on dreaming. Oliver Fox (1962) describes numerous lucid dreams over a period of years. Interestingly, Fox also experienced many out-of-the-body experiences,* but he carefully distinguishes these from his lucid dreams. Garfield (1974b) briefly describes several of her own lucid dreams as part of a general discussion of lucid dreams and ways of inducing them. Green (1968) analyzes the characteristics of lucid dreams collected from a presumably large, but not very well-specified, sample of dreamers. The Marquis de Saint-Denis (1867) described many lucid dreams: his book was presumably known to Freud, or at least Freud included it in the references to his *The Interpretation of Dreams*, without really discussing lucid dreaming or its implications. Ram Narayana (1922a,b), the Indian medical editor, described many lucid dreams he experienced and the philosophical questions they raised, with particular and interesting emphases on viewing them from

---

*I am slowly building up a case collection of lucid dreams to analyze later for internal characteristics, and I would welcome accounts of personal lucid dreams from readers. They may be mailed to me c/o Psychology, UC Davis, Davis, CA 95616.

*Out-of-the-body experiences are experientially like a lucid dream except that the experiencer believes his environment is real, rather than illusory: see Tart (1974b,c, 1977) for a review of this phenomenon.

the point of view of traditional Indian philosophy.   The Russian philosopher P. D. Ouspensky (1960) described various degrees of lucidity in dreams, lucidity he deliberately induced in himself as part of an exploration of the experiential nature of dreaming.   Sparrow (1976, 1978) describes some of his lucid dreams in two brief articles.   Frederick van Eeden presented some data on his lucid dreams in fictional form (van Eeden, 1918), as well as in the scientific article mentioned earlier (van Eeden, 1913).   And, J. M. H. Whitman, a physicist, describes lucid dreaming in a book about his mystical experiences (Whitman, 1961).

There has been very little experimentally oriented work on lucid dreaming. Garfield, as part of a home study on influencing various aspects of dream content (Garfield, 1974a), discussed earlier, also tried inducing lucid dreaming. She reported a change from a few brief instances in the one-month baseline period to four prolonged lucid dreams in the nine-month experimental period.

In a second study of attempts to induce lucid dreaming in herself, Garfield (1975b) was able to attain a steady increase to a terminal frequency of three lucid dreams per week.   Based on a sample of 30 lucid dreams over an 18-month period, Garfield found that her lucid dreams: (a) were more likely after a very busy day, regardless of affective tone; (b) were more likely to occur following sexual intercourse in the middle of the night; (c) occurred almost exclusively after several hours of sleep, between 5 A.M. and 8 A.M.; (d) were often preceded by ordinary dream imagery of swimming or flying or activities that seemed to symbolize the imminence of a shift in consciousness to lucidity; and (e) occurred most often when she slept on her back, rather than her side.   She was able to prolong or end these lucid dreams at will.

Belicki and Hunt (1978) approached the study of lucid dreaming indirectly by looking for differences between two groups of students, one who claimed to have had lucid dreams with some frequency (N = 20), and a second group who had not (N = 38).   The two groups did not differ on various personality test measures, their estimates of how often they recalled dreams, or their beliefs in the personal meaningfulness of dreams.   Each group recorded their dreams at home for four weeks.   Two measures of hallucinations and confused thoughts in the dreams showed no differences between the groups, but the self-reported lucid dreamers did show significantly higher dream recall than the nonlucid controls (mean of 14.6 vs. 10.9 dreams in the four-week period).   It is not clear from the abstract of this paper whether any lucid dreams occurred during the dream collection period.   The lack of relation between lucid dreaming and importance attached to dreaming is somewhat at variance with Hiew's (1976b) finding that subjects who attached more importance to dreaming showed more ability to dream about a suggested topic, but the higher recall frequency of lucid dreamers does parallel Hiew's findings.

Some data from my own laboratory that are still in the process of being analyzed suggest that posthypnotic suggestions may have some potential in inducing lucid dreaming.

WHY IS DREAM CONTROL IMPORTANT?

Developing presleep control over the content of nocturnal dreams, and/or developing the concurrent control that occurs with lucidity is scientifically interesting; but would such development be of any practical importance?

In considering this question, we must remind ourselves that we typically do not ask from a neutral position: our general cultural bias is that dreams are trivial mental aberrations, of no practical importance, and probably tainted with the pathological. Even within our psychotherapeutic and psychoanalytic subcultures, dreams are seen primarily as a *reflection* or indicator of important unconscious processes, rather than as important processes themselves.* We are aware that other cultures have often regarded dreams as important, but we usually consider them "primitive" cultures; indeed, the importance they give to dreams is usually considered one of the marks of "primitivity"! Most of this cultural bias we have against considering dreams important is not a scholarly or scientific attitude based on study or data, but simply a result of irrational and a-rational historical processes which affected our socialization; so we must be especially aware of the possible distorting effects of our biases here.

I shall not attempt to survey the many cultures that have assigned a positive function to nocturnal dreaming, but shall focus on one culture that seems to have had the most positive attitude toward and most developed "technology" for dream control, the Senoi of Malaysia. I regretfully use the past tense in describing this culture. The Senoi were a peaceful and isolated series of small, related groups, protected by their isolation in the jungles of Malaysia; but their culture was largely destroyed by successive waves of modern, mechanized warfare, with both Japanese and Allied invasions of their territory in World War II, as well as consequent continuous guerrilla warfare and accompanying forced conscription of the Senoi. Our knowledge of Senoi dream control techniques is thus historical knowledge, taken from a few articles written by Kilton Stewart (now deceased) a number of years after he actually visited them before World War II (Stewart, 1943-54, 1954, 1962, 1969), and some tangentially relevant writings by some travelers (Holman, 1958; Noone and Holman, 1972).

Briefly, the Senoi believed all normal persons could attain lucidity in many of their dreams and thus exercise volitional control over dream events. Since

---

*A partial exception is the psychoanalytic theory that dreams serve a "safety valve" function by allowing discharge of unconscious tension, but this is seen as an automatic function, beyond conscious control.

dreams were viewed as representing real events in some nonphysical continuum and/or as representing deep psychological events (Stewart interprets their beliefs as the latter), dreams were seen as both reflecting ongoing life events and as presaging developing life events. Dreaming of a quarrel with a known friend in an ordinary dream, e.g., would be seen as reflecting unconscious psychological tensions between the dreamer and his friend, even if those tensions were not yet manifested overtly in ordinary life. The proper response to such a dream would include discussing the dream with the dreamer's family group and with the friend, giving a gift to the friend to make up for any slights that might have occurred but not been recognized in ordinary life, and attempting to have a lucid dream in which friendship would be manifested to the dream image of the friend. Stewart believed the Senoi had a basic understanding of the dynamics of the un-conscious, but had gone beyond Western understanding by developing dream control and lucid dreaming so that they dealt *directly* with potential conflicts on the unconscious level as they arose, thus efficiently dealing with them *before* they reached the stage of overt problems in everyday life.

I can attest to the validity of one aspect of Senoi dream technique through personal experience. The Senoi teach their children that any unpleasant, fright-ening, or threatening image in a dream represents a part of themselves that they have not come to grips with, and rather than run from it or wake up, they should confront it. The child should try to dream about the frightening image again in his next dream, and either fight and conquer it, make friends with it, or allow himself to be conquered by and absorbed by it, as a third way of healing the split. I discovered this technique myself as a young child of about eight, when I was troubled by nightmares. Feeling that the nightmares were *my* dreams and so should be responsive to me instead of frightening, I taught myself to go back to sleep and into the dream as quickly as possible, and either conquer the fright-ening image or make friends with it. After fewer than a dozen dreams where I did this, nightmares became a very rare occurrence with me and my dreams took on a very positive, happy tone. I taught the technique to my son when he was having frightening dreams around age four, and it quickly worked for him. Stu-dents in my classes who have heard of the technique from me have also reported that they taught it to their children with successful results.

Many other sophisticated techniques of dream control, as well as uses for dreams (creative inspiration, e.g.), were employed by the Senoi but cannot be reviewed here. The reader is referred to Stewart's writings.

Stewart describes the Senoi as an incredibly civilized people, with practically no obvious cases of mental illness, and with warfare unheard of. His description is idyllic enough to make some people wonder if the Senoi were really like that or whether Stewart exaggerated his material. The destruction of Senoi culture makes any definitive answer impossible, but regardless of the literal truth of

Stewart's reports, the central ideas of dream control and lucidity in dreams have taken hold in our culture. Several therapists (Corriere and Hart, 1977; Garfield, 1975a; Greenleaf, 1973; Johnston, 1978; Latner and Sabini, 1972; Reed, 1976; Sabini, 1972a; Wallin, 1977) have applied these ideas in their therapeutic practice and report quite positive results, not only in patients occasionally showing control over difficult or unpleasant situations in their dreams (with or without accompanying lucidity), but in terms of positive carryovers to their life situations.

It is difficult to draw any precise conclusions from a few anthropological/ psychological reports and clinical reports; but even if the claims made are scaled down considerably, deliberate control of dream content, with or without lucidity, will have considerable therapeutic use.

CONCLUSIONS

In reviewing the literature on various techniques for affecting the content (and the process) of nocturnal dreaming almost 14 years ago (Tart, 1965a), I concluded that sleeping and dreaming were not passive states where things "just happened" to people, but rather that sleepers could respond selectively to external stimuli, both in terms of incorporation into dreams and in making overt motor responses, with some control over dream content being possible as well. The studies reviewed in this chapter, almost all published subsequent to that earlier review, further confirm that some control over the content of State 1–REM dreaming (and, in some cases, NREM activity) is quite possible.

I further concluded in the earlier review that posthypnotic suggestion seemed to be the most powerful technique for content control via presleep suggestion, and that conclusion is now stronger than ever. Studies using implicit or overt presleep suggestion with subjects in their ordinary waking state seem to have a peak effect of about one or two suggested content elements per dream, whereas the studies utilizing posthypnotic suggestion have reported peak effects of up to 25 elements in a single dream, and average effects in the 5–15 element range. A very high degree of control is possible with posthypnotic suggestion.

Lucid dreaming is a form of concurrent content control, rather than presleep control. It may be the most powerful form of content control, although the sparse data we have on lucid dreaming at present are too qualitative to allow any precise comparison with presleep suggestions in the waking or hypnotic d-SoCs.

As I emphasized in the methodological section, our present data allow only a pointing-out of possibilities rather than any firm drawing of conclusions about effects of specific parameters. Yet these possibilities are very intriguing: posthypnotic suggestion and lucid dreaming, for example, are clearly large effects of great potential psychological significance, not just statistically significant trivia that are only of arcane scholarly interest. Given a few years of development and refinement of techniques for control of the content of dreams, especially the development of lucidity, we may enter an era of deliberate and controlled phenomenological and scientific exploration of dreaming (including the development of state-specific sciences of dreaming: Tart, 1972b, 1975) which promises great excitement as well as great significance.

REFERENCES

Agnew, H., Webb, W., and Williams, R.   The first night effect: An EEG study of sleep. *Psychophysiology*, 3: 263–266, 1966.

Arkin, A.   Sleep-taking: A review. *J. Nerv. Ment. Dis.*, 143: 101–122, 1966.

Arnold-Forster, J.   *Studies in Dreams.* London: Allen & Unwin, 1921.

Aserinsky, E., and Kleitman, N.   Regularly occurring periods of eye motility and concomitant phenomena during sleep. *Science*, 118: 273–274, 1953.

Barber, T.   Toward a theory of "hypnotic" behavior: The "hypnotically induced dream." *J. Nerv. Ment. Dis.*, 135: 206–221, 1962.

Barber, T., Walker, P., and Hahn, K.   Effect of hypnotic induction and suggestions on nocturnal dreaming and thinking. *J. Abnorm. Psychol.*, 82: 414–427, 1973.

Belicki, D., and Hunt, H.   An exploratory study comparing self-reported lucid and nonlucid dreamers. Paper, Assoc. Psychophysiol. Study of Sleep, Palo Also, California, 1978.

Belvedere, E., and Foulkes, D.   Telepathy and dreams: A failure to replicate. *Percept. Mot. Skills*, 33: 783–789, 1971.

Brown, J., and Cartwright, R.   Locating NREM dreaming through instrumental responses. *Psychophysiology,* 15: 35–39, 1978.

Brunette, R., and De Konick, J.   The effect of presleep suggestions related to a phobic object on dream affect. Paper, Assoc. Psychophysiol. Study of Sleep, Palo Alto, California, 1977.

Cartwright, R.   The influence of a conscious wish on dreams: A methodological study of dream meaning and function. *J. Abnorm. Psychol.*, 83: 387–393, 1974.

Castaneda, C.   *A Separate Reality: Further Conversations with Don Juan.* New York: Simon & Schuster, 1971.

Castaneda, C.   *Journey to Ixtlan: The Lessons of Don Juan.* New York: Simon & Schuster, 1973.

Castaneda, C.   *Tales of Power.* New York: Simon & Schuster, 1974.

Castaneda, C.   *The Second Ring of Power.* New York: Simon & Schuster, 1977.

Corriere, R., and Hart, J.   *The Dream Makers: Discovering Your Breakthrough Dreams.* New York: Funk & Wagnalls, 1977.

De Koninck, J., and Koulack, D.   Dream content and adaptation to a stressful situation. *J. Abnorm. Psychol.*, 84: 250–260, 1975.

Delage, Y.   *La réve.* Paris: Les Presses Universitaires de France, 1919.

Dement, W., Kahn, E., and Roffwarg, H.   The influence of the laboratory situation on the dreams of the experimental subject. *J. Nerv. Ment. Dis.*, 140: 119–131, 1965.

Domhof, B., and Kamya, J.   Problems in dream content study with objective indicators. *Arch. Gen. Psychiat.*, 11: 519–524, 1964.

Eliade, M.   *Shamanism: Archaic Techniques of Ecstasy.* New York: Pantheon, 1964.

Evans, F.   Hypnosis and sleep: Techniques for exploring cognitive activity during sleep. In Fromm, E., and Shor, R. (Eds.), *Hypnosis: Research Developments and Perspectives.* Chicago: Aldine-Atherton, 1972.

Faraday, A. *Dream Power*. New York: Berkeley Publishing, 1973.

Fischer, C. Studies on the nature of suggestion: Part 1. Experimental induction of dreams by direct suggestion. *J. Am. Psychoanal. Assn.*, **1**: 222–255, 1953.

Fischer, C. Dreams and perception: The role of preconscious and primary modes of perception in dream formation. *J. Am. Psychanal. Assn.*, **2**: 389–445, 1954.

Fischer, C. Subliminal and supraliminal influences on dreams. *Am. J. Psychiat.*, **116**: 1009–1017, 1960.

Foulkes, D., Belvedere, E., Masters, R., Houston, J., Krippner, S., Honorton, C., and Ullman, M. Long distance "sensory bombardment" ESP in dreams: A failure to replicate. *Percept. Mot. Skills*, **35**: 731–734, 1972.

Foulkes, D., and Griffin, M. An experimental study of "creative dreaming." *Sleep Research*, **5**: 129, 1976.

Fox, O. *Astral Projection*. New Hyde Park, New York: University Books, 1962.

Fox, P., Kramer, M., Baldridge, B., Whitman, R., and Ornstein, P. The experimenter variable in dream research. *Dis. Nerv. System*, **29**: 298–301, 1968.

Freud, S. *The Interpretation of Dreams*. London: Allen & Unwin, 1954.

Garfield, P. Self-conditioning of dream content. Paper, Assoc. Psychophysiol. Study of Sleep, Jackson Hole, Wyoming, 1974(a).

Garfield, P. *Creative Dreaming*. New York: Ballantine, 1974(b).

Garfield, P. Using the dream state as a clinical tool for assertion training. Paper, Assoc. Psychophysiol. Study of Sleep, Edinburgh, 1975(a).

Garfield, P. Psychological concomitants of the lucid dream state. Paper, Assoc. Psychophysiol. Study of Sleep, Edinburgh, 1975(b).

Green, C. *Lucid Dreams*. Oxford: Institute of Psychophysical Research, 1968.

Greenleaf, E. Senoi dream groups. *Psychotherapy: Theory, Research, and Practice*. **10** (3): 218–222, 1973.

Griffin, M., and Foulkes, D. Deliberate presleep control of dream content: An experimental study. *Percept. Mot. Skills*, **45**: 660–662, 1977.

Hadfield, J. *Dreams and Nightmares*. Baltimore: Penguin, 1954.

Hall, C. Representation of laboratory setting in dreams. *J. Nerv. Ment. Dis.*, **144**: 199–208, 1967.

Hall, C., and Van de Castle, R. *The Content Analysis of Dreams*. New York: Appleton-Century-Crofts, 1966.

Hiew, C. The influence of pre-sleep suggestions on dream content. Paper, Brunswick Psychological Assoc., Bathurst NB, Canada, 1976(a).

Hiew, C. Individual differences in the control of dreaming. Paper, Assoc. Psychophysiol. Study of Sleep, Cincinnati, 1976(b).

Hiew, C., and Short, P. Emotional involvement and auditory retrieval cues in presleep dream suggestion. Paper, Assoc. Psychophysiol. Study of Sleep, Houston, 1977.

Holman, D. *Noone of the Ulu*. London: Heinemann, 1958.

Johnston, J. Elements of Senoi dreaming applied in a Western culture. *Sundance Community Dream J.*, **2** (1): 50–61, 1978.

Kales, A., Jacobson, A., Kales, J., Kun, T., and Weissbuch, R. All-night EEG sleep measurements in young adults. *Psychonomic Sci.*, **7**: 67–68, 1967.

Keith, C. Some aspects of transference in dream research. *Bull. Menninger Clinic*, **26**: 248–257, 1962.

Latner, J., and Sabini, M. Working in the dream factory: Social dreamwork. *Voices: The Art & Science of Psychother.*, **8**, No. 3: 38–43, 1972.

Lee, P., Ornstein, R., Galin, D., Deikman, D., and Tart, C. *Symposium on Consciousness*. New York: Viking, 1975.

Malamud, W., and Linder, F. Dreams and their relationship to recent impressions. *Arch. Neurol. Psychiat.*, **25**: 1081-1099, 1931.

Mendels, J., and Hawkins, D. Sleep laboratory adaptation on normal subjects and depressed patients (first night effect). *EEG Clin. Neurophysiol.*, **22**: 556-558, 1967.

Moss, C. *The Hypnotic Investigation of Dreams.* New York: Wiley, 1967.

Moss, C. Innovations in the experimental manipulations of dreams. *Progress in Clinical Psychology.* New York: Grune & Stratton, 1969.

Nachmansohn, M. Ueber experimentell erzeugte Traeume nebst kritischen Bemerkungen ueber die psychoanalytische Methodik. *Zeitschrift fur die gesamte Neurol. Psychiat.*, **98**: 556-586, 1925. In Rapaport, D. (Ed.), *Organization and Pathology of Thought.* New York: Columbia University Press, 1951.

Narayana, R. *The Dream Problem and its Many Solutions in Search after Ultimate Truth: A Symposium*, Vol. I. Delhi, India: Practical Medicine, 1922(a).

Narayana, R. *The Dream Problem and its Many Solutions in Search after Ultimate Truth*, 2nd vol., part 1. Delhi, India: Practical Medicine, 1922(b).

Noone, R., and Holman, D. *In Search of the Dream People.* New York: Wm. Morrow & Sons, 1972.

Ogilvie, R., Hunt, H., Sawicki, C., and McGowan, K. Searching for lucid dreams. Paper, Assoc. Psychophysiol. Study of Sleep, Palo Alto, California, 1978.

Orne, M. On the social psychology of the psychological experiment: With particular reference to demand characteristics and their implications. *Am. Psychologist*, **17**: 776-783, 1962.

Ouspensky, P. *A New Model of the Universe.* London: Routledge & Kegan Paul, 1960.

Ramsey, G. Studies of dreaming. *Psychol. Bull.*, **50**: 432-455, 1953.

Rechtschaffen, A. The psychophysiology of mental activity of during sleep. In McGuigan, F., and Schoonover, R. (Eds.), *The Psychophysiology of Thinking.* New York: Academic Press, 1973.

Rechtschaffen, A., and Verdone, P. Amount of dreaming: Effect of incentive, adaptation to the laboratory, and individual differences. *Percept. Mot. Skills*, **19**: 947-958, 1964.

Reed, H. Dream incubation: A reconstruction of a ritual in contemporary form. *J. Humanistic Psychol.*, **16** (4): 53-70, 1976.

Roffwarg, H., Herman, J., Bowe-Anders, C., and Tauber, E. The effects of sustained alterations of waking visual input on dream content. In Arkin, A., Antrobus, J., and Ellman, S. (Eds.), *The Mind in Sleep.* New York: Lawrence Erlbaum Assoc., 1978, pp. 295-350.

Sabini, M. The dream group: A community mental health proposal. Unpublished Ph.D. dissertation. San Francisco: California School for Professional Psychology, 1972.

Saint-Denis, H. (Marquis de). *Les rêves et les moynes de les diriger.* Paris: Cercle du Livre Précieus, 1964 (orig. 1867).

Schrötter, K. Experimentelle Träume. *Zentralblatt für Psychoanalyse*, **2**: 638-648, 1912. In Rapaport, D. (Ed.), *Organization and Pathology of Thought.* New York: Columbia University Press, 1951.

Silverman, I. *The Human Subject in the Psychological Laboratory.* New York: Pergammon Press, 1977.

Sparrow, S. Personal testimony: Developing lucidity in my dreams. *Sundance Community Dream J.*, **1** (1): 4-17, 1976.

Sparrow, S. Lucid dreams: Some examples. *Sundance Community Dream J.*, **2** (1): 45-49, 1978.

Stern, D., and Saayman, G. A methodological study of the effect of experimentally induced demand characteristics in research on nocturnal dreams. *J. Abnorm. Psychol.*, in press.

Stewart, K. Dream theory in Malaysia. *Complex*, 9: 3–30, 1953–54.

Stewart, K. Culture and personality in two primitive groups. *Mental Hygiene*, 38: 387–403, 1954.

Stewart, K. The dream comes of age. *Mental Hygiene*, 46: 230–237, 1962.

Stewart, K. Dream theory in Malaya. In Tart, C. (Ed.), *Altered States of Consciousness: A Book of Readings*. New York: John Wiley, 1969.

Stoyva, J. Posthypnotically suggested dreams and the sleep cycle. *Arch. Gen. Psychiat.*, 12: 287–294, 1965.

Stoyva, J., and Budzynski, T. The nocturnal hypnotic dream: Fact or fabrication? Paper, Assoc. Psychophysiol. Study of Sleep, Denver, 1968.

Tart, C. The influence of the experimental situation in hypnosis and dream research: A case report. *Am. J. Clin. Hypnosis*, 7: 163–170, 1964(a).

Tart, C. A comparison of suggested dreams occurring in hypnosis and sleep. *Int. J. Clin. Exp. Hypnosis*, 12: 263–289, 1964(b).

Tart, C. Toward the experimental control of dreaming: A review of the literature. *Psychol. Bull.*, 64: 81–91, 1965(a).

Tart, C. The hypnotic dream: Methodological problems and a review of the literature. *Psychol. Bull.*, 63: 87–99, 1965(b).

Tart, C. Some effects of posthypnotic suggestion on the process of dreaming. *Int. J. Clin. Exp. Hypnosis*, 14: 30–46, 1966.

Tart, C. The control of nocturnal dreaming by means of posthypnotic suggestion. *Int. J. Parapsychol.*, 9: 184–189, 1967.

Tart, C. *Altered States of Consciousness: A Book of Readings*. New York: John Wiley & Sons, 1969(a).

Tart, C. Influencing dream content: Discussion of Witkin's paper. In Kramer, M. (Ed.), *Dream Psychology and the New Biology of Sleep*. Springfield, Illinois: Charles C. Thomas, 1969(b).

Tart, C. Self-report scales of hypnotic depth. *Int. J. Clin. Exp. Hypnosis*, 18: 105–125, 1970.

Tart, C. Measuring the depth of an altered state of consciousness, with particular reference to self-report scales of hypnotic depth. In Fromm, E., and Shor, R. (Eds.), *Hypnosis: Research Developments and Perspectives*. Chicago: Aldine/Atherton, 1972(a).

Tart, C. States of consciousness and state-specific sciences. *Science*, 176: 1203–1210, 1972(b).

Tart, C. On the nature of altered states of consciousness, with special reference to parapsychological phenomena. In Roll, W., Morris, R., and Morris, J. (Eds.), *Research in Parapsychology 1973*. Metuchen, New Jersey: Scarecrow Press, 1974(a).

Tart, C. Some methological problems in out-of-the-body research. In Roll, W., Morris, R., and Morris, J. (Eds.), *Research in Parapsychology 1973*. Metuchen, New Jersey: Scarecrow Press, 1974(b).

Tart, C. Out-of-the-body experiences. In Mitchell, E., and White, J. (Eds.), *Psychic Exploration*. New York: Putnams, 1974(c).

Tart, C. *States of Consciousness*. New York: Dutton, 1975.

Tart, C. The basic nature of altered states of consciousness: A systems approach. *J. Transpersonal Psychol.*, 8, No. 1: 45–64, 1976.

Tart, C. *Psi: Scientific studies of the psychic realm*. New York: Dutton, 1977.

Tart, C. A systems approach to altered states of consciousness. In Davidson, J., Davidson, R., and Schwartz, G. (Eds.), *Human Consciousness and its Transformations: A Psychobiological Perspective*. New York: Plenum, in press.

Tart, C., and Dick, L. *Conscious Control of Dreaming:* I. The posthypnotic dream. *J. Abnorm. Psychol.*, **76**: 304–315, 1970.

Van de Castle, R. Sleep and dreams. In Wolman, B., Dale, L., Schmeidler, G., and Ullman, M. (Eds.), *Handbook of Parapsychology.* New York: Van Nostrand Rheinhold, 1977.

van Eeden, F. A study of dreams. *Proc. Soc. Psych. Res.*, **26**: 431–461, 1913. Reprinted in Tart, C. (Ed.), *Altered States of Consciouness: A Book of Readings.* New York: John Wiley, 1969.

van Eeden, F. *The Bride of Dreams.* New York: Mitchell Kennerley, 1918.

Walker, P., and Johnson, R. The influence of presleep suggestions on dream content. *Psychol. Bull.*, **81**: 362–370, 1974.

Wallin, D. Intentional dreaming, An active approach to the imagery of sleep. Doctoral Dissertation, Wright Institute, 1977.

Weitzenhoffer, A., and Hilgard, E. *Stanford Hypnotic Susceptibility Scale, Form C.* Palo Alto, California: Consulting Psychologists Press, 1962.

Whitman, J. *The Mystical Life.* London: Faber & Faber, 1961.

Whitman, R., Kramer, M., and Baldridge, F. What dream does the patient tell? *Arch. Gen. Psychiat.*, **8**: 277–282, 1963.

Whitman, R., Pierce, C., Maas, J., and Baldridge, B. The dreams of the experimental subject. *J. Nerv. Ment. Dis.*, **134**: 431–439, 1962.

Whitman, R., Ornstein, P., and Baldridge, B. An experimental approach to the psychoanalytic theory of dreams and conflicts. *Comprehensive Pyschiat.*, **5**: 349–363, 1964.

Witkin, H. Influencing dream content. In Framer, M. (Ed.), *Dream Psychology and the New Biology of Dreaming.* Springfield, Illinois: Charles C. Thomas, 1969.

Witkin, H., and Lewis, H. The relation of experimentally induced presleep experiences to dreams: A report on method and preliminary findings. *J. Am. Psychoanal. Assn.*, **13**: 819–849, 1965.

Witkin, H., and Lewis, H. *Experimental Studies of Dreaming.* New York: Random House, 1967.

Part II

THEORIES AND APPLICATION

8

Freudian and Post-Freudian Theories of Dreams

Richard M. Jones

But he would have us remember most of all
To be enthusiastic over the night
    Not only for the sense of wonder
    It alone has to offer, but also

Because it needs our love: for with sad eyes
Its delectable creatures look up and beg
    Us dumbly to ask them to follow;
    They are exiles who long for the future

That lies in our power. They too would rejoice
If allowed to serve enlightment like him, . . .

               From *In Memory of Sigmund Freud*
               d. September 1939
               W. H. Auden

PART I. FREUD

Freud composed our first *scientific* story of dreams, and he placed it at the center of our first *scientific* story of human development—individual and collective. The story has been opposed, revised, extended, and amplified in the light of much subsequent clinical and experimental research. In introducing the chapter on Freud's theory in this way I mean to emphasize the pointlessness of evaluating it in its original form. Its value is unique: it *began* the composing of *scientific* theories about what dreams are, why people have them, and what they may do with them. As far back in human evolution as we know of, these questions have stimulated religious, magical, and poetical stories. Only science avoided them, until forced by Freud to confront them.

There is, I think, an awesome significance in the fact that it was on dreams that Freud chose to center the psychoanalytic theories of human development. Dreams are stories. The only thing that all dreams have in common (excepting some schizophrenic ones) is that they are remembered and expressed in storied form. One of the formative experiences of my life occurred around the age of eight. As I was walking to school I chanced to remember a dream. I have forgotten its contents, but I can still vividly recall being awed by the recognition that in my sleep, without any awareness of having been thinking—much less composing—my mind had made up a remarkably interesting story. Now, 44 years later, I am still astonished by these elemental facts about dreams: (1) that they happen in our heads, (2) that they do so by themselves of their own accord, and (3) that they always assume the form of more or less interesting stories. (There was this bicentennial butterfly munching on the American flag. Its camouflage was remarkable: white stars against a blue background on its body, and white stripes on its red wings. It was really remarkable. And then its parents flew by . . .)

Historical Perspective

So, what we have in the psychoanalytic theory of human development, centered as it is on its theory of dreams, is a scientific story about the making of stories. Alexander Marshack has taught me that I may use "scientific story" and "scientific theory" interchangeably, without insinuating anything about scientific theories except that they represent a form of cognition which is probably distinctive of humans: *storied thinking*.

Marshack is best known for the persuasive case he has made—on the basis of microscopic and photographic analysis of inscribed bones and stones from the Neolithic, Magdalenian, and Mesolithic periods—that prehistoric peoples developed a sophisticated tradition of notation, in relation to precise observations of the lunar cycle; and that it was out of this tradition, embellished by artistic developments, that there "suddenly" emerged the hieroglyphic writing, the mathematics, the astronomy, the agriculture, and the religions and mythologies which launched history during the several millenia before Christ. The central hypothesis which Marshack draws from this research puts Freud's choice of dreams as the center of his theories of human development in a newly enhanced perspective, one that Freud could only have dimly intuited. The hypothesis is that considerations of language, social organization, and technology, while obviously essential in order to describe cultural evolution, are not, in themselves, sufficient to *explain* cultural evolution. Only a more general condition,

Marshack contends, a propaedeutic cognitive mode which had been evolving all along the hominid line leading to *Homo sapiens*, and which every *Homo sapiens* has possessed, can *explain* cultural evolution. This cognitive mode is visual, kinesthetic, symbolic, time-factored, and *storied*.

> I am not here discussing the origins of specific words or any language but rather the origins of "story" and the uses and meaning of "story" . . . .
>
> What then is "story"? The simplest definition is that it is the communication of an event or process—that *is* happening, *has* happened, or *will* happen. There is a beginning, something happens, and there is a change or result, an understood solution: act one, act two, act three. It is in the nature of the "story equation" that it must always be told in terms of someone or something. There is, in fact, no other way to tell a story. This holds whether one uses words, mime, dance, ritual, or refers to the symbolism of dream and trance. It holds in the more primitive "storied" communications of lower forms of life, and it holds in the evolved and specialized human "story" categories: magic, religion, ceremony, rite, lore, reportage, history, science. In the hominid on the way to becoming man, the time-factored and time-factoring content and complexity contained in story would have evolved as the brain itself and human culture evolved. . . .
>
> Let me repeat, for the concepts are crucial: every process recognized and used in human culture becomes a story, and every story is an event which includes characters (whether spirit, god, hero, person, "mana," or in modern terms, element, particle, force, or law) who change or do things in time. Since every story can potentially end in a number of ways, efforts would be made to participate in the story, and, therefore, to change or influence the story or process or to become meaningfully a part of it. When such acts become traditional, we can sometimes call them "magic" or "religious." The specific content of these storied efforts would vary from culture to culture. But the cognitive, symbolizing processes would not change, and the basic nature of the storied equation would remain. (Marshack, 1972, pp. 117–119 and p. 283.)

To my knowledge, Marshack has yet to become cognizant of the singular contributions to the support of his hypothesis that may come from recent psychophysiological studies of sleep and dreams. Here I can only suggest a hint: All of the "story categories" to which Marshack refers—magic, religion, ceremony, rite, lore, reportage, history, science—are, to an extent, influenced by the conative experiences of waking life, and, therefore, by the physical and psychological constraints of waking life. Dreams are stories that indulge the human genius for storied thinking *purely*. Moreover, we know from REM sleep research that dreams occur in lavish abundance. Every night of everyone's life more or less exactly 150 minutes' worth of them is composed effortlessly and involuntarily in REM sleep, when anti-gravity muscle potential is totally disengaged by a subcortical region of the brain. What stronger phenomenonological evidence could there be for Marshack's thesis, that storied thinking—visual, kinesthetic, symbolical, time-factored, storied thinking—*is* what the human cortex does, than that when not constrained by the demands of regulating waking behavior by means of practical knowledge, it dreams.

We are thus led, by a confluence of Marshack's archeological research and modern knowledge of the psychophysiology of sleep, to wonder whether remembered dreams may not have served as a kind of capital fund in the economics of storied thinking over the course of human evolution, practical knowledge serving, as it were, as the operating fund—with perhaps the development of history out of prehistorical evolution pivoting around the dawning of conscious awareness that there is a difference, i.e., that a story is "only" a story, a dream "only" a dream. As Marshack puts it:

> We cannot assume that the ice age hunter himself would have been able, consciously and in words, to separate his stories from his hard, factual knowledge. For he probably used one to understand and teach the other, and the words and names he used would have had a storied content. The story might, in fact, seem to him to be the definition of the phenomena, since it would be his only way of explaining or describing it, even while its practical cues and uses were unstoried. (Marshack, 1972, p. 133)

Susanne Langer has allowed herself a similar set of speculations:

> Imagination, I think, begins in this fashion; its lowest form is this organic process of finishing frustrated perceptions as dream figments. In primitive stages of hominid specialization dreams may not have occurred exclusively or even mainly in sleep. For eons of human (or proto-human) existence imagination probably was entirely involuntary, as dreaming generally is today, only somewhat controllable by active or passive behavior, in the one case staving it off, in the other inviting it. But what finally emerged was the power of image-making. This, too, must have had its evolutionary course, starting with . . . dream . . . . None of these hominid creatures in the heyday of fantasy is likely to have suspected any difference between imagination and fact. (Langer, 1972, p. 283)

In the words of Lewis Mumford:

> We shall not go too far astray, I submit, if we picture this proto-human as a creature pestered and tantalized by dreams, too easily confusing the images of darkness and sleep with those of waking life, subject to misleading hallucinations, disordered memories, unaccountable impulses: but also perhaps animated occasionally by anticipatory images of joyous possibilities . . . . From the beginning, one must infer, man was a dreaming animal; and possibly the richness of his dreams was what enabled him to depart from the restrictions of a purely animal career . . . . This brings us back to a paradoxical possibility, namely that consciousness may have been promoted by the

strange disparity between man's inner environment, with its unexpected images and exciting, if disordered, events, and the outer scene to which he awakened. Did this breach between the inner and the outer world not merely cause wonderment but invite further comparison and demand interpretation? If so, it would lead to a greater paradox: that it was the dream that opened man's eyes to new possibilities in his waking life. (Mumford, 1966, pp. 48–51)

Freud did not have the knowledge that Marshack, Langer, Mumford, and I have, with which to speculate on the possible roles of dreams and dreaming in the evolution of man. We know, though, that when he turned his studies away from the neuroses, he often browsed in the archeology of his day. One such scholarly diversion (into the work of Karl Abel) led him in 1910 to write *The Antithetical Meaning of Primal Words*. What especially impressed Freud about Abel's analyses of the eccentricities of the early Egyptian language was the correspondences they revealed (to Freud) between prehistoric language and the dream work, particularly as regards their respective tendencies to disregard negation, their regular trading in antithetical double meanings, and their reversals of representational materials and sounds. In a statement which suggests that he was at least intuitively aware of the future, larger significance of his theory of dreams, he concluded this paper as follows:

> In the correspondence between the peculiarity of the dream-work ... and the practice discovered by philology in the oldest languages, we may see a confirmation of the view we have formed about the regressive, archaic character of the expression of thoughts in dreams. And we psychiatrists cannot escape the suspicion that we should be better at understanding and translating the language of dreams if we knew more about the development of language. (Freud, 1957b, p. 148)

So much for Freud's theory of dreams in historical perspective, which, I believe is the only meaningful perspective within which to view it. To ask if it was right or wrong is a superfluous question. Had it been right or wrong it would not have been a theory. A theory *is* a story. A story is interesting or not interesting. If it is not interesting, it will be forgotten. If it is interesting, it will beget other stories, as Freud's theory of dreams certainly did. To ask why Freud's theory of dreams didn't anticipate Jung's theory or French's theory or Ullman's theory is like asking why Chaucer didn't write *Hamlet*, or why Shakespeare didn't write *Moby Dick*, or why Melville didn't write *Catch-22*.

Dream Formation

What I propose to do in the rest of this chapter, therefore, is to reread Freud's theory of dreams with a contemporary eye, that is, with an eye to denoting those parts of it that had, necessarily, to beget other theories. Compared to some of its progeny, Freud's theory is an unpretentious one, deriving its interest-value as much from what it leaves out as from what it includes; and as much of its heuristic power from its inconsistencies as from its consistencies.

Before we begin, it is of crucial importance to note that Freud's theory of dreams was a theory of dream *formation*. His method of *interpreting* dreams, from which he partially derived the theory of dream formation, is of another conceptual order—an observation that is singularly important for understanding the historical significances of both the theory and the method, as we shall see.

Freud summarized the theory of dream formation as follows:

> The situation is this. Either residues of the previous day have been left over from the activity of waking life and it has not been possible to withdraw the whole cathexis of energy from them; or the activity of waking life during the course of the day has led to the stirring up of an unconscious wish; or these two events have happened to coincide . . . . The unconscious wish links it-self up with the day's residues and effects a transference onto them; this may happen either in the course of the day or not until the state of sleep has been established. A wish now arises which has been transferred onto the recent material; or a recent wish, having been suppressed, gains fresh life by being reinforced from the unconscious. This wish seeks to force its way along the normal path taken by thought processes, through the preconscious. But it comes up against the censorship, which is still functioning and to the influ-ence of which it now submits. At this point it takes on the distortion for which the way has already been paved by the transference of the wish onto the recent material. So far it is on the way to becoming an obsessive idea or a delusion or something of the kind—that is, a *thought* which has been intensi-fied by transference and distorted in its expression by censorship. Its further advance is halted, however, by the sleeping state of the preconscious . . . . The dream process consequently enters on a regressive path, which lies open to it precisely owing to the peculiar nature of the state of sleep, and it is led along that path by the attraction exercised on it by groups of memories; some of these memories themselves exist only in the form of visual cathexes and not as translations into the terminology of the later systems . . . . In the course of its regressive path the dream process acquires the attributes of representability . . . it has now completed the second portion of its zigzag journey. The first portion was a progressive one, leading from the un-conscious scenes or fantasies to the preconscious; the second portion led from the frontier of the censorship back to perceptions. But when the con-tent of the dream process has become perceptual, by that fact it has, as it were, found a way of evading the obstacle put in its path by the censorship and by the state of sleep of the preconscious . . . . It succeeds in drawing attention to itself and in being noticed by consciousness. (Jones, 1970, pp. 15–16)

The method of dream interpretation sought to reverse this supposed process as follows: The dreamer reports to the analyst what it is that has succeeded in "drawing attention to itself and in being noticed by consciousness" by way of "evading the obstacle put in its path by the censorship"—i.e., the manifest content. The dreamer proceeds to associate freely to the various segments of the dream. Scanning these associations, and drawing on his knowledge of the ways in which the "censorship" works under the regressed conditions of sleep—displacement, condensation, regard for representability, regard for intelligibility—the analyst seeks to undo this "dream work" and to infer from the results of this undoing the thoughts wherein "the unconscious wish (had linked) itself up with the day's residues and (affected) a transference onto them"—i.e., the latent content. The sole aim of the interpretive process is to reformulate the manifest content of the dream back into the latent thoughts which, it is assumed, provoked the dream in the first place.

Dream Interpretation

A classic example of this interpretive method is Freud's analysis of Norbert Hanold's dream, as included in Wilhelm Jensen's novel: *Gradiva: A Pompeiian Fantasy*. The dream is as follows:

> The dreamer is in Pompeii on that day which brought destruction to the unfortunate city, experiences the horror without himself getting into danger, suddenly sees Gradiva walking there, and immediately understands as quite natural that, as she is a Pompeiian, she is living in her native city and "without his having any suspicion of it, was his contemporary." He is seized with fear for her and calls to her, whereupon she turns her face toward him momentarily. Yet she walks on without heeding him at all, lies down on the steps of the Temple of Apollo, and is buried by the rain of ashes, after her face has changed color as if it were turning to white marble, until it completely resembles a bas-relief. On awakening, he interprets the noises of the big city which reach his ear as the cries for help of the desperate inhabitants of Pompeii, and the booming of the turbulent sea. The feeling that what he has dreamed has really happened to him persists for some time after his awakening and the conviction that Gradiva lived in Pompeii and died on that fatal day remains from this dream as an addition to his delusion.

We know from the context of Jensen's story that, as a boy, Hanold had developed a close relationship with a female playmate, Zoe Bertgang, which probably included the mutual enjoyment of erotic pleasures; and that, as a man whose scientific interests have taken the place of his sexual interests, he has ceased to recognize Zoe, even though he encounters her regularly in the city in which they both live. Freud continues:

> Hanold learned in the dream that the girl he is looking for lives in the city and in his own day. That is, of course, true of Zoe Bertgang, only that in his dream the city is not the German university city, but Pompeii, the time not

the present, but the year 79, according to our reckoning. It is a kind of distortion by displacement; Gradiva is not transported to the present, but the dreamer is to the past; yet even this way we are given the essential and new fact that he shares locality and time with the girl sought. Whence, then, this dissimulation and disguise which must deceive us as well as the dreamer about the real meaning and content of the dream? Well, we already have means at hand to give us a satisfactory answer to this question . . . .

To interpret a dream . . . means to translate the manifest dream-content into the latent dream-thoughts, to undo the distortion which the latter had to suffer at the hands of the resistance censorship. If we bring these considerations to bear upon the dream occupying us, we find that the latent dream-thoughts must have been as follows: "The girl who has that beautiful walk you are seeking really lives in this city with you . . . ."

In Hanold's dream there is conspicuous another component of the content, whose distortion is easily removed so that one may learn the latent idea represented by it. This is a part of the dream to which the assurance of reality at the dream's end can also be extended. In the dream the beautiful walker, Gradiva, is transformed into a bas-relief. That is, of course, nothing but an ingenious and poetic representation of the actual procedure. Hanold had indeed transferred his interest from the living girl to the bas-relief; the beloved had been transformed into a stone relief. The latent dream-thoughts, which must remain unconscious, want to transform the relief back into the living girl. In connection with the foregoing they say something like this to him: "*You are interested in the bas-relief of Gradiva only because it reminds you of the contemporary Zoe who lives here.*" But this insight, if it could become conscious, would mean the end of the delusion. (Freud, 1956, pp. 82–83)

Now, it is indeed remarkable, as Freud repeatedly observes in *Delusion and Dream*, that Jensen, although unacquainted with psychoanalysis, "knew" what Freud knew concerning the latent contents of dreams, for, in the novel, he has Zoe Bertgang cure Norbert of his delusion, and restore herself to his affections, by artfully confronting him with exactly these two pieces of unconscious knowledge! Equally remarkable, however, is the fact that when Freud wrote to Jensen and informed him of his psychoanalytic prescience, Jensen's reply was, in effect, poppycock!—wherein is reflected the first identifying characteristic (I refuse to say limitation) of Freud's theory, which must beget other theories: its lack of an aesthetic dimension. Certainly, Freud's inferences regarding the latent dream thoughts are on the money. And, certainly, Jensen had to have been prescient of them to have written the novel he wrote. *But*, had Jensen, the artist, acknowledged the latent thoughts *in connection with the dream*, an average work of art would have immediately devolved into a piece of literary trash. For, however "true" the thoughts proved to be, and however important they were for the curing of Hanold's delusion, they simply are not very interesting in their analyzed form. For the artist, then, it is the manifest content of a dream which communicates, which *does not* disguise.

Theory of Dreams

Freud's sole and exclusive intention was to compose the first *scientific* theory of dreams. Recalling of what science consisted in 1900, this meant that he had to focus on the *causes* of dreams. If dreams had interesting purposes, or effects, they had to be overlooked until dreams were scientifically proved to be meaningful objects of study. Other kinds of stories about dreams had been, and would continue to be, told by other kinds of story tellers—an observation that was lost on many of Freud's students, but not on Freud:

> Storytellers are valuable allies, and their testimony is to be rated high, for they usually know many things between heaven and earth that are not yet dreamt of in our philosophy.
> In psychological insights, indeed, they are far ahead of us ordinary people, because they draw from sources that have not yet been made accessible to science. (Freud, 1956, p. 27)

Another identifying characteristic of Freud's theory of dreams stems from the fact that while he intended the theory of dream formation to develop into *the* scientific theory, the method of interpretation on which the theory was significantly founded was but *a* method, as many of his followers began almost immediately to demonstrate. Moreover, the method was defined in its inception by the goals and constraints of psychiatric treatment, where the enjoyable, the humorous, the artful must often be ignored in favor of the healing powers of truth. On many occasions, Freud demonstrated that his method of interpretation could be applied to the dreams of normal people as well as to those of neurotic people. However, each such demonstration is like the interpretation of Hanold's dream: correct, but comparatively uninteresting. The experience of living through Pompeii's destruction is, I contend, far more interesting than having it brought to one's attention that one has forgotten a childhood playmate. The implications of this memory lapse are, of course, more important to a man suffering from a delusion. But most dreams are dreamt by people who do not suffer from serious mental illness. For the vast majority of humans, as Alfred North Whitehead (1973) said: "It is more important that a proposition be interesting than that it be true. The importance of truth is that it adds to interest." If this is so of philosophical propositions, how much more so must it be of dream interpretations? As I have noted elsewhere, Freud based his theory of dream formation on sources other than interpreted dreams, but these were the major source and, to that extent, certain ways of perceiving dreams and certain ways of theorizing about dreams had to be excluded.

For example, the only function of dreaming that Freud's theory can hypothesize is the catharsis or safety-valve function. Repressed infantile wishes are given periodic opportunities for partial fulfillment in the safety of sleep, thus preventing them from building up intolerable states of psychological tension in waking life. This is a very important function, possibly the most important, but it hardly closes the book on the subject, as the section on post-Feudian dream theorists will show.

Close inspection of the safety-valve hypothesis reveals an important inconsistency in the theory. The wishes that are partially fulfilled must, by definition, be *repressed infantile* wishes. That is, in the theory of dream formation this must be so. But in Freud's dream interpretations the repressed infantile wish is almost never identified. The wish to recognize that Zoe Bertgang is alive and well, and still living across the street, simply does not qualify as a repressed infantile wish. It could without much difficulty be traced to a repressed infantile wish (no doubt related to their childhood "games"). But the translation of the dream's manifest content into its latent content *does not do this tracing*. As reported in a former work, when this observation first dawned on me, I reread *The Interpretation of Dreams* with the sole purpose of counting how many times Freud's interpretations included identifications of repressed infantile wishes, which his theory of dream formation assumed were always a dream's motive source of energy. The finding? None. Not one. It was a sobering experience, and had the salutory effect of ensuring that I would never again confuse the theory of dreaming with the method of interpreting dreams.

A related source of confusion concerns the connotations which have come to be projected onto the terms latent content and manifest content. Latent has come to suggest "deep." "Deep," in psychoanalytic circles, tends to suggest the primary processes of the system unconscious. Consequently, the latent content is frequently, however erroneously, understood to be the product of the primary process. Conversely, manifest content has come to carry connotations of shallowness and unimportance, probably because in the actual practice of strict psychoanalytic dream interpretation it is given attention only for the purpose of extracting the latent content from it. The realities of these matters are exactly the opposite. "I wish to recognize that Zoe Bertgang still lives across the street," while an unconscious thought, is not a deep thought, and it is not the product of the primary process. It is a rational thought, couched in the language of the secondary process, and is obviously the product of Freud's impeccably logical secondary thought processes. Living in Pompeii in the year 79, and seeing a beautiful woman turn into a white marble bas-relief is not, on the other hand, an unconscious thought (because it was remembered), and it *is* a deep thought, in the sense that it is a product of the primary process, i.e., the dream work. If, therefore, we wish to study dreams for the purpose of better understanding the ways of unconscious thinking, it is the manifest content, not the latent content, which we should study.

To summarize this very slippery point: The latent content of a dream is unconscious in the *descriptive* sense that it is not, and cannot of itself become, conscious. The manifest content of a dream is conscious (because it has been remembered) but is the product of the unconscious in the *dynamic* sense of having been symbolized by way of displacement, condensation, regard for representability, and secondary revision. This, of course, is precisely why Freud lavished so much attention on dreams: they *are* the royal road to the unconscious, because they *are* the unconscious made conscious. Indeed, in my reading of the literature on dreams, only one prominent psychoanalytic student kept a clear head as to these distinctions: their author.

> A psycho-analyst can characterize as dreams only the products of the dream-work: in spite of the fact that the latent dream-thoughts are only arrived at from the interpretation of the dream, he cannot reckon them as part of the dream, but only as part of the preconscious reflection.
> ... now that analysts at least have become reconciled to replacing the manifest dream by the meaning revealed by its interpretation, many of them have become guilty of falling into another confusion which they cling to with equal obstinacy. They seek to find the essence of dreams in their latent content, and in so doing they overlook the distinction between the latent dream-thoughts and the dream-work. At bottom, dreams are nothing other than a particular form of thinking, made possible by the conditions of the state of sleep. (Jones, 1970, p. 8)

We come now to the most fertile limitation of all, fertile in the sense that it begs for the composing of other theories of dreams: the metaphor of the dream censor. As is well known, Freud derived this metaphor from his perception of an analogous relation between dreams and neurotic symptoms.

> I have been engaged for many years ... in unravelling certain psycho-pathological structures—hysterical phobias, obsessional ideas, and so on .... It was in the course of these psychoanalytic studies that I came upon dream-interpretation. My patients were pledged to communicate to me every idea or thought that occurred to them in connection with some particular subject; amongst other things, they told me their dreams and so taught me that a dream can be inserted into the psychical chain that has to be traced backwards in the memory from a pathological idea. It was then only a short step to treating the dream itself as a symptom and to applying to dreams the method of interpretation that had been worked out for symptoms.
> In view of the complete identity between the characteristic features of the dream-work and those of the psychical activity which issues in psycho-neurotic symptoms, we feel justified in carrying over to dreams the conclusions we have been led to by hysteria. (Jones, 1970, pp. 9–10)

We are as close, here, as I think we can get to the heartbeat of Freud's genius. A serious scientific enterprise should not be launched on a metaphor drawn from an analogy. It should not have worked. Nothing scientifically credible should have come of it. But it did. In Freud's intrepid hands something scientifically revolutionary came of it. Not only a theory of dreams, but, ultimately, a comprehensive theory of individual and collective human development.

Meanwhile, however, I hear Norbert Hanold replying to Freud's interpretation of his dream: "Ah, so that's what the dream means: that I have forgotten the good times with Zoe, have even forgotten Zoe and I want to realize that she still lives across the street. Very interesting, and thanks. But tell me, Doctor, were you ever in Pompeii in the year 79, on the big day; and have you ever seen a beautiful woman turn into a white marble bas-relief? Probably not. Let me tell you those are things I don't wish to forget either. Could you explain to me how I happened to have those experiences? And might you suggest something interesting or useful that I might do with them?"

These, I submit, are valid questions, and Freud could not have answered them. Or, rather, according to my reading of Freud's works, he would have refused to try, as he refused on repeated occasions (most notably in his book on jokes) to apply psychoanalysis to the aesthetic dimension of the human condition. Having drawn the enormous power that he did from the metaphor of the dream censor, he had the intellectual honesty to accept its limitations. Censorship is not an adaptive process, nor is it given to providing enjoyment. It is a restrictive process and a permissive process—perfect for a story about how dreams serve as guardians of civilized mental health; but mute in response to Norbert's questions as to *what else* his dream may have to tell him, and *what else* he may have to tell it.

Freud's theory, then, is about the dream's therapeutics. It is not about the dream's adaptive or aesthetic achievements. For these stories we must look elsewhere. Fortunately, we can do so. And we shall, in Part II of this chapter, on post-Freudian dream theorists, and in the chapter on dreams and education, respectively.

PART II. POST-FREUDIAN THEORIES

One of the most puzzling statements Freud ever made was: "Everything that is repressed is unconscious; but we cannot assert that everything unconscious is repressed." One could have expected him to introduce at this point certain unconscious processes that are not repressive, but something else. But he does not go on to do this. Instead, he expands the statement in the following way:

"Unconscious" is a purely descriptive term, in many respects indefinite and, so to speak, static. "Repressed" is a dynamic expression which takes into consideration the play of psychic forces and denotes that there is present an effort to express all psychic activities, among them that of becoming conscious, but also a counter-force, a resistance, which is able to prevent a part of these psychic activities, including, again, that of becoming conscious. It is characteristic of the repressed material that, in spite of its intensity, it cannot break through into consciousness. (Freud, 1956, p. 70)

Is that all he meant when he said " . . . but we cannot assert that everything unconscious is repressed?" That the descriptive unconscious should not be confused with the dynamic unconscious?

The post-Freudian dream theorists whose ideas I shall discuss in this chapter are the theorists who have assumed that dreams serve *adaptive* functions, over and above the cathartic function which Freud deduced. In the order in which I shall discuss them they are Carl Jung, Herbert Silberer, Samuel Lowy, Thomas French, Montague Ullman, and Richard Jones.

I shall follow the format, used previously, of interpreting a dream of my own from these respective points of view. The dream, from the night of June 10, 1974, is as follows: "A world convention had been called to recalibrate the calendar. As a result of this recalibration I was now 52 instead of 49. I thought: 'Gee, that's pretty neat—adding three years of age just like that—like finding some change in the pocket of an old pair of pants. On the other hand, I was looking forward to feeling what it's like to turn 50. I'll miss that experience.' " The day residues were immediately self-evident: (1) June 10, 1974 was my forty-ninth birthday, and I fleetingly, the day before, wondered what it would be like to turn 50, an age which, in younger days, I considered vastly more ancient than I now see it. (2) A close friend had moved to California the day before, and I had spent a good part of the day missing her.

Some of my associations were as follows:

A World Convention.   My friend and I had attended a meeting of the American Orthopsychiatric Association several months before, where we jointly presented a paper on the uses of dreams in education. There were sides to our relationship that were *un*conventional. The idea of it being a *world* convention has a presumptuous feeling to it, as though the dream was trying to inflate my importance. I do have a world reputation among a small circle of oneirologists, yet I have chosen to devote most of my time and energy to teaching in an almost unknown experimental state college. I know it was a good decision, and I would do it again, but it does pose a challenge to my sense of identity at the level of vanity. Another thing about its being a *world* convention: something wildly overoptimistic about that. As if *this* world of divisiveness and conflict could ever agree to a change of such universal scope!

Recalibrate the Calendar.   First, you don't recalibrate calendars; you recalibrate *instruments.* No, you *cali*brate instruments; you don't *re*calibrate them. Calibrate used to be a very familiar part of my vocabulary when, during World War II, I served as an aerographer in the Navy. One of my jobs was regularly to check the calibration of the meteorological instruments, but I'm sure I haven't used the term since that time. My thoughts turn to a critical two-year period (my eighteenth and nineteenth years) that I spent at a remote weather station on the coast of California. During those years, with lots of spare time, I discovered the joys of reading books. Previously, I had only read what was assigned in school, and had never considered going to college. Now I found myself spending almost my whole monthly salary on books, on every subject that caught my eye. Walt Whitman became my favorite. I must have read *Leaves of Grass* 20 times. Among other things, it finished me as a practicing Catholic. It was, in many ways, a sublimely happy two years. I had discovered what I wanted to do with my life: learn. As soon as the war was over, I was going to go to college. Meanwhile, I was content to wait it out, reading books and writing 30-page letters about what I was reading to my girl friend at home, who didn't understand them.

But there was another "discovery" during this period of my life, which was as devastating as the discovery of books was uplifting. An older married woman, whose husband was overseas, took a fancy to me at a party and invited me to her bed. I had not previously "gone all the way," as it was called in those days, but I'd had the normal range of fantasies, and thought I knew what to do. I didn't, and the woman wasn't much of a teacher. We tried on three different occasions, and then she gave up on me. You can imagine the depths of torment to which this experience subjected me. Suffice it to say that I came close to ending my life over it.

Another association came from the rhythm of the phrase "recalibrate the calendar": two Johnny Mercer songs that were popular during the weather-station years—"Accentuate the Positive" and "Don't Fence Me In." I tried to recall the words of "Accentuate the Positive": "You've got to accentuate the positive; eliminate the negative; latch on to the affirmative . . . . " And then I blocked, and guessed the next line to be: "That's what love is all about." What we have here is, of course, a classic Freudian slip, for, in reality, the last line is "Don't mess with Mr. In Between," which, as it happens, was precisely what my mother had said to me in a dozen different ways, in response to my masturbatory play as an oedipal boy. Thoughts, now, of the many times during my psychoanalysis when my impressionable brush with sexual impotence at age 18 had been traced to the phallic anxiety instilled in me by my mother around the age of 5. My mother's name is Marie, but when I was learning to speak I could only manage "Ree." It stuck, and to this day she is called Ree by the family. Which may explain why the dream used recalibrate instead of calibrate.

Calendar is one of the very few words I have difficulty spelling correctly. Otherwise, I am an exceptionally accurate speller. I always won the spelling bees in school. Spelling came naturally to me; I couldn't understand how some of the other children couldn't learn it.

Now 52 Instead of 49.   What comes to mind is that the first intimate conversation I'd had with the close friend who had moved to California was about death. I happen to be one of those people who thinks about death a lot. I genuinely enjoy thinking about it. Not only do I not fear my own ultimate death; I look forward to it. The worst death, for me, would be an instantaneous one, which offered no opportunity for reflection on it. Very few people seem to understand this; so I tend to keep my thoughts about death to myself. My friend was an exception; she seemed to understand.

She is considerably younger than I am. Twenty-seven years younger. This age difference was one of the exciting aspects of the relationship, and also one of its frustrating aspects. The May-December subtleties were something neither of us had experienced before, nor was it likely that either of us would experience them again. On the other hand, there were many experiences we might have shared, had we been closer in age, that were precluded by the age difference.

Like Finding Some Change in the Pocket of an Old Pair of Pants.   That's an experience that doesn't do anything for me now. When I was a boy it was cause for celebration. Many things like that lose their special charge of delight with the passing of time. In some ways that boyhood memory is a good metaphor for the relationship with my young friend. Neither of us intended it; it took us both by welcome surprise.

Looking Forward to Feeling What It's Like to Turn 50. I'll Miss that Experience. This happens to have been true. In reality, I didn't miss the experience, and enjoyed it immensely. I felt it quite palpably as the beginning of becoming an old man. It's quite a change, and I'm getting a kick out of it.

These were not all of my associations to the dream, but they should be sufficient for the purpose of illustrating the various post-Freudian adaptive theories of dreams.

Freud.   Having analyzed Freud's approach to dreams, I shall give the dream but a brief psychoanalytic interpretation: The latent dream thoughts, which could not have become conscious at the time, were probably something like: "Good, I'm glad she's gone. Now, I can get on with my life, without the distractions she brought to it." Consciously, at the time, I was only aware of missing her, partly because her departure had been more abrupt than expected. But the dream censor had found a way of making this sudden change a subject for merely mixed feelings, some welcome, some unwelcome. The repressed infantile wish which found partial fulfillment in the dream was very likely an auto-erotic one.

All of the post-Freudian theorists whose views I shall now apply to this dream have two things in common: (1) they all ascribe an adaptive function to dreaming, and (2) they all work directly with the manifest content of the dream.

Jung appears to have understood Freud's cryptic statement about the unrepressed unconscious much as did I, for he assumed the interactive relationship between unconscious and conscious processes to be compensatory, not oppositional.

> I expressly used the word compensatory and not the word opposed because conscious and unconscious are not necessarily in opposition to one another, but complement one another to form a totality which is the self . . . . The unconscious processes that compensate the conscious ego contain all those elements that are necessary for the self-regulation of the psyche as a whole. On the personal level these are the not consciously recognized personal motives which appear in dreams, or the meanings of daily situations which we have overlooked, or conclusions we had failed to draw, or affects we have not permitted, or criticisms we have spared ourselves. (Jones, 1970a, pp. 75–76)

Accordingly, Jung's method of dream interpretation follows these guidelines: (1) The dream should be amplified by way of exigesis, in respect to specific manifest dream symbols, rather than by way of association. (2) One should be concerned with the dream's purposes rather than with its causes. Thus, we should ask of the dream "what for?" rather than "why?" (3) The dream should be regarded as real, i.e., as having actually happened, rather than as a merely symbolic experience—so as to increase the chances that the compensatory influences of the unconscious will be consciously assimilated.

Following these guidelines in respect to the world-convention dream, I am moved to dwell on the specific symbol of *change*, as in the dream element "like finding some change in the pocket of an old pair of pants." The dream means monetary change, i.e., coins, but a brief exigetical reflection on the sound of the word immediately reveals considerations of another kind of change, i.e., change of life. In my conscious life I had been resisting change, especially the change in the status of the friendship. And I had been vague as to how I might experience turning 50. In the experience of the dream, however, I am encouraged to welcome change, indeed to delight in the discoveries that accompany change.

Actually, this interpretation is not inconsistent with the latent content revealed by the Freudian interpretation. It does, however, broaden the scope of the Freudian interpretation by viewing the dream in a more holistic perspective.

Silberer, although he subscribed to Freud's theory of dreams, chose to focus on the states of mind in which the dreams were apparently formed (what he termed the "functional symbols") rather than on the actual content of the dream (what he termed the "material symbols"). Dreaming occurs under conditions of "apperceptive deficiency" when we are unable to maintain rational mastery of intellectual achievements that are normally routine. Under these circumstances, as the psyche seeks to maintain a semblance of control at regressed levels (per Freud), the affective tone of the dreamer's overall outlook on the situations symbolized by the dream—its leitmotiv—may be revealed.

> ... even though I am in accord with the theory of hidden wishes and their disguised appearance, my formula in essence is: the stimulus of the dream is always an emotional factor of high valence which arouses our interests with lustful or unlustful coloring. It incites in us gay expectation, complacent self-mirroring, anxious apprehension, worried reflections, bitter accusations, or any other inner reaction animated by affect. (Jones, 1970a, p. 83)

A dream's "functional symbolism," then, reveals not *what* the dreamer is thinking about in the dream but *how* he is doing so.

Applying this point of view to my dream, I am impressed by its very distinctive mood of easygoing, almost philosophical, detachment and quiet humor. I confess I am at a loss to evaluate this mood, i.e., to determine whether it was serving my neurosis or my health. I recognize it as one of the leitmotivs characteristic of my approach to life, and can remember times when it served growth needs, as well as other times when it served neurotic needs; but, in the situational contexts revealed by the Freudian and Jungian interpretations, I cannot be sure which is the case here. Perhaps it is the singular value of Silberer's approach to dreams that it requires the articulation of such questions.

Lowy's dream psychology is one of the most original and most heuristic to have been formulated—and yet his novel contributions are almost never encountered in the contemporary literature on dreams. Lowy conceived the process of dreaming to be an emotion-producing and emotion-regulating process ("psycho-affective homeostasis"), thus combining, as it were, the core insights of Silberer and Jung. However, unlike Jung, he does not conceive of dreams as being intended to influence the conscious ego, and it is this novel attitude toward the relationship (or, nonrelationship) between the dreaming ego and the waking ego that I find so refreshing in Lowy's theory.

> The recollection of the dream has always to surmount some resistance, some counter-pressure of varying intensity .... This, surely, is a strange phenomenon! Why do we possess at all a faculty for remembering our dreams in the waking state, if complete remembering is impeded in this way? It seems almost as if dreams were not destined for the knowledge of our waking consciousness .... This fact seems to constitute a certain argument against the view held by some that the dream is a finger-post for the waking life, a guide for the correct solution of the various problems of one's existence. However fitting and clever many of the examples may be, which are quoted in support of this view, the fact that dreams are usually forgotten speaks strongly against it.

Dreams which appear to be of such an "advising and warning" kind might be actually something different, something more. They contain not a mere plan for later life, not a counsel, nor a purely theoretical principle; but they represent a self-contained, concrete process within the compass of the psyche. When, for instance, we refuse to see some real difficulty, some threatening complication, and exorcise it from our conscious thoughts, and then this reality appears in our dreams, this is probably not mere exhortation, or warning, but a sign that the subconscious psyche is usefully dealing with the difficulty in question, that it is mobilizing and integrating the thought-processes relating thereto, that it is preparing itself for and against the eventuality, forming, as it were, "antibodies," and thus making up for what our conscious thinking neglected to do because it was unable to cope with it. If, then, the real difficulty actually occurs, the psyche, the nervous system, the personality are not unprepared, not quite without mental "antitoxins" . . . Eventual memory constitutes a secondary gain. (Jones, 1970a, pp. 86–87)

Lowy's contribution to dream interpretation pertains less to matters of method than to a certain attitude of largesse with which he approaches dreams.

Although . . . the dream is not primarily destined for conscious memory, it is clear, on the other hand, that it is definitely destined for being "consciously" experienced during sleep. What the subconscious puts at the disposal of the dream-ego is meant to become "conscious" during dreaming. These two different modes of becoming "conscious" ought not to be confounded.

Moreover:

The world of dreams appears as dissociated only in comparison with the world of conscious thought, in relation to the world of logical reality. But why assume and take for granted that the world of dreams wants to be compared with, and related to, the world of reality and realistic thinking? The contrary is much more probable. The world of dreams is a world apart. (Jones, 1970a, p. 87)

If, then, the adaptive functions of dreaming are performed in the consciousness *of sleep* and the mental health benefits achieved, therefore, *whether or not the dream carries over into waking memory*, why, then, all conceivable ways of responding to remembered dreams are luxuries of a sort, which we may learn to learn from and enjoy, up to the limits of our motivation to pay them attention. This perspective on dreams, which has been made exceedingly persuasive by modern REM sleep research, has the liberating effect of encouraging the involvement of dreams in other than therapeutic pursuits. For, it says that we may choose to dwell on the *effects* of a dream, either aside from, or in addition to, trying to understand its presumed causes and/or purposes.

In the dream at hand, for example, the most memorable event involved in remembering it, and reflecting on it, was the moment when I realized that the line from "Accentuate the Positive" which I had difficulty recalling was not "That's what love is all about," but "Don't mess with Mr. In Between"—and the consequent further realization that the sound "re," as in recalibrate, is also the sound of my mother's diminutive name. What made this moment a memorable one? Not its therapeutic effects, but its aesthetic effects. Three years later those memories still come with a smile. I seriously doubt, with Lowy, that the dream was "intended" to have those effects; but if it was, it would be of less interest to me than that my reflections on the dream did have them. Furthermore, even though the dream was "my" dream, I cannot take personal credit for its having had these effects, as I know I am incapable, in waking consciousness, of so artful a feat of dissemblance as to "remember" my mother's sexual prohibitions by way of inventing a phrase whose rhythm would remind me of a song which included a line that I would misremember, so that I could discover a humorous way of recalling the prohibition. It is this ego-less quality of appreciating dreams that Lowy invites when he says:

> But why assume and take for granted that the world of dreams wants to be compared with, and related to, the world of reality and realistic thinking? The contrary is much more probable. The world of dreams is a world apart. (Jones, 1970a, p. 87)

Being a world apart, the world of conscious thought may bring itself into commerce with the world of remembered dreams in any way that may prove to be meaningful, instructive, or enjoyable. (For more on this line of thought, see the chapter on dreams and education.)

French's central assumption is that dreaming serves the purpose of seeking solutions to interpersonal problems by embedding a recent emotional dilemma of the dreamer (the "focal conflict") in a network of analogous problems and solutions from the past, and related problems in the present. The pattern of analogous problems from the past is the dream's "historical background." The constellation of defensive and integrative mechanisms which relate the dream's historical background to its focal conflict and to the dreamer's present life situation is the dream's "cognitive structure." Often the succession of episodes which make up the story of a manifest dream reveals an initial attempt to deny the focal conflict by means of a reassuring hallucination, followed by further symbolic representations of the focal conflict, and subsequent attempts to imagine more realistic solutions. In the process of interpreting a dream, French follows Freud's free association method but relies much more heavily than did Freud on intuition and "empathic imagination" in identifying the focal conflict, and in making inferences as to the dream's historical background and cognitive structure.

French's suggestion that a dream's opening scene often depicts a hallucinatory denial of the focal conflict, plus the prominence in my associations to the world-convention dream of reading, writing, words, and books, provides just the clues needed to identify intuitively the dream's focal conflict: namely, whether or not I should commit myself to the writing of another book. For, if, indeed, at that time in my life, I had awakened one morning to discover that I had magically become three years older, that would have been the conflict with which I would not have had to deal. For several years prior to the dream I had been aware that I had the thoughts and materials for the writing of another book on dreams: *The Dream Poet*. All that was needed was to think through the ideas with precision, and to relate them to pertinent other ideas in the literature, and to marshal and organize the evidential materials for the writing of the book—a lot of work, at which, in earlier years, I would have jumped. Now, although I wanted the book to be written, I did not wish to write it. During the academic year that preceded the dream, I had been engaged in a full-time educational program with three colleagues and 60 students, the aim of which was to produce the book, collectively. My fondest wish, through most of the year, was that my students and colleagues, after learning the basic theory and methods from me, would proceed, as they had agreed, to produce the book. It was an impressively successful year for all concerned, from an educational point of view. But a publishable book was not produced. And the departure of my friend perfectly symbolized the irreversible nature of this "failure." I had now to decide whether to see the book go unwritten, and some of my best thoughts die with me, or to write the book myself.

I should explain why this was an emotional dilemma. I enjoy writing, when I am doing it, and do not begrudge the time and energy it requires, but I have had to recognize that the writing of books is not good for me personally, i.e., for my ego strength and mental health and so forth—in my interpersonal life. It erodes my already limited access to spontaneity; it takes me away from my wife and children more than is good for any of us. In short, it turns my life into a project. Therefore, I had deeply hoped to see the book written as a collaborative effort, in company with my friends and students. At the time of the dream I had had to acknowledge that this hope had been unrealistic—perhaps even selfish. And I was seriously debating whether I was willing to pay the interpersonal price which I knew would be necessary for the personal pleasure of writing the book alone.

The dream's historical background and cognitive structure now reveal themselves readily enough in the associations to the dream: At the meeting of the American Orthopsychiatric Association my friend and I did jointly *present* the paper, thus leaving the interpretation open that we had jointly written it; in fact, I had written the paper in the form of a dialogue, after we had both had to concede that her writing attempts were less than adequate. The tension that is generated by my reputation as a scholar and my decision to teach in a small state college expresses this same ambivalence in another contemporary context. The pessimism about the world situation may be the beginning of a rationalization: what good will another book do? The references to my eighteenth and nineteenth years portrays the same conflict between personal adequacy and interpersonal inadequacy in one of its most acute earlier phases. The memories of my spelling accomplishments in grammer school portray the conflict in an even earlier setting (I enjoyed winning the spelling bees, but it made me no friends). And the references to my mother's response to my infantile masturbatory pleasures manage to represent the focal conflict about as far back as it may go.

I am not in a good position, at this distance from it, to speculate as to the dream's success in contributing to the resolution of the focal conflict—if, indeed, it has been resolved. I can only report that my family and I are three years older, and that the book is written and in press. I shall refer to it again, in the chapter on dreams and education.

Ullman's theory of the adaptive function of dreams, although independently conceived (indeed, the first major such theory to be derived from both clinical and experimental research) parallels French's theory in all but one aspect. French tends to emphasize the *defensive* resolutions of the focal conflict; Ullman tends to emphasize the *revelational* resolutions of the focal conflict.

> The content of dreams can best be viewed as a dialectical unity in which new perceptions leading to new levels of self-revelation are struggling to gain expression in an area where outmoded techniques of self-deception are beginning to weaken and crumble.
>
> The remarkable feature of the dream content lies in the dreamer's ability to express in symbolic or metaphorical terms the connection between a present problem and aspects of the past experience related to the problem and culled from all levels of the longitudinal history of the individual. The dream states more about the problem and the healthy defensive reactions evoked by it than is immediately accessible to waking consciousness.
>
> The affective overtones of the dream are direct, though often subtle, clues to the objective truths involved in the problematic situation. If anything, self-deception is more difficult to effect in a dream than in waking life. This is so because the individual has to explain in depth—that is, in a more complete and historically or genetically integrated fashion—the nature of the threat or upset that besets him. (Jones, 1970a, pp. 100–101)

Thus, Ullman might add to the interpretations given so far that a dialectical unity may be perceived in the world-convention dream, in which the dreamer finds himself personally affected by an event of world significance, and is, as a consequence, faced with a situation he cannot have both ways—as long as he persists in perceiving it exclusively in a *personal* perspective. Why, Ullman might ask, does the dream create a *world* convention? And why the tone of resignation that pervades the dream throughout? Is it possible that, as a consequence of having to perceive the conflict, as Ullman says, "in a more conplete and . . . . genetically integrated fashion than is accessible to waking consciousness" the dreamer sees that a conflict which the dreamer has always perceived from personal and interpersonal points of view must now *also* be perceived from a *cultural* point of view? That the question can no longer merely be whether the writing of the book is good or bad *for him*? Perhaps responsibilities to people with whom he will never have interpersonal relations should count in the decision?

I confess that it was thoughts of this kind which led to the decision to write the book, although I am not conscious now, nor was I then, that the dream— much less Ullman's possible interpretation of it—had any bearing on the decision. As I recall them, the conscious thoughts were more like: "All right, the metaphor of the dream poet is my conception. It has been extraordinarily productive, not only in my hands but in those of many colleagues and students. If it is to have a public birth it must be as my baby. Maybe it will do the world some good, and maybe it won't, I can't really say that I care. But *it* might, and *it* deserves the chance." As I said, I cannot be sure that the dream had any part in producing these (presumably adaptive) thoughts, but who can be sure that it did not?

My own contribution to the view that dreaming may serve adaptive purposes is not as original as those discussed above. It merely seeks to show one way in which the adaptive functions attributed to dreaming by Jung, Silberer, Lowy, French, and Ullman may be understood along the adaptive dimension of psychoanalytic theory, as formulated by Erik Erikson. I call it the epigenetic method of dream analysis. The hypothesis, which the method was invented to test, was suggested by Erikson as follows:

> In addition to a dream's striving for representability, then, we would postulate a style of representation which is by no means a mere shell to a kernel, the latent dream; in fact, it is a reflection of the individual ego's peculiar time-space, the frame of reference for all its defenses, compromises, and achievements. (Jones, 1970a, p. 102)

The hypothesis states that in addition to the parts played in dream formation by repressed wishes, the psychological conditions of sleep, and the defense ego, a dream is partially a product of the *synthesis ego*, which so governs the setting, style, and rhythm of the dream's remembrance as to support a subsequently adaptive state of wakefulness. I have described the work of the synthesis ego as that of preconscious re-differentiation and re-integration of previous epigenetic successes and failures in the context and under the pressure of contemporary (phase-specific) developmental crises.

The method presumes intimate familiarity with and mastery of Erikson's epigenetic theory of individual human development (which is more complex than it appears to some). Here I can only present its structural outline in the form of a previous attempt of mine to combine Erikson's various charts and diagrams (Jones, 1968, pp. 130–131). (See Table 8-1).

We are now prepared to observe that the setting, style and rhythm of the world-convention dream, as illuminated by the interpretations of Jung, Silberer, Lowy, French, and Ullman, were quite precisely oriented to support an adaptive state of wakefulness in a man whose life cycle is predictably pivoted between the last two phases: generativity/self-absorption and integrity/despair. Will the dreamer write a book because it might have a value of its own, or will he choose not to write it because the experience might be bad *for him*? Will his approach to "being a has been" be informed by those experiences he has lived or by those experiences he has missed? I invite you to review the dream and the various adaptive interpretations of it from the points of view of the various psychosexual, cognitive, imaginal, social, psychosocial, and societal qualities that Table 8-1 ascribes to the life stages of adulthood and senescence, in order to judge for yourself the accuracy of this analysis.

So much for the developmental crises in the context and under the pressure of which the synthesis ego must have been working. Can any evidence of this synthesis work be observed? Yes, readily: the references to the aborted friendship carry reminiscences of successes and failures at the level of intimacy/isolation. The associated memories of finding myself, as an adolescent, to be a reader of books and possibly sexually inadequate carry reminiscences of successes and failures at the level of identity/diffusion. The associated memories of the spelling-bee days of grammer school carry reminiscences of successes and failures at the level of industry/inferiority. The excitement of finding some change in the pocket of an old pair of pants carries reminiscences from the level of initiative/guilt. The thoughts of having inflated my sense of self-importance carry to the phase-specific conflict reminiscences from the level of autonomy/shame-doubt. The tone of ambivalent calmness that pervades the dream may carry reminiscences from the level of basic trust/mistrust.

What has been added to the other theories of adaptive dreaming by these exercises? Only a note of credibility. For, Erikson's epigenetic theory of healthy development was designed to complement, in strictly psychoanalytic terms, Freud's theory of neurotic development. It was not designed to support the analysis of dreams. That Erikson's theory does, readily, support the analysis of dreams suggests to me that the Freudian and post-Freudian dream theories need not be viewed in adversarial relations.

TABLE 8-1.

A	B	C	D	E
				Qualities of Reciprocity in Expanding Radius of Significant
Life Stages	Psychosexual Stages	Cognitive Skills	Imaginative Themes	Relations
Infancy	Oral-sensory-respiratory-kinestheic Zones	attention observation inspection	incorporation total embracement or absorption "oceanic" proportions	Trustworthy Maternal Persons (implicit faith)
Play Age	Anal-urethral-muscular Zones Eliminative-retentive Modes	affirmation negation exclusion postponement	disappearance reappearance power magic control impotence	Judicious Parental Persons (implicit justice)
	Infantile-genital-locomotor Zones Intrusive-inclusive Modes	investigation contemplation scrutiny reflection	exploration discovery metamorphosis origination	Exemplary Basic Family (implicit morality)
School Age	Latency Period	representation transcription paraphrase metaphorical thought	invention construction achievement	Instructive Adults (implicit technological ethos)
	Puberty and Adolescence	intuition generalization insight individuation	justice revolution reformation utopias	Confirming Adults and affirmative peers (implicit ideological verification)
Young Adulthood	Genitality	paradox enigma dialectic	true love	Mates and Partners in search of shared identity (implicit social selection)
Adulthood	Genitality and Generativity	tolerance preception	generation regeneration	Progeny and Products in need of generative ingenuity (implicit social mutation)
Senescence	Physical and Mental Decline	"ultimate concern"		New Generation in need of integrated heritage

F	G	H	I
Psychosocial Modalities	Nuclear Growth Crises	Qualities of Awareness	Related Social Structures
To get To take	Trust and Mistrust	Hope (Drive)	Organized Faith
To hold (on) To let (go)	Autonomy and Shame-doubt	Will (Control)	Law and Order
To "make" (= going after) To "make like" (= play)	Initiative and Guilt	Purpose (Direction)	Moral Law
To turn to To know how	Industry and Inferiority	Skill (Method)	Technology
To be (one-self)	Identity and Identity Diffusion	Devotion (Fidelity)	Ideology
To share (one-self)	Intimacy and Isolation	Love (Affiliation)	Organized Cooperation and Competition
To let be To make be To take care of	Authority and Self-absorption	Care (Production)	Education and Tradition
To face not being To be a has been	Integrity and Despair	Wisdom (Renunciation)	Literature and Philosophy

BIBLIOGRAPHY

Part I

Auden, W. H. In Memory of Sigmund Freud, d. September 1939. In *Collected Shorter Poems*, New York: Random House, 1975.

Freud, S. *The Interpretation of Dreams*. In *Standard Edition of the Complete Psychological Works of Sigmund Freud*, Vol. 4, J. Strachey, Ed. London: Hogarth Press, 1953.

Freud, S. *A Metapsychological Supplement to the Theory of Dreams*. In *Standard Edition of the Complete Psychological Works of Sigmund Freud*, Vol. 14. London: Hogarth Press, 1958 (a).

Freud, S. *An Evidential Dream* (1913). In *Standard Edition of the Complete Psychological Works of Sigmund Freud*, Vol. 12. London: Hogarth Press, 1958 (b).

Freud, S. *Jokes and Their Relation to the Unconscious*. In *Standard Edition of the Complete Psychological Works of Sigmund Freud*, Vol. 8, J. Strachey, Ed. London: Hogarth Press, 1957 (a).

Freud, S. *The Antithetical Meaning of Primal Words*. In *Standard Edition of the Complete Psychological Works of Sigmund Freud*, Vol. 12, J. Strachey, Ed. London: Hogarth Press, 1957 (b).

Freud, S. *Delusion and Dream*. Boston: Beacon Press, 1956.

Jones, R. M. *The New Psychology of Dreaming*. New York: Grune & Stratton, 1970.

Langer, S. K. *Mind: An Essay on Human Feeling*, Vol. 2. Baltimore: The Johns Hopkins Press, 1972.

Marshack, A. *The Roots of Civilization*. New York: McGraw-Hill, 1972.

Mumford, L. *Technics and Human Development*. New York: Harcourt Brace Jovanovich, 1966.

Whitehead, A. N. Quoted in *Two Kinds of Teaching* by Huston Smith, *The Key Reporter*, Vol. 38, No. 4, 1973.

Part II

Erikson, E. The dream specimen of psychoanalysis. In Knight, R., and Friedman, C. (Eds.), *Psychoanalytic Psychiatry and Psychology*. New York: International Universities Press, 1954, pp. 131-170.

French, T. *The Integration of Behavior. II. The Integrative Process in Dreams*. Chicago: University of Chicago Press, 1954.

French, T. M., and Fromm, E. *Dream Interpretation*. New York: Basic Books, 1964.

Freud, S. *The Interpretation of Dreams*. In *Standard Edition of the Complete Psychological Works of Sigmund Freud*, Vol. 4, J. Strachey, Ed. London: Hogarth Press, 1953.

Freud, S. The Unconscious, *Collected Papers*, Vol. 4. London: Hogarth Press, 1949.

Freud, S. *Delusion and Dream*. Boston: Beacon Press, 1956.

Jones, R. M. Epigenetic reconstruction in dreaming. *Percept. Mot. Skills*, **13**: 32, 1961.

Jones, R. M. *Ego Synthesis in Dreams*. Cambridge, Massachusetts: Schenkman, 1962.

Jones, R. M. *Fantasy and Feeling in Education*. New York: New York University Press, 1968.

Jones, R. M. An epigenetic approach to the analysis of dreams. In Kramer, M. (Ed.), *Dream Psychology and the New Biology of Dreams*. Springfield, Illinois: Charles C. Thomas, 1969, pp. 379-398.

Jones, R. M. *The New Psychology of Dreaming*. New York: Grune & Stratton, 1970 (a).

Jones, R. M. The manifest dream, the latent content and the dream-work. In Hartmann, E. (Ed.), *Sleep and Dreaming*. *International Psychiatry Clinics*. Boston: Little, Brown, 1970 (b).

Jones, R. M. The functions of dreaming. In Hartmann, E. (Ed.), *Sleep and Dreaming*. International Psychiatry Clinics. Boston: Little, Brown, 1970 (c).

Jones, R. M. *The Dream Poet*. Cambridge, Massachusetts: Schenkman Publishing Co., 1979.

Jones, R. M., Daugherty, L., Maddox, T., and Sinclair, L. Dreams and poetry (unpublished manuscript).

Jung, C. G. *Modern Man in Search of a Soul*. New York: Harcourt, Brace & World, 1933.

Jung, C. G. *Two Essays on Analytical Psychology*. New York: Meridian Books, 1956.

Lowy, S. *Foundations of Dream Interpretation*. London: Kegan Paul, Trench, Trubner, 1942.

Silberer, H. Report on a method of eliciting and observing certain symbolic hallucination-phenomena. In Rapaport, D. (Ed.), *Organization and Pathology of Thought*. New York: Columbia University Press, 1951, pp. 195–207.

Silberer, H. The dream. *Psychoanal. Rev.*, **42**: 361–387, 1955.

Ullman, M. The dream process. *Am. J. Psychother.*, **12**: 671–690, 1958.

Ullman, M. The adaptive significance of the dream. *J. Nerv. Ment. Dis.*, **129**: 144–149, 1959.

Ullman, M. Dreaming, altered stages of consciouness and the problem of vigilance. *J. Nerv. Ment. Dis.*, **133**: 529–535, 1961.

Ullman, M. Dreaming, life style and physiology: A comment on Adler's view of the dream. *J. Individ. Psychol.*, **18**: 18–25, 1962.

9

C. G. Jung's Theory of Dreams

Thayer A. Greene

THEORY

One can raise the question of whether, in fact, Jung does have a theory of dreams. His instinctive response to the phenomenon of the dreaming process was pragmatic and empirical. He received the impact of the imagery and drama of the dream with as open a mind and psyche as possible. He rigorously sought to exclude any preconceived theory or attitude from imposing itself upon the phenomenology of a particular dream.

> I have no theory about dreams, I do not know how dreams arise. And I am not at all sure that my way of handling dreams even deserves the name of a "method." I share all your prejudices against dream-interpretation as the quintessence of uncertainty and arbitrariness. On the other hand, I know that if we meditate on a dream sufficiently long and thoroughly, if we carry it around with us and turn it over and over, something almost always comes of it. This something is not of course a scientific result to be boasted about or rationalized; but it is an important practical hint which shows the patient what the unconscious is aiming at . . . . I may allow myself only one criterion for the result of my labors: does it work?[1]

Although Jung does have a profound suspicion of any rational system that would attempt to codify the task of dream interpretation in too rigid a schema, his own lifelong interest and preoccupation with dreams and their significance indicates that, despite his disclaimer, he did have operative theoretical assumptions which guided him in his approach. It was the reading of Freud's *The*

Interpretation of Dreams which first led Jung to the older man. In their early encounters, they were of one mind that the dream was the "royal road to the unconscious." The essential link which bound them together at that time was their common discovery and awareness of the tremendous dynamic importance of the theory of the unconscious for an understanding of individual and collective human psychology. The fact that these two pioneers of depth psychology were later divided by significant theoretical and practical differences, which still greatly affect their followers, should not obscure the essential fact that both the Freudian and Jungian approaches are founded upon a common appreciation for the absolute centrality of the unconscious in any therapeutic approach to the dream and psyche. "Obviously," Jung contended, "if a person holds a view that the unconscious plays a decisive role in the aetiology of neuroses, he will attribute a high practical importance to dreams as direct expression of the unconscious."[2]

It is a misunderstanding of Jung and of Jungians to believe that the Freudian, Adlerian, Existentialist, and Gestalt approaches to the dream are not valued. Quite the contrary, in fact, since the richness and variety of psychic experience made Jung skeptical of any one theory of the dream process which claimed to be definitive.

> Everyone who analyses dreams of others should constantly bear in mind that there is no simple and generally known theory of psychic phenomena, neither with regard to their nature, nor to their cause, nor to their purpose. We therefore possess no general criterion of judgement .... The sexual theory and the wish theory, like the power theory, are valuable points of view without, however, doing anything like justice to the profundity and richness of the human psyche. Had we a theory that did, we could then content ourselves with learning a method mechanically .... It would then be simply a matter of reading certain signs that stood for fixed contents, and for this it would only be necessary to learn a few semiotic rules by heart.[3]

Inflexible rules of dream interpretation quickly become a bed of Procrustes which sacrifices uniqueness and individuality of imagery and meaning for the sake of uniform theory. In this regard one wonders whether Jung would not be most impatient with some of his own disciples who use his method of dream interpretation in a stereotyped and unimaginative manner. It was the *uniqueness* of the dream as an *experience* of the individual psyche that he sought always to hold in the foreground of his awareness.

The Dream as a Product of Nature

In his autobiography, *Memories, Dreams, Reflections*, Jung writes, "I was never able to agree with Freud that the dream is a 'façade' behind which its meaning lies hidden."[4]   The Jungian approach sees the dream as a product of nature, and "nature commits no errors."[5] Jung writes:

> *I take the dream for what it is.* The dream is such a difficult and compli-
> cated thing that I do not dare to make any assumptions about its possible
> cunning or its tendency to deceive. The dream is a natural occurrence, and
> there is no earthly reason why we should assume it is a crafty device to lead
> us astray. It occurs when consciousness and will are to a large extent ex-
> tinguished. It seems to be a natural product which is also found in people
> who are not neurotic . . . . Nature is often obscure and impenetrable, but
> she is not like man, deceitful. We must therefore take it that the dream is
> just what it pretends to be, neither more nor less.[6]

The consequence of such a view is that no dream censor is assumed to have garbled and disguised the message from the unconscious presented by the dream. The distinction between the manifest dream and the latent dream content, so central to the Freudian approach, is perceived from a different perspective by Jungians. *The problem is not so much one of repression and therefore willful disguise, as it is a failure on the part of the rational mind to speak and understand the primitive, symbolic language of the unconscious.* To someone totally untrained in the native tongue of a particular land, the most genuine attempts by its inhabitants to communicate and reveal their thoughts will appear confusing and incomprehensible. The difficulty is created not by a desire to deceive, but by the absence of a common vocabulary and grammar.

Jung argues that the language of the dream is rooted in the experience of the ancient, the primitive, and the child. The symbolic imagery of myth, fairy tale, legend, and fantasy reveal a way of thinking and experience that stands in contrast to the focused, directed, verbal, and conceptual thinking of modern, scientific man. Directed, verbal thinking is oriented primarily toward adaptation to the reality of the objective world of things, persons, and events. The fantasy or image thinking of the child and primitive is rooted in imagination and subjectivity. It has a spontaneous and autonomous quality which demands little effort from the ego. Directed thinking, on the other hand, has been won only through enormous effort by the conscious ego. A great price has been paid for that victory, moreover, for it has separated rational man from the forgotten language of the instincts.

> Just as the body bears the traces of its phylogenetic development, so also
> does the human mind. Hence there is nothing surprising about the possibility
> that the figurative language of dreams is a survival from an archaic mode of
> thought.[7] . . . It is characteristic that dreams never express themselves in a
> logical, abstract way but always in the language of parable or simile. This
> is also a characteristic of primitive languages, whose flowery turns of phrases
> are very striking. If we remember the monuments of ancient literature,

we find that what nowadays is expressed by means of abstractions was then expressed mostly by similes.[8]

From the Jungian perspective, the apparent illogic of the dream is an expression of archaic but superior wisdom from the instinctive layer of the psyche. The language of metaphor and image, of allegory and symbol, reveals a remarkable precision for the communication of insight when we have come to understand their imaginal logic. The task of the analyst is to meet the dream at this level, to bring his own instinctive awareness and imagination receptively into play with the particular symbolism of the dream.

In his understanding of the function of unconscious imagery, Jung makes an important distinction between *sign* and *symbol*. An expression that represents a known thing remains merely a sign and is never a symbol. Those images and numbers which guide us on our highway journeys are signs, since they stand for known destination, distances, and directions. A symbol, on the other hand, has a living quality. It is an expression for something that cannot be portrayed in any other or better way. The symbol itself embodies that which it symbolizes, and, therefore, its precise form and quality have a particular significance for the meaning which it seeks to convey. It is quite possible for the same image to be merely a sign in one context and a numinous symbol in another. The image of the caduceus worn on the jacket of a medical officer is a *sign* of his particular role and function, just as a silver bar or two stars would be a *sign* of his rank. A patient who has a vivid dream of two snakes winding themselves along a staff may well experience that image as a living *symbol* of some unknown element emerging from the unconscious. Jung writes:

> The symbol is only alive so long as it is pregnant with meaning . . . . It is, therefore, quite impossible to create a living symbol, i.e., one that is pregnant with meaning, from known associations. For what is thus produced never contains more than was put into it. Every psychic product, if it is the best possible expression at the moment for a fact as yet unknown or only relatively known, may be regarded as a symbol, provided that we accept the expression as standing for something that is only divined and not yet clearly conscious . . . . Once its meaning has been born out of it, once that expression is found which formulates the thing sought, expected, or divined even better than the hitherto accepted symbol, then the symbol is *dead* i.e., it possesses only an historical significance.[9]

For the Jungian approach, no dream symbol ever bears a fixed meaning. Consequently, the encounter between the understanding of the analyst and the dream of the patient always has the character of unique dialogue. All the dream images are important in themselves, each one having a special significance of its own, to which it owes its inclusion in the dream. In this regard, the Jungian view is akin to that of existential phenomenology. The particular meaning of the image must be uncovered and extracted from the context of the individual dream and the individual life of the dreamer. The very issue of *meaning* will have at least as much to do with intuitive understanding and emotional response as with conceptual abstraction. If dream symbols do not bear a fixed meaning, then concrete sexual imagery in a dream, for example, may or may not have to do with some personal sexual conflict of the dreamer. As is well known, Jung considered Freud's sexual aetiology of the libido to be too one-sided and limiting an understanding of the nature of psychic energy. From the Jungian perspective, therefore, one may be led in surprising directions in following the imagery of a dream to its source meaning. A dream with religious or banal imagery may lead through the associative context into the realm of unconscious sexual conflict in the dreamer's personal life. Likewise, a dream full of the most blatant sexual images may be discovered to be expressing a religious issue in the dreamer's life of which he is unaware.

> The sexual language of the dreams is not always to be interpreted in a concretistic way—it is, in fact, an archaic language which naturally uses all analogies readiest to hand without their necessarily coinciding with real sexual content. It is therefore unjustifiable to take the sexual language of dreams literally under all circumstances, while other contents are explained as symbolical. But as soon as you take the sexual metaphors as symbols for something unknown, your conception of the nature of dreams at once deepens.[10]

The Dream as Compensatory

In Jung's view, the psyche is a self-regulating system that maintains its equilibrium just as the body does. Every process that goes too far immediately and inevitably evokes a compensatory response. Through his work with patients and his own research, Jung came to the formulation that the nature of psychic process is a dialectical interplay between pairs of opposites, most especially that between ego consciousness and the unconscious. Consequently, the dream is understood as a primary mode by which the unconscious expresses in symbolic form a balancing or homeostatic reaction to the one-sided position of the conscious attitude. Somatic symptoms, compulsive fantasies, and behaviors are other ways by which the compensatory reaction of the unconscious may manifest itself. The more rigidly one-sided and repressive the conscious attitude, the more likely it is that the dreams will be vividly nightmarish in quality and repetitive, with a strongly contrasting but purposive content.

> Never apply any theory, but always ask the patient how *he* feels about his dream images. For dreams are always about a particular problem of the

individual about which he has a wrong conscious judgement. The dreams are the reaction to our conscious attitude in the same way that the body reacts when we overeat or do not eat enough or when we ill-treat it in some other way. Dreams are the natural reaction of the self-regulating psychic systems.[11]

Such an approach necessarily implies that the analyst give careful attention to the conscious situation and attitude of the dreamer. To work only with the dream and not appreciate in detail the existential experience of the one who dreamed it will make the unconscious imagery incomprehensible, or worse yet, lead to superficial and mistaken interpretations. Jung insisted that one of the most helpful rules of dream interpretation was to ask: What conscious attitude does it compensate? For the hard-driving, work-obsessed, self-made businessman, to dream of being a child sitting in the lap of the therapist would have a very different meaning from what it would have for a passive, drug-dependent, aimless adolescent. A graphically sexual dream from the unconscious of a highly spiritual and celibate priest might have an entirely different meaning from what it would have if dreamed by an actor in pornographic films. In itself, a dream image can mean anything or nothing. Only when seen contextually in the dialectical tension with the conscious attitude does its particular meaning emerge.

Objective and Subjective Level of Interpretation

Related to Jung's theory of compensation and his appreciation of the bipolar character of psychic process was his creatively original insight that the dream has both an objective and a subjective level of interpretation. In more recent years, Fritz Perls and other Gestalt therapists have provided us with a method of dream work in which the subjective relation of the ego to the dream contents is developed in a most creative way. What may not be realized or appreciated is that Jung had a very similar understanding of dream work and dream interpretation as early as 1912.

> I call every interpretation which equates the dream images with real objects an *interpretation on the objective level*. In contrast to this is the interpretation which refers every part of the dream and all the actors in it back to the dreamer himself. This I call *interpretation on the subjective level*. Interpretation on the objective level is analytic, because it breaks down the dream content into memory-complexes that refer to external situations. Interpretation on the subjective level is synthetic, because it detaches the underlying memory-complexes from their external causes, regards them as tendencies or components of the subject, and reunites them with that subject .... In this case, therefore, all the contents of the dream are treated as symbols for subjective contents.[12]

Jung's subjective level of interpretation was and remains a major contribution to the theory and practice of analytic psychotherapy. As one who developed the concepts of extraversion and introversion, and was himself a markedly introverted personality, he had a particular sympathy and appreciation for the subjective factor in psychic experience. What some other psychologists of a more extraverted or object-related bias were often inclined to describe as "schizoid" or "autistic," Jung perceived to be a personality with a primarily subjective response to the stimuli of the object world. Such a subjective bias toward external reality was not, in Jung's view, to be equated necessarily with pathology but was rather to be understood as another, totally legitimate mode of psychic experiencing. His own autobiography provides a notable illustration of a life lived with a subjective depth and richness that few persons of this or any age could equal. It is no surprise, therefore, that the Jungian approach lays great stress upon the intrapsychic and intrapersonal dimension of experience and of the dream process. "One should never forget," Jung observes, "that one dreams in the first place, and almost to the exclusion of all else, of oneself."[13]

Causal and Prospective Aspects

Jung's understanding of Freud's apprach to the dream was that it was retrospective and reductive in its assumption that the dream content would lead the interpreter back into repressed childhood instinctual conflict. The aetiology of the dream, like the aetiology of the neurosis, was rooted in the events of childhood. The purpose of the dream was essentially to open a path along which the free associative method could bring the dreamer face to face with forgotten memories and repressed feelings of a much earlier time. The essence of this approach is that past experience represents itself through the present experience of the dream. The Jungian approach does not disagree with such an argument as an accurate description of the basis and function of some, but by no means all, dreams. Jung was also impressed, as was Adler, with the prospective function of the dream. He sensed that the unconscious was not only seeking to call attention to the forgotten past, but was also pointing toward future possibility.

> Considering a dream from the standpoint of finality, which I contrast with the causal standpoint of Freud, does not—as I would expressly like to emphasize—involve a denial of the dream's causes, but rather a different interpretation of the associative material gathered around the dream. The material facts remain the same, but the criterion by which they are judged is different. The question may be formulated simply as follows: What is the purpose of the dream? What effect is it meant to have?[14] . . . The prospective function is an anticipation in the unconscious of future conscious achievements, something like a preliminary exercise or sketch, or a plan roughed out

in advance . . . . The occurrence of prospective dreams cannot be denied. It would be wrong to call them prophetic, because at bottom they are no more prophetic than a medical diagnosis or a weather forecast. They are merely an anticipatory combination of probabilities which may coincide with the actual behavior of things but need not necessarily agree in every detail.[15]

The practical therapeutic value for such a prospective function is that it mobilizes a sense of potentiality and hope for the ego life of the dreamer. In the Jungian view, the unconscious itself has a center, what Jung calls the Self, and this center has a teleological relation to the life of the whole personality. In other words, there is a purposiveness to the psyche itself, and its purpose is wholeness, i.e., to become complete and unified rather than dissociated or fragmented. The prospective function of the dream is one expression of that forward-looking energy which seeks a synthetic re-integration of those psychic elements which have been damaged and divided in the life history of the individual.

Personal and Archetypal Layer of the Dream

It is not appropriate to the purpose of this chapter to describe in detail Jung's thesis that the unconscious is divided into two discernible layers or levels. It may be enough to say that his research and work as an analyst, as well as his own self-exploration, led him to the conclusion that beneath that layer of personal developmental history and experience which has been forgotten or repressed by the individual in his or her struggle for adaptation, there is another layer that has a collective, universally human character. Jungians describe this level as "archetypal" because, similarly to Plato's original use of the term, the archetypes represent a universal, ageless, nonindividual patterning of energy that manifests itself in certain typical forms of behavior and imagery. For example, in developing his theory of the oedipus complex, Freud, himself, was in fact drawing upon a particular archetypal pattern of energy and interaction which is constellated universally between the child and the parents and is not simply the consequence of particular events in individual development. That is not to say, of course, that the specific character of an individual's developmental history does not mediate the archetypal energy and pattern in a particular way, depending upon the personality of the parents.

In his autobiography, Jung tells of a vivid dream which he had in 1909 that led him to his understanding of the levels of the unconscious psyche:

I was in a house I did not know, which has two stories. It was "my" house. I found myself in the upper story, where there was a kind of salon furnished with fine old pieces in the rococo style. On the walls hung a number of precious old paintings. I wondered that this should be my house, and thought,

"Not bad." But then it occurred to me that I did not know what the lower floors looked like. Descending the stairs, I reached the ground floor. There everything was much older, and I realized that this part of the house must date from about the fifteenth or sixteenth century. The furnishings were Medieval; the floors were of red brick. Everywhere it was rather dark. I went from one room to another, thinking, "Now I really must explore the whole house." I came upon a heavy door, and opened it. Beyond it, I discovered a stone stairway that led down into the cellar. Descending again, I found myself in a beautifully vaulted room which looked exceedingly ancient. Examining the walls, I discovered layers of brick among the ordinary stone blocks, and chips of brick in the mortar. As soon as I saw this, I knew that the walls dated from Roman times. My interest by now was intense. I looked more closely at the floor. It was of stone slabs, and in one of these I discovered a ring. When I pulled it, the stone slab lifted, and again I saw a stairway of narrow stone steps leading down into the depths. These, too, I descended, and entered a low cave cut into the rock. Thick dust lay on the floor, and in the dust were scattered bones and broken pottery, like remains of a primitive culture. I discovered two human skulls, obviously very old and half disintegrated. Then I awoke.[16]

Jung comments on this remarkable dream in these words:

It was plain to me that the house represented a kind of image of the psyche—that is to say, of my then state of consciousness, with hitherto unconscious additions. Consciousness was represented by the salon. It had an inhabited atmosphere, in spite of its antiquated style.

The ground floor stood for the first level of the unconscious. The deeper I went, the more alien and the darker the scene became. In the cave, I discovered remains of a primitive culture, that is, the world of primitive man within myself—a world which can scarcely be reached or illuminated by consciousness. The primitive psyche of man borders on the life of the animal soul, just as the caves of prehistoric times were usually inhabited by animals before men laid claim to them.[17]

For Jung these various levels of his descent revealed past stages of psychic life and human consciousness. For the interested reader who is curious to examine a thorough exposition of this approach to collective psychic development, Erich Neumann's work *The Origins and History of Consciousness* provides a valuable source. Jung's archetypal theory has great importance for the interpretation of a dream. It suggests that any dream may have a meaning for the dreamer which is primarily personal and developmental, primarily collective or universal, or, very often, a complex interweaving of the two levels of unconscious psychic life. The task of the analyst is to differentiate these two layers and to relate them relevantly to the conscious life situation of the dreamer. Such a skill requires of the analyst that he or she be well read and deeply familiar with the images and motifs of religion, mythology, folklore, fairy tale, drama, and the arts. When such images and motifs appear in dreams, the archetypal layer is impinging upon the personal "story" of the dreamer.

> Every individual problem is somehow connected with the problem of the age, so that practically every subjective difficulty has to be viewed from the standpoint of the human situation as a whole. But this is permissible only when the dream really is a mythological one and makes use of collective symbols.[18]

APPLICATION

In the clinical practice of dream interpretation, the Jungian attitude, learned from Jung's own example, is to treat the dream as though it were a totally unknown object. An open, naive receiving of the dream and its contents without preconceived opinion is the initial requirement.

> So difficult is it to understand a dream that for a long time I have made it a rule, when someone tells me a dream and asks for my opinion, to say first of all to myself: "I have no idea what this dream means." After that I can begin to examine the dream.[19]

Such an approach by no means ignores the necessity for wide knowledge and trained skills. Quite the contrary, in fact, since Jungian analytic training takes an average of six years at most institutes, and dream interpretation is a major subject. Most important to creative work with a dream, however, is the capacity to experience it, not only for the dreamer but also for the analyst—to let it in in its own terms, to enter into its drama, to be affected by its numinousity. In such a way one establishes a genuine basis for dealing with a dream.

> To *experience* a dream and its interpretation is very different from having a tepid rehash set before you on paper. Everything, about this psychology is, in the deepest sense, experience; the entire theory, even when it puts on the most abstract airs, is the direct outcome of something experienced.[20]

Dramatic Structure of the Dream

The basic elements in the composition of classical drama are by no means arbitrary. They have evolved because they embody inherent, archetypally formed ways in which the human drama is perceived and understood. The inevitability of conflict, its development, and its resolution are universal aspects of life, both individual and collective. Through the centuries the theater has provided an arena for the elucidation of these themes in great variety. Similarly, the dream has dramatic structure that underlies its variety and complexity. The basic elements are: (1) exposition; (2) plot or development; (3) crisis, peripeteia; (4) lysis or catastrophe. In a lengthy and involved dream, the analyst's appreciation of the basic structure can prevent him or her from getting bogged down in the details and provide a sense of the dream's movement, a vision of the whole. It is also remarkable how often one structural element of a particular dream will turn out to offer the key to the meaning of the total dream.

The exposition of a dream refers to its setting, its dramatis personae, its mood or atmosphere, its time, and so forth. Much like the first act of a play when the curtain parts, we are confronted with a particularity of space and time and persons that are the beginning of something, that will lead somewhere even if that somewhere is nowhere. One man of 38 who had great difficulty in establishing an individual basis for his own life had dream after dream that placed him in the setting of his parental home. No matter what direction the dreams took, they almost always began in that setting of his boyhood. The repetition of this expositional theme provided both analyst and dreamer with a clear experiential sense of the extent to which a rather successful man in mid-life was still unconsciously contained by his own childhood origins and parental complexes. There was, of course, other material in the dreams to support this view, but the repetition of the same exposition was in itself an emphatic statement by the dream process, as was the dream in which the same patient finally moved all his belongings into a newly constructed and furnished house of his own.

The plot or development portion of a dream refers to the action and events that grow out of the original exposition and lead to the final denouement or crisis. We say "the plot thickens," for example, in relation to a play or a mystery. The development section of a dream corresponds roughly to the second act of a three-act play where the characters that have been presented in the first act engage with each other in ways that lead to some sort of conflict or situation of tension by the end of the second act. Take for example the following dream of a woman with a tyrannical father complex that ruled her life and prevented her from expressing her true feelings or experiencing enough security within herself to allow her to be close to anyone.

> I am talking with my father on the telephone. We were arranging to meet each other, but I had called him names or "drop dead" or something like that over the phone. He said he was coming to meet me immediately and left the phone. Then, suddenly, he was there at the meeting place, an outdoor cafe in the evening. He was going to yell at me, but I did not let him and really expressed angry feelings. Then there was warmth between us.

The exposition of this dream is simply that the dreamer is talking on the phone with her father. That is the setting out of which everything else develops. The plot or development would be the arrangement to meet and her calling him names, telling him to "drop dead," and his announcement that he was coming to meet her at once.

The crisis or peripeteia, i.e., sudden turn of events, is that point in the drama when things come to a head, when the essential and fateful confrontation occurs, when the crucial choice or action is taken or not taken. In the dream above, the crisis happens when the dreamer's father appears, ready to yell at her. In the history of her past relationship with him, that prospect had always intimidated her to the point of paralysis. In the dream, however, she meets the crisis with direct, autonomous action. She restrains his habitual temper tantrum and instead expresses her own anger, a strikingly new behavior for her. Frequently the crisis point in a dream can be identified by the use of the term "suddenly" or some equivalent expression that indicates a dramatic turn or surprise in the course of events. The game has played itself out, and now the cards are being called. It is the moment at the masked ball when all the dancers unmask and reveal their true identities. Such a moment presents crisis, i.e., choice, to the dream ego.

The lysis or catastrophe in a dream concerns that result which ensues from the crisis and how it has been confronted by the dream ego. In the present dream we are told that following the dreamer's refusal to permit herself to be yelled at and the expression of her own anger, "then there was warmth between us." The lysis or resolution is a somewhat changed relationship with her father which allows for greater affective connection and intimacy, a condition that had not existed for years in the dreamer's actual life, but which began to become possible in the months following the dream and its assimilation by the conscious ego. Many dreams do not end with a positive resolution but with images of catastrophe or interminable inconclusiveness: being pursued endlessly by strange and menacing figures; taking an examination over and over for which one is never prepared; following a trail that leads to a locked door which will not open, or an empty room, or a well whose water cannot be reached. Earthquakes, tidal waves, volcanoes, atomic explosions, or devastating radiation sometimes conclude the drama of the dream process and may provide the analyst with diagnostic and prognostic indications of the patient's potential difficulties.

Many dreams do not correspond totally to the dramatic structure that has just been described. Some dreams may include no more than one element, such as the dream setting, or a plot development that aborts itself without ever reaching a crisis. Very frequently a dream leaves the dreamer with no lysis, as though the potential consequences of the dream situation were still too unknown or veiled for the unconscious to comment on them. Such dreams have a fragmentary or partial quality about them, similar to the fragments of an ancient manuscript which the archaeologist can only partly decipher. Occasionally such a brief fragment or even a single image can open up a wealth of meaning through the personal associations that it evokes or the archetypal background which, through amplification, gives to the single image far more significance than one would at first imagine.

Association, Explanation, Amplification

Central to the practice of Jungian dream interpretation is the associative method of working with the imagery presented.

> The psychological context of dream-contents consists in the web of associations in which the dream is naturally embedded . . . . It should be an absolute rule that every dream, and every part of a dream, is unknown at the outset, and to attempt an interpretation only after carefully taking up the context. We can then apply the meaning we have thus discovered to the text of the dream itself and see whether this yields a fluent reading, or rather whether a satisfying meaning emerges.[21]

Associations are the thoughts, feelings, memories, moods, even bodily reactions that pop up into conscious awareness as the dreamer plays with or meditates upon particular images or events in the dream; for instance, "candy bar: when I was very good, my mother would give me a candy bar." By means of the personal associations of the dreamer the image-logic of the dream can be translated, in part, into conceptual forms and language that can be genuinely understood by the consciousness of the dreamer. When this happens, one feels it "clicks"—it fits. There is often an "aha" sense of recognition as the personal relevance of the dream sinks in, a "touché" experience of sudden insight. For example, a woman of 40 with an overly proper and constricted life style dreamed that she had left her handbag in the family ancestral home and felt terribly insecure without it. To her handbag she associated personal feminine items such as perfume, lipstick, her dream journal, and also her driver's license and credit cards. To the ancestral home she associated a succession of stern Calvinist clergy and their straight-laced women who had lived there and whose stony portraits had looked down at her during childhood visits. The dream imagery can be conceptualized, then, as revealing that her sense of her own personal feminity and her social identity and power in the world are not available to her, causing a feeling of great insecurity. These values are still contained and under the power of a stern and stony religious and cultural bias rooted in her family history which constricts her present life and does not allow her to be her own person. Such a translation from image into conceptual statement must be carefully faithful to the particular associations of the patient and not be contaminated by the projection and bias of the analyst's own unconscious. In this way the dreamer discovers an intelligible, if partial, meaning to his or her material. That such meanings will be "partial" is based upon the fact that a genuine symbol embodies the unknowable, and therefore no single understanding will be complete.   Some dreams, especially those from the archetypal layer of the psyche, take years of pondering and walking around before the central meaning opens to conscious understanding.

The associative method used in Jungian dream work is quite different than the free associative method of Freudian psychoanalysis, where the manifest dream content is seen as a façade which can be a springboard for free association that penetrates below the censorship and leads finally to repressed primary process material.   In contrast, the Jungian method stays with the dream itself as being an authentic statement from the unconscious.   One considers associations to be much like daisy petals, all attached to a common center.   Jung insisted that the dream is seeking to reveal the unconscious situation directly, and that the interpreter's task is to learn its specific language, i.e., the associations, in order to make it available to consciousness.

The use of explanation in dream work is for the purpose of establishing a functional definition of a dream image or object.   Such definitions are largely consensual and objective; for instance, "automobile: a means of individual travel; typewriter: a precise mechanical method for expressing oneself by writing; telephone: a means for personal communication and connection at a distance."   All such explanations of an image will be greatly colored by the personal associations and emotional attitudes of the dreamer.   For one person, a car may mean simply "wheels" to get there; but for another, it may be a status symbol, and for a third an expression of driving skill, autonomy, or ambition.   A dream in which the dreamer is a buck private being drilled by a top sergeant would tell us functionally that the dream message is about this person's relation to authority, but the personal association would reveal the particualr feeling tone or memory-attitude of the dreamer.   The combination of explanation with association provides a more precise reading of the personal and subjective reactions of the dreamer to objective, functional objects, persons, and events in his or her life experience.

Amplification is the art of relating a particular dream image to the symbolic and mythic treasury of the past experience of humankind.   Art, literature, religion, myth, fairy tale, folklore can all be brought into play at this point, for they contain a rich storehouse of archetypal patterns and images from which the well-read and discriminating analyst can select those that may directly relate to the material of the dream and the life situation of the dreamer.   For instance, a psychologically naive and innocent young man who refused to take responsibility for his own life and looked to the authority of others dreamed that he entered an orchard full of beautiful orange trees.   He was very thirsty and wanted to pick an orange to eat, but was so fearful of the owner of the orchard that he could not do it. He associated oranges with a "wake-up fruit" he had for breakfast. He had no association with the orchard or the owner. Amplification by the analyst called his attention the universal motif of the picking of the forbidden fruit, most familiar to us in the Eden story of Genesis. From that archetypal perspective, the dream pointed to the dreamer's inability to commit the necessary theft of his own consciousness, his own "knowledge of good and evil." He was too fearful to take that step which would wake him up to his own responsibility for his existence.

Whereas a Jungian analyst withholds his or her own personal associations to a patient's dream image, the addition by the analyst of amplificatory background to an understanding of the dream is considered legitimate and necessary if the dream's larger meaning and significance are to be uncovered. Jung's conviction that the deeper level of the human unconscious has a universal character leads logically and practically to the requirement that a professional therapist who interprets dreams as a central therapeutic tool should be well grounded in the archetypal foundations of the human psyche so that he may help the patient relate his individual experience to the larger whole.

Object and Subject Level

Jung discovered that a dream could have either an objective or a subjective reference and frequently both. At the object level, the dream is providing information and potential insight about something or someone who is part of the dreamer's external reality. Moreover, the information being provided is a compensation for the dreamer's conscious attitude. Jung gave an example of a man who came shortly before he was to be married to a woman he had known only briefly but loved with a passionate idealism. This man brought Jung a disturbing dream in which his beloved fiancée was portrayed as a lady of pleasure working in an elegant house of prostitution. Although there was an obvious dissociation in the man's own psychology between his spiritual idealism and his sexuality, Jung told his patient to take the dream seriously as an objective message and check into the background and present life of his bride-to-be. The man did so and discovered to his horror that the dream was a truthful statement of the facts he had been too blind to see.

Whenever a dream has to do with people or objects in one's immediate life situation, such as spouse, child, sibling, boss, analyst, friend, and so on, there is a reasonable possibility that the unconscious may be trying to provide information about the other "out there" in order to compensate for a distorted or one-sided attitude by the conscious ego. A too-trusting man may dream that his brother is embezzling the family fortune. A wife may dream her husband is having an affair. A patient may dream that her therapist is ignoring her telling of an important dream while he checks through his wallet. Each dream may be stating something not yet realized about the interpersonal reality of the dreamer's life. When the dream presents images of persons and events from the distant past (the homeroom teacher in fourth grade) or fanciful material (a dragon or unicorn) or objects and places unrelated to the dreamer's own history, the most fruitful interpretive approach is almost surely to be an exploration of the subjective dimension of the dream message.

Jung writes of the subjective level of the dream:

> If our dreams reproduce certain ideas these ideas are primarily *our* ideas, in the structure of which our whole being is interwoven. They are the subjective factors, grouping themselves as they do in the dream, and expressing this or that meaning, not for extraneous reasons but from the most intimate promptings of our psyche. The whole dream work is essentially subjective, and the dream is a theatre in which the dreamer is himself the scene, the player, the prompter, the producer, the author, the public, and the critic.[22]

The view that every aspect of a dream refers back to the dreamer is similar to the Gestalt approach as developed by Perls and others. What gives the Jungian method a different cast is the recognition that a dream is always a compensation. It is presenting some inner piece of truth not known or not yet adequately trusted by consciousness. Rarely, if ever, does a dream simply parallel an already existing viewpoint of the conscious ego. A variety of approaches to the same dream may be called for in order to determine which one "hits the mark" most exactly. For instance, a dream in which Mr. A. dreams that his brother, Mr. B., is deceiving him and embezzling the family fortune may in fact be revealing an objective fact of which Mr. A. is totally unaware. He may believe his brother to be a most admirable fellow who could not possibly do such a thing. In such a case, the dream would be compensating for the unrealistically virtuous perception that Mr. A. has of his thieving brother. If Mr. B. is in fact an absolutely honest man who is not stealing the family fortune, then the deceptive embezzler in Mr. A's dream must be related to some aspect of himself which he has denied or dissociated from his own conscious self-image of virtue and integrity. If Mr. A. knows his brother to be a cheat and has been watching him like a hawk for the least sign of dishonesty, the dream is all the more likely to refer to Mr. A's inner brother who cheats and deceives, i.e., an aspect of his own behavior that he has not faced. In yet another variation, it is possible that Mr. B. is totally honest and fair in his dealings but that the embezzling brother image in Mr. A's unconscious shadow is being projected onto the actual brother. In Jung's understanding, projection is not a deliberate defense but an original choiceless illusion caused by unconsciousness. An activated unconscious complex is most likely to appear as though it adhered to an external object or person. A major clue to the presence of such a projection is the intense affect often connected with it, i.e., strong positive or negative feelings.

The structure of a dream does not of itself indicate whether one should interpret at the object or the subject level. Where it touches on the relational life and actual environment of the dreamer, the object level should always be considered. In the great majority of dreams, however, it will be the subject level of interpretation that will provide a compensatory and healing effect, perhaps especially in a culture such as our own where the libido of most persons is so extraverted and attached to external phenomena. The subjective reality, the inner truth, is more likely to be ignored and hence in need of expression by means of the compensatory function of the dream.

When the interpretation of a dream seems obvious and to be expected, we have usually missed the point. A true reading of a dream carries an element of surprise, of being caught off guard, as though we were waiting for its meaning at the front door and it sneaked in through the cellar. A recently divorced man whose wife had been extremely punitive and hostile during the separation and divorce process dreamed: "My ex-wife and I are in a room. She has a knife and is trying to cut me with it but I use all four of my extremities by stretching them out like a cross and that neutralizes her power." At first, the man was sure he had dreamed about his actual wife and her continuing efforts to "cut me up." His conscious attitude, however, was already well aware of her hostile intentions and behavior. He hardly needed a dream to remind him. When asked what he associated with his ex-wife, he replied that she was supercritical, was extremely petty, needed to control, and never trusted anyone. When it was also uncovered that he had dreamed this particular dream the night following a difficult encounter in his professional work wherein he had been caught in a very critical and cutting reaction to a colleague who had felt his integrity was not being trusted, the message of the dream took on a very different meaning. It was as though the dreamer were under attack by a critical, cutting, petty, and controlling reactive quality in his own behavior (similar to that of his ex-wife), which had popped out in his interaction with his colleague, and for which he had later felt remorse. The dream encouraged him to hope that he had a potential capacity to neutralize the tendency and relate differently in the future. What at first seemed to deal with his marital woes took a surprising turn and revealed a part of his own personality that needed to be faced.

Personal and Archetypal Level

The Jungian appreciation for the relevance of myth and symbol adds a dimension of meaning to the interpretation of many dreams. The dream above, for instance, contains the ancient image of the anthropos (human figure with arms and legs extended in form of a cross) and also refers to the number four. Both the number and the image have a long history in the mythic experience of mankind and refer to the principle of wholeness, of a totality that transcends the partial and fragmented condition of the human ego. It suggests a potential for a whole humanity where a new level of self-realization is present. Viewed from such an archetypal perspective, the sense of the dream deepens and enlarges the meaning of the man's encounter with his colleague, and more importantly, his painful encounter with himself. There is in him a capacity for being fully human and an ability to carry his own destructiveness without unconsciously wounding others as he, the dreamer, had been so often wounded.

In the early stages of analysis, one is likely to find dreams that are concerned primarily with the developmental history of the patient. Such material Jung saw as belonging to the personal unconscious and is to be dealt with as personal complexes, related to sex, aggression, parents, siblings, work, authority, and all such basic elements of human development from child to adult. The common misperception of Jungian therapy as being too "mystical" ignores the extent to which a well-trained analyst of the Jungian tradition gives careful attention to a full anamnesis of the patient's life and seeks to relate present neurotic symptoms and behavior to early development. Where the Jungian approach differs is in the tested conviction that forces beyond the personal and the social are at work in the psyche. Through the images of fantasy, spontaneous art, visionary experience, and most especially the dream, the most common, ordinary individual may encounter levels of psychic life that connect him with the human drama of other ages and lands. Sometimes that awareness can have an impressive healing effect upon the immediate clinical situation. The initial dream of a young man who had just started therapy was that he was performing fellatio on himself, and that when he climaxed, he spit out his semen. The dreamer was a theological student with a history of anxiety and inhibition about his own sexuality. He was so shocked and embarrassed by the imagery of the dream that he could not speak of it and seriously considered stopping the therapy he had just begun. The imagery of the dream obviously had relevance to his own sexual anxieties, but it also was an exact parallel to an ancient Hindu myth of creation in which a male God sucks his semen forth and then blows it out of his mouth, thereby creating the world. This archetypal point of reference made it possible to see that underneath the personal level of the dream, his entrance into therapy had set in motion a creative introverted process that would make possible the creation of a new life in the world for him. His own self-fertilization was the precondition for a realization of creative power. With such an understanding he was more ready to face his own sexual conflicts and inhibition.

Resistance

Resistance by the patient to the analyst's interpretation of a dream is to be treated with respect and sensitivity. In Jung's view, "a dream that is not understood remains a mere occurrence; understood, it becomes a living experience."[23]

For that reason, the dreamer remains the final arbiter of his own dream and his own truth.

> It makes very little difference whether the doctor understands or not, but it makes all the difference whether the patient understands. . . . Understanding should therefore be understanding in the sense of an agreement which is the fruit of joint reflection . . . . The patient does not need to have a truth inculcated into him—if we do that, we only reach his head; he needs far more to grow up to this truth, and in that way we reach his heart, and the appeal goes deeper and works more powerfully.[24]

When an interpretation is incorrect or misses some part of the message of a dream, the unconscious of the patient may be trusted to provide further dreams that will attempt to correct the misinterpretation. In this sense, the compensatory function is at work in the analytic process itself. If the dreams of a patient are consistantly misinterpreted, the analysis will begin to show signs of sterility and lack of movement. Jung comments, "Just as the reward of a correct interpretation is an uprush of life, so an incorrect one dooms (patient and doctor) to deadlock, resistance, doubt, and mutual desiccation."[25]   Sometimes the resistance of the patient to the analyst's interpetation is due to a wide discrepancy in their typology. An extraverted feeling-type patient might have great difficulty in accepting the interpretations of an introverted thinking analyst. The interpretations might be quite accurate and germane, but the way they are presented might be so alien and offensive that the inherent relevance is never acknowledged. When working with an opposite type, it is the analyst's responsibility to find a mode of approach that is congenial to the patient's capacities for understanding.

Other Aspects of Dream Work

A number of other aspects of dream work are of significance for clinical practice and need to be mentioned. Transference dreams are given a priority of attention by Jungians, since they present a commentary upon the therapeutic relationship from the unconscious of the patient. The subject-object and compensatory methods of approach are particularly useful in deciphering the meaning of such dreams. Initial dreams in analysis are often looked into with especial care because they are likely to reveal diagnostic and prognostic information as to the ego potentials of the patient and the character and strength of his or her most pressing complexes. Childhood and repetitive dreams prior to the inception of the analysis are often asked for as another diagnostic tool for assessing the parameters of the patient's conflict. Series of dreams in the course of the analysis are followed with attention. A single dream rarely unlocks a major complex in one night of dreaming. More often, a series of dreams over a period of days, weeks, or even months will fill in the outline of the course of change and development taking place in the unconscious. A patient is likely to have a succession of dreams circling around many different facets of his ego relation to the mother complex which may continue for half a year until one or more dreams signal a stage of resolution has been reached, at which time the dreams may suddenly focus on the father or some other central theme in the dreamer's psychology.

Jungians tend to involve their patients as active participants in the task of interpretation and self-discovery. To that end, the analysand is encouraged to keep a dream journal in which every night's dreams are recorded in the morning. Some patients learn to continue the dream process by way of a method developed by Jung which he termed "active imagination." It is a process that has the quality of a waking dream experience. Many patients are also encouraged to represent particularly vivid or significant dreams and images through some form of artistic expression. This has the effect of consolidating and making more real and concrete the often illusive and evanescent quality of the dream imagery. Frequently also the Gestalt method of dream work is employed so that the dreamer can "be" the various figures and objects in his or her dream, thereby gaining an ego-syntonic relation to an image that might otherwise seem of little immediate value or relevance.

In this brief review of Jung's theory and practice of dream interpretation, it should be clear that the dream process is the major bridge of relationship between conscious and unconscious. The dream is the doorway to the symbolic life and hence to that restoration of balance to the psyche which brings healing change and renewal.

> Together the patient and I address ourselves to the 2,000,000-year-old man that is in all of us. In the last analysis, most of our difficulties come from losing contact with our instincts, with the age-old unforgotten wisdom stored up in us. And where do we make contact with this old man in us? In our dreams.[26]

FOOTNOTES

1. Jung, C. G. *Collected Works*. Princeton: Princeton University Press, 1966, Vol. 16, p. 42.
2. Ibid., p. 139.
3. *C. W.*, Vol. 8, p. 259.
4. *Jung. C. G. Memories, Dreams, Reflections*. New York: Vintage, 1965, p. 161.
5. *C. W.*, Vol. 18, p. 86.
6. *C. W.*, Vol. 11, p. 26.
7. *C. W.*, Vol. 8, p. 248.
8. Ibid.
9. *C. W.*, Vol. 6, p. 474.
10. *C. W.*, Vol. 8, p. 263.

11. *C. W.*, Vol. 18, p. 110.
12. *C. W.*, Vol. 7, p. 84.
13. *C. W.*, Vol. 10, p. 151.
14. *C. W.*, Vol. 8, p. 243.
15. Ibid., p. 255.
16. *Memories, Dreams, Reflections*, pp. 158–59.
17. Ibid., p. 160.
18. *C. W.*, Vol. 10, p. 152.
19. *C. W.*, Vol. 8, p. 283.
20. *C. W.*, Vol. 7, p. 117.
21. *C. W.*, Vol. 12, p. 44.
22. *C. W.*, Vol. 8, p. 266.
23. *C. W.*, Vol. 16, p. 123.
24. Ibid., p. 146.
25. *C. W.*, Vol. 7, p. 112.
26. "Roosevelt 'Great' in Jung's Analysis," *New York Times*, October 4, 1936.

10

Adler's Theory of Dreams: An Holistic Approach to Interpretation

Leo Gold

Alfred Adler viewed dreams as purposeful. He saw the dream as an integral part of the thought process and stressed its congruent relationship to the life style of the individual. Adler based his theory of dream interpretation on the concept that everyone is continually preparing himself for the future. Dreams reflect the dreamer's view of life in terms of the here and now combined with his fictional goals, whereby he plans guidelines for moving toward his goals.

In understanding the dream one must stress the unity of the personality. Adler (1956) stated: "The dream can thus only be understood as an expression of the life style and serves as an integral part of the mental functioning of the individual" (p. 358). The dream, being the creation of the dreamer, always reflects his basic personality. In evaluating dreams we get a comprehensive view of the individual not only in terms of his objective nature and relationship to life, but also in regard to his private logic, biases, and mistakes. The Adlerian interpretation of dreams does not preoccupy itself with unconscious strivings but is directed to the total experiential nature of the dreamer. The dream gives us a direct access to the inner ideation of the dreamer, and can serve as a rich source for grasping the motivations, judgments, and aspirations of the individual. It offers insights into his characteristic attitudes and emotions and clarifies the kinds of logic the individual brings to bear on the nature of his self-percept in relation to the interpersonal process. His typical modes of movement become clarified, and the unique nature of his reasoning becomes apparent.

If we believe in the purposive nature of the dream, then we also understand the subjective nature of its problem-solving functions. Since we seek to solve problems in a manner consistent with our life style, in the dream we create solutions that will gratify our subjective desires. The dream permits us to do this privately without the limitations set by external reality. In dreams we can create a range of solutions satisfying to our private logic which in waking life, if we are reasonably well adjusted, we can either accept or reject on the basis of consensual validation.

We confront the problems of everyday life in keeping with our unique life style and the underlying goals toward which it is directed. The dream becomes a stimulus or means of reasoning that seeks to move us toward these goals. A goal can be a long-term or an immediate one. Both types are reflected in the dream. The value of recognizing the basic life style of the individual is that it clarifies the unique nature of that person's dream structure and greatly facilitates the interpretation of the dream. Once we have a unified view of the individual, we can see the direction the thinking is taking and are better able to assess the quality of the dreamer's judgments as well as the kinds of mistakes his biased view might create. This has rich therapeutic implications.

How one perceives oneself, what one's consistent view of self is, creates a cohesive pattern of how one relates to the world. This gives one a consistent sense of role in the dream process. We can perceive ourselves in a range of roles from the ideal to the most negative. Each individual thus has a unique inner construct of self along which he can fit a series of imaginary events in dream form, which he subjectively draws from his life experience. The dreamer then experimentally creates a series of movements or scripts that enable him vicariously, in sleep, to test out or experience life situations in keeping with his special capacity to comprehend the nature of his reality. The script does not have to agree with external reality but follows the life style and intention of the dreamer. In the wish-fulfillment dreams we perceive the aspirations of the dreamer, the way that he hopes to attain them, and, in waking, the judgment of how likely this solution is when tested against the reality of waking life.

To illustrate, let us postulate that a given dreamer has the life style of a "getter." In other words, in his relationship to others the individual is always expecting to get rather than to give. Since the odds are that his approach to life is based on being deprived or never having enough, his expectation is that others should be constantly available to supply his needs. His goals are always geared to acquisition, and in the dream life this is a consistent pattern. He dreams as follows:

> I was in a great hall standing to one side. I was feeling alone and very hungry. At first others did not realize who I was and passed me by. Then an older man came by and recognized me and took me to a large well-lit chamber. People surrounded me and placed a beautiful robe on my shoulders. I was led

to a banquet table and all kinds of food were brought to me. The older man kept urging things on me. He said, "Here you can take anything you want." I felt a great sense of contentment.

The dream lends itself to quick interpretation. It states simply that the dreamer feels uncertain, a little frightened and empty. When others pay attention to him and give him many things, he feels better. When the dreamer can easily get what he wants and others bend to his service, he feels great. When he is told he can have what he wants, he feels more secure. He states, "I can only understand where I fit in life when I can take or be given what I want." What is of interest in the dream is the passivity of the dreamer. He does not initiate but rather expects others to take the initiative in supplying his needs. This position is consistent with the concept of the life style of the "getter"; it describes the kinds of movements he utilizes and reflects the passive mode he follows in seeking to achieve his goal of getting.

If we look closer at the dream, it is also possible to see him expecting his parents or parent surrogate (authority) to cater to his needs. From this it is possible to create a hypothesis about how he relates to others and the kinds of difficulties he can get into as he stresses his need to get in his social milieu. A picture of his life style having been achieved, subsequent dreams become more readily understandable, and a base is achieved from which we can assess future change when in a therapeutic process.

Adler (1956) clearly stresses the unity of the personality in dream interpretation. He states: "The property of belonging to this unity must also characterize the dream" (p. 358). The dream, like all other aspects of human behavior, is unitary and reflects the dreamer's style of life. Every aspect of the dream, since it is the creation of the dreamer, reflects the dynamic functioning of the individual both subjectively and socially as an expression of the life style. In keeping with a concept of purposefulness Adler (1938) says that "the dream has a forward aim, that it 'puts an edge' on the dreamer for the solution of a problem in his own particular way" (p. 259).

The dream in part represents unfinished business. The dreamer carries into sleep the full range of thoughts and events that preoccupied him during the day. From the holistic point of view there is, therefore, continuity of thought and feeling from waking into sleeping. The process is ongoing, and the dreamer continues to wrestle with his preoccupations through the night. A basic question of dream interpretation deals with what happened during the day prior to the dream.

For Adler the dream continues to address the future and creates a range of ideational experience that attempts clarification of those events which puzzle us or those areas of uncertainty which cloud our path toward meaningful goals.

The dream represents a preoccupation in sleep that occurs as well during waking hours. The human condition is always geared to thinking about possible solutions to the everyday demands of life as well as long-term goals.

In dreams one is more aware of one's inner ideational process, since external stimuli are at a minimum. The dream is not significantly different from our waking thoughts. If we follow the process of reverie introspectively, when we are awake, we can recognize structures of thought and imagery identical to those of the dream process. In essence we use the same shortcuts and imagery in waking thought as we do in sleep. Our need to communicate or to be consensually logical makes us less aware of this process in waking life though we use it actively and are so familiar with it while dreaming.

If we can agree that all human behavior is purposive, then the dream contributes to that purpose and helps clarify the directions the dreamer is pursuing both in fact and in feeling. The dream, like all thought, becomes part of the process of transition toward the achievement of the future. As Adler has pointed out, a dream comes true because, in fact, the dream was preparation for something the individual desired and worked out. As Shulman (1973) has indicated: "It is therefore one function of the dream to make plans for future behavior" (p. 62). The dreamer is preoccupied with choice and changes, considers alternatives, calculates risks, tries on roles, and makes choices and decisions in keeping with his goals.

To evaluate this purposeful direction let us look at a dream of transition. The dreamer relates:

> I am on a boat sailing down a narrow channel. It is a beautiful day. The sun is shining and everything appears serene. The boat sails out onto a large lake. In the center of the lake there is a beautiful island; green; peaceful; empty. On the shore of the lake there is great activity. I see cities, towns, factories, people, farms, war, trains, and all the activities that characterize civilization. I have to make a decision as I am in control of the boat. Though the island appears most attractive, I choose to sail to the mainland and steer my boat to the shore.

The aim and thrust of the dream are clear. The dreamer, in a period of well-being, is finally confronting the reality of his life situation. He perceives two choices: withdrawal from his life situation or direct participation in the hurly-burly of life with an awareness of all the risks entailed in day-to-day living. He states in the dream that it is better to risk and pursue reality in achieving a meaningful existence than to isolate himself in a fantasy never-never land devoid of human contact. He, in essence, recognizes that to achieve meaningful goals in life he must be a participant feeling all the emotions, painful and pleasant, involved in relating to his fellow human beings. The dream deals with both short-term and long-term purpose. The dream says that at a time when he is feeling at peace with himself, it is time to make decisions that eventually will make him a full and productive member of society. He is willing now to risk his serenity in order to reach his full productivity and creativity as a human being. He recognizes that this cannot be achieved in a greenhouse but only in the crucible of life. It is a dream of choice and defines the kinds of movements he will embark on in order to achieve his life goals. He establishes a guiding philosophy of being a participant in life as his direction, and by sailing to the shore in the dream begins to practice and experience what he will do the next day and in the future. He has a sense of direction based on his own choice once he was in the lake rather than in the narrow channel, which gave no choice and, therefore, required less independent responsibility.

Such a dream is extraordinarily important in therapy because it clarifies prognosis, and indicates the significant point of change and transition from withdrawal to social participation. It indicates the client's willingness at last to be a participant in life. It also indicates for him an awareness that he is not a victim but rather an individual who has choice. The dream is a trial solution which he experiences first in sleep and which he later translates into significant actions in life. The dream, in essence, effectively helps him prepare for the future. In keeping with Adler's construct of the dream as a bridge that connects the problem to the goal of the dreamer, we see in this dream how he rehearses and prepares himself for the future.

The concept of rehearsal is most useful in Adler's system. The purpose of rehearsal is to enable us to give a good performance when we confront life and must play out our roles in reality. We constantly, in one form or another, train ourselves for future situations. If we do it well and reasonably correctly, we adjust adequately to life. If we do it poorly, we make mistakes and our performance suffers so that we find ourselves in increasingly neurotic or emotionally disturbed situations. In the dream, as in waking life, we are seeking to orchestrate our thoughts and emotions toward achieving effective ends in life. In life, as in the theater, a performance requires ample rehearsal time. The dream, with its direct expression of our private logic, becomes a significant ground for that rehearsal. Tonight's dream is practice for tomorrow's activity. It contributes toward our choosing attitudes and feelings during the following day. It gives us trial situations and enables us to calculate ahead, correctly or incorrectly, how to cope with the life situations we expect. In the above dream the coping mechanism is clear. The dreamer is stating that the only way to understand life is to get into it and let it happen. The way one achieves it is to reduce distance and become an active participant.

PROBLEM SOLVING

The dream is geared to view humans as problem-solving creatures who are continuously evolving new solutions as the daily social demands of living vary and change. This creates a meaningful construct in relationship to Adler's theory of goal-directedness. The dream deals with ongoing and continuous problems of one sort or another. These problems cannot be thought of as only serious difficulties or major events but rather as the entire fabric of our everyday living. The nature of a problem is not based on degree of difficulty but is concerned with the concept of uncertainty, and the seeking of clarification enables the individual to achieve a better grasp of the expectations of the next day. Problem solving has a number of functions. Within a single dream a number of different problems can be dealt with simultaneously concerning the past, the present, and the future. The individual creates a set of hypotheses about what the future might be like and the kinds of results he is expecting to achieve. In the dream he plays with these concepts in order to see if he can find a direction that will facilitate his attaining any of these possibilities.

In the previously mentioned dream we see the individual exploring the nature of the world he is about to enter and in which he is going to participate. He views its positives and negatives, which reflect his own hopes and aspirations about what he wants to accomplish. The dream becomes a kind of road map where the individual seeks to establish guide points that will help him resolve problems which prevent him from achieving significant goals in his life. As we note from the structure of the dream, the mode of thinking and of working through does not follow literal patterns of actual events or situations but uses a more fanciful approach, which allows a much richer range of facts, information, ideas, fantasies, feelings, emotions, excitement, and passivity to interplay to create a fairly rich fabric not literally true to life but rather containing within it enough material to make possible a solution that everyday living would not ordinarily allow. Peculiarly, the dream is able to create a perspective in relationship to those things which preoccupy the individual that is not available within the limitations of logical thought. It is the broader illogical or greater logical structure of the dream which reflects the inner thought process that makes it possible to achieve this kind of understanding.

The results of problem solving in the dream process are variable and relative because of the basic nature of the unique life style. The results the dreamer comes up with, dependent on the nature of his understanding, private logic, intelligence, and sensitivity, may vary from effectiveness through intermediary possibilities to total ineffectiveness. For the therapist this type of information is invaluable in that it makes it possible to ascertain the kinds of characteristic mistakes the dreamer is likely to make in dealing with his life situations. It also reveals the modes of thinking used by the dreamer in his approach to life, such as optimism vs. pessimism, sureness vs. doubt, anticipation of success or failure, and so on, thus enabling us to assess the degrees of judgment and attitude basic to the individual.

As in life, the end goal is not as important as the process we use to achieve it because until or unless it is achieved, it remains simply a fiction we use to guide our actions in a consistent direction. In the problem-solving dream above, we see the use of choice operating in keeping with the dreamer's preparing himself for full participation in everyday life. We see how he anticipates the kinds of forces he will have to face as a result of his decision.

This does not mean that he knows what the result of his choice will be. It only signifies that he is prepared to take risks. We cannot, despite our favoring the choice, be certain that it is a wise choice, since we cannot know what subsequent life events will occur. The therapist works from a theory of change that favors moving toward greater social participation and interprets accordingly. However, for this theory to be true, there must be subsequent benefits to the dreamer that sustain this hypothesis, a result that is not so readily predictable. It is only where subsequent choices are congruent with the goals underlying the dream, where the therapist perceives growth and maturation on the part of the client, that the guiding function of the dream in problem solving can be sustained. It is necessary in this construct to differentiate between problem solving and wishful thinking.

The dream construct uses analogy as a means for clarifying and enhancing the range of feelings that the dreamer may experience but cannot fully express in waking life. In a sense the dream makes a poet of the dreamer, since its expression is reflective of the same process involved in poetic creation. The dream, as does poetry, uses analogy and metaphor to intensify the emotional impact the dreamers intends to exert on himself. In this sense the experience within the dream is larger than life. It enables the dreamer to utilize a private language of symbol and metaphor to create the structure of thought that exaggerates or expands what one can normally experience in everyday life. Thought process does not follow the usual logic of waking common sense. Rather, it creates a broader fictional world where even the impossible can happen. If the dream in part deals with problem solving, this becomes extremely important, since by going beyond the framework of common sense, the dreamer is also able to create new perspectives on seemingly unsolvable situations in waking life. Thought does not require consensual validation. It is the application of the results of thought to life situations that must fit within the framework of common sense.

Adler (1956) states: "In dreams we reproduce the pictures which will arouse the feelings and emotions which we need for our purposes, that is, for solving the problems confronting us at the time of the dream, in accordance with the particular life style which is ours" (p. 361). There is a heightened emotionality in the dream which creates those psychological elements that project the individual into attempts at solutions. Implicit in this construct is the role of feeling and emotion in creating the momentum that encourages the individual toward some method of problem resolution. The emotions generated in the dream, whether correct or incorrect, can affect the mood of the following day and can determine how the dreamer relates and feels toward others.

The following dream by a man who is contemplating divorcing his wife might illustrate the foregoing. Prior to going to sleep he had made the decision to leave his wife, being quite certain that he could continue a good and responsible relationship with his children. He dreams:

> I am in the country with my girl friend. The fields are beautiful and the weather is warm and sunny. We are walking hand in hand very contentedly. We see some children playing in the distance. The sky begins to darken and clouds begin to amass in a most alarming manner. The children continue playing, ignoring the danger of the storm. We begin to run toward the children. No matter how fast we run, we cannot seem to get any nearer. It gets darker and darker and I become more and more frightened. There is an enormous flash of lightning and I wake up shaken.

The dream is essentially a nightmare that reflects the highly ambivalent state the dreamer is in regarding the contemplated divorce. The predominant theme of the dream is guilt and reflects his feeling that if he divorces his wife he will be unable to reach his children and to sustain and help them in their development. The dream becomes a nightmare because he cannot achieve a resolution. The setting of the dream dramatized his situation and created a highly ambivalent situation, and it sets a base for preventing the change he is contemplating. He imagines a fictional danger which reflects his fear of change. It is the intensity of feeling which is important in the dream because, by its outsized nature, it creates feelings that might continue his marriage rather than risk the frightening difficulties and consequences of divorce.

The dream is a nightmare because his need for security and comfort outweighs the idea of the divorce, which was symbolized by the dark clouds and the storm. We might also guess that, though he is not prepared to confront it, he is also ambivalent about his relationship to his girl friend and uses his children as an excuse for a future decision about terminating this relationship. The appearance of the children in the dream leads to the destruction of the romantic idyll represented in the first part of the dream. The heightened emotion here becomes a way in which the dreamer intoxicates himself into a rationale for ending the relationship, not on the basis of his fear of the consequences of his earlier decision, but rather because of the needs of his children. It becomes a nightmare because his feelings and emotions are not in accord with his conscious desires.

The mood of the following day is, of necessity, anxious and without the clarity and certainty of his decision the night before.

The process of thought inherent in dreams deals with unresolved problems. As Adler (1938) states: "Every attempt to solve a problem that confronts the individual sets the fantasy to work, since, in seeking a solution, he has to deal with an unknown future" (p. 244). The dream becomes a means of examining the problem, trying out possible solutions without the necessary risk of doing so in life. In the dream facts are organized in a variety of ways, logically or bizzarely as the case may require, with the purpose of finding a solution consonant with the life style and goals of the individual.

SELF-DECEPTION

Adler and Shulman (1973) have suggested that there is a self-deceptive element in the dream. Adler (1956), as we have noted, stated that in dreams we produce pictures which will arouse the feelings and emotions needed for our purposes, for solving the problems confronting us at the time of the dreams, in accordance with our particular life style. While there is a self-deceptive element within dreams, it is necessary to see it from a purposive point of view. If the idea is to enable the individual to deal with an area, if it serves as a basis for confronting a situation he might otherwise avoid, if it creates a false perspective that may eventually lead to a more correct one, there is certainly value in this mode of thinking. The self-deception in the dream can be thought of as negative only when the ideas are carried forward into waking life and consensuality is ignored. The heightened emotionality of this process has as its goal a stimulus to action and resolution which is a most important aspect of effective human functioning. Adler further postulates that self-deception is part of the intent of the dream because one's private goals are usually not consonant with immediate realities. The dreamer seeks to find a solution to an unresolved problem which represents his wishes.

A common business situation can well illustrate this. A young woman holds a junior executive position in a company. She is highly ambitious and wishes to climb higher in the hierarchy. It has been announced that the head of her department will move out of his position, which will now be open. Besides herself, there are three male junior executives who could be considered for the job. She dreams:

> I am in a large room. In the center there is a large empty chair. Many people seem to be circling it. Those nearest the chair are men and the women form a circle on the outside. I hide behind a screen, wipe off my makeup and put on a man's suit. I move out into the crowd and no one recognizes me. I move through the group of men and sit in the chair. Everyone applauds.

The dream is self-apparent. In the dream she says, "If I can fool people, I can achieve my goal." It also states, "If I behave more like a man, I could get the job." Essentially her reality makes her resent the inequality of her position in relationship to men and clearly underlines her feeling of women being treated as second class citizens. Since she cannot change her gender, the dream addresses itself to her private goals and creates a fiction reflecting her desire to find a way to obtain the position of department head.

Characteristically, this dreamer's is a life style of a doer who actively seeks solutions to problems. The dream also reflects her need for recognition (the people applaud), and the strong ambition that motivates her actions. While the dream solution is not realistic, it has the components of direction in it whereby she begins to define how she will attempt to achieve her goal. She is aware of the sexist dilemma in her company, and she structures a methodology whereby she will borrow attributes of her male competitors' façades that might enable her to bypass them. The dream begins to create a ground plan toward achieving her goal. There is an excitement in the dream which encourages her optimism through the belief that she can get away with it. The dream content, in its use of fiction, creates a stimulus for future action.

The symbol of the chair becomes the guiding point she keeps in mind as the end goal of her ambition, as she experiences it subjectively and expresses it through her private logic. She utilizes a simple, direct set of symbols to express the forces operating in her emotions and displays her characteristic way of moving through life in dealing with her ambitions, going from the outer circle of women to the inner group of men and finally achieving the goal she sets for herself. In essence, the guiding philosophy that she will use is that she must transcend the limits and biases set by sexist concepts of role if she is to achieve success. She also sets an implication that for a woman to achieve success she has to fool others into seeing her as possessing masculine rather than feminine traits.

SYMBOLS

The content of the dream reflects the private logic of the individual, and it is impossible to establish universal symbols in dream interpretation. Each dreamer has his own unique language, which is consistent with the uniqueness of his life style. The dreamer, utilizing his immediate cultural setting, creates the contents of the dream in a symbolic, idiosyncratic fashion. These symbols are translatable by the therapist if he understands the dreamer's life style, or if they are shared by their common culture. However, no symbol is fixed in its meaning. Thus, while a dream of flying upward might generally reflect a sense of optimism in many dreams, in others it may simply relate concretely to flying because the individual may be anticipating going somewhere. Shulman (1973) has stated: "The dreamer, therefore, uses a private language and private logic, valid only for himself and not subject to consensual validation" (p. 63). The dream language or symbolism can be drawn from any aspect of the dreamer's life experience. It is not inherent in the individual, as suggested by Jung and Freud, but rather derives from the socio-cultural matrix.

Symbols become the basic keystone in establishing the language of the dream. The art of interpretation lies in our ability to translate the particular language utilized by the dreamer. As each individual has a unique life style, so each individual has his characteristic mode of thinking and creates his own unique symbolic structure for expressing his preoccupations, perceptions, and emotions. The symbols serve a pragmatic purpose in that they facilitate our making a large range of inductive leaps and connections.

The interplay of symbols facilitates this thought process. The Adlerian system does not perceive the symbol as universal; every dreamer gives it his own specific meaning. There is no such thing as a phallic symbol, but rather a symbol which may or may not be interpreted phallically, depending on the need of the dreamer and on a particular unitary symbolic system of logic each specific dreamer has created. This, of course, does not occur in a vacuum but is related to the socio-cultural matrix in which the dreamer exists and interreacts.

SOCIO-CULTURAL FACTORS

The fact that we all share in a socio-cultural interreactive process is what makes it possible to understand and decipher another person's dreams. It is the communality among a group of people that makes such understanding possible; groups or societies establish a series of agreements called language, values, and so on, that they hold in common. We are not going to have difficulty with the elements of the dream, but we are going to have difficulty in terms of calculating to some degree the unique way in which the individual dreamer will use these elements. If every human being were so uniquely different that there were not enough commonality, the interpreter would have no way of understanding the particular symbols a dreamer was using. Therefore, in the private logic of our thought, we share symbols because we learn and borrow these symbols from the environment. In this sense, all symbolic ideation is internalized from the outside world and given its own special meaning in our private logic.

As each individual becomes adept in his use of language to communicate, he becomes equally adept in manipulating symbols in his dreams to think through the life situations that confront him. He has a private language of words, feelings, and imagery that enables him to reason beyond the confines of ordinary language. The dreamer has a unique way of utilizing the usual. There is nothing in the dream that actually violates what occurs in reality. It merely expands the parameters to achieve broader levels of perspective to achieve goals more effectively.   The play of symbolism in this process is always geared to seemingly pragmatic ends.   As interpreters of the dream we also seek to translate the directions of the dream to the practical reality of the dreamer based on his dealing with the here and now.

Basic symbols exist in dreams which can be interpreted within the conditions of a given society. In American culture the automobile is a very common symbol. It can be used as a symbol of how we move through our daily existence and the type of role we fulfill therein. Within the interpretive/associative context, let us examine how it is used as a standard symbol.   A dreamer says, "I am sitting behind the wheel driving"; as compared to a dreamer who says, "I am sitting in the back seat and a stranger is driving"; as compared to a dreamer who says, "I am sitting in the back seat and there is no one at the wheel." Each dreamer uses the car as a vehicle for describing how he moves through life. The first dreamer indicates that he has control of the way he moves. The second dreamer indicates that he feels that others are in the driver's seat and control his destiny. The third dreamer indicates that he has no control and that he may be in a basically dangerous or chaotic situation, since he cannot see how to control or direct his movement in life. The symbol itself is excellent, since it is common to our society, plays a significant role in our everyday living, and lends itself readily to a broad expressive range of human experience that can be easily understood.

Let us expand each of the dreams and see what else can be drawn from the basic structure. The first dreamer says: "I am sitting behind the wheel driving. An older person sitting next to me keeps telling me which way to go. I am not happy with her instructions because they seem to be in the wrong direction. I ask her to be still and go the way I want to." The dreamer here is in control of the situation and describes how he utilizes that control in relationship to authority. He prefers to trust his own judgment and moves consistently with his own goals.   Based on our knowledge of the client's life style, this can positively reflect the courage to follow his own judgment or negatively reflect stubbornness because of his need to be right no matter what authority says.   Either interpretation indicates an assertive orientation toward life, which is in keeping with the dream.

In the second dream, the dreamer says: "I am sitting in the back seat of the car and a stranger is driving it. We are driving along the shore and passing through one fishing village after another. There is a lively conversation going on between us and I am feeling very comfortable." The mood of this dream would suggest that the dreamer is enjoying being taken care of and that, in all likelihood, he looks to and expects others to make the world safe and comfortable for him. Certainly one of his priorities is comfort, and the other is to look toward others to take care of things and make life attractive. The dreamer also expects to be stimulated by authority or significant undefined others. The dream is clearly not one of conflict and suggests more a willingness to let things be if nothing disturbing is occurring. There is a pleasant passivity about the dream.

In the third dream, the dreamer states: "I am sitting in the car and there is no one at the wheel. It is hurtling along a dark road. I cannot imagine what I am doing there or how I got there. It is very frightening and I huddle in the corner uncertain as to what to do next. I cannot see out and can only feel the motion of the car. My heart begins to pound and I wake up in a sweat." Here the comment is about "life is!" Life is frightening. Life makes me feel helpless. If only I could hide in a corner, but even that doesn't help. The dreamer experiences life as a victim of unseen forces. He feels he has no control over what is happening, and what is even worse, he has no concept of anything being in control. The events of his life are perceived as chaotic, and what frightens him most is that he can see no way out and can find no one to guide him. It is indeed a nightmare.

The car in all three dreams represents for each dreamer a symbol of the way he moves through life. This is the commonality. How it is utilized is unique to each dreamer, reflecting his life style and private logic in keeping with the immediate events of his life.

The private logic of the dreamer directly affects the use of symbol in the dream. Therefore, as we ascertain the nature of the private logic of each dreamer, the specific use of the symbol becomes clarified. In the above dreams each dreamer is preoccupied with a goal, and in each dream at different levels, the same as in waking life, thought is moving in a direction. The car serves the purpose remarkably well. In the dream, to move in any kind of direction, we have to have a range of symbols to interpret and explain both to ourselves and to others where we are going, even if the goal itself is not clear. Each society creates a series of symbols which may become standard in that society because of their high degree of effectiveness, or temporary because, while they may meet the fashions of the moment, they soon go out of date. In the modern world the car has replaced the coach-and-four of the last century as a symbol of speed and movement. The symbol is not universal but practical to the need of the individual in his immediate world. Certain symbols remain constant through history, such as fire, water, mountains, and so on, because they remain constant in human experience. It should also be noted that primitives who live on plains or deserts where there are no mountains do not dream of mountains. All symbols are learned or created by the dreamer.

The symbol is used because it effectively describes those facts that are continuous in the human experience. The symbol condenses that range of human experience and permits the dreamer to manipulate it in a large variety of ways going beyond the limitations of logical thought. The symbol is generally multi-determined. The car can reflect the self-percept of the individual. It can also represent the small world the dreamer occupies, such as the family as compared to the larger world of society. It can simply be a car. How it is interpreted is dependent on how it is used in the dream.

Not only is it important to note what symbols appear in the dream but also what symbols are absent. What about the dreamer who never reports people in the dream? What is he telling you? Basically he is saying that he is terribly isolated from others and has great difficulty in terms of intimacy. He is likely to be fearful of contact with others, and the odds are that his anticipation in social situations is probably that of pain or humiliation.

PURPOSE OF DREAMS

Within Adler's concept of the unity of the personality there also exists the concept of the unity of the dream. He (1938) sees the dream life as a variant of waking life and then states: "The supreme law of both life forms, sleep and wakefulness alike, is this: the ego's sense of worth shall not be allowed to be diminished" (p. 255). Here, he develops the purposeful nature of the dream as safeguarding the ego of the dreamer, who has to cope with the pressures and demands of external reality. Each individual has a vested interest in protecting his own personality and sense of self-worth, both in the present and in the future. The dream seeks to reinforce that sense of integrity without consistent regard to reality but rather on the basis of the private needs of the individual. This would suggest that the dream is less geared to the individual's social interest in his interaction with others but is rather self-serving. Within such a framework it becomes necessary for the individual to deceive himself as to the validity of his position, and in the dream he is led to abandon common sense.

The effect of the ideation of the dream does not, therefore, generally lead to direct solutions but, according to Adler, serves a more important function. He asks what is left when the dream has ended, and he (1938) states: "There remains what is always left when one indulges in fantasy: feelings, emotions and a frame of mind" (p. 259). The dream arouses the individual emotionally and stimulates him to pursue more actively the aims of the life style even if this requires the elimination of common sense should it interfere with the dreamer's goal of superiority. If the purpose is, therefore, to arouse the individual, then it is preferable that the individual not understand the meaning of his dream, since this would be antithetical to his being able effectively to deceive himself consonant with his fictional goals. It is generally the purpose of the dream to justify the individual's position, rightly or wrongly, so that he feels strengthened in his attitude and behavior. Adler points out that though we often forget dream contents, the feelings they arouse nevertheless remain. The purpose of dreams, he says, lies in these heightened feelings, which form a bridge between the problems confronting the individual and his life style. Adler (1956) states: "In a dream the individual's goal of achievement remains the same as in waking life, but a dream impels him toward that goal with increased emotional power" (p. 361). These heightened emotions then aid the individual in his pursuit of his goals consistent with his life style.

DREAMS AND THERAPY

The interpretation of dreams sets a series of tasks for the therapist. The attempt to utilize standard symbols is understood as simply a matter of probability in Individual Psychology. The interpretation of a given dream is also only probable and is based fairly strictly on what the interpreter grasps and understands of the nature of the life style of the individual.

Given a reasonable degree of knowledge of the life style of the dreamer, we make sophisticated guesses about what the symbol is revealing. It is not our intention to make a perfect interpretation of the symbol but rather to come to a reasonable calculation of what the dreamer is expressing. Since we postulate that the symbol represents a kind of "shorthand" of ideas preoccupying the dreamer in his dealings with life, as we master the dream language it can be interpreted at several levels of meaning. The interpretations are hypotheses that only the logical/affective response of the dreamer clarifies. Here the skill of the interpreter becomes extremely important. His ability logically and empathically to respond to the productions or associations of the dreamer becomes a significant factor, particularly in those dreams where Adler has postulated the dreamer's intention to deceive himself.

The interpretation of a symbol at several levels is important, since it gives us several perspectives into the nature of the dreamer's experience. For example, a client states: "I am in a courtroom. A judge is sitting on the high bench looking down at me with a rather severe and disapproving look." In therapy the client has been berating himself over his inability to complete some work. In this fragment of the dream the primary theme is one of criticism and negative self-judgment. At level one the judge represents authority; how will others, such as his employer, react to his lack of productivity? At level two the judge represents himself putting himself down because of his lack of productivity. Self-censure is his mode of dealing with his feelings of inferiority. At a third level he associates his father with the judge. His comment here is that with his father there is no use in trying because no matter how much or how well he did, his father would always demand more and was never satisfied. At the fourth level it produces a view of life where, no matter what he does, it won't be right, and he is always destined to fit into an inferior position. Associated with this is a predominant sense of guilt, resulting in an anticipation of being subtly and negatively judged one way or another by a condemning society, which is symbolized by the judge.

From the holistic viewpoint all symbols can serve a multiple purpose in tying together a range of events and feelings. In the interpretation of dreams each aspect can best be understood in its overall relationship to the entire dream. Thus, the same element appearing in the dreams of two different people may have different meanings. Adler clearly stresses a flexible approach to dream interpretation, which does not bind itself to fixed rules. Dream interpretation cannot be based on universals, but on an understanding of the individual dreamer with the awareness that each individual is unique and therefore different from others.

Adler sought to elicit associations from the dreamer in order to determine the significance that each aspect of the dream has to the dreamer. Since the content is often expressed allegorically, it must be translated into meaningful structures. Though the dream may appear to violate common sense, the interpretation itself must not. The dream interpretation should clarify how an individual thinks and feels, what his biases are, and the kinds of mistakes he may be making when he overstresses his private logic at the cost of common sense. If one understands the attitudes the dreamer takes toward life in general, it is possible to come to reasonable and effective interpretations of the dream content. One seeks, in the dream material, the quality of movement that characterizes a given individual's life style. The tortuous path of a dream may readily reflect the tortuous way in which an individual moves through life. The dream can reflect reality in a heightened poetic form, which must then be translated back into common sense. The greater the degree of unwillingness on the part of the dreamer to cooperate with the therapist in this, the greater are the distortions of his private logic. Implicit in such an attitude is an unrealistic or mistaken attempt to overcome one's sense of inferiority.

In order for the details of dream thought to be effectively interpreted, they must be understood as a particular mode of presenting one's experience. Adlerians, by stressing the unity of the personality, seek out the modes of movement the individual uses in a particular current life situation.

In the aforementioned dream of the judge, the particular way in which the dreamer moves is clear. His movements are geared to a direction that will avoid censure by others. Thus, when faced with certain situations, we can predict avoidance as a primary means of coping. What is not done cannot be judged. He will choose the path of a follower rather than that of a leader. He will avoid his own creative impulses, since he will see them as provoking criticism rather than as meaningful self-expression. Authority and fear are linked in his mind and leave him vulnerable. We might even predict that he moves toward comfort by selecting relations with others whom he feels are inferior to himself and away from those whom he perceives as above him. Within such a situation he can rarely find what he experiences as a peer relation. It can also be assumed that he will make basic mistakes in such judgments because he will act on initial impressions without judging the correctness of them. His subjectivity overwhelms his objectivity and pushes him in the wrong direction.

Important in Adlerian dream interpretation is the care not to bend the client's thought to a rigid theory of personality but rather to see it in terms of how the individual responds to the processes. In this sense, interpretation is dealt with in direct application to the immediate life of the individual and how he deals with others, rather than in vague theoretical concepts or stereotypes.

Keeping in mind that the language of dreams is uniquely individual, it is then possible to make certain generalizations about contents that appear in dreams. These are then, at best, generalizations and must be modified or shaped by the interpreter to fit the schema of the dreamer. In this sense, Adler perceives the interpretation process as an art requiring skill, sensitivity, and a creative imagination. These requisites are the same as for any other aspect of the therapeutic process.

Symbolic material creates strong affective imagery, causing a richer response and awareness than the more usual process of logical thought, which conforms more rigidly to the demands of everyday reality. In the dream, hanging from a cliff creates a core of feeling that is easily recognizable. One can grasp the anxiety and fear present in the dreamer coupled with the degree of uncertainty implied in hanging over an abyss. One can also recognize the element of uncertainty as to how one will survive a difficult situation. One could generally agree that within Western civilization this meaning would be relatively consistent, even though the unique cause might vary from individual to individual.

The freedom from the standards of consensuality increases the capacity to assess consequences without the actual risk of waking life. No matter how dangerous the experience, the dreamer survives. Even falling from the cliff produces no real danger, since invariably the dreamer survives. But, within the dream the difficulties are symbolically exaggerated or magnified, more in keeping with what we feel about a situation in life rather than how it, in fact, appears logically. This is in part in keeping with how we feel about things in life as compared to how they are from an objective point of view. Invariably, in many life situations, our emotional reactivity is beyond what is going on. Society trains us to inhibit our reactions, and it creates the concept of judgment whereby we temper our emotionality.

The cliff most dramatically expresses this intensity of feeling. The symbol illustrates the "as if" construct of human feeling. For example: An individual has been informed during the day that there is going to be a cut in staff because of economic difficulties. He does not as yet know who or how many will be let go. One can readily imagine his anxiety and uncertainty. While on the surface he appears as his usual self, what kinds of thoughts run through his mind? He begins to worry about money, the effect on his family, what the job market is going to be like, who will hire him at his age, whether he will be one whose job will be all right, and so on. At night he dreams:

> I am walking along a path through some fields. I come to a high cliff over-looking the sea. While admiring the view, I come too close to the edge and the ground crumbles under me and I slip. As I fall, I grab hold of some vege-tation and hang partially suspended over a steep fall. I call for help and hear people coming. The vegetation is not very strong and I feel as though I am about to fall to the bottom. I wake up very upset.

The basic theme of the dream is of someone falling from a high place. The cliff symbolizes the level of position he has achieved in life. The edge symbol-izes the danger extant in his current work situation. The fall and holding on are the vicarious experiencing of the danger should he, in fact, lose the "foothold" in his work situation. Emotionally, the consequence of being fired would be like being killed. The loss is symbolized by the concept of violent death. The experience is dealt with through symbols of emotionality rather than solely through the common sense of waking logic. There is an important value in this flow of symbols. By its seeming dramatization of the event, not only does it stimulate and express the dreamer's fear, but the emotion generated may moti-vate the individual to consider alternative possibilities in the event that the loss of position becomes a reality. The emotions are geared to a concept of survival which is reflected in the dreamer's call for help. The symbols are marshaled to express the intensity of the individual's feelings, and lead, at this point, toward an ill-defined hope for rescue, which would logically be the first hope necessary for him to work out of the situation.

It is interesting, in the dream, that he utilizes a high place as a concept of security or success. Concepts of height in terms of upward movement, such as climbing or flying, take on the meaning of optimism or stimulation for success. Dreams involving downward motion or falling can signify the reverse in terms of uncertainty geared to concern with, or fear of, failure. The movement each type of dream content produces, in essence, becomes a means of creating an attitude to deal with impending life situations, in order to sustain a sense of integration through spurring toward action or safeguarding from failure.

The setting of a dream may reflect how an individual experiences his social matrix. For example: If an individual regularly dreams of jungles, this is a commentary about how he sees life. If he perceives the jungle negatively, as a dangerous place, it tells how he creates danger in his life setting and then reacts as if it were so. If he perceives the jungle as an exciting, colorful place where he is overcoming odds, it may be a commentary on how he creates artificial dangers in his life so that he can achieve a sense of superiority through overcoming.

Let us take as another example the individual who regularly dreams of being in a theater. Sometimes he is in the audience and sometimes on the stage. The setting itself becomes a significant symbol because it expresses his view of life. He follows Shakespeare's adage that life is a stage and we but actors on it. He perceives himself in a variable position, as being actively a performer or passively an observer in life. There is a guarded element in such a symbol: in his active phase he is playing a role, and one could suspect that he is obsessed with the idea of what his real self is, since, invariably, he is playing a role in relation to others; in the part of the observer, he is no longer the center of attention, and the combination suggests a mode of life where recognition by others is of major importance, and he ambivalently seeks to be the center of attention as a form of compensation for some felt inadequacy. The specific contents of each of the dreams show us the variations that are played on this theme based on what specific events occur in his daily living.

He shapes his behavior to meet the demands of the audience, and his major goal becomes the approbation of others. To understand his more subjective feeling of self, we examine his experiences as a member of the audience in contrast to his behavior on the stage. His role of actor follows the ancient Greek tradition of wearing a mask. The actor never reveals himself, but creates a role that will move his audience to respond to him as he wishes. Acting becomes a way of being someone other than who one is. This also has its roots in feelings of inferiority, which we keep in mind in the interpretation of the theater that the dreamer occupies.

The structure of the dream gives one a flavor of the characteristic functioning of the dreamer. One sees, in the dream, the mode in which the individual moves through life, and thus the characteristics of the life style. The interpretation of this, where offered to the client, must be comprehensible to him if it is to have therapeutic value. Overinterpretation or cultish interpretation should be avoided, since this confuses, rather than advances, the understanding of the client.

The interpretation of the dream should not reflect the esoteric knowledge of the interpreter. To be effective, it must be presented in keeping with the language and understanding of the client. We are not so much concerned with the drives or forces in communicating the interpretation of the dream, but rather with how the dreamer directly perceives and reacts to life situations. In keeping with this, we relate his feelings to function in a direct and understandable fashion. The use of the interpretive art is a practical process. Its goal is the clarification for the individual of his private logic and the emotions generated in an inter-reactive social process. We do not seek to clarify the concept of self in isolation but as it is experienced in the full range of relationship to others.

A young man dreams the following:

> I am sitting at the foot of a large statue. It has the feeling of the Lincoln Memorial and yet I have the feeling that it is Zeus. I have the feeling that it is alive and responsive to me though I am unable to see it clearly or entirely. I feel that I have a special relationship to him. There is a feeling of warmth tha permeates the atmosphere and I have the feeling of being loved and at peace.

In the interpretation it can be pointed out how the dreamer relates to author-ity, particularly male authority. One can point out to him how he is drawn to male authority in a seemingly worshipful fashion. At the same time, one can also point out that he doesn't perceive this clearly. The idea could be raised, since he cannot fully make out the entire figure, that perhaps he holds this attitude only because he tends to imbue people with qualities which might not stand the test of clear perception. Gods directly perceived may quickly lose their godlike status. One might suggest to him that one of the difficulties he might have in life is that he makes certain male or authority figures more than human, which leaves him prone to disappointment. At the same time we can clearly see that as long as he doesn't see his idol's clay feet, it appears noble. This makes him special and gives him a sense of elevation he may ordinarily not find in himself. He needs the god as a mirror for his self-esteem. There is a special kind of dependency coupled with optimistic expectations about how he deals with life. He is a believer in luck and, in this phase of his life, expects that authority will work beneficently in his favor.

These concepts in the dream open up a whole broad spectrum of investigation at various levels regarding how he experiences life. The areas of inferiority vs. superiority, large vs. small, how one achieves acceptance in relationship to others, passivity vs. assertiveness in a range of life situations, can all be directly explored with him. We should also be interested in whom the Zeus-like figure is as-sociated with and explore the subtle, affective ways in which he deals with this directly in the interpersonal process and in his private logic. It leads us to ex-plore the kinds of fantasies and expectations he has about certain male figures in his life or, from a goal position, whom he would like to meet in the future.

The clear force of the dream is directed to his feeling very special and to his seeking favored treatment. At the same time, in the dream, we note how at peace he is with himself, and we would begin to investigate what elements in his current life are working to create this sense of well-being. Is he perennially in search of a loving father, or has he come to terms with such a need in his current life situation? We explore this, not from an historical theoretic construct of oedipal identification, but, directly, in his present-day relationship to significant older males.

The dream content is to be understood as the creation and part of the creativity of the dreamer. As the dreamer, in essence, is the artist of himself, his dream clearly reflects the kind of creativity he brings to his everyday living. The concept of creativity is important, since it clarifies for us the process used by the dreamer in problem solving. It displays the unique combinations of imagery he utilizes in order to better grasp and tackle the ideas that preoccupy him in his daily living. The creative element is essential, since it is the basis of unorthodox juxtaposition of events and images in the dream that seek to achieve clarification. The dream is always geared to greater experiential clarification regardless of whether the dreamer does this correctly or incorrectly. It reveals, in this sense, the resources available to the dreamer in his coping behavior toward society.

In commenting on the skill of interpretation, Adler (1938) stated: "Once again I refuse to lay down rules for the interpretation of dreams, since that requires more artistic inspiration than is needed for the pedantic systems of a Beckmesser" (p. 262).

Yet, as Freud and others have indicated, one can approach the dream systematically in order to reach its core of possible meanings. The dream must also be considered as multi-determined rather than dealing with a single event so that in its interpretation one may well look for several levels of meaning. Here, rather than speak of the latent aspects of the dream, it is better, from the holistic point of view, to recognize that one is simultaneously preoccupied with a broad range of ideation carried over from the previous day which is associatively connected in the dream process. Each preoccupation enters into the dream to a greater or lesser extent, depending on the priorities of the dreamer, in keeping with his goal orientation. It is generally a safe rule to assume that dreams are multi-determined in the same fashion as our waking ideation is influenced.

Another good assumption is that each dreamer sets up a standard idiosyncratic structure of symbols which is utilized routinely in his dreams. This language can readily be learned by the interpreter and, once mastered, facilitates his understanding of the client's use of symbol. In the aforementioned dream, the use of the stage as a symbol clearly alerts the interpreter as to the area of the dreamer's preoccupation in regard to his role in relationship to others. When it occurs in his dreams, we are immediately alerted to what preoccupation he has in dealing with the interpersonal process. It brings to the fore his engrossment with the goal of recognition and, in terms of the way it is used in the dream, clarifies how he is currently reacting and dealing with it in his life situation. Also, in the symbols of the boat and the island as they reappear in different dreams by the same dreamer, we recognize the recurrent theme of "escape from" vs. "integration with" reality. They cue us quickly as to how he is dealing with current pressures and how well he applies past knowledge in dealing with them.

The symbol, in this sense, can be compared to the musical themes used by Wagner in *Das Rheingold*. It is immediately recognized, it points to a specific area and mood, and the whole flows to a resolution. As in opera where the music creates a whole mood and atmosphere, so too in the dream one looks for this integration. As the interpreter observes the flow and play of symbols in the libretto of the dream, he also pays attention to the kind of affect or atmosphere in the dream which represents the score. It is the affective states in the dream that lead to the clarity of the intention of the dreamer. The symbol can be used for several elements or individuals in the life situation of the dreamer, since it follows primarily the basic life style of the individual.

The dream plays an important role in Adlerian therapy. However, Adler is clear that much of the information may be derived from other aspects of the therapeutic process. This is consistent with the holistic approach where, because of the basic unity and interrelatedness of every part of the individual and his relationship to the environment, the same information may come from other sources such as early recollections, body movements, attitudes, and so forth. Adler, in agreement with Freud, saw the dream as a rich source of understanding the nature of the individual. Where, however, Freud perceived the dream as the royal road to the unconscious, Adler, from the holistic point of view, might have seen it as the royal road to consciousnes.

In defining the practical role of the interpreter of dreams, Shulman (1973) stated:

> The Adlerian therapist, thus asks for dreams from the patient, uses them to understand and define problem areas, to predict the near future direction of movement of the patient, to fill out his understanding of the patient's characteristic lines of movement (the life style), to alert himself to the patient's movement in the therapeutic relationship, to show the patient these aspects of himself, and to teach the patient to observe and understand his own dynamics. (p. 71)

The dream becomes a superb source of self-awareness. As the client examines his dreams, he becomes more conscious of what motivates his behavior, what simplifies or blocks his achievement of goals, and what conceptual constructs interfere with or encourage interpersonal relationships. During seemingly unproductive periods of therapy, dream material readily stimulates exploration of subjective experience and opens new possible sources of observation in the treatment process. It brings one directly into contact with the private logic of the dreamer and presents us with a range of material normally not available through the more familiar process of communicable speech. As the dreamer confronts the nature of his private logic more directly, the potential for significant change becomes greater.

BIBLIOGRAPHY

Adler, A. *Social Interest: Challenge to Mankind.* London: Faber and Faber, 1938.

Adler, A. *The Practice and Theory of Individual Psychology.* Paterson: Littlefield, Adams, 1959.

Adler, A. *What Life Should Mean to You.* New York: Capricorn, 1958.

Ansbacher, H. L., and Ansbacher, R. R. *The Individual Psychology of Alfred Adler.* New York: Basic Books, 1956.

Ansbacher, H. L., and Ansbacher, R. R. *Superiority and Social Interest of Alfred Adler.* Evanston: Northwestern University Press, 1964.

Bonime, W. *The Clinical Use of Dreams.* New York: Basic Books, 1960.

Freud, S. *The Interpretation of Dreams.* New York: Basic Books, 1962.

Mullahy, P. *Oedipus Myth and Complex.* New York: Heritage, 1948.

Orglen, H. *Alfred Adler: The Man and his Work.* New York: New American Library, 1963.

Shulman, B. H. *Contributions to Individual Psychology.* Chicago: Alfred Adler Institute of Chicago, 1973.

11

Dreaming: Horney, Kelman, and Shainberg

Susan Knapp

KAREN HORNEY

Karen Horney was a German psychiatrist, psychoanalyst who at the age of 47 years came to teach and work in the United States. While she had been trained by classical Freudian psychoanalysts, she went on to develop her own theories based on the conviction that ". . . sickness is a form of ordering intrapsychic and interpersonal experience into environmental domains" (Kelman and Shainberg, 1975, p. 581). Influenced by concepts of organism (Goldstein), holism (Smuts), process (Whitehead), and system (von Bertalanffy), Horney spoke in terms of the organism's creative growth capacities and the environmental factors that either foster or block this growth (Kelman and Shainberg, 1975, p. 581).

Horney's philosophical roots included (1) Hegel's notion of dialectic process as transcending the dichotomies of any dualistic theory and (2) existentialism with its emphasis on how the person experiences himself in his world. In addition to these philosophical influences, Horney was also exposed to twentieth century developments in science. Freud, with whom Horney had studied, had based his theories of behavior on nineteenth century philosophical and scientific notions of biological materialism. Thus he saw the organism as organized in such a way as continually to free itself from tension created by inner or outer stimuli. Horney, however, had the advantage of being able to work from the rather dramatic developments in such areas as embryology:

> Embryology has demonstrated modes of development in which different functions and parts spontaneously evolve spatially and temporally in relation

to each other in fascinating and unique ways; that the biological system is not passive and exhibits an inherent capacity for ordering and extending itself when the relationship with the environment provides the necessary nutriment and proper conditions (Waddington). (Kelman and Shainberg, 1975, p. 582)

Grounded in these philosophical and scientific positions, Horney evolved a theory of personality based on the assumption that striving toward self-realization is inherent in the biological system of the organism and that out of these strivings the unique attitudes and values arise:

> For her, distortions of equilibrium and balance are not constitutionally built-in oppositions; rather they are developments that block the functioning of the flexible and plastic organism. They represent forms (miscreations) or organizations that have emerged ontogenetically, phylogenetically, histor-ically, and culturally. (Kelman and Shainberg, 1975, 583)

Thus Horney developed a system which differed from that of Freud.

In describing personality Horney postulated two core systems: the *real self*, a central inner force which represents our deepest source of growth or ". . . free healthy development in accordance with the potentials of one's generic and individual nature" (Kelman and Shainberg, 1975, p. 583), and the *real self-dynamism* or the integrating system ". . . moving and unifying the organism in the persistent expression of its nature" (Kelman and Shainberg, 1975, p. 583). In a reasonably good environment, these systems interact intrapsychically and interpersonally in a flexible and spontaneous fashion. In an impoverished or destructive environment they become rigid, static, compulsive, and often at odds with self and others.

The Concept of Solution

Horney felt that of Freud's findings, the most basic and significant were his doctrines that ". . . psychic processes are strictly determined, that actions and feelings may be determined by unconscious motivations, and that the motiva-tions driving us are emotional forces" (Kelman and Shainberg, 1975, p. 585). Horney, however, believed that a *basic anxiety* or an increasingly pervading sense of being alone and helpless in a hostile world is *the* central emotion which determines neurotic conflict, whether it be intrapsychic or interpersonal. In addition to this basic conflict, Horney proposed that there are other levels of anxiety which arise dialectically out of our attempt to deal with this basic anx-iety. For example, a primary response to anxiety is the neurotic solution or organized pattern of responses developed by the individual in order to preclude the experience of basic anxiety. Yet further anxiety is then generated by at-tempts to maintain these solutions or by conflicts between solutions. So the process continues, often with more and more disastrous consequences in terms of the individual's increasing alienation from himself as he really is in his world as it actually exists.

Theoretical Consideration of Dreams

In contrast to Freud's concept of the dream as an expression of wish fulfillment, Horney saw the dream as a significant expression of an attempt at solution of conflict in either healthy or neurotic ways. (Horney later began to use the word solution to signify a neurotic activity and resolution to signify a neurotic or healthy working through of a conflict.)

Wanda Willig (1951), in a paper based on lectures on psychoanalytic technique given by Karen Horney during the years 1946, 1950, and 1951, states that Horney was deeply impressed by the work of P. Bjerre. Bjerre, felt that the dream should be viewed in terms of its constructive forces toward personality integration rather than as an attempt at libidinal satisfaction on an infantile level. In his book *Dreaming as the Healing Process of the Mind*, Bjerre (1936) compared these constructive forces with other inherent biological healing tendencies, such as the formation of white blood cells in an abscess. This concept of inherent growth-promoting processes is at the core of Horney's theory. "She felt that healing is always in the service of self-realization and the undermining of neurotic positions occurs simultaneously" (Willig, 1951, p. 131).

Thus, in the tradition of Jung and Bjerre, Horney and her contemporaries such as Fromm developed an approach to dreams and the analyst's work with them which differed fundamentally from that of Freudians. In her early writings Horney retained such notions as manifest and latent, displacement and condensation, and so on; but as her overall theory of personality organization came together, these concepts no longer fit. Yet, like Freud, she continued to see the dream as an invaluable aid to the analytic process. She felt the dream to be one of our most valuable means of gaining a deeper awareness of ourselves, especially of our feelings of which we are often so unaware in our waking life. Horney summarized her view of the dream as an analytic tool by saying:

> The greatest help at the beginning, as well as later on, comes from the patient's dreams. I cannot develop here our theory of dreams. It must suffice to mention briefly our basic tenets: that in dreams we are closer to the reality of ourselves; that they represent attempts to solve our conflicts, either in a neurotic or in a healthy way; that in them constructive forces can be at work, even at a time when they are hardly visible otherwise.
>
> From dreams with constructive elements the patient can catch a glimpse, even in the initial phase of analysis, of a world operating within him which is

peculiarly his own and which is more true to his feelings than the world of his illusions.   There are dreams in which the patient expresses in symbolic form the sympathy he feels for himself because of what he is doing to himself.   There are dreams which reveal a deep well of sadness, of nostalgia, of longing; dreams in which he is struggling to come alive; dreams in which he realizes that he is imprisoned and wants to get out; dreams in which he tenderly cultivates a growing plant, or in which he discovers a room in his house of which he did not know before. The analyst will of course help him understand the meaning of what is expressed in symbolic language. But in addition he may emphasize the significance of the patient's expressing in his dreams feelings or longings which he does not dare to feel in waking life. And he may raise the question of whether, for instance, the feeling of sadness is not more truly what the patient does feel about himself than the optimism he displays consciously. (Horney, 1950, pp. 349–350)

Symbols

Freud had postulated that the dream itself represents a breakdown in the censoring process, and that the symbolic representations within the dream itself are manifestations of further efforts to disguise the wish which the dream seeks to express.   Horney, however, differed with Freud, maintaining that the symbols within the dream, like metaphors and analogies in our speaking and writing, exemplify our creative efforts to capture the essence of previously unspoken or unexpressible aspects of ourselves at a specific point in time.   Willig (1951) quotes Horney as saying that the meaning of the dream could not be expressed more concisely and precisely than in the appearing symbol (p. 130).

Horney stressed that a key aspect of neurosis is the degree of alienation from the real self. This alienation is generated by both our exaggerated pride and self-deprecation and by other neurotic processes which become almost statically reified as a result of our inability to confront and resolve the inevitable intrapsychic and interpersonal conflicts that arise in our daily lives. Because of the self-deceiving function of the various neurotic systems, the individual is often unaware of the host of conflicts that he manifests in both his actions and his attitudes. Yet the inevitable existential confusion is expressed rather blatantly, such as when the individual dreams that he has lost his passport or is unable to identify himself when asked to do so. However, more often the dreamer is less concerned with identity per se. Rather, he expresses his confusion by presenting himself in terms of divergent symbols: different people, animals, plants, or inanimate objects. Clearly Horney is suggesting that we are in one way or another everyone and everything in our dream. This particular point is one that is often hard to accept, and yet how could any creative process not be a reflection of aspects of its creator? In any particular dream, the dreamer can be both jailer and prisoner, torturer and tortured, and it is the analyst who can then assist the patient in the process of coming to terms with these conflicting trends.

> The dreamer's tendency toward resignation, for instance, may be expressed by a resigned person playing a role in the dream; his self contempt, by cockroaches on the kitchen floor. But this is not the entire significance of self-dramatization. The very fact of its occurrence . . . also indicates our capacity to experience ourselves as different selves. The same capacity also shows in the often blatant discrepancy between the way a person experiences himself in daily life on the one hand and in his dreams on the other. In his conscious mind he may be the mastermind, the savior of mankind, for whom no achievement is impossible; while at the same time in his dreams he may be a freak, a sputtering idiot, or a derelict lying in the gutter. (Horney, 1950, pp. 187–188)

Harold Kelman, in response to Horney's lecture on this issue of self-presentation in the dream, evolved through his own work, which will be discussed later in this chapter, the following position:

> The subject of all my dreams is me in my world. My universe includes all that is subsumed in the creation of my symbolic self and is analogous to the existential domains of *Eigenwelt, Mitwelt,* and *Umwelt.* When Peter talks about Paul he is really talking about Peter. He is seeing Paul through Peter's eyes, no matter how many people consensually validate the accuracy of his perception of Peter.
>   Every symbol has an I, or subject aspect, and another, or object aspect. This means that the moment there is awareness, in sleeping, waking, or any form of consciousness, the moment there is an I who is aware, my awareness will have an internal and external reference. No symbol is pure I, pure subject, or pure other, pure object. The predominant aspect may be an I aspect or other aspect. All symbols should be looked at from both viewpoints. (Kelman, 1971, p. 255)

Kelman goes on to point out that the meanings that any particular symbol seeks to convey are not based on any imminent, inherent qualities in the self or object but are determined by the position that they hold in the system of the whole as it is presented in the dream. He then makes a point that seems to come out of working dream research data:

> One factor determining the extent to which a symbol will be expressive of the subject aspect is the depth of sleep at which the dream was dreamed, namely, the degree to which the organism is being moved autonomously. As sleep becomes lighter, and as we are moved toward waking and being awake, the ratio changes in the direction of increasing heteronomous influences. Total

separability of organism and environment is impossible, because the organism cannot exist in isolation. (Kelman, 1971, p. 255)

Technique

In order to do any valid work with the dream, Horney felt that the analyst must not only take into consideration the patient's whole character structure with both his neurotic and constructive systems but must also ask himself specific questions about the dream. These include:

What is the disquieting factor from which the dream arises?
What is the essential characteristic of the dream?
What is the evoking factor, and in what way does the dream deal with it? (Willig, 1951, p. 131)

These preparations serve to orient the analyst, but it is equally crucial to involve the patient in working with his own dream. For a variety of reasons patients are often quick to disown their dreams and tend to see them as visitations from outside which are in no way connected to or emanating from within. This is particularly true with the more disturbed or alienated person whose dreams are often weird or terrifying. Obviously, with these patients the analyst must move slowly, but his underlying position is that eventually the patient must reclaim what has been disowned. Horney expressed this position by saying:

We have to say to the patient, "But this is your dream!" so that he begins to feel, in a spirit of search and not of blame, "I am responsible; this is my dream and I must recognize that this is going on in me." In this way the patient learns about himself from them. (Willig, 1951, p. 132)

When this approach is adopted with supportive curiosity, the patient will gradually come to ask spontaneously of himself why that particular symbol? Or besides the fact that X is a son of a bitch in real life, what's he doing in my dream, and how does he stand for something in me that I would rather not own? The analyst can aid in this self-inquiry by questions, suggestions, and tentative interpretations, which can help the patient to understand the language of his dreams. Most important, the analyst must pick up on constructive aspects of the dream, especially with patients who are particularly depressed or caught up in overwhelming self-hate. Yet, for the most part the patient in a facilitating environment will come actively to engage in appreciating his own creative process.

The following is an example of this process in action:

A man dreamed that a female dwarf was sitting at a table. Another woman the same size came up to the table and started climbing onto a chair. The dwarf asked, "Are you a dwarf?" The woman replied, "No, I am short."

The patient felt that the dream dramatized "two frames of reference." He needed to be a cripple, an excuse for evading life's challenges. Being crippled meant being shrunken, which defined a stage on the way toward self-obliteration, hence total conflict avoidance.

He felt the two frames of reference communicated contrasting possibilities for living. Crippled meant being weak, dependent, and taken care of like a woman. The dream portrayed conflict process. He had moved from the pull to conflict obliteration, to conflict definition, conflict emergence, and possible future conflict resolution. The movements in the dream process define both neurotic and healthy conflict. (Kelman and Shainberg, 1975, p. 596)

HAROLD KELMAN

Harold Kelman, in his book *Helping People* (1971), describes his relationship with Karen Horney by saying: "My meeting with her significantly altered the rest of my life" (p. 21). He began his supervision with her in 1939, three years after he had begun his psychoanalytic career by entering the New York Psychoanalytic Institute, and worked closely with her until her death in 1952. Yet, despite the clear indebtedness that Kelman readily acknowledges, he cautions, ". . . influence, indebtedness, and regard do not equal abrogation of convictions" (p. 21). Thus Kelman describes a cooperative and uniquely productive relationship which has brought a richness to theoretical understanding and clinical work with dreams.

Kelman, like Horney, feels that the dream is an invaluable vehicle in psychoanalytic treatment. He states that:

> Dreams are not the *via regia* to the unconscious, but they are one of the better ways of contacting it. Dreams (and fantasies) are extremely helpful for moving a patient toward freer associating, toward greater openness to the prelogical. The patient is helped to metaphorically move down the symbolic spiral to pure fact, to his ground of being. His acquired distortions can thereby be moved quickly and effectively resolved and creative processes freed. Through focus on here-now experiencing, the patient's need to see a dream as a thing, as unconnected with him, something that happened in another place and time, can be more quickly resolved so that he begins to experience the dream's meaning in the ongoing context. (Kelman, 1971, p. 251)

Early Concepts

In an early paper, Kelman (1944) expresses his agreement with Horney's assertion that dreams represent an attempt to solution of neurotic conflict. (Horney defined conflict as consisting of drives of a compulsive quality, unconsciously motivated and of a contradictory and irreconcilable nature.) In an effort to clarify what the concept of solution entails, Kelman presents a method of thinking that he calls dialectic. He describes Horney as having gained from Hegelian philosophy a profound appreciation for the concept of dialectic process, a process that transcends dichotomies inherent in theories which deal in concept of opposing forces such as ego vs. id. Thus the thrust of Horney's theory became a focus on the transformations that emerge out of the organism's interactions. "Dialectically produced new forms are directly influenced by previous dilemmas, which they transcend in evolving reorganizations" (Kelman and Shainberg, 1975, p. 582).

In describing how the dialectic approach underlies his concept of dreams, Kelman (1944) proposes that first we must appreciate the fact that the analyst cannot mirror the patient with so-called objectivity because he is as much a part of the analytic situation as the patient. "Both are functioning dynamic processes within the process of analysis. This is true process in process—namely dialectics" (p. 89). Kelman believed that once the dialectic method of thinking has been adopted, an understanding of a person's way of living in life and reacting to it can best be understood through an appreciation of his character structure. Here he is using character structure as it is defined by Horney, i.e., ". . . the sum total of the interactions between the various attitudes in an individual, as well as the interactions between himself and others all simultaneously interacting in a dynamic process" (p. 92). In all of these interactions there are both neurotic and healthy components which the organism struggles to integrate in an effort to maintain a state of equilibrium. This applies not only to each feeling, thought, or action in waking life but also to dreaming. For, unlike Freud, who maintained that the dream represents wish fulfillment, a concept that describes an accomplished fact, a static, finite event, Kelman talks instead of *attempts* at solutions. "Our idea of solution being attempted is that of dynamic processes in interrelated actions, moving toward goals of a constructive or destructive nature" (p. 96).

The Symbolizing Process

With his emphasis on dynamic process and with his appreciation for Horney's conviction that both analyst and patient can only live and therefore must work in the *now*, Kelman pushed toward a description of what would represent human process as it is. Neither we nor our dreams are static entities; rather, we are ever moving, interrelating processes. While dreaming we are involved in a creative process that represents an integrating of stimuli from within and without. The dream that we later report is representative of the state of our physical and psychic economy at a specific moment. This report, which includes not only visual images but olfactory, gustatory, auditory, and kinesthetic ones as well, is organized in the same way as all other reports which we make. In order to describe aspects of this process of organizing from moment to moment, or the universal forming process, Kelman developed a concept that he called the *symbolizing process* (Kelman, 1950, p. 77).

This concept, in expressing the nature of the ever moving *now*, helps to clarify the nature of the transitions, the organismic happenings of the patient and therapist, as they are occurring in the therapeutic hour and in all that goes on between hours. Time that takes place between sessions is most often starkly captured by the dream (Kelman and Shainberg, 1975, p. 593).

> Symbolizing is considered to be a mode of human integrating. It is biological action expressing the flow and healing of the organism. Kelman describes it metaphorically as a spiral that begins in the basic event of being of which there is not awareness.
> *The now moment.* The pure essence of any moment for any person is a silence in which his particular life history is an instantaneous connection to how and what he is in the world. It is an event before words. Then there is immediately a possibility for making forms that express this experience. The number of forms that can emerge are myriad. No single form can ever capture all the possibilities that can come from this pure experience. However, as forms do merge, they represent the person's attempts to integrate his pure moment.
> *The symbolic spiral—lower levels.* The lowest levels of this metaphorical spiral are prerationative, that is, before intellection is possible. Because fluidity is greatest at these levels there is a maximum potential for creating many different forms of imagery, metaphor, flash feeling, and the processes of empathy, intuition, and insight. They may be subliminal or subverbal, being forming waves of immediacy. They often penetrate areas of the patient and his reality of which he and his analyst have been unaware in themselves and in each other in the unitary process they are and share. The processes that pertain between mother and infant, namely of human communing, obtain at these levels. There are no words and no particular structure, but an ongoing process that is undifferentiated, widely connecting, and forming.
> *The symbolic spiral—higher level.* At the higher levels of the metaphorical spiral, we have thought, abstract ideas, and dreams. Experience is integrated in forms that have more rigid connections and more relationship to public forms. In compulsive processes of neurosis, we see a tendency to move automatically into these forms and to avoid the more open spontaneous possibilities of the lower levels of the spiral. (Kelman and Shainberg, 1975, pp. 593–594)

Technique

In 1965 Kelman started a series of papers about dreams in which he presented his evolving position with regard to dreams. "A dream is not a static, objective something that you can pick up and examine from all sides. Dreaming is a process" (1965a, p. 4). With this concept as a basic premise, Kelman begins to redefine many of the traditional terms that are used in relation to work with dreams. In the first of these papers, "Techniques in Dream Interpretation," he presents what might be called a philosophy of technique. He states that the word "technique" generally refers to an explicit manipulation, a specific procedure, a mechanical method of doing something to an object with the expectation of a predictable effect. Kelman, however, wants to change this definition:

> Technique is no longer seen as what to do but an attitude in and of a process which points at what and how to be, feel, think, and act. It is no longer something on top and at the surface of, but that which arises from the totality of processes and is immediately relevant to what the situation is requiring. (1965a, p. 4)

The technique most often associated with dreams is that of interpretation. Yet, interpretation is often conceived of in the same restricted sense that technique is. It implies a static closed system of explanatory hypotheses. "The focus is on deciphering. The dream is seen as a question, the interpretation the correct answer" (1965a, p. 3). This particular approach to the dream is extremely popular, especially among beginners who feel they must answer for their patients and who are fearful of process, depth, openness, effort, and rigor. Therefore, the need to slow and even undercut this compulsive need to answer the question of "What does it mean?" is essential to a holistic approach to the dream. In the spirit of this approach, the analyst must begin to ask rather than tell. His questions must direct the patient to the how and what of his experience and allow for the emergence of the spontaneous and creative as opposed to the compulsive intellectualizing of experience that typifies the neurotic condition (1965a).

To express the essence of this approach, Kelman uses the word *illuminator* to express the kind of intervention through open-ended questioning that furthers the patient's experience of his own processes.

> This happens as questions function as pointers saying look here, as guides indicating possible directions, as illuminators lighting the way. Rather than techniques of interpretation mechanically explaining, interpretation becomes its root meaning, exposition. (1965a, p. 4)

When interpretation is redefined in this way, it becomes that which:

> ... helps here-now experiencing toward the end of furthering straighter growing, by affirming it as it emerges and by identifying and resolving blocks to this possibility. (1965a, p. 4)

Yet, while Kelman redefines the word "interpretation" so that it better expresses his position, gradually he drops the term altogether in favor of the terms "illuminators" and "questions."

Kelman has suggested that the analyst:

> ... offer the patient not interpretations but *illuminators*. "What I call illuminators function to sharply light up nuances of the what and how of compulsive and spontaneous processes." They call attention to, point at, and suggest that in that direction the patient will be able to open up more areas of connecting and developing more different ways of seeing himself and feeling into himself. In that way he will begin the process defined by Kelman as "creative vision," only partially covered by the concept of insight. In creative visioning he will experience "the unity of insight and outsight, of feeling-thinking, and thinking-feeling," In this there will be the inward and outward connecting of his relating to the experiencing process and the world forms. There will be a creating in that there will be more resolving of the compulsive processes and an encouragement of the awareness of the integrative processes that are being manifested in the healing of the forming action (Kelman and Shainberg, 1975, pp. 595–596).

On hearing the dream, Kelman states that if he feels that more can be gained from the dream than what has emerged from the telling and the patient's spontaneous associations, he might ask some of the following questions. "What did you feel in the dream? When you woke? As you tell it now?" (Kelman, 1965a, p. 5). Kelman emphasizes feelings because he sees them as crucial to our experience of ourselves. Therefore, questions as to our feelings deepen our connectedness with our dreams. This is not to say that our capacity to think is unimportant. Here in the West, however, our capacity to experience through thinking has been consistently overemphasized at the expense of our capacity to experience through feeling. Similarly, Kelman almost never asks "why" or "who" questions because they so quickly prompt an intellectualized answer which short-circuits the capacity for deeper levels of experiencing. "My questions are not actions to cause reactions but stimuli to prompt reponses, processes to move other processes" (1965a, p. 5).

A good question or statement serves as a guide or direction which helps the patient to find his own meaning; a poor one focuses him on the analyst as the authority or author of the patient's own experiences. There are no set questions that the beginning analyst can learn. Rather, they arise spontaneously from the analyst's own experience of and response to the dream, a process which Kelman describes by the phrase "analyst as instrument." "Through his own analysis and self analysis the analyst should become familiar with and have experienced moving up and down the spiral. This means he will be sensitive to the forming process in himself and in his patient" (Kelman and Shainberg, 1975, p. 594). What is important is the attitude, form, and direction of the question as opposed to the content. Examples of such questions are:

What do you feel about this or that?
What else comes to you about Mr. X in the dream?
What else about saying no to your mother?
Anything further you can say about your feeling like a bystander?
(Kelman, 1965a, p. 5)

Sometimes a formal question is not necessary. It is enough to prompt the patient through the use of "Yes," "Ah-huh," and a restatement of a key word or phrase, and then allow the patient to further his own experience of the dream (1965a, p. 5). Thus it can be clearly seen that Kelman views the dream not as a puzzle to be deciphered but as a tool with which to aid further growth.

... the main aim of dream analysis, hence of all therapy, is to widen and deepen here-now experiencing. We can form symbols of past, present, and future, of here and of all other places called "there," but the only time we can experience is now, the only place we can be is here, and the only feelings we can be, not have, are here-now feelings. Likewise, symbol forms may seem to reflect feelings identical with ones we had in the past, there-then, but what looks like, is, or appears to be similar or equivalent to is not identical with. We cannot step into the same stream twice. Not only are children incapable of symbol forms of the dimensions which adults can have, but the meanings of the identical symbol to that person as a child and as an adult must be vastly different because of the lived life between the two periods. (Kelman, 1965a, pp. 10–11)

Kelman finishes this excellent article with many clinical examples, which illustrate the clinical issues raised by specific kinds of dreams.

Phenomenology

In the second of the series of the 1965 dream papers, "A Phenomenological Approach to Dream Interpretation, Part I: Phenomenology—An Historical Perspective," Kelman presents a comprehensive exposition of the nature of phenomenology as an introduction to an experimental way of working with dreams that he felt would open up our understanding and engagement with our patients. Essentially the phenomenological stance, as it is presented by Ellenberger in his discussion of the work of Husserl, requires that the observer:

... exclude from his mind not only any judgment of value about the phenomena but also any affirmation whatever concerning their course and background; he even strives to exclude the distinction of the object and the observing subject. With this method, observation is greatly enhanced: the less apparent elements of phenomena manifest themselves with increasing richness and variety, with finer gradations of clarity and obscurity, and eventually previously unnoticed structures of phenomena may become apparent. (Kelman, 1965b, p. 189)

When we think about what modern neurological research has demonstrated about the myriad of events that go on in our brains at any one moment, we see that we must go beyond thinking in terms of meaning and interpretation.

In Part II of the series "A Phenomenological Approach to Dream Interpretation: Clinical Examples," Kelman (1967) describes his implementation of this approach. He lists three major determinants of the approach: (1) the historical evolution of phenomenology and existentialism, (2) developments in psychoanalysis, and (3) his experience in teaching the theory, technique, and practice of dream interpretation. Kelman points out that not only do students understandably lack knowledge and experience, they bring to their patients assumptions and preconceptions which prevent them from experiencing their patients as anything other than things (p. 75).

> Only by bringing to light these presuppositions, which requires special techniques in teaching and specifically in teaching the experiencing of process in therapy, in learning, and in life, can the dreaming process in its own true nature be exposed to be confronted, experienced, and described. (Kelman, 1967a, p. 75)

Among these burdens are assumptions that there are *right* theories and *right* techniques with which the analyst can *make* the patient *change* into a *healthy* person. It appears all too easy for us to forget we are ". . . first and last people, simple human beings interacting with other human beings" (Kelman, 1967, p. 77). Much of this difficulty comes from our naive notion that through intellection we can find right answers, and we are all but oblivious to the fact that we are trapped by our own history and culture. We forget that the ". . . subject/object perception of the cosmos is a creation of the Western mind and that its languages are an expression of it" (Kelman, 1967, p. 77). Moreover, we are frightened when confronted with radically different philosophies or paradigms for organizing experience. Thus, the work of the teacher must focus on fostering a movement, in the student, from explaining to describing as a means to coming to an understanding of the other:

> In order for describing to obtain, there must be openness to and immediacy of contact with, without assumption or presupposition, the processes in observing, seeing, experiencing, reflecting and producing into forms, as words, the products of neutral describing, solely according the values as to fact, used quantitatively and qualitatively. (p. 78)

When this occurs, the analyst is able to go beyond the objective aspects of dreams and dreaming; and terms such as manifest and latent, terms which are embedded in a motivational theory, which are dualistic, based on closed-system thinking and created by and belonging specifically to Freudian theory, become no longer relevant (p. 78).

As an alternative to traditional approaches to the analysis of dreams, Kelman proposes a phenomenologic analysis emphasizing the descriptive, relying heavily on the language of process and guided by the generative notion of form. He postulates a universal forming process through which "... forms are continually being produced while simultaneously emerging, being manifest, and being reabsorbed" (p. 78). These forms are of and in a context of the moving matrix from which they emerge as manifestations and into which they are reabsorbed. In themselves forms have no values; they only acquire value from the position they hold in the system. During the process of reabsorption the forms disappear as they are transformed back into their sources. This patterning of the form in process in and its producing of sequences of forms in arrangements may be called integrating in the sense of forming into wholes. This integrating is phasic with sequences of integrating, disintegrating, and reintegrating continuously (pp. 78–83).

All structures and systems including the human one are in tension, and processes as structures and systems are both tension-producing and tension-reducing. Tension is not only natural but essential to and part of the essence of the living organism. What we must see is not that the organism is in a state of tension, for not to be would be the equivalent of death. Rather, what is important is the ranges from moment to moment that are physically and psychologically supportive to well-being or expressive of ill-being. We can think of the tension level of the organism as oscillating around a mean that when exceeded results in the cueing off of anxiety (p. 83).

Three dimensions, those of length, breadth, and height, and their various degrees, describe the extent of forms and their relationships to each other. The terms "fast" and "slow" express the rhythm of system changes, while the duration of these changes is described as either long or short. Time and space can also be used to describe phenomena, but when we introduce such concepts as those of time, space, matter, and cause, it must be remembered that they bring with them theoretical constructs based on systems of thought which impose values on the phenomena (p. 84).

To neutrally describe forms in arrangements we can look at them from the perspective of their being emotive, conative, cognitive, and behavioral. These attributes pertain to forms and arrangements of forms in context, and both to subsystems within the whole and to the systems of the whole. What must be remembered is that this describing can take place before and without recourse to ascribing any of the values which are derived from motivational theories. "The more rigorously we learn to describe neutrally, the greater the harvest from the motivational and non-motivational theories to be subsequently utilized" (p. 84).

Having outlined his philosophical premises, Kelman suggests the adoption of a phenomenological analysis of dreams as a way of undercutting our tendency to stay with familiar theories of human motivations at the expense of new discoveries. Such a phenomenological approach would include questions about various aspects of the dream including time, spatiality, emotion, conation, cognition, behavior, and so on. When this approach is used, previously overlooked attributes of the patient come to the fore (p. 84).

Kelman demonstrates this form of analysis with the following dream:*

"I dreamed that my grandmother was where she used to live. She was quite elderly. I was about twenty feet away from her. She did not want me to come over to her. She was afraid I might contract something from her. I couldn't understand it. I put my place near her. I asked my stepmother, who was standing behind me, if I could go over to my grandmother and she said yes. So I went over and my grandmother wouldn't let me near her. She had her arm double, indicating that she didn't want me to come near her. She said she was going to leave me her rings and some valuable stones, meaning that she felt that she was so ill that she was going to die soon.

I will start with the most obvious and easily identifiable and describable aspect of phenomena, *spatiality*, as it is manifest in this dream. "My grandmother was *where* she used live. I was about *twenty feet away* from her. She did not want me to come *near* her. I put my place *near* her. I asked my stepmother who was *behind* me if I could *go over* to my grandmother. So I *went over*. She didn't want me to come *near* her."

Simultaneously we can describe the dream from the viewpoints of emotion, conation, cognition and behavior with conation being the more prominent. We have: "my grandmother . . . did not *want* me to come over to her. I asked my stepmother. My grandmother wouldn't *let* me near her. She didn't want me to come near her. She said she was going to leave me her rings, etc." As cognition we have "I couldn't *understand* it," and all the conceptualizations in the implied and explicit conversation between the three figures in the dream as well as all the behaviors. The most explicitly stated emotion was: "She was afraid," but mounting tension and agitation run through the dream.

The space positions of the three persons in the dream and their positions with reference to each other go through many dysintegrations and reintegrations with the concomitant changes in values as to fact, aesthetics, morality and spirituality invested in the forms as to emotion, conation, cognition and

*Reprinted by permission of the Editor of *The American Journal of Psychoanalysis*, 1967, Vol. XXVII, No. 1, 84–94.

behavior. This is saying that there are many phases of dysintegrating and reintegrating with concomitant dyspositioning and repositioning, dystensioning and retensioning, dysproportioning and reproportioning, dysorienting and reorienting, dysbalancing and re-equilibrating. All of these assume new and different dimensions as we follow the sequences from the viewpoint of time. There is not only chronological, objective, mathematical, undirectional time, which the Greeks referred to as *chronos*, but also experienced, immediate, concrete, filled, subjective, lived time, which the Greeks referred to as *kairos* and which can be experienced unidirectionally or bidirectionally. . . .

Past time comes up in the dream in "where she—[my grandmother—] used to live"; future time, in her anticipated death; and present time, in the many ongoing events. We have much kairotic time, as the lived time in the three generations of a grandmother, and in "the place she used to live." We have time as death: in the past of her mother, because she has a stepmother; in the future, as the anticipated death of her grandmother; and in the patient's fear of illness and possible death from something "I might contract from her." In the dream there is much additional happening in time as moment-to-moment duration (chronological) and experiencing (kairotic).

We can strongly infer that the dreamer is female from the form and content of her feelings, their intensity, her expression of them and her behavior with reference to them. We also have her grandmother "going to leave me rings and valuable stones." The analysis of the dream as experienced in terms of the patient's feelings and of her relations to her grandmother and stepmother, suggests she is still an unmarried female in her early twenties.

The dream starts with her grandmother in a place "where she used to live," namely, in a location in which, over time, many forms of relating participated, with a segment of which the dreamer was associated. The implied, condensed, retrospective life panorama could have prompted many responses producing increasing tension. After being told that twenty feet separate, and definitely do not connect or join her with her grandmother, we are quickly made aware that the distance was requested. This the patient experienced as being enforced by her grandmother, still further heightening the level of tension.

While early in the dream there were less obvious pattern breaks, with dysintegrations and reintegrations, at this point there is an obvious disintegration of the patterns, positions and relationships. We can infer that spatially, and definitely emotionally, the dreamer turns her back on her grandmother and her face toward her stepmother. This new integration is immediately followed by a quick series of dysintegrations during which the dreamer faced back, narrowed the distance between herself and her grandmother to such a close proximity that she is warded off by her grandmother's "arm double." The possible temporary lowering of tension, through action, now suddenly mounts again through the abrupt ending of the dreamer's action, as locomotion, by the grandmother's arm. The tension rises abruptly and is dealt with by indicating the seriousness of her illness, also implying early death.

We see how the patient deals with the gradual and sudden tension-increases and that she must suffer a radical dysbalance and dysequilibrium of her world, as *eigenwelt* and *mitwelt*. Her *umwelt* is not so obviously and immediately involved in the dream, but it is inferred. She deals with her accessions of tension mainly by moves in the physical and cognitive spheres. She attempts to move away from her feelings of increased tension by physical moving away, by working off the tension in action, and by the explanation: "She was afraid I might contract something from her." But all this is still not enough to deal with the sudden and greatly increased tension. There are evidences of imminent anxiety, identity, disruption and confusion expressed in "I couldn't understand it." She holds herself together by an anxious insistence expressed in the statement "I put my place near her."

Guided by the human attribute or function of conation, we can describe many dimensions of movement in this dream. Under conation are subsumed wanting, willing, desiring, urges, impulses and the feeling of having to. I use conation for purely neutral descriptive purposes and imply no theory or theories of motivation. This would be in the spirit of descriptive phenomenology. We can also use the genetic-structural viewpoint if we separately or concomitantly with conation, organize the patterning of this dream according to the guiding schema of accepting/rejecting.

"She did not want me to come over to her" tells us that the dreamer's wish, urge and impulse had been toward moving toward her grandmother. She was responding to her grandmother's conative moves as being rejected by one by whom she wanted to be accepted. Implied had been an earlier expression of her wanting to move close to her grandmother to which her grandmother negatively responded. The insistent quality of the dreamer's wanting and willing came in her statement "I put my place near her," and by the evidence of the breaking through of disruptive anxiety at her moves being blocked.

The mounting tension, motoring her urges and impulses, turns her around to face her stepmother. We can imply that it is but for a moment and that while doing so her back is turned to her grandmother. She thus rejects her grandmother to turn to her stepmother, "behind," asking for and receiving her acceptance of the dreamer's mounting wish to reject her grandmother's wishes.

We next find her being even more forcibly rejected by her grandmother who had explained her rejection of the dreamer's proximity. She thereby expressed her acceptance of the dreamer, in wishing for and being concerned for her welfare and health. Now her grandmother is physically rejecting the dreamer's proximity asserting even more forcefully her acceptance of the dreamer. She emphasizes and explains it, while showing affection through promises of giving and through informing the dreamer of the seriousness of her illness and expected death. The depth of the grandmother's acceptance, while rejecting the dreamer's proximity, parallels the dreamer's rejecting of her grandmother's wishes while insisting on being accepted on her terms, as proof of her acceptance, love and concern for her grandmother.

This brief phenomenologic analysis of this dream reveals how much can be learned by such a methodology before resorting to any attempts at so-called understanding, explaining and interpreting the dream . . .

I have limited myself to a phenomenologic analysis of the three dreams mentioned to focus on and explore this way of studying the dreaming process. For several reasons I have not given what we refer to as interpretations. The main one was that I felt I could communicate what I had to say by devoting myself to the one area of phenomenologic analysis. There is also the issue of space. Likewise having given material relating to life history, the analytic process, the process in dreaming, and some associations to each of the dreams, the readers can make their own conjectures and, finally, I have dealt elsewhere with "Techniques in Dream Interpretation." (Kelman, 1967, pp. 84-94)

In this example of Kelman's use of the phenomenological approach to work with the dream we have seen how much the approach has to offer. Yet, it must be remembered that Kelman's adoption of a phenomenological approach did not represent a disavowal of other approaches but rather an enrichment.

Rigorous phenomenological analysis of the evolving dreaming process leads to meaning which emerges through experiencing the interconnectedness of patternings. Further dimensions of meaning accrue through using the existential and psychodynamic approaches. Meaning has been measurably enhanced through these approaches after phenomenological analysis, and is greater than if either of the latter is used alone. (Kelman, 1971, p. 251)

DAVID SHAINBERG

David Shainberg, who with Kelman experimented with teaching the phenomenological kinds of dream analysis, found that when students are asked to feel into the time, space, temperature, and movement of the dream as it is presented by the patient, the group almost invariably connects with some of the basic individual forms of processing the patient uses. "The dream is a patient confronting uncertainty with his characteristic patterns. At every nodal point of the dream he operates characteristically." (Shainberg, 1971, pp. 21-22)

Shainberg feels that this kind of approach to the dream represents our changing understanding of man and his mental forms, part of what he calls the third psychiatric revolution. We are coming to view nature as an eventing process as opposed to being a function of mind autonomous in action and evolution, an old notion going back to Descartes but one that is still prevalent in almost all theories of human behavior.

Dreaming, not dreams, is the focus, with man as a processing phenomenon emerging as an aspect of nature. One feature of this hierarchical eventing structure is the self-conscious self . . . . The dream is an abstract forming level of integration and an orienting response. When an organism experiences novelty and discordance, it seeks meaning through the personal language available, the day residue, previously incompletely comprehended and inadequately organized into the total structure of the organism . . . . The novelty is first physiologically experienced, second integrated visually, and third organized in specific forms in a specific form in a specific way. (Shainberg, 1971, pp. 20-22)

REFERENCES

Bjerre, P. *Das traümen als heilungweg der seele* (*Dreaming as the Healing Process of the Mind*). Zurich: Rascher Verlag, 1936.

Horney, K. *Neurosis and Human Growth*. New York: W. W. Norton, 1950.

Kelman, H. A new approach to dream interpretation. *American Journal of Psychoanalysis*, **4**, (1): 89-107, 1944.

Kelman, H. Movement in dreams. Abstract Author. *American Journal of Psychoanalysis*, **10**, (1): 77-79, 1950.

Kelman, H. Techniques of dream interpretation. *American Journal of Psychoanalysis*, **25**, (1): 3-10, 1965a.

Kelman, H. A phenomenological approach to dream interpretation, Part I: Phenomenology, an historical perspective. *American Journal of Psychoanalysis*, **25**, (2): 188-202, 1965b.

Kelman, H. A phenomenological approach to dream interpretation. Part II: Clinical examples. *American Journal of Psychoanalysis*, **27**, (1) 75-94, 1967.

Kelman, H. *Helping People: Karen Horney's Psychoanalytic Approach*. New York: Science House, 1971.

Kelman, H., and Shainberg, D. Karen Horney. In Freedman, A. M., Kaplan, H. I., and Sadock, B. J. (Eds.), *Comprehensive Textbook of Psychiatry*, 2nd ed. Baltimore: Williams & Wilkins Co., 1975, pp. 581-597.

Shainberg, D. Discussion. Cognitive patterns in dreams and daydreams, Beck, A. T., The semantic and aesthetic analysis of dreams, Schimel, J. L. In Masserman, J. H. (Ed.), *Science and Psychoanalysis*, **19**: 20-23, 1971.

Willig, W. Dreams. *American Journal of Psychoanalysis*, **28**, (1): 127-137, 1951.

12

Dreams in Psychopathology

Milton Kramer and Thomas Roth

A careful review of the dream literature was undertaken (see Table 12-1). From this review, studies of the major psychopathologic entities were selected and examined (see Table 12-2).

SCIENTIFIC ADEQUACY OF THE STUDIES

Type, Nature, and Site of the Studies (see Table 12-3)

Studies rather than case reports account for over three-quarters of the periodical literature on the dream life of the patient groups. This is an encouraging recognition that case reports will not provide the data base to answer the basic questions about the dream in psychopathologic states.

About one-third of the studies on dreams in these psychopathologic conditions are purely descriptive in nature, and appropriately some 88% of the case reports are descriptive in nature. As these descriptive studies utilize no comparison groups, no definitive statements about the dream content of the psychopathologic group reported in such a descriptive study is possible. However, the essential value of a descriptive report is in its generating hypotheses about, not its contributing to our knowledge of, a patient group's dreams. The hope would be that the hypotheses generated in a descriptive study would be explored more explicitly utilizing other modes of study, e.g., separate group and repeated measures designs. Interestingly, 82% of the descriptive studies are non-laboratory in nature. Apparently, there has been almost no interest in utilizing the laboratory-collected

**TABLE 12-1. EXTENT OF PERIODICAL
LITERATURE SEARCH FOR DREAMS IN
PSYCHOPATHOLOGIC STATES.**

	Number
Citations Found	2,503
Citations Requested	1,410
Citations Obtained	1,359
Citations Unavailable	51
Citations Reviewed	71
Citations Not Reviewed	17

dream as an observational base to generate hypotheses about the dreams of patients.

A bit more than half of the studies we examined utilized a *separate group design* in which the dreams of the patient group of concern were compared to the dreams of some other group of patients or subjects. None of these studies were case reports, and almost three-quarters of these separate group studies were done on non-laboratory-collected data. Separate group designs have been the major method utilized to characterize a patient population's dreams.

Separate group comparisons can serve to delineate a patient group's dreams, but the comparison group must be appropriately chosen. In 29% of the separate group comparisons, the comparison group is a non-ill group. Comparisons in these studies are open to the alternative explanation that any difference discovered may reflect not the dreams of the particular psychopathologic entity under study but the difference between ill and non-ill groups. Some separate group studies confounded the problem by comparing the index group to a group that is resident outside of a hospital while the index group is in a hospital. The

**TABLE 12-2. PSYCHOPATHOLOGIC CATEGORIES WITH
REPORTED DREAM CONTENT.**

Reviewed Category	Number of Articles	References
Schizophrenia	30	12–41
Disturbing Dreams	17	42–58
Depression	14	24, 25, 33, 59–69
Alcoholism	5	23, 70–73
Chronic Brain Syndrome	5	74–78
Mental Retardation	4	79–82
TOTAL	75	

TABLE 12-3. TYPE, NATURE, AND SITE OF STUDIES.

A, B, C

	Schizophrenia	Disturbing Dreams	Depression	Alcoholism	Chronic Brain Syndrome	Mental Retardation	Total	Percentage
A. Type of Report								
1. Study	22	11	11	5	5	4	58	77%
2. Case Report	8	6	3	0	0	0	17	23%
B. Nature of Report								
1. Descriptive	9	13	3	0	1	2	28	37%
2. Separate Groups	16	2	10	4	4	2	38	51%
3. Repeated Measures	5	2	1	1	0	0	9	12%
C. Site of Data Collection								
1. Sleep Laboratory	11	5	4	1	3	0	24	32%
2. Non-Laboratory	19	12	10	4	2	4	51	68%

D. Type × Nature × Site

	Schizophrenia Lab (S-CR)	Schizophrenia N-Lab (S-CR)	Disturbing Dreams Lab (S-CR)	Disturbing Dreams N-Lab (S-CR)	Depression Lab (S-CR)	Depression N-Lab (S-CR)	Alcoholism Lab (S-CR)	Alcoholism N-Lab (S-CR)	Chronic Brain Syndrome Lab (S-CR)	Chronic Brain Syndrome N-Lab (S-CR)	Mental Retardation Lab (S-CR)	Mental Retardation N-Lab (S-CR)	Total Lab (S-CR)	Total N-Lab (S-CR)	
1. Descriptive	0 1	3 5	2 1	5 5	0 0	0 3	0 0	0 0	1 0	0 0	0 0	2 0	3 2	10 13	= 28
2. Separate Groups	5 0	11 0	0 0	2 0	3 0	7 0	0 0	4 0	2 0	2 0	0 0	2 0	10 0	28 0	= 38
3. Repeated Measures	3 2	0 5	2 0	0 5	1 0	0 0	1 0	0 0	0 0	0 0	0 0	0 0	7 2	0 0	= 9
	8 3	14 5	4 1	7 5	4 0	7 3	1 0	4 0	3 0	2 0	0 0	4 0	20 4	38 13	= 75

E. Subject-Control in S.G.

	Schizophrenia Lab	Schizophrenia N-Lab	Disturbing Dreams Lab	Disturbing Dreams N-Lab	Depression Lab	Depression N-Lab	Alcoholism Lab	Alcoholism N-Lab	Chronic Brain Syndrome Lab	Chronic Brain Syndrome N-Lab	Mental Retardation Lab	Mental Retardation N-Lab	Total Lab	Total N-Lab	Total	Percentage
1. Sick-Sick	1	7	0	1	1	5	0	3	0	0	0	2	2	18	20	53%
2. Sick-Well	3	2	0	0	2	0	0	1	1	2	0	0	6	5	11	29%
3. Sick-Both	1	2	0	1	0	2	0	0	1	0	0	0	2	5	7	18%
	5	11	0	2	3	7	0	4	2	2	0	2	10	28	38	

problem is further confounded when comparisons are also made to groups not taking medication while the index group is on medication. All of these parameters, illness (100), place of residence (101), and medication (102), are believed to effect dream content, and if not controlled, provide alternative explanations for any differences in dream content that may be found.

It is important to recognize that separate group designs, even when appropriate comparison groups have been used, cannot delineate whether any difference which may have been found is a concomitant of the illness under study or is an aspect of patients who are prone to such an illness. Another way of putting this is to recognize that one cannot tell if a content difference found in a separate group study reflects the trait or state aspects of the patient. A study utilizing a repeated measures design would be appropriate to resolve this question. As descriptive studies provide leads to be pursued in separate group studies, the latter provide leads to be pursued in repeated measures studies.

Repeated measures designs in which some aspect of the dream content, which may or may not be unique to the psychopathologic group under study, is examined at two different points in time is the least-utilized approach to studying dreams. Only 12% of all the reports have used this approach, and almost one-fourth of them are case reports. It is indeed unfortunate that this approach has not been more vigorously explored, as it would provide a most convincing insight into any potential relationship dreams might have to the nature of a psychopathologic condition. All of the repeated measures studies have utilized laboratory-collected dreams, and it is in this more precise approach to characterizing the relationship between dreams and psychopathology that the laboratory-collected dream may have the most to offer.

Description of the Sample

The Patient Sample (see Table 12-4):

Sample Size. Looked at from an overall point of view, and certainly for the major functional entities, the mean total patient sample size of 171 and median of 15 appear adequate. However, as the total figure is a mixture of case reports and studies, the range of one to 3,850 reflects the high variability in sample size. Further, as might be expected, the mean total patient sample size in the laboratory studies is considerably less, 12, than in the non-laboratory studies, 246.

Patient Selection. In only 31% of the studies could the basis for patient selection be determined. In 69% of the studies no mention was made as to whether the patient population was randomly selected. The omission of the basis for patient subject selection would seriously limit both the replicability and generalizability of any results obtained.

TABLE 12-4. DESCRIPTION OF THE PATIENT SAMPLE.

	Schizophrenia		Disturbing Dreams		Depression		Alcoholism		Chronic Brain Syndrome		Mental Retardation		Total (Percentage)	
	Lab	N-Lab	Lab	N-Lab	Lab	N-Lab	Lab	N-Lab	Lab	N-Lab	Lab	N-Lab	Lab (24)(17)	N-Lab (51)(46)
A. Patient Sample Size														
1. Total	137	1,011	75	10,351	41	458	14	155	30	21	0	235	$\bar{X}$ 12 297	$\bar{X}$ 246 12,528
2. Original	106	936	63	4,201	21	453	14	120	30	21	0	235	$\bar{X}$ 14 234(79%)	$\bar{X}$ 130 5,966(48%)
	Yes	No	Yes	No	Yes	No	Yes	No	Yes	No	Yes	No	Yes	No
B. Basis of Selection	9	21	6	11	2	12	5	0	1	4	0	4	23(31%)	52(69%)
C. Basis of Diagnosis	14	16	5	12	8	6	4	1	3	2	0	4	34(45%)	41(55%)
D. Specificity of Diagnosis	21	9	3	14	5	9	4	1	2	3	1	3	36(48%)	39(52%)
E. Drugs or Physical Treatment	9		4	13	3	11	1	4	1	4	0	4	18(24%)	57(76%)
F. Demography														
1. Sex	27	3	12	5	14	0	5	0	3	2	3	1	64(85%)	11(15%)
2. Age	22	8	8	9	11	3	5	0	2	3	4	0	52(69%)	23(31%)
3. Race	10	20	0	17	6	8	4	1	0	5	0	4	20(27%)	55(73%)
4. Education	8	22	2	15	5	9	4	1	1	4	—	*	20(29%)	51(72%)
5. Marital Status	9	21	2	15	7	7	4	1	0	5	0	4	22(29%)	53(71%)
6. Socioeconomic Class	7	23	2	15	4	10	5	0	1	4	0	4	19(25%)	56(75%)
G. General Health	2	28	1	16	0	14	0	5	1	4	0	4	4 (5%)	71(95%)
H. Original Sample	23	7	14	3	12	2	3	2	5	0	4	0	61(81%)	14(19%)
I. Site of Patient Residence														
1. In-Patient	25		21		6		3		3		4		43(57%)	
2. Out-Patient	1		11		5		2		2		0		21(28%)	
3. Both	2		4		2		2		0		0		8(11%)	
4. Not Given	2		0		1		0		0		0		3 (4%)	

*Not appropriate for this group.

Basis of Diagnosis.   In over half of the studies, no mention is made of the basis on which the clinical diagnosis of the patient group was made. There is no way to know if the categorization of the patient sample was accomplished on reasonable and reproducible grounds. Comparison among studies becomes a difficult if not impossible task when the basis for defining the patient population is absent in 55% of the studies.

Specificity of Diagnosis.   The delineation of the subtypes that make up the total patient group is provided in from one-third to two-thirds of the studies, depending on the diagnostic group being studied. Unfortunately, as occurred in the reporting of the basis for diagnosis, the operational basis for subtype classification is not likely to be provided.

Drugs or Treatment.   In only one-quarter of the reports is any mention made of whether the patient group is receiving any drugs or other types of physical treatment. As medication (103) and other somatic treatments (104) are likely to effect the psychology and physiology of dreaming, the absence of any comment on whether patients under study are receiving any treatment clouds the meaning of any results reported. The problem is one of not knowing whether to attribute any results obtained in the study to the psychopathological condition, the treatment, or an interaction between the two.

Demography.   The description of the patient sample reflects an awareness of the impact on dream content of the two major demographic variables, sex and age (105). A description is made of the sex of the patient sample in 85% of the reports and of the age of the patients in 69%. The other four demographic variables, race, education, marital status, and socioeconomic class, are described much less frequently, i.e., about a quarter of the time. These latter four variables do play less of a role in influencing dream content, and their absence, although unfortunate, is not as crucial as that of the two major demographic variables.

General Health of the Patient Sample.   In only 5% of the reports is any comment made on the general health of the patients under study. As the incidence of physical disease is generally higher in psychopathologic groups (106), a comment on the general health of the patient sample would be desirable. If the patient sample does indeed suffer with more physical illness than the comparison group (separate group design), or if the patient sample is less physically ill at one of the points in the psychopathologic process from which dreams are collected (repeated measures design), then a clear confounding with physical illness would exist. Any content differences discovered could just be attributed to the differences or changes in the physical status of the patient group rather than to their index psychopathology.

Original Sample.   Some 81% of the studies were performed on original patient samples. This figure reduces the overall patient pool only modestly, and a reasonably large patient group, at least in the major functional psychopathologies, has been the object of investigation. However, the original laboratory studies of psychopathologic groups became significantly reduced or nonexistent, especially in studies that used a repeated measures design. Again, note should be made that the sleep laboratory has only been minimally utilized to explore the dreams of psychopathologic groups.

Site of Patient Residence.   The major focus of these dream studies of psychopathologic conditions has been on patients who were hospitalized at the time the dream studies were conducted. This is especially the case for studies of the dreams of schizophrenic patients. As it is reasonable to assume that the more severely impaired members of a patient group are likely to be available in the hospital, the results obtained from studies of hospitalized patients may not generalize to nonhospitalized patients of the same entity. Further, comparing the results of studies of the same entity from hospitalized and nonhospitalized patient samples may be confounded by the impact of hospitalization on dream content.

The Control Sample (see Table 12-5).   It is only in the separate group studies that a control group is required. It has already been noted that these studies make up about half of the total number of studies. The major problem in these studies is that an ill group in a hospital on medication is compared to a non-ill group resident outside the hospital and not taking any medicines. These confounded studies cannot contribute to our knowledge of the dream life of the index psychopathology.

The control samples overall suffer from the same descriptive inadequacies that we discussed above for the patient samples. If anything, the descriptive shortcomings are more severe in the case of the control samples. An especially glaring lack is the absence of comment in 95% of the separate group studies on whether the control sample is taking any medication.

The Process of Dream Collection and Analysis

The Method of Dream Content Collection (see Table 12-6).   The original data base which indicates the nature and extent of the sampling of the dream life of a given psychopathologic population is reflected in information about the number of nights (laboratory study) or days (non-laboratory study) dream collection was attempted, the number of dreams collected, and the percentage of dream recall achieved. This basic information, necessary to establish the adequacy of the sampling process in a given study and whether comparability of sampling exists across studies, is given inconsistently in 35–57% of the studies.

The interpersonal setting (107) and mode of dream inquiry (108) have been shown to influence not only the nature of the content obtained but whether any dream content is recovered at all. The who, when, and where of the dream collection process is described directly or indirectly in 37–67% of the studies. In only

TABLE 12-5. DESCRIPTION OF CONTROL SAMPLE (SEPARATE GROUPS ONLY).

	Schizophrenia		Disturbing Dreams		Depression		Alcoholism		Chronic Brain Syndrome		Mental Retardation		Total (Percentage)	
	Lab	N-Lab	Lab	N-Lab	Lab	N-Lab	Lab	N-Lab	Lab	N-Lab	Lab	N-Lab	Lab (10) (8)	N-Lab (28) (23)
A. Patient Sample Size														
1. Total	115	730	0	518	34	238	0	185	17	62	0	110	$\overline{X}$ 17 166	$\overline{X}$ 66 1843
2. Original	105	655	0	518	21	238	0	120	17	62	0	110	$\overline{X}$ 18 143	$\overline{X}$ 74 1703(92%)
	Yes	No	Yes	No	Yes	No	Yes	No	Yes	No	Yes	No	Yes	No
B. Basis of Selection	6	10	1	1	2	8	4	0	1	3	0	2	14(37%)	24(63%)
C. Basis of Diagnosis	4	12	0	2	2	8	3	1	1	3	1	1	10(26%)	28(74%)
D. Specificity of Diagnosis	4	12	1	1	0	10	2	2	1	3	1	1	9(24%)	29(76%)
E. Drugs or Physical Treatment	1	15	0	2	1	9	0	4	0	4	0	2	2 (5%)	36(95%)
F. Demography														
1. Sex	13	3	1	1	7	3	4	0	2	2	2	0	29(76%)	9(24%)
2. Age	12	4	1	1	5	5	4	0	2	2	2	0	26(68%)	12(32%)
3. Race	2	14	0	2	1	9	4	0	0	4	0	2	7(18%)	31(82%)
4. Education	5	11	1	1	2	8	3	1	1	3	1	—*	12(33%)	24(67%)
5. Marital Status	2	14	1	1	2	8	4	0	0	4	0	2	9(24%)	29(76%)
6. Socioeconomic Class	2	14	1	1	0	8	4	0	1	3	0	2	10(26%)	28(74%)
G. General Health	3	13	1	1	8	10	0	4	0	4	0	2	4(11%)	34(89%)
H. Original Sample	12½	3½	2	0	8	2	2	2	4	0	2	0	30½(80%)	7½(20%)
I. Site of Subject Residence														
1. In Hospital	7		0		4		2		1		2		16(42%)	
2. Out of Hospital	5		1		3		2		2		0		13(34%)	
3. Both	4		1		3		0		1		0		9(24%)	

*Not appropriate for this group.

TABLE 12-6. DREAM CONTENT COLLECTION VARIABLES.

	Schizophrenia		Disturbing Dreams		Depression		Alcoholism		Chronic Brain Syndrome		Mental Retardation		Total (Percentage)	
	Yes	No	Yes	No	Yes	No	Yes	No	Yes	No	Yes	No	Yes	No
A. Number of Days or Nights	13	17	11	6	7	7	2	3	3	2	3	1	39(52%)	36(48%)
B. Number of Dreams	17	13	6	11	12	2	3	2	4	1	1	3	43(57%)	32(43%)
C. Percent Dream Recall	11	19	3	14	7	7	1	4	3	2	1	3	26(35%)	49(65%)
D. Who Collected Dreams	17	13	15	2	10	4	3	2	3	2	2	2	50(67%)	25(33%)
E. When Dreams Were Collected	18	12	5	12	10	4	4	1	3	2	1	3	41(55%)	34(45%)
F. Where Dreams Were Collected	13	17	5	12	5	9	2	3	3	2	0	4	28(37%)	47(63%)
G. Mode of Awakenings S*	3	8	4	1	0	4	1	0	1	2	0	0	9(38%)	15(62%)
H. Protocol for Obtaining Dreams	5	25	1	16	2	12	0	5	2	3	1	3	11(15%)	64(85%)
I. Mode of Recording Dreams	24	6	14	3	13	1	5	0	5	0	4	0	65(87%)	10(13%)
J. Associations Were Obtained	11	19	7	10	5	9	0	5	4	1	1	3	28(37%)	47(63%)

*Only applicable in laboratory studies.

15% of the studies is a protection against interviewer bias attempted by specifying a protocol for the elicitation of the dream content. Yet, the mode of recording the data elicited is specified in 87% of the studies. Clearly, the investigators of dream content in psychopathologic states have been insensitive to important variables while slavishly reporting less significant ones.

The application of the new technology, the sleep laboratory, has not lead to a heightened awareness of variables that are known to influence the availability of dream content for recovery from subjects. It is known that the mode of awakening will influence the percentage of dreams recalled in the laboratory (109). In only 38% of the laboratory studies is the mode of dream awakening reported.

The major problems in dream collection in these studies relate to not reporting the basic sampling parameters, not utilizing a fixed manner of eliciting the dream, and failing to specify, in laboratory studies, the mode of awakening the patient. The neglect of these crucial parameters contributes significantly to our difficulty in assessing the adequacy of a study, in comparing the results from one study to another, and to our all-too-frequent inability to resolve discrepancies between studies.

The Method of Scoring the Dream Content (see Table 12-7). The manner of preparing the protocol for scoring the establishment of scorer reliability with the dream content rating system to be utilized, and the utilization of more than one rater "blind" to the hypothesis of the study and the source of the data occurs in just less than one-third of the studies. The preference for the more "difficult" inferential thematic dream rating rather than item scoring is reflected in the use of such thematic scoring alone in 69% of the studies. Standard rating scales are utilized in just over one-quarter of the dream studies.

Given the recognized problem with bias in the evaluation of verbal material, only those studies that utilized blind raters would meet the minimal requirements for scientific acceptability. Further, the assumption that raters do not need to be appropriately calibrated, i.e., have their rating reliability established and checked periodically, attributes a consistency to human performance greater than what we expect from less variable mechanical devices.

The limited use of standard scales in these studies underlines a core problem in the entire field of dream research. The failure to describe the basic elements in the manifest dream report with a standard device and then build special and inferential scoring from these identifiable parameters limits severely the development of a body of knowledge in which one study builds on another and in which any given study is potentially relatable to another (110).

The Nature of the Statistical Analyses (see Table 12-8). In 41% of the total studies some statistical analyses were reported. Even recognizing that 37% of

TABLE 12-7. DREAM CONTENT SCORING VARIABLES.

	Schizophrenia Yes	Schizophrenia No	Disturbing Dreams Yes	Disturbing Dreams No	Depression Yes	Depression No	Alcoholism Yes	Alcoholism No	Chronic Brain Syndrome Yes	Chronic Brain Syndrome No	Mental Retardation Yes	Mental Retardation No	Total (Percentage) Yes	Total (Percentage) No
A. Protocol Preparation	14	16	2	15	3	11	1	4	1	4	0	4	21(28%)	54(72%)
B. Reliability Reported	13	17	0	17	7	7	1	4	0	5	0	4	21(28%)	54(72%)
C. "Blind" Raters	11	19	1	16	7	7	0	5	1	4	0	4	20(27%)	55(73%)
D. Number of Scorers Used														
1. One	17		15		6		5		4		4		51(68%)	
2. Two	9		2		8		0		1		0		20(27%)	
3. Three	4		0		0		0		0		0		4 (5%)	
E. Type of Scale Used														
1. Item	4		3		1		1		1		0		10(13%)	
2. Thematic	19		14		11		2		3		3		52(69%)	
3. Item and Thematic	5		0		2		2		1		1		11(15%)	
4. Other	1		0		0		0		0		0		1(1.5%)	
5. Not Given	1		0		0		0		0		0		1(1.5%)	
F. Scale Source														
1. Standard	5		0		3		2		2		0		12(16%)	
2. Ad Hoc	20		17		7		1		3		4		52(69%)	
3. Standard and Ad Hoc	2		0		0		1		0		0		7 (9%)	
4. Sorting	1		0		0		0		0		0		1(1.5%)	
5. Ad Hoc and Sorting	1		0		0		0		0		0		2 (3%)	

all of the studies are descriptive in nature and would not require statistical analysis, the extent of statistical treatment in the remaining studies is disappointing, being present in only two-thirds of the nondescriptive studies.

In those studies reporting statistical treatment of the data, 81% report the number of tests done, and in a similar percent the statistics are appropriate to the design. In only a little over a half of the studies is the statistic used appropriate to the data.

Clearly it is only from studies with acceptable statistical treatment of the data collected that an understanding of dreams in psychopathologic states can be developed. This necessary parameter will be applied to sort out the potentially acceptable results in each psychopathologic group to be discussed in the next section.

THE DREAM CONTENT RESULTS OBTAINED

Schizophrenia

Descriptive Studies:

Non-laboratory (12–19).   The descriptive studies suggest that the form of the dream in schizophrenia is more primitive in nature, i.e., less complex, more direct, more sexual, and less repressed than in normals. In addition, the schizophrenic seems more interested in his dreams than the nonschizophrenic.

The relationship between the dream and waking life has been another area of interest in these descriptive studies. It has been observed that patients are able to distinguish their hallucinations from dreams and perceptions, but that the hallucinations can enter the dream and the content of the dream and the hallucination are often relatable.   Further, it has been observed that a compensatory relationship exists between the direction of threat in the dream— toward the patient or by the patient toward others—and activity and passivity in waking life.

Laboratory (20).   Study suggests that the degree of paranoia a patient exhibits in therapy sessions and dreams tends to covary positively. This observation is particularly interesting as it comments on waking dream relationships and is diametrically opposed to Freud's observation (111).

Separate Group Studies:

Non-laboratory (21–31).   The overall impression one gets from the six studies (21–26) in this group which obtain statistically significant results from a comparison of a schizophrenic patient group to another "ill" nonschizophrenic group is that the dreams of schizophrenics are more negatively toned, especially in

TABLE 12-8. NATURE OF THE STATISTICAL ANALYSIS.

	Schizophrenia		Disturbing Dreams		Depression		Alcoholism		Chronic Brain Syndrome		Mental Retardation		Total (Percentage)	
	Yes	No	Yes	No	Yes	No	Yes	No	Yes	No	Yes	No	Yes	No
A. Are Statistical Tests Reported?	14	16	1	16	9	5	4	1	1	4	2	2	31(41%)	44(59%)
B. Are the Number of Tests Reported?	11	3	1	0	8	1	3	1	1	0	1	1	25(81%)	6(19%)
C. Are the Statistics Appropriate														
1. To the Design?	13	1	1	0	6	3	2	2	1	0	2	0	25(81%)	6(19%)
2. To the Data?	8	6	1	0	5	4	1	3	1	0	1	1	17(55%)	14(45%)
D. What is the Nature of The Statistical Comparison?														
1. Pre-Planned	8		1		5		1		0		0		15(48%)	
2. Post-Hoc	6		0		4		3		1		2		16(52%)	

having more hostile and destructive content. One study (26) found more sexual content but less affect. Further, the characters in the dreams of schizophrenics are more often strangers than family members, and the schizophrenic more often reports dreams in which he is not the central character.

From a form point of view, evidence of the schizophrenic thought disorder has been discerned more often in their dreams than in nonschizophrenics. This observation is supported by reports of a higher incidence of bizarreness and implausibility in their dreams. Additionally, the dreams of schizophrenics are shorter, with one study reporting more (25) and one fewer (26) scene changes in their dreams than for nonschizophrenics.

Two studies (22, 26) addressed the question of whether judges are able to discriminate (sort) the dreams of schizophrenics from those of nonschizophrenics. One reported that they could (26), and the other that they could not (22). This "sorting" approach most closely approximates the clinical situation, and further work to test the discriminability at the "clinical level" would be desirable.

Laboratory (32–36). Only two (32, 33) of the five laboratory, separate group studies utilized an appropriate control group and reported statistically significant results. One (33) of the studies offers some confirmation and support to the non-laboratory studies, namely that schizophrenics show more aggression and apprehension in their dream reports and have more strangers as well as males and groups of characters in their dream reports. The other study (32) points out that the schizophrenics have fewer laboratory references in their dream reports than normals. This latter study is an effort at exploring an aspect of waking–dream content relationships, an aspect of dream studies suggested by the descriptive studies but not explored in the non-laboratory separate group studies.

Repeated Measures Studies (Laboratory) (37–41). Only one (37) of the five studies utilizing a repeated measures design reported statistically significant results. This study was directed at testing judges' ability to discriminate (sort) dreams from different patients and from different nights from the same patient. Discriminability was achieved. This study would lead one to speculate that judges ought to be able to discriminate dreams from schizophrenics and non-schizophrenics, an unresolved issue discussed under the non-laboratory separate group studies.

There have been no successful attempts (41) to study changes in parameters identified in the separate group studies across time, i.e., in repeated measures design. Clearly, this is a crucial focus for research in the dream life of schizophrenics.

If one were to establish a standard of verifiability such that to accept a result as verified required that two independent investigators report in studies utilizing appropriate methodologies the same or essentially the same result, the findings in schizophrenia would indeed be very limited.

We would be able to accept only three findings at most: (1) that hostility (conflict) was more common in the dreams of schizophrenics; (2) that reflections of the schizophrenic thought disorder (implausibility, bizarreness, and so on) occurred more frequently in their dreams: and (3) that there is more anxiety and apprehension in their dreams, although one study found less feeling in the dreams of schizophrenics.

Disturbing Dreams (Anxiety Dreams, Nightmares, and Traumatic Neuroses)

Descriptive Studies:

Non-laboratory (42-51).   There are ten articles that are non-statixtical, non-laboratory descriptive examinations of anxiety dreams or nightmares.   Five articles (42-46) are case reports, and five (47-51) are studies.

The five case reports suggest several points.   One, they suggest that hypnotic and spontaneous nightmares are equivalent and are related to the state of the patient.   Two, they call attention to the possibility that water and suffocation themes in dreams are related to the birth trauma.   Three, they give examples of nightmares and attempt to illustrate their wish fulfillment and mastery of trauma function.   The five studies describe dreams of rape victims and soldiers. The dreams of rape victims suggest a mastery of trauma function.   The dreams of soldiers suggest that the traumatic dream serves a wish fulfillment, mastery function, but points out that the disappearance of the traumatic dream does not necessarily covary with an improvement in the clinical condition of the patient.

Three studies (49-51) are directed at distinguishing three types of anxiety dreams—falling, fear of attack, and threat to a loved one.   Falling dreams relate to loss of love and a history of being unable to show defiance, especially to mother.   Attack dreams relate to a fear of castration and occur in individuals who express emotions naively and are self-protective of their self-esteem.   In the dreams of psychiatric patients, parents are typically the threatened loved ones. In non-patients' dreams, peers are usually the threatened loved ones.   The threat to loved ones is the least frightening and least common of the three disturbing dream types and occurs more frequently in women.

Laboratory (52-54).   There are three articles that are nonstatistical laboratory descriptive examinations of anxiety dreams and nightmares, one of which is a case report (52) and two of which are studies (53, 54). The case report observes that traumatic dreams are rare in the sleep laboratory.   The two descriptive studies suggest that recall from arousals and nightmares is the same, and that the themes of the latter are unpleasant, relate to threats to people by the dreamer, and are linked to non-laboratory concerns of the dreamer.

The leads provided by these appropriately nonstatistical descriptive reports and studies are basically in two directions. First, these articles raise the question of whether the Freudian dream theory is potentially confirmable in regard to disturbing dreams subserving a wish-fulfilling and/or mastery function. Second, the descriptive studies begin to explore the hypothesized difference between disturbing dreams that come out of Stage 4 and Stage REM, particularly in terms of frequency of the recall of content. Subsidiary issues to these basic ones are also commented on, namely, the frequency of occurrence of disturbing dreams in the laboratory and the content of disturbing dreams. It will be of great interest to see if the basic leads provided in these relatively numerous articles are pursued in more systematic studies.

Separate Group Studies (Non-laboratory) (55, 56).   There are two non-laboratory separate group studies, one of which (55) is directed at the frequency of disturbing dreams but is unfortunately nonstatistical in nature. At least it was an attempt to pursue a question raised in the descriptive studies.

The other separate group study (56) is also nonstatistical. It contrasts the mothers and solutional modes of patients with attack and falling dreams, following up on the non-laboratory descriptive studies in this area. Mothers of patients with attack dreams were more involved with their children and obtained more gratification from them. Mothers of patients with falling dreams were more independent of their children. Patients with attack dreams solved separation problems by defending against the need for attachment, while patients with falling dreams solved their separation problems by substitution and rage.

The series of non-laboratory studies of disturbing dream types is systematic, provocative, and worth pursuing. The lack of statistical treatment of the data is extremely unfortunate. It is hoped that the study of these types of dreams will be pursued more strenuously.

Repeated Measures Studies (Laboratory) (57, 58).   There are two laboratory repeated measures studies. In one of them (57) disturbing dreams from Stage 4 and Stage REM are compared (in the same subject populations). Differences are described, e.g., more no content from Stage 4, more elaborate dreams from Stage REM, and so on. However, these observations cannot be accepted, as there is no statistical treatment of the results on which to base an acceptance or rejection of the findings.

The one repeated measures study (58) with adequate statistical treatment of the results is a study of the treatment of Stage 4 night terrors with diazepam. This study reports a significant reduction of the frequency of the episodes with diazepam treatment.

It is clear that systematic study of the many interesting problems related to disturbing dreams in patients has not been pursued. The basic problem areas have been delineated but not specified. Studies of the frequency, content, type, function, stage distribution, clinical covariance, and treatment of disturbing dreams remain to be done. Not a single verified finding, i.e., one properly demonstrated by two separate investigators, exists in this entire area.

Depression

Descriptive Studies (Non-laboratory) (59-61).   There is a very meager literature of a descriptive nature directed at providing clues about the nature of the dream in depressed patients. Historically, the three papers of a descriptive sort on the dreams of the depressed do not precede the studies utilizing the more definitive designs.   Nevertheless, these descriptive contributions, all nonstatistical case reports, do suggest important issues that are worthy of further study.

The two issues addressed in these reports relate to the frequency of the dream experience and the nature of the dream content in the depressed. These studies suggest that the depressed dream as frequently as the nondepressed; that while their manifest dreams contain a striking paucity of depressive material, their latent dream content is depressive in nature; and last, that the depressed have as much masochistic material in their manifest dreams when depressed as when they are nondepressed.

It would be worthwhile to follow the leads these studies suggest. For example, if dreams are a clue to the nature of a psychopathology, then an alteration in the frequency of the dream experience might suggest that the "absence" of the dream contributes to the psychopathologic state. The paucity of depressive material in the dreams is not congruent with the waking state in depression and thus suggests that dreams might bear a compensatory relationship to waking. This day-night relationship might provide clues to the mechanism of depression, e.g., a shift in the relationship might occur when the clinical depression lifts. The conclusion could be "if depressed asleep, nondepressed awake, and vice versa."   This concept is identical to the relationship Freud reports (111) for dream-waking life relationships in cases of paranoia, i.e., delusional awake, nondelusional asleep, and vice versa.   The similar frequency of masochistic themes in depressed and nondepressed phases would be at odds with Beck's work to be described later on.

Separate Group Studies:

Non-laboratory (24, 25, 62-66).   The five (24, 25, 62, 63, 66) non-laboratory studies that use an appropriate control group and report statistically significant results do follow up on the frequency and content issues in the dreams of the depressed and add some other findings. For example, several studies report essentially the same frequency of dream experience in the depressed and nondepressed.

The nature of the dream experience in depression is characterized as barren and nontraumatic in keeping with the descriptive suggestion of a paucity of depressive content in the dreams of the depressed. However, when hostility is present, it is directionally different from that in schizophrenia, i.e., in depression half the time it is directed by the dreamer at another, while in schizophrenia it tends to be directed primarily at the dreamer.

The equal frequency of masochistic content in a patient's dreams depressed and nondepressed is not directly tested in these studies. It has been reported that the incidence of masochism continues unchanged post-depression. However, depressed patients have a higher incidence of masochism than the nondepressed, and patients who are highly depressed have more masochistic content in their dreams than those with minimal depression.

Relationships between manifest and latent content are not pursued in any of the separate group or repeated measures studies in depression. Interestingly, we found no study in any diagnostic category that successfully related the manifest and latent content.

Additional content observations deal with the type of characters in the dreams of the depressed and the association between a history of suicide attempt and the current dream content of the patient. Family members have been reported as being more frequent in the dreams of the depressed than in other patient groups. In those depressed patients who have made a suicide attempt, there are more themes of death, destruction, and violence in their dreams.

There is a consistent observation about the form of the dream in depressed patients, related to the length of their dream reports. Two studies (24, 25) indicate that the length of the dream report is shorter for depressed patients than other psychiatric patient groups.

Laboratory (33, 67, 68). The one separate group laboratory study (33) of depressed patients' dreams that reports statistical results and compares the index group to another "ill" group provides a mixed picture in regard to whether depressed patients have more or less depressive content in their dreams than other groups, and confirms the character type frequency noted in the nonlaboratory studies. Unfortunately, the issue of masochism is not pursued in this report.

The dreams of the depressed have more friendly and fewer aggressive interactions than schizophrenics, observations that could be considered as consistent with the view of there being less "depressive" material in the dreams of the depressed. However, the depressed have more failure and misfortunes in their dreams than do schizophrenics, findings potentially at odds with the notion of their having less depressive material in their dreams. A study comparing the waking and dreaming fantasy contents of the depressed would be the most appropriate method to confirm or reject the thesis hypothesized in the descriptive studies of a compensatory relationship between depressive content awake and asleep.

The observation in the non-laboratory separate groups studies of a higher incidence of family members in the dreams of the depressed is confirmed in a laboratory study (33). Whether the family member character type covaries only with the depressed phase is unfortunately not explored in the one repeated measures study to be reported below.

Repeated Measures Studies (Laboratory) (69).   One study, which utilizes the same data base as in the laboratory separate groups comparison, applies a repeated measures design to study the effect on dream content of successful treatment with antidepressant medication.   Unfortunately, the measures applied to the content do not pursue the issues developed in the descriptive and separate group studies.   Rather, the dreams are scored for the effect on dream content parameters noted to be affected by psychotropic drugs in a study (102) in normal persons.

The results of this study indicate that with an improvement in depression, hostility is decreased while intimacy, heterosexuality, and motility are increased. As the initial observation about these dimensions being different in depression was not suggested in a descriptive dream study or demonstrated as being quantitatively or qualitatively different in a separate groups design study, these statistically significant results exist as an isolated result.

The limited number of findings that have independent verification in any study of the dreams of a psychopathologic group is impressive, and depression is no exception.   The increased frequency of family members in the dreams of the depressed and their dreams being shorter than those of nondepressed patients are the *only* two verified findings.   The greater frequency of masochism in depressed or formerly depressed patients has not been verified.

Alcoholism

Separate Group Studies (Non-laboratory) (23, 70-72).   Although there are no descriptive studies, three (23, 70, 71) of the four separate group studies do report statistically significant results from a comparison of alcoholics to another "ill" group.   The one repeated measures study (73), which is a laboratory study, reports no statistical results.

The three separate group studies indicate that judges can discriminate the dreams of alcoholics from those of nonalcoholics.   As might be expected, alcoholics have more dreams of oral incorporation, see themselves in the dreams more often as objects of aggression than do nonalcoholics, and have fewer sexual interactions.   Those alcoholics who dream about drinking are more likely to abstain from drinking than those alcoholics who do not. The latter observation is especially interesting as it suggests the use of the dream as a prognostic tool and provides clues about a possible functional role the dream may play.

Note should be taken of the lack of studies on the dream life of alcoholics. It is worth observing that not a single study replicates the results of another study, and no investigator has reported more than one dream study in this group. The results obtained from the study of the dream in alcoholics are provocative and potentially of high value, both theoretically and practically.

Chronic Brain Syndrome

Descriptive Studies (Laboratory) (74).   In essentially a physiological study of Korsakoff's patients (74), the observation is made that the patients showed poor recall of dreams and that the quality of their dreams was impaired. This study would invite an examination of recall rates in this patient group and a description of the form, if not the content, of their dreams.

Separate Group Studies (Non-laboratory and Laboratory) (75-78).   There are four separate group studies, two laboratory (75, 76) and two non-laboratory (77, 78). However, only one of the laboratory studies makes an appropriate comparison and reports statistically significant results.

The one acceptable study reports that aged patients with a chronic brain syndrome have a lower dream recall rate than middle-aged patients with a similar condition. The severe chronic brain syndrome patients had more characters in their dreams than the less severely ill.

The results do, at least partially, address the questions raised in the descriptive study. One issue addressed was the question of recall rates, and some related answer was provided. Clearly, no verified data exist.

Mental Retardation

Descriptive Studies (Non-laboratory) (79, 80).   The descriptive studies suggest that the theme of being at home is very common for institutionalized retarded patients.   Their dreams are simple, contain day residues, and are primarily visual, but without color, variety, or vividness. Their dream and T.A.T. content appeared to be quite similar in one study (80).

Separate Group Studies (Non-laboratory) (81, 82).   The high frequency of dreams about home suggested in the descriptive studies was demonstrated in a separate group study (81). Further, a sex difference has been observed. Male retardates have more aggressive dreams, and dream more about males, sports, finding money, and eating. Female patients with mental retardation have more color in their dreams, and dream more about falling and being chased.

The exploration of the dreams of the mentally retarded has only minimally begun. No verifiable results could be found. As with all of the psychopathologic groups, a large arena for investigation remains.

DISCUSSION

Our extensive search of the periodical literature for work relating to the nature of the dream in psychopathologic patient groups uncovered a surprisingly small number of articles. It seems highly unlikely from so few studies, e.g., 22 in schizophrenia, 11 in disturbing dreams, 11 in depression, 5 in alcoholism, 5 in chronic brain syndrome, and 4 in mental retardation, that a meaningful characterization of the dream life of any psychopathologic group could be developed. Further, many patient groups of high importance have not had any studies of their dream life reported. Clearly, from a purely quantitative point of view, we have only begun in our efforts to explore the dreams of the emotionally disturbed.

If, in order to accept a description of the dream content of a patient group, the description had to meet a standard of verifiability, i.e., the finding must be reported in two scientifically acceptable studies by two independent investigators, our knowledge of the dream content of patient groups would be even more compromised. The impact of utilizing a verifiability standard can be illustrated by comparing the summary of dream content in schizophrenia and depression we attempted in our 1970 article in which the findings of various studies were uncritically accepted and the summary of verified dream content we established in the present critical review.

In our 1970 article (8), we described the dreams of schizophrenics as "unrealistic, affectively neutral, openly hostile with the hostility directed at the dreamer, less blatantly sexual than the patient's waking life, with the dream action focused on the dreamer who finds himself most of the time with strangers." Based on our present review, utilizing a verifiability standard, we would limit our description of the dreams of schizophrenics to their being more hostile, more affective, and containing more evidence of the schizophrenic thought disorder, i.e., unrealistic, bizarre, and so on, than those of nonschizophrenics. An important "loss of information" about the dream life of schizophrenics obviously takes place when only verifiability standards are applied.

In a similar fashion, comparing our uncritical summary of the dream content in depression to our verified findings in the present report leads to a similar reduction in our knowledge of the dream life in depression. In 1970, we summarized the dreams of the depressed as being "either depressive or nondepressive in tone." They "have hostility present in their dreams about half the time, and the hostility is equally divided between being directed at or away from the dreamer." They show an increase in sexuality in their dreams associated with clinical improvement. They have more realistic dreams than schizophrenics but less than normal persons, and quite often have family members and themes of escape in their dreams. The only two verified findings in regard to the dreams of the depressed that resulted from our current review is that they have shorter dreams and more family members in their dreams than the nondepressed.

It strikes us rather forcibly that the major shortcoming in the study of the dream life in psychopathologic patient groups is that lack of a systematic strategy for approaching the problem. It would seem reasonable to utilize a sequence of studies that would capitalize on the known value of various research designs. We would recommend an approach that would use a descriptive study to generate or support a hypothesis about the nature of the dream content of the index patient group. This should be followed by a separate group study which would ensure that the aspect of the index group's dream life in question was indeed specific to the index group. Then a repeated measures study should be performed to demonstrate that the particular aspect of the index patient group's dream life covaries either with the intensity or the presence of the illness or both. If the aspect of dream life in question does not covary with the presence or the intensity of the illness, but is specific to the index group, then we may be dealing with a dream content that is related to proneness to the index illness but not the illness itself. Prospective studies would be one approach to pursuing this issue.

Assuming that we have achieved separate group specification and repeated measures covariation of an aspect of a patient group's dream life, what should the next steps be? The individual investigator should attempt to replicate his or her specification and covariation findings. For colleagues, the attempt would be to confirm and thereby verify the findings. Clearly, the replication-verification step could just as well come in two steps, once after the specification study, and again after the covariation study. The last phase would be an attempt to manipulate the dream content in question in order to cause both a negative and a positive change in the index illness. If this is achieved, and replicated, then verifying confirmation by an independent investigator would complete the process.

Our genuine knowledge of the dream life of various psychopathologic patient groups is either too meager or does not exist, and therefore is unavailable to help us understand the nature of the patient groups' distress or to have it provide the necessary clues to unlock the riddle of their illness. It seems reasonable to call for greater application of scientifically rigorous programmatic investigation by more researchers into the nature of the dream in psychopathologic groups.

BIBLIOGRAPHY

1. Freud, S. *The Interpretation of Dreams, Standard Edition*, Vols. 4 and 5. London: Hogarth, 1900.
2. Jung, C. *Two Essays on Analytical Psychology*. New York: Meridian Books, 1956.
3. Jackson, J. *Selected Writings of John Hughlings Jackson*, Taylor, J. (Ed), Vol. 2. New York: Basic Books, 1958.
4. Bonime, W. *The Clinical Use of Dreams*. New York: Basic Books, 1962.
5. French, T. *The Integration of Behavior*, Vols. 1, 2, 3. Chicago: University of Chicago Press, 1952, 1954, 1958.
6. Aserinsky, E., and Kleitman, N. Regularly occurring periods of eye motility, and concomitant phenomena, during sleep. *Science*, 188: 273, 1953.
7. Ramsey, G. Studies of dreaming. *Psych. Bull.*, 50: 432, 1953.
8. Kramer, M. Manifest dream content in normal and psychopathologic states. *Arch. Gen. Psychiat.*, 22: 149, 1970.
9. Kramer, M., Winget, C., and Roth, T. Problems in the definition of the REM dream. In Levin, P., and Koella, W. (Eds.), *Sleep 1974*, Proceedings of the Second European Congress on Sleep Research. Rome, 1974.
10. Winget, C., and Kramer, M. *Dimensions of the Dream*. Gainesville, University of Florida Press, in press.
11. Foulkes, D., and Vogel, G. The current status of laboratory dream research. *Psychiat. Ann.*, 4: 7, 1974.
12. Framo, J., Osterweil, J., and Boszormenyi-Nagy, I. A relationship between threat in the manifest content of dreams and active-passive behavior in psychotics. *J. Abn. Psych.*, 65: 41, 1962.
13. Hendrick, I. Dream resistance and schizophrenia. *J. Am. Psychoanal. Assn.*, 6: 672, 1958.
14. Kant, O. Dreams of schizophrenic patients. *J. Nerv. Ment. Dis.*, 95: 335, 1942.
15. Kass, W., Preiser, G., and Jenkins, A. Inter-relationship of hallucinations and dreams in spontaneously hallucinating patients. *Psychiat. Quart.*, 44: 488, 1970.
16. Martin, P. A psychotic episode following a dream. *Psychoanal. Quart.*, 27: 563, 1958.
17. Noble, D. A study of dreams in schizophrenia and allied states. *Am. J. Psychiat.*, 107: 612, 1950.
18. Trapp, C. Dream studies in hallucinated patients. *Psychiat. Quart.*, 11: 253, 1937.
19. Karpman, B. Dream life in a case of hebephrenia. *Psychiat. Quart.*, 27: 262, 1953.
20. Grand, S., Freedman, N., and Jortner, S. Variations in REM dreaming and the effectiveness of behavior in group therapy. *Am. J. Psychother*, 23: 667, 1969.
21. Brenneis, C. Features of the manifest dream in schizophrenia. *J. Nerv. Ment. Dis.*, 153: 81, 1971.
22. Brenneis, C. Factors affecting diagnostic judgments of manifest dream content in schizophrenia. *Psych. Rep.*, 29: 811, 1971.
23. Hall, C. A comparison of the dreams of four groups of hospitalized mental patients with each other and with a normal population. *J. Nerv. Ment. Dis.*, 143: 135, 1966.
24. Kramer, M., Baldridge, B., Whitman, R., et al. An exploration of the manifest dream in schizophrenia and depressed patients. *Dis. Nerv. Syst.*, 30: 126, 1969.
25. Langs, R. Manifest dreams from three clinical groups. *Arch. Gen. Psychiat.*, 14: 634, 1966.

26. Richardson, G., and Moore, R.   On the manifest dream in schizophrenia. *J. Am. Psychoanal. Assn.*, **11**: 281, 1963.

27. Boss, M.   The psychopathology of dreams in schizophrenia and organic psychoses. In DeMartino, M. (Ed.), *Dreams and Personality Dynamics*. Springfield, Illinois: Charles C. Thomas, 1959.

28. Carrington, P.   Dreams and schizophrenia. *Arch. Gen. Psychiat.*, **26**: 343, 1972.

29. Cappon, D.   Morphology and other parameters of phantasy in the schizophrenias. *Arch. Gen. Psychiat.*, **1**: 33, 1959.

30. Chang, S.   Dream-recall and themes of hospitalized schizophrenics. *Arch. Gen. Psychiat.*, **10**: 119, 1964.

31. Doust, J.   Studies in the physiology of awareness: The incidence and content of dream patterns and their relationship to anoxia. *J. Ment. Sci.*, **97**: 801, 1951.

32. Arey, L.   First night dreams of normals, neurotics, and three groups of schizophrenics. Paper presented at meeting of the Association for the Psychophysiological Study of Sleep, Gainesville, Florida, 1966.

33. Kramer, M., and Roth, T.   A comparison of dream content in laboratory dream reports of schizophrenic and depressive patient groups. *Compr. Psychiat.*, **14**: 325, 1973.

34. Cartwright, R.   Sleep fantasy in normal and schizophrenic persons. *J. Abn. Psych.*, **80**: 275, 1972.

35. Dement, W.   Dream recall and eye movements during sleep in schizophrenics and normals. *J. Nerv. Ment. Dis.*, **122**: 263, 1955.

36. Okuma, T., Sunami, Y., Fukama, E., et al.   Dream content study in chronic schizophrenics and normals by REMP-awakening technique. *Fol. Psychiat. Neur.*, **24**: 151, 1970.

37. Kramer, M., Hlasny, R., Jacobs, G., et al: Do dreams have meaning? An empirical inquiry. *Am. J. Psychiat.*, **133**: 7, 1976.

38. Kramer, M., Whitman, R., Baldridge, B., et al.   Dream content in male schizophrenic patients. *Dis. Nerv. Syst.*, **31**: 51, 1970.

39. Ornstein, P., Whitman, R., Kramer, M., et al.   Drugs and dreams IV: Tranquilizers and their effects upon dreams and dreaming in schizophrenic patients. *Exp. Med. Surg.*, **27**: 145, 1969.

40. Freedman, N., Grand, S., and Karacan, I.   An approach to the study of dreaming and changes in psychopathologic states. *J. Nerv. Ment. Dis.*, **143**: 399, 1966.

41. Kramer, M., Clark, J., and Day, N.   Dreaming in schizophrenia. In Zikmund, V. (Ed.), *The Oculomotor System and Brain Functions*.   Proceedings of the International Colloquium, Smolenice, Czechoslovakia, 1970.

42. Schneck, J.   Observations on the hypnotic nightmare. *Am. J. Clin. Hyp.*, **16**: 240, 1974.

43. Fodor, N.   Nightmares of water. *An Imago*, **4**: 140, 1948.

44. Fodor, N.   Nightmares of suffocation. *J. Nerv. Ment. Dis.*, **101**: 557, 1945.

45. Garma, A.   The traumatic situation in the genesis of dreams. *Int. J. Psychoanal.*, **27**: 134, 1946.

46. Loewenstein, R.   A posttraumatic dream. *Psychoanal. Quart.*, **18**: 449, 1949.

47. Burgess, A., and Holmstrom, L.   Rape trauma syndrome. *Am. J. Psychiat.*, **131**: 9, 1974.

48. Lidz, T.   Nightmares and the combat neuroses. *Psychiat.*, **9**: 37, 1946.

49. Harris, I.   Observations concerning typical anxiety dreams. *Psychiat.*, **11**: 301, 1948.

50. Harris, I.   Characterological significance of the typical anxiety dreams. *Psychiat.*, **14**: 279, 1951.

51. Harris, I. The dream of the object endangered. *Psychiat.*, 20: 151, 1957.
52. Greenberg, R., Pearlman, C., and Gampel, D. War neuroses and the adaptive function of REM sleep. *Brit. J. Med. Psych.*, 45: 27, 1972.
53. Fisher, C., Kahn, E., Edwards, A., et al. A psychophysiological study of nightmares and night terrors. *J. Nerv. Ment. Dis.*, 158: 174, 1974.
54. Kahn, E., Fisher, C., Edwards, A., et al. Mental content of stage 4 night terrors. *Proc. Am. Psych. Assn.*, 8: 501, 1973.
55. Cason, H. The nightmare dream. *Psych. Monogr.*, 46: 1, 1935.
56. Harris, I. Typical anxiety dreams and object relations. *Int. J. Psychoanal.*, 41: 604, 1960.
57. Fisher, C., Byrne, J., Edwards, A., et al. A psychophysiological study of nightmares. *J. Am. Psychoanal. Assn.*, 18: 747, 1970.
58. Fisher, C., Kahn, E., Edwards, A., et al. A psychophysiological study of nightmares and night terrors: Suppression of stage 4 night terrors with diazepam. *Arch. Gen. Psychiat.*, 28: 252, 1973.
59. Hes, J. Depression and dreams. *Am. J. Psychiat.*, 122: 1067, 1966.
60. Shtoffer, S. Analysis through dream analysis. *Quart. Rev. Psychiat. Neur.*, 6: 158, 1951.
61. Esman, A. The dream screen in an adolescent. *Psychoanal. Quart.*, 31: 250, 1962.
62. Beck, A., and Hurvich, M. Psychological correlates of depression. *Psychosom. Med.*, 21: 50, 1959.
63. Beck, A., and Ward, C. Dreams of depressed patients. *Arch. Gen. Psychiat.*, 5: 66, 1961.
64. Raphling, D. Dreams and suicide attempts. *J. Nerv. Ment. Dis.*, 151: 404, 1970.
65. Miller, J. Dreams during varying stages of depression. *Arch. Gen. Psychiat.*, 20: 560, 1969.
66. Sethi, B. Relationship of separation to depression. *Arch. Gen. Psychiat.*, 10: 486, 1964.
67. Kramer, M., Whitman, R., Baldridge, B., et al. Drugs and Dreams III: The effects of imipramine on the dreams of depressed patients. *Am. J. Psychiat.*, 122: 411, 1965.
68. Hauri, P. Dream content in patients remitted from neurotic depression. *Sleep Res.*, 4: 185, 1975.
69. Kramer, M., Whitman, R., Baldridge, B., et al. Dreaming in the depressed. *Canad. Psychiat. Assn. J.* (special supplement), 11: 178, 1966.
70. Choi, S. Dreams as a prognostic factor in alcoholism. *Am. J. Psychiat.*, 130: 699, 1973.
71. Moore, R. The manifest dream in alcoholism. *Q. J. Stud. Alcohol.*, 23: 583, 1962.
72. Scott, E. Dreams of alcoholics. *Percept. Mot. Skills*, 26: 1315, 1968.
73. Wolin, S., and Mello, N. The effects of alcohol on dreams and hallucinations in alcohol addicts. *Ann. New York Acad. Sci.*, 215: 266, 1973.
74. Greenberg, R., Pearlman, C., Brooks, R., et al. Dreaming and Korsakoff's psychosis. *Arch. Gen. Psychiat.*, 18: 203, 1968.
75. Looney, M. The dreams of heroin addicts. *Soc. Work*, 17: 23, 1972.
76. Jelliffe, S. Two morphine color dreams with a note on the etiology of the opium habit. *Psychoanal. Rev.*, 31: 128, 1944.
77. Shaskan, D., Miller, E., and Sears, D. Does noludar (methyprylon) change dreams? *Behav. Neuropsychiat.*, 1: 22, 1970.
78. Kramer, M., Roth, T., and Trinder, J. Dreams and dementia: A laboratory exploration of dream recall and dream content in chronic brain syndrome patients. *Int. J. Aging Hum. Develop.*, 6: 169, 1975.

79. Walsh, W. Dreams of the feeble-minded. *Med. Rec.*, 97: 395, 1920.
80. Sarason, S. Dreams and thematic apperception test stories. *J. Abn. Soc. Psych.*, **39**: 386, 1944.
81. DeMartino, M. Some characteristics of the manifest dream content of mental defectives. *J. Clin. Psych.*, 10: 175, 1954.
82. Sternlicht, M. Dreaming in adolescent and adult institutionalized mental retardates. *Psychiat. Quart. Suppl.*, 40: 97, 1966.
83. Freedman, A., Luborsky, L., and Harvey, R. Dream time (REM) and psychotherapy. *Arch. Gen. Psychiat.*, **22**: 33, 1970.
84. Gershman, H. Dream power. *Am. J. Psychoanal.*, 33: 167, 1973.
85. Grand, S., and Pardes, H. The transition from sleep to wakefulness: Implications of a study of the organization of laboratory dream reports for the psychoanalytic situation. *J. Am. Psychoanal. Assn.*, 22: 58, 1974.
86. Kaplan, D. The emergence of projection in a series of dreams. *Psychoanalysis Psychoanal. Rev.*, 49: 37, 1962.
87. French, T. Physiology of behavior and choice of neurosis. *Psychoanal. Quart.*, 10: 561, 1941.
88. Izner, S. On the appearance of primal scene content in dreams. *J. Am. Psychoanal. Assn.*, 7: 317, 1959.
89. Lorand, S. Fairy tales, lilliputian dreams, and neurosis. *Am. J. Orthopsychiat.*, 7: 456, 1937.
90. Stamm, J. Infantile trauma, narcissistic injury and agoraphobia. *Psychiat. Quart.*, 46: 254, 1972.
91. Freidemann, M. Representative and typical dreams with emphasis on the masculinity-feminity problem. *Psychoanal. Rev.*, 44: 363, 1957.
92. Kremer, M., and Rifkin, A. The early development of homosexuality: A study of adolescent lesbians. *Am. J. Psychiat.*, 126: 129, 1969.
93. Roos, A. Psychoanalytic study of a typical dream. *Psychoanal. Quart.*, 29: 153, 1960.
94. Goldhirsh, M. Manifest content of dreams of convicted sex offenders. *J. Abn. Soc. Psych.*, 63: 643, 1961.
95. Hanks, L. An explanation of the content of dreams through an interpretation of dreams of convicts. *J. Gen. Psych.*, 23: 31, 1940.
96. Selling, L. Effect of conscious wish upon dream content. *J. Abn. Soc. Psych.*, 27: 172, 1932.
97. Gold, M. An individualized 24-hour therapeutic approach to a psychotic child. *Child Psychiat. Hum. Develop.*, 3: 115, 1972.
98. Gold, M., and Robertson, M. The night/day imagery paradox of selected psychotic children. *J. Am. Acad. Child Psychiat.*, 14: 132, 1975.
99. Emonds, E. Treatment of a severe chronic phobic neurosis in general practice. *Brit. J. Med. Psych.*, 20: 393, 1944.
100. Jenkins, R., and Groh, R. Mental symptoms in Parkinsonian patients treated with L-dopa. *Lancet*, 2: 177, 1970.
101. Domhoff, W. Home dreams versus laboratory dreams. In Kramer, M. (Ed.), *Dream Psychology and the New Biology of Dreaming*. Springfield, Illinois: Charles C. Thomas, 1969, p. 199.
102. Whitman, R., Pierce, C., Maas, J., et al. Drugs and dreams II: Imipramine and prochlorperazine. *Compr. Psychiat.*, 2: 219, 1961.
103. Firth, H. Sleeping pills and dream content. *Brit. J. Psychiat.*, 124: 547, 1974.
104. Cohen, H., and Dement, W. Sleep: Suppression of rapid eye movement phase in the cat after electroconvulsive shock. *Science*, 154: 396, 1966.

105. Winget, C., Kramer, M., and Whitman, R. Dreams and demongraphy. *Canad. Psychiat. Assn. J.*, 17: 203, 1972.
106. Brodan, K., and Erdmann, A. *Cornell Medical Index Health Questionnaire*. New York Hospital and Departments of Medicine (Neurology) and Psychiatry, Cornell University Medical College, 1949.
107. Fox, R., Kramer, M., Baldridge, B., et al. The experimenter variable in dream research. *Dis. Nerv. Syst.*, 29: 698, 1968.
108. Berger, R. The sleep and dream cycle. In Kales, A. (Ed.), *Sleep: Physiology and Pathology*. Philadelphia: J. B. Lippincott Company, 1968.
109. Goodenough, D., Lewis, H., Shapiro, A., et al. Dream reporting following abrupt and gradual awakenings from different types of sleep. *J. Pers. Soc. Psych.*, 2: 170, 1965.
110. Clark, J., Trinder, J., Kramer, M., et al. An approach to the content analysis of dream content scales. *Sleep Res.*, 1: 118, 1972.
111. Freud, S. *Some Neurotic Mechanisms in Jealousy, Paranoia, and Homosexuality. Standard Edition*, Vol. 18. London: Hogarth, 1922.

13

Dreams and Schizophrenia

Benjamin B. Wolman

The term schizophrenia is often loosely used to describe a variety of symptoms and, in some instances, even different clinical entities. In a paper on autism and childhood schizophrenia, I wrote as follows:

> I would like to start with a modified version of the story of the blind men and the elephant. The three blind men touched different parts of the elephant's body and, therefore, their descriptions of the elephant differed from one another. I am adding to the story a fourth man who touched, instead of an elephant, a rhinoceros.
>
> Something similar has happened to autism. Every student of this issue seems to have come across another aspect of this syndrome, and some of us apparently describe totally *different* clinical entities. The fact that some children display autistic symptoms does not necessarily mean that all of them belong to the same category. Not all people who have high temperatures are suffering from pneumonia and not all depressed moods are an indication of the manic-depressive psychosis (Wolman, 1976a).

I believe that all mental disorders with the exception of clearly organic cases are sociogenic. They can be divided into three distinct clinical types and five levels of severity. All sociogenic mental disorders are caused by noxious interaction with the environment. The human neonate interacts with parents and other individuals from the day he is born. Unless his organism was impaired by hereditary factors or by prenatal, natal, or postnatal physicochemical noxious factors, the mental disorder is started by his interaction with the social environment.

One may distinguish three patterns of observable social interaction (Wolman, 1956, 1974). Whenever an individual enters a social relationship with the objective of having his own needs satisfied, it is an *instrumental* social pattern. The individual is a *taker* and uses others for the satisfaction of his needs. All business relationships are instrumental; a man sells goods, hires service, or looks for a job in order to satisfy his own needs.

The second type of relationship is *mutual* or mutual acceptance. Whenever an individual enters a social relationship with the objective to give and to take, to satisfy his own needs and to satisfy the needs of others, it is a mutual relationship. Friendship, partnership, and marriage are usually mutual relationships.

Certain relationships belong to the third, *vectorial* type. True charity, i.e., giving without expecting anything in return, is vectorial. So is one's dedication to religion, homeland, or any other ideal.

The infant-toward-parent relationship is the prototype of instrumentalism; the husband-and-wife relationship is the prototype of mutualism; the parent-toward-infant relationship is the prototype of vectorialism. The normal adult acts in a balanced manner in all three types of relationship; he is instrumental in his breadwinning activities, mutual in regard to his marital partner, friends, and relatives, and vectorial toward his children and toward those who need his help.

Severe distortion or imbalance in social interaction is indicative of mental disorder. One may, therefore, classify sociogenic mental disorders using as a criterion the patterns of maladjustment.

Observing mentally disturbed people, one can discern, despite the diversity of symptoms, three fairly consistent patterns of abnormal social interaction. These are so pervading, so apparent, so easily observable, that they can be used also as diagnostic clues (Wolman, 1965 and 1978).

HYPERINSTRUMENTAL TYPE

Some mentally disturbed individuals are hyperinstrumental. They always want something for nothing; they show no consideration for fellow men, not even for their own parents, marital partners, or children; they act convinced that the world owes them a living, but they don't owe anything to anyone in return. They treat life like a bank to be robbed or an oil field to be exploited. They have no love for anyone except themselves. They are exploitative, selfish, brutal to others, and sentimental for themselves. They feel sorry for themselves but have no mercy for anyone else. They never blame themselves, but always blame others. They believe themselves to be innocent and surrounded by selfish and unfair enemies.

The type of individual belonging to the *hyperinstrumental type* corresponds to what has been often called psychopath or sociopath. Hyperinstrumentals are selfish, dishonest, and disloyal. Yet they believe in their own innocence. They believe the world is hostile, and they are resentful whenever others refuse to serve them. Hyperinstrumentals are very sensitive to their own sufferings and deprivations, but have no empathy or sympathy for anyone else. They have no moral restraints, no consideration, no compassion for their fellow man. They may or may not become criminals, depending on whether they fear retaliation. The hyperinstrumental symptom formation offers both primary and secondary gains; it alleviates the feeling of being weak and helpless and also helps to win privileges from the environment.

DYSMUTUAL TYPE

The second type is an epitome of inconsistency. Sometimes the dysmutuals overdo in love for others as hypervectorials do, and sometimes they feel no love for others and are as selfish as hyperinstrumentals. When the dysmutuals love, they expect their love objects to return love with a high interest rate; when in love they are hyperaffectionate, showering with protectiveness and tenderness, and are ready for any self-sacrifice. When not repaid in full (with interest), they turn love into hate with the ease with which one turns on cold and hot water in a faucet. Their assumed great, unselfish love turns into a selfish, brutal hostility. But not only does their object love turn so easily into hostility; the same happens also with their attitude toward themselves. Usually they love themselves very much, but often their self-directed love turns into hate and leads to suicidal attempts. Their changing, cyclic moods reflect their libido and destrudo imbalance. When they feel loved, they believe themselves to be great, strong, and wonderful; and their mood is elated. When they feel rejected, they believe themselves to be weak, small, destitute, and hostile; and their mood is depressed. These fluctuations of mood gave rise to the name *manic-depressives*. Actually they are the type torn by exaggerated feelings of love and hate toward others and themselves. In a loving mood they are Dr. Jekyll; in a hating mood they are Mr. Hyde. Since none of these moods is lasting, they give the impression of being insincere, dishonest comedians. Actually they swing from extreme honesty to dishonesty, from love to hate, from heroism to cowardice.

HYPERVECTORIAL TYPE

The third group of disturbed individuals are extreme opposites to the first type. They are hypervectorial even in situations in which people are usually instrumental. They are always ready to give, to protect, to sacrifice themselves. In their childhood they did not act as all other children did, i.e., in a naturally instrumental way, but as if they were the protectors of their parents. As adults they seem to believe that they owe everything to the world, and no one owes them anything. Unless they are badly deteriorated, they seem to believe life is an obligation to be honored, a ritual to be followed, or a mission to be fulfilled. They have sympathy for everyone except themselves. Once in love they are exceedingly loyal, overprotective, often domineering and despotic in their over-protectiveness. When their exaggerated self-controls fail, they may regress into autistic seclusion.

The *hypervectorial type* covers all that is called schizophrenia and related conditions. Symptom formation in hypervectorialism offers mainly primary gain. The hypervectorials are unselfish, hyperethical though often self-righteous; they often believe that they are not as good as they should be and fear their own hostility. Their libido is object-hypercathected, their destrudo overre-pressed. Their superego is overgrown and dictatorial.

THE CONCEPT OF INTERINDIVIDUAL CATHEXIS

The above classification is based on two isomorphic factors, namely, balance of cathexes and social interaction. Freud's concept of cathexis offers considerable methodological advances: loving someone is conceptually presented as investing, changing, cathecting one's emotional energy, libido, into the image of the be-loved person.

Freud's model of personality can be adapted to interindividual relations by a broadening of Freud's term cathexis. While Freud dealt with the individual who cathects his libido in objects, I suggest including the cathected objects in our study. Thus one can make full use of the important contributions made by the neoanalytic schools without abandoning the Freudian system.

The concept of interindividual cathexis is a *theoretical construct*. There are neurological or physiological counterparts to it. One may find some similarity to Pavlov's explanation of reflex. An external stimulus, wrote Pavlov (1928, p. 121), is "transformed into a nervous process and transmitted along a circuitous route (from the peripheral endings of the centripetal nerve, along its fibers to the apparatus of the central nervous system, and out along the centrifugal path until, reaching one or another organ, it excites its activity)." Pavlov's description can be explained in terms of cathexis of physical energy; the external stimulus somehow transmits a part of its energetic load in the peripheral endings of the centripetal nerve and thus cathects or charges this nerve ending and, through the circuitous route, cathects the nerve center also.

By analogy, and it is nothing more than an analogy, one may speculate about the interindividual cathexes of mental energy. It has to be stated clearly, how-ever, that I neither have evidence nor know how to find it, that mental energy is cathected and that it follows the analogy with physical energy. Thus, I have to say that at the present time I use the term "interindividual cathexis" as a theoretical construct and nothing else.

Cathexis and the Power-Acceptance Theory.   This construct is introduced because of its methodological flexibility and usefulness. The term interindividual cathexis allows one to make full use of Freud's model of personality which offers so many methodological advantages and has been tested in the vast experience of psychoanalytic therapy. While being faithful to Freud's principles, we are able to understand interpersonal relations better, for the cathected object is included in our studies. Furthermore, the concept of interindividual cathexis permits us to build a bridge between the body of psychoanalytic studies and experimental research in social psychology in terms of the theory of power and acceptance.

Consider the instrumental type of relationship. It is a "getting" type of relationship. The individual's aim is to receive libido cathexes from others. His libido is self-cathected, and he expects the libido of others to be object-cathected into him. An infant wants to be loved, or accepted (Horney), or approved (Sullivan). In accordance with Freud's personality model, the infant wishes to receive cathexes and to become a libido-cathected object. The same applies to any other instrumental relationship, such as the desire to be supported, to be popular, and to be appreciated and admired.

In a mutual type of relationship, the individual wishes to receive libido cathexes as well as to give them to those from whom he desires to receive. It is a give-and-take relationship. Satisfactory sexual intercourse is usually such a relationship. So is true friendship. Each partner desires to object-cathect his libido (aim-inhibited, if it is a nonsexual relationship) in his partner and expects his partner to have the same aim.

In a vectorial type of relationship, the individual aims to invest, to object-cathect, to give to others. Parenthood is the prototype of such a giving-without-receiving, one-way-object-libido cathexis. It is an aim-inhibited cathexis, of course. So is psychotherapy.

Instrumental, mutual, and vectorial attitudes are normal human attitudes. A well-adjusted adult is instrumental in his breadwinning behavior; is mutual in friendship, sex, and marriage; and is vectorial in parenthood and in charitable and idealistic activities. A dysbalance in these attitudes gives rise to psychopathological behavior, namely hyperinstrumental (sociopaths), dysmutual (hysterics and manic-depressives), and hypervectorial (phobias, compulsives, and schizophrenics). A dysbalance in social attitudes can be presented in the conceptual system of dysbalance of libido cathexes, as follows: a self-hypercathexis is hyperinstrumental; a shifting from object hyper- to hypocathexis and vice versa is dysmutual; and an object hypercathexis is hypervectorial.

An individual who will become schizophrenic starts his life like any other child, in a state of primary narcissism with all his libido invested in himself and all his destrudo ready to be directed against threatening objects. In a normal development, the loving and protecting (vectorial) parents satisfy the child's needs and enable him to grow and gradually develop the instrumental, mutual, and vectorial attitudes. The preschizophrenic child, however, is exposed to a love-demanding, pseudo-vectorial mother who is actually instrumental and hostile-parasitic, and to an overtly instrumental father. The child begins to feel that his parents are not protective, and, unless he protects them, he may lose them. The schizophrenic paradox reads as follows: "I want to live, but I must sacrifice my own life to protect those upon whom my survival depends." This attitude leads to an abundant, hypervectorial cathexis if the child's libido in his parents and extreme efforts on his part to control his self-protective out-bursts of destrudo directed against those whom he must protect at his own expense. The schizophrenic fears that his inadequate love of parents and loss of control over his own hostility may kill them, and then he will be lost forever. All schizophrenics are panic-driven by the fear of their own hostility (Arieti, 1974; Sullivan, 1962), which may lead, so they believe, to the death of love objects and to their own death.

Schizophrenia is, essentially, an *irrational struggle for survival*. The fear of losing the love object forces the individual to care more for the object, to pro-tect him, to invest more and more libido into him. This hypervectorial object cathexis reduces the individual's own resources and prevents an adequate self-cathexis (cf. Federn, 1952). When the shrinking amount of libido left for self-cathexis is unable to protect the individual, destrudo takes over. It is the "panic" type of hostility of an animal that flees mortal danger, or "terror" type of a wounded animal.

This is, in essence, the core of the paranoid and catatonic hostility. Hostility serves survival, and the frightened schizophrenic fights for life. Of course, he fights in an irrational way. Yet as long as he fights for life, the prognosis is better as compared with withdrawal and resignation. In the more regressed types of schizophrenic behavior (I believe the simple and hebephrenic types are more regressed), the schizophrenic acts as if he were saying: "I want to live a normal life, but I had to pay too high a price. Now I am trying to survive while giving up self-control, responsibilities, and my conscious mind. Perhaps I can survive if I live an infant's life." Undoubtedly the symptomatology of the sim-ple and hebephrenic schizophrenias brings about a passive and energy-saving pattern of living (Wolman, 1967).

LEVELS OF DISORDER

My assumption is that the normal personality is a balanced one. Once an im-balance in cathexes starts, the ego, in accordance with Freud's "constancy principle" and its main task of protection of the organism, tries to counteract the maladjustive processes. The struggle of the ego against pressures from within creates profound feelings of anxiety with a great variety of ego-protective symptoms. Although the nature of the symptoms depends on the nature of the threat or damage and is specific in each of the three types of disorder, the common denominator for this level of all three types is anxiety and ego-protective symptoms. As long as the ego is capable of asserting itself using a galaxy of defense mechanisms, the disorder level is *neurosis*. It can be a hyperinstrumental neurosis, a dysmutual neurosis, or a hypervectorial neurosis; they are different *types* of neurosis, but are the same, first level of mental disorder.

When the ego, so to say, comes to terms with the neurotic symptoms and the neurotic symptoms or attitudes become "included in the ego" or "blended into personality" (Fenichel, 1945, p. 463ff.), then neurosis becomes "*character neurosis*," or "character disorder," or "personality disorder." These three names describe the same category, the same second level of mental disorder.

Sometimes the defenses are inadequate, and a neurosis or a character neurosis may turn into a latent or manifest psychosis. A neurosis does not have to become first character neurosis and then a latent psychosis and later on a manifest psychosis. Character neurosis serves as a "protective armor" (Reich, 1949), a rigid set of ego-protective symptoms that prevents further deterioration into psychosis; but sometimes even armor may break. Yet, in some cases, in spite of a severe psychotic deterioration the individual still is not manifestly psychotic. He somehow continues functioning on a slim margin of ego controls; a mild noxious stimulus may throw him into a manifest psychosis. As long as his ego keeps on and a contact with reality is preserved, it is a *latent* and not a manifest psychosis.

The main difference between neurosis and psychosis lies in the strength of the ego. As long as the ego controls the id and preserves the contact with reality, the disorder is neurosis. *Psychosis* is a neurosis that failed; it is a defeat of the ego that lost the contact with reality and a victory of the id.

The victory of the id does not destroy the ego. The three *types* and five *levels* of mental disorders yield 15 clinical entities, presented in Table 13-1.

According to Freud, the entire id belongs to the province or layer of the unconscious, while only parts of the ego and superego are unconscious. Normally, unconscious wishes are partly repressed, partly sublimated, and partly incorporated in, and subordinated to the conscious purposes of the ego. The repressed parts come up in a disguised manner in dreams, slips of tongue and pen, misplacing things, and forgetting.

The unconscious part of human personality plays a significant role in life. It gives the overall "tone" of personality, colors the moods and desires, and forms the basis for one's likes and dislikes.

TABLE 13-1. CLASSIFICATION OF PSYCHOGENIC MENTAL DISORDERS.

	Sociopathic Hypersinstrumental Type (I)	Depressive Dysmutual Type (M)	Schizo-Hypervectorial Type (V)
Neurotic Level	Hyperinstrumental neurosis (Sociopathic neurosis)	Dysmutual neurosis (Dissociations, hysterias, and depressions)	Hypervectorial neurosis (Obsessional, phobic, and neurasthenic neurosis)
Character Neurotic Level	Hyperinstrumental character neurosis (Sociopathic character)	Dysmutual character neurosis (Depressive and hysteric character)	Hypervectorial character neurosis (Schizoid and obsessional character)
Latent Psychotic Level	Latent hyperinstrumental psychosis (Sociopathic borderline psychosis)	Latent dysmutual psychosis (Borderline depressive psychosis)	Latent vectoriasis praecox (Borderline and latent schizophrenia)
Manifest Psychotic Level	Hyperinstrumental psychosis (Sociopathic psychosis)	Dysmutual psychosis (Manifest depressive psychosis)	Vectoriasis praecox (Manifest schizophrenia)
Dementive Level	Collapse of personality structure.		

Normally the ego keeps the unconscious id processes under rational control. While doing it, the ego also satisfies the legitimate demands of the id in a rational manner. While the unconscious id presses for an immediate action (pleasure principle), the ego weighs the consequences and then acts cautiously (reality principle). Part of the ego itself is unconscious, and some individuals have "wisdom dreams" that warn them against attempted or planned misdeeds. When the conscious ego yields to the irrational pressures of the id, the unconscious part might have better preserved its protective functions and expressed them in dreams.

The relationship between the three mental layers, the conscious, preconscious, and unconscious, is not a matter of a simple or a static stratification. Creative minds use their unconscious; persons of genius, among them Sigmund Freud, have often relied on what they have called intuition. Every psychotherapist utilizes this talent for an unconscious perception of the feelings of his patients; this talent, called *empathy*, is a *sine qua non* for psychotherapist (Wolman, 1956). Individuals who have undergone psychoanalysis have acquired a greater access to their unconscious than they ever had before, and their life has become richer in content and deeper in its emotional refinement.

Mental health does not require shutting off the wells of the unconscious. Well-balanced individuals use the deep waters of the unconscious without causing a flood; or, to use Freud's comparison, it is the ego that rides on the back of a horse, the id. The neurotic fights his horse; the psychotic is overthrown by the horse and stepped on. The well-adjusted individual controls the horse and uses it for transportation.

A breakdown of the barriers dividing the conscious (primary) from the unconscious (secondary) processes is one of the outstanding signs of psychosis. Reasonably mentally healthy individuals can perform reality testing, that is, distinguish between stimuli coming from within and without. They know that their wishes are not fact but merely wishes. They are aware of their reactions to outer stimuli and do not confuse dreams with real experiences.

More of these characteristics of confusion apply to psychotics. In psychosis the line dividing conscious from unconscious processes is broken down or, in milder cases, punctured (Wolman, 1965).

The schizophrenic process is characterized by desperate efforts to control unconscious impulses. A failure of these efforts leads to a full-blown psychotic breakdown.

There are two weighty reasons for the desperate repressive measures taken by the ego. The first reason is the weakness of the ego common to preschizophrenics. The ego grows and thrives on contacts with reality, on testing reality, and on playing an active part in interindividual relationships. The overprotective parasitic-symbiotic attitude of mother reduces the child's outer contacts to a minimum. The child's emotional involvement with his parents leaves little room for interindividual relationships with people outside the family circle.

The second reason for the increased fear of the unconscious is the content and intensity of the unconscious wishes. The peculiar family situation strengthens and magnifies the unconscious incestuous and aggressive impulses.

These impulses, latent in all persons, have been stirred up, tormented, and brought to a pitch by the unfortunate interindividual relationships in schizogenic families. Normally the incestuous, heterosexual, Oedipal impulses become aim-inhibited and desexualized in the latency period, and in adolescence nonincestuous heterosexual desires develop. Hostility toward the parent of the same sex is mitigated by love, and finally the child "introjects" the parental image and identifies with the parent of the same sex.

This process is highly distorted in preschizophrenics. Mother's pseudovectorial and actually parasitic-instrumental attitude and father's overtly instrumental attitude prevent a normal distribution of libido-cathexes in the child. Hetero- and homosexual impulses are confused, and there is no way to renounce the hypercathected parent of the opposite sex or to identify entirely with the parent of the same sex. No schizophrenic ever comes close to the solution of the Oedipus complex, and all of them are not too clear in regard to their own sex and age role. The incestuous heterosexual, and the even more socially disapproved homosexual impulses come easily to the conscious surface, carrying the threat of social ostracism.

Even more threatening are the aggressive impulses. Parental attitudes usually create some degree of resentment in children; part of this resentment is repressed, part acted out in little rebellious acts against the parents, part sublimated, and part stored in the superego. There is much more resentment in the forced hypervectorial development than in a normal childhood. Furthermore, the preschizophrenic is much too involved emotionally to be able to sublimate, and too afraid to lose his parents to act out his hostility. As a result, he carries the dynamite of destrudo in his heart, partly repressed in the id, partly stored in the superego, and his impoverished ego has to mobilize all its resources to prevent explosion.

Thus begins the typical schizophrenic process that either goes through the neurotic, character neurotic, latent psychotic, manifest psychotic, and dementive stages, or skips some of them. The story of schizophrenia is the story of the ego's desperate struggle to control the unconscious impulses. The results of that struggle will determine whether a stop will be made on a milder level, or the individual will go all the way down toward a complete dismemberment of personality (Wolman, 1957).

DREAMS

Arieti (1974) noticed that the dreams of schizophrenics are quite bizarre. Anxiety and/or despair are pronounced with no resolution, and finally, the latent, unconscious latent dream elements are less covered up by secondary processes. The last remark agrees with my observation of the openness of the primary processes, which come through poorly inhibited or totally open.

Dreams of latent schizophrenics often point to their fear of psychotic breakdown. One of my patients brought the following dream to one of the earliest psychotherapy sessions:

> I am driving my car. Suddenly the breaks fail and the car accelerates more and more. I panic. I lost control over the car. The car is moving toward a black curtain. I know there is a precipice behind the curtain. I woke up screaming. I felt I am losing my mind.

Boss (1977, pp. 123-126) described two dreams of latent schizophrenics. The first dreamer concluded his dream as follows: "I was . . . growing weaker by the moment. I dissolved into dust, disintegrating completely." The second dream ended in a similar vein: "I turn into a skeleton, my head changing into a grinning skull."

Both dreams express the fear of loss of consciousness and of a total collapse of ego controls. Quite often the dreams of latent schizophrenics express struggle between the unconscious impulses and the ego, which desperately tries to regain control and prevent the breakdown.

A 40-year-old patient, mother of two, dreamed that she was in a car with her sister-in-law, the mother of three, and the car burst into flames. She did not worry about herself being burned, but about her two children, who played safely on the lawn. The dreams of schizophrenics are usually very lucid and apply classic symbols. Fire meant sex, in this case homosexual, and the patient worried about what would happen to her children if she gave in to her homosexual impulses. A 30 year-old patient, who blamed himself for his father's poor health, told a dream:

> Father is very, very ill, and no one wants to help. He badly needs a surgical operation on his chest or he will die. The patient feels desperate; he is a little boy and does not know what to do, but everybody seems to expect him to perform the operation. So he does it, restrains various veins, and saves father, but he knows that he did a poor and unsanitary job and father may still die.

Sometimes dreams of schizophrenics do not require interpretation. Their content is obvious, sometimes void of symbols. Many patients reported dreams of being beaten, raped, kidnapped, lost, rejected, left alone, and brutally assaulted. The fear of death was the prevailing theme of these dreams.

Schizophrenics often dream of neglecting their duties, forgetting to do things, missing appointments, failing to prepare homework for school, breaking things, being blamed and accused for all kinds of transgression and misbehavior.

These dreams often represent their own aggressive impulses and fear of them. One patient had a dream in which she was supposed to watch lions in cages, but the lions broke loose and attacked people. The patient woke up screaming for help. Another patient saw reptiles and tried to fight them off in his dream.

Dreams about wild animals, usually representing their own sexual and aggressive impulses, frequently occur in latent and manifest schizophrenics. One patient reported the following dream about her hated stepmother: "My stepmother and father fought. Father killed her. I cut my stepmother into pieces and we ate her. I woke up in horror, and was upset all day. I must be a very mean person. I hate my stepmother, but it was terrible to eat her."

There is no limit to regression in dreams. The most hostile dreams point to profound regressive tendencies, thus supporting the hypothesis that destrudo is more primitive than libido.

A 30-year-old patient dreamed about an infant burned alive. She woke up and felt that she was the child destroyed by flames. Another patient dreamed that people poisoned him. Another dreamed that someone came to strangle him. Still another reported a dream in which she was hiding behind several doors and a gorilla (her father) broke through and raped her.

Schizophrenics often report dreams in which their fathers, mothers, spouses, and friends disappear. They call and no one answers. Sometimes they dream of running after lost love-objects and not being to catch them; then they wake up in utter despair.

Sometimes they dream that their parents or other love objects are dying, and the dreamers cannot help. They wake up in the middle of the night, unable to fall asleep again. Many of them are afraid to go to sleep, fearing they may lose self-control and something terrible will happen. They desperately strive to master their impulses and are in panic when their impulses break through.

Often in dreams patients identify themselves with a parental figure and practice incestuous sex. A 26-year-old woman dreamed that she gave birth to her younger sister. Many women dream about sex with a duke, a noble, or other authority figures representing father. Sometimes the symbolism does not apply to the father, but to the intercourse. A female patient reported she was "climbing" with her father; another was sliding and gliding with her father. The psychoanalytic symbolism is obvious in all these cases, and obvious to the patients themselves.

A man reported a dream in which he had intercourse with a woman who had two sons. His first reaction: "my mother."

The more the patients deteriorate, the less sharp is the line dividing dreams from the waking state. Ultimately, in a severe deterioration the dream wins, and reality disappears. They dream while awake; they hallucinate.

Dreams of manifest schizophrenic cases in all four syndromes (paranoid, catatonic, hebephrenic, and simple deterioration) point to discontinuity in self-awareness (Boss, 1977) and frequently convey their unconscious power cravings (Wolman, 1966a). The hypervectorial attitude makes one wish to have superhuman powers to help one's weak parents, and many schizophrenics see themselves in dreams as omnipotent creatures.

The fear of their own hostility makes them dream of themselves as devils, warlocks, and witches, full of destructive power.

HALLUCINATIONS

When the ego-controls fail, and the barrier between conscious and unconscious breaks down, schizophrenics hallucinate. They dream while awake. They are unable to distinguish between stimuli coming from within and those coming from without. Once a schizophrenic patient spoke to me as follows:

> I know that you are Doctor Wolman but I am not sure about it. Now you are my father who died last year. Why did you die? I took care of you. Don't blame me! You are not my father. Are you Uncle Henry? Are you critical of me? Doctor Wolman, please, help me! . . .

When the unconscious takes over, the schizophrenic often feels omnipotent. He may believe he is an inventor, a king, a dangerous person, a prophet, or a monster, but always an omnipotent super-parent figure. He believes others try to steal his ideas; they hate him or fear his power, or try to read his mind. Thus his paranoid accusations of persecution, ideas of reference, delusions and hallucinations of grandeur, and world-saving or world-destroying devices originate.

The drama of the schizophrenic personality overinvolved with and overdevoted to his parents evolves in a spectacular manner in delusions and hallucinations. What is carefully hidden and desperately repressed in the prepsychotic stages breaks through with an irresistible clarity in the display of the unconscious in manifest schizophrenia. Schizophrenics are not the rejected children; they are the "overdemanded," overcriticized, and overinvolved ones. When rational controls break down, the conflict between the demand for perfection and the failure to meet this demand leads to one of the possible outcomes. Consider Harry's delusions: "Everybody in my office laughed at me. They said I was a coward and did not seek Suzie. They whispered that I was unfaithful to her. So I had to find her, to chase her, come what may." Harry, 30 years old, did not stop even before the sign "Ladies Room." He entered in search of Suzie and "took" the law into his hands." In his lucid moments he knew that Suzie, his college sweetheart, was presently married, had a child, and lived hundreds of miles away. When driven by delusions, Harry had "to prove" that he was faithful, that he was courageous, and that he would not betray Suzie, who had a baby and was merged in his mind with his mother. He was seeing her face wherever he went, and he tried to talk to her about his love.

George, a 28-year-old schizophrenic, told the following story:

> My boss gave me a look that meant a demand. He demanded my friendship. But I didn't feel I owed him anything, so I gave him a harsh look. Then he began to mimic me whenever he saw me. He made people call me on the phone and hang up. Next day I gave him a very hostile look. Then he said loudly to another man, "Let's forget it." I am sure he said it intentionally loud so I could hear him. His words meant, "I do not demand anything from George." You see, I won. He cannot force me to be his friend. But now I am afraid I hurt his feelings and he may abandon me.

George's father had tried to win George over as an ally against his hated wife, the boy's mother. The father acted seductively with a poorly veiled homosexual undercurrent. George feared his own homosexual thoughts and was trying to repress them. But there is the typical schizophrenic conflict with no way out. If you yield to a homosexual temptation, you are a bad person; if you fight it off, you will be forsaken. You feel trapped. The desperate situation leads into a more morbid, more confused, and more irrational state of mind.

In a state of utter confusion ideas come and go; impulses emerge and get lost in a senseless effort or lack of effort. Sometimes parts of the rational personality remain relatively intact, even after years or decades in a custodial type hospital. Too often, however, the whole mental structure falls apart, thoughts become more and more bizarre, ruminations of shreds of past events become confused with present experiences, sensations coming from within, and the unconscious primary processes flood whatever was preserved from the conscious development.

NEUROPHYSIOLOGICAL CORRELATES

Gladys was a latent schizophrenic with several manifest psychotic episodes and periods of remission. After childbirth she felt very elated and began to hallucinate. She was now a mother and saw God-Father. God spoke to her; God loved her. She was to become omnipotent and omniscient, a God herself. She was entrusted by God to protect Russia and America (father and mother) and make peace between them. She felt she could control the world and feared nothing. As a God she finally overcame her perplexing fear of death. Now she would never die.

Feinberg et al. (1964), Gulevitch et al. (1967), and Kupter et al. (1970) noticed that more-disturbed schizophrenics have shorter REM periods than the milder ones and those in remission. It seems that schizophrenics dream less in sleep because part of their waking state is sort of a dream. Delusions and hallucinations possess dreamlike features. Primary processes normally experienced in dreams are experienced in schizophrenics while they are awake.

Studies of REM and non-REM sleep phases (Dement, 1969; Rechtschaffen et al., 1972; Watson et al., 1976) have shown that the periorbital phasic integrated potentials (called PIP), are usually associated with dreamlike processes. In normal individuals the PIP phenomena occur in REM phases of sleep. In schizophrenics these periorbital phasic discharges take place in non-REM sleep phases, and often in the waking state when they are associated with dreamlike processes such as delusions and hallucinations.

It seems, therefore, plausible to follow the suggestion made by Watson et al. (1976) and Fiss (Chapter 2 in the present volume) that normally, phasic discharges are limited to REM sleep, but psychotic deficiency of some sort of "safety valves" permits a "leakage" of these discharges into non-REM sleep and also into the waking state. Whether this leakage causes hallucinations or is a by-product of them is as controversial as the somatic origin of schizophrenia (Wolman, 1966a, 1966b, 1976b, 1970, 1978).

The idea that dreaming of normal individuals and schizophrenic reveries are physiologically identical or very similar was refuted by Rechtschaffen et al. (1964), who studied the waking EEG, electromyographs, and eye movements of schizophrenic patients. My clinical observations (Wolman, 1966a, 1973, 1976a) confirm Rechtschaffen's views.

For one, no schizophrenic is schizophrenic all the time, and no one incessantly hallucinates. I have noticed on several occasions that the most disturbed schizophrenics are at least partially aware of who they are and who the therapist is, and at the end of therapeutic session they always go back to the ward. Feinberg et al. (1964) have observed a higher rate of eye movements in hallucinating schizophrenics as compared to the nonhallucinating ones, which again supports the view that extreme instances of hallucinating come close to a dreaming state, but this need not be interpreted to mean that schizophrenics' hallucinations correspond to normal dreaming. Analogously, schizophrenia is a state of severe regression, but while the behavior of an adult schizophrenic might be infantile, it does not resemble the behavior of a normal infant.

DREAMS AND PSYCHOTHERAPY

Interpretation of dreams of latent and manifest schizophrenics is, in most cases, unnecessary and in some cases it may be harmful. For one thing, latent and manifest schizophrenics have an uncanny insight into their own dreams, and interpretation is unnecessary. My schizophrenic patients themselves usually have offered a correct interpretation of dreams, making superfluous any further comments.

In many cases the interpretation of dreams might be unadvisable and even dangerous. When the unconscious, morbid wishes are piercing the weak defenses, an interpretation could bring a total collapse of personality structure and turn latent schizophrenia into a manifest one. My method, called interactional psychotherapy (1966b, 1976b), implies gradual improvement by substituting lesser symptoms for more dangerous ones. In some cases helping a manifest schizophrenic to become a hypervectorial neurotic (see Table 13-1) may be all that could be accomplished. My policy has been *One step up*, and in many instances supporting neurotic defenses may prevent further deterioration.

The main aim of interactional psychotherapy is to strengthen the patient's ego. In neurosis the ego is struggling against undue pressures from within; the *ego-protective*, neurotic symptoms bear witness to the struggle. In psychosis the ego has lost the battle, and psychotic, *ego-deficiency* symptoms develop, such as loss of reality testing (delusions and hallucinations, loss of control over unconscious impulses, deterioration of motor coordination, and so on).

Ego-therapy means the strengthening and reestablishment of the defeated ego. Thus, the therapist must never become part of the irrational transactions of the psychotic mind, be they delusions, hallucinations, or anything else. He must never offer support to erroneous perceptions of reality. The therapist must not interpret unconscious motivation processes if this interpretation may weaken the patient's ego (Wolman, 1957, 1977).

For example, the aggressive and obstinate Mrs. Hart is not treated (as she was at home) as the crazy Betsy, but as Mrs. Hart who happens to be presently disturbed and therefore hospitalized. The psychotherapist, the nurses, the attendants must not make her regress further and perceive herself as the nasty little Betsy, the "black sheep" as she was in her childhood. Presently, Mrs. Hart is Mrs. Hart; she is a mental patient, but an *adult* patient, and enhancement of her self-esteem is a necessary part of treatment.

Physical appearance and bodily cleanliness are important factors in one's self-image. Uncombed hair, untidy clothing, unshaved face, and dirty hands foster the patient's feeling that he is what he deserves to be. Scratching of one's own face or banging one's head against the wall are clear indications of an inadequate self-cathexis and lack of self-esteem. Vectorial attitude of the therapist will increase self-love of the patient and will reduce self-depreciation. For love and respect from without enhance love and respect from within.

Control of instinctual impulses is one of the most severe issues in schizophrenia; a catatonic patient in remission describes this inner struggle:

> "I want to be strong to be able to control myself and here I am again doing terrible things."
>
> A gifted latent schizophrenic woman said once: "I can't do what I want to do. I feel like expressing my feelings with quick motions of the brush over the canvass, but something holds me back and I paint silly little houses that I detest. I would like to let myself go in nonobjective art, but something tells me it must be a composition, a plan. Maybe I am afraid to let myself go, for I may do something wrong. So I sit for hours, as if paralyzed, afraid to move . . . ."

Inability to make decisions and restraint of motor freedom are typical for the schizophrenic type. This conflict between the desire to "let go" and the fear of one's own impulses may, in some cases, lead to catatonic mutism and stupor. One could not therefore encourage the young painter to follow her need for a free expression that would have inevitably led to a panic state and perhaps even to a catatonic episode. Nor would it be wise to enhance self-restraint that would produce an unbearable tension. Thus the best method was to foster self-esteem; with the increasing self-confidence the painter was less afraid to express her feelings on the canvass. She began to believe in herself, despite her past experiences.

Moreover, an overt disapproval of delusions and hallucinations, and even efforts to undermine them by rational reasoning, was doomed to failure. A too-early interpretation might have caused, in this case, deeper regression and withdrawal.

When one hospitalized patient told me how she discovered God and spoke to him, I did not comment; my attentive listening to her was apparently very reassuring. I began to talk to her about her daily life and chores, and she replied in a realistic way. Instead of challenging her hallucinatory omnipotence, I brought her closer to reality. When we talked about occupational therapy, her real achievements in work pushed aside the hallucinatory daydreams of omnipotence.

Even the most disturbed patient is at least partially aware of what is going on. He knows who is the patient and who is the therapist; he knows when the therapeutic session comes to an end, and he leaves the office to go back to the ward.

It is not advisable to deny flatly or to contradict the content of delusions and hallucinations, but it is never advisable to join the patient and to share or support the delusions. The therapist may not interpret the content of delusions and hallucinations until he is reasonably sure that the interpretation will help the patient restore his reality testing.

While I am rather cautious in interpreting dreams of my schizophrenic patients, I eagerly listen to them. Interpretation of dreams might be contraindicated in severe cases of latent schizophrenia and certainly in manifest ones, but the content of dreams has a high diagnostic value. The above-quoted dreams of latent schizophrenics pointed to an imminent danger of psychotic breakdown and call for the utmost therapeutic effort to prevent it. Schizophrenic dreams are usually transparent and point to what is going on in the patient's mind, and their content may offer the therapist valuable hints as to how to proceed in psychotherapy.

A schizophrenic dream is usually a call for help. Its message reads: "Doctor, see what is going on with me. I am running away from real life because it is too frightening. But the world of unreality I am escaping into is even more frightening. Please, help!"

The call for help must not be ignored. The dream may point to a highly significant aspect of the disorder. It may also indicate an emergency, such as an intent to commit suicide.

In several instances, after listening to patients' dreams, I have adjusted my therapeutic strategy. Sometimes a dream indicated that the patient was ready for a remission; in other cases the dream called for a slowdown of the therapeutic intervention. In practically all cases patients' dreams forced me to rethink my therapeutic plans.

Sometimes schizophrenics' dreams reveal uncanny telepathic experiences. On several occasions my patients have told me details of my life they could never have read or heard about.

REFERENCES

Arieti, S. *Interpretation of Schizophrenia* (2nd ed.). New York: Basic Books, 1974.
Boss, M. *"I dreamt last night..."* New York: Gardner Press, 1977.

Dement, W.   The biological role of REM sleep.   In Kales, A. (Ed.), *Sleep Physiology and Pathology*.   Philadelphia: Lippincott, 1969.

Federn, P.   *Ego Psychology and the Psychoses*.   New York: Basic Books, 1952.

Feinberg, I., Koresko, R., Gottlieb, F., and Wender, P.   Sleep encephalographic and eye movements pattern in schizophrenic patients.   *Comprehensive Psychiatry*, 5: 44-53, 1964.

Fenichel, O. *Psychoanalytic Theory of Neurosis*.   New York: Norton, 1945.

Gulevitch, G., Dement, W., and Zarcone, V.   All night sleep recordings of chronic schizophrenics in remission.   *Comprehensive Psychiatry*, 8: 141-149, 1967.

Kupter, D., Wyatt, R., Scott, J., and Snyder, F.   Sleep disturbance in acute schizophrenic patients.   *American Journal of Psychiatry*, 126: 1213-1223, 1970.

Pavlov, I. P. *Lectures on Conditioned Reflexes*.   New York: Liveright, 1928.

Reich, W. *Character Analysis*.   New York: Noonday Press, 1949.

Rechtschaffen, A., Schulsinger, F., and Mednick, S. A.   Schizophrenia and physiological indices of dreaming.   *Archives of General Psychiatry*, 10: 89-93, 1964.

Rechtschaffen, A., Watson, R., Wincor, M., Molinari, S., and Barta, S.   The relationship of phasic and tonic periorbital EMG activity to NONREM mentation.   Paper presented at Lake Minewaska, New York, Association for the Psychophysiological Study of Sleep, 1972.

Sullivan, H. S. *Schizophrenia as a Human Process*.   New York: Norton, 1962.

Watson, R., Liebman, K., and Watson, S.   Comparison of NONREM PIP frequency in schizophrenic and non-schizophrenic patients.   Paper presented in Cincinnati, Ohio, Association for the Psychophysiological Study of Sleep, 1976.

Wolman, B. B.   Remarks on C. C. Thompson's "The role of analyst's personality."   *American Journal of Psychotherapy*, 10: 363-366, 1956.

Wolman, B. B.   Explorations in latent schizophrenia.   *American Journal of Psychotherapy*, 11: 560-588, 1957.

Wolman, B. B.   Mental health and mental disorders.   In Wolman, B. B. (Ed.), *Handbook of Clinical Psychology*.   New York: McGraw-Hill, 1965.

Wolman, B. B. *Vectoriasis Praecox or the Group of Schizophrenias*.   Springfield, Illinois: Charles C. Thomas, 1966 (a).

Wolman, B. B.   Interactional psychotherapy with schizophrenics.   *Psychotherapy: Theory, Research, and Practice*, 3: 61-70, 1966 (b).

Wolman, B. B.   The socio-psycho-somatic theory of schizophrenia.   *Psychotherapy and Psychosomatics*, 15: 373-387, 1967.

Wolman, B. B. *Children without Childhood: A Study in Childhood Schizophrenia*.   New York: Grune & Stratton, 1970.

Wolman, B. B.   Power and acceptance as determinants of social relations.   *International Journal of Group Tensions*, 4: 151-183, 1974.

Wolman, B. B. *Call No Man Normal*.   New York: International Universities Press, 1973.

Wolman, B. B.   Infantile autism.   In Sankar, D. V. S. (Ed.), *Mental Health in Children*.   Westbury, New York: PJD, 1976 (a).

Wolman, B. B.   Treatment of schizophrenia.   In Wolman, B. B. (Ed.), *Therapist's Handbook*.   New York: Van Nostrand Reinhold, 1976 (b), pp. 325-357.

Wolman, B. B.   New ideas on mental disorders.   *American Journal of Psychotherapy*, 31: 546-560, 1977.

Wolman, B. B.   Classification and diagnosis of mental disorders.   In Wolman, B. B. (Ed.), *Clinical Diagnosis of Mental Disorders: A Handbook*.   New York: Plenum, 1978.

14

The Experiential
Dream Group

Montague Ullman

DEFINITION

An experiential dream group is one in which people come together for the purpose of helping each other work out the feelings and metaphors conveyed by the imagery of their dreams. It is best thought of as an exercise in dream appreciation. It is analogous to the appreciation at a feeling level of the metaphor of a poem.

There is no a priori theoretical base in experiential dream work that guides the response to the images. There is only the general assumption that the images convey meaning to the dreamer through their metaphorical construction. The concept of dream appreciation places the emphasis on the feeling response that comes with the recognition of the connections between the metaphorical image and the relevant life situation of the dreamer. There is an opening-up quality to the experience which goes beyond any specific meaning that can be assigned to the image. Once these connections are made, the dreamer's relationship to the image changes from one of mystery and estrangement to one of relief and appreciation at the way in which levels of personal meaning are so creatively expressed.

Although the analogy to poetry is valid, there are significant differences between a dream and a poem. The poetic metaphor is a communication that can be understood and appreciated by others without knowing anything about the personal life of the poet. The visual metaphor of the dream, on the other hand, is a purely personal communication of the dreamer to himself. It cannot be appreciated in its separateness from the immediate life context of the dreamer. The dreamer and no one else is the proper audience to the dream. The process in experiential dream work involves the group as a catalytic agent which supports the dreamer in the role of expert in relation to his own dream.

BACKGROUND

From time immemorial people have shared their dreams in the hope of penetrating their meaning. Perhaps they merely have sought solace in the sharing of an awesome experience. In some preliterate societies there is still much social support for dream sharing. This is so, for example, among the Senoi Indians of Malaysia and the Hopi Indians of Arizona. For the most past, however, activities around dreaming in Western societies have followed a pattern, also laid down earlier, of bringing a dream to an expert who offers an interpretation. The psychoanalytic context is the current version of this earlier model.

Some degree of interest in dream sharing has persisted and has erupted into greater prominence in the past decade as part of the general interest in consciousness-raising activities. Growth centers have promoted small-group dream sharing, spontaneous and sponsored dream groups have sprung up, and a literature on the benefits and technology of dream work has addressed itself to the needs and interests of people who wish to work with their dreams. The Gestalt approach to dream work has become increasingly popular. It stresses the advantage of role playing the elements of a dream in the company of another or others (Perls, 1969). There have been notable efforts to demystify dreams to make them accessible to the nonprofessional (Faraday, 1973, 1974; Ullman and Zimmerman, in press). A number of doctoral theses on the subject of dream sharing have appeared in recent years (Randall, 1977; Sabini, 1972). A new publication, *The Sundance Community Dream Journal*, has appeared and is devoted to the encouragement of dream work, particularly in group settings. An excellent review of these developments appears in a recent volume by McLeester (1976).

We know that dreaming is a universal aspect of human existence, and we also know that dreams contain significant personal meanings. It is all the more surprising that dreams have been accorded so low an order of social priority and have remained so little valued and appreciated. We suffer from a syndrome that I term *dreamism*, signifying an irrational prejudice against dreams. It seems that two kinds of social influence sustain this prejudicial attitude. On the one hand there is the emphasis on the mastery and control of events and forces outside the individual, with human subjectivity and potential subordinate to achieving these ends. Since dreams have no commercial value and simply reflect our subjectivity, they rank relatively low among things that count in our society. Dreams are not worth bothering about.

An opposite message comes to the public from the psychoanalytic profession. Here dreams are elevated to a very special place in human affairs, a place so special that highly technical psychoanalytic knowledge is necessary to penetrate their mystery. Here the message is that dreams are valuable but that dream work should remain in the hands of an expert because the factor of disguise requires psychoanalytic decoding and because of the potential danger of tampering with the unconscious.

There have been two unfortunate consequences to this socially reinforced estrangement from our dreams. We end up less sophisticated about how to relate to the expressive potential of our dream imagery than might have been the case if dream sharing and dream work had been an integral part of our lives from early childhood. But more important, we lose out on an important need to share intimate and private aspects of ourselves in the context of an interested and responsive support system. Outside of structured therapeutic situations, there are few arrangements in life where that degree of honesty in self-disclosure can be risked in the presence of others. It is precisely this level of honesty that must be reached if one is to move beyond the constraints of one's personal emotional limitations. People in a dream group seem to sense this, a fact that opens the way to greater and greater freedom in self-disclosure. Sharing of oneself at this level is a basic unmet need in our society.

The followers of Freud tended to perpetuate the idea that dream work had best be left to professionals because of the risks involved and the special theoretical knowledge that was needed. Jung's notions about dreams could be more readily understood apart from any particular psychoanalytic orientation to personality conflict. Dreaming experience stood in a complementary relationship to waking life, and the elements that made up the manifest content of the dream could gain meaning through a process of amplification rather than through efforts to get at a disguised latent content. Jung meant by amplification allowing the images and the qualities and properties connected with them to come into focus as expressive and revealing statements about the dreamer's life. This emphasis on the revelatory power of the manifest content has been the leverage used to move dream work from a restricted professional setting to a more general public setting.

My own experience with dreams and the role they play in our lives (Ullman, 1969, 1977, in press; Ullman and Zimmerman, in press) left me convinced that dream sharing in small groups is a feasible route to serious dream work. What one can do with a dream depends neither on professional credentials nor on one's mastery of psychoanalytic theory. It evolves out of one's interest in dreams and on one's readiness to engage in self-disclosure in the context of a supportive social response system. Resistiveness to dream work diminishes rapidly once a group gets under way. This is not to say that it melts away completely, but rather that there is a good deal of variation in the degree of comfort that people feel as they engage in the self-disclosure intrinsic to dream work and that for each person the freedom grows greater with experience.

AXIOMS AND PRINCIPLES

There are certain axioms and principles that underlie the operation of an experiential dream group.

Axioms:

1. A remembered dream has a useful application to waking life.
2. The imagery of the dream is generated as part of an intrinsic self-healing process. This relates to the root-meaning of the verb "to heal," meaning "to make whole."
3. When a dream is recalled, the dreamer is ready to be confronted with the information it contains. There may be varying degrees of resistance to such confrontation, but, at some level, there is a readiness to come to terms with the issues presented. Our dreams are always efforts at self-orientation to our current predicament.
4. Dreams may appear mysterious, but they are not intrinsically inaccessible. Given a basic knowledge about the metaphorical nature of dream imagery and a supportive social context, the necessary connections can be made between dream images and the realities they express.

It is in the nature of dream work that it can be carried on most effectively in the presence of one or more other people. It seems somewhat paradoxical that this most private of all communications requires some kind of public airing for its message to be apprehended fully. This is so because of the resistance we all have to facing certain truths about ourselves. It is easier for others to recognize such truths and to offer the support needed to bring us closer to self-recognition. The dream is a remarkably honest reflection of who we are and how we react to situations. It is not easy to achieve that same degree of honesty about ourselves by ourselves when we are awake. We tend to ward off unpleasantness and fall into more expedient ways of seeing ourselves. The group relates to and respects the level of honesty displayed in the dream. This facilitates greater honesty on the part of the dreamer as he learns to trust the intentions of the group. Further trust develops in the act of trusting.

Principles. There are three main principles that govern experiential dream work:

1. The dreamer remains in control of the process from beginning to end. The dreamer decides to share a dream, modulates the level of self-disclosure engaged in response to the group's input, sets the limits of the exploratory dialogue, and has the option of terminating the process at any point.
2. The group is there to serve as a catalyst by stimulating and supporting the dreamer's effort to relate to the dream. No one, including the leader, assumes an authoritative stance vis-à-vis the dreamer. No one tells the dreamer what the dream means. The members of the group project their own feelings and content into the imagery in the hope that some of it resonates with the dreamer.
3. The dreamer is respected as the expert in relation to his dream. It is the dreamer who experiences at a feeling level the correctness of the fit of what the group has to offer. The dreamer is the ultimate source of validation and has the last word in accepting or rejecting the contributions of the group. It is the dreamer who has to experience a sense of closure before the process can come to a successful end.

BASIC CONCEPTS FOR DREAM WORK

Emotional growth is contingent on the discovery of who we are and the real impact we make on others. It involves the gradual shedding of illusions as to who we are and what we think our impact is on others. Where there are illusions, there are vulnerable areas. Our dreams reflect back to us the tensions generated when events in our daily life expose some of these vulnerable areas. In our dreams we seem capable of assessing these events against the backdrop of our past experience and, in so doing, arrive at a felt sense of their importance and the impact they may have for our future.

Emotional growth also takes place by another route. Tension results when the novelty and strangeness of a reality event test the limits of our competence. When tension of this kind triggers a dream, we again resort to a backward scanning of our past to explore the possible resources we can mobilize to meet the challenge. Inventive and creative solutions may be the result.

In both instances the backward scanning makes available a rich memory store of experience out of which the dreamer culls whatever is needed to assess and cope with the immediate tension confronting him. When the resources thus mobilized are not adequate to the task, and the tension rises rather than abates, awakening occurs. From the point of view of an adaptive maneuver, this means that further waking experience is necessary before this particular issue can be adequately dealt with.

In sum, our dreams serve as corrective lenses which, if we learn to use them properly, enable us to see ourselves and the world about us with less distortion and with greater accuracy. It is in this sense that dreams may be said to serve a healing function. To allow oneself to be confronted clearly and honestly with an issue is the first step in coming to terms with it. Our dreams are a way of helping us take this first step.

These general ideas about the nature of dreaming are shared with the group. They represent a point of view about dreams that defines the essentials without a commitment to any particular metapsychological superstructure. They are developed in greater detail elsewhere (Ullman, 1973; Ullman and Zimmerman, in press).

Precipitating Event

I prefer the term "intrusive novelty" to "day residue" to refer to the event that determines the content of the dream. This term defines the two characteristics of the prior event that make it apt to resurface as the nuclear focus in a dream sequence. The event has the quality of novelty in the sense that it catches the person off guard. At the time it is encountered, there are no immediately available ways of coping with it. The event is intrusive to the extent that it is linked to earlier unsolved emotional issues from the past. Alternatively, it may be experienced as novel on the basis of its being truly new and outside the range of past experience. In the first instance the element of novelty lies in the unexpected exposure of some defensive strategy related to unresolved emotional residues from the past. In the second instance the element of novelty lies in the nature of the event itself and the challenge to personal growth that it offers. In either instance the intrusiveness results in the need to explore past stores of experience in order to mobilize the resources needed to deal with the impact of the precipitating event.

Longitudinal Scanning

This term refers to the remarkable way in which a precipitating event taps into our remote memory stores and mobilizes bits and pieces of past experience that are affectively related to it. This is a mechanism available to the dreamer that enables him to explore the implications of any tensions associated with the day residue and to assess his coping resources, healthy and defensive, in dealing with them. The range of data thus made available is much greater than that at his disposal at the time the event was initially confronted. In effective dream work it becomes necessary to clarify and understand the present context in order to understand the relevance of the references to past experience.

Visual Metaphor

The images of the dream can be understood as visual metaphors. This is so for physiological reasons having to do with the need to process information at a concrete level as a way of influencing the arousal system (Ullman, 1956), and for psychological reasons having to do with the expressive function served by metaphor (Ullman, 1969). Through the use of visual imagery a great deal of information is organized in highly condensed form and presented at a glance, so to speak, instead of linearly. As metaphorical statements the images are intended to communicate the feelings behind them.

The Tripartite Structure of the Dream

Dreams can be thought of as three-act dramas with the dreamer looking for the answer to a specific question in each act. The opening act setting begins with the dreamer's concern with the question: What is happening to me? The affective residue associated with the recent event has registered a tension now being experienced by the dreamer. As he moves into the second act, his concern is with the question: What is the history of this tension, and what resources can I mobilize to deal with it? In the final act, he is concerned with the question of how to move toward some kind of resolution. At this point he is faced with the possibilities of a binary decision. Can the tension be contained without disrupting the sleep cycle, or is it great enough to result in awakening?

Dilemmas and Predicaments

There are only a limited number of dilemmas which people find themselves in that preoccupy them while dreaming. Some of the more frequent ones include:

Authenticity vs. sham
Activity vs. passivity
Dependency vs. self-reliance
Defiance vs. compliance in relation to authority
Adequacy vs. inadequacy
Confrontation vs. denial
Self-definition vs. definition by others
Being vs. having
Being for oneself vs. being for others

Defining the dilemma in relation to the specific predicament that the dreamer is in at the moment is helpful in extending the range of meaning of the dream.

GUIDELINES

After the group is introduced to the general information outlined above, specific guidelines for the work to follow are set forth.

1. The decision to share a dream rests solely with the dreamer. No one should ever be made to feel under constraint to share a dream.
2. A recent dream is preferable to an older dream because the more recent the dream, the easier it is to identify the precipitating life context. With dreams that are several days or a week or more old, this may be more difficult except in those instances where the context was so unusual that it was clearly remembered.
3. Short dreams are preferred to longer ones for reasons of expediency with regard to time. Dream work proceeds slowly and should progress at a leisurely pace. A very long dream may prove too cumbersome to manage in any reasonable time period.
4. The process is explained, and the roles of the dreamer, the group, and the leader are defined. Any questions concerning the process or the various roles are clarified at this point.
5. The prerogatives of the dreamer are emphasized. He is given to understand that he is in control of the process throughout the session and has the option of stopping the process at any point at which he wishes to carry it on by himself.
6. The leader indicates that he holds the option of considering several dreams before settling on a choice. This is generally of importance only in a beginning group. The leader is concerned with working with a dream that might readily and clearly lend itself to illustrating the process. He also must remain sensitive to the possibility of a dream's being offered, not for the purpose of sharing, but as an acting out of some manipulative need.
7. Issues of confidentiality are discussed and clarified. These include the use of tape recorders, the need for permission for any published material, and the general question of respecting personal disclosures.
8. There is an opportunity for the airing of general questions about dreams, problems connected with remembering dreams, special kinds of dreams such as repetitive dreams, and so forth.

THE PROCESS

First Stage

Presentation of the Dream.   A group member presents a recent dream. Even though he may have written the dream down, the dreamer is asked to tell it from memory and then fill in from notes. The account is limited to the manifest content, and no associative data are presented. The other participants listen and take notes if they wish. When the dreamer has finished, there is an opportunity to ask questions limited to clarifying the content of the dream.

Roles. The dreamer's role is clear. He is simply to recount the remembered dream and not go beyond that. Knowing that they will be expected to respond, the members of the group listen and remain sensitive to any feelings they experience as they listen. The main task of the leader is to preserve the integrity of the process. At this stage it involves seeing that the dreamer does not go beyond the simple recounting of the dream, and alerting the group to attend to every detail. As the group becomes more experienced, it will also begin to take into account any qualifying statements that the presenter might make before introducing the dream.

Rationale. By limiting the dreamer's presentation to the manifest content alone, we are minimizing the degree to which the dreamer will influence the subsequent responses of the group. It may seem paradoxical that we should want to do this inasmuch as our goal is to get at the meaning the dream has for the dreamer. Why are we injecting an intermediate step before we explore the dreamer's personal connection to the dream? That step is necessary to ensure that the response of the group can evolve in the freest way possible. Were the dreamer to begin the process of relating to his dream at this point, it would not only have the expected effect of sharpening the responses of the group, but it would also have the constraining effect of having these responses move along tracks laid down by the dreamer. By first operating in a clear field, without the dreamer's intervention, the group avoids any limiting biases the dreamer may unconsciously communicate. When the dreamer does have the opportunity to tell his side of it in the third stage, then the full unconstrained response of the group has already been set before him.

Second Stage

The group members are asked to "move into" the dream and try to make it their own. They are asked to respond at two levels, first to the feelings the dream evokes, and second to the images. They have free reign in exploring the limits of their response and are under no obligation to defend or justify it. They are to speak to each other rather than to the dreamer. They are told that what they come up with is to be considered their own projections until and unless there is later validation by the dreamer. As much time as is needed is allowed for each of these responses to run its course.

The group's responses will be a mixture of feelings evoked by the dream as it is being presented, by the dreamer who is presenting it, by what they already know about the dreamer, and by feelings flowing from their own efforts to take over the dream. Regardless of the source of these reactions, they are considered presumptively projective until checked out with the dreamer. Group members are asked to describe feelings in personal terms and to avoid putting them in terms of what they think the dreamer felt.

The concept of the visual metaphor having been explained, the group now explores each of the images as well as the relationship of each image to each other one for its possible metaphorical meaning. Again, the group is encouraged to report whatever occurs to it. We are seeking out what each one has to contribute. At this stage we are not concerned with contradictions, differences of opinion, and so on. The goal is to display the broadest possible spectrum of personal responses to the metaphorical potential of the imagery and to do it without "laying" an interpretation onto the dreamer.

Roles. The dreamer's role is to listen as impassively as possible to the input being generated. Some of it will connect; some of it will be wide of the mark. What does connect will stimulate a flow of feelings and ideas about the image and bring him closer to a feeling of its bearing on his life. Even group responses that appear incongruous or wrong may be helpful. By defining what the image is not, the dreamer may get closer to defining what it is. As he begins to resonate with the input from the group, it becomes increasingly difficult for him to remain impassive, as his face and gestures will betray the feelings of inner discovery.

The group's activity at this point is best described as an exercise that may or may not be helpful to the dreamer. The members are encouraged to come out with whatever they feel, regardless of how unrelated or purely personal it may at first appear. This is not easy to do. It takes some effort and experience to move away from the comfortable stance of focusing on what they think the dream is telling the dreamer to working with the dream in terms of what it is telling them.

The leader's ability to preserve the integrity of the process is tested in various ways in this stage. It requires some effort to keep the group focused on their feeling responses initially. This is so because the images are so challenging and stimulating that there is the temptation to begin to work directly with the metaphors. The leader must be on guard against anyone slipping into the role of dream interpreter and telling the dreamer what the dream means. His role is to support everyone's right to say what he thinks, no matter how far out it may seem. Finally, he must respond as a member of the group with his own feelings and metaphors.

After all the projective responses have been developed, the leader may attempt to bring them into a more organized relationship to the manifest content, in order to emphasize that the sequence of images is as important as the images themselves. Comparisons, contrast, and other clues to meaning emerge when this is taken into consideration. An image that appears puzzling when looked at by itself may assume meaning when examined in its relationship to the preceding and succeeding images. The leader's efforts at orchestrating the group's input and checking it against the manifest content also provide the opportunity to call attention to any details in the dream that might have been overlooked or not given sufficient attention.

Rationale.   All of the group's contributions are considered as projections. This is so regardless of the degree to which there may be an admixture of accurate perceptions of the dreamer. The ultimate test of the relevance of any contribution is validation by the dreamer. The fact that the group is working on this premise has a freeing impact on both the group and the dreamer. The members of the group, through the act of projecting onto a foreign body, are able to tap deeply into their own unconscious fantasies in their response to the imagery. On the other hand, the dreamer is exposed to a range of feedback under circumstances when he is under no constraint to respond, and therefore has little need to defend himself against any projections from the group that may strike home. It is a freeing experience to be exposed to public input of this kind while, at the same time, being able to deal with it privately and having complete say over how much of it will ultimately be shared.

What accounts for the fact that some of the responses of the group at feeling and metaphorical levels resonate with the dreamer?   The group's ability to pick up feelings the dreamer may be unaware of is, I think, due to the fact that images arise out of feelings in the first place, and through their selection and arrangement they often convey the source of their origin. As for the group's coming upon metaphorical translations of the imagery that strike a chord with the dreamer, it is not a surprising development. We all swim about in the same social sea so that any particular image may convey similar metaphorical meaning to the dreamer and to one or more respondents in the group.

Third Stage

This stage is devoted to the dreamer's effort to find the connecting links between the imagery of the dream and the immediate life situation giving rise to the dream. It unfolds in three phases.

Phase I.   The dreamer is given all the time needed to respond to the input from the group and to develop his own view of what the dream now means to him. He can go about it in any way he wishes; either he may stress those parts of the dream that were opened up by the group, or he may begin with where he was in relation to the dream before the group work began.

Phase II.   When the dreamer is finished, the group then enters into a dialogue with him to help explore any images that remain unclear and to help identify the relevant life context. This is done in the form of open-ended questions which any member of the group may put to the dreamer, at the same time recognizing that the dreamer remains in control of the level of self-disclosure he wishes to make. When the dreamer finds it difficult to identify any recent events related to the dream, it may be helpful to ask him to try to recall his last thoughts and preoccupations before falling asleep. This often yields a direct clue to the focus of the dream. If the dreamer is unable to do this, he may be asked to recount the events of the day before. Doing this often leads quite unexpectedly to the identification of the significant precipitating event. The dreamer is also encouraged to explore the connections to the past suggested by the imagery.

Phase III. The dreamer has the last word. He assesses the degree of "closure" he now feels about the dream. If it is not sufficient, he can encourage the group to continue with the exploration. He is free to stop the process at an earlier time if, for any reason, he should wish to.

Roles. The dreamer is expected to respond to the group's efforts only if he is genuinely touched by them. What should be guarded against are compliant responses—particularly in people who are highly suggestible—which are rather infrequent because of all the safeguards provided for the dreamer to ensure that he has the feeling of being the authority about his own dream. When a compliant rather than a genuine response occurs, it is easily detected. A feeling of passive agreement betrays this response and is in sharp distinction from the "eureka" feeling and sense of liberation that comes with a true response.

At this stage the group must again be careful to respect the dreamer's authority and not use their questioning to challenge it. The questioning, like the group's participation in the second stage, should be an instrument that helps the dreamer in his exploration of the dream. It should not be used in a confronting or challenging way or as a way of getting agreement.

People with a background in therapy unconsciously tend to step into an interpretive stance at this stage, something the leader must be alert to counteract. The task of the leader is also to sense and check with the dreamer when "closure" has taken place. It is at this point that the dreamer feels that he owns his dream. He is now ready to engage in further exploration of the impact of the dream by himself.

Rationale. By the time the third stage is reached, a feeling of trust and rapport has developed between the dreamer and the group. A genuinely concerned, helpful, and supportive response is elicited when someone has had the courage to share a dream and seek help with it. There is an important though implicit aspect of the process that further nurtures this trust. It stems from the fact that the process evolves dialectically into one of mutual self-disclosure. The dreamer defines himself by offering a dream. This in turn leads to the group members defining themselves through the projections they offer. In the final stage all parties become better known to themselves and to each other. The dreamer gains from those parts of the group's projections that are relevant to him. The group members gain from the discovery that aspects of their responses that they thought related to the dreamer were really their own projection. They learn by being confronted with their own biases as the images fall into place in the dreamer's life.

The dreamer needs the group's help in the exploration of the images. It is the group's interest, support, and probing that help close the gap between what the image is conveying and what the dreamer may be defending himself against. Our dreams offer us the opportunity of growing more whole. This is an aspect of emotional healing that requires the concerned support of others.

EXPERIENTIAL DREAM WORK AND GROUP PSYCHOTHERAPY

To someone unfamiliar with experiential work as carried out in a group, the question often arises: How is it different from group psychotherapy? There are major differences, which can be defined by a number of criteria. These can best be presented in tabular form, as shown in Table 14-1.

To summarize, we are dealing with two processes that have a similar endpoint, namely, the healing of the individual. Each process gets there by different routes, using different ground rules and assigning different roles to the partici-

TABLE 14-1.

Criteria	Experiential Dream Group	Group Psychotherapy
1. Nature of the communication.	The dream is an intrapsychic communication from a part of one's being to oneself. It is the dream that is being communicated.	Waking behavior is a communication to others. It is waking behavior that is being communicated.
2. Focus of the group.	The focus of the group is on the impact of the dream on the dreamer. The focus is on an intrapersonal field.	The focus of the group is on the impact of the behavior on an interpersonal field.
3. Nature of the task.	The nature of the task is to establish the meaning the dream images hold for the dreamer by seeking to close the intrapersonal distance between the image and the real-life context of the dream.	The nature of the task is to seek meaning in the behavioral expression of a tension as it becomes manifest in an interpersonal field (past or present).

TABLE 14-1. (*Continued*)

Criteria	Experiential Dream Group	Group by Psychotherapy
4. Expectational set.	The expectations of the group are secondary to its task of helping the dreamer realize his own expectations with regard to the dream. One set of expectations, those of the dreamer, dominates the interplay.	The expectations of all the members of the group and of the therapist gain expression and seek realization. Manifold expectations are at play.
5. Nature of the process.	The process brings into the open the unknown messages embedded in the imagery of the dream.	The process brings to light the unknown messages embedded in interpersonal behavior.
6. Source of the expectations.	The dreamer and the group work along intuitive and shared experiential levels with no specific theoretical orientation.	The leader works from a theoretical base involving personal and group dynamics.
7. Source of change.	The support and trust developing between dreamer and group liberate the healing power dream images have, once their concrete connections to waking life are established.	The leader and group members engage in a number of strategies to work through personal defenses and stimulate change. These include interpreting, confronting, modeling, and so on.
8. Mechanism of change.	Using the projections of the group to free up the dreamer's connection to the dream.	Unmasking the projections of the various participants.
9. Tempo	The group moves at the tempo of the dreamer.	The tempo is a reflection of combined needs.
10. Role differences.	*Leader:* Plays a dual role. In leadership position he assumes the responsibility for ensuring the integrity of the process. As a participant he engages in the same level and degree of self-disclosure and dream sharing.	*Leader:* Assumes responsibility of a leader but level of self-disclosing participation is considerably less.
	Dreamer: The dreamer remains in control of the process including the right to stop at any point.	*Dreamer:* The control is largely in the hands of the therapist.
	Group: The group works with the metaphor as depicted in the dream and helps redefine it in terms of personal life context.	*Group:* The group experiences the roles assigned unconsciously by the patient and seeks to redefine those roles in terms of the present interpersonal reality.

pants. It is important to bear this in mind in assessing the relative indications and advantages of each. It is also important to avoid slippage from one process to the other without taking cognizance of the fact that the ground rules have changed.

EXPERIENTIAL DREAM GROUPS AND INDIVIDUAL THERAPY

Implicit in the distinctions drawn above between group psychotherapy and the experiential process are features that distinguish it from individual psychotherapy. A number of participants in groups I have worked with have been in individual therapy at the same time, which gave me the opportunity of observing the impact of one on the other. Despite some concern originally about problems that might arise relating to the possibilities for competitiveness and manipulativeness, there were surprisingly few situations when any difficulties arose. In almost all cases the two processes complemented each other, with the patient learning to make the best use of each.

Aspects of group work on dreams that were most helpful to those in individual therapy were:

1. *The time factor.*   There is an unhurried, leisurely approach when a group sets out to work on a dream. It is the only item on the agenda, and it may occupy the group for the entire time they spend together. Dream work has its own tempo, which is more apt to unfold naturally when other constraints on time are absent.

2. *The diversity of input.*   The diversity of response from a group to the feelings and meanings expressed by the images presents a broader range of possibilities to the dreamer than any one person can offer. Although in individual therapy the range is more limited, it is generally more accurate on matters within that range because of the amount of information available to the therapist.

3. *The control exercised by the dreamer.*   This allays fears and anxieties that might otherwise heighten defensive operations.

4. *The leveling out of hierarchical arrangements.*   The fact that the leader shares dreams and does not assume any special therapeutic role minimizes defensive operations. It also lessens the likelihood of issues arising relating to transference and resistance.

5. *The deprofessionalization of the process.*   A sense of the normality of the experience is conveyed by the absence of any allegiance to a technical or theoretical system. A feeling of competence evolves along with a respect for the healing potential of dream images and a lessening fear of what the images might convey.

6. *The ludic quality of dreams.*   The ludic or play aspect of dreams has a greater chance of surfacing in a group setting than in the dyadic relationship.

The group accepts the dream as a challenge, a mystery to be solved. As the group works with the images, there is an exciting and playful quality. This does not mean that they are taken more lightly; their meaning comes through in the excitement of engaging with their subtlety and inventiveness.

The best arrangement seems to be to use the group experience to get the leverage on the dream necessary to pursue it in greater depth in the private sessions. Quite often the pressures in the therapeutic hour do not allow for the time necessary to work through a dream, in which case it may be brought to the group. There are also instances when transferential and countertransferential issues arising in therapy are clarified through group work.

PRACTICAL CONSIDERATIONS

Some of the optimal conditions for any small group process are the same for dream groups. Some are different.

Size.   The optimal number of participants is six to eight.

Frequency.   There is some flexibility here. I prefer groups that meet weekly for two hours.

Homogeneity.   The groups are self-selective and generally result in a mix of professionals, nonprofessionals, patients, nonpatients. Groups work well despite differences in age, education, background, and cultural disparities. Groups that are heavily professional tend to feel more comfortable working with others of comparable educational level. Sensitivity, freedom in self-disclosure, and the capacity to be in touch with internal processes count for more than credentials.

Duration.   The contract can be for any duration. Four weeks gives a newcomer a feeling and grasp of the process. My groups tend to be ongoing on the basis of renewing the contract for four weeks at a time. As participants get to know each other better, more of their interaction becomes reflected in their dreams, and the growing knowledge of one another sharpens the accuracy of the contributions.

Group Process.   There are occasions, though relatively rare, when the integrity of the process is jeopardized. Then more time has to be devoted to group process in order to deal with tensions that may arise within the group. If the dream process is adhered to, tensions of this kind are minimal.

Deviations from the Process.   Once the group understands the importance of identifying the immediate life context that gave rise to the dream, there can be more flexibility about presenting older dreams and repetitive dreams, provided enough of the context can be recalled, or if the dream is so important that the dreamer is willing to risk the loss of specificity that occurs when the context eludes us.

Changes in the Group.   At the end of each four-week period the makeup of the group may change because of turnover. Although these changes may have some impact on the growing sense of intimacy and trust among the participants, they also provide the compensatory feature of fresh new input. The group joins in the decision to bring in newcomers.

APPLICATIONS

The process lends itself to training and general educational purposes. It has been introduced into a college curriculum (Jones, 1979) and into the training of psychiatric residents and psychoanalytic candidates (Ullman, 1977). Experiential dream work can be extended to all age groups with whatever changes may be needed to accommodate the special needs of selected populations. Training programs to assure competence in leadership will ultimately be necessary in larger numbers than are now available.

SUMMARY

Dreams are a normal dimension of human experience. The experiential dream group is one way of helping a dreamer realize in a feeling way the relevance of the images he creates at night to the issues he faces during the day. A social process has been presented that helps put the dreamer in touch with these images while, at the same time, respecting his privacy and authority over the dream. Although the goal of the process is one of healing, it differs in strategy and structure from group psychotherapy. The process can be used advantageously in conjunction with individual therapy. It has application in psychiatric training programs as well as in educational and other programs geared to personal growth.

REFERENCES

Faraday, A. *Dream Power.* New York: Berkley Publishing Corp., 1973.
Faraday, A. *The Dream Game.* New York: Harper & Row, 1974.
Jones, R. *The Dream Poet*, Boston: G. K. Hall, 1979.
McLeester, D. *Welcome to the Magic Theater.* Worcester, Massachusetts: Saltus Press, 1976.
Perls, F. *Gestalt Therapy Verbatim.* Lafayette, California: Real People Press, 1969.

Randall, A. Dreaming, sharing, and telepathy in a short term community. Unpublished doctoral dissertation. New York: Teachers College, Columbia University, 1977.

Sabini, M. The dream group. A community mental health proposal. Unpublished doctoral dissertation. San Francisco: California School for Professional Psychology, 1972.

Ullman, M. Physiological determinants of the dream process. *J. Nervous and Mental Disease*, **124**: 45–48, 1956.

Ullman, M. Dreaming as metaphor in motion. *Arch. General Psychiatry*, **21**: 696–703, 1969.

Ullman, M. A theory of vigilance and dreaming. In Zikmind, V. (Ed.), *The Oculomotor and Brain Functions*. London: Butterworths, 1973.

Ullman, M. Experiential dream groups. Paper presented before Academy of Psychoanalysis, December, 1977.

Ullman, M. The transpersonal dimensions of dreaming. In Boorstein, S., and Speeth, K. (Eds.), *Explorations in Transpersonal Psychology*. New York: Jason Aronson, in press.

Ullman, M. and Zimmerman, N. *Working with Dreams*. New York: Delacorte/Eleanor Friede, in press.

15

Dreams and Education

Richard M. Jones

The world-convention dream, reported in the chapter on post-Freudian dream theories, was not interpreted in a clinical setting. Nor was it analyzed for the purpose of writing the chapter. It was, first, the subject of a *dream reflection seminar*, which is a technique I have developed to enhance the reading of, and writing about, good literature in college. This is the way it goes:

1. We first read a work of literature and discuss it in a seminar, from the points of view of the meanings possibly intended by the author, the meanings suggested by the text, and our personal responses to the work.

2. On a subsequent morning someone (usually a student; in this instance the teacher) brings to the seminar a dream and his or her written reflections on it—typed and dittoed, so that everyone has a copy.

3. The dreamer reads the dream and the reflections.

4. As we close our eyes and try to visualize our own versions of the dream's imagery, the dreamer reads the dream again. This has the effect of calming inevitable personal jitters and getting us into a studious frame of mind.

5. For approximately the next two hours we discuss the dream from two points of view: what it may be saying to us and what we may be prompted to say back to it. Thus, our objectives are to understand the dream *and* to enjoy it. In this latter venture we learn to respond to the dream's play on words and images, its sound symbolisms and flourishes of synesthesia, its visually alliterative sequences, its deployments of the figurative and the literal, its double entendres, stagings, artifices, puns, and jokes. The discussion is guided by the rule that we are free to advance any hunch, speculation, or intuition, ask any question, offer

any interpretation or outright guess which may help us to achieve the two objectives: understanding and enjoyment. This freedom is limited only by the common acknowledgment that the dreamer will be the ultimate judge as to corrections of the understanding and the tastefulness of the enjoyment.

6. We then go off individually, and write for two hours. The dreamer's writing usually consists of summarizing the highlights of the discussion, and extending his reflections on the dream. The rest of us write something—a poem, an essay, a letter, a story, a play—which links our reflections on the dream to our understanding of the week's common reading assignment. This is the most challenging step in the sequence; and, when successful, the most rewarding.

7. We then reconvene as a seminar, and read to each other what we wrote. The writings tend to be of such startlingly liberated quality as to generate a mood of uncommon mutual respect—sometimes falling not far short of shock. Here are some samples of it:

The Text of

MOBY-TRICK:

or

THE TALE

"There are certain queer times and occasions in this strange mixed affair we call life when a man takes the whole universe for a vast practical joke, though the wit thereof he but dimly discerns, and more than suspects that the joke is at nobody's expense but his own."

"Though in many of its aspects the visible world seems formed in love, the invisible spheres were formed in fright."

—Melville in Moby Dick

"A great big old log three-story house up on stilts"—the beginning of Linda's dream—strikes me with the same feeling tone as the classical opening of fanciful stories, tall tales: viz., "Once upon a time . . . ," a line that seems an implicit and an apt prefix to the dream.

What is the activity proper to one whose spirit is informed by the sense of the world as a vast joke, dim and oblique as that intimation may be? Why, to plunge into the play of energies, surrendering the greatest part of the self to go with the flow, so as not to miss the point of pointlessness; to remain buoyant in accepting the part of the joke that falls to one's lot. What of the rest of the self, not so involved? That is the observing self, whose equable detachment is bred of understanding; it has no fixed locus, but instead can rove in imagination to different spaces and times, bringing new perspectives to bear on happenings in the present. In short, by a certain detachment from the immediate, the observing self can reflect, and so enrich the here-and-now.

But what if the joke has a malevolent cast, if indeed the invisible spheres were formed in fright? Or, which is worse, if there is no joke at all, no objective relief from the serious matter of inhabiting a universe behind which lurks only an unthinkable horror? Perhaps the natural impulse will allow of nothing but recoiling, or a willed forgeting. Then, to fill the void left by such repudiation, we spin out our names and stories and dreams in large letters, populating the vacuity with our new creations, embellishing the malign order of the world with mythological constructs fashioned of our own sweat and blood. In a a deep and not unambivalent sense, we learn to play, to entertain ourselves— which amounts in the end to another kind of joke.

—Frank Greenhalgh

*   .*   *

COUNTER FEAT*

The computer
Escalates
Picking its mountains
Out of Helen's teeth
While the goy on the bicycle
Incestuously
With rings on his fingers and clubs on his heels
Writes up four dollar bills
On ancient plates
Carved out of looted slabs
Which the Byronic hero
Interpreted as sexual allegories
(At hyperbole velocities)
To initiate schizoid fission
In the fourfold genetic temple
Where the hermaphroditic Athena
Protects the spiral strands
Of the terminal memory bank
From serpent spirochetes
And Aurora unfolds her mushroom chandelier
In the pentalic temple
Signaling to the Parthian cock
That Atlantis is within

And when evening sets on the fever
Of the earth-exiled poet
The temple of the virgin
Will become an open vehicle

*The reading was William Blake's *The Mental Traveler*.

(Mistress to an apocalypse)
The brother of the Rebel
Shall sign for the Tao
And the guilty lame duck diplomat
Shall come bicycling infinity
Till his keys are tangled in the red tape
Of immaculate calculation

—Edward Ketcham

*   *   *

Catch Two Plus Two*

Missing the crux, the crotch. I'd say your aim ain't so good. You'll smile a little crooked indulgence, because I'm a woman. But all the same you're caught in the catch. You know you can if you want, but if it matters, and you want, you can't. Maybe we should ask the Muse, but her cunt's made of gold. I read somewhere that "she is idealized sex, which has as much (and as little) to do with 'real sex' as white goddesses have to do with real women." Look, you're humpin the wrong ladies for the wrong things, is all I'm sayin. You want the blood to be wine and transubstantiate into verse, thinking you won't be impotent as a poet because you promised not to be impotent as a man. Well, the son won't rise to that cause when the gold is cold it don't cuddle like the mother's womb you've forgotten. I'm ready to kick and I'm aimin low. But you put me here. "Gimme, gimme," says the favorite son, "I want to be pregnant too." But that won't catch the Muse for you cause $2 + 2$ is 2 too many. You need to see your penis at eye-level in a warm steamy shower.

—Mary Jo Eloheimo

*   *   *

I would like to live in a circle
become androgynous
walk in an alley
between brick buildings
both hands occupied
and both of those hands
occupied
looking in all directions
simultaneously
comprehending
roundness.†

—Steven Weinberg

*The reading was Joseph Heller's *Catch 22*.
†The reading was Robert Frost's *The Road Not Taken*.

8. The writings are then typed and printed, so that each week everyone receives copies of the previous week's writings.

The tone of the seminar tends to be one of scholarly good humor. Therapeutic gains in self-knowledge are expected and accepted, but the prevailing expectation is that personal insights will be extended to grace some aspect of our academic commitments with personal meaning. Here is the way one student described the experience:

> We come in alone and we go out alone, but in between we have each other; the tight throats, the full and empty days, the tears, the unions of minds and hearts, the laughter, the limbo of chaos—the magic. Feeling the moment as it breaks on the nerve of the heart, turns time timeless, as here and now cease to matter and we grope for the mysteries—the magic. Of sharing and knowing, and sharing the knowing and knowing the sharing.
>
> Hear a quiet woman talk of her life and feel the thread that binds her to me, as though we'd loved. Hear a tender man who turns his dreams—and mine—into wriggling flashing poetry. To find a watch pocket we thought the world had taken from us, or a blue tin cup we thought our childhood had lost, or a new blue streetcar named desire, or a hidden hinge hitched to integrity, or the real thing in a coke bottle . . . .
>
> All of us have been burned. We have a common past but it gives us no cohesion. Each alone. No village anymore. No more we . . . only the slide toward un-we.
>
> No mythology sought in unison. No common bond with the strength of history in it. Forced, all of us, in this way or that, to create our mythologies from personal experience, lived or dreamed; having, like it or not, ready or not, to make heroes of ourselves.
>
> "You, whoever you are," is probably the most repeated phrase in *Leaves of Grass*. Whitman saw us coming. No, he was already one of us. Is there an "other" to whom the modern poet can speak? If there is no "other"—no beloved, no audience, no God—what is the point, the possibility even, of turning private vision into public song? . . .
>
> The uncertainty is still there within each of us, every Friday. But rather than holding us back, spontaneity stifled, we become instead almost child-like in freedom and vitality of mind. And then the afternoon writing shows that we are anything but children. The quality of uncertainty characteristic of the dream reflection seminar seems to act as a catalyst freeing our thoughts from their usual musty pathways. The integrity and quality of "the play" becomes the prevailing concern. Everyone becomes more sensitive to everyone, more civil, more thoughtful, more human. And, as is true of a good play, the sign of a good dream reflection seminar is always lots of hearty laughter.

—Lloyd Houston

With this artful statement I want to join a scientific statement of Freud's, which will identify the foresights that I think we are following in this work:

> Co-operation between a preconscious and an unconscious impulse, even when the latter is subject to very strong repression, may be established if the situation permits of the unconscious impulse operating in harmony with one of the ego's controlling tendencies. The repression is removed for the occasion, the repressed activity being admitted as a reinforcement of the one intended by the ego. In respect of this single constellation the unconscious becomes ego-syntonic, falls in line with the ego, without change taking place in the repression otherwise. The effect of the Ues in this co-operation is unmistakable; the reinforced tendencies reveal themselves as, in spite of all, different from the normal—they make possible achievements of special perfection, and they manifest a resistance in the face of opposition similar to that of obsessional symptons. (Freud, 1949, p. 127)

I may now describe the process by which the world-convention dream became understood and enjoyed. I and 16 students had read and discussed Virginia Woolf's novel *Orlando*. I read the *dream* and the reflections reported in Chapter 8. As the seminar began, it occurred to me that the play on the sounds "re" and "cal" might be a clever way of reminding myself that I do have occasion, from time to time, to return to California where my friend now lived. The students were much taken with the imagery of recalibrating the calendar. It carried the *Cal*ifornia reference, of course, and references to the passage of time and age—but what else? The best I could manage at first was that "calendar" is one of the very few words I have regular difficulty in spelling. I can never remember whether it is calender or calendar or calander; I am not sure which is correct. This led one of the students to ask whether, in dealing with the change in my relationship with the friend who had moved to California, my anticipations were on the side of *ending*, i.e., of its ending with the passage of time, or on the side of *anding*, i.e., of its being sustained in some new combination of events. I had, indeed, thought about it, although not in those words. Very astute . . . and we all felt ourselves warming to the dream poet's presence. "You don't calibrate calendars," someone noted, "you calibrate *instruments*." Was I aware of this bit of foolery in the dream? Very much so, since it had in fact been one of my tasks as an aerographer at a weather station in California during the war, around the time of the unfortunate sexual escapade, to calibrate the various meteorological instruments. Strange that I should mistake something that I knew so very well, even in a dream. Then, as I mentally revisited the weather station at which I had lived my impressionable eighteenth year, the rhythm of the phrase caught my attention and I sounded it out in my mind's ear: re *caal* ibrate the *caal* endar: re *caaal* ibrate the *caaal* endar. And this brought back the old Johnny Mercer tune that is sung to the same beat: Ac *ceeen* tuate the *Pooos* itive; Ac *ceeen* tuate the *Pooos* itive. That was a very popular song back then, as was the other

Johnny Mercer hit—what was it? Oh yes, "Don't Fence Me In." Were the students familiar with these songs, I wondered, or did my memories of them date me? No, they had heard them both many times. "Let me see if I can remember some of the lines," I went on: "You've got to accentuate the positive; eliminate the negative, latch on to the affirmative . . . ah . . . , that's what love is all about?" A few snickers, then some chuckles and then, as embarrassed eyes failed to avoid their counterparts around the room, a crescendo of uproarious laughter, with me the only one in the dark. "OK, OK, what's funny?" "Richard, do you really recall that last phrase as 'that's what love is all about'?" "Well, I'm not sure, but it's what came to mind as I tried to let my memory follow the rhythm." More snickers. "Do you want to know what the last phrase really is?" "Yes, damn it, what is it?" "You had the first parts right, but the whole thing goes (and they proceeded to sing it in unison): 'You've get to accentuate the positive; eliminate the negative; latch on to the affirmative; DON'T MESS WITH MR. IN BETWEEN!'" . . . "My God, my mother! That's exactly what she was telling me as a kid: don't mess with Mr. In Between! Incredible." And then another round of belly laughs, including mine this time . . . .

"OK," I continued, "but what about the 're-'? We got something from calendar and from calibrate but what about the 're-'? Why *re*-calibrate and not just calibrate? . . . Wait a minute. Wait a minute. My mother! . . . Do you folks know what I call my mother? I call her *Ree*, and have all my life. Her name is Marie, but when I was very young, probably around the time she was getting across to me not to mess with Mr. In Between, I couldn't say Marie. All I could get out was Ree. And it stuck. The whole family started calling her Ree and still does." . . . "What about 'Don't Fence Me In'? Anything there?" "Well, yes, maybe. Let me think a minute . . . . Yes, I'd been thinking the evening before of our book seminar on *Orlando*. Remember how impressed we were with the way Virginia Woolf managed to dispel the normal constraints of time, space, and sex and make us believe it? How she made the utterly fantastic seem credible? Even when she had Orlando change sex the character remained the same; the story just gets another dimension." . . . And then we went on to re-discuss the artistry with which Virginia Woolf managed, in *Orlando*, to write a fictional historical novel in which nothing is ever historical and everything is experienced in the present tense—only this time referring to this feat of Woolf's as one of not fencing us in, by way of recalibrating the calendar.

During the course of this seminar, which lasted some three hours, two of the students reported that they had recently passed what for them were critical birthdays. We had recently spent a seminar on a dream of one of these students in which there were images of flying and of swimming, symbols of the cross and of army tents and a prevailing sense of not knowing where he was. So, in the writing period which followed the seminar on my dream, I set myself the tentative task of composing something that tried to bring into aesthetic resonance my dream, his dream, the three birthdays, the various dream images, and Virginia Woolf's *Orlando*. In another three hours I had the following:

25–27 and Who's Counting?

Welcome to the next generation!

Ready?

 Arms outstretched?

  Legs together?

   Body straight?

Now!

Across the cross
(For what more terrifying revelation can there be than that it is the present moment? That we survive the shock at all is only possible because the past shelters us on one side, the future on another.) (p. 195)

    Braced for the impact
    Of the present tents
    The past on one side
    Thinking it my fault
    The future on the other
    A road in the making
    Surprise! Surprise!

    Happy birthday to me
    In the middle
    Half way up
    Half way down
    "Sometimes I take a great notion
    to jump into the river
     and drown."

(The true length of a person's life, whatever the Dictionary of National Biography may say, is always a matter of dispute. Indeed it is a difficult business—this time keeping . . . .) (p. 200)

    Am I half way up
    Or half way down?
    Do I even know my ass from a hole in the ground?
    Am I too far out
    Or too far in?
    And how long before the double chin?

Ready?
    Get Set?
        Now!

("Time has passed over me," she thought, trying to collect herself; "this is the oncome of middle age. How strange it is! Nothing is any longer one thing . . . .") (p. 199)

Welcome then, men
To the next generation
Here in the summer of
Nineteen hundred and seventy four
and flying . . . .

(. . . something . . . which is always absent from the present—whence its terror . . . something one trembles to pin through the body with a name and call beauty, for it has no body, is as a shadow and without substance or quality of its own, yet has the power to change whatever it adds itself to . . . .   Yes, she thought . . . I can begin to live again . . . I am about to understand . . . .) (pp. 210–211)

I am proud of that piece of writing, although as poetry I know it would not amount to much without the parenthetical assists from Virginia Woolf. The students were impressed with their writing too, as was I, although polished literature it was not. One of the reasons why I chose to share this particular experience with dream reflection was to make clear what the source of the pride is in this kind of teaching and learning. In this instance it was not in our growing prowess as interpreters of dreams, although that was a source of satisfaction and feelings of competence. It was not in the bit of homespun psychotherapy that I and the two young men experienced, although we welcomed that. It was that we were able as author *and* audience to respond to this tidbit of a dream in such ways as to enable us to reperceive, to renovelize, in some ways to re-create a great literary work we had previously read, discussed, and (so we thought) properly claimed as a part of our education. Through the agency of this second effort, in other words, we were enabled to make Woolf's novel truly our own. Along the way we got to know one another better than do most students and teachers when reading a book together, and our own writing was livelier and more enjoyable than it would otherwise have been.

Recall, now, that Freud's theory of dreams was centered on a metaphor drawn from an analogy: the metaphor of the dream censor drawn from a perception of dreams as analogous to neurotic symptoms. This choice of metaphor predetermined the parameters of the theory: preoccupation with the disguised *causes* of the dream; a predilection to conceive the transformative processes of dream formation as *work*; the attributing of greater importance to what can be deduced from the *associations* to a dream than to the dream itself; the investing of authority as to questions of relevance in the *objectivity* of the analyst; and the assumption that dream interpretation must be a comparatively *private* enterprise, a confidential dialogue between a patient and his analyst.

As I have sought over the past five years to involve dreams in the educational process, I have been guided by a companion metaphor, that of the *dream poet*. As the dream censor is drawn from a perception of dreams as analogous to neurotic symptoms, the dream poet is drawn from a perception of dreams as analogous to artistic visions. As the dream censor invites preoccupation with the disguised causes of a dream, the dream poet courts the liberating *effects* of dreams. As the dream censor invites the view of the transformative processes of dream formation as one of work, the dream poet invites the view of the same processes as one of *play*. As the dream censor requires that we place the locus of authority as to questions of relevance in the objectivity of the analyst, the dream poet requires that we place this locus in the *subjectivity* of the dreamer. And, as the dream censor insists that dream interpretation be a private enterprise, the dream poet requires that dream reflection be a *public*, collective enterprise.

I do not—and I cannot emphasize this too strongly—I *do not* conceive of these two metaphors, and the approaches to dreams that they suggest, as in any way competitive. They are *companion* metaphors. They coexist, not in reality, of course, but in our contemporary theory of dreams. Their compatible coexistence suggests that dreams seek as they hide, reveal as they conceal, beautify as they mystify, play as they work, communicate as they dissemble. There is nothing new in this view. Homer had it when, in the *Odyssey*, he sang:

> For fleeting dreams have two gates: one is fashioned of horn and one of ivory. Those which pass through the one of sawn ivory are deceptive, bringing tidings which come to nought, but those which issue from the one of polished horn bring true results when a mortal sees them.

Geza Roheim notes, in respect to this quotation, that the Greek word for ivory is a play on the Greek word "to deceive," and that the Greek word for horn is a play on the Greek word "to fulfill."

In comparing the two metaphors, I am prepared to go only so far as the obvious: the dream censor is more fruitful in considering the dreams of patients; the dream poet is more fruitful in considering the dreams of students. Even this may be an overstatement, insofar as there are times in therapy when a dream may be enjoyed, and there are times in dream reflection seminars when a dream should be analyzed.

One of the more noteworthy and welcome consequences of perceiving dreams as productions of a dream poet, whose effects we seek to understand, enjoy, and respond to in writing, is that dreams cease to be the special preserve of psychological experts, and become, as they were for millenia before the scientific revolution, objects of public interest, approachable by anyone who can articulate that interest. Of the dozens of my colleagues and former students who now conduct dream reflection seminars, few have much formal training in psychology. Here is the way, for example, that my friend Dr. Leon Sinclair, a Medievalist and seasoned conductor of dream reflection seminars, expresses his understanding of the dream poet:

> The metaphor that opens up all the other metaphors is that of the dream poet. While working on the dream, the dreamer must assume the existence of another consciousness, a dream poet not himself. The dream poet must be assumed to have command of his materials (memories, "olde bokes" as Chaucer says) and an intention (the truth, the poet's intention). Also, the poet must be shameless, must be willing to steal from anywhere, as the Middle English lyric poets would steal from sexual love in order to worship Mary and vice versa, as Joyce steals from the mass to write Ulysses.
>
> That doesn't mean the dream poet doesn't operate within boundaries: the accidents of day residue, the current tension configuration of the dreamer, the dreamer's memory (which is after all finite even if you hypothesize a "racial memory"), not many words, a biologically set amount of time, and other parameters we haven't yet perceived. You'll recognize these as having their counterparts in the poet's freely chosen or at least freely accepted limitations. Yet, like the poet, the dream poet seems mainly to break rules: rules of logical sequence, cause and effect, proximity in space and time, relevance, grammar and usage, decorum, audience expectation.
>
> The dream poet is fundamentally lawless. He has an insatiable rage for chaos when dream perception is compared to waking perception. That is, chaos as opposed to order. It is when you think of chaos as meaning not only without order, but also without function, that you discover the outlaw to be Robin Hood stealing from the riches of metaphor to give to the impoverished world of ordered perception. The dream poet is frantically active; Freud thought in terms of enormous amounts of psychic energy and used the term dream work. But the dream poet is also totally noncommitted to the dreamer. I have mentioned above his shamelessness, but it goes beyond poor socialization. In vain you search the structure of the dream for advice, for decision, for answers. I have wanted to call the dream poet delicate, courtly, as most anybody must who enjoys their dreams. What this amounts to I think is that the dream poet is totally nonjudgmental. When we think of his amazing access to memory, it hardly seems possible that he could be nonjudgmental. It seems to us that if we knew that, all that, we would know the meaning of it all. Isn't this urge to know the meaning of it all exactly Freud's most basic premise, the very wellspring of his genius and his work? But in fact the dream poet neither approves nor disapproves. He is, therefore, totally without means to mean. He intends nothing. His function is total

homonomy, total autonomy, total vicariousness, total noncommitment, and nothing more can be said. Purpose, intention as we ordinarily understand those terms, are the business of waking life.

Of what use is the dream poet metaphor then? I counter with a question. Did Freud's metaphor, the dream censor, call up the same response? It's not that anybody's afraid that, in either metaphor, people will start believing in little-men-in-the-head—not really. Where an objection to the dream poet comes from is that most people are more inclined to pay attention to Thoreau's, "Most men live lives of quiet desperation," than to Nietzsche's, "The fair illusion of the dream sphere, in the production of which every man proves himself an accomplished artist . . . ." It can't be denied that somewhere between sleep and waking the accomplished artist becomes our desperate, unaccomplished selves, and what better metaphor than the censor for explaining how and why? In opting for the dream poet rather than the dream censor we choose engagement over defense and revelation over concealment.

Taking one's dreams seriously is the art of integrating memory and perception, which is the same art that must be performed in reading or writing a poem. The dream poet, like the poet, turns memory into perception. The poet also turns perception into memory. The dream poet doesn't do that; the dreamer does, with the help of the reflectors. Then the reflectors turn the new memory into art, new perception. The dream poet is valued for his competence. It is an uncommitted competence. Such a thing does not exist in waking life. In the dream all visual imagery is best taken as symbolic, while words mean what they say—everything that they say. In waking life the opposite usually rules. We feel that we see what we see, and are seldom able to say what we mean and equally seldom are able to mean what we say. The poet is like the dream poet but with greater commitment. Finally, the dream poet and the poet have one function exactly in common, the aesthetic function. Simply stated, none of it is worth it, no significant action will be undertaken if life cannot be perceived to be beautiful.

In Chapter 8, on the psychoanalytic theory of dreams in this handbook, I focussed on the psychological functions that have been attributed to dreaming: Freud's "sanity preservation" or "safety valve" function, in which psychic tensions, caused by recently reactivated noxious memories and wishes, are safely neutralized by way of the disguised expression engineered by the dream work or censor; and the various adaptive functions conceived by Jung, Silberer, Lowy, French, Ullman, and Jones, in which, by way of various reintegrations and reorganizations of recent problematic experiences with analogous problematic experiences from the past, the mind appears to be preparing itself to cope adaptively with future challenges to personal development. For the sake of simplicity, let us call the first the *mental health function* and the second the *learning function*. For example, it is clear that in my world-convention dream the oblique references to the sexual traumas of my adolescence and childhood were working in the service of my mental health, while the references to my advancing years and to whether or not I should write another book were working in the service of my learning processes.

Against this background, how shall we regard the attempts, reported in this chapter, to involve dreams in education? I propose that we are in the process of discovering (perhaps rediscovering) that dreams may, in addition, serve a *re-creative function*, in which the novelties generated by the dream poet *in remembered dreams* are made the objects of consciously effortful aesthetic perception, with the expectation that such efforts will have renovelizing effects on the formal learning processes of the dream's author and of the dream's audience.

In my forthcoming book, *The Dream Poet*, I have described this educational method in detail, and have sought to provide the dream poet's archeological, anthropological, historical, philosophical, aesthetic, and psychological credentials. Permit me, here, to summarize all of that cryptically: I was once asked by my friend Dr. Eli "Mike" Bower to participate in a symposium addressed to the question, "To what extent can the primary and secondary processes be integrated in a school setting?" I began my presentation as follows:

> The answer to your question, Mike, is yes, the primary and secondary processes can be integrated in a school setting to a very impressive extent. And we have found one very direct and simple way of bringing this about. Dreams, as we all know, are the purest expressions of the primary process it is possible for normal people to experience, which is why dreams are so hard to remember, and, once remembered, so elusive to the waking mind.
>
> Reading and writing in school, the way we tend to go about them, tend to be as excessively weighed down by the secondary process as anything we ever do in life, which is why we tend to find doing them so deadly dull.
>
> So, find an enjoyable and productive way of making the two—dreams and school work—pay attention to each other, and you have found a way of integrating the primary and secondary processes in a school setting. Simple. No mysteries. No psychodynamic hijinks.

Finally, I want to acknowledge my indebtedness to Samuel Lowy for making possible this third approach to dreams, retrospective though the indebtedness is, since I was not conscious of it until recently. If, as I interpret Lowy to contend, the mental health and learning functions of dreaming are achieved whether or not the dreams are remembered (bearing in mind that the vast majority of them are not remembered), then it only seems right to look for something else to do with those few that are remembered—something other than pondering what they have done *for us*—something more on the order of what we can do *with and for them*. For, as W. H. Auden so exquisitely said:

> But he would have us remember most of all
> To be enthusiastic over the night

Not only for the sense of wonder
It alone has to offer, *but also*

Because it needs our love: for with sad eyes
Its delectable creatures look up and beg
    Us dumbly to ask them to follow;
    They are exiles who long for the future

That lies in our power. They too would rejoice
If allowed to serve enlightenment like him, . . .
(my underscore)

From *In Memory of Sigmund Freud*
d. September 1939

BIBLIOGRAPHY

Auden, W. H. In Memory of Sigmund Freud, d. September, 1939. In *Collected Shorter Poems*. New York: Random House, 1975.

Freud, S. The Unconscious, *Collected Papers*, Vol. 4. London: Hogarth Press, 1949.

Jones, R. M. *The Dream Poet*. Cambridge, Massachusetts: Schenkman Publishing Co., 1979.

Jones, R. M., Daugherty, L., Maddox, T., and Sinclair, L. Dreams and poetry (unpublished manuscript).

Lowy, S. *Foundations of Dream Interpretation*. London: Kegan Paul, Trench, Trubner, 1942.

Roheim, G. *The Gates of the Dream*. New York: International Universities Press, 1952.

Woolf, V. *Orlando*. New York: Harcourt, Brace, Jovanovich, 1973.

Name Index

Subject Index